Politics in the European Union

Develop your understanding of the European Union with our range of textbooks from the New European Union Series, created to give you clear and comprehensive coverage of a range of essential topics in EU politics.

THE NEW EUROPEAN UNION SERIES

Series Editors: John Peterson and Helen Wallace

The European Union is both the most successful modern experiment in international cooperation and a daunting analytical challenge to students of politics, economics, history, law, and the social sciences.

The EU of the twenty-first century continues to respond to expanding membership and new policy challenges—including the Eurozone crisis, climate change, energy security, and relations with Russia, Ukraine, and the Middle East—as well as the challenges to its legitimacy presented by the global financial crisis and the rise of Eurosceptic political parties in Europe. The result is an ever-evolving European Union that requires continuous reassessment.

THE NEW EUROPEAN UNION SERIES brings together the expertise of a community of leading scholars writing on major aspects of EU politics for an international readership. Build your knowledge with regularly updated editions on:

ORIGINS AND EVOLUTION OF THE EUROPEAN UNION

POLICY-MAKING AND THE EUROPEAN UNION

THE EUROPEAN UNION: HOW DOES IT WORK?

THE INSTITUTIONS OF THE EUROPEAN UNION

THE MEMBER STATES OF THE EUROPEAN UNION

INTERNATIONAL RELATIONS AND THE EUROPEAN UNION

For more information on the titles available in the New European Union Series visit the OUP website at

http://ukcatalogue.oup.com/category/academic/series/politics/neu.do

Make your voice heard: join the OUP politics student panel

To help us make sure we develop the best books for you, the student, we've set up a student panel.

To find out more visit www.oxfordtextbooks.co.uk/politics/studentpanel

Politics in the European Union

Fourth Edition

Ian Bache, Simon Bulmer,
Stephen George & Owen Parker

OXFORD
UNIVERSITY PRESS

OXFORD

UNIVERSITY PRESS

Great Clarendon Street, Oxford, OX2 6DP,
United Kingdom

Oxford University Press is a department of the University of Oxford.
It furthers the University's objective of excellence in research, scholarship,
and education by publishing worldwide. Oxford is a registered trade mark of
Oxford University Press in the UK and in certain other countries

1st edition 2001
2nd edition 2006
3rd edition 2011

Impression: 2

Published in the United States of America by Oxford University Press
198 Madison Avenue, New York, NY 10016, United States of America

British Library Cataloguing in Publication Data
Data available

Library of Congress Control Number: 2014941345

ISBN 978–0–19–968966–8

Printed in UK by
Bell and Bain Ltd, Glasgow

Contents in Brief

Contents in Detail

Map of Europe

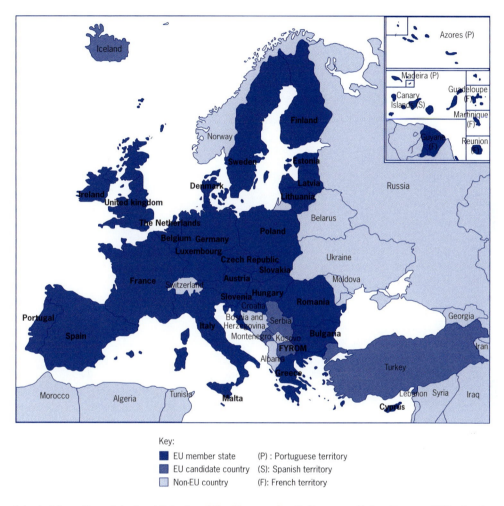

Key:
- ■ EU member state
- ■ EU candidate country
- ☐ Non-EU country

(P) : Portuguese territory
(S): Spanish territory
(F): French territory

Adapted from the original published on http://europa/eu © European Union. Responsibility for the adaptation lies entirely with Oxford University Press.

About the Authors

Ian Bache is Professor of Politics at the University of Sheffield. He has published widely on the European Union and related issues, including: *The Politics of European Union Regional Policy*, UACES/Sheffield Academic Press, 1998; *Politics in the European Union* (co-authored), Oxford University Press, 1st edition 2001, 2nd edition 2006; 3rd edition 2011; 4th edition 2015; *Multi-Level Governance* (co-edited), Oxford University Press, 2004; *The Europeanization of British Politics* (co-edited), Palgrave Macmillan, 2006; *Europeanization and Multilevel Governance*, Rowman and Littlefield, 2008; *Cohesion Policy and Multi-level Governance in South East Europe* (co-edited), Routledge, 2011; *Multi-Level Governance, Carbon Management and Climate Change* (co-authored), Rowman and Littlefield, forthcoming; *The Politics and Policy of Wellbeing* (co-authored), Edward Elgar, forthcoming: *Multi-level Governance* (co-edited) Edward Elgar, forthcoming.

He has published in a range of academic journals, including: the *British Journal of Politics and International Relations*; *Current Politics and Economics of Europe*; *Governance*; *Journal of Common Market Studies*; *Journal of European Public Policy*; *Journal of Public Policy*; *Journal of Southeast European and Black Sea Studies*; *Local Government Studies*; *Political Studies*; *Public Administration*; *Public Policy and Administration*; *Regional and Federal Studies*; *Scandinavian Political Studies*; and *West European Politics*. Between 2003 and 2005, he convened the UACES Study Group and ESRC Seminar Series on The Europeanization of British Politics and Policy Making and he is currently convenor of the ESRC Seminar Series on The Politics of Wellbeing.

Ian is an experienced teacher, having taught numerous undergraduate and post-graduate courses, and has supervised thirteen PhD students to completion. In 2008, he received a University of Sheffield Senate Award for Sustained Excellence in Teaching and Learning.

Simon Bulmer has been Professor of European Politics at the University of Sheffield since September 2007. Having held prior lectureships at Heriot-Watt University and the University of Manchester Institute of Science and Technology (UMIST), he moved to the University of Manchester in 1989, was appointed Professor of Government from 1995, and served as Head of Department 2001–04. He has held a Jean Monnet *ad personam* chair since 1999 and has been an Academician of the Social Sciences since 2001. He has been a Visiting Professor at the College of Europe Bruges, the Autonomous University of Barcelona, and the Stiftung Wissenschaft und Politik (the German Institute for International and Security Affairs), Berlin. From 1991 to 1998 he co-edited the *Journal of Common Market Studies*.

Simon has written or edited fourteen books on European politics, working with a range of co-authors. His most recent monograph (with Martin Burch) is *The Europeanisation of Whitehall: UK Central Government and the European Union*, Manchester

University Press, 2009. His most recent edited book (with Charlie Jeffery and Stephen Padgett) is *Rethinking Germany and Europe: Democracy and Diplomacy in a Semi-Sovereign State*, Palgrave, 2010. With Christian Lequesne he co-edited the textbook *The Member States of the European Union*, Oxford University Press, 2nd edition, 2013. He has published on European politics in leading academic journals, has taught on the EU in the United Kingdom, Spain, Belgium, Germany, and the USA, and has supervised twelve PhD students to completion.

Stephen George taught in the Department of Politics at the University of Sheffield for thirty years, the last ten as Professor. During that time he authored or co-authored four major books on the European Community/European Union, two of which—*Politics and Policy in the European Union* and *An Awkward Partner: Britain in the European Union*—went into multiple editions. He also edited books on Europe, and contributed some two dozen chapters to edited books and articles to several academic journals, including *The Annals of the American Academy of Political and Social Science*, *The British Journal of International Studies*, *Contemporary Record*, *Current Politics and Economics of Europe*, *European Access*, *International Affairs*, *Journal of European Integration*, *Journal of European Public Policy*, *Millennium: Journal of International Studies*, *Modern History Review*, *West European Politics*, and *The World Today*. He has given innumerable talks, guest lectures, and conference papers throughout the world, mostly on aspects of the European Union. Between 1997 and 2000, he was Chair of the University Association for Contemporary European Studies (UACES). As a teacher he successfully supervised eight PhD students, and devised innovative teaching materials on the European Union for undergraduate students, including a simulation exercise in European decision making. Since 2003, he has been Emeritus Professor of Politics, retired from active teaching and administration, but still involved in research and writing.

Owen Parker has been Lecturer in European Politics at the University of Sheffield since April 2012. Previously he was a Research Fellow in the Centre for the Study of Globalisation and Regionalisation (CSGR) at the University of Warwick. Before becoming an academic, Owen worked for the European Commission in the Enlargement Directorate General (2003–06) on Turkey's bid for EU membership.

Owen is the author of *Cosmopolitan Government in Europe: Citizens and Entrepreneurs in Postnational Politics*, Routledge, 2013. His work on European and international politics has been published in a range of journals, including: *Journal of Common Market Studies*, *Journal of European Public Policy*, *International Theory*, *International Studies Quarterly*, *Constellations*, *New Political Economy*, and *Co-operation and Conflict*. He is supervising a number of PhD projects on topics related to the EU and has taught a variety of EU politics courses at both undergraduate and postgraduate levels. As a teacher he seeks to emphasize the sometimes unacknowledged political and normative debates at the heart of European integration.

About the Book

This is a textbook on the study of the European Union (EU) within the cognate disciplines of political science and international relations. It reflects both the most significant contributions to the study of the EU within these disciplines and the gaps in existing research. It is designed to be used by students as part of a university course or module, although we hope it works well for the independent reader also.

While we would argue that there is no easy separation between economics and politics, or between law and politics, this book is explicitly concerned with politics in the EU. Thus, we address some of the standard issues of the disciplines of political science and international relations. Is the EU developing into a super-state of some sort? If so, of what sort? Have national governments voluntarily surrendered sovereignty to European institutions, or have there been forces at work dragging member states towards ever closer union against the will of the governments? Is the process driven by vested interests that stand to benefit from it, or by ideas that place a positive value on international integration? Does the process have legitimacy in the eyes of the people who are being brought into an ever closer union? If so, why? If not, why not?

These questions are relevant not because of their practical importance—although they do have a great deal of practical importance—nor because they figure in the coverage of the EU in the media—although because of their practical importance they do so figure—rather, they are relevant because they are questions generated by the theories of political scientists and students of international relations about the nature of European integration and of the EU. Academic disciplines are formed when scholars are brought together by shared concerns, and they are forged by academic debates, which are fiercest when they are between advocates of different theories. That is why the textbook begins with theory. It is theory that provides our criteria of relevance. Many eclectic textbooks do exist in politics and international relations, books that never mention theory—and we are not thinking here exclusively of books on the EU. Our view is that theory is very important. It shapes what is studied and what is not, what is included and what is excluded. We see it as central to the study of the EU and not as an optional extra. However, for those who wish to know something of the EU before approaching theoretical issues, it is possible to read the 'History' section of the book first without having read the 'Theory' section: it is primarily the conclusions to the 'History' chapters that refer back to the theories in Part One.

This edition was written in the context of a sustained economic and financial crisis that began in 2008 and whose effects were still being felt in the EU in 2014. Crisis for the EU is not new, as we have observed in previous editions. However, the scale and intensity of the eurozone crisis has presented the EU with arguably its greatest political challenges to date. Euroscepticism is at a record high, the UK is having serious debates about a referendum on withdrawal, and the nature of the EU that will finally emerge from this crisis is still unclear.

Change happens not only in the field of study, but also in the study of the field. Between the first and third editions of the book (2001–11), the study of the EU expanded tremendously and it continues to do so. In the area of theory, the developments have continued to be rich and varied, and this section has expanded to include approaches that have relatively recently been applied to the EU. The notion of 'disintegration' has taken its place in the lexicon of the EU scholars alongside that of 'integration' and critical approaches have become more prominent. Our expanded theory section reflects these developments in the field.

Obviously the output did not just stop when we finished writing, so there will be more for the student to explore, but we think that this edition is as up to date on the academic literature as it could be. The strong rooting of the text in the research literature is one of the distinctive features of this book.

As the task of producing a comprehensive and up-to-date textbook on the EU expands, so has the authorship team expanded to meet this challenge. For this edition, Ian, Simon, and Stephen welcome on board their Sheffield colleague, Owen Parker, as a co-author for the fourth and subsequent editions of the book.

New to this Edition

Owen Parker joins Ian Bache, Simon Bulmer, and Stephen George as a new author for the fourth edition.

The theory chapters have been updated taking into account, in particular, a broader range of 'critical' approaches to the study of the EU.

There is a revised and restructured history section with additional material on the eurozone crisis.

Chapters on institutions and policy reflect the practice of the Lisbon Treaty over the four years since its implementation.

The Online Resource Centre, which accompanies the text, has also been updated with new materials for students and lecturers.

Acknowledgements

This is the fourth edition of a textbook that appeared previously in 2001, 2006, and 2011. In revising it we have been helped enormously by the comments of colleagues and students who used these previous editions or acted as anonymous referees.

We would like to thank Paul Cardwell, Wyn Grant, Tammy Hervey, and Gabriel Siles-Brügge for their help and advice on various points. We have tried to incorporate as many of the comments received as possible, but some we have not been able to accommodate for reasons of time and space.

We would like to thank all of the production staff at Oxford University Press, and in particular Martha Bailes and Suzy Armitage for their advice, skill, and patience.

We have been tremendously encouraged by the positive feedback that we have received from users of our previous editions. We hope that it will continue to prove a stimulating textbook for all who use it and will lead to stimulating and critical debates in the classroom.

Ian Bache
Simon Bulmer
Stephen George
Owen Parker
March 2014

Copyright disclaimer

Guided Tour of Textbook Features

We have developed a number of learning tools to help you develop the essential knowledge and skills you need to study EU politics. This guided tour shows you how to get the most out of your textbook.

Chapter overviews

Chapter overviews set the scene for upcoming themes and issues to be discussed, and indicate the scope of coverage within the chapter.

Chapter 1
Theories of European Integra

Chapter Overview

The dominant approaches to understanding the early phase of European integra international relations (IR). In particular, the study of integration was dominated ing approaches of neofunctionalism and intergovernmentalism. Although neofun neatly fitted events in the 1950s and early 1960s, subsequent events led to its rise of intergovernmentalist explanations. While theorizing European integration significantly from these early approaches, much of what followed was either debate or developed as a rejection of it. The debate about whether the EU is intergovernmentalism or supranationalism still informs much of the academ subject.

Insight boxes

Throughout the book, insight boxes provide you with extra information on particular topics and define and explain key ideas, helping you to build on what you have learned from the main chapter text.

Insight 3.4 Input–Output Democracy

Scharpf (1997: 19) argued that:

On the *input side*, self-determination requires that political choices should be derived, directly or indirectly, from the *authentic preferences of citizens* and that, for that reason, governments must be held accountable to the governed...

On the *output side*, however, self-determination implies *effective fate control*. Democracy would be an empty ritual if the political choices of governments were not able to achieve a high degree of effectiveness in achieving the goals, and avoiding the dangers, that citizens collectively care about. Thus, input-oriented authenticity and output-oriented effectiveness are equally essential elements of democratic self-determination.

Glossary terms

Key terms appear emboldened in blue in the text and are defined in a glossary at the end of the book, helping you to understand technical terms as you learn, and acting as a useful prompt when it comes to revision.

> Ordinary Legislative Procedure (Co-Decision). The crucial breakthrough was the introduction of the co-operation procedure in the Single European Act (SEA). This was insisted upon by the governments of those states—especially Germany and Italy—that were most convinced by the federalist arguments and concerns regarding the democratic deficit (Rittberger 2003: 220). Consensus gradually emerged between the governments that, for the single market to be created, they would have to accept **qualified majority voting (QMV)**, otherwise every individual measure would be vetoed by the government of the state that stood to be most adversely affected. This implied, though, that national parliaments would no longer be able to reject a proposed measure by instructing their government's representative to veto it in the Council. The democratic deficit argument implied that the loss of control by the national parliaments should be made up by an increase in the role of the EP.
>
> Once the principle of a larger role for the EP in the legislative process had been established, the extension of that role followed; as experience of operating the new system made it clear that co-operation was a clumsy procedure, and that the EP would use its powers to improve legislation, not just to be obstructive. Subsequent Treaty reform increased the number of policy issues on which co-decision applies and the co-operation procedure was abolished by the Lisbon Treaty. The move to the co-decision process provoked an academic debate as to how far that increased the effective influence of the EP in the legislative process.

Key points

Each chapter concludes with a set of key points that reinforce your understanding and act as a useful revision tool.

> lacks transparency, its legitimacy is called into question. Attempts to regulate lobbyists' access to the institutions have been the response to this concern.
>
> **KEY POINTS**
>
> **The Growth of Interest-Group Activity at the EU Level**
> - Interest-group activity in Brussels has increased greatly since the mid-1980s.
> - Factors in this growth are: the growing policy competence of the EU; the perception of a shifting balance of institutional power in Brussels, most notably in favour of the EP; the receptiveness of EU officials to interest-group representations; and the 'snowballing' effect of groups following the lead of others so as not to risk being disadvantaged.
>
> **Types of Interest Group**
> - There are several different types of interest organization active in Brussels.
> - Business interests were the first to locate in Brussels, and still account for the largest number of groups.
> - Interest groups representing workers, consumers, environmental interests, and other parts of civil society have become increasingly active.
>
> **Forms of Interest Representation**
> - Five forms of interest representation coexist in the EU: 'corporatist'; 'neo-corporatist'; pluralist; informally institutionalized policy networks; and legal representation.
> - Of these five, pluralism and informal institutionalization predominate.
>
> **Resources**
> - The most effective interest groups in a pluralist system are generally those that control key resources such as information and expertise, economic muscle, and status.
> - Small organizations can pool resources, but they may then find problems in agreeing on priorities and tactics.
> - The three types of information sought by the institutions are expert knowledge, information on the needs and concerns of actors in the relevant sector across Europe, and information on the needs and concerns of national actors in the sector.

Further reading

Annotated recommendations for further reading at the end of each chapter identify the key literature in the field, helping you to develop your interest in particular topics.

> **FURTHER READING**
>
> The most comprehensive review of the external trade policy of the EU is provided by **S. Meunier**, *Trading Voices: The European Union in International Commercial Negotiations* (Princeton, NJ: Princeton University Press, 2007). A useful recent literature review is offered by **A. Poletti and D. De Bievre**, 'The Political Science of European Trade Policy: A Literature Review With a Research Outlook', *Comparative European Politics*, 12 (2014): 101–19.
>
> The common commercial policy of the EU is analyzed as a multi-level game in **S. Collinson**, '"Issue Systems", "Multi-Level Games" and the Analysis of the EU's External Commercial and Associated Policies: A Research Agenda', *Journal of European Public Policy*, 6 (1999): 206–24. The increasing complexity of trade policy is well set out in **A. R. Young and J. Peterson**, 'The EU and the New Trade Politics', *Journal of European Public Policy*, 13 (2006): 795–814.
>
> The chapters in **G. Faber and J. Orbie (eds)**, *Beyond Market Access for Economic Development: EU Africa Relations in Transition* (Routledge, 2009), address the emergence of EPAs in the context

Guided Tour of the Online Resource Centre

www.oxfordtextbooks.co.uk/orc/bache4e/

The Online Resource Centre that accompanies this book provides students and instructors with ready-to-use learning and teaching materials. These resources are free of charge and have been created to take student learning further.

The Online Resource Centre Resources have been updated by Dr. Mary Murphy of University College Cork.

For students

Interactive map of Europe

An interactive map provides a wealth of social and political facts about each EU member state. Simply click on the state you are interested in and the information appears in a separate window.

Interactive timeline

Use the interactive timeline to improve your knowledge of the history of European integration. Key events are summarized when you click on each date.

Multiple-choice questions

A bank of self-marking multiple-choice questions has been provided for each chapter of the text to reinforce your understanding, and act as an aid to revision.

Flashcard glossary

A series of interactive flashcards containing key terms allows you to test your knowledge of the terminology of EU politics.

Web links

A selection of annotated web links, which accompanies each chapter, will point you in the direction of important treaties, working papers, articles, and other relevant sources of information on EU politics.

For registered adopters of the book

PowerPoint slides

PowerPoint slides complement each chapter of the book and are a useful resource for preparing lectures and handouts.

Essay and seminar questions

A range of essay and seminar questions has been devised to be used in assessment, or to stimulate class debate.

Boxes, tables, and figures from the text

Boxes, tables, and figures from the text have been provided in high-resolution format for downloading into presentation software or for use in assignments and exam material.

Part One
Theory

This part of the book consists of four chapters. Its purpose is twofold: first, to review the main theories used in the study of the European Union (EU); and second, to identify themes that will inform our analysis of subsequent chapters. We do not see this exercise as being an optional extra for a textbook: it is fundamental to understanding the academic study of the EU.

Our understanding of the world is guided by our particular conceptual lenses or theoretical frameworks, whether we are aware of them or not. The theoretical frameworks we adopt determine the questions we ask, and so the answers that we find. As Rosamond (2013: 86) suggests: '... being conscious about the theoretical propositions chosen by authors is vital because alternative "readings" of the EU and European integration follow from alternative theoretical premises.'

There has been no shortage of theoretical models and frameworks applied to the study of EU politics and we provide an overview of what to us appear to be the most important. One way of considering the wide variety of approaches considered in these chapters is in terms of different phases of theorizing and the central questions that were asked during these phases. Table I.1 summarizes these phases and should serve as a useful reference point for students throughout their engagement with these theory chapters and other chapters. It should be noted that these phases and the questions posed are not mutually exclusive, but overlapping in a variety of ways. The table makes clear the wide variety of approaches that have sought to engage with the EU (and its antecedents) as an object of study.

The first phase of study, during the early stages of co-operation between western European states, was dominated by approaches from the study of international relations (IR). From the end of World War I, academics had grappled with the question of how to achieve peace in war-torn Europe, and such issues became even more acute following World War II. In particular, federalist and functionalist theories identified the ways in which nationalism in Europe might be overcome and peace achieved. Federalists in particular were politically active in *promoting peace* via a federal Europe. As the EU's antecedent organizations evolved, albeit not along strictly federalist lines, IR scholars became increasingly interested in *explaining integration* as a potentially generalizable phenomenon. In the 1960s, neofunctionalists and intergovernmentalists placed the accent on, respectively, non-state and state actors in driving processes of integration. The question of how integration occurred and its key drivers has remained central for scholars of the EU and many have followed in the footsteps of these early or classical theories of integration. Liberal intergovernmentalism (LI), for instance, offered a refined version of early intergovernmentalism in the 1990s and various contemporary 'supranational' accounts build on the insights of neofunctionalism. These theoretical approaches are considered in Chapter 1, 'Theories of European Integration'.

As the EU became more established and institutionalized, IR approaches were increasingly accompanied by insights from the study of domestic and comparative politics which asked, in particular, *how does the EU and its governance work?* The most straightforward way of understanding this theoretical shift is to see it as a move away from treating the EU as an international organization similar to others (such as the North Atlantic Treaty Organization—NATO) to seeing it as something unique, with some features more akin to those of national political systems. While there were important precursors to such work as early as the 1970s, it was in the 1990s that those with backgrounds in the study of domestic and comparative politics really became dominant in the study of the EU. Such work analysed the institutions and governance of the EU, adopting a variety of approaches that had been applied to domestic politics. Also in the 1990s, scholars from similar backgrounds began to consider *the consequences of the EU* on its member states. They did so by asking how it had impacted upon or 'Europeanized' its member states' domestic polities in various domains. Scholars also considered age-old questions about legitimacy and democracy in the context of the new governing realities precipitated by the developing

Table I.1 Phases in Theorizing and Key Questions

Phase	When	Main questions	Main Theories	Chapter
Promoting peace through integration	1920s onwards	How can peace be achieved in Europe (and beyond)? How can nationalism be overcome?	Federalism Functionalism	1
Explaining integration	1950s onwards	How can integration processes be explained? What are the drivers of European integration?	Neofunctionalism (late 1950s) Intergovernmentalism (1960s) Liberal intergovernmentalism (1990s)	1
Analyzing the EU as political system	1990s onwards	How does the EU and its governance work? How do its institutions work? What kind of political system is it? How can political processes be described?	New institutionalism Policy networks Multi-level governance	2
Analyzing consequences of EU	1990s onwards	What is the impact of the EU on member states? What are the consequences of the EU for democracy and legitimacy?	Europeanization Normative/ democratic theories	3
Critiquing EU and/or 'mainstream' approaches to its study	Late 1990s onwards	Which ideas /ideologies predominate in the EU? How and why? Where does power lie within the EU? In whose interest does the EU act and with what political and social consequences?	Social constructivism Critical political economy Critical social theory Gender approaches Post-structural approaches	4

Adapted from Diez and Wiener (2004: 7).

EU. Theories based primarily on domestic and comparative politics approaches are set out in Chapter 2, 'Theories of EU Governance', and in Chapter 3, 'Theorizing Consequences', we consider the contribution of the *Europeanization* literature and approaches to understanding the challenges for *democracy*.

While these approaches continue to provide important contributions to the study of the EU, they have been joined by a wide range of more critical perspectives that question many of the assumptions on which these approaches are based. Such approaches are disparate but all tend to question the positivist assumptions upon which other theories are largely based (see Chapter 4 and Table 4.1). The majority of these approaches have also been critical of various aspects of the EU status quo although that is not to say that they are anti-EU per se. They ask such questions as: *which ideas or ideologies* have prevailed in EU governance? *Which actors have been most powerful* and *whose interests* has integration served, and whose has it undermined? In Chapter 4 we consider five approaches that offer a flavour of this emerging critical work: social constructivism, critical political economy, critical social theory, critical feminism, and post-structuralism.

In later chapters we refer back to these theory chapters where relevant. We would encourage students to consider the connections between these theoretical positions and the material discussed in other parts of the book.

Chapter 1

Theories of European Integration

Chapter Overview

The dominant approaches to understanding the early phase of European integration came from international relations (IR). In particular, the study of integration was dominated by the competing approaches of neofunctionalism and intergovernmentalism. Although neofunctionalist theory neatly fitted events in the 1950s and early 1960s, subsequent events led to its demise and the rise of intergovernmentalist explanations. While theorizing European integration has moved on significantly from these early approaches, much of what followed was either framed by this debate or developed as a rejection of it. The debate about whether the EU is characterized by intergovernmentalism or supranationalism still informs much of the academic work on the subject.

European Integration and the First Attempts to Theorize It

The signing of the Treaty of Paris in April 1951 by the governments of Belgium, France, Germany, Italy, Luxembourg, and the Netherlands (see Chapter 5, The Schumann Plan for Coal and Steel) began the process commonly referred to as European integration (see Insight 1.1). This process has meant that the economies of participating states, and subsequently other areas, have been increasingly managed in common. Decisions previously taken by national governments alone are now taken together with other governments, and specially created European institutions. Governments have relinquished the sole right to make legislation (national sovereignty) over a range of matters in favour of joint decision making with other governments (pooled sovereignty). Other tasks have been delegated to European institutions.

It was something of a surprise to academic theorists of IR when governments in western Europe began to surrender their national sovereignty in some policy areas. For the first half of the twentieth century, the nation state seemed assured of its place as the most important unit of political life in the western world, especially in Europe. As such, the process of European integration constituted a major challenge to existing theories and generated an academic debate about the role of the state in the process. The two competing theories that emerged from IR to dominate the debate over early

Insight 1.1 European Integration

European integration has a number of aspects, but the main focus of Chapter 1 is on *political* integration. Ernst Haas (1968: 16) provided a definition of European political integration as a *process*, whereby:

> political actors in several distinct national settings are persuaded to shift their loyalties, expectations and political activities toward a new center, whose institutions possess or demand jurisdiction over the pre-existing national states. The end result of a process of political integration is a new political community, superimposed over the pre-existing ones.

Implicit in Haas's definition was the development of a European federal state. More cautiously, Lindberg (1963: 149) provided a definition of political integration as a process, but without reference to an end point:

> political integration is (1) the process whereby nations forego the desire and ability to conduct foreign and key domestic policies independently of each other, seeking instead to make *joint decision*s or to *delegate* the decision-making process to new central organs; and (2) the process whereby political actors in several distinct national settings are persuaded to shift their expectations and political activities to a new center.

The first part of this definition refers to two 'intimately related' modes of decision making: sharing and delegating. The second part of the definition refers to 'the patterns of behaviour shown by high policy makers, civil servants, parliamentarians, interest group leaders and other elites' (Lindberg 1963: 149), who respond to the new reality of a shift in political authority to the centre by re-orientating their political activities to the European level.

developments in European integration were neofunctionalism (Haas 1958; Lindberg 1963) and intergovernmentalism (Hoffmann 1964, 1966).

Before discussing these two main positions in the debate, it is necessary to consider the intellectual context from which the idea of European integration emerged. Below we look first at the functionalist ideas of David Mitrany on how to avoid war between nations, then at the ideas of the European federalists, and finally at the 'federal-functionalism' of Jean Monnet. We then turn to look first at neofunctionalism and then at intergovernmentalism, before looking at two later contributions to this debate: liberal intergovernmentalism (LI) and supranational governance.

The Intellectual Background

To understand the ideas that fed into the first attempts to theorize European integration, it is useful to consider some important theoretical predecessors, which were prominent in the period after World War II. Particularly important among these were functionalism and federalism. While these theories differed in important respects, both were geared towards ending war and achieving peace in Europe (see Table I.1). As described in this section, while functionalists such as David Mitrany emphasized primarily technical solutions, federalists such as Altiero Spinelli saw the solutions as primarily political in nature. The pragmatic and political ideas of the functionalists and the federalists respectively were brought together in the 'functional-federalism' of Jean Monnet, which in turn provided one important source of intellectual inspiration for the neofunctionalist theory of European integration.

Mitrany and Functionalism

David Mitrany (1888–1974) was born in Romania, but spent most of his adult life in Britain and the United States. He was not a theorist of European integration. His concern was with building a *Working Peace System*, the title of his Fabian pamphlet (Mitrany 1966; first published 1943). For Mitrany, the root cause of war was nationalism. The failure of the League of Nations to prevent aggression prompted debate about a new type of international system even before the outbreak of the Second World War. For those who blamed the failure of the League on its limited powers, the response was the development of an international federation. In other words, the League had not gone far enough and the same mistake should not be repeated: henceforth, nations should be tied more closely together.

Mitrany did not agree with the idea of federation as the means of tying states together. He opposed the idea of a single world government because he believed that it would pose a threat to individual freedom. He also opposed the creation of regional federations, believing that this would simply reproduce national rivalries on a larger scale. Any political reorganization into separate units must sooner or later produce the same effects; any international system that is to usher in a new world must produce the opposite effect of subduing political division.

Instead of either of these possibilities—a world federation or regional federations—Mitrany proposed the creation of a whole series of separate international functional agencies, each having authority over one specific area of human life. His scheme was to take individual technical tasks out of the control of governments and to hand them over to these functional agencies. He believed that governments would be prepared to surrender control because they would not feel threatened by the loss of sovereignty over, say, health care or the co-ordination of railway timetables, and they would be able to appreciate the advantages of such tasks being performed at the regional or world level. As more and more areas of control were surrendered, states would become less capable of independent action. One day, the national governments would discover that they were enmeshed in a 'spreading web of international activities and agencies' (Mitrany 1966: 35).

These international agencies would operate at different levels depending on the function that they were performing. Mitrany gave the example of systems of communication. Railways would be organized on a continental basis; shipping would be organized on an intercontinental basis; aviation would be organized on a universal basis. Not only would the dependence of states on these agencies for their day-to-day functioning make it difficult for governments to break with them, but the experience of the operation of the agencies would also socialize politicians, civil servants, and the general public into adopting less nationalistic attitudes and outlook.

Spinelli and Federalism

A completely different approach to guaranteeing peace was devised during World War II in the ranks of the various Resistance movements. It was a specifically European movement, and whereas Mitrany aimed explicitly to depoliticize the process of the transfer of power away from national governments, federalists sought a clear transfer of political authority.

The European Union of Federalists (EUF) was formed in December 1946 from the war-time Resistance movements. It was particularly strong in Italy, where the leading figure was Altiero Spinelli. Federalism appealed to the Resistance groups because it proposed superseding nationalism. It is important to bear in mind that whereas in Britain (and Russia) the Second World War was a nationalist war (in the former Soviet Union, it was 'the great patriotic war'), in countries such as France and Italy it was an ideological war. Resistance fighters drawn from communist, socialist, and Christian democratic groups were in many cases fighting their own countrymen—Vichy supporters in France, Italian Fascists in Italy.

While being held as political prisoners of the Fascists on the island of Ventotene, Spinelli and Ernesto Rossi (1897–1967) produced the Ventotene Manifesto (1941), calling for a 'European Federation'. It argued that, left alone, the classes 'most privileged under old national systems' would seek to reconstruct the order of nation states at the end of the war. While these states might appear democratic, it would only be a matter of time before power returned to the hands of the privileged classes. This would prompt the return of national jealousies and, ultimately, to renewed war between states. To prevent this development, the Manifesto called for the abolition of the division of Europe into national, sovereign states. It urged propaganda and action to bring together the separate national Resistance movements across Europe to push for the creation of a federal European state.

The EUF adopted the Ventotene Manifesto, and began agitating for an international conference to be called that would draw up a federal constitution for Europe. This ambitious proposal was designed to build on what Milward called 'the wave of hope for a better world and a changed future for the human race which had swept across Europe' and which included an 'extraordinary wave of enthusiasm for European federation' (Milward 1984: 55).

The strategy of the EUF was to exploit the disruption caused by the war to existing political structures in order to make a new start on a radically different basis from the Europe of national states. They aimed to achieve a complete break from the old order of nation states, and to create a federal constitution for Europe. Their Congress took time to organize, though. It eventually took place in The Hague in May 1948 (see Chapter 5, The End of War, Federalism, and the Hague Congress). By that time, the national political systems had been re-established, and what emerged from the Congress was an intergovernmental organization, the Council of Europe, not the new federal constitutional order for which the federalists had hoped. Many federalists then turned to the gradualist approach that was successfully embodied in the European Coal and Steel Community (ECSC).

Monnet and Functional-Federalism

The plan for the ECSC was known as the Schuman Plan because it was made public by the French Foreign Minister Robert Schuman, but it is generally accepted that it was drawn up within the French Economic Planning Commission (*Commissariat du Plan*), which was headed by the technocrat Jean Monnet. It was the task of the Planning Commission to guide the post-war reconstruction and modernization of the French economy, and it was through his experiences in this task that Monnet came to appreciate the economic inadequacy of the European nation state in the modern world. He saw the need to create a 'large and dynamic **common market**', 'a huge continental market on the European scale' (Monnet 1962: 205). He aimed, though, to create more than just a common market.

Monnet was a planner: he showed no great confidence in the free-market system, which had served France rather badly in the past. He placed his faith in the development of **supranational institutions** as the basis for building a genuine economic community that would adopt common economic policies and rational planning procedures. Coal and steel were only intended as starting points. The aim was to extend integration to all aspects of the western European economy—but such a scheme would have been too ambitious to gain acceptance all at once. There had been a clear indication of this in the failure of previous efforts to integrate the economies of France, Italy, the Netherlands, Belgium, and Luxembourg.

There was also a new factor in the equation, the key factor prompting Monnet's plan: the emergence in 1949 of a West German state. For Monnet, the existence of the Federal Republic of Germany posed two problems in addition to that of how to create an integrated western European economy. The first problem was how to organize Franco–German relations in such a way that another war between the two states would become impossible. To a French mind, this meant how to control Germany. The pooling of coal and steel production would provide the basis for economic development as a first step towards a 'federation of Europe'. Stimulating the expansion of those industries for peaceful purposes would provide an economic alternative to producing war materials for those regions of Europe that had been largely dependent on providing military material. The second problem facing Monnet was the very practical one of how to ensure adequate supplies of coking coal from the Ruhr for the French steel industry. The idea of pooling Franco–German supplies of coal and steel would tie the two states into a mutual economic dependency, in addition to taking out of the immediate control of the national governments the most basic raw materials for waging another war.

Mitrany (1966) described Monnet's strategy as 'federal-functionalism'. It is not clear, though, how far Monnet was a federalist at all. He might be seen as a supreme pragmatist who proposed the ECSC as a solution to the very practical problems described above. To solve these problems, Monnet adopted a solution similar to that of Mitrany: remove control of the strategically crucial industries—coal and steel—from the governments and put it in the hands of a free-standing agency. This was the High Authority of the ECSC, and in Monnet's original plan it was the only institution proposed. The development of other supranational institutions came from other pressures (see Chapter 7). The High Authority was the prototype for the later Commission of the European Economic Community (EEC), which became central to the neofunctionalist theory of European integration.

International Relations Theories of European Integration

As noted, the thinkers considered in the previous section were politically active in the promotion of peace in the post-war context. In contrast, for the generation of IR theorists of integration that emerged in the 1950s and 1960s European integration had already begun and their primary purpose was to consider how it might be explained and what were its key drivers (see Table I.1). In many ways these theorists were responding to realism, the dominant approach to explaining IR in the 1950s. It assumed that sovereign states formed the fundamental units of analysis for understanding IR. The appearance of the European Community (EC) was an anomaly from this perspective and prompted the emergence of alternative analyses. Neofunctionalism was the name given to the first attempt to understand European integration. Its implied critique of realism led to a counter-theory from within a broadly state-centred perspective, which became known as intergovernmentalism. The debate between these two broad positions has evolved over time, but the central issues of dispute remain much the same today as they were in the 1950s.

Neofunctionalism

Starting with the analysis of the ECSC by Ernst Haas (1958), a body of theorizing about European integration known as neofunctionalism was built up in the writings of a group of US academics (see Insight 1.1). These theorists drew on the work of Mitrany and Monnet in particular. In addition to Haas, the main figures in this school of analysis were Leon Lindberg (1963, 1966), and Philippe Schmitter (1970).

Neofunctionalism was a **pluralist** theory of international politics. In contrast to the more traditional realist theories, it did not assume that a state was a single unified actor; nor did it assume that states were the only actors on the international stage. In the concepts that it used, it anticipated later writings on global interdependence (Keohane and Nye 1977).

In the first period of European integration, neofunctionalism appeared to be winning the theoretical debate. Neofunctionalism sought to explain 'how and why they (states) voluntarily mingle, merge and mix with their neighbours so as to lose the factual attributes of sovereignty while acquiring new techniques for resolving conflict between themselves' (Haas 1970: 610). There were four key parts to the neofunctionalist argument, as follows.

(1) The concept of the 'state' is more complex than realists suggested.

(2) The activities of interest groups and bureaucratic actors are not confined to the domestic political arena.

(3) Non-state actors are important in international politics.

(4) European integration is advanced through 'spillover' pressures.

In contrast to realists, neofunctionalists argued that the international activities of states were the outcome of a pluralistic political process in which government decisions were influenced by pressures from various interest groups and bureaucratic actors. In common with the general tenor of US political science at the time, it was often assumed that these pressures constituted the complete explanation for government decisions. So, if the analyst could identify the strength and direction of the various pressures accurately, it would be possible to make predictions about government behaviour in IR.

Using the concepts that were later called 'transnationalism' and 'transgovernmentalism' (Keohane and Nye 1977: 129–30), neofunctionalists expected nationally based interest groups to make contact with similar groups in other countries (transnationalism), and departments of state to forge links with their counterparts in other states, unregulated by their respective foreign offices (transgovernmentalism).

Neofunctionalists pointed to the activities of multinational corporations to illustrate their argument that non-state actors are important in international politics. However, for neofunctionalists, the European Commission was the most important non-state international actor. The Commission was believed to be in a unique position to manipulate both domestic and international pressures on national governments to advance the process of European integration, even where governments might be reluctant. This contrasted with realist explanations of IR, which focused exclusively on the international role of states.

Neofunctionalists used the concept of spillover to explain how, once national governments took the initial steps towards integration, the process took on a life of its own and swept governments along further than they anticipated going. As Lindberg (1963: 10) put it:

> In its most general formulation, 'spillover' refers to a situation in which a given action, related to a specific goal, creates a situation in which the original goal can be assured only by taking further actions, which in turn create a further condition and a need for more action, and so forth.

Two types of spillover were important to early neofunctionalist writers: functional and political. The notion of 'cultivated spillover' was added by later theorists to explain the part played by the Commission in fostering integration (Tranholm-Mikkelsen 1991) and the concept of 'exogenous spillover' was added to explain enlargement (Niemann 2006).

Functional spillover argued that modern industrial economies were made up of interconnected parts. As such, it was not possible to isolate one sector from others. Following this understanding, neofunctionalists argued that, if member states integrated one functional sector of their economies, the interconnectedness between this sector and others would lead to a 'spillover' into other sectors. Technical pressures would prompt integration in those related sectors, and the integration of one sector would only work if other functionally related sectors were also integrated. For example, if a joint attempt were made to increase coal production across member states, it would prove necessary to bring other forms of energy into the scheme. Otherwise, a switch by one member state away from coal towards a reliance on oil or nuclear fuels would throw out all of the calculations for coal production. In addition, any effective planning of the total energy supply would involve gathering data about future total demand, implying the development of overall plans for industrial output across member states.

To this technical logic of functional spillover, the neofunctionalists added the idea of political spillover, and set perhaps more store by this than by functional spillover in explaining the process of integration. Political spillover involved the build-up of political pressures in favour of further integration within the states involved. Once one sector of the economy was integrated, the interest groups operating in that sector would have to exert pressure at the supranational level, on the organization charged with running their sector. So the creation of the ECSC would lead to the representatives of the coal and steel industries in all of the member states switching at least a part of their political lobbying from national governments to the new supranational agency, the High Authority. Relevant trade unions and consumer groups would follow suit.

It was argued that, once these interest groups had switched the focus of their activity to the European level, they would rapidly come to appreciate the benefits available to them as a result of the integration of their sector. Further, they would also come to understand the barriers that prevented these benefits from being fully realized. As the main barrier would be that integration in one sector could not be effective without the integration of other sectors, these interest groups would become advocates of further integration and would lobby their governments to this end. At the same time, they would form a barrier themselves against governments retreating from the level of integration that had already been achieved. This was important because such a retreat would be the one alternative way in which pressures caused by functional spillover could be resolved. In addition, governments would come under pressure from other interest groups who would see the advantages accruing to their counterparts in the integrated sector and realize that they could profit similarly if their sectors of the economy were also integrated. For Haas, the driving force of political integration was the calculated self-interest of political elites:

> The 'good Europeans' are not the main creators of the regional community that is growing up; the process of community formation is dominated by nationally constituted groups with specific interests and aims, willing and able to adjust their aspirations by turning to supranational means when this course appears profitable.

(Haas 1966: xxxiv)

Neofunctionalists looked for spillover pressures to be encouraged and manipulated by the Commission. It was expected both to foster the emergence of EC-wide pressure groups and to cultivate contacts behind the scenes with national interest groups and with bureaucrats in the civil services of the member states, who were another group of potential allies against national governments (Tranholm-Mikkelsen 1991). This was the third type of spillover, which was known as cultivated spillover because it involved the Commission cultivating the contacts and the pressure on governments.

While Haas (1958) mentioned the concept of 'geographical spillover', in particular to draw attention to the external effects of integration on Britain, the main contributions to neofunctionalism paid little attention to enlargement—understandably, given that these were produced before the first enlargement in 1973 (see Chapter 7, The Hague Summit). More recently, Niemann (2006) has argued that neofunctionalism does provide tools for understanding this process: integration leads to some contradictions and demands that cannot be satisfactorily resolved by increasing the intensity or policy scope of integration, but instead requires territorial expansion (see also Niemann and Schmitter 2009: 62).

In the 1950s, neofunctionalist theory neatly fitted events, particularly in explaining the transition from the ECSC to the EC. Events in the 1960s were less supportive. The beginning of the end for neofunctionalist theory in its original manifestation came in the early 1960s and in particular the use of the veto by de Gaulle, leading to the 'empty chair' crisis of 1965–66 (see Chapter 7, The 1965 Crisis). National governments had power and were clearly prepared to use it to determine the nature and pace of integration:

> By 1967 Haas was already attempting to cope with the possibility that De Gaulle had 'killed the Common Market' by revising his theory to account for the prospect of 'disintegration', and by 1975 he was announcing the 'obsolescence of regional integration theory'.
>
> (Caporaso and Keeler 1995: 36–7)

Intergovernmentalism

In response to the neofunctionalist analysis of European integration, a counter-argument was put forward by Stanley Hoffmann (1964, 1966). This argument drew heavily on realist assumptions about the role of states, or, more accurately, the governments of states in IR. Essentially, there were three parts to Hoffmann's criticism of neofunctionalism.

(1) European integration had to be viewed in a global context. Regional integration was only one aspect of the development of the global international system. The neofunctionalists predicted an inexorable progress to further integration— but this was all predicated on an internal dynamic, and implicitly assumed that the international background conditions would remain fixed. This criticism became particularly relevant in the light of changes in the global economic situation in the early 1970s.

(2) National governments were uniquely powerful actors in the process of European integration: they controlled the nature and pace of integration guided by their concern to protect and promote the 'national interest'.

(3) Although, where 'national interests' coincided, governments might accept closer integration in the technical functional sectors, the integration process would not spread to areas of 'high politics' such as national security and defence.

Hoffmann rejected the neofunctionalist view that governments would ultimately be overwhelmed by pressures from elite interest groups to integrate. However, his argument departed from classical realism, in which states were treated as unified rational actors, with little importance attached to domestic politics. Hoffmann's intergovernmentalist position was more sophisticated than that of realists in this respect, and his political awareness was also greater than that of the neofunctionalist writers, who tended to adopt a rather simplified pluralist view of political processes.

Hoffmann claimed the neofunctionalist argument was based on 'false arithmetic' that assumed that the power of each elite group (including national governments) was approximately equal, so that if the governments were outnumbered they would lose.

In addition, he argued that government decisions could not be understood simply as a response to pressure from organized interests, but that, often, political calculations led governments to take positions to which powerful groups were hostile (Hoffmann 1964: 93). These political calculations were driven by domestic concerns, particularly in relation to the impact of integrative decisions on the national economy and on the electoral implications for the governing party.

Hoffmann acknowledged that actors other than national governments played a role in the process of integration. He recognized that in the 'low-politics' sectors (for example, social and regional policy) interest groups did influence the actions of governments—but, as he pointed out, they were not the only influence. Other influences included government officials (particularly on economic matters) and also the electoral considerations of the party or parties in office (Hoffmann 1964: 89). However, he considered national governments to be the ultimate arbiters of key decisions. The governments of states were said to be uniquely powerful for two reasons: first, because they possessed legal sovereignty; and, second, because they had political legitimacy as the only democratically elected actors in the integration process. In this view, where the power of supranational institutions increased, it did so because governments believed it to be in their national interest.

In Hoffmann's picture of the process of European integration, governments had much more autonomy than in the neofunctionalist view. The integration process therefore remained essentially intergovernmental: it would go only as far as the governments were prepared to allow it to go. However, Hoffmann also pointed to the fact that European integration was only one aspect of the development of international politics. That insight led to a more restrictive view of government autonomy. In this respect, Hoffmann, like the realists, stressed the external limitations on autonomy: states were seen as independent actors, but their governments were constrained by the position of the state in the world system.

Liberal Intergovernmentalism

Building on Hoffmann's work, Andrew Moravcsik (1993) developed a subsequent version of the intergovernmental explanation of the integration process. Like Hoffmann, Moravcsik started from a critique of neofunctionalism. He restated the argument that neofunctionalism failed to explain developments in the EC itself, but he put more weight on a theoretical critique. In particular, he argued that the self-criticisms of the neofunctionalists themselves had to be taken seriously. He identified three such self-criticisms (Moravcsik 1993: 478–80), as follows.

(1) Theories of European integration had to be supplemented (or even supplanted) by more general theories of national responses to international interdependence.

(2) The development of common policy responses needed to be looked at as much as did institutional transfers of competence; the emphasis on formal transfers of authority to the EC often concealed a failure to effect a real surrender of sovereignty.

(3) Unicausal theories were inadequate to deal with the phenomenon under consideration; more than one theory was needed to grasp the complexity of EC policy making.

Instead of reviving neofunctionalism, Moravcsik argued that these criticisms should be taken seriously, and a theory constructed that took account of them. He believed that all of the points could be accounted for if the analysis of the EC was rolled into what he called 'current theories of international political economy' (Moravcsik 1993: 480).

Moravcsik's approach, like that of Hoffmann, assumed that states were rational actors, but departed from traditional realism in not treating the state as a **black box**. Instead it was assumed that the governments of states were playing what Putnam (1988) called 'two-level games'. A domestic political process determined their definition of the national interest. This constituted the first part of the analysis and determined the position that governments took with them into the international negotiation.

This approach built on the undeveloped argument of Hoffmann about the role of domestic politics, but in some ways it was less sophisticated in its account of domestic politics than Hoffmann's. Moravcsik's 'liberal' view of domestic politics was that the primary determinant of the preferences of a government was the balance between economic interests within the domestic arena—a narrow conception of domestic political process that has been frequently criticized (for example, see Wincott 1995: 601; Forster 1998: 357–9; Caporaso 1999: 162; Wallace 1999: 156–7).

The second part of the analysis was to see how conflicting national interests were reconciled in the negotiating forum of the Council of Ministers. This process was divided into two logically sequential stages. The first stage was to reach agreement on the common policy response to the problem that governments were trying to solve. The second stage was to reach agreement on the appropriate institutional arrangements. Moravcsik (1998: 21–2) gave the example of monetary union: it would be impractical to try to understand the negotiations over the constitution of a European Central Bank without first understanding the objectives that the bank was being set up to achieve.

The analytical framework of liberal intergovernmentalism was applied by Moravcsik (1998) to five key episodes in the construction of the EU:

- the negotiation of the Treaties of Rome (1955–58);
- the consolidation of the common market and the Common Agricultural Policy (CAP) (1958–83);
- the setting up of the first experiment in monetary co-operation and of the European Monetary System (EMS) (1969–83);
- the negotiation of the Single European Act (SEA) (1984–88);
- the negotiation of the Treaty on European Union (TEU) (1988–91).

On the basis of these case studies, Moravcsik came to the following conclusions:

(1) The major choices in favour of Europe were a reflection of the preferences of national governments, not of the preferences of supranational organizations.

(2) These national preferences reflected the balance of economic interests, rather than the political biases of politicians or national strategic security concerns.

(3) The outcomes of negotiations reflected the relative bargaining power of the states; the delegation of decision-making authority to supranational institutions

reflected the wish of governments to ensure that the commitments of all parties to the agreement would be carried through rather than federalist ideology or a belief in the inherent efficiency of international organizations.

However, he was criticized for his choice of case studies. As Scharpf (1999*a*: 165) put it:

> Since only intergovernmental negotiations are being considered, why shouldn't the preferences of national governments have shaped the outcomes? Since all case studies have issues of economic integration as their focus, why shouldn't economic concerns have shaped the negotiating positions of governments? And since only decisions requiring unanimous agreement are being analysed, why shouldn't the outcomes be affected by the relative bargaining powers of the governments involved?

The alternative would have been to look at the smaller-scale day-to-day decisions that constitute the bulk of the decisions made within the EU. Here, the picture might be very different. Supranational actors might have more influence, and national preferences might be less clearly defined and less vigorously defended. We look at some of these arguments later in the book (Chapters 13, 14, 15). Moravcsik and Schimmelfennig (2009) provided a response to such criticisms, which were said to have 'small kernels' of theoretical truth, but be generally 'overstated'. Thus, while it was accepted that LI 'works best when decision-making is taking place in decentralized settings under a unanimity requirement rather than in settings of delegated or pooled sovereignty under more complex and nuanced decision rules', it was also suggested that 'the theory applies far more broadly than is commonly supposed, including much everyday EU decision-making' (Moravcsik and Schimmelfennig 2009: 74). Further, while Moravcsik and Schimmelfennig (2009) acknowledged that economic issues are not always predominant, they suggested that to read Moravcsik's earlier work as arguing this was to misunderstand it.

Supranational Governance

Starting from the intergovernmentalism versus supranationalism debate, a team of scholars claimed to offer an alternative that cut through the dichotomy (Stone Sweet and Sandholtz 1997; Sandholtz and Stone Sweet 1998; Stone Sweet et al. 2001). Supranational governance was an approach that drew on the transactionalism of Karl Deutsch (Deutsch 1953; Deutsch et al. 1957) and on new institutionalism as applied to the EU (see Chapter 2, New Institutionalism), although the authors themselves located the origins of their approach in neofunctionalism.

Fundamental to the approach was the argument that, if the EU was to be analysed as an international regime, as Moravcsik insisted it could be, then it had to be seen not as a single regime but as a series of regimes for different policy sectors. The authors therefore sought to explain the different levels of supranationalism that existed in different policy sectors. The three key elements in their approach were the development of transnational society, the role of supranational organizations with meaningful autonomous capacity to pursue integrative agendas, and a focus on European rulemaking to resolve what they called 'international policy externalities'. By this last phrase, the authors meant the unintended effects on one country of policies being followed in another country, such as the pollution of the air in one country by smoke from factories in a neighbouring country.

Following Deutsch, Stone Sweet and Sandholtz (1997) argued that transactions across national boundaries were increasing. As they increased, so a supranational society of relevant actors would emerge. These actors would favour the construction of rules to govern their interactions at the supranational level because nationally based rules would be a hindrance to them. If companies that operated across national boundaries were to have to comply with different rules in every member state, this would impose additional costs on their activity. A good example here is merger control (see Insight 1.2).

Another example of what the authors call the emergence of supranational society is provided by the case of the emergence of a supranational telecommunications regime (see Insight 1.3).

Insight 1.2 Supranational Governance 1: The Emergence of Supranational Society—Merger Control

Two companies in the same sector operating across national borders might decide to merge so as to rationalize their operations and reduce their costs. To do so, they might have to get the approval not only of national monopoly and merger authorities in their two states of origin, but also in all of those states where either company or both combined had a significant proportion of the relevant market. To avoid this situation of 'multiple jeopardy', we would expect to see considerable support from large companies for the transfer of merger approval to the supranational level, giving them a one-stop approval procedure to negotiate, and this is what has actually happened (Cini and McGowan 1998).

Insight 1.3 Supranational Governance 2: The Emergence of Supranational Society—Telecommunications

In the 1980s, the sector was dominated by national monopoly suppliers, the nationalized post, telegraph, and telephone companies (PTTs). These national suppliers formed parts of policy communities consisting of the PTTs, the officials in the relevant national ministries, and the suppliers of switching equipment, who were also nationally based and who had a guaranteed market from the PTTs. Sandholtz (1998) showed how the domination of the sector by these national policy communities came to be challenged by a coalition of users of telecommunications who demanded cheaper and more technically advanced services than were provided by the PTTs. These users formed a supranational coalition for change, allying with the Commission and with the British government, which had liberalized its own telecommunications market and wished to extend liberalization to the other national EC markets. Gradually, the pressure from this coalition eroded the hold of the PTTs on the policy preferences of national governments and opened a window of opportunity for the Commission to get proposals through the Council of Ministers for opening up national markets to competition.

The construction of rules at the supranational level would result in the 'Europeanization' of a sector: that is, the regulation of the sector would be at the EU level. Once the initial step is taken in the Europeanization of a policy sector, Stone Sweet and Sandholtz argued that the consolidation of the supranational regime would proceed through the emergence of European rules. Actors working within the new framework of European rules would start to test the limits of those rules. They would seek clarification from the adjudicators—administrators and courts. These clarifications would not only establish the precise meaning of rules, but would also, and at the same time, modify them. The actors would then face a different set of constraints, which would be tighter (and more precise) than the previous constraints, and the actors would adjust their behaviour accordingly. As rules became more precise, so they would tend to develop away from the original intentions of the member states, and would simultaneously become more difficult to modify in any different direction. This pointed to the same process as in the historical institutionalist concept of path dependence (see Chapter 2, The New Institutionalism).

Branch and Øhrgaard (1999) argued that Stone Sweet and Sandholtz had not succeeded in escaping the intergovernmental–supranational dichotomy, but had instead offered a mirror image of Moravcsik's liberal intergovernmentalism. In particular, they argued that both theories privileged certain types of actor, and therefore certain types of decision, and that both theories classified actors as either intergovernmental or supranational in a way that ensured that they would oversimplify the complexity of the nature of the EU. According to Branch and Øhrgaard, Moravcsik gave a privileged role in his theoretical framework to national actors and intergovernmental bargains. He therefore concentrated on episodes, the grand bargains, which were highly likely to demonstrate the value of these concepts. On the other side of the mirror, Stone Sweet and Sandholtz gave a privileged role to transnational business actors and supranational actors, and to the operation of supranational rules of governance. They therefore concentrated on routine decision making in policy sectors that were concerned with economics and trade, which were highly likely to demonstrate the value of these concepts.

Branch and Øhrgaard also argued that both Moravcsik and Stone Sweet and Sandholtz equally made the mistake of treating evidence of influence on policy decisions by supranational actors as necessary and sufficient evidence of supranational integration, and evidence of decisions remaining in the hands of national governments as necessary and sufficient evidence of intergovernmentalism. In contrast, Branch and Øhrgaard argued that not all European integration was driven forward by transnational and supranational actors. In fields such as social policy, the process had been driven by national governments anxious to correct for the effects of the economic integration that *had* been driven by transnational and supranational actors. They further argued that European integration could not simply be equated with the influence of supranational actors. In the field of the Common Foreign and Security Policy (CFSP) (see Chapter 26), although the mechanisms remained intergovernmental and the formal power of the supranational institutions remained limited, academic experts agreed that the process involved much more than just diplomatic consultation. CFSP was a form of European integration that did not involve supranational governance.

A further criticism of Stone Sweet and Sandholtz's approach is that the framework of analysis ignored the wider context within which the process of 'Europeanization' takes place. This criticism points to an omission that is curious given the association of one of the authors, Sandholtz, with a seminal analysis of the emergence of the single market (Sandholtz and Zysman 1989) that put particular stress on the wider context of global capitalism in explaining the emergence of the policy. This study is examined in the single market chapter (Chapter 20, Project 1992: Freeing the Internal Market). In the empirical studies contained in the book that they edited (Sandholtz and Stone Sweet 1998), the influence of the wider capitalist system did not emerge very clearly. For example, Sandholtz (1998) explained the emergence of the supranational European society in the telecommunications sector without referring to the deregulation of US telecommunications, which both put European-based companies who were consumers of telecommunications at a disadvantage in comparison with their US competitors, and led to intense pressure from the US government for the European market to be opened to entry by US telecommunication providers (Dang-Nguyen et al. 1993; Fuchs 1994). This inadequacy in the analysis reflected the inadequacy in the theory.

Recent Contributions

One recent contribution to the integration debate comes from authors closely associated with the concept of multi-level governance, which has strong antecedents in neofunctionalism (see Chapter 2, Multi-Level Governance). Liesbet Hooghe and Gary Marks (2008) emphasized the importance of identity in the process of European integration. They shared with intergovernmentalists and neofunctionalists the view that European integration is triggered by a mismatch between efficiency and existing structures of authority, but differed from them in believing that the outcome of this process would reflect functional pressures. Instead, they suggested that political conflict is a crucial part of the explanation and that communal identities are central to this conflict. Thus, theorizing needs to move beyond the intergovernmentalist–neofunctionalist preoccupation with economic interests. They argued that:

> Functional pressures are one thing, regime outcomes are another. Community and self governance, expressed in public opinion and mobilized by political parties, lie at the heart of jurisdictional design.

(Hooghe and Marks 2008: 23)

Reflecting on the post Maastricht Treaty (TEU) period, another group of scholars has recently highlighted the emergence of what they term 'the new intergovernmentalism' (Bickerton et al. forthcoming). Their central point is that while significant integration has occurred since this treaty in a range of policy areas—including, among others, monetary union, justice and home affairs, and common foreign and security policy (see Chapters 21, 24, and 26)—the tendency has often been not to delegate significant decision-making responsibilities nor regulatory responsibilities in these areas to supranational EU institutions.

In other words, co-operation in certain policy areas has occurred without a clear reduction in national authority or a clear increase in supranational authority, but we might nevertheless regard this as integration. Integration, from this perspective, has meant the institutionalization of intergovernmental exchanges and mutual oversight at the EU level based on 'soft law' or 'new governance modes' such as the 'open method of co-ordination' (see Chapter 18, The EU Policy Process, and Chapter 12). These authors suggest that, while such governance modes have been dealt with extensively in EU literatures, they have tended to be treated as exceptional. However, it is suggested that in fact they have come to constitute an increasingly normal way of pushing EU-level involvement in particular policy areas.

The notion that integration can be rooted in this 'new intergovernmentalism' is at odds with preceding theories such as neofunctionalism, intergovernmentalism, or liberal intergovernmentalism, which, notwithstanding their differing explanations for the process, all conceive of integration in terms of a gradual shift of authority from member states to supranational EU institutions, usually via the adoption of the so-called 'Union Method' of decision making (see Chapter 12, The Decision-Making Institutions). Although these arguments are relatively new in the literature, they point to the importance of considering integration in different ways in relation to the contemporary EU. While the emphasis here is on the emergence of intergovernmental forms of co-operation, there is some resonance with the injunction of some of the 'supranational governance' scholars to consider different kinds of integration in relation to different policy areas (see also Chapter 18).

One obvious critique of this approach would be that any integration that is dependent upon an intergovernmental form of governance is destined to be limited or ineffective. However, such a critique is likely to be more or less pertinent depending on the particular policy area that is considered.

CONCLUSION

Essentially the same 'intergovernmental–supranational debate' about the process of European integration has been going on since the very early stages of the process. Central to this continuing debate is a disagreement over the central drivers of the integration process. In intergovernmental perspectives, European integration is a process whereby national governments are the central actors: they voluntarily enter into agreements to work together to solve common problems. The alternative supranational perspective—associated with neofunctionalism and supranational governance approaches—suggests that, although governments started the process, integration soon took on a life of its own that went beyond the control of the governments. This intergovernmental–supranational debate forms the first of the themes that recur throughout this book. Although, as highlighted in this chapter, these theories are primarily explanatory, they have not been neutral in their effect (some scholars would argue that no theory can be—see Chapter 4). In the 1950s and 1960s, neofunctionalist ideas were eagerly embraced by members of the Commission as a blueprint for constructing a united Europe. Today, opponents of further integration implicitly invoke the neofunctionalist idea that the process is no longer under control and threatens national identity. Conversely, intergovernmentalist arguments are more likely to be voiced by the advocates of further steps, who echo Hoffmann and Moravcsik in reassuring hesitant European public opinion that the governments of states remain in charge: that sovereignty is only 'pooled', not lost.

While, as will be discussed in subsequent chapters, theorizing about the EU has in many ways moved beyond the intergovernmental–supranational dichotomy, a number of themes that are central to this debate—state power, the role of organized interests, and the influence of supranational institutions—continue to resonate in much research.

KEY POINTS

European Integration and the First Attempts to Theorize It

- European integration involved national economies being managed in common.
- This partial surrender of sovereignty by the participating states led to a reassessment of existing theories of IR.

The Intellectual Background

- Functionalism and federalism are two important precursors to European integration theory. Both addressed the problem of how to overcome war between nations.
- A key proponent of functionalism, David Mitrany sought to prevent war between states by taking routine functional tasks out of the hands of national governments and giving them over to international agencies.
- Mitrany argued that world government would limit freedom, and that regional federations would reproduce on a larger scale the conditions that produced wars between states.
- European federalism attracted strong support among Resistance groups in war-time Europe. The leading intellectual figure was Altiero Spinelli, who advocated a 'constitutional break' at the end of the war to supersede the system of sovereign states with a federal constitution for Europe.
- By the time the Congress aimed at adopting this new constitution had been arranged, national political elites were re-established in European states. While the (Hague) Congress did produce the Council of Europe, this was an intergovernmental body that fell far short of federalist aspirations.
- The Schuman Plan for the ECSC was devised by Jean Monnet, the head of the French Economic Planning Commission, who believed the European nation state was inadequate as an economic unit in the modern world and argued for a Europe-wide economy.
- The pooling of coal and steel resources was the first step towards a Europe-wide economic zone. It also removed strategic industries from German control and ensured adequate supplies of coal for the French steel industry: both were concerns for Monnet.

International Relations Theories of European Integration

- IR theory in the 1950s was dominated by realism. This theory treated nation states as the fundamental units of IR. It did not lead to any expectation that governments would voluntarily surrender their sovereign control over policy. As such, the first European integration theorists posed a direct challenge to realist assumptions.
- *Neofunctionalism* suggested that European integration was a process that, once started, would undermine the sovereignty of states beyond the expectations of governments.
- Neofunctionalism argued that states are not unified actors, but that national interests are determined through a pluralistic process in which governments interact with organized interests. Organized interests were also seen to be important transnational actors.
- The concept of spillover was central to the neofunctionalist theory. Functional spillover, political spillover, and cultivated spillover would lead the process of European integration to run out of the control of national governments. The concept of 'exogenous spillover' was added later to theorize enlargement.
- Hoffmann's *intergovernmentalism* argued that neofunctionalists had made three mistakes: regional integration was not a self-contained process, but was influenced by a wider

international context; governments were uniquely powerful actors because they possessed formal sovereignty and democratic legitimacy; and integration in low-politics sectors would not necessarily spill over into high-politics sectors.

- Moravcsik's *liberal intergovernmentalism* incorporated the neofunctionalist insight that national interests are defined as part of a domestic pluralist political process; within this domestic process, economic interests were seen to be dominant.

- Moravcsik proposed a two-level analysis of EU bargaining, in which governments' preferences were determined at the domestic level and were then used as the basis for intergovernmental negotiations at the European level.

- Moravcsik denied the importance of supranational actors as independent actors in EU decision making and insisted that governments remained in control of the process of European integration.

- The approach of *supranational governance* was located in neofunctionalism, but also drew on transactionalism and new institutionalism. Stone Sweet and Sandholtz argued that the EU should be studied not as one international regime, but as a series of regimes for different policy sectors, and that increased transactions across national boundaries would create a supranational society that favoured the creation of supranational rules to govern its behaviour.

- Branch and Øhrgaard argued that this approach did not escape the intergovernmental–supranational dichotomy. Rather, it privileged certain types of actor and also classified actors as either intergovernmental or supranational in a way that oversimplified the complexity of the EU. The approach was further criticized for not placing the analysis in a global context.

- Hooghe and Marks emphasized the importance of identity in the process of European integration and the need to go beyond the preoccupation with economic interests and functional pressures that has characterized much of the intergovernmental–supranational debate.

- Bickerton et al. argued that mainstream integration theories may need to reconsider how integration is conceptualized in light of what they term *a new intergovernmentalism* that has emerged in EU politics since the early 1990s.

FURTHER READING

The key texts on the early development of neofunctionalist theory are: **E. B. Haas**, *The Uniting of Europe: Political, Social and Economic Forces 1950–57* (London: Library of World Affairs, 1958); **E. B. Haas**, *The Uniting of Europe: Political, Social and Economic Forces, 1950–1957*, 2nd edn (Stanford, CA: Stanford University Press, 1968); and **L. Lindberg**, *The Political Dynamics of European Economic Integration* (Stanford, CA: Stanford University Press; London: Oxford University Press, 1963). On intergovernmentalism, the main early contributions are: **S. Hoffmann**, 'The European Process at Atlantic Crosspurposes', *Journal of Common Market Studies*, 3 (1964): 85–101; and **S. Hoffmann**, 'Obstinate or Obsolete? The Fate of the Nation State and the Case of Western Europe', *Daedalus*, 95 (1966): 862–915.

Neofunctionalism is elaborated, expanded, and defended in **J. Tranholm-Mikkelsen**, 'Neofunctionalism: Obstinate or Obsolete? A Reappraisal in the Light of the New Dynamism of the European Community', *Millennium*, 20 (1991): 1–22; a further development of neofunctionalism can be found in **A. Niemann**, *Explaining Decisions in the European Union* (Cambridge: Cambridge University Press, 2006). A review of the criticisms applied to neofunctionalism and subsequent revisions can be found in **A. Niemann and P. Schmitter**, 'Neofunctionalism', in

A. Wiener and T. Diez (eds), *European Integration Theory*, 2nd edn (Oxford: Oxford University Press, 2009). 45–66.

The earliest statement of liberal intergovernmentalism is in **A. Moravcsik**, 'Preferences and Power in the European Community: A Liberal Intergovernmentalist Approach', *Journal of Common Market Studies*, 31 (1993): 473–524. A later statement of the theory, which differs subtly, is given in **A. Moravcsik**, *The Choice for Europe: Social Purpose and State Power from Messina to Maastricht* (London: UCL Press, 1998). Of interest most recently is **A. Moravcsik and F. Schimmelfennig**, 'Liberal Intergovernmentalism', in **A. Wiener and T. Diez (eds)**, *European Integration Theory*, 2nd edn (Oxford: Oxford University Press, 2009), 67–87, which includes a response to criticisms of Moravcsik's earlier work.

Supranational governance is outlined in **A. Stone Sweet and W. Sandholtz**, 'European Integration and Supranational Governance', *Journal of European Public Policy*, 4 (1997): 297–317. It is developed in **W. Sandholtz and A. Stone Sweet (eds)**, *European Integration and Supranational Governance* (Oxford: Oxford University Press, 1998), and contested in **A. P. Branch and J. C. Øhrgaard**, 'Trapped in the Supranational-Intergovernmental Dichotomy: A Response to Stone Sweet and Sandholtz', *Journal of European Public Policy*, 6 (1999): 123–43.

The postfunctionalist theory of integration is set out in **L. Hooghe and G. Marks**, 'A Postfunctionalist Theory of European Integration: From Permissive Consensus to Constraining Dissensus', *British Journal of Political Science*, 39 (2008): 1–23. On the concept of 'new intergovernmentalism' see **C. Bickerton, D. Hodson, and U. Puetter (eds)** *European Politics in the Post Maastricht Period: States, Supranational Actors and the New Intergovernmentalism* (forthcoming).

 online resource centre **Visit the Online Resource Centre that accompanies this book for links to more information on theories of European integration: http://oxfordtextbooks.co.uk/orc/bache4e/**

Chapter 2

Theories of EU Governance

Chapter Overview

As European integration progressed, the academic focus began to shift from explaining the integration process to understanding the European Union (EU) as a political system (see Table I.1). As such, EU scholars increasingly drew on approaches from the study of domestic and comparative politics. While some attempts to escape the supranational–intergovernmental dichotomy have proved more successful than others, these contributions broadened the study of the EU considerably beyond the traditional international relations (IR) debate and many scholars have spoken of a 'governance turn' in EU studies in the 1990s. This chapter surveys a number of approaches that focus on the EU as a political system. These approaches fall within the broad categories of 'new institutionalism' and 'governance and networks'. While they diverge in some important ways, there is also considerable overlap between the approaches.

A Shift of Focus

The theoretical stand-off between intergovernmental and supranational interpretations remains significant in the study of the EU. However, alongside this debate other voices have emerged that move beyond the supranational–intergovernmental dichotomy. Approaches from the study of domestic and comparative politics turn away from the focus of IR theories on the process of European integration, and instead treat the EU as a political system that is already in existence, and try to explain 'the nature of the beast'.

A shift away from the exclusive use of IR paradigms to concerns with institutional and policy analysis first appeared with Lindberg and Scheingold's book *Europe's Would-Be Polity* in 1970 (Bulmer 2009). It gathered pace with the acceleration of integration in the 1980s through the single market programme (see Chapter 20), and culminated in Simon Hix's (1994) call to scholars within the discipline of comparative politics to wake up to the existence of the EU as a suitable subject for study using their established concepts. Instead of asking questions such as how far the EU was dominated by the member states and how far it operated as an autonomous entity, Hix (1999: 1) asked questions that derived from the study of comparative politics:

> How is governmental power exercised? Under what conditions can the Parliament influence legislation? Is the Court of Justice beyond political control? Why do some citizens support the central institutions while others oppose them? How important are political parties and elections in shaping political choices? Why are some social groups able to influence the political agenda more than others?

The approach succeeded in shifting the focus away from the study of European integration as a process to '*how the EU works today*' (Hix 1999: 1; emphasis in original).

An increasing number of concepts are applied to the EU that originated from the study of comparative and domestic politics. Here, we look at two influential sets of approaches that come under the headings of 'new institutionalism' and 'governance and networks'. While we identify these as separate approaches, and there are variants within each approach, there is also a significant overlap between the two categories, and a close relationship between these approaches and other concepts increasingly applied to the study of the EU.

New Institutionalism

One adaptation of an approach that was originally applied to the study of domestic and comparative politics that found favour among EU scholars was new institutionalism (March and Olsen 1984, 1989, 1996). This was a reaction to the behavioural approaches that had come to dominate political science in the 1960s and 1970s. Behaviouralism had been a reaction against formal institutional analyses of government and politics that had lost sight of the real political processes that lay behind the formal structures of government—in particular, the influence of societal groups. New institutionalism argued that the reaction against the old, formal institutional analyses had gone too far: that the importance of institutions in structuring political action had been lost.

Bulmer (1993) set down a marker in arguing that institutions matter in the EU context, identifying the different institutions and instruments of EU governance. This article further argued that the profile of instruments and institutions differed within discrete 'governance regimes' situated within an overarching EU structure that had pronounced regulatory characteristics.

From the mid-1990s, new institutionalism became more prevalent in the literature on EU governance. It not only argued that institutions matter in understanding EU politics and policy making, but also sought to explain how they matter. Moreover, one thing that was new about this reassertion of institutionalism was that institutions were not only defined as the formal organizations that the old institutionalism had recognized—such as parliaments, executives, and judicial courts—but also extended to categorize informal patterns of structured interaction between groups as institutions themselves. These structured interactions were institutions in the sense that they constrained or shaped group behaviour.

At the same time, new institutionalism argued that formal institutions were more important than behaviouralists had suggested. Behaviouralists treated formal institutions as neutral arenas within which the struggle for influence between the different societal actors was carried out. New institutionalists disagreed with this perspective in two ways. First, they argued that formal institutions were not neutral arenas, since formal institutional structures and rules biased access to the political process in favour of some societal groups over others. Second, they argued that institutions could be autonomous political actors in their own right.

While, collectively, this reassertion of institutionalist perspectives is known as new institutionalism, it is now common to distinguish between three varieties: rational choice institutionalism; historical institutionalism; and sociological institutionalism (Hall and Taylor 1996). These approaches emerged at around the same time, but in relative isolation from each other.

Rational Choice Institutionalism

Rational choice institutionalism focuses on the constraints that formal institutional structures impose on actors. It suggests that, in trying to understand the behaviour of political actors, it is important to identify the parameters that are set by the fact that they are acting within a specific framework of rules. So, for example, the activities of interest groups reflect the procedures that prevail for the passage of the legislation that affects them, the access points that are available to them in that process, and the previous relationships that they have established with key decision makers. Thus, in the case of the EU, whether interest groups choose to try to influence legislation through national governments or through the Commission and the European Parliament (EP) would reflect:

- the relative openness to those groups of the national government actors compared with the supranational actors;
- the extent to which the process is intergovernmental (for example, what decision rules applied within the Council of Ministers);
- what role the EP has in the final decision.

If national decision making were dominated by other interest groups, then 'outsider' groups trying to influence EU policy might turn to the **supranational institutions** because they would be more likely to get their voices heard there. In competition policy decisions, for example, national monopoly suppliers that have a close working relationship with national government officials would tend to work through national channels. In contrast, potential competitors, who want to see the dismantling of the advantages that the national monopoly suppliers enjoyed at the national level would be more likely to turn to the Commission because it would be difficult for them to obtain access to the national decision makers and easier for them to obtain access to the supranational institutions.

Were unanimity to apply in the Council of Ministers, it would be more important to lobby at the national level because one vote against a proposal could block it; were **qualified majority voting (QMV)** to apply, the potential influence of the Commission would be greater, making it a more attractive target for lobbying. In areas in which the powers of the EP were extended under the Single European Act (SEA), the Treaty on European Union (TEU), and the Treaty of Amsterdam (see Chapter 15), interest groups began to lobby the EP more extensively than they had previously, and to do so more than did interest groups in policy sectors in which the powers of the EP remained restricted to the consultation procedure.

Rational choice institutionalists have also made a significant contribution to understanding the ways in which supranational actors might obtain a degree of autonomy from national governments, allowing them to make their own input to the policy process (Pollack 1997). Applying what is known as **principal–agent theory**, rational choice institutionalists have highlighted the difficulties of principals (the national governments) in keeping control over the activities of their agents (the supranational institutions).

- As the range of delegated tasks has increased, so the difficulties of monitoring what the agents were doing has increased.
- As the number of principals increases with successive enlargements of membership, so the agents may play off the preferences of different coalitions of principals against the attempts of other principals to restrain them.
- As QMV has expanded, so the constraints on the Commission in constructing a winning coalition in support of its proposals have been reduced.

Mark Pollack (2003) applied rational choice theory to test hypotheses about the delegation of power by the member states to the EU's supranational organizations (mainly the Commission, the Court of Justice, and the Parliament) and the efforts of these organizations to shape the process of European integration. Pollack's first concern was with the types of function that governments delegate to supranational organizations and the conditions under which greater or less discretion is allocated to these agents. Here, principal–agent theory suggested that governments would delegate to supranational agents to reduce the transaction costs of EU policy making. The evidence suggested that this was the case with the Commission and Court of Justice, but delegation to the EP was motivated more by governments' attempts to reduce the EU's democratic deficit (see Chapter 3, Democracy) and was thus more effectively explained in terms of the logic of appropriate behaviour identified by sociological institutionalists (below), rather than by rational choice explanations.

The principal–agent debate extends beyond a concern with how national governments maintain control over supranational institutions to a concern with how formal institutions of government maintain control over regulatory agencies that are a key component of modern governance in the EU and beyond (see Insight 2.1). The

---

Insight 2.1 The EU as a Regulatory System

The idea of the EU as a regulatory system is most closely associated with the work of Giandomenico Majone (1996). Rather than a single analytical approach, it offers a terrain of study focusing on the EU's increased use of regulatory instruments to secure policy objectives. This focus accompanied the changing character of the EU from the late 1980s, with the extensive regulatory activity aimed at completing the single market, and it continues to be important for a polity with limited budgetary policy instruments (see also Chapter 20, Evaluating the Single Market).

proliferation of agencies in the EU context has been important to the development of governance approaches to understanding the EU (see this chapter, Governance and Networks) and has also raised important issues relating to the accountability of EU decision making (see Chapter 3, Democracy).

Historical Institutionalism

Historical institutionalists place emphasis on the argument that political relationships have to be viewed over time. Their approach argues that decisions are not made according to an abstract rationality, but according to perceptions and within constraints that are structured by pre-existing institutional relationships. While rational choice institutionalism focuses its analysis primarily on formal institutions, historical institutionalism takes a broader definition of institutions to incorporate also informal constraints on behaviour such as values and behavioural norms.

> **They can range from the rules of a constitutional order or the standard operating procedures of a bureaucracy to the conventions governing trade union behaviour or bank-firm relations. In general, historical institutionalists associate institutions with organizations and the rules or conventions promulgated by formal organization.**

(Hall and Taylor 1996: 938)

Central to historical institutionalism is the concept of 'path dependence'. This is the argument that once one decision is made, it tends to make it more likely that policy continues to develop in the same direction. Or, as Hall and Taylor (1996: 941) put it, 'forces will be mediated by the contextual features of a given situation often inherited from the past'. In extreme cases, path dependence can turn into 'lock-in' (Pierson 1996), whereby other avenues of policy are entirely blocked off by the bias towards the existing route that is built into the system. This could be one explanation of why policies such as the Common Agricultural Policy (CAP) proved so resistant to reform even after their negative effects had become obvious (see Chapter 19).

Applying historical institutionalism to the EU led to a further critique of intergovernmental analyses, and revealed further reasons for thinking that national governments might not be entirely in control of the process of integration. Intergovernmental analyses tended to focus on the historic decisions, represented mainly by revisions to the Treaties (see Chapter 1, International Relations Theories of European Integration). Intergovernmentalists treated what happened between these historic decisions as simply the working through of the decisions. Historical institutionalists argued that, after the decision had been taken, it would be likely to produce unanticipated and unintended outcomes. This might be because of a simple failure to think through the implications—but it might be for one or both of two other reasons (Pierson 1998: 41).

First, the preferences of governments might change over time. For example, the preference for a CAP based on price support might have been a rational response to conditions in the 1960s in Europe, when security of food supplies was a paramount concern, but no longer appropriate in the changed circumstances of the 1990s, when technological advances had removed this concern. Also, national governments might change. For example, the EC directives on social policy to which a British Labour government had agreed in the 1970s were not to the liking of the Conservative governments between 1979 and 1997. However, even where preferences change, governments would find it extremely difficult to change decisions: policy sectors became institutionalized and various incentives emerged for maintaining the status quo.

A second reason why governments find it difficult to change decisions is because the voting rules in the Council of Ministers make it difficult to get agreement to move back from a policy once it has been agreed. Where the rule is unanimity, it is impossible to retreat so long as one member state benefits from the status quo and refuses to move from it. This is sometimes referred to as 'the ratchet effect'. Even where QMV applies, in order to effect change, it is necessary to construct a coalition representing more than a simple majority of states (the exact number depending on the weighting of the votes of the members of the coalition, and therefore on the identity of the states involved: see Chapter 14, The Council of Ministers).

Sociological Institutionalism

The emergence of sociological institutionalism is closely linked with the 'constructivist turn' in the study of the EU and international politics, which is dealt with in Chapter 4. Like constructivism, sociological institutionalism takes as its starting point a rejection of the rationalist approach to the study of politics that characterizes rational choice institutionalism and some contributions to historical institutionalism, and places more emphasis on broadly 'cultural' practices (see Chapter 4 for more on this debate).

Hall and Taylor (1996: 947) identified three features of sociological institutionalism that distinguished it from the other new institutionalisms. First, the definition of what constitutes 'institutions' is considerably broader than in the other approaches, so that it includes not only formal rules, but also 'symbol systems, cognitive scripts, and moral templates that provide the "frames of meaning" guiding human action'. This definition blurred the lines traditionally separating the notions of 'institutions' and 'culture'.

Second, sociological institutionalism takes a distinct position on the relationship between institutions and individual action that flows from the 'cultural' approach. In particular, it suggests that institutions do not simply influence the 'strategic calculation' of actors, but have a deeper effect on their preferences and very identity. As Hall and Taylor (1996: 948) put it:

> **The self images and identities of social actors are said to be constituted from the institutional forms, images and signs provided by social life.**

This does not mean that actors are not 'rational' in the pursuit of the goals and objectives; rather, it means that these goals and objectives are constituted differently (that is, socially) and are more broadly defined than rationalist theory would suggest.

Finally, sociological institutionalism contrasts with rationalist explanations on how institutions are formed and developed. For rational choice institutionalists, institutions are developed by rational actors to meet particular ends efficiently, such as reducing transaction costs. For sociological institutionalists, institutions are often created and developed because they contribute to social legitimacy rather than efficiency. In some cases, this may mean that the formal goals of an organization are overridden by these broader social goals. Here, a distinction is made between the rationalist 'logic of instrumentality' with the sociological 'logic of appropriateness'. Thus, in the case of delegation to supranational institutions discussed above, it may not be in the instrumental interests of national governments to enhance the EP's powers, but the need to enhance the democratic legitimacy of the EU provides a powerful logic of appropriateness.

Rosamond (2003) suggested that the application of sociological institutionalism may be particularly useful in understanding why the Commission's Directorates-General operate in very distinct ways. It may also provide insights into whether 'formally inter-governmental processes … conform to established patterns of interstate interaction, or whether they bring about new norms of exchange between the envoys of member states' (Rosamond 2003: 117). As with historical institutionalism, this variant of new institutionalism is making an important contribution to explaining the domestic media-tion of Europeanization (see Chapter 3, Europeanizaton and the New Institutionalisms).

New Institutionalism Assessed

Put concisely, new institutionalism in its three variants reveals that, respectively, rules matter to rational action (rational choice institutionalism), time matters to policy and institutional evolution (historical institutionalism), and social context matters to polit-ical behaviour within institutions (sociological institutionalism).

For Hall and Taylor (1996: 95), none of the new institutionalisms is particularly 'wrong-headed' or 'substantially untrue'; rather, 'each seems to be providing a partial account of the forces at work in a given situation or capturing different dimensions of the human action and institutional impact present there'. The three approaches rest on different assumptions about the world that led them to focus on different questions. This is illustrated in relation to EU enlargement (see Chapter 27, Explaining Enlargement), where sociological institutionalists have placed more emphasis on why the EU decided to enlarge and how we can account for the subsequent negotiations, while rational choice institutionalists have devoted greater attention to the impact of enlargement on the EU's institutional arrangements and historical institutionalists on the process of reform in central and eastern Europe (Pollack 2004: 151).

The various strands of new institutionalism are increasingly being refined, through both empirical research and through engagement with the other strands and with other conceptual approaches to the EU. In particular, new institutionalism has made a significant contribution to the burgeoning literature on Europeanization (see Chapter 3) by providing sensitivity to how domestic institutions (formal and informal) mediate EU pressures. The new institutionalisms link closely to research on constructivism (see Chapter 4) and to governance and network approaches, to which we now turn.

Governance and Networks

While we distinguish between 'governance' and 'network' approaches here to reflect labels assigned by particular scholars, these two concepts are very closely linked.

Definitions of governance abound (for different perspectives, see Pierre 2000). Jachtenfuchs and Kohler-Koch (2004: 99) provide a broad definition of governance as 'the continuous political process of setting explicit goals for society and intervening in it in order to achieve these goals', and suggest that 'networking is the most characteristic feature of EU governance' (2004: 100). Common to more specific definitions of governance is the view that public policy making is increasingly characterized by wide participation of public, private, and voluntary sector actors. In the context of the EU, the multi-level governance framework (see Multi-Level Governance section, this chapter) brings together this increased 'horizontal' mix of actors from different sectors with increased 'vertical' interactions between actors organized at different territorial levels (supranational, national, and sub-national).

Policy Networks and Epistemic Communities

Richardson (1996) took up Hix's call to approach the EU from different disciplinary directions, but instead of organizing the study around the concepts of comparative politics, he advocated organizing it around the concepts that he and others had been using for some time to study the policy-making process within member states. He argued in particular for the application of two concepts: policy networks and epistemic communities. The first of these concepts was originally developed in studies of public policy making in the United States and later became prominent in Britain, particularly through the work of Rhodes (1981, 1988). Ironically, the second concept originally arose from the study of IR and then fed back into domestic policy analysis before being applied to the EU. Both concepts are mid-range or 'meso-level', aimed at explanations of particular policy sectors or issues rather than the characteristics of the political system as a whole (the 'macro level').

According to the 'Rhodes model', a policy network is a set of resource-dependent organizations, meaning that each of the groups that makes up the policy network needs something that the others have in order to fulfil its own objectives (Rhodes 1988). The types of resource that organizations bring to a policy network to exchange in the process of bargaining include constitutional-legal, organizational, financial, political, and informational resources. These 'resource dependencies'—the extent to which organizations depend on each other for resources—are the key variable in shaping policy outcomes. As Peterson and Bomberg (1993: 28) put it: 'They set the "chessboard" where private and public interests manoeuvre for advantage.' However, interdependence between network participants is 'almost always asymmetrical' and in some cases it is possible to talk of 'unilateral leadership' within networks (Rhodes 1986: 5).

The policy-networks approach does not constitute a predictive theory of policy making, but is seen to contribute to explaining policy outputs. For Peterson and Bomberg (1993: 31):

> Policy networks are essentially descriptive theoretical tools which simply help order facts and evidence in novel ways. However, policy networks can be used to anticipate and explain policy outputs by providing insights into how and why decisions were taken which produced them.

One way in which the approach contributes to anticipating and explaining outputs is by outlining the importance of different structural characteristics of different types of network. Rhodes (1988) distinguished between different types of network, ranging from highly integrated policy communities to loosely integrated issue networks (see Insight 2.2). These different 'structural characteristics' of networks have different effects on both the internal dynamics of the networks and on the ability of networks to resist external pressures for change. However, policy outputs are generally not just a

> ### Insight 2.2 Policy Communities and Issue Networks
>
> A *policy community* is marked by:
>
> - limited membership;
> - stable membership over long periods of time;
> - a high level of interaction between the members;
> - shared values between members;
> - some degree of equality in the distribution of resources;
> - a relative balance of power and influence between members.
>
> An *issue network*, in contrast, is marked by:
>
> - large and diffuse membership;
> - frequent shifts in the membership;
> - fluctuating frequency of contact between members;
> - lack of shared values;
> - marked inequality in the distribution of resources;
> - marked inequality in power and influence within the network.

function of internal network characteristics, but are shaped also by changes in the broader political and economic environment (Rhodes et al. 1996). As such, the approach is often at its strongest when used in conjunction with a macro-level theory of politics or policy making that seeks to explain the broader political context within which the network is situated.

A particular strength of the policy-networks approach is its emphasis on policy implementation as an important phase in policy making: a phase in which policy 'is actually made in the course of negotiations between the (ostensible) implementers' (Rhodes 1986: 14). This aspect of the approach is particularly important in the context of the EU, in which the Commission is heavily dependent upon domestic actors for effective policy implementation.

Policy Networks and the Study of the EU

The applicability of the policy-networks framework to the analysis of the EU was questioned by Kassim (1994). He argued that EU processes were not settled enough to allow policy networks to emerge. Interest groups used different channels to influence decisions: sometimes national; sometimes at EU level. The multinational character and institutional complexity of the EU made it difficult to delimit policy networks, and particularly to identify the relevant public sector actor. Sometimes national agencies would be key; sometimes the Commission; sometimes other EU level institutions. The institutions themselves often acted as lobbyists in the EU in pursuit of their own objectives.

One of the scholars who had advocated the use of policy networks replied to Kassim (Peterson 1995*a*). He questioned Kassim's insistence on the fluidity of EU policy-making procedures, arguing that while some sectors remained fluid, others were settling into more stable patterns. Indeed, he argued that the Commission was so under-resourced that it had to try to enter into stable relationships with partners that it could trust, which had information that it could use. While he accepted Kassim's points about the complexity of the role of institutions in the EU in comparison with national institutional arrangements, he argued that the policy-networks approach was perfectly compatible with new-institutionalist analyses of the EU, which allowed theorization of the working of institutional relations. While he accepted that the delineation of policy networks at the EU level was a difficult task, Peterson insisted that this did not make it a less important one.

Peterson's most interesting observation, though, was the need to be clear about the level of the policy-making process that was being analysed. He argued that the policy-networks model was best able to explain what he called 'the policy-shaping decisions', when proposals were being formulated and before a political decision was taken that 'set' the policy (Peterson 1995a: 400). In a subsequent article, the same author expanded on this argument (Peterson 1995b). He here identified three 'levels' of analysis in EU decision making. The highest level he termed the 'super-systemic' or 'history-making' decisions. These were mainly decisions taken by national governments in the European Council or at intergovernmental conferences (IGCs), and were most fruitfully analysed using intergovernmental ideas. The second level he termed the 'systemic' or 'policy-setting' stage. At this level, a combination of intergovernmental and inter-institutional analysis was needed to understand outcomes. The third level he called the 'sub-systemic' or 'policy-shaping' stage. At this level, policy networks were a useful concept for understanding how policy options were formulated in bargaining between the Commission Directorates-General, national civil servants, and private actors (see Table 2.1).

Subsequently, Peterson (2009: 109) put his case more strongly, suggesting that 'policy network analysis is never more powerful an analytical tool than when it is deployed at the EU level'. He set out a three-pronged argument for the applicability of the policy-networks approach to the study of the EU: first, that there is considerable variation in how different EU policy sectors operate; second, that much of the EU's policy

Table 2.1 Levels of Analysis in EU Decision Making

Level	Type of decision	Dominant actors	Rationality
Super-systemic	History-making	European Council, national governments in IGCs, Court of Justice	Political, legalistic
Systemic	Policy-setting	Council of Ministers, Committee of Permanent Representatives (COREPER)	Political, technocratic, administrative
Sub-systemic/ meso-level	Policy-shaping	Commission, committees, Council groups	Technocratic, consensual, administrative

Source: Reproduced from *Journal of European Public Policy*, 2 (1995): 71. Reprinted with the permission of the Taylor & Francis Group.

making is highly technical; and, third, that EU policy making is 'underpinned by an extraordinarily complex labyrinth of committees that shape policy options before policies are "set" by overtly political decision makers such as the college of Commissioners, Council of Ministers, or European Parliament' (Peterson 2009: 118).

Jachtenfuchs (2001: 254) made a complementary case for the advantages of network analysis:

> It appears that, on the whole, the fragmented and fluid institutional structure of the EU and the lack of a strong power centre lead to an increase of channels of access and a larger variation of participants in the policy-making process as compared to governance systems in territorial states.

Network Governance

Parallel to the Anglo-American policy-networks literature, exemplified by the work of Rhodes, is a related strand of conceptual and empirical literature on network governance that is most strongly associated with German scholars—especially Beate Kohler-Koch and her associates (see Kohler-Koch 1996; Kohler-Koch and Eising 1999). The key difference is that, while the British approach is primarily an analytical model seeking to understand state–society relations in a given policy area, the German approach treats networks as an alternative form of governance to states and hierarchies (Börzel 1998). The network governance material tends to be more normative than does the Rhodes model of policy networks, and views networks as a potential solution to the co-ordination challenges posed by the increased complexity of public policy making—different actors can be mobilized, and bring different resources to the table in seeking to meet these challenges. Here, the links with multi-level governance are very clear, and officials in the EU and beyond have embraced these notions of network and multi-level governance. Indeed, in 2009, the EU's Committee of the Regions (Chapter 12, The Decision-Making Institutions (the Union Method)) launched a White Paper on multi-level governance (Committee of the Regions 2009).

However, while network governance is seen as a potential solution to co-ordination challenges in the EU, it has both strengths and weaknesses. For example, in the field of environmental policy, Jordan and Schout concluded that networked forms of governance 'while in vogue, are by no means a panacea' (Jordan and Schout 2006: 274). While network governance connects the relevant actors, who can bring different skills and resources to a specific policy challenge, it can also mean that responsibility for policy co-ordination becomes dispersed and no one takes overall responsibility.

Epistemic Communities

Whereas policy networks are held together by resource interdependence, epistemic communities are knowledge-based groups. An epistemic community was defined by Peter Haas (1992: 3) as:

> a network of professionals with recognised expertise and competence in a particular domain and an authoritative claim to policy-relevant knowledge within that domain or issue-area.

The members of an epistemic community share both normative beliefs and causal beliefs: that is, they hold a common set of values about what is right and desirable, and a common set of assumptions about how to achieve those goals. They also agree on notions of validity, so they have a common basis for settling differences of opinion between themselves, and they share a common policy enterprise, so that they are all involved in efforts to solve the same problems.

Epistemic communities are likely to exercise particular influence over policy when policy makers face conditions of uncertainty about the likely consequences of policy choice. Such uncertainty is thought to be particularly high where international co-ordination of policy is concerned. Success in such situations is heavily dependent on the actions of other states. There is also a high degree of uncertainty about the possible unforeseen consequences. In these circumstances, state actors are highly likely to turn to epistemic communities because they are not sure how to define the national interest.

Members of transnational epistemic communities can influence state interests either by directly identifying them for decision makers or by illuminating the salient dimensions of an issue from which the decision makers may then deduce their interests. The decision makers in one state may, in turn, influence the interests and behavior of other states, thereby increasing the likelihood of convergent state behavior and international policy co-ordination, informed by the causal beliefs and policy preferences of the epistemic community.

(Haas 1992: 4)

Haas's perspective suggested that epistemic communities are useful as a means of helping governments to think their way through situations of uncertainty, and to provide a common framework of analysis that could act as a guarantee that states that try to co-ordinate policy will all work along the same lines. However, going beyond Haas's arguments, epistemic communities might also be used by supranational actors such as the European Commission as a means of furthering the Europeanization of policy. The expert analysis that they provide, and the policy prescriptions that they advocate, if they point in the desired direction, could form a powerful lever for supranational actors to move states in the direction of common European solutions to problems that confronted them.

While developed separately from the Rhodes model of policy networks, the notion of epistemic communities is a compatible approach that provides a way of understanding how professionals can come to dominate policy making. Sabatier's advocacy coalition framework, which offers an explanation for how policy change is brought about by coalitions within networks bound together by a shared belief system, has similar potential (Sabatier 1988, 1998). Moreover, Peterson (2004: 121) suggested that alliances of epistemic communities and advocacy coalitions may form to influence policy making and provides the example of the EU's 'quite radical liberalization of its agricultural sector during the Uruguay Round which gave birth to the WTO in the early 1990s'. Such contributions also inform approaches that theorize how issues rise up the EU's agenda.

Agenda-setting

The agenda-setting literature asks two main questions: where do issues on the political agenda come from and under what conditions do actors succeed in getting those issues on the agenda (Princen 2007)? Much of this work on the EU draws on Kingdon's (2011) classic study in which he identified three separate processes or 'streams'—of problems, policies, and politics—that develop largely in isolation from each other, but which must ultimately come together for significant policy change to occur.

Problems can rise up the political agenda through a high-profile event or crisis (e.g. an economic recession), or through a shift in respected indicators (e.g. on climate change). *Policies* generally emerge away from the political spotlight through the exchanges of 'experts', such as academics, statisticians, and civil servants. Ideas in this stream may 'float around' for years before finding their moment—often after a 'softening up' of policy makers has taken place. *Political* processes, such as elections, leadership changes, and shifts in public opinion, also shape the agenda. While first developed in the study of US politics, the multiple-streams approach has been applied to an increasing range of EU issues including sugar reform (Ackrill and Kay 2011), regulation of hedge funds (Moschella 2011), and measuring quality of life (Bache 2013).

Complementing the agenda-setting literature has been a focus on 'venue shopping', which attributes policy change to changes in venue, image, and social mobilization (Baumgartner and Jones 1993). Again originating in the US, and influenced by the presence of a federal system, it focuses on how the EU has created opportunities for actors to exploit different policy venues (e.g. national or European) and has been applied to cases including European Immigration policy (Guiraudon 2002) and Justice and Home Affairs (Bulmer 2011).

Multi-Level Governance

Multi-level governance (MLG) has antecedents in neofunctionalism, but is less concerned with explaining the process of European integration and more with explaining the nature of the EU that has emerged from that process. In that respect, it is entirely in line with the approach advocated by Hix (1999).

MLG was first developed from a study of EU structural policy (see Chapter 22, Explaining Cohesion Policy) and was later developed and applied more widely. An early definition by Gary Marks (1993: 392) spoke of:

> the emergence of *multi-level governance*, a system of continuous negotiation among nested governments at several territorial tiers—supranational, national, regional and local.

While accepting that integration involved intergovernmental bargains, MLG theorists reasserted the neofunctionalist critique of realism that individual governments were not as firmly in control as suggested.

Marks et al. (1996) made three key points against the intergovernmental view, as follows:

(1) Collective decision making involves loss of control for the governments of individual states.

(2) Decision-making competencies in the EU are shared by actors at different levels, not monopolized by the governments of states.

(3) The political systems of member states are not separate from each other, as Moravcsik assumed (see Chapter 1, International Relations Theories of European Integration), but are connected in various ways.

While Marks et al. accepted the central role of the Council of Ministers in EU decision making, they pointed to a number of constraints on the ability of individual governments to control the outcomes of such collective decision making. The use of QMV in the Council was an obvious constraint: any individual government might be outvoted. The Luxembourg Compromise (see Chapter 7, The 1965 Crisis) did allow a government to exercise a veto if it felt that its vital national interests were threatened, but the prevailing culture in the Council worked against frequent use of this option, making it a rather blunt instrument for maintaining national sovereignty. So, while it was true that governments might be able to attain desired objectives by pooling their sovereignty, this was not the same as arguing that their control of decision making remained intact.

Supranational institutions might be created by member governments to assist them, as Moravcsik argued, but these did not remain under close national government control. For intergovernmentalists, national governments could ultimately choose to rein in the power of these institutions. For MLG theorists, this was difficult in practice because changes to the role of supranational institutions required unanimous agreement, which was difficult to secure with so many member states.

Marks et al. criticized Moravcsik's argument that national interests were determined purely through the interplay of domestic actors (see Chapter 1, International Relations Theories of European Integration). Instead, they argued that component parts of national governments, and also non-state actors, could form alliances with their counterparts in other member states, which influenced national governments' negotiating positions on EU matters. These alliances would not be under the control of the core institutions of the central government, such as the Foreign Office or the Prime Minister's Office, and the Commission in particular would be able to exploit the existence of these **transgovernmental and transnational networks** of actors to promote its policy preferences within the 'domestic' politics of member states.

Rather than a coherent theory, MLG was initially an amalgamation of perspectives that were primarily directed at what its advocates saw as the misrepresentation of the nature of the EU by the intergovernmental theorists. It did contain some elements of an explanation for the development of the EU, but it was primarily concerned with the analysis of the *nature* of the EU. As such, it lacked the basis for the analysis of political dynamics that was present in neofunctionalism.

Andrew Jordan (2001) identified seven key criticisms of MLG:

1. MLG was nothing new, but an amalgam of existing theories;
2. it provided a description of the EU, but not a theory;
3. it overstated the autonomy of sub-national authorities (SNAs);
4. it adopted a 'top-down' view of SNAs;
5. it focused on SNAs to the exclusion of other sub-national actors;
6. it mistook evidence of SNA mobilization at European level as evidence of SNA influence;
7. it ignored the international level of interaction.

Stephen George (2004) argued that Jordan's criticisms were of 'variable validity'. He agreed with the first claim, but suggested that it was 'scarcely a criticism'. More significantly, George (2004: 125) suggested that MLG went beyond description to offer a theory of what sort of organization the EU is: 'It is hypothesized to be an organization in which the central executives of states do not do all the governing but share and contest responsibility and authority with other actors, both supranational and subnational.' Of course, the validity of this theory was contested, but MLG offered counter-hypotheses to those of (liberal) intergovernmentalism.

George agreed that work adopting the MLG perspective had tended to focus on SNAs to the exclusion of other actors, but had not sufficiently addressed the question of whether the mobilization of SNAs had made a real difference to outcomes in the policy process. It had also not been applied sufficiently to the international level, where the EU itself stands in the role of potential gatekeeper between different arenas.

In a development of the approach, Hooghe and Marks (2003; Marks and Hooghe 2004) developed a twofold typology of MLG to capture the EU (see Table 2.2). Type 1 MLG effectively describes the formal institutions of government at various territorial levels (supranational, national, sub-national), which have multiple tasks and responsibilities and have jurisdictions that are clearly distinct from each other. In other words, Type I MLG describes the system-wide governing architecture. Co-existing with Type I MLG, Type II describes the many smaller bodies of governance that are generally set up with a specific purpose, sometimes for a limited time period, and which are deliberately flexible in membership and organization to deal with specific public policy challenges.

Other contributions focused on the normative dimension of MLG. Peters and Pierre (2004) suggested that the flexible and informal modes of co-ordination of MLG might bring dangers. In particular, they argued that MLG could be a type of 'Faustian bargain' in which the purported advantages of MLG in terms of functional efficiency are traded for core democratic values as authority seeps away from the formal institutions in which democratic accountability is exercised, or as political actors use these informal and opaque processes to escape accountability for their decisions (see also Chapter 3, Democracy).

In a similar vein, Jan Olsson (2003) considered the 'democracy paradoxes' in MLG in relation to structural policy, the policy area from which the concept first emerged. He suggested that one way in which to address the democratic challenges inherent in the partnership arrangements established to deliver structural policy (see Chapter 22, The 1988 Reform) would be to allocate a greater role to the formal institutions in the

---

Table 2.2 Types of Multi-Level Governance

Type I	Type II
General-purpose jurisdictions	Task-specific jurisdictions
Non-intersecting memberships	Intersecting memberships
Jurisdictions at a limited number of levels	No limit to the number of jurisdictional levels
System-wide architecture	Flexible design

Source: Hooghe and Marks (2004: 17). Reprinted with the permission of Oxford University Press.

region, which were directly elected. This could be done by both abolishing the institutions of MLG (multi-level and cross-sectoral partnerships) and allocating their functions to elected institutions, or, more realistically, by allowing elected institutions to play a greater role in regulating partnerships.

Building on Olsson's work, Bache and Chapman (2008) put forward three models of democracy—electoral, **pluralist**, and elite-democratic—through which to evaluate the democratic credentials of MLG. Their case study of the structural funds in South Yorkshire (UK) illustrated that, among the expected complexity and technocracy at this stage of policy making, there were also experiments in local democracy that had not previously been identified in the academic literature. As such, in the context of deep MLG, there is evidence that, while traditional mechanisms of accountability may be undermined, other mechanisms may provide a valuable alternative.

In summarizing the state of the debate, Bache and Flinders (2004: 197) identified four common strands in the literature on MLG that raised hypotheses for future research:

(1) that decision making at various territorial levels is characterized by the increased participation of non-state actors;

(2) that the identification of discrete or nested territorial levels of decision making is becoming more difficult in the context of complex overlapping networks;

(3) that, in this changing context, the role of the state is being transformed as state actors develop new strategies of co-ordination, steering, and networking to protect, and in some cases to enhance state autonomy;

(4) that, in this changing context, the nature of democratic accountability has been challenged.

CONCLUSION

Approaches beyond the intergovernmental–supranational debate yield a number of insights about the EU, particularly in relation to the more routine decision making. Such decisions may not be as monumental as the 'history-making decisions', but, as Richardson (1996: 29) said, they constitute 'the nine-tenths of the policy iceberg that is below the water line', and 'some means has to be found of analysing it'.

If theories of EU governance were relative latecomers to the study of the EU, their proliferation has more than made up for lost time. There are a number of overlapping and related approaches competing for the same space in analyzing the operation of the EU system. For organizational purposes, we have made a distinction between the categories of 'new institutionalism' and 'governance and networks'. However, the reality is less clear-cut, not only between these categories, but also within them. A key theme that cuts through these categories is the emphasis on interests versus ideas, alternatively viewed as the 'rationalist vs reflectivist' dichotomy, which has become very prominent in the study of the EU. However, as the summary of approaches provided here suggests, this dichotomy has a long lineage in theorizing on the EU and provides a thread running through both the 'newer' theories of EU governance and the long-standing theories of integration covered in Chapter 1.

The governance and networks category of approaches raises again the theme that was prominent in Chapter 1: that of the role of interest groups. In the policy-networks approach, the emphasis is squarely on the links between interest groups and policy makers. This approach reproduces at the sectoral level the insight of neofunctionalists that European integration would be driven forward more by interests responding in a rational, self-serving manner to the changed circumstances produced by the existence of the EC than by an idealistic commitment such as that shown by the federalists. Liberal intergovernmentalism also emphasizes interests rather than ideas as the key to analyzing the EU. However, the concept of the epistemic communities (and also the advocacy coalition framework) modifies this emphasis on interest, and brings knowledge and ideas back into the analysis. Here, the key actors in networks coalesce and bring about change through shared values, ideas, and knowledge.

Sociological and historical institutionalists also bring ideas back in, while rational choice institutionalists analyse the logical responses of actors to the institutional rules that they face. Sociological and historical institutionalists put a great deal of emphasis on the values and norms that actors develop within institutionalized relationships over time. These values and norms can be interpreted as ideas that actors hold, perhaps not fully consciously, that affect and at least partially explain their behaviour. While rational choice theorists, neofunctionalists, and liberal intergovernmentalists would all tend to argue that the existence of the EU structures the responses of actors because it provides a new set of rules within which they pursue their interests, sociological and historical institutionalists would tend to argue that the existence of the EU affects the way in which the actors perceive their interests, their aims, and their objectives. The theme of the role of interests in the EU is therefore also about the role of ideas.

Moving beyond the rationalist–reflectivist dichotomy, one problem with the application to the EU of concepts that were originally derived from the study of domestic political systems is that they tend to underemphasize the influence of the wider international system. An appreciation of the impact of the wider international system is the strength of some approaches derived from IR. The absence of such a dimension was one of the most telling criticisms made by Hoffmann of neofunctionalism, although Hoffmann may himself be criticized for having under-theorized this aspect (see Chapter 1). So, approaches originating in the study of domestic politics are not alone in this failing; the point remains important though, as the effects of globalization show no signs of abating. Of the theories discussed here, MLG perhaps has the greatest potential for effectively conceptualizing the relationship between developments 'internal' and 'external' to the EU. There is nothing inherent in the framework that would exclude its propositions being applied to governance beyond the EU; indeed Type 2 MLG (see Table 2.2) appears partly designed to meet that challenge.

Finally, we should keep in mind that, MLG apart, the approaches and theories discussed in this section are primarily mid-range: they seek to explain developments at a sub-system or sectoral level and are not attempts at theorizing the EU system more broadly. Moreover, as the EU becomes more complex, there may be greater application of mid-range theories. The possibilities for applying the policy-network approach to the EU are borne out by an increasing number of sectoral studies highlighted by Peterson (2004: 129–30), particularly in the domains of cohesion policy, research policy, and the CAP. Governance theories more broadly defined may become more prominent with the increased use of more informal modes of governance in the EU, such as the Open Method of Co-ordination (see Chapter 10, The Lisbon Strategy and Chapter 12, Implementation).

KEY POINTS

A Shift of Focus

- Approaches from the study of domestic and comparative politics turn away from the focus of IR theories on the process of European integration, and instead treat the EU as a political system that is already in existence, and try to explore 'the nature of the beast'.

New Institutionalism

- New institutionalism argues that analysts have lost sight of the importance of institutions in structuring political action.
- Three varieties of new institutionalism can be distinguished: rational choice institutionalism, historical institutionalism, and sociological institutionalism.
- *Rational choice institutionalism* emphasizes the argument that the behaviour of political actors is shaped by the specific framework of rules within which they operate.
- *Historical institutionalism* emphasizes the argument that political relationships have to be viewed over time and that decisions are shaped by the nature of pre-existing institutional relationships.
- *Sociological institutionalism* emphasizes the argument that the behaviour of political actors is shaped by informal norms and values.

Governance and Networks

- Definitions of governance commonly emphasize the proliferation of non-state actors in the policy process.
- Richardson advocated the application of two concepts from the study of domestic politics: policy networks and epistemic communities.
- A *policy network* is a set of resource-dependent organizations. The approach advocates analysis of sectoral policy networks that range from tightly knit policy communities to loosely bound issue networks.
- As a 'meso-level' approach, policy-network analysis is often most effectively used in conjunction with broader theories. It places emphasis on policy implementation, which is particularly relevant in the context of the EU.
- Kassim argued that EU processes were not settled enough for policy networks to emerge. Against this, Peterson argued that while some EU policy sectors remained fluid, others had developed into policy networks. He later argued that the networks approach was particularly relevant to studying the EU.
- The literature on network governance tends to be more normative than does the Rhodes model of policy networks and views networks as a potential solution to public policy dilemmas rather than being aimed at analyzing sectoral decision making.
- *Epistemic communities* are knowledge-based groups that are most likely to be influential when policy makers face uncertainty over policy choices. This approach is complementary to the policy-networks approach.
- The agenda-setting literature asks where issues on the political agenda come from and under what conditions these issues get onto the agenda, while 'venue shopping' focuses on how the EU has created opportunities for actors to exploit different policy venues.

Multi-Level Governance

- MLG has strong antecedents in neofunctionalism, but is a theory of the nature of the EU rather than a theory of the process of European integration.
- While accepting that integration involved intergovernmental bargains, MLG theorists argued that individual governments were not in control of the process. Actors at supranational and sub-national levels played a key role also.
- While initially established by national governments, supranational EU institutions develop a degree of autonomy from the control of governments.

- Transnational and transgovernmental alliances mean that states are open to external influences. The Commission is able to exploit this situation to promote its own agenda.

- MLG has been criticized on a number of counts, not least for its analysis of the role and significance of sub-national actors.

- Hooghe and Marks have developed a twofold typology of MLG that addresses both analytical and normative concerns.

- Peters and Pierre have warned of a 'Faustian bargain' in which the purported gains in efficiency from MLG are traded for core democratic qualities.

- Bache and Flinders identified four common strands in the literature on MLG that raised hypotheses for future research.

FURTHER READING

In relation to the adoption of governance approaches in EU studies, see **B. Kohler-Koch and B. Rittberger**, 'The "Governance Turn" in EU Studies', *Journal of Common Market Studies*, Annual Review, 44 (2006): 27–49, and **S. Bulmer**, 'Institutional and Policy Analysis in the European Union: From the Treaty of Rome to the Present', in **D. Phinnemore and A. Warleigh-Lack (eds)**, *Reflections on European Integration: 50 Years of the Treaty of Rome* (Basingstoke: Palgrave Macmillan, 2009), 109–24. A clear statement of dissatisfaction with approaches to the EU based on theories of IR is **S. Hix**, 'The Study of the European Community: The Challenge to Comparative Politics', *West European Politics*, 17 (1994): 1–30.

Significant applications of the new-institutionalist approach to the EU are to be found in: **P. Pierson**, 'The Path to European Integration: A Historical and Institutionalist Analysis', *Comparative Political Studies*, 29 (1996): 123–63; **S. Bulmer**, 'New Institutionalism and the Governance of the Single European Market', *Journal of European Public Policy*, 5 (1998): 365–86; and **M. Pollack**, *The Engines of European Integration: Delegation, Agency and Agenda Setting in the EU* (Oxford: Oxford University Press, 2003). See also **M. Pollack**, 'The New Institutionalisms and European Integration', in **A. Wiener and T. Diez (eds)**, *European Integration Theory*, 2nd edn (Oxford: Oxford University Press, 2009), 129–41, for an overview of applications of new institutionalisms to the study of the EU. For a discussion of the historical institutionalist research agenda on the EU, see **S. Bulmer,** 'Politics in Time Meets the Politics of Time: Historical Institutionalism and the EU Timescape', *Journal of European Public Policy*, 16 (2009): 307–24.

Epistemic communities are explained in **P. Haas**, 'Introduction: Epistemic Communities and International Policy Coordination', *International Organization*, 46 (1992): 1–35. For an overview of the policy networks approach and its application to the EU, see **J. Peterson**, 'Policy Networks', in **A. Wiener and T. Diez (eds)**, *European Integration Theory*, 2nd edn (Oxford: Oxford University Press, 2009), 105–24. On the distinction between the Anglo-American and German approaches to policy networks, see **T. Börzel**, 'Organizing Babylon: On the Different Conceptions of Policy Networks', *Public Administration*, 76 (1998): 253–73.

On network governance, see **B. Kohler-Koch and R. Eising (eds)**, *The Transformation of European Governance* (London: Routledge, 1999) and **A. Jordan and A. Schout**, *The Coordination of the European Union: Exploring the Capacities of Networked Governance* (Oxford: Oxford University Press, 2006). On agenda-setting, see **S. Princen**, *Agenda-Setting in the European Union* (Basingstoke: Palgrave Macmillan, 2009).

On multi-level governance, the most complete statement of the approach is contained in **L. Hooghe and G. Marks**, *Multi-Level Governance and European Integration* (London: Rowman and Littlefield, 2004). The collection by **I. Bache and M. Flinders (eds)**, *Multi-Level Governance* (Oxford: Oxford University Press, 2004) undertakes a critical assessment of both the potentialities and limitations of MLG, drawing both on theoretical contributions by scholars from different academic traditions and fields, and on different policy studies. A more recent collection is **H. Enderlein, S. Wälti, and M. Zürn (eds)**, *Handbook on Multi-level Governance* (Cheltenham: Edward Elgar, 2010). For a substantial theoretical treatment see **S. Piattoni**, *The Theory of Multi-level Governance: Conceptual, Empirical, and Normative Challenges* (Oxford: Oxford University Press, 2010).

The relationship between multi-level governance and policy networks is explored in **A. Warleigh**, 'Conceptual Combinations: Multi-Level Governance and Policy Networks', in **M. Cini and A. Bourne (eds)**, *Palgrave Advances in European Union Studies* (Basingstoke: Palgrave Macmillan, 2006), 77–95, and is developed further by **I. Bache**, *Europeanization and Multilevel Governance: Cohesion Policy in the European Union and Britain* (Lanham: Rowman and Littlefield, 2008).

 online resource centre **Visit the Online Resource Centre that accompanies this book for links to more information on theories of EU governance: http://oxfordtextbooks. co.uk/orc/bache4e/**

Chapter 3

Theorizing Consequences

Chapter Overview

As the European Union (EU) has increasingly been understood as a political system in its own right, so academic attention has shifted to understanding the implications of this development. This chapter brings together what have usually been presented as separate 'consequences' of European integration: Europeanization effects and challenges to democracy. However, there are clear links between the two, particularly when Europeanization is understood as a process through which domestic politics and polities are changed by their engagement with the EU. Most obviously, the process of Europeanization can challenge domestic democratic structures and processes by transferring responsibilities and obscuring lines of accountability. More positively, Europeanization may add to what is termed 'output democracy' by increasing the policy-making capacities of governments through collective action.

Europeanization

The concept of Europeanization has become a key theme in studies of the EU. However, it has been defined and applied differently in different studies. For example, some scholars refer to Europeanization as an EU-related phenomenon, while others see it as a phenomenon broader than, or largely separate from, the EU. Generally, though, the main application of the concept has been to highlight the changing nature of relations between the EU and its member (and accession) states. Here, we outline the range of uses before focusing on the development of Europeanization studies that relate specifically to the EU.

Meanings of 'Europeanization'

While Europeanization became a key theme in studies of the EU, in the 2000s in particular, it is not a new term. Rather, its importance grew as scholars sought to give more precise meaning to a term that had previously been used quite loosely to indicate a range of issues and processes. In the debates over the meaning and relevance of the term, the extent to which it has been applied in different contexts with different purposes has become evident. Buller and Gamble (2002), Olsen (2002), and Bache and Jordan (2006a) have each identified five uses of Europeanization, some of which overlap, while others do not. Drawing on these contributions, we summarize the ways in which various scholars have used the term 'Europeanization', and distinguish between those uses that relate specifically to the EU and those that are not EU-specific (see Table 3.1 and Table 3.2).

Table 3.1 Uses of Europeanization: EU-Specific

Usage	Focus on
A top-down process of change deriving from the EU	The effects of EU membership on domestic politics, policies, and polities (Héritier et al. 2001; Buller and Gamble 2002). Later research highlighted issues of culture, discourse, identity, and norms (Bulmer and Radaelli 2013).
The creation of new EU powers	The development of EU structures of governance and the accumulation of EU competences (Risse et al. 2001). This usage is similar to the notion of European integration.
The creation of a European lodestar of domestic politics	The idea of the EU as an increasingly important reference point for the political activities of domestic actors, such as sub-national governments and interest groups (Hanf and Soetendorp 1998; Fairbrass 2003).
An increasingly two-way interaction between states and the EU	States seeking to anticipate and ameliorate the effects of top-down Europeanization pressures by 'uploading' their preferences to the EU level. As such, the EU both affects and is affected by domestic processes (Bomberg and Peterson 2000; Börzel 2002).
Changes in external boundaries	The expansion of Europe as a political space, particularly through the process of enlargement (Grabbe 2001, 2003; Olsen 2002, 2003; Schimmelfennig and Sedelmeier 2004, 2005).
A 'smokescreen' for domestic manoeuvres	A process in which domestic actors 'hide behind' the EU to legitimize domestic action (or inaction) that may be unpopular (Dyson and Featherstone 1999; Buller and Gamble 2002; Radaelli 2004; Woll and Jacquot 2010).

Table 3.2 Uses of Europeanization: Non-EU-Specific

Usage	Focus on
Horizontal transfer or 'crossloading' between states	The movement of ideas and practices between European states (whether EU members or not). The EU *may or may not* play a role in facilitating these movements. This usage is linked to ideas of policy transfer (Bomberg and Peterson 2000) and is also referred to as 'crossloading' (Burch and Gomez 2003; Howell 2003).
Exporting forms of political organization	The transfer of European political ideas and practices beyond Europe (Olsen 2002, 2003).

The Development of the Field

Attempts to give a more precise meaning to 'Europeanization' date back to the 1990s. An early and influential contribution was Robert Ladrech's study of the EU and France, in which Europeanization was defined as, 'an incremental process reorienting the direction and shape of politics to the degree that EC political and economic dynamics become part of the organizational logic of national politics and policy-making' (Ladrech 1994: 69). In other words, domestic politics was being changed by the response of domestic organizations to the changing context brought about by EU membership.

Yet, while Ladrech observed Europeanization effects in France, he did not suggest that the effects of the EU would be the same across all member states. Thus, fears of harmonization or homogenization were unfounded. Instead, domestic factors played an important role in shaping the nature of the Europeanization effects in France, and would do so elsewhere. There would be 'national-specific adaptation to cross national inputs' (Ladrech 1994: 84). Ladrech's arguments about the importance of domestic mediating factors were borne out in subsequent studies.

In their study of Britain, Bulmer and Burch looked at the effects of EU membership on the machinery of central government and argued that 'while change has been substantial, it has been more or less wholly in keeping with British traditions' (Bulmer and Burch 1998: 603). At key points in Britain's relationship with the EU, the administrative response had been shaped by the way in which important political actors had perceived the integration process. So, 'the construction of the issue of integration interacts with the prevailing characteristics of national governmental machinery to explain the different starting points for national adaptation' (Bulmer and Burch 1998: 606).

Uploading, Downloading, and Crossloading

While early studies focused on the downward flow of pressures from the EU to the national level, later studies increasingly highlighted the interactive two-way relationship between member states and the EU. As well as being 'downloaded' by the member states from the EU level, ideas and practices are also 'uploaded' from member states to the EU level. The focus on uploading had antecedents in the 'domestic politics' approach developed by Bulmer (1983), while downloading resonated with the even earlier work by Puchala (1975) on post-decisional politics: the processes and politics involved in securing compliance with European decisions. Both emphasized the importance of domestic politics in understanding the dynamics of European integration, which is central to Europeanization research.

The incentive for states to upload is that if they can get their existing policy preferences accepted as the preferences of the EU, they will have less trouble adapting to the EU policy when it comes into force. As Mény et al. (1996: 5) noted: 'Often, the most effective results are achieved through controlling the initial stages of the development of a policy... The advantages accrue to those leading countries which succeed in convincing the Community institutions and public opinion that their options or solutions are the best.'

A study of environmental policy by Börzel (2002) emphasized how national executives tried to minimize the domestic implementation costs of EU environmental initiatives by seeking to upload their own preferred policy models to the EU level. Different states' executives had different uploading strategies, according to both their policy preferences and their capacity to participate at the EU level. A distinction was made between the *pace-setting* strategies of those state executives actively seeking to promote their preferences at EU level, and the *foot-dragging* strategies of those seeking to delay or block EU action so as to avoid heavy implementation costs. A third strategy of *fence-sitting* described those states that did not seek to advance or block policies, but worked opportunistically with both 'pace-setters' and 'foot-draggers' to trade their support on environmental policy for reciprocal support in other policy areas.

While this interactive dynamic of Europeanization was widely recognized, much empirical research continued to focus on downward pressures. Of particular note was a multi-state study by Cowles et al. (2001), which focused on the downward pressure from the EU level on 'domestic structures'. The study looked at two categories of domestic structure: *policy structures*, a concern extending beyond policy content to changes in the political, legal, and administrative structures of policy; and *system-wide domestic structures*, relating to changes in the nation state, its society, and economy. The findings of this study echoed those of Ladrech (1994) on the importance of national factors in shaping outcomes. In particular, they emphasized the importance of the degree of 'fit' between EU-level changes and existing domestic structures, policies, and practices. Poor fit implies strong pressure to adapt: good fit implies weak pressure. The extent to which adaptational pressure leads to domestic change depends on five intervening factors: multiple veto points in the domestic structure; facilitating institutions; domestic organizational and policy-making cultures; the differential empowerment of domestic actors; and learning (Risse 2001: 2).

This theme of domestic adaptation was developed further by Olsen (2002: 932), who, drawing on the new-institutionalist arguments of March and Olsen (1989), argued that:

> the most standard institutional response to novelty is to find a routine in the existing repertoire of routines that can be used. External changes are interpreted and responded to through existing institutional frameworks, including existing causal and normative beliefs about legitimate institutions and the appropriate distribution, exercise and control of power.

Olsen provided two broad explanations for different patterns of Europeanization across member states. The first related to the nature of the pressures 'coming down' from the EU—specifically, that EU pressures are more likely to have an impact in the domestic arena under the following circumstances: 'the more precise their legal foundation; when they are based on hard law rather than soft law; when the affected parties (constituent units) have been involved in developing the arrangement; the greater the independence of their secretariat; if the secretariat is single-headed rather than multiple-headed; and the greater the financial autonomy of the institution or regime' (Olsen 2002: 933). The second explanation pointed to different responses to adaptive pressures across member states because 'the (West) European political order is characterized by long, strong and varied institutional histories, with different trajectories of state- and nation-building, resources and capabilities' (Olsen 2002: 934).

The studies summarized above employed different definitions of Europeanization (see Insight 3.1), but common findings emerged. Most obviously, these studies

> ### Insight 3.1 Definitions of Europeanization
>
> Definitions of Europeanization abound. Perhaps the most comprehensive definition of Europeanization comes from Radaelli, who defined it as:
>
> ... processes of a) construction, b) diffusion, and c) institutionalization of formal and informal rules, procedures, policy paradigms, styles, 'ways of doing things', and shared beliefs and norms which are first defined and then consolidated in making of EU public policy and politics and then incorporated in the logic of domestic discourse, identities, political structures and public policies.
>
> (Radaelli 2003: 30)
>
> For framing empirical research with primarily a top-down focus, Bache and Jordan defined Europeanization as:
>
> the reorientation or reshaping of politics in the domestic arena in ways that reflect policies, practices and preferences advanced through the EU system of governance.
>
> (Bache and Jordan 2006a: 30)

illustrated divergence in the domestic effects of EU membership across different dimensions (for example, institutions and policies). This was explained by variations in the nature of the EU initiative or decision, and in the degree of fit between this and domestic preferences and practices. Despite the focus on downward causation, there is agreement that Europeanization is a two-way process in which states also seek to upload their preferences to the EU level. However, there is a persuasive argument that, '[i]f Europeanization entails both the evolution of European integration and its domestic impact, it ceases to be a researchable subject matter' (Börzel and Risse 2007: 495). As such, much Europeanization research continued to focus on the downloading aspect (for example, Cowles et al. 2001; Dyson and Goetz 2003; Schmidt 2006; Bache 2008; Featherstone and Papadimitriou 2008).

The notion of *crossloading* adds a horizontal dimension to Europeanization mechanisms. Crossloading refers to the transfer of ideas or practices from one state to another. Such transfer may involve the EU as a facilitator, for example through funding 'twinning exercises' that promote learning between policy makers in different states or co-operation promoted through the open method of co-ordination (see Chapter 18, The EU Policy Process). Equally, transfer may be bilateral and developed through long-standing relations that may indeed pre-date EU membership or be simply the result of one state being seen to offer best practice in a particular activity that other states seek to emulate (see Harmsen 1999; Radaelli 2000; Kassim 2003; Bulmer 2007).

Dyson and Goetz (2002) distinguished between first-generation and second-generation Europeanization studies to illustrate differences between those studies that emphasized the more formal, observable consequences of EU membership and those that focused on less formal and less observable changes. While first-generation Europeanization studies can be traced back to the early 1970s, the second generation emerged in the 1990s and was consistent with a broader sociological turn in EU

> **Insight 3.2 Interests, Institutions, and Ideas**
>
> - *Interests* are causally important because they directly shape policy responses by establishing a distribution of societal preferences that national officials take into account as they seek to build electoral coalitions capable of winning and then holding political power.
> - *Institutions* influence what actors do or do not do by allocating power to some actors but not others, structuring the content and sequence of policy making, and providing opportunities for and constraints on the state as its officials seek societal support for their policy choices.
> - *Ideas* matter because they enable actors to manage uncertainty about the expected consequences of alternative choices, and they provide actors with a symbolic and conceptual language to advance their causes. In the context of strategic interaction among numerous actors, shared ideas can bring about the convergence of expectations and strategies facilitating agreement and co-operative outcomes.
>
> *Source:* Anderson (2002, 2003).

studies around that time. In the perspective of second-generation studies, Europeanization is not limited to changes in political–administrative structures and policy content, but also focuses on the effects on ideas, discourses, and identities.

Anderson (2002: 9) captured the broader concerns of second-generation analyses through the categories of interests, institutions, and ideas (see Insight 3.2). These categories are often separated for analytical purposes, but the point is to understand their relationship: that is, for example, how the motivations and values of political actors are shaped by the institutional context in which they operate; or how the ideas held by political actors shape what they perceive their interests to be. This is significant in 'isolated' domestic contexts, but in the context of EU membership, such isolation is not possible. As such, the EU 'matters' because it 'automatically entails multilayered interactions of interests, institutions, and ideas at and across the national and supranational levels' (Anderson 2002: 10).

The key features of first-generation and second-generation Europeanization research are summarized in Table 3.3. It should be noted that while this generational division provides a useful way of distinguishing between the differing emphases of different Europeanization studies, many cover aspects contained in both categories.

Europeanization and the New Institutionalisms

As Europeanization research has become more fine-grained, it has been characterized by a new-institutionalist agenda, including the various sub-branches of that theoretical literature (see Chapter 2, New Institutionalism). However, the main variants of the new institutionalisms—rational choice, sociological, and historical—have not been utilized to the same degree, with the application of pure rational choice institutionalism limited (Bulmer 2007). The picture is blurred because authors do not always place themselves neatly in one of the categories identified above. For example, Börzel and Risse (2003),

Table 3.3 Summary of Dyson and Goetz (2002) on the 'Two Generations of Europeanization Research'

First generation	Second generation
• Generally top-down approaches, seeking to explain domestic change from EU 'pressures'.	• Emphasizes more complex interactions (top-down, bottom-up, and horizontal).
• Assumed 'misfit' between European and domestic levels—particularly formal institutional.	• Greater emphasis on the 'political' dynamics of fit: interests, beliefs, values, and ideas.
• Emphasis on reactive and involuntary nature of adaptation.	• Greater emphasis on voluntary adaptation through policy transfer and learning.
• Focus on policy and polity dimensions.	• Greater emphasis on politics, e.g. identities, electoral behaviour, parties, and party systems.
• Expected increasing cross-national convergence.	• Emphasizes differential impact of Europe.
• Defined Europeanization in substantive terms—focus on the 'end state' effects.	• Emphasizes impact of Europeanization on domestic political, institutional, and policy dynamics.

Note: An earlier version of this table appeared in Bache and Marshall (2004).

two significant contributors to this literature, have many affinities with historical institutionalism while attempting to synthesize from the other two main variants. Moreover, the choice of theoretical framework utilized in Europeanization research is inevitably influenced by the definition that is adopted. Despite these caveats, the new institutionalisms retain a prominent place in the theorization of Europeanization research and it remains inconclusive which variant carries most causal weight (Börzel and Risse 2007: 493).

Europeanization Assessed

Interest in the concept of Europeanization remains central to the study of the EU, with studies being published from an increasing variety of angles. There are studies of:

- individual member states across politics, polity, and policy dimensions (for example, Dyson and Goetz (2003) on Germany; Bache and Jordan (2006*b*) on Britain; and Featherstone and Papadimitriou (2008) on Greece);

- specific policy areas in a number of states (for example, Jordan and Liefferink (2004) on the environment; Faist and Ette (2007) on immigration; and Bache (2008) on cohesion policy);

- institutional effects across different states (for example, Knill (2001) on national administrations; Hughes et al. (2004) on regionalization) or within a single state (for example, Bulmer and Burch (2009) on Britain).

Other studies focus on particular parts of Europe (for example, Schimmelfennig and Sedelmeier (2005) on central and eastern Europe; O'Brennan (2008) on the western Balkans), and some studies cover a range of states and topics (for example, Cowles (2001); Featherstone and Radaelli (2003)).

As suggested by some of the literature cited above, the scope of Europeanization research has moved beyond the boundaries of the EU membership to shed light on the dynamics of the process of enlargement both in terms of the acceptance and assimilation of the formal *acquis communautaire* by accession states, and in terms of the pressures on accession states to conform to less formal, but nonetheless important, norms of democratic behaviour—that is, acceptance of both the 'regulatory pillar' and the 'normative pillar' (Bulmer and Radaelli 2013: 359).

Radaelli (2006) suggested that, while it was difficult to map and summarize the diverse range of empirical studies to date, a number of results stood out. In particular, the evidence for the Europeanization of public policies was more robust than the evidence for the effect of Europeanization on political competition, state structures, or the polity. Moreover, while Radaelli was clear that Europeanization did not lead to uniform convergence across Europe, there was evidence of 'clustered convergence' as states with similar characteristics or preferences in a given domain responded in similar ways to particular pressures or opportunities.

Mair (2004: 342) argued that there had been significant 'informal' Europeanization in terms of cross-cultural convergence, although this might not be directly the result of the EU (for similar arguments see Chapter 4, Critical Social Theory). While this argument is slightly beyond our EU focus here, it is important in drawing attention to notions of 'Europeanization as convergence' that are long established in the study of comparative politics and which may have implications for the study of the EU. In this academic tradition, Europeanization is equated with the older historical process of 'nationalization': a polity-building process. The logic of this process is that:

> Through 'coercion' or through 'authoritative allocation' in the case of more formal processes, and through education, communication, and sheer imitation and diffusion in the more informal cases, certain rules, practices and forms of behaviour become increasingly standardized throughout a given political and social system. And where this once applied and led to the more or less wholesale 'nationalization' of state territories, we now appear to witness it being applied and leading to the—admittedly far more uneven—'Europeanization' of a spreading transnational territory.

(Mair 2004: 342)

Most recent contributions to the literature have diversified the theoretical frames and raised issues in relation to the scope and methodology of Europeanization research.

Drawing on historical sociology, Trine Flockhart (2010) argued that Europeanization should be understood in terms of a longer time frame. She identified five phases of Europeanization starting with 'European Self-Realization' in the period up to 1450. Only her fifth phase covered the period since 1945. Drawing on critical theoretical frames (see Chapter 4), Woll and Jacquot (2010) looked at 'usages of Europe'—how the EU is something that domestic actors appropriate and exploit for strategic purposes in their own debates.

A key issue in the methodological debate has been the extent to which research design in this area has adequately allowed scholars to assess whether Europeanization—as opposed to other possible factors, domestic or international—is the cause of domestic change. This issue of *causality* was emphasized by Haverland (2005) and subsequently picked up by Exadaktylos and Radaelli (2009), who identified a lack of consistency in research designs and later brought together a number of scholars to look at this issue (Exadaktylos and Radaelli 2012). A central aim of this work was to respond to the criticism that Europeanization research privileges Europe (or the EU) as the explanation for domestic change.

This methodological reflection on Europeanization research raised fundamental issues relating to underlying theoretical assumptions. Bache et al. (2012) suggested that there had been little explicit reflection on such issues in Europeanization research and argued for a more critical approach, including in research methods. Their argument pressed the claims for critical perspectives (see Chapter 4) to be deployed in Europeanization research.

These debates suggest that Europeanization remains a useful concept, although, as Bulmer and Lequesne (2013) suggest, the slackening of the long-standing 'twin dynamics' of deepening (integration) and widening (enlargement) that lay behind the emergence of Europeanization research may shift some focus away. That said, in line with other theoretical currents graining greater traction in light of the eurozone crisis (see Chapter 4), it is possible that the critical turn already evident in some recent contributions on Europeanization research may be further strengthened.

Democracy

For a long time, European integration proceeded with relatively little public or political debate on the implications for democracy and legitimacy. Decisions were taken by elites in the context of a 'permissive consensus'—the absence of public debate and protest on developments was taken as evidence of consent. European integration appeared to have low salience for most people. Economic integration was relatively uncontroversial in the context of a globalizing marketplace, and unanimous voting procedures were in place to protect perceived national interests.

However, as the EU's reach extended into a wider range of activities, and decision-making procedures changed, reducing the use of unanimous voting, European publics increasingly signalled their objections to further integration, most obviously through negative votes in referenda on treaty reforms. The contentious ratification of the Maastricht Treaty was a particularly significant moment (see Chapter 9, After Maastricht). In this changing context, debates about popular control over the integration process and the accountability of EU elites have grown. These debates intensified with the fifth enlargement and they were a prominent feature of the deliberations of the Constitutional Convention (see Chapter 10, The Constitutional Treaty) that led to the Constitutional Treaty and ultimately to the Treaty of Lisbon. The subsequent problems in ratifying these treaties heightened debate on the democratic dimension of the EU. More recently, the eurozone crisis further undermined the 'permissive consensus', with the EU responses to it regarded in many national contexts as further damaging democracy (see Chapter 11).

While public debate on democracy in the EU was limited until the 1990s, there has been a long-established academic debate over the EU's perceived 'democratic deficit'. This debate has taken a significant twist in recent years, with an increasing number of academics arguing that the democratic deficit has been overstated and, indeed, that it may not actually exist. Alongside the debate on the democratic deficit has been a related interest in the concept of legitimacy. In some cases, democracy and legitimacy are used somewhat interchangeably, although it is more usual to view legitimacy as a broader concept.

Democracy and Legitimacy

Birch (2001: 72) argued that 'the term "democracy", in its modern sense, came into use during the course of the nineteenth century to describe a system of representative government in which representatives are chosen by free competitive elections and most male citizens are entitled to vote'. However, the term has been used in various ways by political theorists, leaving the concept somewhat contested. The same is true for the concept of legitimacy. In simple terms, democracy is concerned with the public control over their leaders exercised by citizens with broadly equal rights (see Insight 3.3), while legitimacy is a broader concept that can be understood as the public acceptability of the exercise of power (Lord 2001: 187). Democracy is an important source of legitimacy, but not the only source.

Beetham and Lord (1998) pointed to three liberal-democratic criteria of legitimacy that are relevant to the authority of the EU. These are performance, democracy, and identity. The concept of a legitimacy deficit relates to all three, not simply the democratic dimension. *Performance,* defined as 'effectiveness in the attainment of agreed ends or purposes of government', is considered 'an important component of legitimacy' rather than as something separate from it (Beetham and Lord 1998: 25). In terms of *democracy,* EU institutions are seen to be deficient in each of the three aspects of direct democratic legitimacy: authorization, accountability, and representation. However, extending direct democratic legitimacy in the EU depends on the development of a more robust common European *identity* among the EU electorate, which is generally considered, at best, to be embryonic (Smith 1992).

The notion of a 'democratic deficit' has been the focus of much scholarly work in this area. The key concern here has been the lack of public accountability of the EU's institutions. More broadly, the concept of a 'legitimacy deficit' is used to describe the gap between the principles and practice of decision making. It is concerned with the difference between 'the moral authority or normative standing *required* by a public

---

Insight 3.3 Democracy

Christopher Lord (2001: 166–7) suggested that democracy, defined as 'a system of government in which the people rule themselves', can be reduced to two core attributes: 'The first is that the public must be able to control those who make decisions on its behalf, even where it does not directly assume the reins of government; and, second, citizens should exercise such control as equals, since a condition in which some decide on behalf of others is paternalism, not democracy ...'.

Albert Weale (1999a: 14) defined democracy as a condition in which 'important public decisions on questions of law and policy depend, directly or indirectly, upon public opinion formally expressed by citizens of the community, the vast bulk of whom have equal political rights'.

Insight 3.4 Input–Output Democracy

Scharpf (1997: 19) argued that:

On the **input side**, self-determination requires that political choices should be derived, directly or indirectly, from the *authentic preferences* of citizens and that, for that reason, governments must be held accountable to the governed...

On the **output side**, however, self-determination implies *effective fate control*. Democracy would be an empty ritual if the political choices of governments were not able to achieve a high degree of effectiveness in achieving the goals, and avoiding the dangers, that citizens collectively care about. Thus, input-oriented authenticity and output-oriented effectiveness are equally essential elements of democratic self-determination.

authority engaged in the production of binding rules and allocations, and that which it is *actually able* to command' (Beetham and Lord 1998: 126). For Beetham and Lord (1998: 3), legitimacy in the EU system 'has to be understood as a process of interaction between the EU and member state levels'. For traditional international organizations, legitimacy is secured through the recognition of their authority by other legitimate authorities (member states): an indirect rather than direct form of legitimacy, which is dependent on the pre-existing legitimacy of the member states. However, the nature of the EU is seen by many as different from other international organizations and in some respects to resemble domestic systems of governance (see Chapter 2). From this perspective, the EU requires a legitimacy that is wider than the indirect legitimacy provided by the consent of national elites.

As will be seen below, the relationship between notions of democracy and legitimacy, and how and why they are in 'deficit' in the EU, is not always clear in the academic literature. For example, the performance dimension of legitimacy outlined by Beetham and Lord is similar to the notions of *output democracy*, while their democratic accountability dimension is echoed by the notion of *input democracy*. Thus, for Scharpf (1997: 19), democracy is a 'two-dimensional concept, relating to the *inputs* and to the *outputs* of the political system at the same time' (see Insight 3.4).

The Democratic Deficit

The notion of the democratic deficit has been defined in a number of ways, but is essentially concerned with the degree to which the EU adequately represents and is accountable to European citizens (see Insight 3.5).

Insight 3.5 The Democratic Deficit

- This refers to the idea that EU decisions are 'in some ways insufficiently representative of, or accountable to, the nations and the people of Europe' (Lord 2001: 165).
- It is said that the EU suffers from 'deficiencies in representation, representativeness, accountability and support' (Eriksen and Fossum 2002: 401).

Lord (1998: 11) referred to a number of features contributing to the perceived democratic deficit:

> the unelected character of the European Commission, the alleged weakness of the European Parliament, the withdrawal of powers from national parliaments, lack of a European political identity or 'demos', low voter participation in European elections, the absence of strong democratic intermediaries such as political parties, the remoteness and obscurity of the Union's decision-making procedures, and doubtless much else besides ...

A lot of the early literature on the democratic deficit focused on the relative weakness of the European Parliament (EP) within the EU's institutional balance. Strengthening the EP, the only directly elected EU body, has been widely viewed as an appropriate means through which to close the democratic deficit. To some extent, this particular deficit has been addressed, as the EP's powers have increased dramatically since direct elections were introduced in 1979 (see Chapter 15, The Struggle for Power). However, it remains only one of four influential organizations and, by most accounts, it is still not the most powerful. Moreover, the contribution of the EP to correcting the democratic deficit remains limited because elections tend to be fought on national rather than European issues and turnout is generally low (see Chapter 15, Debates and Research). This is because European electorates do not perceive themselves as being part of an EU-wide democratic community in the same way as they do see themselves being part of a national democratic community. So, the EU still lacks the popular authority of national assemblies. The absence of a strong common European identity, or 'demos', remains a central challenge for those seeking to address the problem of the democratic deficit by strengthening further the powers of the EP. As van der Eijk and Franklin (1996: 7) put it: 'It is true that the European Parliament lacks certain powers in comparison with modern-day national parliaments—but what it lacks most is not power but a mandate to use that power in any particular way.'

However, some scholars have suggested that the notion of the democratic deficit is something of a 'non-problem'. Andrew Moravcsik (2002) argued that the EU has been unfairly judged in democratic terms. Specifically, it has been judged either against ideal standards of democracy or compared with national standards and practices, neither of which is appropriate:

> Comparisons are drawn between the EU and an ancient, Westminster-style, or frankly utopian form of deliberative democracy. While perhaps useful for philosophical purposes, the use of idealistic standards no modern government can meet obscures the social context of contemporary European policy-making—the real-world practices of existing governments and the multi-level political system in which they act.

(Moravcsik 2002: 605)

Moravcsik (2002: 603) argued that, rather than acting in an unfettered way, as much of the democratic-deficit argument suggests that they do, the EU's institutions are 'tightly constrained by constitutional checks and balances: narrow mandates, fiscal limits, super-majoritarian and concurrent voting requirements and separation of powers'. Moreover, the EU's appearance of being relatively insulated from democratic accountability reflects the nature of its main functions, such as central banking, constitutional adjudication, and economic diplomacy, which are generally low-key affairs in national systems, and are often delegated to non-governmental or quasi-governmental actors. So, the EU's system should not be singled out for criticism on these grounds.

Concerns over the institutional balance, and the EU's procedures for ensuring accountability, are heightened by the perception of some scholars that the EU fails to deliver on the 'output' side of the equation. Scharpf (1999b) argued that the economic focus of the European integration project, and the relative underdevelopment of effective European social and welfare policies, provide an output imbalance that favours business and economic actors. In the context of intensified market competition, states could face a 'race to the bottom' in terms of welfare spending, which would be accelerated by the neoliberal bias within the EU. The consequence of this is the alienation of those social groups that benefit least from the EU's system—the poor, women, and recipients of welfare benefits.

Moravcsik (2002: 617) recognized Scharpf's argument as 'the most empirically and theoretically nuanced criticism of the EU's democratic deficit that currently exists', but suggested that it should be qualified on a number of grounds—in particular, that there 'is little evidence of a race to the bottom'; that 'the level of social welfare provision remains relatively stable'; and that there is 'little evidence that the EU is driving social protection downward' (Moravcsik 2002: 618). Scharpf and many others would disagree with Moravcsik's assertions. For such scholars the neoliberal orientation of the EU *has* led to the reconfiguration of traditional welfare settlements in its member states, at least since the single market project (see Chapter 20, Evaluating the Single Market) and certainly in the context of monetary union (see Chapter 21, Critical Voices; also see Chapter 4, Critical Political Economy). This erosion has been particularly acute in the context of the eurozone crisis and increased EU pressure to adopt policies of austerity (see Chapter 11).

Moravcsik's position on the democratic deficit flows logically from his argument that the EU is largely characterized by liberal intergovernmentalism (see Chapter 1, Liberal Intergovernmentalism). In this view, national governments dominate the policy process, so the outputs of the system are legitimized primarily by the democratic accountability of those governments. The key point for critics such as Scharpf (1998) is that even if, like Moravcsik, we do not believe that the EU itself needs to meet the standards of democracy associated with the nation state, it is crucial that we consider the *effects* of the EU on such standards *within* member states (see also Wincott 2006).

Such critiques point to the link, highlighted at the start of the chapter, between Europeanization of member states and concerns with the democratic deficit. They argue that, intentionally or not, member states have been complicit in eroding key aspects of national authority in politically salient policy areas, such as welfare, as they delegated powers to EU institutions. This is particularly the case for those member states with more well developed models of welfare capitalism. As Scharpf (1998, 2010) explains, this is not easily compensated for at the EU level due to a structural bias in favour of 'negative integration' geared towards the removal of barriers to free markets.

Schmidt (2006: 22) has usefully described this situation as one characterized by 'politics without policy' at the national level and 'policy without politics' at the EU level (see also Chapter 4, Critical Political Economy and Critical Social Theory for similar arguments). From this perspective, at the national level there has been a 'hollowing out' of politics—including party competition (Mair 2009)—as a consequence of Europeanization. EU policy and law has, in effect, reduced the range of policies that national actors such as political parties are able to propose or adopt, limiting the choice for national electorates. While, at the EU level, the politicization of policy making remains limited (and, for instance, the EP does not adequately make up for a perceived democratic erosion at the national level—see Chapter 15).

The lack of greater input democracy—or Schmidt's 'policy without politics'—at the EU level is, unsurprisingly, unacceptable for many of those who regard the EU as resembling a national polity in important respects (see Chapter 2, A Shift of Focus). For instance, Hix (2006) argues that competitive elections provide for the direct accountability of policy makers, bringing a number of advantages. First, they ensure that decision makers respond to citizens' preferences. Second, party-political competition stimulates public debate, which forms public opinion on the EU and, in so doing, provides political elites with a mandate to undertake reform. Third, competitive elections play a role in identity formation, so rather than waiting for the emergence of a common European identity before democratizing the EU's institutions further, introducing electoral competition now could assist in the development of this identity.

Vectors of Legitimation

Lord and Magnette (2004) considered whether the existence of very different views on how the EU ought to be legitimated might in itself add to its overall legitimacy. In doing so, they identified four 'vectors of legitimation' in the EU: indirect, parliamentary, technocratic, and procedural legitimacy.

- *Indirect legitimacy* depends on the existing legitimacy of the EU's member states, on the EU's respect for the sovereignty of the member states, and on the ability of the EU to serve the purposes of the member states.

- *Parliamentary legitimacy* depends on both an elected EP and the representation of the member states via the Council system. This dual legitimation reflects the co-existence of both a single people that relates to and is affected by the EU in broadly the same way, and a series of peoples with separate identities.

- *Technocratic legitimacy* depends on the ability of the EU to meet the demands and improve the quality of life of its citizens—that is, that it has problem-solving efficiency.

- *Procedural legitimacy* rests on the observance of particular procedures—such as transparency, balance of interests, proportionality, and consultation. Beyond the observance of 'due process', procedural legitimacy is also derived from the observance of given rights, and the capacity to generate new rights (Lord and Magnette 2004: 184–7).

Lord and Magnette (2004) then drew on the distinction between *input legitimacy* and *output legitimacy* to illustrate the different vectors of legitimacy evident at two broad stages of policy making (see Table 3.4). The authors pointed out that these vectors provide 'ideal types', which do not exist in pure form in the EU context, but provide the basis for analyzing and understanding the nature of legitimacy in the EU. Table 3.4 offers a useful schema for considering the different dimensions of legitimacy in relation to EU institutions, decision-making practices, or policy areas. It might also be

Table 3.4 Input and Output Legitimacy under the Four Vectors of Legitimation

	Input	Output
	EU policies are legitimate to the extent that they are based on the following:	EU policies are legitimate to the extent that they deliver the following:
Indirect	Authorization by states	State preferences
Parliamentary	Elections	Voters' preferences
Technocratic	Expertise	Efficiency
Procedural	Due process and observance of given rights	Expanded rights

Source: Lord and Magnette (2004: 188). Reprinted with the permission of John Wiley and Sons.

used as the basis for making qualitative assessments about the democratic legitimacy of the contemporary EU more generally (for instance, we might consider the input and output dimensions of Table 3.4 in the context of the eurozone crisis and reforms described in Chapters 11 and 21).

Ways Forward?

While there is disagreement over the nature and extent of the democratic challenges facing the EU, there is continued debate over how the EU's democracy and legitimacy might be enhanced (for example, Follesdal and Hix 2006; Lord and Harris 2006; DeBardeleben and Hurrelmann 2007; Kohler-Koch and Rittberger 2007; Tsakatika 2007; Ehin 2008; Habermas 2001a. Chryssochoou (2007)) identified five models of democracy that might aid democratization of the EU: the parliamentary, the confederal, the federal, the consociational, and the republican.

- The *parliamentary model*, as the name suggests, emphasizes the role of the elected assembly as legislator within a political system, and would democratize the EU through the enhanced role of elected representatives. However, this model would imply the extension of majority rule to all policy areas, which would be highly unlikely, and also rests on a degree of European social unity that is not yet present.

- The *confederal model* brings states together into a form of union that does not compromise their national identity or political sovereignty. It is a model that does not rest on the development of a new polity or demos, but is based on a *unity of states* rather than a *unity of peoples*. This model would democratize through national channels by 'renationalizing' some issues to provide a greater role for national parliaments, which would be unpalatable to many European and domestic actors involved in the integration process.

- The *federal model* rests on the creation of a unity of people rather than simply a union of states. This model seeks to reconcile the requirement of greater political union with the demands of the component states. In doing so, it aims to 'establish a co-operative democratic ethos in relations between the centre and the subunits' (Chryssochoou 2007: 366). The model has been criticized for its emphasis on the need for clearly demarcated competencies in an age in which more flexible forms of governance are required (on types of multi-level governance, see Chapter 2, Multi-Level Governance). In some respects such thinking harks back to early federalist thinking on Europe (see Chapter 1, The Intellectual Background) and has affinities with certain cosmopolitan thinking (see Chapter 4, Critical Social Theory).

- The *consociational model* has generally been attempted where there are conflicting demands from different societal groups and, in particular, to prevent the abuse of minority rights. It has four features: a grand coalition (such as a council containing elites from the different groups), proportionality (representation of societal groups reflects their size), segmental autonomy (some group control in specific areas), and mutual vetoes (on important decisions). Chryssochoou (2007: 367) suggested that each of these features is evident within the EU. Its main limitation is that it is essentially an elitist approach to seeking compromise and, as it reflects much of the present EU system, it would not appear the likeliest candidate for enhancing democracy.

- The *republican model* stresses the need for greater civic participation in EU affairs in the absence of a formal European constitution and the underdeveloped European demos. Central to the republican model is the idea of 'balanced government', which is developed in two related ways: through a 'proper institutional balance', and through promoting deliberation among different groups that make up civil society (Chryssochoou 2007: 369). This model also has affinities with some cosmopolitan ideas (see Chapter 4, Critical Social Theory).

Chryssochoou (2007: 373) noted that elements of all five models were evident in the workings of the EU, although the models that most closely captured the EU's character were confederal and consociational; a state of affairs that he deemed unsatisfactory as this was likely to hinder the development of a European demos.

One explicit intention of the Lisbon Treaty, ratified in 2009, was to enhance democracy in the EU (see Chapters 10 and 12). It strengthened the powers of the EP, enshrined the republican principle of democratic equality between EU citizens, gave the national parliaments new control powers, boosted the powers of EU-level parties, and introduced a new form of participatory democracy, the 'citizens' initiative' (whereby EU citizens can initiate legislative action with a petition requiring a million supporters from at least one-quarter of the member states). These measures address several of the above models of democracy. Supporters and opponents of the Treaty, however, were fiercely divided about some of these measures. For supporters, democracy was enhanced by strengthening the role of the EP in a number of policy areas, and by granting enhanced powers to national parliaments. Opponents of the Treaty questioned the legitimacy of the EP (see also Chapter 15) and suggested that the enhanced powers for national legislatures were insignificant.

Whatever one's view on the Lisbon Treaty, the eurozone crisis which unfolded shortly after it came into effect certainly dealt a significant blow to public perceptions of EU legitimacy and democracy (see Chapter 11). At the same time it further opened the study of EU politics to a range of critical scholarship on the fundamental nature and purpose of the EU (further discussed in Chapter 4; see also Table I.1).

CONCLUSION

This chapter has brought together what have usually been presented as separate 'consequences' of European integration: Europeanization effects and challenges to democracy. However, as noted throughout, there are clear links between the two, particularly when Europeanization is understood as a process through which domestic politics and polities are changed by their engagement with the EU. Most obviously, the process of Europeanization may obscure lines of political accountability, so that citizens are unsure whom to hold to account on particular issues. Alternatively, political elites may use 'Europeanization' as a smokescreen that conceals their own activities and deliberately misleads voters if it is expedient for them to do so. Equally, political elites may themselves be unclear about where responsibility, and thus accountability, should lie.

On a more positive note, Europeanization effects may enhance output democracy. Common action at the level of the EU may bring 'performance' benefits to citizens: for example, through more efficient management of environmental policy. However, for this to enhance legitimacy, it is necessary that the increased efficiency is recognized and that it is recognized as an effect of membership of the EU. It is perhaps a problem for Europhiles that some of the main benefits of European integration are relatively intangible, while some of its failings are not. Moreover, the EU's supporters have the problem of proving the counterfactual: how do we know that member states and their citizens would not have fared as well, if not better, without EU membership? Such questions become even more pertinent at times of political and economic crisis, such as in the context of the eurozone crisis (see Chapter 11).

According to most commentators, the outstanding problem facing democratic development in the EU is the absence of a shared identity that would produce a genuine demos. **Eurosceptics** often argue that democracy cannot be established at the European level because there is no such thing as a European people: democracy can only operate within national cultures. If an attempt is made to force the diverse peoples of Europe into an artificial union, nationalism will be stirred up rather than be abolished. Here also, Europeanization processes may be crucial. However, this may be less to do with changes in formal institutions and policy through member-ship of the EU, and more to do with the diffusion of informal norms and values among EU citizens.

KEY POINTS

Europeanization

- The concept of Europeanization has been defined and employed in a variety of ways. For some, Europeanization is a phenomenon that is broader than or separate from the EU but is generally used to conceptualize the changing relationship between the EU and its member (and accession) states.

- Ladrech provided an influential early conceptualization of Europeanization. He highlighted the importance of domestic factors in mediating Europeanization effects and argued that fears of harmonization or homogenization across European states were unfounded.

- Europeanization became increasingly understood as a two-way relationship between the EU and its member states, involving both the *uploading* of ideas and practices from member states to the EU level, and the *downloading* of ideas and practices from the EU level to member states. However, the focus of most research has been on the downloading effects.

- The notion of *crossloading* refers to the transfer of ideas or practices from one state to another: a process in which the EU may or may not play a role.

- *First-generation* studies tended to focus on observable changes through Europeanization and explained variations in relation to the degree of fit or misfit between EU decisions and domestic practices and preferences.

- *Second-generation* studies placed greater emphasis on the changes in ideas, values, and identities rather than more immediately observable effects of Europeanization.

- As Europeanization research became more fine-grained, it was increasingly characterized by a new-institutionalist agenda.

- Most recent contributions to the literature have diversified the theoretical frames and raised issues in relation to the scope and methodology of Europeanization research.

Democracy

- For a long time, European integration proceeded with little public debate about the democratic dimension. This changed as the EU's competencies expanded and was given particular impetus through the controversial ratification processes of various treaties.

- Democracy and legitimacy are contested concepts and their relationship is not always clear in the EU literature. In essence, democracy is concerned with public control over the exercise of power, while legitimacy is understood as public acceptability of the exercise of power.

- The notion of the democratic deficit has been central to much scholarly work in the area, focusing on the lack of accountability of the EU's institutions and the relatively weak position of the EP as the only directly elected body.

- Moravcsik (2002), among others, argued that, when judged against reasonable criteria, concerns over the EU's democratic deficit are misplaced. However, critics such as Scharpf (1998) and Schmidt (2006) drew attention to the adverse effects of the EU on democratic politics within the member states. Hix (2006) emphasized the importance of democratic institutions at EU level and identified a number of advantages for the EU of competitive elections.

- Lord and Magnette (2004) identified four vectors of legitimation in the EU: indirect, parliamentary, technocratic, and procedural legitimacy. They also distinguished between *input* and *output* legitimacy to illustrate how the four vectors are evident at different policy-making stages.

- Chryssochoou (2007) identified five models of democracy that might aid democratization of the EU: the parliamentary, the confederal, the federal, the consociational, and the republican. Of these, the confederal and consociational models most closely capture the EU's character.

- An explicit aim of the Lisbon Treaty was to enhance democracy in the EU. It addressed several deficiencies according to Chryssochoou's models, although its provisions for doing this were interpreted very differently by supporters and opponents. The eurozone crisis dealt a significant further blow to an already negative public perception of EU democratic legitimacy.

FURTHER READING

Europeanization

An important early contribution was **R. Ladrech**, 'Europeanization of Domestic Politics and Institutions: The Case of France', *Journal of Common Market Studies*, 32 (1994): 69–88. A more recent key reference point is **J. Olsen**, 'The Many Faces of Europeanization', *Journal of Common Market Studies*, 40 (2002): 921–52.

P. Graziano and M. Vink (eds), *Europeanization: New Research Agendas* (Basingstoke: Palgrave Macmillan, 2007) provide the most comprehensive collection on Europeanization, with twenty-five contributions from experts in their respective fields, covering theory, methods, politics, polity, and policies. **S. Bulmer and C. Lequesne (eds)**, *The Member States of the European Union*, 2nd edition (Oxford: Oxford University Press, 2013) explore how the EU impacts on a selection of member states, with a final thematic section of the book that examines the impact of Europeanization on institutions, politics, policy, and political economy.

There are several very good broad-ranging overviews of the topic, including: **T. Borzel and T. Risse**, 'The Domestic Impact of European Union Politics', in **K. E. Jørgensen, M. Pollack, and B. Rosamond (eds)**, *Handbook of European Union Politics*, (London: SAGE Publications, 2007), 483-504; **S. Bulmer**, 'Theorizing Europeanization', in **P. Graziano and M. Vink (eds)**, *Europeanization: New Research Agendas* (Basingstoke: Palgrave Macmillan, 2007), 46–58; and **C. Radaelli**, 'Europeanization: Solution or Problem?' in **M. Cini and A. Bourne (eds)**, *Palgrave Advances in European Studies* (Basingstoke: Palgrave Macmillan, 2006), 56–76. A valuable book-length treatment is provided by **R. Ladrech**, *Europeanization and National Politics* (Basingstoke: Palgrave Macmillan, 2010).

Democracy

For an introduction to EU democracy and the notion of the democratic deficit, see: **D. Chryssochoou**, 'Democracy and the European Polity', in **M. Cini (ed.)**, *European Union Politics* (Oxford: Oxford University Press, 2007), 359–74; **A. Follesdal**, 'Normative Political Theory and the European Union', in **K. E. Jørgensen, M. Pollack, and B. Rosamond (eds)**, *Handbook of European Union Politics* (London: SAGE Publications, 2007), 317–35; or **C. Lord**, 'Democracy and Democratization in the European Union', in **S. Bromley (ed.)**, *Governing the European Union* (London: SAGE Publications, 2001), 165–90.

An analysis of key debates and suggested ways forward can be found in **A. Warleigh**, *Democracy in the European Union* (London: SAGE Publications, 2003). On legitimacy, see **D. Beetham and C. Lord**, *Legitimacy and the European Union* (London and New York: Longman, 1998). The most comprehensive coverage of relevant debates is the collection by **B. Kohler-Koch and B. Rittberger (eds)**, *Debating the Democratic Legitimacy of the European Union* (Lanham, MD: Rowman and Littlefield, 2007).

Other helpful book-length treatments are: **C. Lord and E. Harris**, *Democracy in the New Europe* (Basingstoke: Palgrave Macmillan, 2006), and **J. DeBardeleben and A. Hurrelmann**, *Democratic Dilemmas of Multi-level Governance: Legitimacy, Representation and Accountability in the European Union* (Basingstoke: Palgrave Macmillan, 2007).

Europeanization and Democracy

V. Schmidt, *Democracy in Europe* (Oxford: Oxford University Press, 2006) provides an authoritative study of the relationship between Europeanization and democracy, focusing in detail on the domestic effects in Britain, France, Germany, and Italy. **F. Scharpf** has also made important contributions on this theme. See, in particular, his *Governing in Europe: Effective and Democratic?* (Oxford: Oxford University Press, 1998), and, more recently, 'The Double Asymmetry of European Integration, or why the EU Cannot Be a Social Market Economy', *Socio-Economic Review*, 8 (2010): 211–50.

 online resource centre   **Visit the Online Resource Centre that accompanies this book for links to more information on theorizing consequences, including papers on Europeanization: http://oxfordtextbooks.co.uk/orc/bache4e/**

Chapter 4

Critical Perspectives

Chapter Overview

If the 'governance turn' of the 1990s heralded the arrival of significant new voices in the European Union (EU) debate (see Chapter 2), there is now an even wider chorus. The perspectives and theories covered in this chapter are long established in the study of politics, but have only relatively recently become visible in the mainstream study of the EU. Critical perspectives, although very different from each other, are united in challenging key assumptions about how the EU should be studied, and what we can hope to know. They are generally concerned with exposing which actors and ideas are dominant in the EU and highlighting the less obvious manifestations of power that pervade the interrelated worlds of political action and political theorizing (see Theory Introduction, Table I.1). They tend to concur with the assertion of critical political economist Robert Cox (1981: 128) who said that, 'Theory is always for someone and for some purpose'.

The range of critical perspectives now applied to the EU is too great to cover in a single chapter. Here we focus on five perspectives which provide a flavour of the variety of critical approaches that have been used to study aspects of the EU. *Social constructivism* offers a critique of rationalist approaches that have dominated much of the study of the EU (see Chapters 1 and 2). *Critical political economy* considers the EU in the context of broader dynamics of global capitalism, often building on earlier Marxist scholarship. *Critical social theory* emphasizes the ways in which the EU has transformed European society and politics in ways that are often unrecognized. *Critical feminism* points to the ways in which the issue of gender has been marginalized in the EU and in mainstream approaches to the study of the EU. Finally, *post-structuralism perspectives* seek to question the prevailing wisdom associated with the EU and its ideals.

Critical of What?

All of the theories considered in the preceding chapters are in their own ways critical of something, often a competing theoretical perspective. However, the 'critical' perspectives considered in this chapter are united in their critique of mainstream 'rationalist' or 'positivist' approaches to the study of the social and political world. 'Positivist' approaches are those that assume a fixed social reality (**ontology**) and understand knowledge of that social reality to be obtained via the neutral observation of an objective scholar (**epistemology**). Many of the approaches considered in the previous chapters fall within this positivist mainstream. Thus, for example, intergovernmental approaches assume that states remain key actors in driving integration (ontology) and that scholars can acquire knowledge about integration by objectively studying the actions of states (epistemology).

In contrast, the critical—often termed 'post-positivist'—approaches discussed in this chapter emphasize the constructed and changeable nature of the social and political world. Many such approaches do not consider that social reality can be objectively observed and believe that various agents, including policy actors and scholars themselves, are involved in its construction. Critical scholarship often seeks to highlight which actors, ideas, or theories are either dominant or excluded in the politics of the EU at particular historical junctures or in particular policy areas. In so doing they point to the less obvious manifestations of power that pervade the interrelated worlds of political action and political theorizing (for the sorts of questions posed by such approaches see Theory Introduction, Table I.1). Implicitly or explicitly, critical work of this kind suggests that 'another Europe is possible' (Manners 2007).

That said, the extent to which 'mainstream' theories are tied to a fixed ontology is itself debatable. For instance, neofunctionalist texts (see Chapter 1, Neofunctionalism) refer to interest groups' 'loyalties' *moving* to the EU (or its antecedents) as a new centre, in a manner that we might associate with processes of 'learning' within social constructivism (see this chapter, Social Constructivism). Indeed, the father of neofunctionalism, Ernst Haas (2001: 22), stated that '[a] case can easily be made' that neofunctionalism is a precursor to constructivism. It could be argued that several other theories considered in the foregoing chapters, such as historical and sociological institutionalism (see Chapter 2, New Institutionalism), also sit somewhere between positivist mainstream and post-positivist critical approaches. Moreover, social constructivism, discussed in this chapter, in certain guises explicitly seeks to offer a middle way between these positions. Risse and Wiener (1999: 776) have noted, for instance, that certain strands of social constructivism concur with the positivist epistemology of an objectively observable world even as they reject a fixed ontology.

Positivist and post-positivist positions are consequently best visualized as ideal types on a continuum, with individual scholarly contributions lying somewhere along this continuum. Table 4.1 represents an attempt to map a selection of the theories considered in this, and previous chapters, onto this continuum, although it is important to note that it is a matter for significant debate as to where these are most appropriately placed. Moreover, individual scholars identifying with any given approach may consider their own work to be positioned differently and have a far more nuanced understanding of their ontology and epistemology than the table suggests. Critical approaches that lie towards the post-positivist end of this continuum (those in bold on the table) are the focus of this chapter. These have become increasingly prominent in the study of the EU in recent decades, both due to developments in political theorizing more broadly and due to events in EU politics (Rosamond 2007).

Social Constructivism

Social constructivism entered the debate on the EU not to dispute either the intergovernmental or supranational interpretation of integration, but rather to challenge the

Table 4.1 Mapping Approaches on a Positivist/Post-Positivist Continuum

	ONTOLOGY Nature of (social) reality	**EPISTEMOLOGY** How knowledge acquired	**CONTINUUM** (from positivist to post-positivist)
Positivism	FIXED	Objective observation. Separation of object and observer	Liberal intergovernmentalism Rational choice institutionalism
Between Positivism and Post-Positivism	(MOSTLY) CONSTRUCTED	Objective observation possible. Some interest in discourse/ideas	Neofunctionalism Historical institutionalism Sociological institutionalism
Post-positivism	CONSTRUCTED	Focus on shifting discourse/ideas. Subjective/normative observation. Observer likely to impact upon object of study	**Social constructivism** **Critical political economy (neo-Gramscian)** **Critical social theory** **Critical feminism** **Post-structuralism**

(rationalist) assumptions on which the dominant integration theories were built. As such, it should be understood as an 'ontological approach to social inquiry' (Cowles 2003: 110) which regards social and political reality as constructed, rather than as a theory of EU politics or integration. While critical of rationalist approaches, constructivists in both IR and EU studies tend to situate themselves at different points on the positivist/post-positivist continuum. Many who would associate with the constructivist label would see their approach as an attempt to bridge the two extremes, taking seriously social construction while maintaining a commitment to scientific positivism and objectivity.

The social constructivist approach is closely related to sociological institutionalism. Both approaches emphasize that actors' behaviour is influenced by the 'logic of appropriate behaviour' or norms, which Katzenstein (1996: 5) defined as 'collective expectations for the proper behaviour of actors with a given identity'. In this view, political actors internalize social norms, which shape their identities and thus their interests. This is what constructivists refer to as the 'constitutive effects' of norms.

The constructivist view that the actions of individuals cannot be understood in isolation from their social environment contrasts with the rationalists' emphasis on 'methodological individualism', in which the central focus is on 'individual human action' (Risse 2009: 145). However, while constructivists emphasize that individuals' interests and identities are shaped by the social environment in which they exist, equally they argue that the social environment is shaped over time by the actions of individuals. This relationship—sometimes described in terms of **structure and agency** (Hay 2002: 81–134)—is one of two-way interaction and thus, in the words of constructivists, 'mutually constitutive'.

The essential constructivist critique of rationalist approaches is that a focus on material interests (such as economic interests or security) alone offers an inadequate explanation of key developments in European integration. Such an explanation ignores the role played by deeply-embedded cultures that shape national positions, and the role of ideas and values that connect political leaders or other actors one with another. As such, a constructivist history of the EU would:

> focus on the ongoing struggles, contestations, and discourses on how 'to build Europe' over the years and, thus, reject an imagery of actors including governments as calculating machines who always know what they want and are never uncertain about the future and even their own stakes and interests.

(Risse 2009: 147)

Constructivist Work on the EU

As noted, constructivism is not a theory as such and constructivist scholars differ significantly in terms of the focus and purpose of their analysis. Drawing on Saurugger (2013: 152), we focus here on two interrelated constructivist research themes: socialization and learning and the social construction of European identity.

Many constructivist scholars have studied how identities evolve through learning and socialization, often with a focus on such processes within European institutions. Socialization refers to the process by which actors develop common understandings and internalize common norms in response. For example, many scholars have considered socialization in relation to relatively new EU governance processes such as the 'open method(s) of co-ordination' (OMC) that are explicitly based on the exchange of best practice between member states and thus learning (see Chapter 12, Implementation; see also the discussion of New Intergovernmentalism in Chapter 1). For instance, Radaelli (2008) has noted that three forms of learning can take place in this context: 'learning at the top' between EU civil servants, 'hierarchical learning' from EU to domestic level, and 'bottom up learning' whereby non-state actors and local actors diffuse their knowledge.

Several constructivists have considered the ways in which ideas about Europe or the EU have been constructed and with what consequence. Such analyses often highlight the ways in which ideas produce outcomes, which a consideration of material factors (alone) cannot easily explain. For instance, Risse argued that the EU's decision to enlarge to twenty-five members in 2004 was largely a function of the member states' socialization into a particular conception of 'Europe'. Commission officials acted as 'norm entrepreneurs' to promote a sense of shared community values (democracy, human rights, and market economics) between the fifteen, which generated a normative obligation towards the applicant states who shared these values. In this way, '[r]hetorical commitment to community values entrapped EU member states into offering accession negotiations to the CEE [central and eastern Europe] and other Eastern European countries despite the initial preferences against enlargement' (Risse 2009: 157). It was noted, however, that once negotiations began, rationalist accounts provided a more fitting explanation of the strategic bargaining by national governments. This acceptance of the differential appropriateness of forms of explanation is evidence that certain strands of constructivism do not seek to displace rationalist theories entirely, but to contribute to a more complete picture of how the EU works.

Rosamond (2002) has similarly discussed the ways in which concepts such as the 'European economy' and related concepts such as 'European firms' or 'European competitiveness' have been socially constructed. While they may seem like common sense notions, Rosamond draws attention to the ways in which the Commission, along with networks of interest and advisory groups, was instrumental in constructing them over time and the ways in which significant economic actors came to identify with them (note some similarities here with neofunctionalist ideas about spillover, see Chapter 1, Neofunctionalism). Just as with the case of enlargement highlighted above, such use of discourse was important in determining particular possible policy responses and excluding others. In the case of 'European competitiveness' the concept worked alongside others such as 'globalization' to present the EU within a global context that required a particular, rather narrow, set of 'neoliberal' policy responses (Rosamond 2002: 172). We have arguably seen such responses in the adoption of strategies such as the Lisbon Agenda, in 2000, and Europe 2020, in 2010 (see Chapters 10 and 11; also see this chapter, Critical Political Economy). There are important affinities between aspects of Rosamond's argument and the work of the Critical Political Economists discussed below.

Ideas about the EU may also be purposefully deployed for strategic reasons in national politics (see also Chapter 3, Europeanization). Hay and Rosamond (2002) highlighted how *ideas associated with* either European integration or globalization may, even in the absence of solid evidence, be presented by political actors as external imperatives to justify unpopular domestic reform measures, particularly to the political economy. As they note (2002: 148):

> In a number of contemporary European contexts, it is the process of European integration (often in the immediate form of the Maastricht convergence criteria) which is (or has been) invoked as the proximate cause of often painful social and economic reforms elsewhere legitimated in terms of globalization.

Whether political actors invoke European integration as the reason for such reforms has depended on the extent to which the EU is popular in a given national polity and likely to aid in legitimating unpopular reforms.

Constructivism Assessed

Risse (2004: 151) usefully highlighted three main ways in which social constructivism contributes to our understanding of the EU:

1. By highlighting the mutually constitutive nature of agency and structure it allows for a deeper understanding of the impact of the EU on its member states and particularly on statehood.

2. By emphasizing the constitutive effects of EU rules and policies it facilitates study of the ways in which EU membership shapes the interests and identities of actors.

3. By focusing on communicative practices it highlights both how the EU is constructed discursively and how actors come to understand the meaning of European integration.

Conversely, Cowles (2003: 110–11) identified three criticisms of constructivism:

1. that it lacks a theory of agency and shows a tendency to overemphasize the role of structures rather than the actors who help to shape those structures;
2. that much of the early constructivist literature tended to focus its analysis on public actors to the relative neglect of important non-state actors;
3. that there is a tendency of some constructivists to identify the good things that have been socially constructed rather than the bad.

The last of these points is of particular concern to the critical approaches considered in the following sections.

Critical Political Economy

In this section we focus on the work of a group of neo-Marxist scholars who have engaged with the EU. Before considering these, it is important to issue two disclaimers. First, not all approaches that are critical of the EU political economy are explicitly critical of dominant approaches to the study of the EU. Indeed, some traditionally dominant approaches covered in the previous chapters of this book are themselves informed by a political economy perspective. For instance, the critical work of Schmidt and Scharpf considered in Chapter 3 can be associated with the 'new institutionalism' discussed in Chapter 2 (for an excellent introduction to the political economy of the EU, see McCann 2010). Second, a number of scholars interested in critically reflecting on political economy issues may not associate themselves explicitly with a Marxist or neo-Marxist tradition. Scholars have, for instance, deployed broadly constructivist and post-structuralist approaches in order to make claims that are in some respects similar to those made by authors considered in this section (the work of Rosamond and Hay above and the work of Parker considered below are examples). Thus, while this section focuses on neo-Marxist scholars, it is important to highlight that they are not representative of all those who have said something 'critical' in relation to the EU political economy.

Neo-Marxist critical political economy (CPE) is united in its emphasis on the role of capitalism and material factors in shaping the social world in terms of distinct classes. However, there are many disagreements among scholars influenced by the work of Marx. A key disagreement can be understood in terms of the aforementioned debate on **structure and agency**: the extent to which capitalism and the relations of production are fixed, unchangeable structures or potentially shaped and influenced in important ways by mediating agents such as states, institutions or labour movements (for more on this debate see Bieler et al. 2006).

Those neo-Marxists—notably the 'neo-Gramscian' scholars discussed in the next section—who do see some role for agents in shaping political economy have been particularly active in their engagement with the EU as an object of study and will constitute the main focus of this section. This sub-set of neo-Marxist scholars tends to concur with the constructivist assertion that the political and social world is constructed and that ideas and discourses therefore matter in shaping that world.

However, they are critical of what they term 'liberal constructivist approaches', asserting that we ought to take more seriously material or capitalist structures and emphasizing that EU social and political reality is constructed in ways which favour particular interests or classes (Van Apeldoorn et al. 2003). The work of such scholars thus seeks to expose the ways in which particular elite or capitalist interests are constructed and have prevailed in the context of European integration and constituted a 'neoliberal' order. At the same time, they are critical of an 'orthodoxy' in mainstream studies of integration that has failed to critique such an order and been complicit in its constitution (Ryner 2012).

Critical Political Economy Work on the EU

Critical political economists view the EU and its historical evolution in the context of broader developments in the capitalist world economy. They argue that dominant theories of integration serve to obscure deeper underlying explanations and purposes of the EU. Neo-Marxists, such as Peter Cocks and Stuart Holland, were making such arguments in the 1980s. As Cocks (1980: 39) put it:

> Regional integration was a mechanism for accommodating and reinforcing the expansion of European capital while simultaneously protecting it from the possibly excessive rigours of international competition. Ideologically, supranational ideas such as federalism and functionalism provided moral and intellectual justifications at the elite level for European regional organization.

Holland (1980: 89) emphasized the importance of social class and political power to the integration process, suggesting that mainstream accounts excluded these phenomena from their analyses:

> Class analysis has Marxist connotations which raise issues of exploitation and power which are inconveniently disturbing to many of the élites engaged in integration itself. Lifting the lid on class relations opens a Pandora's box of the kind which key exponents and advocates of international integration have been trying to close and bury for some time.

From this perspective, the neofunctionalist theory dominant at the time rested on problematic pluralist assumptions regarding the wide dispersal of power within society, which meant that no single group would be able to dominate the integration process (contemporary theories such as liberal intergovernmentalism could be criticized for similar assumptions). In other words, although neofunctionalism identified the role of elites and interest groups in advancing integration it did not link the interests of these groups to broader class structures in society and politics. Their dominance in advancing integration was simply put down to the fact that they were better organized than labour interests. Holland accepted that capitalist interests were more effectively organized than labour, but suggested that this argument obscured a more important explanation for capitalist influence over the process. What was important was not an observable process of business leaders influencing state actors, but a shared world view—or, as Holland (1980: 91–2) put it, 'the combination of governmental élites and the self-electing élites of private capital, bound on a common venture in fulfilment of a common ideology'.

A later generation of scholars built on the work of these neo-Marxists, but believed their predecessors had overestimated the existence of crisis tendencies within capitalism and had not accounted for the considerable variations in types of capitalism over time and space (Cafruny and Ryner 2009: 229). Yet, the starting point for contemporary neo-Marxist scholars of the EU was essentially the same as that of Cocks and Holland, that the dominant theories of integration have basic flaws that obscure understanding of the nature of power in the EU:

> by their very design they are unable to conceptualize adequately power relations that are constitutive of capitalist market structures. In other words, these mainstream theories fail to account for the structural power that determines the particular trajectory of European integration.

(Van Apeldoorn et al. 2003: 17)

In particular, 'mainstream theories' make assumptions about the inherent rationality of market forces that leave no room for alternative organizing principles. Specifically, they 'assume either explicitly or implicitly that market forces are expressions of an inner rationality of universal human nature that is held to be the essence of the realm of freedom in political affairs' (Van Apeldoorn et al. 2003: 18). Critical political economists dispute the assumption that the market is a reflection of human nature and that its operation equates with freedom in political affairs, and suggest instead that this starting point obscures the uneven distribution of power inherent in the operation of markets. The consequence is that mainstream theories define power narrowly in relation to control by political authorities and thus the empirical focus is on how this power is organized. In the CPE perspective, this view needs to be supplemented with a view of power derived from social forces (generally, class relations) that underpin market relations and shape formal political authority.

To understand the true nature of power in the EU, Van Apeldoorn et al. (2003) proposed a neo-Marxist approach, drawing on the work of Antonio Gramsci. As noted above, there are affinities here with social constructivism, with the role of ideas being central to the understanding of Gramsci's concept of 'hegemony'. Unlike most constructivists, though, ideas here are firmly embedded in a particular (historical materialist) conception of social relations. Gramsci argued that the capitalist class does not rule by force, either exclusively or primarily, but through consent generated by the diffusion of its ideas (via state institutions and organizations in civil society). In this way, the specific interests of the capitalist class become internalized by all as the general interest and thus states only need to use force to govern as a last resort. This notion of hegemony owes something to the Marxist idea of 'false consciousness'; the notion that people are unaware of what is in their true interest. From this perspective it is argued that mainstream theories of the EU not only fail to expose the underlying nature of class power that shapes its emergent political structures, but in doing so also serve to reproduce the consent that legitimizes and thus sustains this state of affairs.

Later analyses from this perspective focused on core aspects of the EU political economy, the single market, and monetary union (EMU). Van Apeldoorn (2002), for instance, focused on the ways in which preference shifts within the European Roundtable of Industrialists—a lobbying group of corporate actors—contributed to the single market agenda in the 1980s. He charted the ways in which actors, who may have once favoured European-level protectionism, gradually came to favour a conception of competition that was global in scope. Horn (2012) discussed how such processes relate to broader shifts in corporate governance in the context of ever-more-liberalized EU capital markets. Such shifts were the result of EU regulatory reforms which, according to Mügge's (2010) analysis, reflected the interests of banks and finance actors. Approaches from this perspective highlight the ways in which the single market project has privileged the interests of certain elites at the expense of citizens and of national democracy (see also Chapter 3, Democracy and Chapter 20, Evaluating the Single Market).

In a similar vein, Gill (1998) considered the ways in which EMU placed constraints on member states and required them to implement a set of neoliberal policy responses. He perceived EU economic and monetary policy as part of a broader trend towards legally embedding or 'constitutionalizing' neoliberal preferences. In the context of the eurozone crisis, such processes of constitutionalization are ongoing according to this perspective and can be associated with the ideas of a particular strand of neoliberal thought, a German **ordo-liberalism**.

The implications of these broader neoliberal trends for traditional conceptions of the European welfare state are made apparent by such scholars in analyses of EU strategies such as the Lisbon Agenda of 2000 and Europe 2020 of 2010 (see Chapter 10, The Lisbon Strategy and Chapter 11, Europe 2020). While these strategies appeal to the importance of social cohesion and a European 'social model', critical political economists have drawn attention to the emphasis on increasingly flexible labour markets and the associated retrenchment of traditional models of welfare (often couched in terms of 'modernization') (Hager 2008; Nousios and Tsolakis 2012).

Other scholars working in this tradition explored the possibilities for resistance by 'counter-hegemonic' movements which might challenge the neoliberal direction of travel. Bieler (2011), for instance, assessed the possibility for transnational labour and social movements to resist these trends.

Critical Political Economy Assessed

Contributions from this perspective raise important questions for mainstream theorists, in particular about the assumptions that underpin dominant theories both of European integration and of the operation of the EU as a political system. In addition to highlighting the role of ideas, CPE contributions raise questions about the nature of power in the EU that have often been ignored entirely by mainstream theorists or dealt with in a cursory manner. In particular, 'critical political economy relates developments in the EU to the constraints and opportunities of capitalism' (Cafruny and Ryner 2009: 237). The eurozone crisis—in many ways a crisis of capitalism manifest in the EU context—has certainly increased the pertinence of such an approach.

Notwithstanding its usefulness, criticisms of this approach are possible. It could be argued that the true interests of different groups and classes are fairly represented in the context of EU politics to a far greater extent than the Gramscian concept of hegemony recognizes (in accordance with the 'pluralist' assumptions in much mainstream theory—see Chapter 1). It could also be argued that the interests and agendas of economic and other elites, including governments, are not as well aligned as certain neo-Marxist narratives would suggest. In other words, many would argue that governments do not so easily become the vehicle for elite or capitalist interests. More generally, other critical perspectives covered in this chapter might argue that such approaches are too pre-occupied with economic (capitalist) forces to the detriment of other important social forces linked to, among other factors, gender, race, culture, and nation. And even those sympathetic to these approaches may argue that, while the attempt to alter 'macro' level structures such as global capitalism is a worthy endeavour, it is excessively idealistic (see also this chapter, Conclusion).

Critical Social Theory

Critical social theory perspectives have become increasingly important in studying the EU. They overlap in many ways with the approaches that we have already considered. They would support the critique of rationalism and the social constructivist notion that political and social reality is constructed rather than fixed. They would generally concur with the idea that language and communication are central to the constitution of social realities. Many critical social theorists would also support the notion that mainstream theories are complicit in constituting the EU in a particular way and some would concur to a large extent with the CPE critique of the neoliberal bias of the contemporary EU.

However, critical social theory approaches differ from the other critical perspectives discussed in two principal respects. First, while their object of study is inclusive of the EU, it encompasses broader dynamics in contemporary European society (Delanty and Rumford 2005). In particular, they frequently point to a so-called 'cosmopolitan' reality in Europe, highlighting the ways in which society has become increasingly complex and transcended national frames of reference and ways of thinking about the world (Beck and Grande 2007). Second, they often seek to promote a particular normative vision. They do not simply describe a cosmopolitan reality, but also champion it in the face of what they regard as less-positive tendencies within European society and mainstream scholarship. In short, they combine a descriptive social theory with normative prescription, although there are differences between scholars within this tradition both in terms of which attributes of the EU are celebrated and in terms of what a 'better' or 'cosmopolitan' Europe should look like.

Critical Social Theory Work on the EU

Beck and Grande (2007) highlighted the way in which social processes fostered what they called a 'cosmopolitan outlook' in Europe. Such processes include the exchange of social, cultural, and linguistic practices, and a 'cross fertilization' of identities. These have been facilitated by the EU through integration and enlargement and have broken down traditional boundaries among Europeans, particularly those rooted in nationalism. That is not to say that all is well in contemporary Europe. Beck and Grande recognized that a cosmopolitan outlook is only a partial reality that remains endangered by, in particular, nationalist outlooks. This threat is not only the case in the 'real world' of European politics, but also in much scholarship. They highlighted the ways in which what they term a 'methodological nationalism' *blinds us to Europe* (2007: 18) or, in other words, undermines the cosmopolitan outlook that they identified and advocated. As Delanty and Rumford (2005: 188) put it:

> A cosmopolitan perspective holds many attractions, not least of them being that a major problem in the way Europe is studied, perhaps *the* problem, is that the political and social science associated with the nation-state still pervades EU studies.

These social theory perspectives are not arguing that mainstream scholarship necessarily promotes or supports the prevailing nation states in Europe. Rather they are arguing that a particular way of understanding and viewing society and politics that draws for inspiration on the model of the nation state still dominates mainstream scholarship. For instance, many mainstream analyses of European integration view it as a process which erodes the sovereignty of prevailing nation states while tending towards a Europe which increasingly resembles a nation state (see Chapter 1). More recent scholarship has treated the EU as a political system modelled on the nation state (see Chapter 2).

A methodological cosmopolitanism advocates a 'both-and' Europe (Beck and Grande 2007: 18) where *both* loyalty to nation *and* loyalty to Europe (and, indeed, globally) is possible. This may involve reconsidering both the aims and logics of the European project and the very notion of integration, which has pushed for the 'harmonization' of policy by all member states. In so doing it has contributed to an abolition of difference through an assumption that 'uniformity is a precondition for unity' (2007: 73). Beck and Grande cited, as realities within the EU that concur with this 'both-and' position, the 'Open Method of Co-ordination' (see Chapter 18) and forms of 'enhanced co-operation' (whereby certain sub-sets of states may co-operate in a policy area—see Chapter 12, Differentiated Integration). For them, these are contexts which make possible *both* co-operation *and* the preservation of some differences (2007: 246).

Manners (2002) similarly argued that it was the EU's cosmopolitan—or, as he sometimes put it, 'post-Westphalian'—characteristics that actors (including scholars and European policy makers) should both emphasize and promote. 'Post-Westphalian' refers to the way in which the EU as an entity has overcome nationalism without reproducing it in the form of a new, European state. He argued that the EU could, in this respect, serve as a model that problematizes realist thinking and practices in IR, showing the possibility of moving beyond traditional practices of sovereignty and power politics. He was critical of efforts to promote the EU as primarily a military or economic power. Instead he emphasized the importance of promoting the EU as what he called a 'normative power'. A significant body of scholarship on EU external relations has engaged with this concept (see Chapter 26, EU Power in World Politics).

Habermas's work on the EU (2001*a*) shared the idea that the EU can be conceived as an emerging or 'immanent' cosmopolitan entity and similarly encouraged this process. Like these social theorists, he was also concerned with the history of nationalism in the EU and promoted the idea of a 'constitutional patriotism' at the European level. This is a patriotism not based on national or ethnic roots, but on a shared belief in constitutional values such as human rights and democracy. However, he departed from the social theorists discussed above in terms of his more explicit critique of processes of neoliberal globalization. Like many critical political economists, he was concerned with these processes and also with the role that the EU had played in reinforcing and promoting them. In particular, he was critical of the detrimental effect that such processes had on the European welfare state and on democracy within the EU (in this sense Habermas has also been an important contributor to debates on the democratic deficit—see Chapter 3).

Habermas nevertheless sought to promote the EU as the agent that might realistically challenge such trends and thus support the preservation of certain features of European social democracy. As he said, 'the challenge before us is not to invent anything but to conserve the great democratic achievements of the European nation-state, beyond its own limits' (Habermas 2001b: 6). This, he noted, would require the establishment of a new, essentially social democratic constitution for Europe, underpinned by a stronger conception of European citizenship and identity. Habermas's vision of a cosmopolitan EU is thus much closer to a federalist vision of EU (see Chapter 1) than certain of the social theorists mentioned above would be likely to support (Parker 2009a).

Critical Social Theory Assessed

Critical social theory makes an important contribution to the study of the EU in as much as it considers the impact of the EU on European society and culture more generally. It highlights some of the important ways in which the EU has contributed to the constitution of an emerging 'cosmopolitan Europe'; in other words a European society that has to some extent transcended a one-dimensional nationalist parochialism and shares a set of common values such as human rights, democracy, and rule of law. Even as it identifies this emerging cosmopolitanism in Europe, it is critical of those political and social forces and those academic approaches that might undermine such tendencies. However, critical social theorists differ in terms of both what they see as the primary adversary of this emergent cosmopolitan Europe and in terms of what they see as the normative ideal of Europe to which we should aspire.

Not only are there important differences within critical social theory, but critical political economists may detect in some strands a complacency in relation to the social and economic inequalities that an ostensibly cosmopolitan EU has precipitated. In other words, they may not take seriously enough the economic foundations of the European project. Moreover, other critical perspectives covered in this chapter have detected in certain celebrations of a cosmopolitan Europe a problematic moral superiority or euro-centrism which potentially blinds us to ethically questionable aspects of the contemporary EU (Parker 2009a; see also this chapter, Post-Structuralism).

Critical Feminism

While CPE might be described as occupying the margins of EU scholarship until the past decade or so, feminist perspectives were even less present. Hoskyns (2004: 33) argued that 'both the core of EU policy making and many of the key concepts of theorizing European integration remain virtually untouched' by feminist and gender analysis. However, feminist scholarship on the EU has grown and diversified in the past decade, most obviously to move beyond a focus on the EU's gender equality policies to analyse the EU and theorizing on the EU in relation to questions of gender more generally.

We briefly cover some of the work that has been done on the EU's gender equality policy, but focus here on the critical strand in the feminist literature, which shares the broad critique of rationalist approaches. Like CPE and social theory, these perspectives combine a critique of the mainstream with a particular normative perspective—in this case, a perspective that emphasizes the importance of accounting for gender both in policy making and in theorizing about the social and political world.

Feminist Work on the EU

Research on gender equality policies is well established in the EU literature. These policies had their origins in Article 119 of the Treaty of Rome (Hoskyns 1996) and developed through subsequent Treaty provisions, directives, Court rulings, and soft-law instruments relating to a range of policy areas including part-time work, parental leave, sexual harassment, childcare, and violence against women (see Hantrais 2000; Ellina 2003). Locher and Prügl (2009: 183–4), who described the EU gender equality regime as 'one of the more astonishing aspects of European integration', identified a three-stage development in the area—from a focus on equal rights, to positive action, to gender mainstreaming—taking into account the gender dimension in all areas and at all stages of EU policy making. Roth (2008: 4) highlighted the ways in which different enlargements led to opportunities and challenges for the development of EU gender equality policies. She cited evidence of the 'uploading' of policies from certain member states to the EU level (particularly from 'Nordic' countries such as Sweden and Finland) and 'downloading' of policy to member states from EU level in cases such as Spain and Ireland. In a comprehensive discussion of the EU and gender issues, Kantola (2010) considered, among other things, the Europeanization of gender policies, focusing on the impact of the 'downloading' of policies in different member state contexts and their impact beyond the EU (on these concepts, see Chapter 3, Europeanization).

While the EU is often seen as progressive in this area, Hoskyns (2004) argued that, despite the growth in scope of gender equality measures over time, major EU decisions continued to be taken without reference to gender or without adequate representation of women (Hoskyns 2004: 223). The Commission's 2001 Governance White Paper (see Chapter 22) was given as an example of an important document that did not mention the word 'gender', and the Constitutional Convention (see Chapter 10) as an example of an important body with a very small proportion of women members (17 per cent).

Kronsell (2005) extended this critique to integration theories themselves, which she argued had done little to encompass gender dynamics. She critiqued six approaches that she saw as representing the 'state of the art' in EU studies: liberal intergovernmentalism, domestic politics approaches, neofunctionalism, multi-level governance (MLG), supranationalism, and constructivism.

At the core of *liberal intergovernmentalism* is the argument that states are the dominant actors in the EU (see Chapter 1). However, from a feminist perspective, this focus on states as the key actors rests upon a narrow conception of the relevant political space and one that excludes consideration of gender dynamics. As Kronsell (2005: 2035) put it:

Liberal intergovernmentalism defines the place of politics as a place where women are not. Moravcsik's idea that states relate to each other and interact in the process of integration—in intergovernmental negotiations—does not take note of the fact that it is and has been almost exclusively men speaking for the state.

The *domestic politics approach*, a variant of which forms part of Moravcsik's liberal intergovernmentalism, offers more scope for incorporating analysis of gender dynamics by opening up the '**black box of the state**' to consider the complex processes at play in shaping national positions on EU issues. However, while this approach considers the role of a range of actors within and beyond the state, Kronsell (2005: 1027) suggested that the approach had been 'less prone to include gender and women's interest organizations within the overall assessment of EU integration'.

Neofunctionalism, like the domestic politics approach, placed a premium on understanding the role of interest groups, but within the transnational as well as the national context (see Chapter 1, Neofunctionalism). Again, this offers the potential for understanding the contribution of organized interests representing women, but is critiqued for its liberal ('pluralist') view of pressure group activity (note the similar line of critique from CPE approaches), which does not draw attention to asymmetries in the resources available to interest organizations of different types. Specifically, in the competition for influence between transnational interest groups, feminist organizations are not recognized to be at a distinct disadvantage in comparison to more powerful lobbies that shape a range of policies with significant gender implications (Kronsell 2005: 1028). Hoskyns (2004: 225) added to this critique, suggesting that neofunctionalism 'has ended up explaining and thus implicitly often promoting a bureaucratic, technocratic model of policy making in the EU, which from the beginning separated the economic from the social', and thus excluded both gender concerns and democratic concerns.

Multi-level governance (see Chapter 2) is seen as complementary to feminist analysis because it goes beyond a focus on the state, interest groups, and supranational norms to emphasize complex interactions involving multiple actors in which power takes multiple forms. However, like the other approaches that emphasize the plurality of actors discussed above, it overlooks the fact that the policy networks central to the notion of MLG tend to be male-dominated and difficult for women to enter. Thus, for MLG to deliver on the promise that it holds for feminist analysis, more empirical research is required on the composition and dynamics of relevant policy networks (Kronsell 2005: 1031–2).

Supranationalism focuses on the EU level of decision making and highlights how national actors learn not only how to co-operate to get deals done, but also come to appreciate the value of common norms by which decisions should be made in particular sectors (see Chapter 1, Supranational Governance). On one level, this approach is helpful for gender analysis in relation to understanding the development and evolution of the EU's gender policies. However, supranationalism ignores the history of EU institutions as shaped and governed by men, and thus its focus on norms and norm dynamics 'needs to be broadened to include also the institutionalization of the male-as-norm' that is inherent in the EU (Kronsell 2005: 1033).

Like supranationalism, *social constructivism* emphasizes the importance of norms and processes of socialization through which national preferences can be transformed. It is an approach that has an obvious appeal for feminist analysis, given its concern with the social construction of sex difference. Indeed, Hoskyns (2004: 228) suggested that 'women academics who have been writing on gender issues in the EU context for many years are now beginning to identify themselves as social constructivists'. However, constructivism is another approach in which power is either 'downplayed or left external to construction' and thus which inadequately deals with the feminist concern that 'institutions not only delimit our world but systematically distribute privilege and thereby create patterns of subordination' (Kronsell 2005: 1035).

In summarizing her critique of dominant theories, Kronsell (2005: 1035–6) highlighted two points: that they ignore the 'male-as-norm' problem, and that they are based on a simplistic view of power. As Hoskyns (2004: 224) put it, a more gender-sensitive analysis of European integration 'brings the imbalance between the social and the economic in EU policy making into focus, puts the emphasis on democratic legitimacy and forms of participation, and prioritizes the analysis of power relations'. In these senses there are clear overlaps with the concerns of a 'post-positivist' or critical feminism and those of a number of the other approaches considered in this chapter.

Critical Feminism Assessed

Critical feminist perspectives draw attention to particular policy developments, and raise questions that are not addressed by mainstream theories of the EU. In policy terms, they reveal an EU that is, on the one hand, relatively progressive in relation to gender equality issues, but, on the other, perpetuates gender inequalities and limits the participation of women in key forums. In theory terms, gender perspectives seek to reveal hidden aspects of the EU: most particularly in this case relating to the gendered effects of EU policy making and the mechanisms through which patriarchal domination is reproduced (Locher and Prügl 2009: 181). While feminists have been critiqued for overstating the importance of gender relative to other issues that determine social relations, many feminist scholars would emphasize the complementarities between gender perspectives and some of the other critical perspectives covered in this chapter.

Post-Structuralism

A variety of post-structural (sometimes called 'post-modern') approaches have engaged with the EU as object of study. Drawing on such thinkers as Michel Foucault, Pierre Bourdieu, and Jacques Derrida, they are particularly attuned to the interactions of knowledge, language, and power in the construction of social and political reality. Post-structural accounts overlap considerably with the foregoing approaches but they are distinct in certain respects.

Like social constructivists, post-structuralists reject positivist ontologies, but they are sceptical of the attempts of some such approaches to reconcile themselves with a positivist epistemology (see Table 4.1). Like CPE and feminist approaches, they are acutely aware of power relations, but are often cautious about giving undue import to any one key structural factor, such as social class or gender in determining such relations. Like critical social theory, they are critical of methodological nationalism, but may equally point to the ethical problems inherent in their 'cosmopolitan outlook'.

From a post-structural perspective, 'critique is not that which seeks out resolution, reconciliation or the smoothing out of difficulty, but rather that which discomforts and unsettles one's sense of certainty' (Amoore 2008: 274). In other words, 'post-structural scholars are seeking to "denaturalize" stories about European integration which are spoken as common sense' (Manners 2007: 87). The attempt to unsettle a sense of certainty or 'common sense' in relation to the EU has been the uniting theme of post-structural analysis. The post-structuralist contribution is particularly focused on highlighting the often concealed work that is done by discourse, language, knowledge, and power in constituting a variety of 'European' or EU realities and identities.

Post-Structuralist Work on the EU

Post-structuralist work has not been limited to a particular facet of the EU, but is an approach that has also been deployed to consider broad themes of identity, governance, and political economy. However, much post-structural work on the EU emanates from the field of IR and reflects an increasing critical interest in the EU as an actor or presence in world politics and as an ostensible 'area of freedom, security and justice' (see, respectively, Chapters 26 and 24).

Among the first to draw on the work of post-structural thought in EU studies, Diez (1999) appealed to the mainstream to account for the ways in which discourses on the EU shape or constitute the reality of the EU. In other words he pointed to the 'performativity' of language in relation to the EU. By way of illustration he noted how, in a relatively Eurosceptic Britain of the 1960s, the European Economic Community (EEC) was often referred to as the 'Common Market', whereas in relatively pro-European Germany it was referred to as the 'Community'. His point is that the language used in these different contexts was not simply the consequence of different pre-existing feelings towards Europe; rather it was also constitutive of those very feelings.

More recently, Diez (2005) has developed a critique of the above-mentioned notion that the EU is a cosmopolitan 'normative power' (Manners), highlighting the ways in which such a portrayal of the EU might in some respects cast the EU as superior to various 'others' in world politics and blind us to some of its less virtuous policies (see also Merlingen 2007). Parker and Rosamond (2013) have also offered a critique of this concept, arguing in particular that the 'post-Westphalian' or cosmopolitan reality that was celebrated by Manners might have overcome certain exclusionary effects of nationalism, but the EU's manifestation as a 'market' project might have had other exclusionary consequences (see also this chapter, Critical Political Economy). Such work can be situated within a broader post-structural critique of the critical social theory discussed above, and in particular its celebration of an ostensibly cosmopolitan Europe/EU (Parker 2009a).

Several post-structural scholars in the sub-field of critical security studies have problematized the relationship between the 'European' ideals of liberty and security, highlighting the paradoxes, even hypocrisies, at the heart of many EU practices and policies (see also Chapter 24, Critiquing the AFSJ). Among other things, they have—with reference to post-9/11 policy on terrorism (de Goede 2008) and immigration policy (Huysmans 2006; Van Munster 2009)—drawn attention to the ways in which security, enacted with the stated purpose of preserving liberty, has paradoxically undermined that liberty in certain respects for both EU 'insiders' and 'outsiders'. The concept of 'the border' is frequently unsettled in such accounts. A range of scholars have articulated the ways in which the EU's practices and policies—in relation, for instance, to free movement, counter-terrorism, and immigration control—have 'multiplied' borders within and beyond EU space (Vaughan Williams 2008).

Drawing together some of the themes discussed above, Walters and Haahr (2005) deployed Foucault's notion of 'governmentality'—an interest in the particular rationalities that lie behind governmental practices—to explore the ways in which various ideas and practices have constituted Europe as an entity in very particular ways and its forms of government. In so doing, they, among other things, challenged histories of integration that suggested a linear progress, pointing to the alternatives that did not become part of the historical legacy of European integration. For example, with reference to the early days of integration, they noted how proposals to place under public ownership the coal and steel industries—which were central to the early steps in European integration—were ultimately not pursued and, instead, Monnet and Schuman's particular ideas prevailed (see Chapter 5) (Walters and Haahr 2005: 15).

Parker (2013, 2012a) deployed Foucault's work on liberalism to point to some important tensions or ambiguities within EU governance. Considering which identities the EU as governing actor seeks either to promote or to exclude, and drawing together some of the themes of interest to both a CPE and a critical security studies, he highlighted the ways in which the EU has, through its governing logics, discourses, and collective knowledge, attempted to constitute individuals as variously postnational market actors or 'entrepreneurs' and postnational political actors or 'citizens'. This work points to the potentially exclusionary effects of both of these agendas. However, in line with Foucault's interest in political resistance, Parker (2013, 2012a) noted that the ambiguous co-existence of these two governing logics in the EU might open the possibility for practical acts of resistance and re-politicization by those excluded and marginalized by either agenda.

Post-Structuralism Assessed

Post-structural accounts have added a new dimension to scholarship on the EU by drawing attention to the important role of language and discourse in constituting the EU in particular ways. This work highlights a range of difficult questions in relation to the common sense ideals that the EU professes to embody, such as peace, freedom, and justice. It also contributes to the broader critique of mainstream approaches and extends this to a critical engagement with some of the other critical approaches, and particularly a normative critical social theory, discussed above. However, those approaches have themselves critiqued post-structural analyses for offering no positive normative vision or agenda (for the EU or more generally) (see Parker 2013: 172–4).

CONCLUSION

This chapter has summarized contributions that can be broadly categorized as 'critical perspectives'. As the discussion shows, these perspectives are not only critical of mainstream theories, but, in many cases, also of each other. Importantly, though, they share an emphasis on the limits of rationalist or positivist approaches.

Several approaches discussed are normative in their intent, seeking to highlight problems with the status quo but also to suggest that 'another Europe' is possible. They are not interested primarily in explaining how integration has taken place or how the EU works. Instead, their purpose is to critically assess these things, pointing in various ways to the often overlooked dynamics of power within the EU, considering both elite and marginalized voices (see Part One, Theory, Table I.1).

To adopt a critical approach is not necessarily to reject a mainstream approach, or vice versa. As noted, there may be important overlaps between and blurring of these positions (see Table 4.1). Moreover, they can be understood in terms of the quite different functions that they perform. Robert Cox (1981) usefully characterized what we have here termed the mainstream as 'problem solving theory'. Such theory views the broad structures of the social and political world as a given, in order to focus on specific problems or issues within that pre-defined world. In contrast, 'critical theory' points to the mutability and alterability of that broader social and political world in an attempt to contemplate more fundamental changes. If we accept the importance of both of these functions, then scholars and students of the EU do not necessarily need to place themselves either definitively within or in opposition to either camp.

It is, however, important to consider why these more critical perspectives have been absent for so long within mainstream studies of the EU. Both their exclusion and their gradual (re-)admittance to the mainstream can be accounted for by factors internal to political studies scholarship—a disciplinary politics—and factors related to the politics of European integration and the EU (Rosamond 2007). Recent political crises in the EU, and the increased openness of mainstream scholarship to alternative perspectives, are therefore interrelated factors that are likely to foster continued interest in critical approaches.

KEY POINTS

Critical of What?

- Critical perspectives have received increasing attention in the study of EU politics in the past decade or so. Collectively they challenge mainstream 'positivist' approaches to the study of the EU.

Social Constructivism

- Social constructivism entered the debate on the EU to challenge the positivist (rationalist and materialist) assumptions on which the dominant integration theories were built.

- In relation to the EU, social constructivism puts particular emphasis on how national positions and perceived national interests are shaped through the socialization of national actors within and with EU levels of government.

- Social constructivist work on the EU has analysed the ways in which 'European' identities and ideas are constructed and shifting over time and with what consequences.

Critical Political Economy

- A broadly neo-Marxist CPE analyses the EU in the context of broader capitalist social relations, often emphasizing the role of elites in driving particular sorts of integration at the expense of subordinate classes. It is critical of a 'liberal' bias in much mainstream theorizing on the EU.

- A contemporary generation of scholars working in this tradition has drawn on Gramsci's concept of hegemony to elucidate the ways in which economic elites have been able to push their 'neoliberal' agendas in the EU, often at the expense of the interests of particular classes and democratic practices.

- Academics working in this tradition have focused their critique on 'economic' areas of EU policy making, such as the single market and monetary union.

Critical Social Theory

- The Critical Social Theory considered in this chapter can be traced to the 'Frankfurt School' of 'Critical Theory' and in particular the work of Jürgen Habermas, who is himself a frequent commentator on EU politics.

- Critical Social Theory emphasizes the ways in which the EU has facilitated the emergence of a cosmopolitan European society and views this as a positive development worthy of scholarly and political support. But Critical Social Theory is not uncritical of the status quo within the EU.

- Theorists such as Beck and Grande have been critical of a residual 'methodological nationalism' within EU politics and EU scholarship. They oppose both member state nationalism and the attempt to re-invent the EU as a unified state, and advocate a 'both-and' EU of plural identities.

- Habermas, like critical political economists, emphasizes the 'neoliberal' bias in the EU status quo. His vision of a cosmopolitan EU more closely resembles a federal Europe built on a social democratic constitution.

Critical Feminism

- There is no single 'gender theory' or 'feminist theory' of the EU, but rather a broad range of perspectives. Such perspectives have often focused on the emergence of gender equality policies at EU level.

- Critical feminists argue that dominant integration theories have done little to develop understanding of gender dynamics in the EU. They are seen to ignore the 'male-as-norm' problem and as based on a simplistic view of power.

Post-Structuralism

- Post-structural approaches draw on the insights of a range of (often French) thinkers including Michel Foucault, Pierre Bourdieu, and Jacques Derrida

- Post-structural work on the EU is diverse in terms of its focus, and includes work on questions of European identity, borders, security, and political economy. There are significant overlaps between post-structuralism and the other critical approaches considered.

- The attempt to unsettle a sense of certainty or 'common sense' in relation to both the EU and strands of EU scholarship has been the uniting theme of post-structural analysis.

- Parker's (2013) work offers an example of the way in which a post-structural approach can critically engage with both the EU as object of study and other approaches considered in this chapter such as CPE and critical social theory.

FURTHER READING

For a wide-ranging review of critical perspectives on the study of the EU, see **I. Manners**, 'Another Europe is Possible', in **K. E. Jorgensen, M. Pollack, and B. Rosamond (eds)**, *Handbook of European Union Politics* (London: SAGE Publications, 2007), 77–95.

On social constructivism, see the influential collection in the special issue of the *Journal of European Public Policy,* 6(4) (1999), edited by **T. Christiansen, K. Jørgensen, and A. Wiener**. Other helpful contributions are: **J. Checkel and A. Moravcsik**, 'A Constructivist Research Programme in EU Studies?', *European Union Politics*, 2 (2001): 219–49.

There are number of useful edited collections encompassing a range of CPE perspectives, including: **A. Cafruny and M. Ryner (eds)**, *A Ruined Fortress? Neoliberal Hegemony and Transformation in Europe* (Lanham: Rowman and Littlefield, 2003); **P. Nousios, H. Overbeek, and A. Tsolakis (eds)**, *Globalisation and European Integration: Critical Approaches to Regional Order and International Relations* (London: Routledge, 2012); **B. van Apeldoorn, J. Drahokoupil, and L. Horn (eds)**, *Contradictions and Limits of Neoliberal European Governance: From Lisbon to Lisbon* (Basingstoke and New York: Palgrave Macmillan, 2008).

Key works in the area of critical social theory include **J. Habermas**, *The Postnational Constellation* (Cambridge: Polity Press, 2001); **U. Beck and E. Grande**, *Cosmopolitan Europe* (Cambridge: Polity Press, 2007); **G. Delanty and C. Rumford**, *Rethinking Europe: Social Theory and the Implications of Europeanization* (Abingdon and New York: Routledge, 2005). For a critical discussion of Habermas's and other critical social theory work on the EU, see, **O. Parker**, 'Why EU, Which EU? Habermas and the Ethics of Postnational Politics in Europe', *Constellations: An International Journal of Critical and Democratic Theory*, 16 (2009): 392–409.

On feminist/gender approaches there are several helpful overview pieces, including: **C. Hoskyns's** 'Gender Perspectives', in **A. Wiener and T. Diez (eds)**, *European Integration Theory* (Oxford: Oxford University Press, 2004), 217–36; **E. Prügl**, 'Gender and European Union Politics', in **K. E. Jørgensen, M. Pollack, and B. Rosamond (eds)**, *Handbook of European Union Politics* (London: SAGE Publications, 2007), 433–48. For a comprehensive overview of the EU's impact on gender policies see **J. Kantola**, *Gender and the European Union* (Basingstoke: Palgrave Macmillan, 2010). For a particular focus on gender and theories of European integration see **A. Kronsell**, 'Gender, Power and European Integration Theory', *Journal of European Public Policy*, 12 (2008): 1022–40.

Key works from a post-structuralist perspective include **O. Parker**, *Cosmopolitan Government in Europe: Citizens and Entrepreneurs in Postnational Politics* (Abingdon and New York: Routledge, 2013) or 'Towards an Ambiguous "Cosmopolitics": Citizens and Entrepreneurs in the European Project', *International Theory*, 4 (2012): 198–232; and **W. Walters and J. Henrik Haahr**, *Governing Europe: Discourse, Governmentality and European Integration* (London: Routledge, 2005)

 online resource centre **Visit the Online Resource Centre that accompanies this book for links to more information on critical perspectives:http://oxfordtextbooks.co.uk/orc/bache4e/**

Part Two
History

Deciding where to begin a history is often difficult, but not really in this case. While there were attempts to integrate Europe before the twentieth century, the end of the Second World War in 1945 provided the catalyst for the phase of European integration with which we are familiar today. There is little dispute among historians that 1945 is the most appropriate starting point for discussing the events leading to the creation of what is today the European Union. Thus, while we reflect briefly on previous attempts to integrate Europe, our point of departure here is the end of the Second World War.

The history we present is largely a familiar account of developments in European integration in the second half of the twentieth century. The history of European integration often told is one that emphasizes individuals, perhaps at the expense of broader social, economic, and political forces that shape events. Our account here generally reflects this dominant approach, not least because it is the function of a textbook to cover the most recognized contributions on the field of study. However, we have sought to add to the dominant narrative in the conclusions to the chapters in this section by drawing on the themes and perspectives discussed in Part One of the book.

We encourage a critical approach to the reading of history. In this respect, readers would be well served by reading Mark Gilbert's (2008) article, which questions many of the assumptions of the way in which the EU's history is often told as the 'progressive story of European integration'. For example, Gilbert (2008: 645) highlights rhetorical devices that are used to present this as a progressive story:

> Choice of terms: construction metaphors abound. References to Europe's 'path', 'march', 'advance', 'progress', are [...] commonplace. Moments of relative inactivity are described as 'stagnation'—the 1970s, for instance, are frequently referred to in this way. The process is always 're-launched' or 'revived' after moments of difficulty.
> Authorial judgements: the standard used to measure whether major decisions were successes or failures is almost always whether they augmented or reduced the overall degree of supranationality within the Community.

Whether we write the history in this way and, if so, how it might be written differently is something for the readers of this book to reflect upon.

Chapter 5

From the End of the War to the Schuman Plan (the late 1940s to the early 1950s)

Chapter Overview

In 1945 the European continent emerged exhausted from the Second World War. It was soon to be divided between the capitalist West and the communist East. Yet, in the west of the continent something happened that was without historical precedent: some of the states took the first steps towards surrendering their sovereignty in pursuit of European integration. Although there had been many previous plans and movements for a united Europe, they had foundered on the unwillingness of the governments of states to surrender their control over important political decisions. This time, though, practicalities suggested to some political leaders that there were more advantages in pooling the sovereignty of their several states than in trying to meet the challenges of the post-war world alone.

This chapter looks briefly at the long history of plans for European unity that came to nothing, before turning to the period immediately after the end of the Second World War, and the ideas of the European federalists. Their vision of a federal Europe did not appeal to the new governments of the post-war period, but there were practical reasons why some moves to European unity found favour with those governments: the threat of communism and the emergence of the Cold War; the problem of what to do about Germany; and the need to ensure adequate supplies of coal for the post-war economic reconstruction. As a solution to these intersecting problems, the French civil servant, Jean Monnet, came up with a proposal for a European coal and steel community. The proposal, national reactions to it, and the negotiations that led to the setting up of the first of the European communities are all reviewed.

Background: The Ideal of European Unity

Our starting point for this discussion of European integration is the end of the Second World War, but the idea of European integration is not unique to this era. Politicians and intellectuals alike aspired to European unity over two centuries. Plans for achieving perpetual peace in Europe by overcoming the division into nation states can be traced back at least to the early eighteenth century, and the *Project for Perpetual Peace* of the Abbé de Saint Pierre (Forsyth et al. 1970: 128). At a practical level, though, moves for European unity took the form of attempts by one nation or another to dominate Europe through conquest. Both France under Napoleon and Germany under Hitler could be accused of trying to forge European unity in this way.

Whereas attempts at enforced European *political* integration foundered, the potential benefits of *economic* integration proved attractive to European political elites. Yet, nineteenth-century experiments with **free trade areas** across nation states were short-lived, while early **customs unions** were specific to regions within nation states. Ultimately, these experiments in economic integration suffered the same fate as attempts at political unity.

Movements in favour of peaceful integration emerged in Europe after the First World War, but the political settlement after the war was based on the peaceful co-existence of nation states rather than integration. The failure of the League of Nations (see Insight 5.1) to sustain peace was rapid and complete, with the resurgence of nationalism in the 1920s and 1930s. The pro-integration groups emerging in Europe after 1918 were unable to offer any practical solutions to this. The outbreak of the Second World War destroyed hopes of European unity. The aftermath of the war, though, provided the origins for the modern movement for European integration.

Emerging from the war physically devastated, Europe began a process of both economic and political reconstruction. The idea of European unity was present in this process from the outset, as the ideology of federalism had attracted a great deal of support during the war. However, the story cannot be told simply in terms of ideals. Although influential figures showed some degree of attachment to the concept of federalism, the steps that were taken were informed by hard-headed realism about what was necessary for reconstruction to succeed. They were also taken in the context of an emerging Cold War that divided the continent on ideological lines.

Insight 5.1 The League of Nations

- The League of Nations was inspired by the vision of US President Woodrow Wilson. Its Covenant was drawn up at the Paris Peace Conference in 1919, but the US Congress refused to ratify the Treaty so the United States never became a member of the League.

- The League Covenant committed the states that signed to respect the sovereignty and territorial integrity of other states and not to resort to force to resolve disputes, but to submit them to arbitration by the League.

- The League's institutional structure consisted of a General Assembly, in which all member states were represented, and a Council. The Council had four, then later six, permanent members—Britain, France, Italy, Japan; then Germany, from 1926, and the USSR, from 1934.

- Between 1931 and 1939 the League failed to deal effectively with aggression by Japan, Italy, Germany, and the USSR. In 1935 Japan and Germany withdrew from membership.

- Although it failed to prevent war, the League did successfully establish a number of special agencies working at a functional level to deal with matters such as health and the protection of labour. The success of these bodies may have influenced the thinking of David Mitrany (see Chapter 1, The Intellectual Background).

The End of the War, Federalism, and The Hague Congress

The war in Europe had extensively destroyed physical infrastructure, disrupted economic production, and caused severe social dislocation. Roads, railways, and bridges had been destroyed by Allied bombing or by the retreating German army in its attempt to slow the advance of the Allied forces. According to Laqueur (1972: 17–18) coal production at the end of the war was only 42 per cent of its pre-war level; pig iron output in 1946 was less than one-third of that in 1938; and crude steel output was about one-third of what it had been before the war. There were millions of refugees wandering around Europe trying to return to their homes, or without any homes to return to.

Accompanying the economic and social dislocation, there was political dislocation as governments that had collaborated with the Nazis were displaced. Germany and Austria remained occupied, and divided between the occupation zones of the Allies. Elsewhere, there was a mood in favour of change; a feeling that there should be no return to the pre-war elites and the pre-war ways.

This mood particularly benefited parties of the left. In Britain, a Labour government was elected in 1945 with a massive majority despite the Conservatives being led by the wartime hero, Winston Churchill. In France, the provisional government that was set up in 1945 was presided over by General Charles de Gaulle, the conservative leader of the Free French forces, which had fought on from outside of the occupied country; but the first elections favoured the parties of the internal Resistance, particularly the communists but also the Socialists and the centre-left Christian party, the *Mouvement Républicain Populaire* (MRP). In Italy, although the Catholic south ensured the emergence of a large conservative Christian Democratic Party, the communists dominated in the industrial north.

The mood for change also fed a strong popular sentiment in the countries that had suffered from fascism, in favour of a decisive move away from nationalism in the post-war reconstruction. Ideas favouring European federalism gained support, particularly in Italy, but also in France, Germany, and elsewhere in continental Europe, although not in Britain or the Scandinavian countries.

The European Union of Federalists (EUF) was formed in 1946 from the wartime Resistance movements. It attempted to exploit the disruption caused to existing political structures by the war to make a new start on a basis radically different from the Europe of nation states, and to create a federal constitution for Europe as part of a more distant plan for global unity. However, it took until 1947 to organize the conference that was supposed to pave the way to the new constitution, by which time national governments had already been restored to office everywhere. The conference, the European Congress, eventually took place in The Hague in May 1948.

The Congress attracted considerable attention at the time. It was attended by representatives of most of the political parties of the non-communist states of Europe, and its Honorary President was Winston Churchill, who had used a speech in Zurich in 1946 to call for a united Europe. Churchill had implied in the Zurich speech that Britain, with its Commonwealth of Nations, would remain separate from the 'United States of Europe' to which he referred. Britain, along with the United States, and possibly the Union of Soviet Socialist Republics (USSR), would be 'friends and sponsors of the new Europe'. The vital development in this project would be a 'partnership' between France and Germany. Beyond this, and the 'first step' of forming a Council of Europe (see Insight 5.2), Churchill did not detail how the process towards European unity should proceed.

The Hague Congress was an occasion for fine speeches, but it gradually became apparent that the British were not interested in being part of a **supranational organization** that would compromise their national sovereignty. While the Congress did lead to the creation of the Council of Europe, this was so dominated by national governments that there was little realistic prospect of it developing in the federal direction that the EUF hoped.

Insight 5.2 The Council of Europe

Founded in 1949 as a result of the 1948 Congress of Europe in The Hague, the Council of Europe is not connected to the EU and should not be confused with the European Council, which is the name of the institutionalized summit meetings of the EU heads of state and government.

The Council of Europe is an intergovernmental organization based in the French city of Strasbourg. It originally had ten members, and by 2014 had forty-seven, including twenty-two countries from central and eastern Europe. Its main institutions are:

- the Committee of (Foreign) Ministers;
- the Parliamentary Assembly, consisting of 321 members of national parliaments, with 321 substitutes;
- the Congress of Local and Regional Authorities of Europe;
- the Secretariat;
- the European Commissioner for Human Rights;
- the European Court of Human Rights.

The Council was set up to:

- defend human rights, parliamentary democracy, and the rule of law;
- develop continent-wide agreements to standardize member countries' social and legal practices;
- promote awareness of a European identity based on shared values and cutting across different cultures.

Since 1989, its main job has become:

- to act as a political anchor and human rights watchdog for Europe's post-communist democracies;
- to assist the countries of central and eastern Europe in carrying out and consolidating political, legal, and constitutional reform in parallel with economic reform;
- to provide know-how in areas such as human rights, local democracy, education, culture, and the environment.

Source: **http://hub.coe.int/**.

The Council of Europe still exists today, and it has many solid achievements to its credit. In particular, it was responsible for adopting the European Convention on Human Rights in 1950, and it maintained both a Commission on Human Rights (replaced by a Commissioner in 1999) and a Court of Human Rights: the former to investigate alleged breaches of such rights by governments, and the latter to rule definitively on whether a violation of rights has occurred. It also serves useful functions as a meeting place for parliamentarians from the diverse member states and promotes Europe-wide cultural activities. This all falls far short of the hopes of the EUF.

European integration was not to be achieved in one great act of political will, because the will was not there. Some blamed the failure of the Council of Europe to develop in a federal direction on the attitude of the British; but the truth is that no national government, once installed, was willing to surrender much of its power. In 1947 the attention of governments was still focused on national economic reconstruction, not on superseding the nation state. Yet, there were soon more insistent pressures on the governments to move away from national sovereignty than those that the federalists could muster.

The Cold War

To understand the origins of the European Communities, which led to the European Union, it is essential to see them in the context of the emerging Cold War between the capitalist West and the communist Soviet Union. Before the Second World War, advocates of a European union had assumed it would stretch to the borders of the USSR. But as relations between the former Allies deteriorated throughout 1946 and into 1947, it became clear this would be a project confined to the western part of the continent.

Agreement was reached at an Allied summit meeting in Yalta in 1945 to divide Europe at the end of the war into 'spheres of influence'. This was intended by the western Allies to be only a temporary arrangement, but the Soviet Union soon started to make it permanent. Regimes friendly to the USSR were installed in those countries of central and eastern Europe that had been assigned to the Soviet sphere at Yalta. This led Churchill to make a speech in Fulton, Missouri, in March 1946 in which he talked about an 'iron curtain' descending across Europe. The speech did not receive a sympathetic hearing in Washington, where the prevailing mood was still in favour of co-operation with the USSR; but this mood changed in the course of 1946.

In September 1946, communist insurgents restarted a civil war in Greece. This was a decision that could not have been taken without the agreement of the Soviet Union. In 1945 Stalin had ordered the Greek communists, who controlled large areas of the country, not to continue with an armed insurrection against the government that the British had installed in Athens. Greece was in the British sphere of influence according to the Yalta agreement, and it seemed that whatever unwelcome moves Stalin might be making in the Soviet sphere, he was at least intent on respecting the limits set at Yalta. The recommencement of hostilities in Greece threw that interpretation into doubt. During 1946, too, the Soviet Union refused to withdraw its troops from Persia, which was also outside its sphere, and made territorial demands on Turkey.

The weather in the European winter of 1946–7 was particularly severe, and put considerable strain on the economic recovery that was underway. This had direct consequences for the emergence of the Cold War. In February 1947, London informed Washington that it could not afford to continue economic and military aid to Greece and Turkey. In response, in March 1947, President Truman asked Congress for $400 million of economic and military aid for Greece and Turkey. To dramatize the situation, he spoke of the duty of the United States to assist 'free peoples who are resisting attempted subjugation by armed minorities or by outside pressures'. This became known as the Truman Doctrine, and it marked a clear statement of intent by the US Administration to remain involved in the affairs of Europe and the wider world, and not to allow isolationist sentiments within the country and within Congress to force a withdrawal from an international role.

Perhaps even more significant in converting the US Administration to Churchill's view, was the collapse of the Four-Power Council of Foreign Ministers, a standing conference to discuss the administration and future of Germany. Soviet intransigence in that forum, and the eventual walk-out of the Soviet representative in April 1947, convinced those who were trying to negotiate on behalf of Washington that it was not possible to work with the USSR. From that point on, the emergence of separate west and east German states became gradually inevitable.

A second direct consequence of the bad winter and economic setback of early 1947 was that waves of strikes spread across France and Italy. In both cases the strikes were supported by communists, who engaged in revolutionary anti-capitalist rhetoric. In the light of events in Greece, this was interpreted as further evidence of the Soviet Union attempting to undermine stability outside its sphere of influence, although in both cases it may have been an incorrect interpretation. Certainly in France, where the Communist Party was part of the coalition government, the strikes appeared to take them by surprise. However, it was very difficult for the French communists not to support their core electorate, and indeed not to interpret the strikes as evidence of the imminent collapse of capitalism. The other parties in the French coalition responded by expelling the communists from the government; the Truman Administration responded with the Marshall Plan.

On 5 June 1947 George Marshall, the US Secretary of State, announced that the United States Administration proposed to offer financial and food aid to Europe to assist in its economic recovery (see Insight 5.3). Suspicious of US motives, the USSR

Insight 5.3 The Marshall Plan

- The European Recovery Programme (ERP) was announced by US Secretary of State George C. Marshall in a speech at Harvard University on 5 June 1947.

- It involved the United States giving a total of $13 billion in financial aid to the states of western Europe. The assistance was offered to the states of eastern Europe, but they declined under pressure from the Soviet Union.

- The European states that accepted held a conference in July 1947 in Paris, and set up the Organization for European Economic Co-operation (OEEC) to facilitate the unified response that the United States required.

and its allies rejected the offer. There were some grounds for this suspicion: the American gesture went far beyond simple altruism to a concern with economic self-interest.

Marshall presented the American people with a vision of Europe in crisis in 1947. People were starving. The economy had broken down. Milward (1984: 3–4) contested this orthodox view. He denied there was a crisis, although he accepted that there was a serious problem about the ability of the west European states to build and sustain international trade because of a lack of convertible currencies to finance it. In his view, the Marshall Plan was entirely political in its conception and objectives, although its means were entirely economic. The misleading representation of the economic position in Europe was designed to get the agreement of the US Congress to the reconstruction programme.

Marshall Aid offered an injection of dollars into the European economy, which would finance trade between the European states and the United States, and trade between the European states themselves. This was a policy much favoured by those sections of US industry that were involved in exporting. It was less favoured by those sections of US industry that were oriented towards the domestic market, and that suspected that they would pay the bill for European reconstruction without gaining the benefits. This section of domestic opinion was strongly represented within Congress, and so it was by no means a foregone conclusion that the Administration would get its plans through Congress. Following the Soviet Union's rejection of aid, Truman and Marshall were able to justify the Plan as part of the same response to the threat of communism as was the Truman Doctrine. Marshall argued that economic conditions in western Europe in 1947 were so serious that they provided a breeding ground for communism. The struggle had to be waged by economic as well as military means.

Whether it was motivated by genuine concern for the condition of western Europe, or by economic considerations that had more to do with lobbying by the larger US corporations, Marshall Aid came with strings attached. The US Administration was committed to the idea of free trade. It was concerned to see what it described as 'European integration', meaning that national economic barriers to trade should be broken down. Both of the motives discussed above would support this position. Given that the Administration genuinely believed that free trade would strengthen the west European economies, integration was compatible with the stated aim of strengthening western Europe against communist expansion. However, it was also compatible with the aim of creating a large and exploitable market for US exports and for investments by US multinational corporations.

The United States insisted that decisions on the distribution and use of Marshall Aid be taken by the European states jointly. To implement this, a body known as the Committee for European Economic Co-operation (CEEC) was set up. Despite the professed aim of allowing the Europeans to make their own decisions on the use of the aid, the United States was represented on this committee, and because it was contributing all the funds, it clearly had economic and political leverage.

The CEEC was transformed in April 1948 into a more permanent body, the Organization for European Economic Co-operation (OEEC). The OEEC initially had fifteen members, but was soon joined by the newly-independent Federal Republic of Germany (1949), while the United States and Canada became associate members in 1950.

For Marshall, and other members of the US Administration, the OEEC was to be the basis for the future supranational economic management of Europe. Nobody was quite clear what 'supranational' meant in this context, but it certainly meant breaking down national sovereignty in economic affairs. In particular, the US view was that western Europe should become a free trade area as the first step towards global free trade.

This was not a vision that appealed to the governments of the European states involved. The British did not particularly want to be tied into any arrangement with the continental European states. The French had already embarked on their own recovery programme, which was based on a much more restrictive view of the role of free trade and the free market. Other governments shared some of the French concern to keep as much control as possible over their own economies, giving away sovereignty neither to a supranational organization nor to the workings of the international free market.

Crucial to the economic and political stance of the European states was the position of Germany. Whether the German economy and state would be reconstituted was still an open question when CEEC began operations. The US wanted the decisions to be made by the OEEC. Germany's neighbours were simply not prepared to see that happen. In particular, they were nervous about the extent of political leverage the United States was able to exercise within the OEEC because of its economic influence as the sole contributor to the reconstruction funds. However, despite its economic leverage, the United States simply did not have sufficient political weight to overcome the combined opposition of Britain, France, and the smaller European states to allowing the OEEC to develop as a powerful supranational organization (Milward, 1984: 168–211).

The body within the OEEC controlling policy and administration was the Council of Ministers, which consisted of one representative from each member state. Decisions taken by the Council were binding on members but each member state retained the right of veto. While effective within its limited remit, the OEEC promised little in terms of further integration.

Despite its limitations, the OEEC continued its work for twelve years and, according to Urwin (1995: 22), 'played a major role in driving home the realization that European economies were mutually dependent, and that they prospered or failed together'. In 1961, the OEEC was superseded by the Organization for Economic Co-operation and Development (OECD), which had a broader remit, concerned with issues of economic development both in Europe and globally, and included the USA and Canada as full members.

The German Problem

The German problem came increasingly to dominate the debate about the future of Europe. For the United States and Britain the future of Germany was inevitably linked to the emerging Cold War. For France and Germany's smaller neighbours it was still a question of how to prevent the re-emergence of a threat to their sovereign independence from Germany itself.

Initially Germany's neighbours tried to protect themselves through a traditional military alliance, in which British participation was seen as crucial. This approach produced the Treaty of Dunkirk between Britain and France in March 1947, and the Treaty of Brussels between Britain, France, and the **Benelux** states in March 1948. Both alliances were directed more at forestalling German aggression than they were at the Soviet Union.

The French government also tried to prevent the emergence of any German state. Ideally the French Foreign Office would have liked to have kept Germany under Allied occupation. Failing that, it wanted the former German state to be divided into a large number of small separate states. By 1949 it had become apparent that this was not going to happen. Again, the crucial dynamic was the rapidly emerging Cold War. In 1948 the Soviet Union walked out of Allied talks on the future of Germany. The United States and Britain responded by starting to prepare the Anglo-American zones for independence. The French were left in no doubt that they were expected to merge their occupation zone into the new west German state, which would be created under the plans for independence. Once the Federal Republic of Germany came into existence in 1949, the French policy had to be rethought.

The Schuman Plan for Coal and Steel

In May 1950 the French Foreign Minister, Robert Schuman, proposed a scheme for pooling the coal and steel supplies of France and Germany, and invited other European states who wished to participate to express an interest. The idea involved a surrender of sovereignty over the coal and steel industries. It was devised by Jean Monnet, a French civil servant (see Insight 5.4), and addressed practical problems for France that

---

Insight 5.4 Jean Monnet

Jean Monnet (1888–1979) was born into a small brandy-producing family in Cognac. He left school at sixteen and, after a period gaining experience of financial affairs in London, he worked for the family business, travelling widely.

In 1915 he was declared unfit for military service, and spent the war in the civil service instead. He rose rapidly to the position of representative of the French government in London.

After the war he was appointed deputy secretary-general of the League of Nations, but he returned to private life when the family firm got into difficulties in 1922. He subsequently became an investment banker and financier.

In the Second World War he worked first for the British government in Washington, then for de Gaulle in Algiers. He was instrumental in preventing the British and Americans from replacing de Gaulle, who, in 1946, appointed him as head of the CdP.

He devised both the Schuman Plan and the Pleven Plan for a European Defence Community (EDC).

He was the first President of the High Authority of the ECSC between 1952 and 1955. Following the defeat of the proposed EDC in the French National Assembly, he resigned from the High Authority to be free to promote further schemes for European integration, setting up the Action Committee for the United States of Europe.

arose from the establishment of the Federal Republic of Germany. The first problem was how to avert the threat of future conflict between France and Germany; the second was how to ensure continuing supplies of coal for the French steel industry once the Ruhr region reverted to German sovereign control. The plan was welcomed by the German Chancellor, Konrad Adenauer, and the Benelux states and Italy indicated that they would wish to participate. The British government declined an invitation to take part. The negotiations between the six states that did wish to participate were marked by hard bargaining in defence of national interests, but eventually agreement was reached on what became the European Coal and Steel Community (ECSC). The Six signed the Treaty of Paris in April 1952, and the ECSC came into operation in July 1952.

National Positions and the Origins of the ECSC

The plan for the ECSC was known as the Schuman Plan because it was made public by the French Foreign Minister, Robert Schuman. He was born in Luxembourg, lived in Lorraine when it was part of the German empire, was conscripted into the German army in the First World War, and only became a French citizen after the war when Alsace and Lorraine reverted to French sovereignty. Thus he had a particular reason for wanting to reconcile the historic conflict between the two countries.

Milward (1984: 395–6) argued that the Foreign Ministry must have played a role in devising the plan, but the more generally accepted view is that it was drawn up within the French Economic Planning Commission (Commissariat du Plan—CdP), which was headed by Jean Monnet. It was the task of the CdP to guide the post-war reconstruction and modernization of the French economy, and it was through his experiences in this task that Monnet came to appreciate the economic inadequacy of the European nation state in the modern world. As he himself put it:

> For five years the whole French nation had been making efforts to recreate the bases of production, but it became evident that to go beyond recovery towards steady expansion and higher standards of life for all, the resources of a single nation were not sufficient. It was necessary to transcend the national framework.

(Monnet 1962: 205)

The wider framework that Monnet had in mind was an economically united western Europe. He saw the need to create a 'large and dynamic common market', 'a huge continental market on the European scale' (Monnet 1962: 205). But he aimed to create more than just a common market. Monnet was a planner: he showed no great confidence in the free market system, which had served France badly in the past. He placed his faith in the development of supranational institutions as the basis for building a genuine economic community that would adopt common economic policies and rational planning procedures.

Coal and steel were only intended as starting points. The aim was to extend integration to all aspects of the west European economy; but such a scheme would have been too ambitious to gain acceptance all at once.

> Europe will not be made all at once, or according to a single plan. It will be built through concrete achievements which first create a *de facto* solidarity.

(Schuman Declaration 1950)

There had been a clear indication of this need for incrementalism in the failure of various post-war efforts to integrate the economies of France, Italy, the Netherlands, Belgium, and Luxembourg. Although negotiations for an organization to be known as 'Finebel' had proceeded for some time, they were on the verge of collapse in 1950. Besides, the new factor in the equation, and the key factor prompting Monnet's plan, was the emergence in April 1949 of a sovereign west German state.

For Monnet, the existence of the Federal Republic of Germany posed two problems in addition to that of how to create an integrated west European economy. The first was how to organize Franco-German relations in such a way that another war between the two states would become impossible. To a French mind this meant how to control Germany. The pooling of coal and steel production would provide the basis for economic development as a first step towards a 'federation of Europe', and would change the future of those regions devoted to producing munitions, which had also been 'the most constant victims' of war.

> The solidarity in production thus established will make it plain that any war between France and Germany becomes not merely unthinkable, but materially impossible.

(Schuman Declaration 1950)

The problem of how to control Germany remained at the heart of the process of European integration throughout the early post-war period.

The second problem facing Monnet was the very practical one of how to ensure continuing adequate supplies of coking coal from the Ruhr for the French steel industry. The idea of pooling Franco-German supplies of coal and steel was not new: similar schemes had been proposed on many occasions previously (Gillingham 1991*b*: 135; Duchêne 1994: 202). In fact the idea of pooling coal and steel supplies had featured in two recent publications, one from the Assembly of the Council of Europe and the other from the UN Economic Commission for Europe (Urwin 1995: 44). These reports were concerned with the very practical problems affecting the coal and steel industries of Europe. There was excess capacity in steel, and a shortage of coal. This combination was of particular concern to Monnet, whose recovery plan for France involved expanding steel-producing capacity. The French steel industry was heavily dependent on supplies of coking coal from the Ruhr.

At the end of the war, the Ruhr region of Germany had been placed under joint Allied control. Its supplies of coal had been allocated between the various competing users by the International Authority for the Ruhr (IAR), which had been established in April 1945. It seemed unlikely that this arrangement could be long continued once the Federal Republic was constituted, which raised the question of how France could ensure that it continued to get access to the supply of scarce Ruhr coal which its steel industry needed. The coal and steel pool had the potential to achieve this.

In summary, Monnet's reasons for proposing the plan to pool Franco-German supplies of coal and steel were a combination of taking a first step on the road to complete integration of the west European economy, finding a way to organize Franco-German relations which would eliminate the prospect of a further war between the two states, and solving the problem of how to ensure continued access for the French steel industry to supplies of coking coal from the Ruhr. That Schuman essentially accepted this thinking, informs the standard explanation for France's participation in the Schuman Plan.

For the Federal Republic of Germany, Chancellor Adenauer accepted the Schuman Plan with alacrity. Yet, if the proposal had been made to serve French interests, why was the German Chancellor so keen on it? As with Schuman, one of the factors was a commitment on the part of Adenauer to the ideal of European integration. Like Schuman, Adenauer came from a border region, in his case the Rhineland. Like Schuman, he was a Roman Catholic and a Christian Democrat. In accepting the Schuman Plan, Adenauer committed himself to Franco-German reconciliation and to European integration. This does not mean, though, that he acted only for idealistic reasons. There were also very practical reasons for Adenauer's acceptance of the Schuman Plan. The Federal Republic needed to gain international acceptance; Adenauer wanted to make a strong commitment to the capitalist West; and the new German government was looking for a way of getting rid of the IAR.

The legacy of the Nazi era and of the war had left Germany a pariah nation. It had also left it divided into two separate states, the Federal Republic in the west and the Democratic Republic in the east. Adenauer wanted to establish the Federal Republic as the legitimate successor to the pre-war German state, but also as a peace-loving state that would be accepted as a full participant in European and international affairs. He also wanted to establish the western and capitalist orientation of the Federal Republic beyond question or reversal. This was important to Adenauer because the Social Democratic Party (*Sozialdemokratische Partei Deutschlands*—SPD) was arguing for the Federal Republic to declare itself neutral in the emerging Cold War in the hope that this would facilitate re-unification of the country. As well as being strongly anti-communist, Adenauer believed that the Democratic Republic was dominated by the Soviet Union, and he feared the cultural influence of Russia would be damaging to the vitality of German culture and to the process of moral renewal in the aftermath of Nazism, which, as a devout Catholic, he believed to be essential (Milward 1992: 329–30).

The importance for Adenauer of getting rid of the IAR was both political and economic. Politically it was important to him that the region be integrated into the Federal Republic. Economically, the Ruhr had always been one of the powerhouses of the German industrial economy, so it was important to the prospects of economic recovery that it be unchained from the restrictions that the IAR placed on its industrialists. There was a risk that, in accepting the Schuman Plan, Adenauer would commit his country to a relationship from which French industry would gain at the expense of German industry. However, Adenauer was confident that German industrialists could stand up for their interests within a coal and steel pool (Gillingham 1991a: 233).

The reason why the Benelux states agreed to enter the negotiations for the ECSC was the same in each case: they could not afford to stay out of any agreement between France and Germany on coal and steel. These commodities were essential to the economies of the three states, and there was a high degree of interdependence between the industries in the border regions of France and Germany, and those in

Belgium and Luxembourg particularly. There was also support in all three states for any moves that promised to reduce the risk of war between their two larger neighbours.

Italian reasons for joining in the negotiations require a little more explanation than the reasons for Benelux participation. Italy is not geographically part of the same industrial region as the other participants, so there was not the same inevitability about its involvement. In many ways the reasons for Italian participation in the negotiations resembled those of Germany more closely than those of the Benelux states.

Like Germany, Italy was governed by Christian Democrats; and as in the case of Adenauer (and of Schuman) the individual who dominated the government was a Roman Catholic and someone who originated in a border region. Alcide di Gasperi came from the Alto Adige region of Italy, which had been part of the Austro-Hungarian empire before the First World War. Like Germany, Italy had to rebuild its international reputation after the war. Mussolini had been Hitler's ally and had ended up as his puppet. Like Germany, Italy was on the front line in the emerging Cold War. Geographically, it had a land frontier with the communist state of Yugoslavia, and only the Adriatic Sea separated it from Albania. At the end of the war there had been a serious risk that the Italian Communist Party would take over the country in democratic elections, and it remained the largest single party in terms of support. Di Gasperi therefore had a similar need to that of Adenauer in Germany to enmesh his country in a complex of institutional interdependencies with the capitalist West, to establish its western and capitalist identity politically, economically, and in the minds of its own people.

The other state that was invited to participate in the conference that followed the Schuman Plan was Britain. The negative attitude of the British government has been extensively analysed (Dell 1995; George 1998: 19–22; J. W. Young 1993: 28–35; H. Young 1998).

All accounts accept that there were certain peculiarities of the British position that made it highly unlikely that its government would welcome the proposal. Whereas, in continental Europe, nationalism had been discredited through its association with fascism, in Britain fascism had never succeeded, and the war had been fought as a national war. Unlike the other states, Britain had neither been defeated nor occupied in the war. There was not the same sense in Britain of discontinuity with the past. The attitude of the British governing elite was that Britain was not just another European state. It was a world power with global responsibilities. Although this attitude has been described as a 'delusion of grandeur' (Porter 1987), it had some basis in reality: Britain still had a considerable empire, British companies had interests in all parts of the world, and British armed forces were globally deployed in keeping the peace, or acting as a bulwark against communist encroachment.

The perception at the time was that Britain was economically far stronger than the other western European states, and that tying the future of the British economy to that of the German and French economies was dangerous. Britain had adequate indigenous supplies of coal, and the Labour government had just completed the nationalization of the coal and steel industries. Having campaigned over many years for nationalization, the Labour Party was unlikely to surrender control once it had been achieved. Also, European integration was at this time particularly associated with the leader of the Conservative Party, Winston Churchill. Although there were some

Labour Party members who participated in The Hague Congress and remained supporters of a united Europe, the idea was associated with the opposition, not the government.

To add to these general factors, Ernest Bevin, the Foreign Secretary, was personally upset that he had no forewarning of Schuman's announcement. Dean Acheson, the US Secretary of State, was told about the Plan in advance by the French Prime Minister, Georges Bidault, and Acheson subsequently met Bevin, but did not mention the Plan. As Acheson had been given the information in confidence, this was reasonable enough; but it led Bevin to see a Franco-American plot to seize the initiative away from Britain in the formulation of plans for western Europe (Young 1998: 52). Bevin's annoyance was increased when the French government insisted that all those who wished to participate in the scheme must accept the principle of supranationalism. This condition was pressed by Monnet, who was concerned that otherwise the outcome would be another intergovernmental organization. He must have known that it would be an impossible condition for the British government to accept, given the strong attachment of the Labour Party to national sovereignty, and perhaps he did not really want British participation at the outset. It was, after all, the British who had been primarily responsible for the watering down of the commitment to supranational institutions in the Council of Europe.

The British government did not immediately reject the demand for a commitment to supranationalism. Instead, the French were asked to specify exactly what they meant by the phrase, to spell out the full extent of the surrender of sovereignty that was envisaged and its effects. After some three weeks of inconclusive discussions of the implications of supranationalism, Schuman announced on 1 June 1950 that the principle was non-negotiable, and that any state that wanted to be involved in the negotiations must accept it by 8.00 p.m. on 2 June. The British Cabinet immediately rejected this condition.

From the Schuman Plan to the Treaty of Paris

Negotiations between the 'Six' began on 20 June, with all delegations supposedly committed to the principle of supranationalism. However, both the Belgians and the Dutch had reservations, as became apparent once the opening session was completed and the substantive negotiations began on 22 June (Duchêne 1994: 209).

Monnet insisted that the French delegation should be hand-picked by himself, and he rigorously excluded representatives of the French coal and steel industries from influence in the process. This was not the case with the other delegations, which consisted of diplomats and officials from the national energy ministries, who were open to influence from the affected industries.

There followed months of hard bargaining during which various departures were made from the original principles set out in Monnet's working document (see Insight 5.5). These concessions were necessary to make a success of the negotiations. That they had to be made reinforces the view that most participants were concerned to use the ECSC to further their own national interests. The biggest concessions were made by the German government, for whom the main potential advantage of the

> ### Insight 5.5 Bargaining Concessions in the ECSC Negotiations
>
> - At the insistence of the Dutch, and supported by the Germans, a Council of Ministers, consisting of representatives of national governments, was added to the institutional structure to curtail the supranationalism of the High Authority.
> - At the insistence of the Belgians, a special 'equalization tax' on efficient coal producers was agreed, which would be used to subsidize the modernization of inefficient mines. In practice, this amounted to a subsidy from Germany to Belgium.
> - At the insistence of the Italians, the Italian steel industry was allowed to maintain tariffs against the rest of the participants for five years, and to continue to import cheap coking coal and scrap metal from outside the ECSC. As with the Belgian coal mines, there was to be an equalization fund to finance the modernization of inefficient Italian steel plants, although this was much smaller than the coal equalization tax.

Schuman Plan was the opportunity it offered to get the removal of the constraints imposed by the IAR.

At the end of the war, the Allies had forced the deconcentration of the coal and steel industries in Germany, and the break-up of the cartels that had restricted competition. From the German point of view this only served to give an artificial advantage to their French competitors. The IAR acted to prevent reconcentration and re-emergence of cartels, so the German industrialists wanted to get rid of it. But they did not want the High Authority of the ECSC to take over those functions from the IAR, whereas Monnet was determined that the High Authority would do exactly that.

From the French point of view, concentration was dangerous because it gave too much political influence to the large industrial concerns. The support of the Ruhr industrialists for Hitler had contributed to the Nazis coming to power. Cartelization was a device that, in Monnet's eyes, acted as a restraint on competition. In this view he was strongly supported by the United States.

The role of the US Administration in the negotiations was vital. Not officially represented at the talks, the United States nevertheless exerted a tremendous influence behind the scenes. A special committee was set up in the US Embassy in Paris to monitor progress, and it acted as a sort of additional secretariat for Monnet. For the United States, the cartel arrangements were an outrageous interference with the operation of market forces and could not be tolerated. There was initially less concern about the concentration issue because the size of the units involved would still be much smaller than those in the United States. However, after the outbreak of the Korean War in June 1950, the US Administration came to the reluctant conclusion that Germany would have to be rearmed. In this context, the issue of not allowing the emergence of the industrial conglomerates that had supported the previous militaristic German regime became more significant in US minds.

After months of hard negotiation, the United States cut through the arguments and forced a settlement. On 3 March 1951 Adenauer was summoned to see John J. McCloy, the US High Commissioner in Bonn, who told him that the delays caused by the Germans were unacceptable, and that 'France and the United States had no choice but to impose their own decartelization scheme' (Gillingham 1991*a*: 280). Despite vigorous protests from the Ruhr producers, Adenauer accepted the ultimatum because, for him, the political gains of the ECSC were paramount and he could not afford to allow the process to collapse.

It appeared, then, that although Monnet's concept had been severely modified, the essential purpose had been achieved of creating a supranational body that could exercise some control over the coal and steel producers in the interests of promoting efficiency and competition.

The High Authority was funded through a direct levy on Europe's coal and steel firms and had a wide brief on taxes, production, and restrictive practices. Alongside it were established a Council of Ministers consisting of national government representatives, and a Common Assembly. In addition, a Consultative Committee to the High Authority was established to represent producers, employers, and consumers. More significantly in terms of future integration, a Court of Justice was set up with judges drawn from the national judiciaries to rule on the legality of the High Authority's actions. These institutional arrangements provided in embryonic form the core of the institutional framework of the European Union as it exists today.

CONCLUSION

The history of European integration can be told as a story of ideas, or it can be told as a story of heroic individuals who led their states into closer unity. Both factors had a role in the rapid movement from the end of the war to the start of the first of the European communities, but circumstances were also crucially important in giving the ideas practical relevance and in inspiring the national leaders to push the project forward.

Like previous attempts at political unity in Europe, the attempts made immediately after the war were initially driven by idealism. As with previous attempts, this would not have been enough to overcome the vested interests of national governments in maintaining the status quo, had there not also been strong practical arguments in favour of closer co-operation between states. Such practical arguments were provided by the circumstances in which post-war European leaders found themselves.

The fear of communism taking over the whole of Europe if the western states could not provide economic recovery quickly put political urgency behind the arguments for closer collaboration. The need for reconstruction to be carried out on a rational basis in the European coal, iron, and steel industries was one of the pressing economic necessities. In the longer term, the need for Europe to compete economically with the much larger economies of the United States and the Soviet Union may also have played a part in the thinking of some of the more far-seeing founders of the experiment in European unity, but the immediate practical problems were in the forefront of minds.

KEY POINTS

Background: The Ideal of European Unity

• Plans for European unity have a long pedigree, but prior to the 1950s none had succeeded.

The End of the War, Federalism, and The Hague Congress

- Federalist groups put the idea of European unity on the immediate post-war agenda and attracted a lot of public support in several European states.
- By the time that the Hague Congress was held, in 1948, new national governments were in control of the states of western Europe and were reluctant to surrender any sovereignty.

The Cold War

- A growing rift between the Soviet Union and its former western allies led to the emergence of fears in western Europe of a communist takeover inspired by Moscow.
- The severe winter of 1946–7 led to unrest in several west European states that was exploited by indigenous communist parties, and prompted the United States to propose the Marshall Plan to feed economic recovery.
- The United States favoured European unity and pressed for movement in that direction.

The German Problem

- Germany's neighbours, particularly France, were concerned to guard against a resurgence of German militarism and initially opposed the re-formation of a German state. After the German Federal Republic was set up in 1949, a new approach was needed.

The Schuman Plan for Coal and Steel

- Proposed by Robert Schuman, but devised by Jean Monnet, the plan proposed the pooling of the coal and steel resources of the European states.
- Monnet was trying to solve two problems with one plan: the problem of containing Germany and the problem of ensuring supplies of coal to French industry.
- Six states took part in the negotiations that led to the ECSC.

National Positions and the Origins of the ECSC

- France: Monnet saw the need for a European common market with coal and steel as the start.
- Germany: Adenauer saw the ECSC as a way to restore Germany's international position, establish the Federal Republic as the legitimate successor to the pre-war German state, and consolidate the western and capitalist orientation of the new state.
- The Benelux States: could not afford to be left out of a community that pooled the coal and steel supplies of France and Germany.
- In Italy Alcide de Gasperi had very similar motives to Adenauer in Germany: he wanted to restore Italy's international respectability and confirm its western and capitalist identity.
- Britain was not interested in participating in a coal and steel pool as it had its own supplies of coal, the new Labour government had just nationalized these industries, and it saw itself as a global power with a strong economy.

From the Schuman Plan to the Treaty of Paris

- Months of bargaining led to modification of Monnet's original ambitious plan.
- There was a struggle between France and Germany over the powers of the High Authority of the ECSC and over the attitude to cartels.
- The United States played a vital role behind the scenes.
- The institutional arrangements established for the ECSC provided, in embryonic form, the basic institutional framework of the European Union as it exists today.

FURTHER READING

D.W. Urwin, *The Community of Europe: A History of European Integration since 1945* (London and New York: Longman, 2nd edn, 1994) and **Urwin**, *Western Europe Since 1945: A Short Political History* (London and New York: Longman, 4th edn, 1985) should be treated as standard reference sources. A particularly controversial account of the early post-war origins of European integration is given by **A. S. Milward**, *The Reconstruction of Western Europe, 1945–51* (London: Routledge, 1984).

For more information on European federalism, see **M. Burgess (ed.)**, *Federalism and Federation in Western Europe* (London: Croom Helm, 1986) and *Federalism in the European Union: Political Ideas, Influences and Strategies* (London and New York: Routledge, 1989).

There is a considerable literature on the Schuman Plan. For a detailed insight into the process, the account given by **F. Duchêne**, *Jean Monnet: The First Statesman of Interdependence* (New York and London: W. W. Norton and Co., 1994) is indispensable and also provides invaluable insights into the origins of the Pleven Plan. Most of **J. Gillingham**, *Coal, Steel, and the Rebirth of Europe, 1945-1955* (Cambridge: Cambridge University Press, 1991) is devoted to the build-up to the negotiations and the negotiations themselves, and **E. B. Haas**, *The Uniting of Europe: Political, Social and Economic Forces, 1950–1957* (Stanford, CA: Stanford University Press, 1968) contains information on the positions of all the main actors, scattered through a book that is organized thematically rather than chronologically. The British failure to take seriously the Schuman Plan is recounted in **E. Dell**, *The Schuman Plan and the British Abdication of Leadership in Europe* (Oxford: Clarendon Press, 1995).

 online resource centre
Visit the Online Resource Centre that accompanies this book for links to more information on the early years of European unity:
http://oxfordtextbooks.co.uk/orc/bache4e/

Chapter 6

The 'Other' European Communities and the Origins of the European Economic Community (the Early 1950s to the 1960s)

Chapter Overview

In this next period the post-war ferment continued, and plans for both practical and less practical moves to closer European unity were generated. As in the earlier period, there were broadly three positions contending: that of the federalists, who were committed to a supranational vision for Europe that would supersede the nation states; that of the defenders of national sovereignty, represented by the governments of the states; and that of the pragmatic problem-solvers, the epitome of which was Jean Monnet.

The creation of the European Coal and Steel Community (ECSC) was analysed in the previous chapter. Negotiations over a plan for a European Defence Community (EDC) ran parallel to those over the ECSC. Connected with the EDC was a proposal to create a European Political Community (EPC) to provide democratic European structures for co-ordinating foreign policies. This chapter looks at the development of the EDC/EPC plan and the ultimate failure to reach agreement in 1954. It then examines the experience of the ECSC up to the merger of the High Authority with the Commission of the European Economic Community (EEC) in July 1967, before turning to the Messina negotiations and the road to the Rome Treaties. It also looks briefly at the experience of the other organization that was created at the same time as the EEC, the European Atomic Energy Community (Euratom), which, like the ECSC, was institutionally merged with the EEC in 1967.

The Pleven Plan

While the development of the ECSC set much of the tone and framework for future developments in European integration, it was largely overshadowed at the time by parallel negotiations on another plan devised by Monnet, the Pleven Plan for a EDC.

This gave federalists another opportunity to pursue their strategy of 'the constitutional break', moving directly from a Europe of nation states to a federal constitution for Europe. However, the feasibility of doing this was no greater in 1953 than it had been in 1948, and for the same reason: governments were not prepared to surrender their sovereignty.

Following the collapse of the four-power administration of Germany (see Chapter 5, The Cold War), the Cold War developed rapidly. In April 1949 a mutual defence pact, the North Atlantic Treaty, was signed in Washington between the United States, Canada, and ten west European states (Britain, France, the **Benelux** states, Iceland, Italy, Norway, and Portugal). This set up the North Atlantic Treaty Organization (NATO). In the same month the Federal Republic of Germany came into existence. In June 1950 communist North Korea invaded capitalist South Korea. The ensuing civil war involved the United States, acting under the auspices of the United Nations, on the side of the South, and the Soviet Union and communist China on the side of the North. It had a profound impact on western thinking about security.

Like Korea, Germany was divided into capitalist and communist states. While Korea was at that time geographically peripheral to the main global balance of power, Germany was not. The fear in the West was that the Korean invasion was a precursor to an invasion of West Germany from East Germany. In this context, and because the United States was committing troops to the Korean conflict, the US Administration decided that the Europeans had to make a bigger contribution to their own defence. In particular, they reluctantly decided that there was no alternative to reconstituting a German army.

This idea alarmed the French. For them it was unthinkable that a German army should come back into existence. Monnet tried to solve the problem with a proposal based on the same principles as his plan for ECSC. Under his scheme for a EDC, instead of having a German army, he proposed to pool the military resources of France and Germany into a European army. There would be German soldiers, but they would not wear German uniforms, and they would not be under German command. The corollary, of course, was that the French army would at least partially disappear into the same European force. Monnet's proposal did, however, allow France and the other participants, except Germany, to have their own national armies alongside the European army.

The plan proposed the creation of a European army consisting of fourteen French divisions, twelve German, eleven Italian, and three from the Benelux states. The command of the army would be integrated, but there would be no divisions of mixed nationality. The EDC would have had a similar institutional structure to the ECSC: a Council representing the member states, with votes weighted according to each state's contribution to the European army, alongside a Commission and an Assembly.

As with the pooling of coal and steel, a European army was not a new idea. A similar proposal had been made by the French representatives in the Consultative Assembly of the Council of Europe in August 1950, and had received the support of the Assembly, but had been blocked in the Council of Ministers. Monnet now formalized the idea, making an explicit link to the ECSC. The plan was publicly launched by the French Prime Minister, René Pleven, an old collaborator of Monnet, on 24 October 1950.

Despite the election in Britain in October 1951 of a Conservative government under Churchill, who professed to be a supporter of European integration, the British were unwilling to become involved in plans for the EDC. The US Administration was initially cautious, but Monnet persuaded the new NATO Supreme Allied Commander in Europe, Dwight D. Eisenhower, and his support swung the Administration behind the scheme (Duchêne 1994: 231). Adenauer welcomed the idea, seeing in it a way of finally ending the Allied occupation of West Germany. The other four states that had joined in the Schuman Plan signed up to talks for essentially the same reasons as they had joined ECSC: the Benelux states did not feel that they could stand aside from such an initiative between their two larger neighbours, and Italy continued to seek acceptance into the European states system.

At Monnet's prompting, Pleven made it a condition of progress on the EDC that the ECSC Treaty be signed first. This was particularly resented in Germany because Monnet had accompanied preparation of the Pleven Plan with a hardening of his attitude towards the position of the German steel cartels in the talks on the Schuman Plan. This had stalled the talks: Adenauer and the German negotiator, Hallstein, felt that they were being railroaded into accepting an unfavourable agreement on the ECSC in order to secure negotiations on the EDC. They were not mistaken. Gillingham (1991b: 146) was clear that these two developments were linked in Monnet's mind. Indeed, the same author (1991a: 264) went so far as to suggest that the Pleven Plan 'saved the Schuman Plan'. This sort of cross-bargaining worked both ways, however. Duchêne (1994: 250) believed that one explanation for Monnet's failure to press home the Treaty provisions against the Ruhr cartels, when he became President of the ECSC High Authority, was that Adenauer warned him that any premature action on this front would jeopardize the ratification of the EDC Treaty in the German parliament.

A problem with the proposed EDC was the plan for a common European army without a common foreign policy. The proposed institutions of the EDC would not be able to provide this. At the insistence of Italy, a clause was inserted into the draft Treaty linking the EDC with the creation of a European Political Community (EPC) to provide a democratic dimension to the project. Plans were to be drawn up by the Common Assembly of the EDC, but as delays in ratifying the Treaty stretched out the process, Paul-Henri Spaak, the Belgian Premier, suggested that the Common Assembly of the ECSC, enlarged in membership so as to resemble the proposed EDC Assembly, should prepare the EPC proposal.

The opportunity to draft a treaty for the EPC was seized on by federalists within the Assembly. In the course of its work, the ECSC Assembly was supplemented by members of the Parliamentary Assembly of the Council of Europe. The draft Treaty was adopted by this ad hoc Assembly on 10 March 1953. It proposed: a two-chamber European Parliament consisting of a People's Chamber that would be directly elected every five years, and a Senate of indirectly elected members from national parliaments; a European Executive Council that would have to be approved by both chambers of the parliament, but, once in office, would have the power to dissolve the People's Chamber and call new elections; a Council of National Ministers; a Court of Justice. The EPC would not be just a third community, 'but nothing less than the beginning of a comprehensive federation to which the ECSC and EDC would be subordinated' (Urwin 1995: 64).

The fate of the EPC was inevitably linked to the fate of the EDC. The EDC Treaty had been signed in May 1952, but it had not been ratified by any of the signatories when the EPC proposals emerged. In fact, the EDC Treaty was 'rotting before the ink was dry' (Duchêne 1994: 233). Its prospects were crucially dependent on French support, but the French government only signed it on the 'tacit condition that no immediate attempt should be made to ratify it' (Duchêne 1994: 233). German rearmament, even as part of a European army, was unpopular in France. Pleven only managed to get approval for his proposal from the National Assembly by 343 votes to 220. By the time that the intergovernmental negotiations were completed, there had been elections in France and the parliamentary arithmetic did not indicate a clear majority for ratification. In consequence, successive prime ministers refused to bring the Treaty to the Assembly for ratification, fearing that its failure would bring down their government.

This prevarication, which went on for almost two years, caused exasperation in the United States, and, in December 1953, led Secretary of State John Foster Dulles to threaten an 'agonizing reappraisal' of policy. Eventually the Treaty was submitted to the National Assembly by the government of Pierre Mendès-France at the end of August 1954, but the government gave it no support, and indicated that it would not resign if the Assembly voted against ratification. The EDC Treaty was not ratified and the demise of the EDC was accompanied by the collapse of the EPC.

The issue of European defence was eventually solved according to a formula proposed by the British government. The Brussels Treaty of 1948 was extended to Germany and Italy; a loose organization called the Western European Union (WEU) was set up to co-ordinate the alliance; an organic link was made with NATO, to which Germany and Italy were admitted. Adenauer achieved his aim of securing an Allied withdrawal from the whole of West Germany (although not Berlin), and a German army was formed, although it was hedged around with legal restrictions on operating beyond the borders of the Federal Republic. The WEU appeared to contemporary observers to be an organization of no particular importance because it was overshadowed by NATO. However, like other organizations that were set up in the post-war period, it was later to acquire functions that had not been envisaged at the time when it was formed (see Insight 6.1).

The other practical significance of the EDC episode, or rather of the related EPC initiative, was that it kept the federalist idea alive. As Gillingham (1991a: 349) put it, it 'kept the cadres in being, dialogue moving, and served as a learning experience'. The importance of this became clear with the 'relaunching of Europe' that followed the collapse of EDC.

Defence was not an obvious next step after coal and steel in the process of building mutual trust through practical co-operation. It was not an issue with a low political profile, but a sensitive issue that struck to the heart of national sovereignty. Had it not been for the international crisis of the Korean War, it would surely not have surfaced at this stage. Monnet himself may have been of this view. Duchêne (1994: 229) reports that several people who were working close to Monnet at the time had the impression that he regarded the EDC scheme as premature. After winning over Eisenhower, Monnet took no further part in the negotiations on the plan, suggesting a lack of further commitment to the project.

With the collapse of the EDC and EPC, the radical federalist strategy of a direct attack on the system of nation states disappeared from this story. The struggle over European integration at this stage became one between nation states who tried to keep control of the process in their own hands, and supranational bureaucracies that tried to push forward the process using means that were later theorized by the neofunctionalists (see Chapter 1, International Relations Theories of European Integration). This strategy was particularly associated with the Commission of the EEC, but it drew on lessons from the experiences of the two other European Communities that did come into existence, the ECSC and Euratom.

The European Coal and Steel Community

The ECSC survived the EDC debacle and began operation in July 1952 under the presidency of Jean Monnet. Although it had considerable powers at its disposal (see Insight 6.2), it proceeded cautiously in using them, but still found itself in conflict with national governments.

In the original plan for the ECSC there was only one central institution, the High Authority. During the negotiations, a Council of Ministers and a European Parliamentary Assembly (EPA) were added to the institutional structure. This reflected concern about the power and possible *dirigiste* nature of the High Authority, but did not allay that concern.

While coal producers were ambiguous about supranational *dirigisme*, most of them hoping for some degree of support for their troubled industry, steel producers were generally hostile to this aspect of the Schuman Plan. German industrialists in particular opposed the *dirigiste* element to the Plan, and the Federal German government supported them. The governments of the Benelux countries also had severe doubts about the role of the High Authority. At the insistence of these governments, a Council of Ministers was included in the institutional structure of the ECSC, alongside the High Authority.

> ## Insight 6.2 The High Authority
>
> The High Authority of the ECSC had nine members, two each from France and Germany and one from each of the other member states, the ninth member to be co-opted by the other eight. Its seat was in Luxembourg. It had five presidents:
>
> - Jean Monnet (1952–5);
> - René Mayer (1955–7);
> - Paul Finet (1958–9);
> - Piero Malvestiti (1959–63);
> - Rinaldo Del Bo (1963–7).
>
> It had the power under the Treaty of Paris to obtain from firms in the coal and steel sectors the information that it required to oversee the industries, and to fine firms that would not provide the information or evaded their obligations (Article 47).
>
> It could impose levies on production, and contract loans to raise finance to back investment projects of which it approved (Articles 49–51), and it could guarantee loans to coal and steel concerns from independent sources of finance (Article 54). It could also require undertakings to inform it in advance of investment programmes, and, if it disapproved of the plans, could prevent the concern from using resources other than its own funds to carry out the programme (Article 54).

Although its independence was reduced from Monnet's original proposal, the High Authority was still given considerable formal powers. Diebold (1959: 78–9) considered that:

> It was truly to be an *imperium in imperio*, wielding powers previously held by national governments and having some functions not previously exercised by governments.

Despite these powers, in practice the High Authority proceeded very cautiously. It was in a constant state of tension with member state governments, who did not take easily to having their sovereignty circumscribed by a supranational body. The Council regularly rejected proposals of the High Authority that conflicted with national interests. For this reason the High Authority needed a strong president who could impose his authority. In their comprehensive history of the ECSC, Spierenburg and Poidevin (1994: 649) argued that the first two presidents, Monnet and René Mayer, fitted this description, as did the last president, Del Bo, although by the time he took office in 1963 the High Authority was already in its twilight years. The two intervening presidents, Finet and Malvestiti, did not carry the same weight (see Insight 6.2).

Even taking account of this difficult relationship with the Council, Haas (1968: 459) considered that, 'in all matters relating to the routine regulation of the Common Market, the High Authority is independent of member governments'. Because of this independence, those governments that were concerned about the possible *dirigisme* of the High Authority took care to nominate as their members people who were not themselves committed to this outlook. For Milward (1992: 105) the most notable feature of the members of the High Authority was that they never liberated themselves from their national governments. Monnet became the first president of the High Authority, but found himself at the head of a group of people who were not in sympathy with his own view on its role. Haas (1968: 459) argued that in 'the ideology of the High Authority, the free enterprise and anti-*dirigiste* viewpoint ... definitely carried the day'.

This way of presenting the issue is perhaps a little misleading. It suggests that Monnet was in favour of intrusive public-sector intervention and was opposed by other members who favoured free competition. In fact, one of the things that Monnet wanted the High Authority to do was prevent the reformation of the coal and steel cartels—organizations of producers that regulated the industries through their collaboration on prices and output. Monnet wanted such regulation as there was to be carried out by the High Authority; but he was also committed to preserving competition between producers. The other members of the High Authority were committed to preventing it from interfering with self-regulation of the markets, not to competition. Perhaps this is what Haas meant by a 'free-enterprise' viewpoint, but the terminology tends to suggest that less-regulated markets were the objective. In any case, Monnet was frustrated in his policy objectives for the High Authority.

He was also frustrated in his organizational objectives. Mazey (1992: 40–1) argued that Monnet wanted a small, supranational, non-hierarchical, and informal organization; but that internal divisions, bureaucratization, and pressures from corporatist and national interests foiled him in this. Internal divisions between members of the High Authority itself were reproduced within the administration, and when combined with the non-hierarchical structure that Monnet adopted, this led to increasing problems of administrative co-ordination, delays, and duplication of effort because of overlapping competence.

However, as the demands for administering the common market for coal and steel grew, so did the bureaucratic nature of the High Authority. Problems of co-ordination increased as the different Directorates of the ECSC developed different links with interests and producers in the member states. The consequence was that in the first three years of its operation, 'the administrative services of the High Authority were ... transformed from an informal grouping of sympathetic individuals into a professional bureaucracy which, in terms of its structure and "technocratic" character, resembled the French administration' (Mazey 1992: 43).

When the ECSC was proposed, coal was in short supply; but by 1959 the increasing use of oil had led to over-capacity in the industry. This became a crisis in 1958 when a mild winter and an economic downturn produced a serious fall in demand. Although economic growth picked up in the second quarter of 1959, stocks of coal at the pit-head continued to accumulate because of a second mild winter, low transatlantic freight costs that allowed cheap imports of US coal, and an acceleration of the switch from coal to oil. The High Authority diagnosed a manifest crisis, and in March 1959 asked the Council of Ministers for emergency powers under Article 58 of the Treaty. However, this request failed to achieve the qualified majority necessary, primarily because neither France nor Germany was prepared to grant the extra powers to the High Authority that it requested.

This was one of a series of crises in the history of the European Communities that shook the collective morale of the central bureaucratic actors. The immediate effect was to make it very difficult for the High Authority to respond to the crisis. It had to resort to palliative measures such as social assistance, and a restructuring plan for the Belgian industry, which was hardest hit by the crisis. More fundamentally:

The High Authority's powerlessness revealed the inadequacy of sectoral integration for which it was responsible and which did not cover competing energy sources—oil and nuclear energy.

(Spierenburg and Poidevin 1994: 652)

The realization that the attempt to integrate in one sector could not be successful unless integration were extended to other sectors might have led to an increase in the competence of the High Authority. The Council of Ministers did ask the High Authority to undertake the co-ordination of energy supplies and to draw up plans for a common energy policy; but by this time the Treaties of Rome had come into effect, creating the two new communities, the EEC and Euratom, each with its own Commission.

The decision to make a new start with new institutions, rather than extending the competence of the High Authority, inevitably produced a conflict between the established bureaucratic actor and the newcomers. Although the High Authority helped the two Commissions to get started by seconding many of its experienced staff, 'there were undeniable jealousies that precluded closer union between the three executive bodies' (Spierenburg and Poidevin 1994: 652).

Finet complained about the 'poaching' of High Authority staff by the Commissions of Euratom and the EEC (Spierenburg and Poidevin 1994: 381) and there were tensions both over issues of responsibility and budgetary matters. The Commissions, one headed by a Frenchman and the other by a German, had the support of the French and German Governments on these matters. More generally, governments were content to see responsibilities of the High Authority transferred to the less supranational new Commissions.

Yet, the ECSC could claim partial success for its activities, for example in limiting restrictive practices in the coal and steel sectors. More importantly, for Monnet, the creation of the ECSC laid vital foundations for further European integration:

It proved decisive in persuading businessmen, civil servants, politicians and trade unionists that such an approach could work and that the economic and political advantages of unity over division were immense. Once they were convinced, they were ready to take further steps forward.

(Monnet 1962: 208)

While the supranational instincts of the High Authority were kept under control by national governments, it was significant for future developments in European integration that both the Assembly and the Court of Justice were supportive of its supranational efforts. The Court in particular 'stamped its imprint on the ECSC, and in doing so built up a body of case law, an authority, and legitimacy that could serve as foundations for the future' (Urwin 1995: 56).

Six years after signing the Treaty of Paris establishing the ECSC, the six parliaments ratified the Treaty of Rome establishing the Economic Community, taking the major step towards the creation of a common market for all goods and services. Monnet (1962: 211) spoke of a 'new method of action' in Europe, replacing the efforts at domination by the nation states 'by a constant process of collective adaptation to new conditions, a chain reaction, a ferment where one change induces another'. (In 2002 the

Treaty of Paris expired. The strategic importance of these two sectors had declined, and the rationale for the ECSC had disappeared.)

Messina

In November 1954, Monnet announced that when his first term as President of the High Authority of the ECSC ended in February 1955, he would not seek a second term. Citing the collapse of the EDC, he said that he wanted to free his hands to work for European unity. He then formed an organization called the Action Committee for the United States of Europe, consisting of leading political and trade union figures from the member states of the ECSC, but also from Britain and other states.

The main proposal to come from the Action Committee was for a European Atomic Energy Community (Euratom). It was accompanied by a plan to extend the sectoral responsibilities of the ECSC to cover all forms of energy, and transport. Nothing came of these latter proposals, although transport was given a special place in the Treaty of Rome (EEC). The member governments were simply not interested in extending the remit of the ECSC.

Also accompanying the proposals from the Action Committee was a proposal from Beyen, the Dutch Foreign Minister, for a general **common market**. Richard Mayne (1991: 115) maintained that this scheme also originated with Monnet, but he offered no evidence for this, and it is a view that is flatly rejected by other writers. Duchêne (1994: 269–72) provided evidence that Monnet actually rejected the idea of a general common market, believing that it was too ambitious, and might produce another EDC debacle.

There was no great enthusiasm for further sectoral integration. In so far as business interests expressed support for further integration, it was for an extension of the market aspect of the ECSC, not for the centralized regulatory functions of the High Authority. The lesson that was learned from ECSC was the limitations of sectoral integration. As *The Economist* (11 August 1956) reported:

> In the last four years the Coal and Steel Community has proved that the common market is not only feasible but, on balance, advantageous for all concerned. But it has also shown that 'integration by sector' raises its own problems of distortion and discrimination. The Six have therefore chosen to create a common market for all products rather than continuing to experiment with the sector approach.

On 4 April 1955, Spaak circulated a memorandum to the governments of the six states of the ECSC proposing that negotiations begin on the extension of sectoral integration to other forms of energy than coal, particularly to nuclear energy, and to transport. The proposal met with a cool response; only the French government supported it. Beyen then pressed the case for a relaunch based on the idea of a general common market.

The Federal German government reacted very positively to Beyen's proposal, but in France the idea of a general common market was strongly rejected by industry, which argued that it would not be able to compete with German industry. French politicians had generally accepted this argument, but there was a growing belief that the excuse could not be used forever, and that French industry would never be competitive until it had to compete. At this stage, though, the mood in France was not conducive to taking such a step, which may explain why Monnet was reluctant to advocate it.

Spaak subsequently met with the Dutch Prime Minister, Joseph Bech, and as a result of that meeting, a formal Benelux initiative was launched combining Monnet's ideas for further sectoral integration with Beyen's idea of a general common market. This proposal was circulated in late April 1955, and was discussed at the beginning of June in Messina in Italy at a meeting of the heads of government of the six, which had originally been called to decide on a successor to Monnet as President of the High Authority of the ECSC.

Agreement was reached at Messina to set up a committee under the chairmanship of Spaak to study the ideas in the Benelux memorandum. The French government was not enthusiastic, and appeared not to expect anything to come of the talks, but it was difficult for France to block them so soon after its rejection of the EDC. Because the agreement to hold talks was reached in Messina, the negotiations took that name. In fact, most of the meetings were held in Brussels. Their success was unexpected, except perhaps by optimistic partisans of integration like Spaak. In fact, the success of the Spaak Committee, which met in Brussels between July 1955 and March 1956, owed a great deal to his energetic and skilful chairing of the proceedings. Also very important, though, were the changed circumstances between the original Messina meeting and the actual negotiations.

One very important change was in the government of France: Guy Mollet, the leader of the Socialist Party, became Prime Minister in 1956. Having originally been sceptical about European integration, Mollet had become convinced that French industry needed to be opened up to competition if it was ever to achieve the sort of productivity gains that lay behind the remarkable German economic recovery. He had also become a member of Monnet's Action Committee, and Duchêne (1994: 287) maintained that a relationship developed between Monnet and Mollet similar to the earlier relationship between Monnet and Schuman.

Mollet was brought to office by the deteriorating situation in Algeria, where French settlers were under attack by the National Liberation Front (FLN) of Algeria. The war that developed there was traumatic for the French, and dominated the nation's attention so that the negotiations in Brussels were able to proceed without attracting much notice from critics. But Algeria was only one of the international events of 1956 that had an effect on the outcome of the Messina negotiations. In October, the Soviet Union invaded Hungary to suppress an anti-communist national movement that had the sympathy of the Hungarian army. Hungary brought home to western Europeans once again the reality of the Cold War that divided their continent. More directly, the Suez Canal crisis also blew up in October.

The nationalization of the Suez Canal by Egyptian President Gamal Abdel Nasser not only caused outrage in France, as it did in Britain; it also offered the French a possible excuse to topple Nasser, whose pan-Arab rhetoric inflamed the situation in Algeria, and whose regime was suspected of sheltering and arming the Algerian rebels. However, once the nationalization had been effected, Nasser gave no further cause for outside intervention. The canal was kept open to international shipping; it was business as usual under new ownership. To foment an excuse to invade, the French government colluded with the Israeli government and hatched a scheme that was subsequently sold to the British government of Anthony Eden. Israel would invade the canal zone;

the French and British governments would demand an immediate withdrawal from the canal by the armed forces of both sides. Egypt would certainly refuse, and the combined Franco-British force would then move in to occupy the canal zone and reclaim the canal. The fall of Nasser was confidently expected to follow.

However, the invasion failed because, in the face of opposition from the Soviet Union and, more significantly, from the United States, the British government decided to pull out. France could not carry through the operation alone. The episode was perceived in France as a national humiliation at the hands of the Americans, but also as a betrayal by the British who were believed to be too subservient to US wishes. It fed support for the nationalist position of Charles de Gaulle, who subsequently came to office as the first president of the new Fifth Republic in May 1958. It also fed into the Messina negotiations, helping them to reach a speedy and successful conclusion.

Directly, Suez underlined much more than events in Hungary the impotence of France in the post-war world of superpowers. It gave support to the concept of France acting with other European states. Indirectly, the clear signs that this episode marked the beginning of the end for the government of Mollet, and the strong indications that he would be succeeded by de Gaulle, who had always opposed European integration, accelerated the efforts to reach agreement. A 'rush to Rome' began in an effort to get the treaties signed before de Gaulle came to office and aborted the whole experiment.

The Road to the Rome Treaties

The agreements reached in the Spaak Committee were a series of compromises between different national positions, particularly those of France and Germany. Central to the agreement detailed in the Spaak Report of March 1956 was the creation of the general common market favoured by the German government. Although Mollet believed that this step would be good for France as well as for Germany, he had to negotiate concessions that would allow him to get the Treaty ratified in the French National Assembly. There were three main areas where the French government extracted concessions: Euratom, agriculture, and relations with France's overseas territories and dependencies.

Euratom was attractive for many French politicians because they saw it as a means of obtaining a subsidy from Germany for the expensive process of developing nuclear energy, which in turn was linked to the development of nuclear weapons. Although Mollet personally believed that France should confine itself to the peaceful use of nuclear energy, the sentiment in the National Assembly in the aftermath of Hungary and Suez was very much in favour of an independent French nuclear deterrent. Euratom offered the opportunity to devote more national resources to the weapons programme, while depriving Germany of a national nuclear capability, and guaranteeing French access to uranium from the Belgian Congo.

Agriculture was given a separate chapter in the EEC Treaty. Its inclusion, not as part of the general common market, but as, in effect, a further extension of sectoral integration, was another factor that was important in ensuring French ratification of the Treaty. For the French governments of the Fourth Republic, agriculture was both politically and economically important. Politically, small farmers had a disproportionate electoral importance under the voting system that was used in the Fourth Republic. The small farmers were inefficient producers, but were determined to retain their independence, which in effect meant that they had to be subsidized by the state through a national system of price-support. By transferring this cost to the common EEC budget, the French state again obtained a subsidy from the more prosperous Germans. Economically, France also had an efficient agricultural sector, and actually produced a considerable surplus of food, so the guarantee of a protected market for French agricultural exports was another concession that helped to sell the EEC Treaty within France.

In the context of decolonization and the war in Algeria, it was very important for all French governments to ensure that the special links with the former colonies were maintained. There were considerable French economic interests that were dependent on trade with these overseas dependencies and territories, and there was a general sentiment in France in favour of the link. The continuation of this special relationship, by guaranteeing preferential access to the common market for the products of the former colonies, was the third important factor to allow the Treaty to obtain ratification in France.

On each of these points the German government made considerable concessions. There was no sympathy for Euratom in German industrial or government circles; the Germans would have preferred to leave agriculture to national management, and to continue to allow food to be imported as cheaply as possible from the rest of the world; and there was no enthusiasm for supporting the last vestiges of French colonialism. However, in order to obtain the considerable prize of the common market in industrial goods, the German government was prepared to make these concessions to France.

The other major bargaining concession was made to Italy in the form of the inclusion in the Treaty of a commitment to reducing the differences between prosperous and poor regions. This was the Italian government's attempt to claim a subsidy from Germany, given that the problems of the south of Italy represented the main regional disparity within the original six member states.

The Spaak Report was agreed by the governments of the six member states in May 1956. The Spaak Committee was transformed into a conference with responsibility for drafting the necessary treaties. In March 1957, two treaties emerged: one for the EEC; the other for Euratom. The treaties were signed by national governments in Rome in the same month, prior to being passed on for domestic ratification. If the failure of the EDC had meant several steps backwards in the process of integration, the Treaties of Rome promised a major leap forward.

Euratom

The Euratom Commission had similar powers and responsibilities to those of its sister institution, the EEC Commission (see Insight 6.3). While the EEC Commission made skilful use of these powers during its first decade to push forward the process of integration, the Euratom Commission failed to make any significant progress. Illness forced the resignation of its first president, Louis Armand, in the first year. Armand was replaced in February 1959 by Etienne Hirsch, a former colleague of Monnet's at the CdP (see Chapter 5, National Positions and the Origins of the ECSC). Delays over recruitment and establishing priorities meant that, by the time the Euratom Commission really began work in 1960, the context in which it had been created had

---

Insight 6.3 The Euratom Commission

The Euratom Commission consisted of five members, one from each member state except Luxembourg, which had no national nuclear-power programme. During its time it had three presidents:

- Louis Armand (1958–9);
- Etienne Hirsch (1959–62);
- Michel Chatenet (1963–7).

   It was charged to ensure that the member states fulfilled the terms of the Treaty:

- it had the sole right to propose measures to this end to the Council of Ministers;
- it had a duty to oversee the implementation of agreements;
- it represented the Community in the negotiation of agreements with the outside world;
- it was answerable to the EPA for the activities of the Community.

---

changed. In particular, the easing of the coal shortage and reduced concern about dependence on oil from the Middle East in the post-Suez period removed some of the urgency on the development of nuclear energy.

The delay in the start of Euratom operations also allowed national rivalries to become embedded. France, with the largest nuclear research programme had expected the bulk of the subsidies available, but Italy and West Germany rapidly developed their programmes following agreement on Euratom. After 1959, France, which was then under the leadership of de Gaulle, was less enthusiastic about Euratom than it had been. The Hirsch Euratom Commission clashed with the French government over both the right of the Commission to inspect French plutonium facilities and the Commission's decision to divert funds to a joint programme of reactor development with the United States. On the first, Hirsch found no support in the Council of Ministers. On the second, however, the Commission won a majority vote in the Council. Yet, even this victory was hollow, as the French government subsequently insisted that budgetary decisions be taken on the basis of unanimity. Thus, in both instances of conflict with the French government, the Commission's position was ultimately weakened. Further, de Gaulle refused to renominate Hirsch as president and his successor, Michel Chatenet, was less assertive in his leadership of the Commission.

From 1962 onwards, Euratom drifted into deeper crisis. In 1964 there was deadlock over the size of the budget, which was eventually resolved only at the cost of the Commission having to make massive cut-backs in the already modest remaining research programme. A second crisis in 1966 meant that Euratom went into the merger year of 1967 having to survive on the system of 'provisional twelfths' which allowed no more than one-twelfth of the previous year's budget to be spent each month until agreement was reached on the new budget.

A number of explanations have been offered for the failure of Euratom (Scheinman 1967). First, because it dealt with a single functional sector, the Commission was unable to offer national governments trade-offs in other policy areas to secure deals on nuclear power. Second, the external environment that favoured the creation of

Euratom had changed by the time it became operative. Moreover, internal rivalry between member states increased and was consolidated with the election of de Gaulle. France was particularly important here because the development of nuclear power was a key issue for the French government and was closely linked to the high-politics issue of nuclear weapons. Perhaps the key weakness of the Euratom Commission was that it failed to develop a **transnational network** of interests around the nuclear energy issue which could create a momentum that would overcome national rivalries. In sum, while the Euratom Commission faced inevitable constraints, it also failed to deploy tactics that were important to the relative success of the EEC Commission.

CONCLUSION

Several persistent themes of the book emerge in this chapter: the influence of the Cold War; the difficulties of any direct attack on national sovereignty; spillover from the initial integrative steps to further steps; the tension between *dirigisme* and free-market approaches to integration; the use of European integration as a vehicle to introduce unpopular policies; and the struggle between supranationalism and national interests.

The influence of the Cold War on the whole EDC episode is clear, as is the role of the United States in the affairs of western Europe during this period of its hegemony of the capitalist world. However, the fate of the EDC is vindication of the functionalist analysis that a head-on attack on sovereignty would be resisted, whereas gradual steps to tie states together might succeed.

It is contestable whether the opening of negotiations on the EEC is vindication of the neofunctionalist argument that spillover would operate to move integration forward once the first steps had been taken (see Chapter 1, International Relations Theories of European Integration). The line of spillover from ECSC to Euratom is clearer, and was the line of progression favoured by Monnet. However, the proposal for Euratom was countered, rather than complemented, by the proposal from the Benelux states for a general common market. In this can be seen the tension between *dirigisme* and free-market approaches to integration. The general common market was designed to open national markets by removing tariffs, at that time the main barrier to free trade. It stood in marked distinction to the Euratom proposal to extend the system of planning of the 'commanding heights' of the economy from coal and steel to what was expected to be the new main source of energy.

Monnet's scheme also reflected the need to gain the acceptance of the French political elite. France was developing nuclear energy as a priority project, so it could be expected to support Euratom, which offered France the prospect of a subsidy from the other member states for its research and development costs. A free market in industrial goods was less likely to find favour in a country where there was less industrial efficiency than in West Germany. However, things were changing in France. There was a growing awareness among the political elite that if France were to keep up with its German neighbour it had to modernize its economy. Euratom, and concessions on agriculture and overseas territories, were necessary sweeteners to sell the package to the French National Assembly; but the assertion, often made, that the EEC was a deal between German industry and French agriculture hides the truth that, for certain sections of the French political elite, the common market was a useful tool to sweep away the protectionism that was stifling French economic growth. Another theme that reappears later in the story emerges here: this is the argument that 'Europe' is used as a smokescreen by governments to hide behind when pursuing domestically unpopular measures (see Chapter 3, Democracy).

There is no strong evidence that a commitment to maintaining the momentum of integration was a motive for the acceptance of the EEC by the political elite in any of the member states.

Events in Algeria, Suez, and Hungary did, though, bring home to them the weakness of European states in an era of superpowers, and made clinging together more attractive. These dramatic incidents also had an effect on public opinion, and reinforced a general sentiment in favour of federalist ideas. Suez and Algeria in particular caused a crisis of identity among the French public that allowed their government to push through the Treaties of Rome behind a rhetoric of maintaining the momentum of integration. At the same time, the account given here shows that the Messina negotiations were no exception to the rule that national interests will be strongly defended in all moves in the direction of integration.

Finally, the assertion of national control over the supranationalism of the High Authority and the Euratom Commission is clear. If we were to focus only on these forerunners of the EC Commission, the lesson to be drawn would have to be that the member states were suspicious of supranational tendencies in the institutions they had created, and were capable of restraining them. But the first stirrings of the supranational European Court of Justice (ECJ) offered a different lesson for the future. The body of case law that the ECJ began to build up was not particularly controversial, and was not widely noted at the time. It was, however, laying the basis for an independent supranational institution of the future (see Chapter 16).

KEY POINTS

The Pleven Plan

- The outbreak of the Korean War led to concern about the future defence of West Germany.
- Monnet proposed the EDC in an attempt to avert the formation of a German army.
- West Germany supported the proposal as a way of ending Allied occupation.
- EDC was linked to EPC by federalists in the Assembly of the ECSC.
- EDC collapsed when France failed to ratify the Treaty.
- European defence was channelled through the intergovernmental WEU.

The European Coal and Steel Community

- The High Authority was not as powerful as originally planned, but still had considerable formal independence.
- There was considerable suspicion of Monnet's *dirigiste* tendencies among national governments, who consequently nominated members to the High Authority who were mostly not sympathetic to Monnet's aims.
- Monnet tried to run the High Authority on informal lines, but it became internally divided and increasingly bureaucratized.
- Excess supply of coal led to a crisis in 1959. The Council of Ministers refused the High Authority emergency powers to deal with the crisis. This precipitated a collapse of morale in the High Authority.
- Despite its shortcomings, Monnet believed that the ECSC pioneered the development of a community method of working.

Messina

- Monnet served one term as President of the High Authority of the ECSC then resigned and formed the Action Committee for the United States of Europe.
- The Action Committee proposed Euratom.

117

- The Dutch and Belgian governments proposed a general common market, a proposal that West Germany seized upon as potentially beneficial to German industry.

- The common market met with strong opposition in France.

- Negotiations were carried out against the background of the Soviet invasion of Hungary and the Franco-British Suez expedition, both in 1956.

The Road to the Rome Treaties

- Negotiations were accelerated when it became obvious that the nationalist de Gaulle was likely soon to come to office in France.

- In return for the common market for industrial goods, France extracted concessions on Euratom, agriculture, and its overseas territories, while Italy got a commitment to reduce regional disparities.

Euratom

- By the time that Euratom began operation, the energy crisis that existed when it was negotiated had disappeared. Instead of a shortage of coal there was a glut.

- Whereas France had the only developed programme of research on nuclear energy in the mid-1950s, by the end of the decade Germany and Italy also had independent programmes in competition with that of France.

- The French government did not fully co-operate with the Euratom Commission and the Commission never managed to build a supportive network of industry groups or technical experts to help it counter French obstructionism.

FURTHER READING

On all of the material covered in this chapter, valuable information is contained in **F. Duchêne,** *Jean Monnet: The First Statesman of Interdependence* (New York and London: W. W. Norton and Co., 1994).

The Pleven Plan and the abortive attempt to create a EDC is less written about than the Schuman Plan, but it is the subject of **E. Fursdon**, *The European Defence Community: A History* (London: Macmillan, 1980).

Several books are devoted to, or contain extensive sections on, the experience of the early communities: **W. Diebold, Jr.**, *The Schuman Plan: A Study in Economic Cooperation: 1950–1959* (New York: Praeger, 1962); **J. Gillingham**, *Coal, Steel, and the Rebirth of Europe, 1945–1955* (Cambridge: Cambridge University Press, 1991); **E. B. Haas**, *The Uniting of Europe: Political, Social and Economic Forces, 1950–1957* (Stanford, CA: Stanford University Press, 1968).

There is one indispensable work on the ECSC: **D. Spierenburg and R. Poidevin**, *The History of the High Authority of the European Coal and Steel Community: Supranationality in Action* (London: Weidenfeld, 1994).

On the Euratom there is less. The most revealing piece is **L. Scheinmann**, 'Euratom: Nuclear Integration in Europe', *International Conciliation*, 563 (1967). There is also a discussion of the adoption of Euratom in **A. Milward**, *The European Rescue of the Nation State* (London: Routledge, 1992), 200–11.

 online resource centre

Visit the Online Resource Centre that accompanies this book for links to more information on the origins of the EEC:
http://oxfordtextbooks.co.uk/orc/bache4e/

Chapter 7

The First Years of the European Economic Community (the 1960s and into the 1970s)

Chapter Overview

The early 1960s were a period of apparent success for the supranational elements within the European Economic Community (EEC). Rapid progress was made towards the creation of both a common market and a common agricultural policy. The only setback during this period was a crisis in 1963 when President de Gaulle vetoed a British application for membership; but in the middle of the decade there was a more serious crisis, when France boycotted meetings of the Council of Ministers in response to proposals for a more supranational method of funding the EEC budget. This crisis and its aftermath took much of the momentum out of the process of European integration for the remainder of the decade, when changes in political leadership in France and West Germany led to a summit meeting in The Hague that gave a renewed mandate for progress. As a direct result of the renewed mandate, the EEC expanded its membership at the start of the 1970s, and made the first moves towards an economic and monetary union and a common foreign and security policy.

The Early Years: 1958–63

It was not obvious in 1957 which of the two new communities, the EEC or Euratom, would become the more important. Within a few years, though, Euratom had lost all momentum. Driven by the vigorous leadership of Commission President Walter Hallstein, the EEC made a successful start and achieved most of its objectives over most of the first decade of its existence.

The institutional arrangements of the EEC followed those of the ECSC, with a supranational Commission as the equivalent of the High Authority, a Council of Ministers, and a Parliamentary Assembly. In addition, an Economic and Social Committee played an advisory role. Finally, the European Court of Justice (ECJ) was established to interpret the provisions of the Treaty of Rome and to act as arbiter in disputes on Community decisions (see Insight 7.1).

> ## Insight 7.1 The Institutional Arrangements of the EEC
>
> The Commission consisted of nine Commissioners appointed by national governments: two each from France, Germany, and Italy, one each for Belgium, Luxembourg, and the Netherlands. While national appointees, Commissioners were not supposed to advocate national interests but to protect the European ideal. The Commission's primary tasks were to make proposals to the Council of Ministers and to implement the Treaty of Rome. (On the Commission see Chapter 13.)
>
> The Council of Ministers consisted of one representative from each member state. Provision was made for it to vote on proposals from the Commission by qualified majority vote (QMV). For these purposes, seventeen votes were allocated among the six member states: four each to France, Germany, and Italy; two each for Belgium and the Netherlands; and one vote for Luxembourg; a qualified majority required twelve votes, ensuring that a decision required the support of at least four states. However, in the first stage, prior to the completion of the common market, it was agreed that all decisions would be taken by unanimity. (On the Council see Chapter 14.)
>
> The EPA of 142 members was a purely consultative body. Although provision was made in the Treaty for direct election, initially the members were nominated by national parliaments from among their own members. (On the European Parliament see Chapter 15.)
>
> The ECJ was made up of seven judges: one from each member state, plus one appointed by the Council. (On the ECJ see Chapter 16.)

For the whole of its separate existence, the Commission of the EEC had only one President. Walter Hallstein had been the State Secretary in the Foreign Office of the Federal Republic of Germany, and had been in charge of the German team during the negotiation of the EEC. Hallstein's appointment was accepted unanimously, a remarkable development only twelve years after the war.

The very lack of a sense of drama in the choice of a German for the most important of the new posts was not only a tribute to Hallstein's achievements and reputation but also proof of giant progress since the Schuman Plan (Duchêne 1994: 309).

Close to Chancellor Adenauer in his views on west European integration, Hallstein was in no doubt about the political nature of the Commission. In a book published in 1962 he made clear that, in his view, the logic of economic integration not only leads on towards political unity, it involves political action itself.

> We are not integrating economics, we are integrating policies. 'Political integration' is not too bold and too grandiose a term to describe this process.
>
> (Hallstein 1962: 66–7)

Hallstein was backed in this view of the role of the Commission by the energetic Dutch Vice-President and Commissioner for Agriculture, Sicco Mansholt. Between them Hallstein and Mansholt gave vigorous leadership to the Commission, which, according to one observer, constituted 'a relatively united, committed partisan organisation' (Coombes 1970: 259).

The morale of the Commission was increased by its success in getting the Council of Ministers to agree to an acceleration of the timetable for the achievement of a customs union in 1962. It went on to broker agreement on the level of the common external tariff (CET), and at the same time to negotiate acceptance of a common agricultural policy (CAP).

The EEC Treaty (Article 14; now removed) specified a precise timetable for the progressive reduction of internal tariffs. On the original schedule it would have taken at least eight years to get rid of all such tariffs. This rather leisurely rate of progress reflected the concerns of specific industrial groups about the problems of adjustment involved in the ending of national protection. However, once the Treaty was signed and it became obvious that the common market was to become a reality, those same industrial interests responded to the changed situation facing them. Even before the Treaty came into operation, on 1 January 1958, companies had begun to conclude cross-border agreements on co-operation, or to acquire franchized retail outlets for their products in other member states. Just as the neofunctionalists had predicted, changing circumstances led to changed behaviour.

So rapid was the adjustment of corporate behaviour to the prospect of the common market that impatience to see the benefits of the deals that were being concluded and of the new investments that were being made soon led to pressure on national governments to accelerate the timetable. Remarkably, the strongest pressure came from French industrial interests, which had opposed the original scheme for a common market.

On 12 May 1960 the Council of Ministers agreed to a proposal from the Commission to accelerate progress on the removal of internal barriers to trade and the erection of a CET, and on the creation of the CAP. Pressure had come only for the first of these to be accelerated. Progress was slow on agriculture, the negotiations having been dogged by disagreements over the level of support that ought to be given to farmers for different commodities. But the issues were clearly linked: progress on the CAP to accompany progress on the industrial common market had been part of the original deal embodied in the EEC Treaty.

It seemed that in keeping the linkage between the two issues in the forefront of all their proposals to the Council of Ministers, the Commission had played a manipulative role that coincided with the view of neofunctionalism about the importance of central leadership. Indeed, it is possibly from the performance of the Commission in this period that the importance of leadership from the centre was first theorized and added to the emerging corpus of neofunctionalist concepts. As described by Lindberg (1963: 167–205), the progress of the EEC between 1958 and 1965 involved the Commission utilizing a favourable situation to promote integration. Governments found themselves trapped between the growing demand from national interest groups that they carry through as rapidly as possible their commitment to create a common market, and the insistence of the Commission that this could only happen if the governments were prepared to reach agreement on the setting of common minimum prices for agricultural products.

These agreements were engineered by the skilful use of the 'package deal': linking the two issues together, and not allowing progress on one without commensurate progress on the other. In that way, each member state would agree to things in which it was less interested in order to get those things in which it was more interested. It was just such a package deal that the French President, Charles de Gaulle, was to reject in spectacular fashion in 1965, plunging the EEC into crisis. However, before that, in 1963, there was a warning of the problems that lay ahead.

The 1963 Crisis

As Urwin (1995: 103) noted:

> To some extent, the Commission could be so active because the national governments, through the Council of Ministers had been content to allow it to be so. Even President de Gaulle had on the whole been quite circumspect about the Commission.

However, the Commission's influence and the apparent smooth progress of the EEC received a setback in January 1963 when President de Gaulle unilaterally vetoed the British government's application for membership. The most comprehensive history of this episode is Ludlow (1997), on which the following account is largely based.

Having declined the invitation to be present at the creation, Harold Macmillan announced in the House of Commons in July 1961 that the British government had decided to apply for membership of the EEC. The development was not welcomed by Walter Hallstein, who saw it as potentially disruptive to the smooth progress of integration among the Six. It was also unwelcome to de Gaulle, who had ambitions to use the EEC as a platform for the reassertion of French greatness in international affairs.

To this end, de Gaulle tried to get agreement between the Six on co-operation in foreign policy, which he believed that France would be able to dominate. From 1960 it was agreed that the foreign ministers of the member states would meet four times yearly. De Gaulle also developed a special relationship with the German Chancellor, Konrad Adenauer. This relationship was important in securing support for de Gaulle's plans to extend political co-operation between the Six. The matter was subsequently considered by a committee chaired by the French official, Christian Fouchet (see Insight 7.2). The Fouchet negotiations on political co-operation were taking place in 1961 when the British application was lodged, but they had already run into some difficulties over proposals for foreign and defence policy.

Insight 7.2 The Fouchet Plan

In 1961 President de Gaulle proposed to the other members of the Communities that they consider forming what he called a Union of States. This would be an intergovernmental organization in which the institutions of the existing three Communities would play no role. It would involve the member states in pursuing closer co-operation on cultural, scientific, and educational matters, and, most significantly, in the co-ordination of their foreign and defence policies.

At summit meetings in 1961 it was agreed to set up a committee under the chairmanship of the French Ambassador to Denmark, Christian Fouchet, and subsequently to ask the committee to prepare a detailed plan for such co-operation.

This 'Fouchet Plan' proposed a confederation of states with a Council of Ministers, a Consultative Assembly of seconded national parliamentarians, and a Commission. However, unlike the Commissions of the EEC and Euratom, this Commission would not be a supranational body with independent powers, but would consist of officials from national Foreign Ministries.

British entry did not fit de Gaulle's plans: it would have provided an alternative leadership for the four other member states, whose governments were suspicious of him and wished to resist French domination. Technically, de Gaulle could have vetoed the application, but politically he was in no position to do so. In addition to Fouchet, there were negotiations proceeding in 1961 on two issues that were of crucial importance to France: the CAP, and new association terms for Africa. Also, de Gaulle did not want to make it more difficult for the pro-French position of his ally Adenauer to prevail in Bonn.

The approach that de Gaulle chose to adopt was to allow negotiations on enlargement to open, but to instruct the French delegation to set the price high in the hope that the terms would prove unacceptable to the British government. The French position was presented as defending the Treaty of Rome and the ***acquis communautaire***. Both had been so strongly influenced by French demands that their defence was almost the same as the defence of the French national interest. Because the French demands were couched in *communautaire* language, it was very difficult for the other member states to resist them. They were torn between support for British membership and a desire not to dilute the achievements of the EEC to date.

The negotiations did not collapse, but they went on so long that de Gaulle was eventually presented with the excuse that he needed to issue his unilateral veto: the deal on nuclear weapons that was reached between Macmillan and US President John Kennedy at Nassau in December 1962. Macmillan persuaded Kennedy to sell Britain Polaris missiles to carry Britain's independent nuclear weapons. This was presented by de Gaulle as clear evidence that the British were not yet ready to accept 'a European vocation', and used as justification for ending negotiations that had stalled in late 1962 anyway.

The other member states reacted angrily to the veto. Given that the negotiations had run into difficulties, the anger was directed less at their enforced ending than at the way in which de Gaulle had undermined the system of collaborative working that had emerged in the Six, and within which the others had operated throughout the negotiations.

The 1965 Crisis

A more fundamental, and considerably more serious, crisis began in July 1965, when de Gaulle withdrew France from participation in the work of the Council of Ministers in protest at a proposal from the Commission concerning the financing of the Community's budget.

Once agreement had been reached on the details of the CAP, the question arose of how the policy would be funded. For the first time, the EEC would have a budget that went beyond the salaries and administrative costs of the central institutions. The Commission proposed that, instead of the cumbersome method of annual contributions negotiated between the member states, the Community should have its 'own resources'. These would be the revenue from the CET on industrial goods and the levies on agricultural goods entering the Community from outside, which would be collected by national customs officials at their point of entry into the EEC and then handed over to Brussels, after the deduction of 10 per cent as a service charge. The justification was that the goods might be intended for consumption in any part of the Community, and it was therefore unreasonable that the revenue should accrue to the state through which the goods happened to enter the common market.

However, the French President questioned another aspect of the proposal. Using the method of the package deal, the Commission linked the idea of having its own resources with a proposal for an increase in the powers of the European Parliamentary Assembly (EPA), giving it the right to approve the budget. The argument for this was that if the revenues passed directly to the EEC without having to be approved by national parliaments, there would be a lack of democratic scrutiny, which could only be corrected by giving that right to the EPA.

President de Gaulle objected to this increase in the powers of a supranational institution, and when discussion became deadlocked he showed how important he held the issue to be by imposing a French boycott of all meetings of the Council of Ministers from June 1965. This action was subsequently termed the 'empty chair crisis'. In essence, the dispute was about the very nature of the Europe that the Six were hoping to build. For de Gaulle, primacy had to be given to the interests of national governments.

The Luxembourg Compromise

After six months an agreement was reached between France and the other five member states in Luxembourg. The so-called 'Luxembourg Compromise' of January 1966 represented a considerable blow to the process of European integration. First, there was agreement not to proceed with the Commission's proposals: funding of the budget would continue to be by national contributions. Second, France demanded that there be no transition to majority voting in the Council of Ministers. This move had been envisaged in the original treaties once the customs union was complete, and completion was on schedule for January 1966. Under the terms of the Luxembourg Compromise, governments would retain their right to veto proposals where they deemed a vital national interest to be at stake. This agreement was a serious blow to the hope of the Commission that brokering agreement on further integrative moves would be easier in the future.

Third, France made four other demands: that the President of the Commission should no longer receive the credentials of ambassadors to the EEC; that the information services be taken out of the hands of the Commission; that members of the Commission should be debarred from making political attacks on the attitudes of member states; and that the Commission should not reveal its proposals to the EPA before they were presented to the Council of Ministers, as it had with the controversial package on the budget.

The terms of the deal precipitated a collapse of morale in the Commission. In particular, the authority of Hallstein and Mansholt was undermined by the episode. Some Commissioners had warned against a confrontation with de Gaulle on supranationality, but Hallstein and Mansholt had overruled them (Camps 1967: 47). Neither was to regain the air of invincibility that he had acquired in the past. Hallstein withdrew his name from the list of nominations for the presidency of the new combined Commission of the ECSC, EEC, and Euratom that was due to take office on 1 July 1967, and simply served out the remainder of his term. Mansholt stayed on as a Commissioner, but did not put his name forward for the presidency.

Into the 1970s

Whereas the 1960s had been an era of high rates of economic growth within a reasonably stable (if militarily threatening) international environment, the 1970s were times of turbulence and flux in the international economic system.

Under these circumstances it was very difficult for the Commission to inject new momentum into the process of European integration. Also, although the Hallstein Commission was initially given tremendous credit for promoting integration in the period following the signing of the Treaties of Rome, subsequent reassessments suggested that, in fact, it had done little beyond fill out the details of agreements that had been made between the member states in the EEC Treaty. If this view is correct, then for the Commission to play an active role in the 1970s required a new mandate from the member states.

Between 1967 and 1977 the Commission had four presidents (see Box 7.1). Neither Jean Rey nor Franco Malfatti had a new mandate, and besides they were both preoccupied with the difficult issues involved in combining the three executive bodies of the ECSC, EEC, and Euratom into a single Commission. When a new mandate *was* given, at a summit meeting in The Hague in December 1969, it involved completion of the financing arrangements for the EC budget, enlargement to take in Britain and the other applicant states, progress to economic and monetary union, and trying to develop a common foreign policy. The first of these was easily accomplished. The second was successfully carried through for three of the four applicants, but at considerable cost in terms of time and resources for the Commission. Economic and monetary union might have been the mandate that the Commission needed to produce a new impetus to integration, but as Tsoukalis (1977) argued, this decision was more akin to the decision to negotiate on the EEC than it was to the Treaty of Rome itself. As we shall see, this proved to be an intractable issue. Progress on co-ordination of foreign policy was made in a purely intergovernmental framework.

Not only were these issues more difficult in themselves: the overall context of the period was unfavourable to further integration. The Luxembourg agreement that ended the French boycott in January 1966 effectively meant that the national veto was

---

Box 7.1 Presidents of the Commission, 1967–77

1967–70	Jean Rey (Belgium)
1970–72	Franco Maria Malfatti (Italy)
1972	Sicco Mansholt (the Netherlands)
1973–77	François-Xavier Ortoli (France)

retained on all matters that came before the Council of Ministers. Although the Commission had operated with a veto system in the 1960s, the further integration progressed, the more likely it was that particular vested interests would come under challenge, and that individual states would try to block measures.

These tendencies were made more acute by changed economic circumstances. Whereas the early progress of the EEC had taken place against a background of sustained economic growth, a recession started in 1971 which really began to bite after the December 1973 decision of the **Organization of the Petroleum Exporting Countries (OPEC)** to force a quadrupling in the price of oil. This context made governments more defensive and less inclined to agree to integrative measures that would weaken their ability to preserve domestic markets for domestic producers. As the economic context changed, the pace of European economic integration slowed and there was no advance towards political union. Uncertainty within member states restricted the scope for Commission activism.

The problems were exacerbated by enlargement, which brought into membership two more states, Britain and Denmark, that were opposed to supranationalism. The cumulative effect of these developments was to ensure that the second decade of the EEC was not marked by the rapid progress on integration that had marked the first decade.

The Hague Summit

The resignation of President de Gaulle in April 1969 appeared to free the way to further integration. De Gaulle was succeeded by his former Prime Minister, Georges Pompidou, who soon let it be known that he did not object in principle to British membership.

Also in 1969 there was a change of government in Germany. The Social Democratic Party (SPD), which had been the junior coalition partner to the Christian Democrats for the previous three years, became the larger partner in a coalition with the Free Democrat Party (FDP). Willy Brandt, the new Chancellor, intended to pursue an active policy of improving relations with the communist bloc, but was anxious to demonstrate that this *Ostpolitik* did not imply any weakening of German commitment to the EC.

As a result of these two changes, a summit meeting of heads of government was convened in The Hague in December 1969 with the explicit aim of relaunching European integration. This Hague Summit declared the objectives of completion, widening, and deepening. Completion meant tidying up the outstanding business from the 1965 crisis: moving the EC budget from dependence on national contributions to a system of financing from its own resources. Widening meant opening accession negotiations with Britain and other likely applicants. Deepening meant taking the next steps in the process of European integration, specifically in the direction of economic and monetary union and closer political co-operation.

Completion was achieved relatively easily. A system was agreed for the EC to have as its own resources the levies on agricultural products entering the EC under the CAP, and the revenues from the common customs tariff on imports of non-agricultural products from outside of the EC. There were the usual compromises, but France did accept some budgetary role for the European Parliament (EP)—as the EPA became—giving it the right to propose amendments to those parts of the budget that were not classified as 'compulsory expenditure' under the treaties, and to propose modifications to the items of 'compulsory' expenditure. The Council of Ministers, acting by qualified majority, could amend the amendments, and could refuse to agree to the modifications, so, in effect, it retained the final say on the budget. The distinction between compulsory and non-compulsory expenditure defined expenditure under the CAP as compulsory, so making the bulk of the budget difficult for the EP to amend. Nevertheless, there was an acknowledgement that the EP should have some role in scrutinizing the budget, and there was the prospect that deepening would lead to a larger budget in which agriculture was not so dominant, so there would be more areas of non-compulsory expenditure.

Widening was also achieved within a few years. Negotiations with four applicant states—Britain, Ireland, Denmark, and Norway—opened in June 1970, and were successfully completed by January 1972. Referendums were then held on membership in Ireland, Denmark, and Norway. The first two produced clear majorities in favour of entry, but in September 1972 the Norwegian people, not for the last time, rejected membership. In Britain, the Conservative government of Edward Heath refused to hold a referendum, which it argued was not a British constitutional instrument; but parliamentary ratification was successfully completed. So on 1 January 1973 the six became nine.

While enlargement achieved the objective of widening the membership of the EC, it was to cause problems as well. The new member states entered at a time when the economic growth of the 1960s had already started to slow and was about to receive a further setback when OPEC quadrupled the price of oil in December 1973. Not having experienced the positive benefits of membership, neither the governments nor the peoples of these new member states had the same degree of psychological commitment to the idea of European integration as had those of the original six members. In addition, in Britain in particular there was considerable scepticism about the merits of the EC. Edward Heath was personally strongly committed to membership, but he never managed entirely to convince his own Conservative Party; and Heath was soon displaced as Prime Minister when he lost the general election early in 1974, and Harold Wilson once again formed a Labour government.

While in opposition, the Labour Party had been riven with dissension, and membership of the EC had been a central issue. Several of Wilson's cabinet ministers from 1964–70 were committed to British membership. Wilson himself was also convinced of the necessity of membership. But a majority in the party was still opposed, and the pressure from this majority meant that Wilson could not give unqualified approval to entry when Heath negotiated it. On the other hand, his own certainty that membership was necessary, and the importance of the pro-membership minority within the leadership of the party, made it impossible for him to oppose entry. The result was an ingenious compromise of opposition to entry on the terms negotiated by the Conservative government. Labour went into the 1974 election committed to a full renegotiation of the terms of entry with a threat (or promise) of withdrawal if 'satisfactory' terms could not be agreed.

The renegotiation involved serious disruption to other business in the EC, at a time when there were several important issues on the agenda. It also involved a great deal of posturing and nationalist rhetoric from the British government. What it did not

127

involve was any fundamental change in the terms of entry. Nevertheless, the renegotiated terms were put to the British people in a referendum in June 1975, with a recommendation from the government that they be accepted, which they were.

The two-to-one vote in the referendum in favour of Community membership was a passing moment of public favour. Soon the opinion polls were again showing majorities against membership. Britain had joined at a bad time, and the continuing economic difficulties of the country could conveniently be blamed on the EC. Although the Labour opponents of membership had to accept, for the time being, the verdict of the referendum, they lost no opportunity to attack the EC, and Wilson was prepared to accept this if it diverted attention away from his failure to solve the country's economic difficulties. He himself continued to take a strongly nationalistic line in EC negotiations, as did his Foreign Secretary, James Callaghan, who succeeded him as Prime Minister in March 1976.

By succeeding in widening its membership, the EC placed another barrier in the way of further integration. Yet, it is a mistake to blame Britain alone for blocking further integration. Certainly Britain became an awkward partner; but as Buller (1995: 36) argued: 'everybody consciously attempts to be obstructive every now and again in European negotiations. It is all part and parcel of politics in this kind of environment.' The degree of awkwardness of all member states increased during this period of economic problems.

While the objectives of completion and widening were achieved, attempts at deepening co-operation between member states met with limited success. The two main objectives agreed at The Hague were 'economic and monetary union by 1980' and the creation of a common foreign policy.

Economic and monetary union was the logical next step in the building of the EC. Economic union meant that the member states would, at most, cease to follow independent economic policies, and at least would follow co-ordinated policies. This would remove distortions to free competition and would help to make a reality of the common market. Monetary union meant, at most, the adoption of a single Community currency, at least the maintenance of fixed exchange rates between the currencies of the member states.

In 1969 there were the first major realignments of member states' currencies since the EC had started, and the prospect of monetary instability threatened to hinder trade within the common market by introducing an element of uncertainty into import and export deals. In this context, monetary union was seen as a means of making the common market effective.

Following The Hague Summit, a committee was set up under the chairmanship of Pierre Werner, the Prime Minister of Luxembourg, to produce concrete proposals on economic and monetary union (EMU). It reported within a few months, and in February 1971 the Council of Ministers adopted a programme for the achievement of EMU in stages between 1971 and 1980. The institutional centrepiece of the scheme was the 'snake-in-the-tunnel', an arrangement for approximating the exchange rates of member currencies one to another while holding their value jointly in relation to the US dollar. It was to be accompanied by more determined efforts to bring national economic policies into line, with Finance Ministers meeting at least three times per year to try to co-ordinate policies. Thus, there would be progress on both monetary and economic union, the two running in parallel.

> ## Insight 7.3 The Collapse of the International Monetary System
>
> The key aspects of the international monetary system were agreed at a conference at Bretton Woods in New Hampshire in 1944. These were the **International Monetary Fund (IMF)** and the International Bank for Reconstruction and Development (the '**World Bank**'). The **General Agreement on Tariffs and Trade (GATT)** was added later. The system worked with the United States playing a leading and directive role, and provided a stability that was central to the prosperity of west European economies. However, the gradual erosion of US economic dominance in this period, culminating with the ending of the convertibility of US dollars to gold in 1971, marked the collapse of the Bretton Woods international system and a less secure international economic context.

The 'snake' did not last long in its original form. It was destroyed by the international monetary crisis that followed the ending of the convertibility of the dollar in August 1971 (see Insight 7.3). Only after the Smithsonian agreements of late 1971 had restored some semblance of order to the world monetary system was it possible to attempt once again a joint Community currency arrangement, this time with the participation of the four states that had just completed the negotiation of their entry to the EC. That was in April 1972; but it took under two months for this second snake to break apart. In June, the British government had to remove sterling from the system and float it on the international monetary markets. Italy was forced to leave in February 1973. France followed in January 1974, re-joined in July 1975, but was forced to leave again in the spring of 1976. In every case, the currency had come under so much speculative pressure that it had proved impossible to maintain its value against the other currencies in the system.

By 1977 the snake had become a very different creature from that which had been envisaged. Of the nine members of the EC, only West Germany, the Benelux states, and Denmark were still members (Ireland had left with Britain, the Irish punt being tied to the pound sterling at that time). In addition, two non-member states, Norway and Sweden, had joined. Yet, during 1977 even this snake was under strain, and Sweden was forced to withdraw the krona.

European Political Co-operation (EPC) was the more successful attempt at deepening, ironically, since it was only included in The Hague objectives as a concession to France. President Pompidou was dependent for his majority in the French National Assembly on the votes of the Gaullist party of which he was himself a member. De Gaulle had opposed giving budgetary powers to the EP, and Pompidou agreed to this at The Hague. De Gaulle had also opposed British entry to the EC. He had made it clear when a second British application was tabled in May 1967 that there was no point in entering into negotiations, because he would veto British membership. Pompidou had made it equally clear that he was prepared to enter into negotiations, and perhaps even to accept British membership if satisfactory terms could be agreed. Both of these departures from Gaullist orthodoxy were controversial in his own party, and he needed concessions at The Hague in order to be able to sell the package to this domestic constituency.

One of de Gaulle's pet projects had been to set up a system of intergovernmental political co-operation between the member states of the EC. This was the basis of the

Fouchet Plan, which had been under discussion at the same time as the first British application, and had finally collapsed as a result of the French veto on British entry. It was therefore unsurprising that Pompidou should look for a commitment to revive this project as part of the price for his co-operation on completion and widening. It was agreed at The Hague to set up a committee under the chairmanship of Viscount Etienne Davignon, a senior official in the Belgian Foreign Ministry, to devise machinery for co-operation between the member states on foreign policy issues. This committee reported in October 1970, and the system that it recommended became the basis for some successful diplomatic initiatives. Indeed, EPC came to be seen as one of the few achievements in the 1970s.

One of the successes was the formulation of a common position on the Middle East, which allowed the EC to pursue its clear interest in improving trade with the Arab OPEC states in the 1970s, through the Euro–Arab dialogue. In 1980 this common policy culminated in the Venice Declaration, which went further than the United States was prepared to go in recognizing the right of the Palestinians to a homeland. The nine member states were also extremely successful in formulating a common position at the Conference on Security and Co-operation in Europe (CSCE) in Helsinki in 1975, and at the follow-up conferences in Belgrade in 1977, and Madrid in 1982–3. Again, the common position adopted by the EC ran somewhat contrary to the position of the United States, which regarded the Helsinki process with some suspicion as running the risk of legitimating communist rule in eastern Europe. Third, the Community states achieved a high degree of unity in the United Nations, voting together on a majority of resolutions in the General Assembly, and developing a reputation for being the most cohesive group there at a time when group-diplomacy was becoming much more common.

Admittedly there were also failures for the policy of European political co-operation. On balance, though, there were more substantive successes than there were failures. However, all of this remained officially intergovernmental, rather than being rolled up into the more supranational procedures of the EC, so there was a question mark over whether it could be considered to be an advance for the process of European integration. On the other hand, the actual working of the system was less strictly intergovernmental than the formal procedures, a point that is explored further in Chapter 26.

CONCLUSION

The struggle between supranationalism and intergovernmentalism is the clear theme of this chapter. The neofunctionalist interpretation of the history of European integration seems to get both its strongest support and its greatest challenge from the period under consideration. The support comes from the story of the acceleration agreement as told by neofunctionalists (see Chapter 1, International Relations Theories of European Integration). The setback came from the actions of de Gaulle in vetoing British entry in 1963 and in boycotting the Council of Ministers in 1965.

Lindberg (1963) took the role of the Commission in the success of the EEC in the 1960s as clear evidence of its centrality to the process. However, this interpretation was strongly contradicted in the intergovernmentalist tradition, notably by Andrew Moravcsik (1998: 159–237; see Chapter 1). Moravcsik's research indicated that the deals were not cut by the Commission but by the governments of other member states. He argued that 'the Commission was ineffective and repeatedly sidelined' (Moravcsik 1998: 233).

The 1965 dispute over the funding of the budget illustrated the continued ability of national governments, even of a single national government, to stop the process of European integration in its tracks.

In the 1970s, when US hegemony began to falter, the EC had to deal with an increasingly turbulent international environment. The theme of the impact of the wider system on developments within the EC is clearly illustrated here, particularly trends in international political economy (see Chapter 4, Critical Political Economy). The retreat into covert national protectionism, to preserve jobs for nationals, was a direct consequence of the shadow that recession cast over the process of European integration.

There seemed little in the period onto which the neofunctionalists could cling as evidence of their theory being vindicated, and the decade from 1966 through to mid-1970s is often presented as the 'dark ages' of European integration.

Later, though, alternative analyses emerged of the so-called 'dark ages' of integration, which emphasized the importance of work behind the scenes of the ECJ in starting to put in place a body of European law that paved the way for subsequent advances in integration (see Chapter 16).

KEY POINTS

The Early Years: 1958–63

- The EEC Commission under the presidency of Walter Hallstein was very proactive in promoting integration.
- Its apparent successes included getting agreement from the member states to accelerate progress on creating the common market and the CAP.

The 1963 Crisis

- In 1961 President de Gaulle proposed intergovernmental political co-operation.
- Negotiations on the 'Fouchet Plan' were ongoing when Britain applied for EC membership.
- De Gaulle did not want to see Britain become a member, but, rather than risk collapsing the Fouchet negotiations, he allowed negotiations on membership to begin while trying to ensure that French demands would make the terms of entry unacceptable to Britain.
- When the Fouchet negotiations came near to collapse, and the entry negotiations did not, de Gaulle unilaterally vetoed British entry.

The 1965 Crisis

- In 1965 the Commission proposed a system of financing the CAP that would have given the EEC its own financial resources. This was linked to a proposal to increase the budgetary powers of the EPA.
- De Gaulle rejected the increase in the powers of the EPA, and, when agreement could not be reached, he withdrew France from participation in the work of the Council of Ministers.

The Luxembourg Compromise

- In January 1966 France resumed its place in the Council in exchange for the planned move to QMV being abandoned.
- The terms of the 'compromise' caused a collapse of morale in the Commission.

Into the 1970s

- For the Commission to play an active role in the 1970s required a new mandate from the member states.
- The context was less favourable to integration in the 1970s than it had been in the 1960s.
- Problems were made worse by enlargement.

The Hague Summit

- Changes of leadership in France and Germany in 1969 appeared to free the way for further European integration. The result was The Hague Summit, which declared the objectives of completion, deepening, and widening.
- *Completion* was achieved through allowing the EC to have its own resources for the first time. The EP was also given some budgetary powers.
- *Widening* was achieved through the entry of Britain, Denmark, and Ireland into the EC in 1973.
- *Deepening* of co-operation on foreign policy through EPC had some success; less so co-operation on monetary union.

FURTHER READING

When we get to the establishment of the EEC, the range of reading extends considerably. For studies by historians, see **A. Milward**, *The European Rescue of the Nation State* (London: Routledge, 1992) and **A. Milward and A. Deighton (eds)**, *Widening, Deepening and Acceleration: The European Economic Community 1957-1963* (Baden-Baden: Nomos, 1999). Also useful is the official history by **M. Dumoulin and M.-T. Bitsch**, *The European Commission, 1958-1972: History and Memories* (Luxembourg: Office for Official Publications of the European Communities, 2007).

The standard political science account of the early years of the EEC is **L. Lindberg**, *The Political Dynamics of European Economic Integration* (Stanford, CA: Stanford University Press; London: Oxford University Press, 1963); but this is rejected by **A. Moravcsik**, *The Choice for Europe* (London: UCL Press, 1998), 158–237.

On the British application in 1961, see **P. Ludlow**, *Dealing with Britain: The Six and the First UK Application to the EEC* (Cambridge: Cambridge University Press, 1997). The official history of British negotiations for entry is available in **C. O'Neill**, *Britain's Entry into the European Community: Report by Sir Con O'Neill on the Negotiations of 1970-1972* (London: Frank Cass, 2000). For the 1973 enlargement in broader context, see **W. Kaiser and J. Elvert (eds)**, *European Union Enlargement: A Comparative History* (London: Routledge, 2004).

 online resource centre

Visit the Online Resource Centre that accompanies this book for links to more information on the first years of the EEC: http://oxfordtextbooks.co.uk/orc/bache4e/

Chapter 8

The Revival of European Integration (the Mid-1970s to the Late 1980s)

Chapter Overview

Despite some progress following The Hague Summit in 1969, European integration was still at quite a low point in the early 1970s; but signs emerged in the late 1970s of the European Community (EC) turning a corner. A revived Commission, led by Roy Jenkins, secured agreement to be involved in international economic summits; the European Monetary System (EMS) was set up; and membership applications from Greece, Portugal, and Spain reflected positively on the external reputation of the EC. The renewed momentum gathered pace under the Commission presidency of Gaston Thorn, when the basis was laid for an initiative to free the internal market of non-tariff barriers to free trade. That initiative was taken up by Thorn's successor, Jacques Delors, and led to the Single European Act (SEA), which was widely seen as the big breakthrough in the revival of European integration.

Leadership Changes: 1974

Mid-way through the 1970s, there were again coinciding changes of government in both France and Germany, which strengthened the Franco-German relationship. Georges Pompidou died in office in 1974, and was succeeded by Valéry Giscard d'Estaing, who was not a Gaullist, although he was dependent on the Gaullist party for a majority in the National Assembly. In Germany, Brandt resigned following the discovery that an east German spy had been part of his personal staff, and was succeeded by his former Finance Minister, Helmut Schmidt.

These changes brought to office two strong national leaders who had an excellent *rapport*, and who dominated the EC for the next six years. They were not, though, particularly committed to reviving the process of supranational integration. Their approach was pragmatic rather than ideological, and they were prepared to use any instruments that presented themselves to deal with the problems that their countries faced.

The European Council

In 1974 Giscard d'Estaing called a meeting of the heads of government of the member states to discuss his proposal that the EC should institutionalize such summit meetings. The smaller member states were suspicious of this proposal, which sounded very Gaullist, but Giscard d'Estaing got strong backing from Schmidt, and it was agreed to hold meetings of the heads of state and government three times every year under the title the 'European Council'. At the same time, as a concession to the fears of those governments who saw in this a weakening of the supranational element of the EC, agreement was reached to hold direct elections to the European Parliament (EP) in 1978. The British government was reconciled to this by concessions on the renegotiation of its terms of entry that was taking place at the same time.

Direct elections were not actually held until 1979 because the British government was unable to pass the necessary domestic legislation in time to hold the election in 1978. In the long run the decision to hold direct elections was far from insignificant. In the short to medium term, though, the creation of the European Council was much the more significant outcome of Paris, 1974.

The European Council was from the outset an intergovernmental body. It had no basis in the treaties until the SEA came into force in July 1987. It became the overarching institution of the EU in the 1992 Maastricht Treaty. In the 1970s it was symbolic of a profoundly intergovernmental era in the history of the EU. However, it later presided over a set of major treaty reforms and policy initiatives (see Chapter 14).

Other Institutional Developments

The authority of the European Commission was strengthened by the presidency of Roy Jenkins between 1977 and 1981. Jenkins was an established political figure with considerable experience in government. He had held all the major posts in the British cabinet other than Prime Minister. As such, his appointment raised great expectations among those who regretted the decline in the authority of the Commission. Perhaps not all of those expectations were fulfilled. However, Jenkins did enhance the position of the president, and therefore of the Commission, by securing agreement from the heads of state and government that he should be present at meetings of the international economic summits, which had previously been restricted to the leaders of the major industrial nations. This development was strongly resisted by French President Giscard d'Estaing, but was strongly supported by the smaller member states, who felt excluded from an important economic decision-making forum, and who therefore wished to see the President of the Commission present to act as a spokesperson for the EC as a whole (Jenkins 1989: 20–2).

Jenkins also undertook a fundamental reform of the internal structure of the Commission, attempting, against considerable opposition from vested interests, to remove some of the causes of the bureaucratization that had been identified as one of the reasons for its decline in influence (Jenkins 1989: 310, 376). Although he was not completely successful, he did have some impact, and the strong leadership he demonstrated in tackling this problem was probably responsible for earning him the nickname 'Roi Jean Quinze', although this was also suggestive of his grand manner.

The other significant institutional development in this period was the introduction of direct elections to the EP in 1979. Until this point, the demands of the EP for greater powers had always been countered by the argument that it lacked democratic legitimacy because it was only an indirectly-elected body. After it became directly elected, the EP was in a much stronger position to extract new powers from the member states. The decision to move to direct elections was made at the Rome European Council in December 1975 (see Chapter 15, The Struggle for Power). Further controversy had followed when the first elections were delayed for a year because of the failure of the British Parliament to pass the necessary enabling legislation in time for the May/June 1978 date agreed at Rome. However, the elections in June 1979 were relatively low-key affairs within the member states, with national parties taking a prominent role in the selection of candidates and campaign organization.

The European Monetary System

In the policy field there was one very significant development in the late 1970s. The decision taken at the Brussels European Council in December 1978 to create the EMS did not exactly constitute a revival of economic and monetary union (EMU), but it did provide a basis for a future step in that direction.

By 1977, the 'snake in the tunnel' had become a system that embraced only five member states of the EC, together with two non-members. During 1977, even this truncated snake was under pressure from international speculation, and Sweden was forced to withdraw. In this far from promising context, Jenkins launched an initiative that met with a certain amount of scepticism about its feasibility even from colleagues within the Commission. In a lecture at the European University Institute in Florence, in October 1977, he called for a new attempt to start the EMU experiment (Jenkins 1977).

The following year Schmidt and Giscard d'Estaing came up with a joint proposal for what became the EMS. In July 1978, the European Council meeting in Bremen agreed to pursue the idea, and in December 1978, meeting in Brussels, agreed to create what looked remarkably like another snake. It would be more flexible than its predecessor, allowing wider margins of fluctuation for individual currencies, and it would be accompanied by the creation of a new European currency unit (ecu), which would take its value from a basket of the national currencies of the member states, and would be used in transactions within the EMS.

In addition to France and West Germany, the Benelux states and Denmark supported the EMS. After initial hesitation, Italy and Ireland agreed to become full participants. But Britain declined to put sterling into the joint float against the dollar, although it was included in the basket from which the value of the ecu was calculated. Despite the scepticism that had greeted Jenkins's initiative, the EMS did get off the ground, and this time the system did hold together, so that the scheme must be judged a relative success in the context of the overall history of attempts to move towards EMU (see Chapter 21, History).

The Southern Enlargements

In 1974 two significant events took place in the Mediterranean: Turkey invaded Cyprus, and a revolution in Portugal overthrew the right-wing Caetano government. Each led to an application for membership of the EC. Subsequently, political developments in Spain led to a Spanish application.

Greece had concluded an Association Agreement with the EC in 1964. This had envisaged eventual membership, but in 1967 Greece entered a period of military dictatorship that precluded an application. The inability of the Greek military to prevent the Turkish occupation of Cyprus precipitated the collapse of the dictatorship, and in June 1975 the new democratic Greek government sought membership of the EC as a means of consolidating democracy. In January 1976 the Commission issued a very cautious Opinion on the ability of Greece to adapt to membership, but political and strategic considerations led the Council of Ministers to accept the application and order the opening of negotiations. Democracy had to be shored up; but also Greece had to be prevented from swinging to the far left and reorienting itself towards the communist bloc. The negotiation of terms of entry for Greece was not easy, and it took up a great deal of the time of the Commission between July 1976 and May 1979, when the Accession Treaty was signed (membership began in January 1981). Nevertheless, the launching of the negotiations gave a new role to the Commission and put it back at the centre of the EC.

An application from Portugal followed the Greek application in March 1977. Again, there were political and strategic reasons for accepting it. The Portuguese revolution threatened to run out of the control of the pro-capitalist forces, and to fall into the hands of extreme left-wing groups that would have emphasized relations with the Third World. The Socialist International, with the German Social Democratic Party (SPD) taking a lead, provided support to the Portuguese Socialist Party (PSP), and so when the PSP was elected to government in 1976 there was not much doubt that it would apply for EC membership, nor that the application would be accepted.

Similar political and strategic considerations applied in July 1977 to the acceptance of an application from Spain following the death of the dictator Franco and the restoration of democracy there. In the Spanish case, membership of the EC was held out as a bonus if it decided also to join the NATO alliance. Given Spain's strategic position in the Mediterranean, this was a vital interest of the Western alliance.

Whereas the first of these applications stimulated a revival of the role of the Commission, handling three sets of difficult negotiations became a problem, and the Portuguese and Spanish Accession Treaties were not signed until 1985 (membership began in January 1986).

The British Budget Rebate

Another issue that caused problems for the EC in the 1980s was the British budgetary rebate. Although budget contributions had been central to the renegotiation, already by 1976, while transitional arrangements still limited the extent of its contributions,

Britain was the third biggest net contributor to the EC budget, behind Germany and Belgium. In 1977, still under transitional arrangements, the British net contribution was the second highest to that of Germany. By mid-1978 it was becoming apparent that once the transitional period of membership ended in 1980, Britain would become the largest net contributor to the budget.

This situation arose because:

(1) Britain imported more goods, especially foodstuffs, from outside the EC than did other member states, and therefore paid more in import levies.

(2) Low direct taxes meant that British consumers spent more in proportion to the relative wealth of the country, and Britain therefore contributed more to the budget in value-added tax (VAT) receipts.

(3) Payments out of the budget were dominated by the common agricultural policy (CAP), and Britain had a small and efficient farming sector that meant that it received less than states with larger agricultural economies.

The developing position was unacceptable to the Labour government. The Foreign Secretary, David Owen, told the House of Commons that the situation whereby 'the United Kingdom has the third lowest per capita gross domestic product in the Community' yet was already the second highest net contributor to the budget, 'cannot be good for the Community any more than it is for the United Kingdom', and promised that the government would 'be working to achieve a better balance, especially in relation to agricultural expenditure, to curb the excessive United Kingdom contribution' (*Hansard*, 14 November 1978, col. 214).

In fact, the Labour government never had the opportunity to work for a better balance because it lost office in the May 1979 election to the Conservatives under Margaret Thatcher. The new government soon took up the same theme concerning the budget. Shortly after coming into office, Sir Geoffrey Howe, the Chancellor of the Exchequer, announced that the size of the problem was far greater than the Conservatives had realized while in opposition, and something would have to be done about it urgently.

Margaret Thatcher raised the issue at her first European Council in Strasbourg in June 1979, soon after her election victory. Her presentation there was moderate and reasonable, and the complaint was offset by an announcement on the first day of the meeting that Britain would deposit its share of gold and foreign currency reserves with the European Monetary Co-operation Fund that had been set up to administer the EMS. The move was widely interpreted as a sign that sterling would soon join the exchange rate mechanism of the EMS. Discussion of the budgetary issue at Strasbourg was brief and limited to agreeing a procedure for analyzing the problem. The Commission was asked to prepare a report by September; this would be discussed by Finance Ministers, and then revised in time for the next European Council in Dublin in late November.

At that November 1979 Dublin European Council, Thatcher adopted an entirely different tone. She insisted that the Commission proposal of a rebate of £350 million was unacceptable, and that she would not accept less than £1 billion. The French said that they would not agree to more than £350 million, which the British would have to accept as full and final settlement of their claim. This provoked an argument that lasted ten hours, during the course of which Thatcher upset her partners by her uncompromising demands for what she insensitively described as Britain's 'own money back'.

This was the tone that Thatcher persistently adopted in negotiations for the next four-and-a-half years. During that time, several temporary abatements of the British contributions were agreed, but a permanent settlement eluded all efforts to bridge the gap between what the British Prime Minister demanded and what the other member states were prepared to pay. British tactics became increasingly obstructionist on other issues, and relations with the other states became increasingly strained.

Relations reached their nadir in May 1982. Britain was blocking agreement on agricultural price increases for 1982–3, linking agreement to a permanent settlement of the budgetary dispute. Finally, the Belgian presidency called a majority vote on the agricultural prices. Britain protested that this breached the Luxembourg Compromise, but the vote went ahead and was passed. Several of the other states, though, appeared shocked at their own behaviour. It seemed apparent that a settlement of the British dispute was necessary before progress could be made in other areas.

Leadership Changes: 1981-82

The confluence of challenges facing the EC at the beginning of the 1980s coincided with the appointment of Gaston Thorn to the Commission presidency in 1981. Member states generally welcomed Thorn's appointment. Although he took over at a difficult time, there was a feeling that he was uniquely well qualified for the job, as few people had a wider experience of the EC. He had served as a member of the EP, and as both Foreign Minister and Prime Minister of Luxembourg, and while in these posts had chaired the Council of Foreign Ministers and the European Council. Early in his presidency there were two significant changes among the national leaderships with which Thorn would have to work.

In May 1981, François Mitterrand defeated Giscard d'Estaing in the French presidential election. This result was consolidated a month later by a victory for Mitterrand's Socialist party in elections to the National Assembly. The change broke apart the Franco-German axis because Helmut Schmidt had less in common with the Socialist president than he had with the conservative Giscard d'Estaing. In particular, the Socialist government came into office committed to tackling unemployment rather than emphasizing low inflation as its predecessor had. However, a U-turn in economic policy in 1983 brought France more into line with the neoliberal and deregulationist tendencies already evident in West Germany and Britain.

The second change in political leadership came in West Germany itself. Although the SPD/Free Democrat Party (FDP) won the 1980 Federal election, dissension within the coalition was increasing in the face of the economic problems facing the country. Within the SPD, the left-wing and the trade unionist membership were demanding some measures of reflation to relieve unemployment, which in 1981 stood at 1.25 million. But, at the same time, the FDP was returning to its basic principles of economic liberalism, represented most strikingly by the Economics Minister, Count Otto Lambsdorff. The clash between the two parties over economic affairs led to the eventual breakdown of the coalition. In 1982 the FDP changed partners and allowed the Christian Democratic Union (CDU)/Christian Social Union (CSU) into office, with Helmut Kohl, the CDU leader, as Chancellor.

Moves to Revive the EC

By the start of the 1980s there was an acceptance within both national governments and the Commission that the response to challenges facing the EC required, in part at least, institutional reform to facilitate easier and more effective decision making.

The first response came in September 1981 from the foreign ministers of Germany and Italy, and was known as the Genscher–Colombo Plan. This plan called for a new European charter that would supersede the Treaties of Paris and Rome as the basic constitutional document of the Communities, and would bring European political co-operation, together with the EC, under the joint direction of the European Council. This would only be a formalization of the existing situation, although Genscher and Colombo also wished to improve the decision-making ability of the Council of Ministers by increasing the use of majority voting, to expand the functions of the EP, and to intensify foreign policy co-operation in security matters.

The Plan received a cool response in the Council, as had an earlier proposal led by Altiero Spinelli—now a senior figure in the EP—that sought to diminish the institutional position of the Council in favour of the Parliament and Commission. Yet, while these two sets of proposals made no immediate impact on integration, they contributed to the European Council beginning a new round of negotiations on the question of political union and possible revision of the treaties.

On the economic front, attempts by Thorn and his Vice-President and Commissioner for the Internal Market, Karl-Heinz Narjes, to highlight the problems faced by industrialists in trading across national borders within the EC met with little response from national governments. Governments were determined to reserve jobs for their own nationals (read 'voters') by tolerating, or even themselves erecting, non-tariff barriers to trade, and by giving public contracts exclusively to national companies. Yet, Thorn, Narjes, and, particularly, Vice-President Etienne Davignon, the Commissioner for Industrial Policy, laid the groundwork for the agreement that was concluded under the following Delors presidency to free the internal market of all these obstacles by the end of 1992.

Thorn and Narjes maintained a constant propaganda campaign against barriers to a genuine internal market. This campaign had an effect in raising awareness of the issue, especially when it was taken up by a group of members of the EP (MEPs) who called themselves the Kangaroo Group because they wanted to facilitate trade that would 'hop over' national boundaries. The work of Davignon was less public, but possibly more influential in persuading governments to accept change. He called into existence a network of leading industrialists involved in the European electrical and electronics industries to discuss their common problems in the face of US and Japanese competition. Out of these discussions came the Esprit programme of collaborative research in advanced technologies; but, more significantly, there also arose the European Round Table of Industrialists, which was to become an influential pressure group pushing governments into taking measures to liberalize the internal market of the EC.

Fontainebleau

The European Council meeting at Fontainebleau in June 1984 marked a turning point in European integration. First of all, the summit resolved the British budgetary question, in the context of an agreement to cut back on agricultural expenditure and to increase the Community's own resources through an increase in VAT contributions by member states. The agreement settled five years of dispute and opened the door for reform of the CAP.

The meeting also agreed to set up an ad hoc committee on institutional affairs, which came to be known by the name of its Chair, James Dooge of Ireland. The report of this committee became the basis for the institutional changes that were later to be made, alongside the fundamental policy commitment to completion of the internal market.

When a new Commission assumed office in 1985, under the presidency of Jacques Delors (see Insight 8.1), it offered a visible symbol of a new start under dynamic leadership. Delors proposed that the EC should set itself the target of removing a whole series of barriers to free trade and free movement of capital and labour that had grown up during the 1970s. This project would be pursued with a target date for completion of the end of 1992, and became known as the '1992 programme'. The economic project was linked to a programme of institutional reform that would have far-reaching implications for the way in which the EC made decisions, although those implications were not all immediately apparent.

The most important institutional reform was the introduction of **qualified majority voting (QMV)** into the proceedings of the Council of Ministers, thus overcoming the blockage to progress imposed by the system that allowed individual governments to veto proposals. It was also intended to revive the momentum of integration, because Delors believed that the freeing of the internal market would lead to spillover into other policy

---

Insight 8.1 Jacques Delors

Jacques Delors was born in Paris in 1925. His father was a middle-ranking employee of the Bank of France, and Jacques went to work for the Bank straight from school. The young Delors was active in Catholic social movements, and became a devotee of the doctrine of 'personalism', a form of Christian socialism associated with the philosopher Emmanuel Mounier. Delors was also an active trade unionist. In the 1960s he moved from the Bank to a senior position in the French Planning Commission, which had been created by Jean Monnet. Although he was an adviser to the Gaullist Prime Minister Jacques Chaban-Delmas at the end of the 1960s and in the early 1970s, he subsequently joined the reformed Socialist party of François Mitterrand, and was elected to the EP in 1979 as a Socialist. When Mitterrand became President of France in 1981, Delors became Finance Minister in the Socialist government. He was instrumental in moving the government away from policies of economic expansion that were not working and were undermining the value of the currency. He played a crucial role in the negotiation of the 1983 realignment of currencies within the exchange rate mechanism of the EMS, and won the respect of the German government in the process. In 1985, with strong support from Chancellor Kohl of Germany, as well as from Mitterrand, he became President of the European Commission, a post that he retained for ten years.

sectors. In particular, he believed that it would not be feasible to have the single market without strengthening the degree of social protection available to workers at the EC level; and that the single market would set up a momentum towards monetary union.

Despite British reluctance to see these related aspects, the Thatcher government wanted to see the single market programme itself put into place. Subsequently, the British Prime Minister tried to block the institutional aspects, but in the meantime the success of Delors's initiative revived the self-confidence of the Commission, which had already begun to recover under Jenkins and Thorn. It also led to a revival of theoretical interpretations of the EC that emphasized the role of the Commission and other supranational actors, thus rekindling the supranational vs intergovernmental debate about the nature of the EC, which had lain dormant during the 'doldrums years' of the 1970s and early 1980s (see Chapter 20, Explaining the Single Market).

1985: A Watershed Year

Delors had been Finance Minister in the 1981–3 French Socialist governments, which had tried to tackle the problem of unemployment in France by reflating the economy. The result had been a serious balance of payments crisis as the reflation did little to restore full employment, but did suck in imports. There had been two views on how to respond to this. One had been to withdraw from the EMS, and to impose import controls, in contravention of France's EC obligations. The other, of which Delors had been the strongest advocate, had been to revert to national policies of balancing the budget by cutting public expenditure, and to develop a European solution to the problem of unemployment. That view had prevailed, and Delors's advocacy of it made him acceptable to both Germany and Britain as a nominee for the Commission presidency. It had been tacitly accepted that the presidency of the Commission would be given to a German candidate if the Federal Government wished to take it up; but Kohl chose to throw his weight behind Delors.

The Brussels European Council of February 1985 instructed the Commission to draw up a timetable for the completion of the single market. Within a few months of taking office, the British Commissioner for Trade and Industry, Lord Cockfield, produced a White Paper listing the barriers that needed to be removed for there to be a genuine single market inside the EC. This listed some 300 separate measures, later reduced to 279, covering the harmonization of technical standards, opening up public procurement to intra-EC competition, freeing capital movements, removing barriers to free trade in services, harmonizing rates of indirect taxation and excise duties, and removing physical frontier controls between member states. The list was accompanied by a timetable for completion, with a final target date of the end of 1992.

At the Milan European Council, in June 1985, heads of government agreed the objectives of the White Paper and the timetable for its completion by the end of 1992. A massive publicity campaign would be organized to promote the project. It was also agreed, against the protests of the British Prime Minister, to set up an intergovernmental conference (IGC) to consider what changes were necessary to the original treaties in order to achieve the single market, and to consider other changes to the institutional structure that had been recommended by the ad hoc committee under

James Dooge that had been set up at the Fontainebleau European Council a year earlier. This IGC drew up what became the SEA, which was agreed by the heads of government at the Luxembourg European Council in December 1985, and eventually ratified by national parliaments to come into effect in July 1987. Thus was born the '1992 programme', which did more than any initiative since the Treaties of Rome to revitalize the process of European integration.

The Single European Act

Although modest in the changes that it introduced in comparison with the hopes of federalists in the EP and within some member states (particularly Italy), the SEA rejuvenated the process of European integration. The intention of the SEA appeared relatively modest, seeking to complete the objective of a common market set out in the Treaty of Rome. By the early 1980s, the need for member states to compete in world markets, especially against the United States and Japan, was an overriding concern. A single European market would increase the specialization of production at company level and allow greater economies of scale, leading to more competitive firms. The issue of monetary union as an accompaniment to the single market was not addressed at this stage of developments.

While ostensibly an economic project, the SEA had implications for a range of policy areas such as social protection and the environment (see Chapter 18 and Chapter 23). More broadly, in its proposals for institutional change, the SEA:

> had potential for revolution, suggesting a shift in the existing balance of power away from the member states towards the Community institutions. The radical political implications of the economic target of a common market—the single internal market—were there for all to read in the document .... while the issues of political and economic integration are closely interlinked, the parallel debates tended to muddy the waters of each.

(Urwin 1995: 231)

In retrospect at least, the political implications of the SEA are clear (see Insight 8.2). At the time, though, the SEA was largely seen as a mechanism for implementing the

---

Insight 8.2 The Political Provisions of the SEA

- It introduced QMV for single market measures.
- It increased the legislative powers of the EP in areas where QMV applied.
- It incorporated European political co-operation (EPC) into a treaty text for the first time.
- It incorporated in the Preamble a reiteration of the objective of an economic and monetary union.
- It incorporated in the Preamble a commitment by the member states to 'transform relations as a whole among their States into a European Union'.

commitment made at Milan to achieve the single market. This goal was not contested by member states. Moreover, the Commission was concerned with emphasizing the practical rather than the political implications of aspects of the reform. Only in the final section of the White Paper did the Commission refer to the wider implications of the internal market project, acknowledging that 'Just as the Customs Union had to precede Economic Integration, so Economic Integration has to precede European Unity' (European Commission 1985: 55). Despite the political implications of the single market being deliberately understated by the Commission, the proposed institutional reforms proved the most controversial aspect of the project.

Institutional Reforms

While the SEA was ostensibly a project to complete the single market, the institutional reforms that it introduced were to be of lasting significance for European integration, in particular the introduction of QMV in the Council of Ministers. QMV was designed to speed-up decision making by reducing substantially the number of areas in which individual states could reject progress by use of their veto. QMV would apply to measures related to the freeing of the internal market, although certain measures, including the harmonization of indirect taxes and the removal of physical controls at borders, were excluded at British insistence. Without the extension of QMV, the internal market project was likely to be delayed and possibly lost through intergovernmental disputes.

The codification of the commitment to QMV as a formal amendment of the founding treaties, and as part of a potentially wider reform of the institutional procedures for making decisions, was resisted strongly by Prime Minister Thatcher. The whole issue of institutional reform was one of several where the British government differed from most of its continental European partners. Mrs Thatcher insisted at Milan that no institutional reform, and so no IGC, was necessary. However, it seems that she was persuaded by her Foreign Secretary, Sir Geoffrey Howe, and her adviser on European affairs, David Williamson, that, unless a legally binding commitment were made to an element of majority voting in the Council of Ministers, the measures necessary to implement the Cockfield White Paper would never be agreed.

The Internal Market

The freeing of the internal market was supported by all the member states, and it coincided with the belief of the British Prime Minister in universal free trade. On the other hand, it was also an excellent issue for the new Commission to make into the centrepiece of its programme. As Helen Wallace (1986: 590) explained:

> The internal market is important not only for its own sake, but because it is the first core Community issue for over a decade .... which has caught the imagination of British policy-makers and which is echoed by their counterparts elsewhere .... The pursuit of a thoroughly liberalized domestic European market has several great advantages: it fits Community philosophy, it suits the doctrinal preferences of the current British Conservative government, and it would draw in its train a mass of interconnections with other fields of action.

Whereas doctrinal preferences may be sufficient explanation for British support of the internal market project, the support of other member states needs further explanation.

One important factor was the support given to the freeing of the market by European business leaders, some of whom formed the European Round Table of Industrialists in 1983 to press for the removal of the barriers to trade that had developed. This pressure occurred in the context of a generalized concern among governments about the sluggish recovery of the European economies from the post-1979 recession in comparison with the vigorous growth of the US and Japanese economies. In particular, the turning of the tide of foreign direct investment, so that by the mid-1980s there was a net flow of investment funds from western Europe to the United States, augured badly both for the employment situation in Europe in the future, and for the ability of European industry to keep abreast of the technological developments that were revolutionizing production processes.

It was in response to the worry that Europe would become permanently technologically dependent on the United States and Japan that President Mitterrand proposed his Eureka initiative for promoting pan-European research and development in the advanced technology industries. This concern also lay behind the promotion by the new Commission of 'framework programmes' for research and development in such fields as information technology, bio-technology, and telecommunications (Sharp and Shearman 1987). But when European industrialists were asked what would encourage them to invest in Europe they replied that the most important factor for them would be the creation of a genuine continental market such as they experienced in the United States.

It was therefore in an attempt to revive investment and economic growth that governments other than Britain embraced the free-market programme. The pressure to break out of the short-termism that had prevented the EC from making progress in the 1970s and early 1980s came partly from interest groups, but also from the economic situation that faced governments. The EC, as only one part of the global capitalist economy, was seeing investment flow away from it to other parts of the global economy, and was already being left behind in rates of economic growth and in technological advance by rival core-areas within the system. It was a calculation of the common national interests of the member states that led them to agree a new contract, in the form of a White Paper and the SEA.

Beyond these economic interests, other member states were happy to see the SEA's introduction of institutional reforms, and the strengthening of other treaty provisions, notably on social policy, the environment, the structural funds, research and technology policy, and economic and social cohesion. The SEA therefore created a much wider package deal beyond the immediate confines of the single market programme.

The Role of the Delors Commission

The emphasis that Delors put on the single market was part of a carefully considered strategy. During the autumn of 1984 he considered a variety of candidates for the role of the 'Big Idea' that would relaunch European integration (Grant 1994: 66). Initially attracted to completion of EMU, following the relative success of the EMS, Delors ultimately decided that the idea of completing the internal market was the best starting point. This project was firmly within the boundaries of integration established by the Treaty of Rome. Even more important, perhaps, with policies of market liberalization adopted by key member states, the single market project stood the best chance of winning the support of even the most Eurosceptic governments, Britain's in particular. Moreover, successful completion of the 1992 project had implications for a wide range of Community policies. Most notably, the project would inevitably prompt reconsideration of the advantages of monetary union as a complement to the single market and would also lead to demands for strengthening EC social and regional policies from the member states most likely to be adversely affected by the internal market.

Few dispute that the Delors Commission played a pivotal role in developing and pushing forward the single market programme as a means to the end of ever closer union. The emergence of the programme and eventually the drive towards full monetary union and the adoption of a social charter, all bore the hallmarks of a plan devised in Paris in the light of the failures of the 1981–4 French economic experiment. Delors and the British Commissioner Cockfield worked together closely on developing and promoting the project. Cockfield faced accusations from the British Prime Minister that he had 'gone native' in his support for wide-ranging European integration, and it was no great surprise when Thatcher chose not to renominate him to the Commission in 1988.

Under Delors the Commission regained the high profile it had under Hallstein, and, irrespective of whether the Hallstein Commission had been the genuine motor of integration, the Delors Commission certainly appeared to play that role by the 1980s. But it was only able to play that role because of the support Delors received from Mitterrand, and because of the diplomatic skill of Mitterrand himself in ensuring that other member states, Germany above all, were carried along with the plan.

Implementing the SEA

While national governments were initially slow to implement the measures detailed in the SEA, businesses began to take advantage of the emerging opportunities offered by the 1992 project. Company mergers accelerated to take advantage of EC-wide economies of scale. The business publication *The Economist* (1988) noted that in 1987 there were 300 major mergers compared with only sixty-eight in the previous year. In comparison, by November 1987 the Council of Ministers had adopted only sixty-four of the measures set out in the White Paper (Dinan 1994: 150).

The core problem of implementation related to accompanying measures to the SEA; in particular, the demands of southern member states for adequate compensatory mechanisms to balance the adverse effects of market liberalization. While a number of member states were reluctant to commit greater resources to Community regional aid, ultimately these demands had to be satisfied to protect the 1992 programme. Subsequently, at the Brussels European Council of February 1988, the heads of government agreed to a doubling in the allocations to the structural funds to promote greater cohesion as a complement to the internal market.

Overall, though, the 1992 project was a tremendous success for the EC. It led to a revival of investment in Europe, which had been stagnating. The EC experienced a

> **Insight 8.3 Objectives of the Social Protocol Annexed to the Treaty on European Union**
>
> • promotion of employment;
>
> • improvement of living and working conditions;
>
> • adequate social protection;
>
> • social dialogue;
>
> • the development of human resources to ensure a high and sustainable level of employment;
>
> • the integration of persons excluded from the labour market.

wave of business euphoria, which ensured that the work of public officials in actually agreeing the necessary measures did not waver. By the target date of the end of 1992, 260 out of the consolidated list of 279 measures that had been identified in the White Paper had been agreed in the Council of Ministers, a staggering 95 per cent success rate (Pelkmans 1994: 103).

However, the freeing of the market was not the end of the project so far as Delors was concerned. He saw it as a first step that implied further extensions of integration. In particular he argued for a social dimension to the project, and for its completion by agreement on monetary union. On both of these issues he had the support of a majority of the governments of the other member states, but was implacably opposed by the British Prime Minister, Margaret Thatcher.

The British government rejected the proposed social charter, which Mrs Thatcher described as 'Marxist' (Urwin 1995: 231). The proposal for worker representatives on company boards was a particular problem for the Thatcher government. Despite subsequent revisions to the proposed social charter, the UK government refused to sign, leaving the remaining eleven governments to sign a protocol on social policy outside of the next treaty (see Insight 8.3).

CONCLUSION

The story told in this chapter is of a gradual recovery of momentum for the EC from the middle of the 1970s through to the success of the SEA and the single market programme. In seeking explanations for these developments, two of the themes of this book are evident: responses to the changing international environment and the revival of some of the neofunctionalist dynamics.

Developments early in the period were primarily responses to problems posed for the west European states by the decline of US hegemony in the context of the continuing Cold War. The EMS, which has been interpreted with hindsight as the start of a process that led to monetary union, was seen at the time more as a response to the chaos in the international monetary system caused by the refusal of the United States to allow the dollar to continue to be used as the corner-stone of the international monetary system. The southern enlargement was primarily a response to the need to stabilize the southern European states as they emerged from right-wing dictatorship so that they did not become subject to communist influence.

Similarly there is general agreement that global economic developments were the catalyst for the acceptance of the single market. The remarkable economic recovery of the United States and Japan from the second oil crisis contrasted starkly with the sluggishness of the west European economies. Not only was there a marked difference in performance; the success of the United States and Japan was based on the adoption of new technologies into their production processes that threatened to leave western Europe with an obsolete industrial base unless investment could be revived.

At the same time, some of the analyses of neofunctionalists seemed to be vindicated by the single market programme. Interpretations of the relevant importance of different factors certainly vary, but there is a considerable body of analysis that attributes a central role to the European Commission under Jacques Delors, and to the European Round Table of Industrialists. Two of the actors whom neofunctionalists had predicted would be influential appeared to be influential in this landmark decision: the Commission and transnational business interests.

Elements of the neofunctionalist analysis also received support from another development: the speed with which businesses responded to the announcement of the 1992 programme to conclude mergers and announce new investment plans vindicated the argument that changed circumstances would lead to changed attitudes and behaviour.

KEY POINTS

Leadership Changes: 1974

- Valéry Giscard d'Estaing became French President and Helmut Schmidt became German Chancellor. They had a good relationship and were able to work well together.

The European Council

- In 1974, Giscard d'Estaing called for the institutionalization of summit meetings of EC heads of state and government. He received support for this from Helmut Schmidt.
- It was agreed that these meetings be institutionalized under the auspices of the European Council and would be held three times each year.
- The creation of the European Council symbolized a profoundly intergovernmental period in the history of European integration.

Other Institutional Developments

- As Commission President, Roy Jenkins managed to secure a place at international economic summits for the Commission for the first time.
- Direct elections to the EP were agreed and the first elections were held in 1979.

The European Monetary System

- Following a call from Jenkins to renew attempts at monetary union, the European Council passed a proposal by Schmidt and Giscard d'Estaing for a EMS in 1978.
- The new EMS would be more flexible than its predecessor, but Britain declined to put sterling in the exchange rate mechanism and play a full role.

The Southern Enlargements

- Following a difficult period of negotiations, the accession of Greece to the Community was agreed in 1979. Portugal and Spain, who applied later, were eventually accepted into the EC in 1985.

The British Budget Rebate

- Britain was set to be the largest net contributor to the Community budget by 1980. The tactics of the Thatcher government over the issue jeopardized progress in other areas until a satisfactory solution was found in 1984.

Leadership Changes:1981–2

- The appointment of Gaston Thorn to the Commission presidency in 1981 coincided with important leadership changes in France and Germany.

Moves to Revive the EC

- The Genscher–Colombo Plan proposed institutional reforms that received a cool reaction from the Council. However, Commission plans for freeing the internal market began to win over national governments.

Fontainebleau

- The resolution of the British budgetary question at Fontainebleau allowed for progress on both the internal market and institutional reform.

1985: A Watershed Year

- In June 1985, the Council agreed the 1992 timetable for completion of the single market.
- An IGC on institutional reform drew up what became the SEA.

The Single European Act

- For Delors the single market programme was the 'Big Idea' that would relaunch European integration. On the whole, governments were persuaded of the need for the SEA by the desire to compete with Japan and the US.
- Companies were quick to take advantage of the opportunities provided by the single market project, but implementation of SEA measures varied across member states.
- The SEA introduced QMV into the Council of Ministers for measures related to the freeing of the internal market, with some exceptions where there were important national sensitivities.
- The freeing of the internal market was an issue with a lot of spillover potential.
- It received strong support from the European Round Table of Industrialists.
- The Commission played a pivotal role in developing and promoting the single market programme.
- It was only possible for the Commission to play its part successfully because of the backing given to Delors by French President Mitterrand.
- Implementation of the single market agreement was delayed by demands from the southern member states for compensatory mechanisms.
- Businesses were quick to prepare for the single market, and became a strong pressure for progress from governments.
- Delors saw it as only the first step, with a social dimension and monetary union to follow. In this he was opposed by Margaret Thatcher.

FURTHER READING

On the 1970s, **K. Middlemass**, *Orchestrating Europe: The Informal Politics of European Union, 1973–1995* (London: Fontana, 1995), 73–110 calls the years between 1973 and 1983 'The Stagnant Decade'. **A. Moravcsik**, *The Choice for Europe: Social Purpose and State Power from Messina to Maastricht* (London: UCL Press, 1998), 238–313 focuses on monetary co-operation and the European Monetary System. For an insider account of part of this period see **R. Jenkins**, *European Diary, 1977–1981* (London: Collins, 1989). The British budget rebate issue is explained more fully in **S. George**, *An Awkward Partner: Britain in the European Community*, 3rd edn (Oxford: Oxford University Press, 1998), 137–65. For general accounts, see **D. W. Urwin**, *The Community of Europe: A History of European Integration since 1945* (London and New York: Longman, 2nd edn, 1995) and **M. Dedman**, *The Origins and Development of the European Union 1945–2008: A History of European Integration* (Abingdon: Routledge, 2nd edn, 2009).

C. Grant, *Delors: Inside the House that Jacques Built* (London: Nicolas Brealey Publishing, 1994) and **G. Ross**, *Jacques Delors and European Integration* (Cambridge: Polity Press, 1995) both give accounts of what went on within the Delors Commission. For the analysis of the Single European Act, begin with **D. R. Cameron**, 'The 1992 Initiative: Causes and Consequences', in A. Sbragia (ed.), *Euro-Politics: Institutions and Policymaking in the 'New' European Community* (Washington, DC: Brookings Institution, 1992), 23–74; continue with **W. Sandholtz and J. Zysman**, '1992: Recasting the European Bargain', *World Politics*, vol. 45, 95–128; and then read **A. Moravcsik**, *The Choice for Europe: Social Purpose and State Power from Messina to Maastricht* (London: UCL Press, 1998), 314–78 or his chapter 'Negotiating the Single European Act', in **R. O. Keohane and S. Hoffmann (eds)**, *The New European Community: Decision- Making and Institutional Change* (Boulder, San Francisco, and Oxford: Westview Press, 1991), 41–84. For an institutionalist account, read **K. Armstrong and S. Bulmer**, *The Governance of the Single European Market* (Manchester: Manchester University Press, 1998), Chapter 1.

 online resource centre **Visit the Online Resource Centre that accompanies this book for links to more information on European institutions during the 1970s and 1980s: http://oxfordtextbooks.co.uk/orc/bache4e/**

Chapter 9

Maastricht and Amsterdam (the Late 1980s to the Late 1990s)

Chapter Overview

Once the single market programme was underway, Jacques Delors set about trying to exploit its spillover potential to push forward towards monetary union. At the same time, the collapse of communism in central and eastern Europe opened up the prospect of the reunification of Germany, and fears that the larger German state would either dominate the European Community (EC) or turn away from its western European commitments to forge a new central European identity in partnership with the central European states that had formed Germany's traditional economic hinterland in the early twentieth century. To address both issues, the governments of the member states signed another treaty in Maastricht at the end of 1991. The reaction to the treaty within member states was worryingly negative; yet, despite that, further treaty reform was deemed necessary if the former communist states were to be offered a prospect of membership of the EC.

Whereas the start of the Cold War had caused a ferment in western Europe out of which emerged the European communities, its end threw things into as much turmoil. The controlled process that Delors had envisaged, pushing forward from the single market to monetary union and beyond was overtaken by the need to consolidate democracy in the successor states to the failed Soviet bloc, and that meant the EC having to accommodate a whole new group of prospective members. The fall-out from this shock gave the initiative back to intergovernmentalism. It also produced a backlash against the pace of change from within the existing member states.

Towards Maastricht

Monetary policy had been largely absent from the Single European Act (SEA), but the logic of the internal market suggested at least some harmonization of taxation policies. Following the SEA there had been growing support for a single currency controlled by a European central bank, but the British government rejected this concept. Despite British opposition, the heads of government agreed in Hanover in June 1988 to set up a committee of central bankers and technical experts, under the chairmanship of Delors, to prepare a report on the steps that needed to be taken to strengthen monetary co-operation. The subsequent 'Delors Report' proposed a three-stage progress to monetary union leading to a single currency by 1999. The report was presented to the June 1989 meeting of the European Council in Madrid, which on a majority vote of eleven to one—Thatcher voting against—agreed to convene an intergovernmental conference (IGC) to prepare proposals for changes to the treaties to allow movement to a monetary union.

The dramatic collapse of communism in the Soviet Union and other central and eastern European countries in the course of 1989 and 1990 added to the complexity of the situation. This forced a serious reconsideration of the political aspects of the EC. The immediate impact was the destabilization of the geographical area immediately to the east of the EC and, more positively for the EC, the opening up of potential new markets and new sites for investment for west European capital. In addition, the collapse of communism raised the prospect of German reunification.

This 'acceleration of history', as Delors called it, had an impact on the EC and on Delors's plans for its development. In particular, the prospect of a reunified Germany caused alarm in the neighbouring states, particularly over a possible resurgence of German nationalism. A more immediate concern was that the new Germany would turn its attention more to the east and become less concerned with its obligations to western Europe.

Chancellor Kohl of Germany shared these concerns. Kohl had not hitherto been noted for providing strong or dynamic leadership, but he seized the opportunity to go down in the history books as the person who reunified his country. At the same time, however, he did not want to be remembered as the Frankenstein who created a new monster in the centre of Europe. Such concerns led directly to the convening of a second IGC on political union to run alongside the one that had already been called on monetary union. Although Delors supported the move, it was not part of his plan. The IGC on political union, together with that on monetary union, meant that the Maastricht Treaty became a very high profile issue: 'a treaty too far' as Lady Thatcher later described it.

The two IGCs met throughout 1991, and their proposals were incorporated into the Treaty on European Union (TEU), which was agreed in Maastricht in December of that year, and which created the European Union (EU). Britain, under the new premiership of John Major, agreed to the TEU only when a chapter on social policy had been removed from the main text, and only when it was agreed that Britain could opt out of the final stage of monetary union if its Parliament so decided.

The Treaty on European Union

Intergovernmental negotiations leading up to the Maastricht Summit of December 1991 were tough and much of what was agreed reflected the lowest-common-denominator bargaining position of governments. The TEU was signed in February 1992 and entered into force in November 1993. It marked a further big step on the road to European integration, with important implications for both internal and external activities (see Insight 9.1). (The TEU was revised subsequently, but the Insights in this chapter utilize the original 'Maastricht' text.)

The name of the 'European Economic Community' was officially changed to the 'European Community' and there were important new areas of co-operation in the fields of Common Foreign and Security Policy (CFSP) (see Insight 9.2) and Justice and Home Affairs (JHA) (see Insight 9.3). The EC, CFSP, and JHA became part of a

Insight 9.1 Extract from Treaty on European Union: Common Provisions, Article B

The Union shall set itself the following objectives:

- to promote economic and social progress which is balanced and sustainable, in particular through the creation of an area without internal frontiers, through the strengthening of economic and social cohesion and through the establishment of economic and monetary union, ultimately including a single currency in accordance with the provisions of this Treaty;

- to assert its identity on the international scene, in particular through the implementation of a common foreign and security policy including the eventual framing of a common defence policy, which might in time lead to a common defence;

- to strengthen the protection of the rights and interests of the nationals of its Member States through the introduction of a citizenship of the Union;

- to develop close co-operation on justice and home affairs;

- to maintain in full the acquis communautaire and build on it with a view to considering, through the procedure referred to in Article N(2), to what extent the policies and forms of co-operation introduced by this Treaty may need to be revised with the aim of ensuring the effectiveness of the mechanisms and the institutions of the Community.

The objectives of the Union shall be achieved as provided in this Treaty and in accordance with the conditions and the timetable set out therein while respecting the principle of subsidiarity as defined in Article 3b of the Treaty establishing the European Community.

Insight 9.2 Extract from Treaty on European Union: Provisions on a Common Foreign and Security Policy, Article J.1

(1) The Union and its Member States shall define and implement a common foreign and security policy, governed by the provisions of this Title and covering all areas of foreign and security policy.

(2) The objectives of the common foreign and security policy shall be:

- to safeguard the common values, fundamental interests and independence of the Union;

- to strengthen the security of the Union and its Member States in all ways;

- to preserve peace and strengthen international security, in accordance with the principles of the United Nations Charter as well as the principles of the Helsinki Final Act and the objectives of the Paris Charter;

- to promote international co-operation;

- to develop and consolidate democracy and the rule of law, and respect for human rights and fundamental freedoms.

(3) The Union shall pursue these objectives:

- by establishing systematic co-operation between Member States in the conduct of policy, in accordance with Article J.2;

- by gradually implementing, in accordance with Article J.3, joint action in the areas in which the Member States have important interests in common.

(4) The Member States shall support the Union's external and security policy actively and unreservedly in a spirit of loyalty and mutual solidarity. They shall refrain from any action which is contrary to the interests of the Union or likely to impair its effectiveness as a cohesive force in international relations. The Council shall ensure that these principles are complied with.

Insight 9.3 Extract from Treaty on European Union: Provisions on Co-operation in the Fields of Justice and Home Affairs, Article K.1

For the purposes of achieving the objectives of the Union, in particular the free movement of persons, and without prejudice to the powers of the European Community, Member States shall regard the following areas as matters of common interest:

- asylum policy;
- rules governing the crossing by persons of the external borders of the Member States and the exercise of controls thereon;
- immigration policy and policy regarding nationals of third countries:

— conditions of entry and movement by nationals of third countries on the territory of Member States;

— conditions of residence by nationals of third countries on the territory of Member States, including family reunion and access to employment;

— combating unauthorized immigration, residence and work by nationals of third countries on the territory of Member States;

— combating drug addiction in so far as this is not covered by (7) to (9);

— combating fraud on an international scale in so far as this is not covered by (7) to (9);

— judicial co-operation in civil matters;

— judicial co-operation in criminal matters;

— customs co-operation;

— police co-operation for the purposes of preventing and combating terrorism, unlawful drug-trafficking and other serious forms of international crime, including if necessary certain aspects of customs co-operation, in connection with the organization of a Union-wide system for exchanging information within a European Police Office (Europol).

three-pillar structure known as the European Union (see Chapter 12, Figure 12.1). While the first pillar remained an area of pooled sovereignty in which the community method of decision making would continue to predominate, the second and third pillars were explicitly areas of intergovernmental co-operation depending largely on unanimous decisions taken by the member governments.

Monetary union was the biggest single policy initiative in the TEU (see Chapter 21, Origins of EMU), but, in addition, the Treaty contained a number of other important provisions. In institutional terms, it strengthened the power of the European Parliament (EP) through the extension of the co-decision procedure, which gave Parliament greater legislative power in a range of policy areas (see Chapter 12, Decision-Making Procedures); and it created a Committee of the Regions and Local Authorities, in recognition of the growing role of sub-national government in EC affairs, and in line with the principle of subsidiarity (see Chapter 12, The Decision-Making Institutions (the Union Method)). The principle of subsidiarity was itself established as a general rule of the Community by the Treaty, having only applied to the field of environmental policy in the SEA (see Insight 16.2 for the current Treaty text).

The Treaty also introduced the concept of European citizenship, and gave the European citizen the following rights: to circulate and reside freely in the Community; to vote and stand as a candidate for European and municipal elections in the state in which he or she resides; to receive protection while in a non-EU country from diplomatic or consular authorities of a member state other than that of his or her state of origin; and to petition the EP or submit a complaint to the Ombudsman (European Union 2005).

In sum, these measures provided a strong political dimension to the economic imperatives that had dominated the integration process to date. More generally, EC competence was established or extended in a number of areas including education and training, environment, health, and industry. Built on compromise, the TEU included something positive for the EC institutions and for each of the member states involved.

After Maastricht

Although agreed by the heads of governments, the decision to move to a single currency raised concerns within member states. Notably, this decision caused a collapse of support for the EU in Germany itself, where the Deutschmark was held in high regard as the factor that had facilitated post-war prosperity. Problems were made worse when the internal German currency union took effect, following the decision to convert East German Ostmarks at an artificially high rate into Deutschmarks. This led to inflationary tendencies in the unified Germany, which were suppressed by the Bundesbank (the German central bank) raising interest rates. This in turn solidified resistance within Germany to European monetary union, and therefore to Maastricht. It also pushed the buoyant European economies into recession, which made it more difficult to sell Maastricht to European citizens, who were already rather alarmed by the pace of change that was being proposed.

It was against this background that the Danish referendum in June 1992 rejected the Treaty by 50.7 per cent to 49.3 per cent. In Denmark, farmers and fishermen had usually been strong supporters of the EC. Danish opposition to membership had been concentrated in Copenhagen and the other urban areas. In 1992, concern about the reforms of the Common Agricultural Policy (CAP) (see Chapter 19, Agriculture in the 1980s and 1990s) and the Common Fisheries Policy reduced the 'yes' vote in rural areas, and may have been sufficient to make the difference between a narrow 'yes' and a narrow 'no'. It was only when concessions were made on monetary union—giving Denmark similar opt-out rights to those of Britain—and on some other issues of concern, that it was narrowly accepted in a second referendum in May 1993.

Perhaps even more significantly, the Treaty was only accepted by the French public by the narrowest of margins (50.3 to 49.7 per cent) in September 1992. Guyomarch et al. (1998: 97–8) identified six factors that shaped this outcome: high unemployment and the argument of the No campaign that, under the TEU, the government would no longer be able to take effective action to create jobs; concern that further integration would lead to a weakening of the level of social security; hostility to the MacSharry reforms of the CAP (see Chapter 19, Agriculture in the 1980s and 1990s); concern at the effects on previously protected sectors of the economy of the opening of the domestic market; concern at what was seen as interference by Brussels with aspects of the traditional French way of life, including the right to produce and eat unpasteurized cheese, and to shoot migrating birds; and splits in all the main parties on their attitude to the TEU, which deprived the electorate of clear leadership. The same authors pointed to the fact that the controversy generated by the referendum led to an increase in interest in the EU. This meant that in the 1994 elections to the EP the turnout in France increased against the EU-wide trend, from 50.4 per cent in 1989 to 55 per cent (Guyomarch et al. 1998: 101).

In Germany there was no referendum, but the strength of public concern about monetary union was such that the Bundestag secured the right to vote on the issue again before any automatic abandonment of the Deutschmark in favour of a common European currency. There was clear evidence of serious public discontent with the Treaty in other member states, not least in Britain.

The Commission after Maastricht

The Commission became caught in this wave of popular discontent about the pace of integration. Delors was personally associated with the proposals on monetary union, which were what caused the greatest concern in Britain and Germany. He had also adopted a very high profile in the run-up to the ratification debacles. In particular, his ill-timed statement shortly before the Danish referendum, to the effect that small states might have to surrender their right to hold the presidency of the Council of Ministers in a future enlarged EC, was seen as a contributory factor in the negative vote in Denmark.

Delors's comments about small states were actually made in the context of an entirely different debate about enlargement of the EC. The success of the 1992 programme had led to concern among the members of the European Free Trade Association (EFTA) that they were not sharing in the investment boom that 1992 precipitated. Led by Sweden, these states began to broach the question of membership of the EC. Delors was against this because he believed that further enlargement would dilute the degree of unity that could be achieved, and he proposed instead a way in which the EFTA states could become part of the single market without becoming full members of the EC. Membership of the European Economic Area (EEA) would involve the EFTA states adopting all the relevant commercial legislation of the EC, without having any say in its formulation. It was never likely to be a satisfactory agreement for the governments of those states, who would thereby be surrendering sovereignty over large areas of their economies; more significantly, it did not convince the businesses that were already diverting their investments from EFTA to inside the EC. In addition, these states had also pursued foreign policies of neutrality, but the end of the Cold War meant their policies were no longer incompatible with full membership. Consequently, a group of EFTA states decided to press ahead with membership applications, but Switzerland withdrew its application after the Swiss people rejected the EEA in a referendum in December 1992; and the Norwegians again rejected membership in a referendum in November 1994.

Sweden, Finland, and Austria became members of the EU on 1 January 1995 (see Chapter 27, History). The EU that they joined was not the self-confident one that they had applied to join. As well as disagreement about the future direction, and signs of public disaffection with the whole exercise, the European Monetary System (EMS) had effectively collapsed during the ratification problems. Britain had withdrawn and floated sterling, and other states had only been able to remain inside because the bands of permitted fluctuation had been widened from 2.25 per cent either side of parity to 15 per cent.

Delors had started his long period as President of the Commission with a considerable triumph in the single market programme. He ended it with that achievement somewhat overshadowed by the hostile reaction of public opinion in much of the EU to the Maastricht Treaty. Yet, whether it was reasonable to blame the Commission for this debacle is very doubtful. Delors had been upset at the extent to which the Commission had been ignored during the IGCs that prepared the TEU, and had opposed several of the provisions of the Treaty. However, he had adopted such a high profile during his period as president that it was easy for the governments of the member states to pass the blame onto him personally and the institution of which he had been president for ten years.

Political Change

Significant domestic political developments in the mid- to late-1990s affected the position of key member states on the EU. In Germany the government of Chancellor Kohl continued uninterrupted, but the authority of the Chancellor was called into question by a number of difficulties on policy and a number of electoral setbacks. In Britain, the Conservative government of John Major experienced a series of defeats in parliamentary by-elections, which reduced its majority. This, combined with the increasingly militant anti-EU position of a significant number of its own MPs, left the government with little room for manoeuvre, and its discourse on the EU became increasingly negative. Just prior to the Amsterdam European Council in June 1997, at which the Treaty of Amsterdam was agreed, the Conservative government lost office in a general election and was replaced by a Labour government under Tony Blair.

In France there were two changes of government. In May 1995 the Gaullist Jacques Chirac was elected president in succession to the Socialist François Mitterrand. There was already a conservative majority in the National Assembly, from which Chirac nominated Alain Juppé as his Prime Minister. However, when the two rounds of parliamentary elections were held in May/June 1997, the Socialist Party won the largest share of seats, and formed a coalition with the Communists.

Chirac's initial actions as president were viewed with some concern in Germany. His decision to permit the testing of nuclear weapons in the Pacific met with protests throughout the EU, including in Germany. Only the British government supported Chirac on this. Together with the common experience of working together in Bosnia, this incident led to a measure of agreement between France and Britain. Chirac at one stage suggested that France might learn something from the British approach to the EU. However, he gradually came back into line with the position of his predecessor.

Mid-way through this decade, Jacques Delors stepped down as president of the European Commission after serving three full terms, more than any previous president. He was widely attributed with having turned around the fortunes of the EC following the 'doldrum years', and presided over the acceptance of the single market programme and the blueprint for monetary union. He operated as a 'policy entrepreneur', initially through the vehicle of the Commission, thereby enhancing its status, then latterly in a more independent role as the *confidant* and ally of the French President, François Mitterrand, and especially the German Chancellor, Helmut Kohl (Lord 2002: 329–30).

Delors was succeeded by Jacques Santer, who was a very different type of president, and is generally considered to have been a weaker one. He did not get off to a good start. He was not the first choice of the heads of state or government. They had agreed that following Delors, who was a socialist from a large member state, the nominee had to be from the centre-right and from a small member state. This meant that the field was limited. Santer, the Prime Minister of Luxembourg, only got the nomination after John Major had rejected Jean-Luc Dehaene, the Prime Minister of Belgium and the first choice of most of his colleagues, and Helmut Kohl had rejected Ruud Lubbers, the Dutch Prime Minister. Santer's nomination was approved in the EP by a majority of only twenty-one (Lord 2002: 336).

Monetary Union

The agreement on monetary union that had been reached at Maastricht represented a compromise between the positions of states with very different perspectives on the issue. Those compromises had to be sorted out in order for the programme for a single currency to go ahead. During 1995, the decisions on the detail of the monetary union began to be settled, generally in favour of German views. These included agreement that the location of the European Central Bank (ECB) would be in Frankfurt, and that the new currency would be called the Euro, not the ecu as the French wished, because that name was not liked by the German public. More significantly, during 1996 it was agreed that the convergence criteria set out in the TEU (see Chapter 21, Origins of EMU) would have to be met precisely, with no fudging of the issue, and that there would continue to be a stability pact after the single currency came into existence. French hopes for more political control over the monetary policy of the ECB were also dashed (see Chapter 21, Putting Maastricht into Operation (1992–2002)).

Continuing economic recession in Europe hindered the efforts to meet the convergence criteria of those member states that wished to participate in the single currency. During 1995, it was decided to abandon the earlier of the two possible starting dates for the single currency, i.e. 1997, because it was obvious that not enough states, if any, would fully meet the convergence criteria by then. There was also doubt about how many would achieve the targets by 1999, the second of the two possible starting dates. In France and Belgium the efforts of the governments to reduce the level of their budget deficits to the target of 3 per cent led to strikes and disruption. The imposition of lower public spending on economies that already had high levels of unemployment was a sure recipe for political problems.

However, in the course of 1996 and 1997 a surprising number of states did manage either to achieve or to approach the targets. This caused concern in Germany, because the idea that Italy in particular could possibly observe the conditions of the stability pact in perpetuity was not considered credible. There was a fear that the German public might reject a Euro of which Italy was a part. As the trend in the Italian economy moved in the direction of the targets, so the insistence of the Germans that the targets be treated as absolutes grew. On the budget deficit, which was treated as the most important criterion, the German Finance Minister, Theo Waigel, and the President of the Bundesbank, Hans Tietmeyer, insisted that 3 per cent meant exactly 3 per cent or less, not even 3.1 per cent. This was clearly an attempt to set the target at a level that Italy would not be able to reach. The irony was that Germany missed the deficit target of 3 per cent in 1996, and looked like missing it again in 1997. A single currency without German participation was inconceivable, yet the continuing problems posed for the German economy by the absorption of East Germany threatened to disqualify it from membership on its own criteria.

All of this caused some glee within the British Conservative government, which found the whole project of monetary union extremely difficult. For domestic political reasons the government could not join the single currency, even if it met the convergence criteria; but if the project went ahead without it there was a risk that British economic interests would be damaged, and that British political influence within the EU would be permanently diminished. So it was with a certain air of wishing rather than predicting that Prime Minister John Major had said in an article in 1993 that 'economic and monetary union is not realisable in present circumstances' (*The Economist*, 25 September 1993). While there might have been some justification for this view in 1993, by the end of 1997 it was apparent that the single currency would start on schedule in 1999, and although it was not clear which states would be members, it began to look as though all those that wished to join, except Greece, would be in a position to do so.

In January 1999, the Euro came into operation for eleven member states—Austria, Belgium, Finland, France, Germany, Ireland, Italy, Luxembourg, the Netherlands, Portugal, and Spain. This meant that the Euro became the official currency of these states, although national notes and coins continued in circulation until 2002. Greece was initially excluded from the eurozone by failing to meet the convergence criteria, while Britain, Denmark, and Sweden chose not to join the single currency. Britain and Denmark had negotiated opt-outs, while Sweden excluded itself on the technicality that it had not been a member of the exchange rate mechanism for two years and as such was not eligible. There were concerns over Italy's use of a one-off 'Euro-tax' to ensure it met the budget deficit criterion in the qualifying financial year; and both Belgium and Italy had debt ratios that appeared to go beyond the criteria (see Chapter 21, Putting Maastricht into Operation (1992–2002)). Despite all of this, the completion of monetary union, almost thirty years after The Hague Summit had made it an explicit objective, was a considerable achievement.

Although the single currency came into existence more smoothly than many economists predicted, it soon ran into difficulties. The external value of the Euro fell steadily against the US dollar, and the eurozone itself began to exhibit some of the problems of having a single interest rate for such a diverse economic area. National economies on the fringes of the zone, particularly those of Spain and Ireland, began to experience the symptoms of repressed inflation, with rapidly rising property prices and shortages of labour. At the same time, the core economies of Germany and France were experiencing sluggish growth.

It was in this context that, as soon as the new currency came into existence, Oskar Lafontaine and Dominique Strauss-Kahn, Finance Ministers of Germany and France respectively, pressed the ECB to lower interest rates to stimulate growth (see Chapter 21, The Single Currency in Operation). The ECB and its President Wim Duisenberg vigorously resisted such interference, though, and the pressure was reduced after Lafontaine resigned in March 1999.

Enlargement

All member states paid lip-service to the principle of enlargement of the EU to the east, but some states were keener than others. For Germany, the enlargement was an absolute priority; it was also strongly supported by Britain and the Scandinavian countries. However, France, Italy, and Spain had reservations. When the shift was made from the general issue of supporting enlargement to the discussion of the detailed steps that were needed to make a reality of the aspiration, even the strongest supporters were not necessarily prepared to accept the full implications.

Germany's commitment to enlargement was based largely on security considerations. Following reunification, Germany was once again a central European state, having borders with Poland and the Czech Republic. Instability in the region would be right on Germany's doorstep, and admitting its nearest neighbours to the EU was seen as a way of guaranteeing their stability. There were also economic considerations. Before the First World War, German companies and banks had been the leading foreign investors in central Europe, and soon after the collapse of communism German investment began to flow into the area. Guaranteeing the security of those investments was another reason for the German government's support of membership for the central European states.

British motives for welcoming enlargement were less immediately obvious, but reflected a combination of security, economic, and political considerations. In terms of security, British governments since the war had continued to support the principle of global stabilization even where British investments were not immediately involved. This was a habit of statecraft that dated back to the period before the First World War when Britain was the hegemonic power in the world and shouldered responsibility for policing the international capitalist system. That responsibility had largely passed to the United States in the period since the Second World War, but British governments had consistently supported such efforts at global stabilization. In the situation after the end of the Cold War, the US administrations of both Bush and Clinton made it clear that they expected the EU states to play a leading role in stabilizing central and eastern Europe, and membership of the EU was specifically pressed by the Clinton Administration as a means of achieving this.

In economic terms, British support for further enlargement reflected the hope that British business would be able to profit from access to a larger market. Politically, however, this enlargement would also imply a looser EU less likely to move in a federal direction. Thus, in both economic and political terms, eastern enlargement suited the Conservative government of John Major.

While the governments of France and the Mediterranean member states could see the arguments for enlargement to the east, and even accepted them, they were apprehensive about the effect that such an enlargement would have on the EU. First, they were concerned that an eastern enlargement would shift the balance of power in the EU decisively to the north, especially coming immediately after the accession of Austria, Finland, and Sweden. Second, and related to the first point, they were concerned that the problems of the Mediterranean, which affected them more than instability in the east, would be relegated to a secondary issue. Instability in North Africa, particularly civil war in Algeria, was already having an impact on them in the form of refugees and threats to their companies' investments in the region. Third, they feared that EU funds that came to them through the CAP and the structural funds would be diverted to central and eastern European economies.

The concern that attention would be diverted from the problems of the Mediterranean was recognized by the German government when it held the presidency of the EU in the second half of 1994. Agreement was reached at the Essen European Council in December 1994 to launch an initiative on North Africa and the Middle East. This assumed more tangible form during 1995 under the successive French and Spanish presidencies, culminating in a major conference in Barcelona from 23 to 29 November 1995 involving the EU member states, the Maghreb states (Algeria, Morocco, and Tunisia), Israel, Jordan, Lebanon, Syria, Turkey, Cyprus, and Malta. The central and eastern European states were also represented. The conference agreed on a stability pact for the Middle East on the model of the Conference on Security and Co-operation in Europe (CSCE) and the EU agreed to contribute $6 billion in aid and $6 billion in **European Investment Bank (EIB)** loans to the economic development of the region.

The problem of accepting the implications of a commitment to enlargement to the east were apparent in November 1995 when the Commission proposed that agricultural imports from six central and east European states (Bulgaria, the Czech Republic, Hungary, Poland, Romania, and Slovakia) be increased by 10 per cent a year. Britain, Denmark, the Netherlands, and Sweden supported the proposal. France and the Mediterranean member states opposed it, indicating that they would only be prepared to accept an increase of 5 per cent a year. Germany, which was ostensibly the strongest supporter of enlargement, joined the Mediterranean states in opposing the Commission's proposal. This indicated the strength of the farming lobby in Germany, and the fragmented nature of decision making in the country, which allowed the Agriculture Ministry to adopt a line so clearly incompatible with the official policy as enunciated by the Chancellor's office.

The same contradiction in policy emerged after July 1997 when the Commission published its *Agenda 2000* report on the future direction of the EU in the likely context of enlargement. The German Farm Minister, Ignaz Kiechle, publicly stated that the proposed reforms of the CAP were unnecessary. He received no reprimand for this from Chancellor Kohl. In addition to the reform of key policies, the eastern enlargement had implications for the decision-making procedures of the EU. This came to be one of the key issues in the IGC that led up to the Treaty of Amsterdam. (On enlargement, see also Chapter 27.)

The 1996 IGC

Originally, the 1996 IGC was intended to review the working of the TEU. Provision for such a review was written into the agreements that were reached at Maastricht in December 1991. However, nobody expected the ratification of the TEU to take as long as it did, with the result that the review started after only two and a half years of experience of the new arrangements. The difficulties in ratifying the TEU also meant that there was little appetite for further fundamental change. Increasingly, the IGC came to be seen as primarily about preparing the ground for the eastern enlargement. There were several institutional issues that needed to be addressed if the EU were to enlarge to over twenty members: the size of the Commission and the EP; the rotation of the presidency of the Council; the extent of **qualified majority voting (QMV)**; and the weighting of votes under QMV.

The Commission had twenty members in 1995, and that was already too many for the number of portfolios available, as Jacques Santer found out when he tried to allocate responsibilities without upsetting either national sensibilities or the *amour propre* of his colleagues in the College of Commissioners. Enlargement threatened to produce an unwieldy organization. The British government offered to relinquish its second Commissioner if the other large states would agree to do so, but this was not an easy concession for the others. For Italy and Spain in particular, having two Commissioners was a matter of national pride, singling out their countries as larger member states on a par with Germany, France, and Britain. Even if there had been unanimous agreement to dispense with the second Commissioners, the problem of too many Commissioners would have remained.

The EP would also become unwieldy if the same rough formula that had been used up to the 1995 enlargement were applied to further member states. Clearly there had to be some limit put on the numbers; but that had implications for the existing distribution of seats.

With twelve member states, and with the presidency of the Council changing every six months, there were six years between presidencies for any one state (see Chapter 14,

The Council Presidency). This meant that all the expertise that had been acquired for one presidency was lost by the time the next one came round. There was also concern that the next enlargement would involve mostly small states, as had the 1995 enlargement. Small states often had problems with servicing the presidency. The problems had been eased since the Troika system had come into operation, whereby the present, previous, and immediate future presidents co-operated (see Chapter 14, The Council Presidency). However, the impending enlargement heralded a situation in which there might not be a large state in the Troika for much of the time.

On QMV, the German and French governments wanted to see an extension to cover areas under the JHA pillar of the TEU, but the British Conservative government was adamantly opposed to any extension of QMV. The British government was also, along with Spain, one of the strongest advocates of a re-weighting of the votes under QMV.

Because the number of votes allocated to a state was not directly proportional to its population, the increase in the number of small member states had produced a situation in which measures could be passed under QMV with the support of the representatives of a decreasing proportion of the total population of the EU. In the original EC of six states, votes representing 70 per cent of the population were needed to pass a measure. By 1995 this had been reduced to 58.3 per cent and, on the basis of some reasonable assumptions about the allocation of votes to future members, the proportion required could be as low as 50.3 per cent with an EU of twenty-six states. The French government supported the idea of a re-weighting of votes, but the German Chancellor was hesitant because of the concern expressed by the smaller member states that this would be yet another step towards downgrading their role.

Beyond these specific institutional issues, each member state went to the IGC with particular issues that it wished to push. Sweden, Denmark, and the Netherlands were concerned to increase the accountability and transparency of Council business, and proposed that a freedom of information clause be written into the Treaty. Sweden was also a leading mover in pressing for a chapter on employment policy to be added to the Treaty. Britain wanted reform to the working of the European Court of Justice (ECJ), having suffered several adverse judgments at its hands. Britain and France both pressed for an enhanced role for national parliaments in the policy-making process. France and Germany pressed for more flexible arrangements that would allow some states to proceed faster than others with integration; they also co-operated in putting forward proposals to move towards incorporating the Western European Union (WEU) (see Chapter 6, Insight 6.1) into the EU, something that was strongly opposed by the neutral member states (Austria, Ireland, and Sweden) and by Britain.

The IGC was preceded by a 'Reflection Group', which met in the second half of 1995 under the Spanish presidency. This consisted of representatives of the Foreign Ministers and two members of the EP. It had a remit to seek the views of other institutions on progress towards European union, and possible amendments to the TEU, and to prepare a report on the issues that should form the agenda of the IGC.

When he reported on the work of the Group in December 1995, the Spanish Foreign Minister Carlos Westendorp said that there was agreement that the IGC should not aim at fundamental reform, but be about necessary changes; in particular it should be seen as one part of the process of eastern enlargement. Werner Hoyer, the German representative on the Reflection Group, indicated publicly that the work of the Group had soon deteriorated into an exchange of national positions, and warned that there was a risk of the IGC turning into a confrontation between integrationists and intergovernmentalists.

The IGC opened officially in Turin on 29 March 1996. The special European Council that was called to inaugurate it was dominated, though, by the ban on exports of British beef. This had been imposed in the aftermath of the announcement that bovine spongiform encephalopathy (BSE) in cattle, with which British herds were particularly infected, could be the cause of Creutzfeldt–Jakob disease (CJD) in humans. As British efforts to get the ban lifted made little progress over the coming weeks, John Major threatened to block progress in the IGC, and to refuse to sign any Treaty that emerged from it until the ban was lifted. His government did in fact veto just about every item of EU business over which it could exercise a veto until an agreement was reached on a phased lifting of the ban.

This incident marked a new low in relations between the British Conservative government and the rest of the EU. Patience was already exhausted before Major threatened to block agreement on a new Treaty unless two changes were made to the existing one. First, he demanded agreement to allow the reversal of a decision of the ECJ that a directive on a 48-hour maximum working week must apply to Britain, despite the British government's opt-out from the social protocol, because it was a health-and-safety issue and so covered by the SEA. Second, he demanded that changes were made to the Common Fisheries Policy, to prevent fishing boats from other member states buying quotas from British fishermen.

There were some indications that the IGC was deliberately prolonged into 1997 in the hope that the British general election would produce a change of government, which it did. The Labour government under Tony Blair indicated immediately that, while its priorities would remain largely those of its predecessor, it would not block a Treaty over any issue other than that Britain must be allowed to retain its border controls. The way was thus cleared for agreement on the text of a new Treaty at the European Council in Amsterdam in June 1997.

The Treaty of Amsterdam

Agreement was reached at Amsterdam on a rather modest Treaty. In particular, no agreement could be reached on the institutional reforms that were believed to be essential to pave the way for enlargement. Also, there was little extension of QMV because Chancellor Kohl retreated from his earlier advocacy of the principle, and actually blocked its extension to cover industrial policy, social policy, and certain aspects of the free movement of labour.

As a result of what may have been an oversight, the failure to extend QMV to these three areas did not lead to withdrawal of the linked proposal to increase the powers of the EP in the same areas. So when the EP was given the right to amend or reject proposed legislation in two-dozen areas that were brought under co-decision for the first time, these areas were still included.

Dutch plans to extend QMV into eleven policy areas, ranging from cultural activities to industrial policy, ran into German resistance. Kohl insisted that these extensions would undermine the position of the German Länder. The only two extensions of

QMV that were agreed were for research programmes and compensatory aid for imports of raw materials. In addition, new areas were agreed in which QMV would apply from the start; namely, countering fraud, encouraging customs co-operation, collating statistics, and laying down rules for the free movement of personal data.

On the number of Commissioners, a compromise was reached that if more than two and fewer than six new members joined the EU, the Commission would continue to have one representative from each member state. However, Spain insisted that it would only surrender its second Commissioner in return for changes in the weighting of votes in the Council, which could not be agreed.

Rules on allowing flexible integration were agreed. In the first (EC) pillar, if a group of member states wanted to proceed with closer integration in a sector, but others did not, those who wanted to go ahead could do so provided that the Council of Ministers agreed to such a proposal by QMV. However, if any member state insisted that the development would jeopardize its vital national interests it could veto the move.

In the second (CFSP) pillar, the system would be 'constructive abstention'. This would allow a group of member states to undertake a joint action in the name of the EU, if those member states that did not feel they could take part were prepared not to vote against but to abstain, on the understanding that they would not then be required to contribute to the action (see Chapter 26, The Common Foreign and Security Policy (CFSP) and European Security and Defence Policy (ESDP)).

In the third (JHA) pillar, complete freedom of movement was pledged for all individuals within the EU, but the UK and Ireland were allowed to retain border controls. Decisions on immigration, visas, and asylum were to be subject to unanimity for at least five years, and then reviewed with a view to introducing more flexible arrangements, but with any member state being allowed to apply a veto on changing the procedure.

On CFSP, it was agreed that the Council Secretary-General would represent the EU to the outside world. QMV would be used on implementing foreign policy measures, but any state that believed its vital national interests were at stake could exercise a veto. The WEU might be incorporated into the EU in the future, but the North Atlantic Treaty Organization (NATO) was reaffirmed as central to Europe's defence. The Amsterdam Treaty also amended the TEU to distinguish between, on the one hand, deciding the principles and general guidelines of the CFSP, and common strategies in pursuit of these, and, on the other, the adoption of joint actions, common positions, and implementing decisions (see Chapter 26).

Finally, it was agreed that a zone of freedom, security, and justice for EU citizens would come into force within five years of ratification. This was the big policy idea of the Amsterdam Treaty and 'communitarized' some of the EU's JHA policies (see Chapter 24, History).

CONCLUSION

Where Chapter 8 told a story of movement from a relatively low point in European integration to a new high point with the SEA, this chapter tells a reverse story. The period started from the new high point reached at the end of the 1980s, but finished with the new EU in something of a crisis once again.

With the very important exception of the agreement on monetary union, the TEU was predominantly an intergovernmental treaty. Its most significant innovations were the second and third pillars, both of which were intergovernmental in nature. In part the problems that it was designed to solve were a consequence of spillover from the SEA: for example, pressures to develop more systematic ways of dealing with effects of greater flows of people across borders caused by the single market programme. In part, though, the problems arose from the international context within which the member states were operating, which is why the CFSP was so central to the TEU.

Enlargement of the EU to the states of central and eastern Europe, which was the biggest item on the post-Maastricht agenda, also received its impetus from the changing international context. The collapse of the Soviet Union posed the threat of instability in the former communist states of Europe. As with the EC and the Mediterranean enlargements in the 1970s, eastern enlargement in the forthcoming twenty-first century was part of the enhanced security role for the EU in the world after the decline of US hegemony.

A definite tension developed, though, between the will of all EU member states to consolidate democracy and capitalism in eastern and central Europe and the willingness of any particular member state to accept economic sacrifices to allow that enlargement to happen. Willing the end did not appear to mean necessarily willing the means. Domestic politics often assumed priority when it came to trying to agree the details of reforms to the common policies and to the central institutions that everyone agreed were necessary to facilitate the enlargement.

Concern to prevent further slippage of powers from the national or sub-national level to the supranational level was apparent throughout the EU by the time of Amsterdam, indicating an increasing emphasis on intergovernmentalism. There were the first indications that a new form of co-operation was emerging, one that cast the Commission in a different role as an impartial arbiter and referee of agreements for co-ordinated national action rather than as enforcer of legally binding commitments, a development that would also have implications for the role of the ECJ.

Yet, despite the intergovernmental emphasis of the new treaties, developments after Maastricht illustrate a theme that had been largely neglected by governments and analysts until then: the importance of legitimacy for the process of European integration. In a majority of member states, the EC had an independent legitimacy of its own because it represented European integration, which was perceived as a 'good thing'. The aftermath of Maastricht raised questions about whether this was still the case, questions that would become more urgent in the light of subsequent developments as explained in the following chapters.

KEY POINTS

Towards Maastricht

- In June 1989, the European Council agreed to Delors's three-stage plan for monetary union by 1999, despite British opposition.

- The collapse of communism in central and eastern Europe and the prospect of a reunified Germany focused minds on the political aspects of European integration.

- In 1991, IGCs were held on both monetary union and political union. The proposals of these IGCs were incorporated into the TEU, agreed at Maastricht in December 1991.

The Treaty on European Union

- The TEU marked a major step on the road to European integration. It committed most of the member states to adopting a single currency, extended EC competence in a range of areas, strengthened the powers of the EP, created a Committee of the Regions, and introduced the concept of European citizenship.

- The Treaty created a three-pillar structure known as the European Union, consisting of the EC pillar and the intergovernmental pillars of the CFSP and JHA.

After Maastricht

- The decision to move to a single currency caused concern within member states, not least Germany, which had a strong attachment to the Deutschmark.
- The TEU was rejected by a majority of the Danish people in a referendum in 1992 and was only accepted in 1993 following major concessions. A referendum in France (1992) was only narrowly in favour.
- By the time Austria, Finland, and Sweden became members in 1995, the EU was not the confident one they had applied to join.

The Commission after Maastricht

- The Commission became caught up in the wave of unpopularity affecting the EU. Delors' high profile presidency ensured that he was the focal point of much of the criticism.

Political Change

- Significant domestic political developments during this period affected the position of key member states on the EU and shaped the prospects for flexible integration.
- In 1995 Delors was succeeded by Jacques Santer as president of the Commission.

Monetary Union

- In 1995, details of monetary union began to emerge. The ECB would be located in Frankfurt and the single currency would be called the 'Euro'.
- In 1999 the Euro came into operation in eleven member states, although national currencies continued in circulation until 2002.

Enlargement

- While member states were generally supportive of further enlargement to include countries of central and eastern Europe, there were a number of concerns over the impact this would have on key policies, and on decision-making procedures.

The 1996 IGC

- The 1996 IGC focused on the institutional changes necessary to prepare for further enlargement. This IGC was also marked by conflict over the British 'beef' crisis, which resulted in the Major government blocking agreement on a range of issues.

The Treaty of Amsterdam

- Resulting from the 1996 IGC, this Treaty was relatively modest in scope. In particular, it did not contain the decision-making reforms most thought were necessary for incorporating several new member states.

FURTHER READING

The negotiation of the Maastricht Treaty is analysed by **M. Baun**, 'The Maastricht Treaty as High Politics: Germany, France and European Integration', *Political Science Quarterly*, 110 (1996): 605–24, and **A. Moravcsik**, *The Choice for Europe: Social Purpose and State Power from Messina to Maastricht* (London: UCL Press, 1998), 379–471. Also see **M. Baun**, *An Imperfect Union: The Maastricht Treaty and the New Politics of European Integration* (Boulder, CO: Westview, 1996).

The aftermath of the signing of the Treaty is analysed in: **B. Criddle**, 'The French Referendum on the Maastricht Treaty, September 1992', *Parliamentary Affairs*, 46 (1993) 228–38; **D. Baker, A. Gamble, and S. Ludlam**, '1846–1906–1996? Conservative Splits and European Integration', *Political Quarterly*, 64 (1993): 420–34, and 'The Parliamentary Siege of Maastricht 1993: Conservative Divisions and British Ratification of the Treaty of European Union', *Parliamentary Affairs*, 47 (1994): 37–60; **H. Rattinger**, 'Public Attitudes towards European Integration in Germany and Maastricht: Inventory and Typology', *Journal of Common Market Studies*, 32 (1994): 525–40.

On the politics that led up to the Amsterdam Treaty, see **G. Edwards and A. Pijpers**, *The Politics of European Treaty Reform: The 1996 Intergovernmental Conference and Beyond* (London, and Washington, DC: Pinter, 1997). Useful guides to the Treaty are **European Commission**, *The Amsterdam Treaty: A Comprehensive Guide* (1999) and **A. Duff**, *The Treaty of Amsterdam: Text and Commentary* (London: Federal Trust/Sweet and Maxwell, 1997).

A reaction to Amsterdam from an intergovernmentalist perspective is given in **A. Moravcsik and K. Nicolaïdes**, 'Explaining the Treaty of Amsterdam: Interests, Influences, Institutions', *Journal of Common Market Studies*, 37 (1999): 59–85. Other analyses are offered by **E. Philippart and G. Edwards**, 'The Provisions on Closer Co-operation in the Treaty of Amsterdam', *Journal of Common Market Studies*, 37 (1999): 87–108, and **Y. Devuyst**, 'The Community-Method after Amsterdam', *Journal of Common Market Studies*, 37 (1999): 109–20.

 online resource centre

Visit the Online Resource Centre that accompanies this book for links to more information on the Maastricht and Amsterdam Treaties: http://oxfordtextbooks.co.uk/orc/bache4e/

Chapter 10

From Amsterdam to Lisbon (2000–2009)

Chapter Overview

The same themes as emerged in the previous chapter continued to dominate the Eurpean Union (EU) throughout the first decade of the new century. Enlargement became the main issue driving forward repeated reforms of the treaties, and national electorates showed themselves increasingly discontented with the pace of change and their sense that they were being taken for granted by the political elites.

Far from the Amsterdam Treaty marking the end of a phase of institutional and constitutional revision in the EU, it had scarcely entered into force before further treaty reform was on the agenda. Throughout the year 2000 a new intergovernmental conference (IGC) met to discuss outstanding institutional issues that had not been settled at Amsterdam. It concluded in December 2000 with the longest European Council in history, which led to the Treaty of Nice. That was followed by the setting up of a Constitutional Convention at the end of 2001, which produced a blueprint for a Constitutional Treaty in 2003 that was signed in October 2004. The Constitutional Treaty was intended to replace the existing treaties, but it was rejected in key national referendums in the course of 2005, precipitating a crisis within the EU that was papered over rather than resolved by the adoption of a less far-reaching Treaty at Lisbon at the end of 2009. This appears to be a story of growing problems for the further extension of European integration, but in between the Treaty episodes, progress was made in some important areas of common policy.

The Nice Treaty

The Treaty of Amsterdam made institutional reform a precondition of enlargement and contained a protocol anticipating further discussions on reform. The Cologne European Council of 1999 referred to this protocol in agreeing to set up an IGC to discuss the outstanding institutional issues that had not been resolved at Amsterdam, particularly in relation to the weighting of votes in the Council, the size and composition of the Commission, and the possible extension of qualified majority voting (QMV).

The IGC opened in February 2000, under the Portuguese presidency, and continued into the French presidency in the second half of the year, but there were major disagreements on all of the outstanding issues identified above, and these had not been resolved by the time the heads of government met at Nice at the end of 2000 to try to agree the final text of the new Treaty.

Nice turned out to be the longest European Council in the history of the EC/EU. For four days the heads of government haggled over the areas that would become subject to QMV, and over the weighting of votes. Membership of the Commission proved less difficult, although really tough decisions were deferred by allowing the size of the College of Commissioners to grow to twenty-seven before there would be a move to having fewer than one commissioner per member state; but in return for giving up their second commissioner the large member states fought even harder on the weighting of votes in the Council. In the end an agreement was reached that just about opened up the prospect of the EU being ready for enlargement. The Treaty strengthened the powers of the President of the Commission and provided for one commissioner per member state from 2005, with the proviso that the maximum number in future should be twenty-six, and from that point onwards a rotation system would ensure parity among states. In relation to the European Parliament (EP), the Treaty extended the co-decision procedure and also changed the allocation of seats between states and set a maximum of 732 Members (MEPs) (see Chapter 15).

The veto was removed from twenty-nine of the seventy Treaty articles where it still applied, but in important areas national interests prevented movement. Britain would not agree to the removal of the veto on tax or social security harmonization. Although QMV for trade negotiations was extended to services, exceptions were made at French insistence for audio-visual services, education, and health. Maritime transport was exempted from QMV at the insistence of Denmark and Greece. At German and French insistence, many aspects of immigration and asylum policy were not transferred to QMV. Perhaps most significantly, though, Spain, with the support of Portugal and Greece, retained the right to veto changes to the cohesion funds until after the conclusion of the negotiations on the 2007–12 Financial Perspective. This cast further doubt on the possibility of keeping the cost of enlargement to the common budget within limits acceptable to the net contributors.

On the weighting of votes under QMV, the large member states seemed to gain an advantage over the small. The re-weighting, which would apply from 1 January 2005, left the small and medium-sized states with a smaller percentage of the total vote relative to the larger states than under the previous system. There was also the insertion of a clause requiring any measure agreed by QMV to comprise the votes of governments representing at least 62 per cent of the population of the EU. The effect was to put Germany, France, and Britain—or any two of these three plus Italy—in a position where they could effectively block progress on any measure on which they agreed to co-operate. In compensation, the small states were allowed a clause that a measure agreed under QMV would also have to have the support of a majority of the member states. The cumulative effect of these two concessions to different coalitions of 'bigs' and 'smalls' was to make the decision-making system much more complex, and also to make it more difficult than previously to achieve a qualified majority, which now required a 'triple majority'—a majority of weighted votes, a majority of member states, and a 62 per cent or higher majority of the population.

The Treaty of Nice was formally signed in the following February, following eleven months of negotiation. Existing concerns over the low level of public support for the EU were raised further when the Irish people rejected the Treaty by a vote of 53.87 per cent to 46.13 per cent in a referendum in June 2001, with a turn-out of only 32.9 per cent. Although this decision was reversed in a second referendum in October 2001, and the Treaty of Nice entered into force in February 2003, the Irish episode reflected the serious challenges facing the EU on the road to further deepening and widening.

The Lisbon Strategy

In March 2000, a special European Council held in Lisbon agreed to a new EU strategy on employment, economic reform, and social cohesion, with the goal of making the EU 'the most competitive and dynamic knowledge-based economy in the world' by 2010. Its adoption was justified with reference to the challenge of globalization:

> The European Union is confronted with a quantum shift resulting from globalization and the challenges of a new knowledge-driven economy. These challenges are affecting every aspect of people's lives and require a radical transformation of the European economy.

(Presidential Conclusions, Lisbon Special European Council, 23–4 March, para. 1)

The outcome subsequently became known variously as the Lisbon Strategy, the Lisbon Process, or the Lisbon Agenda. Success of the Strategy depended on strengthening investment in research and development, reducing bureaucracy to stimulate innovation and entrepreneurship, and improving the employment rate to 70 per cent overall, including a minimum of 60 per cent for women.

Two features of the Strategy were particularly significant. First, economic competitiveness and social cohesion were placed side-by-side as objectives. Critics of the Strategy from the left maintained that the economic competitiveness elements represented a victory for the advocates of an Anglo-Saxon model of capitalism, while critics from the right argued that the social cohesion elements represented a victory for the advocates of a 'social Europe'. It seems more likely that the new approach represented less the victory of one model of capitalism over the other than a political compromise between the positions of the left and right.

Second, the Lisbon Strategy was to be pursued through what the Presidency Conclusions to the summit described as the 'Open Method of Co-ordination' (OMC). The OMC is described in more detail in Chapter 18 (Major Policy Areas). Its main features, as delineated at Lisbon, were common guidelines to be translated into national policies, combined with periodic monitoring, evaluation, and peer review organized as mutual learning processes and accompanied by indicators and benchmarks as means of comparing best practice. In essence, this was an extension of the approach already adopted 'in the procedures for co-ordinating national economic policies under the EMU established in the Maastricht Treaty, and in the employment chapter of the Amsterdam Treaty' (Borras and Jacobsson 2004: 187–8). As such, it was a departure from the 'community method' of decision making, whereby the Commission makes proposals for legislation and the Council of Ministers (increasingly in conjunction with the EP) adopts the legislation, which then supersedes national legislation. Most significantly, it was a departure in the direction of a more intergovernmental process, where policy competence would not be transferred to the EU, but would be retained at the national level, the Commission would play a less prominent role as the facilitator of intergovernmental co-ordination, and the EP and European Court of Justice would have no real role at all. To strengthen this impression of firm national control over the process, it was agreed that one European Council out of three each year—the spring meeting—would be devoted to reviewing progress.

In March 2004, the European Council appointed the former Dutch Prime Minister, Wim Kok, to convene a committee of experts who would carry out a mid-term review of progress towards the commitment made in Lisbon. The Kok report, *Facing the Challenge*, was presented to the European Commission on 3 November 2004, and to the European Council the following day. It confirmed what everyone knew already: that delivery on the process of reform had been 'disappointing'.

Although it was already too late to meet some of the targets that had been set for 2010, the report argued that the date should not be abandoned, as there was a need to instil a sense of urgency into the process, and the embarrassment of reaching 2010 with results that were so bad that Lisbon would become 'a synonym for missed objectives and failed promises' might impart some momentum.

Beyond that, the report pointed to the need to focus on core objectives and to allocate responsibilities more precisely. So long as the Lisbon Agenda remained so broad, it ran the risk of being about everything, and therefore about nothing. The number of key indicators should be reduced from over 100 to just fourteen; and the emphasis should be placed clearly on growth and employment, because they were essential to underpin the social and environmental objectives. While the governments of the member states had to accept the main responsibility for the relative failure to date, the Commission ought to be made the unambiguous co-ordinator of the process. It needed to be prepared to name and shame those member states that were simply not doing enough. To be able to do this without fear it needed to monitor the process closely, and the report recommended that the next President of the Commission should make driving the Lisbon Agenda forward the main mandate for his period in office.

European Security and Defence Policy

Up to September 2001, steady progress was being made on security and defence policy. The smooth progress ran into choppy waters, though, following the terrorist attacks in the US on 11 September of that year (see also Chapter 24, History, on the implications for EU co-operation on internal security matters; and Chapter 26, CFSP and ESDP in Action, on external security and defence).

The initial response from the EU was to declare solidarity with the United States, and this support was maintained during the subsequent US campaign in Afghanistan to unseat the Taliban government, which had harboured and supported the Al-Qaeda terrorists. Nevertheless, the effect of the united EU response was somewhat spoiled by Britain, France, and Germany trying to act independently of the EU as a whole. In

October 2001, their respective leaders—Blair, Chirac, and Schröder—met outside of the EU forum to discuss their responses to 'September 11', and intended to do so again in London in early November. However, on the second occasion vigorous protests by other member states led to the invitation to participate being thrown open to other states and to the EU High Representative, Javier Solana (see Chapter 26, CFSP and ESDP in Action).

The most serious problems for the EU resulted from the determination of the Bush Administration to make Iraq the next target after Afghanistan. There was no evidence that the secular Ba'ath regime of Saddam Hussein supported Islamic terrorism, or had any involvement in the September terrorist attacks. Similarly, there was no more than circumstantial evidence, which subsequently proved to be totally inaccurate, that Iraq possessed weapons of mass destruction with which it could attack the United States or its allies. In the build-up to the eventual invasion of Iraq, the EU split over how to react to the US initiative.

In January 2003, in response to French and German statements implying that the EU was opposed to the US attitude towards Iraq, eight European states signed a letter indicating their support for the United States. Five of the eight were existing members of the EU—Britain, Denmark, Italy, Portugal, and Spain—while the other three were prospective members—the Czech Republic, Hungary, and Poland. Then ten former communist states, seven of them EU applicants, jointly expressed their support for the US position in February, which infuriated the French government. President Chirac publicly rebuked the ten, saying that they had shown bad manners, and had 'missed a good opportunity to keep quiet'. He pointedly went on to remind the prospective members who had already negotiated entry that the decision to admit them to the EU on 1 May 2004 had yet to be ratified by national parliaments; and he indicated that Bulgaria and Romania, who were still in the early stages of negotiating membership, had been particularly foolish to associate themselves with the statement.

In March 2003, France publicly declared that it would veto any resolution in support of military action against Iraq that might be presented by the United States and Britain to the United Nations Security Council. This caused a serious division between the two member states that had been in the forefront of efforts to create the European Security and Defence Policy (ESDP). On 18 March, Tony Blair made a strong attack in the House of Commons on the French position.

Following the invasion of Iraq in March 2003, Franco-British relations were at a very low ebb, and the prospects for an ESDP looked poor. Yet, by the end of the year there were signs of improvement, particularly following Blair's agreement in principle that the EU should have the joint planning capacity to conduct operations without the involvement of NATO, a concession that appeared to alarm the United States. So, the signs were that the British wanted to facilitate the relaunch of the ESDP.

The Constitutional Treaty

In December 2001, the heads of government, meeting in Laeken (Belgium), agreed to move beyond the modest institutional changes agreed in the Nice Treaty. The adoption of the *Declaration on the Future of the European Union* committed the EU to transforming its decision-making procedures to make them more democratic and transparent and to prepare the ground for a European Constitution. The vehicle for moving forward reform was a Constitutional Convention, which brought together representatives of national governments and parliaments from both the member and accession states with representatives of the EU institutions (see Insight 10.1), and which was chaired by the former French President, Valéry Giscard d'Estaing. It would be a unique forum in both its role and composition, designed to secure legitimacy for the reforms by incorporating the views of a broad range of actors. In addition to the formal members of the Convention and observers, various business representatives, non-governmental organizations, academics, and other interested parties would be consulted on specific topics. The Convention's Chair would report on progress at each European Council meeting and receive the views of the heads of government, and the Convention's final report would provide the starting point for discussions and decisions at an IGC scheduled for 2004.

The proposals of the Convention for a Constitution for Europe were submitted by Giscard d'Estaing to the Thessaloniki European Council in June 2003. There followed a formal IGC, at which some of the proposals were amended, but the Treaty establishing a Constitution for Europe was signed by the heads of government and the EU Foreign Ministers in October 2004. Once ratified within member states, it would replace the existing Treaties.

Insight 10.1 Composition of the Constitutional Convention

In addition to its Chairman (Valéry Giscard d'Estaing) and two Vice-Chairmen (Giuliano Amato and Jean-Luc Dehaene), the Convention comprised:

- fifteen representatives of the heads of state or government of the member states (one from each member state);
- thirteen representatives of the heads of state or government of the candidate states (one per candidate state);
- thirty representatives of the national parliaments of the member states (two from each member state);
- twenty-six representatives of the national parliaments of the candidate states (two from each candidate state);
- sixteen members of the EP;
- two representatives of the European Commission.

There were alternates for each full member.

Observers were invited to attend from the Economic and Social Committee (three representatives), the Committee of the Regions (six representatives), the social partners (three representatives), and the European Ombudsman.

The Laeken Declaration provided for the candidate states to take a full part in the proceedings without, however, being able to prevent any consensus emerging among the member states.

Source: http://european-convention.eu.int/

The Treaty that was agreed had implications for the founding principles of the EU, the institutions, the decision-making process, and its policies. It also specified for the first time the areas that would be the exclusive competence of the EU, and those areas that would be shared between the EU and the member states. Both of these were long-standing federalist demands, although national governments had become increasingly aware of the possible protection that a clear demarcation of spheres of competence would offer against the creeping extension of competence that had sometimes occurred as a result of the Commission's **policy entrepreneurship** (Chapter 13, The Commission in the Policy-Making Process).

At the time there was divergent opinion on the significance of the Treaty. On content, some viewed it as a little more than a 'Nice II' or a 'tidying-up' exercise that mainly brought together existing rules and agreements into a single, more comprehensible Treaty. More sceptical observers viewed it as a major step away from the sovereignty of nation states and towards the creation of a European super-state.

As with the earlier treaties, the Constitutional Treaty had to be ratified by the member states before entering into force. Some states chose to ratify through parliament, others by referendum. The ratification process was expected to last for two years and the Constitution expected to come into force on 1 November 2006, but in May 2005 the French referendum returned a 55 per cent vote against. This was followed shortly afterwards by a negative vote in the Netherlands of almost 62 per cent.

The French vote almost certainly let the British government of Tony Blair off the hook, faced as it had been with holding a referendum that most commentators believed it could not win. Although there had been a clear prior agreement by the heads of government that *all* member states would attempt to ratify the Treaty before the position was re-assessed, the British government maintained that there was no point in it proceeding to a referendum after the French and Dutch 'no' votes, and unilaterally announced an indefinite postponement.

Enlargement

In October 2002, the Commission declared that the applicant states—Cyprus, the Czech Republic, Estonia, Hungary, Latvia, Lithuania, Malta, Poland, the Slovak Republic, and Slovenia—were in a position to conclude negotiations successfully by the end of that year and would be ready for membership in 2004. In April 2003 the EP gave its assent to the accession of these states. On 1 May 2004, the EU's biggest enlargement brought in ten new member states and over 100 million more citizens, taking the size of the Union to twenty-five states and increasing its population by 75 million to 450 million.

Two applications from central and east European countries remained outstanding in 2004: Bulgaria and Romania, neither of which was deemed ready for membership.

Negotiations opened with Croatia in 2004, and an application was accepted from the Former Yugoslav Republic of Macedonia (FYROM). Other Yugoslav successor states were expected to apply, and several Soviet successor states expressed an interest in joining, but were ruled out by the EU (see Chapter 27, History). However, the major outstanding issue at this stage was the question of Turkey.

Turkey had had an association agreement envisaging membership since 1963. It was excluded from the enlargement process in 1997, largely through opposition from Greece and Germany. However, it was offered the prospect of future negotiations in 1999 following a change of government in Germany in 1998 and a dramatic improvement in Greek-Turkish relations in 1999. Further, a decision by the EU in 1999 to allow states to negotiate entry at their own pace made it easier to open negotiations with Turkey, and more difficult not to do so. A change of government in Turkey in 2002 produced rapid progress to meeting the Copenhagen criteria. Moreover, the international climate meant that geo-strategic factors were increasingly in Turkey's favour, although opposition to its accession remained strong in some states in 2004, particularly in France (see Chapter 27, Explaining Enlargement).

The European Parliament and the New Commission

In June 2004, in the run-up to the national votes on ratification of the Constitutional Treaty, there were elections to the EP. The date for the enlargement had been set to allow the new member states to take part in the elections. This in turn was the first stage in a new constitutional timetable, which had applied for the first time in 1995, whereby the election of the new EP was followed by the nomination of the new Commission. There was hope among EU leaders that the publicity that enlargement had generated would result in an increased turn-out for the elections in June 2004. In fact turn-out, which had fallen in every election since 1979, declined further to a record low of 45.7 per cent. As noted above, in the new member states it was much lower. It was unclear at this stage what conclusions should be drawn from this. Pat Cox, the President of the EP, expressed the view that the low turn-outs in the new member states reflected the fact that the citizens felt they had already shown their support for the EU in the referendums on accession in 2003.

In line with the new constitutional timetable, the EP elections were followed by the nomination of the new Commission. In June 2004, the European Council nominated Portuguese Prime Minister José Manuel Durao Barroso as the next Commission President. The conservative Barroso was appointed after some dispute within the Council over Romano Prodi's successor. The French and German governments had sought to install the Belgian Prime Minister Guy Verhofstadt, while Britain had backed Barroso. In the end, Barroso's appointment was not only seen as a compromise between federalists and Atlanticists, but also reassured the concerns of smaller states. It was also in line with the expectation of the EP that the nominee would be drawn from the same political 'family' as the majority that had been returned in the elections. This, combined with Barroso's competent and convincing manner in his own confirmation hearing before the EP, resulted in a comfortable majority in favour of his nomination, but the MEPs were highly critical of some of the other nominations and of Barroso's allocation of portfolios to individuals, resulting in the withdrawal of one nominee and some reallocation of responsibilities.

175

The Lisbon Treaty

In the wake of the French and Dutch votes, the European Council of June 2005 called for a period of reflection. The passage of time would allow for the depoliticization of some of the more sensitive issues raised in the referendum campaigns and held the prospect of a change of government in some key states, France and the Netherlands in particular (Christiansen 2010: 24).

For a while, the Treaty fell from public view. Indeed, at one point Commission President Barroso declared that the Treaty would not come back for several years (Church and Phinnemore 2010: 61). However, in June 2006 the European Council asked the incoming German presidency to present a report on how to end the constitutional impasse.

Reflection brought the conclusion that what was needed was separation of the more controversial symbolic (constitutional) aspects of the Treaty from the practical requirements of institutional reform. In January 2007, the new German presidency announced plans to revive the Constitution and began a series of bilateral and multilateral meetings with national leaders to discuss ways forward. The tone of domestic politics revealed in these meetings signalled to the German negotiators that the EU needed to step back from its initial ambitions (Carbone 2010: 222).

In short, the task facing the German presidency was one of reconciling the demands of the maximalist eighteen states who had ratified the Constitutional Treaty and wanted to retain as much of it as possible, with those of the minimalists who wanted simply to amend the EU's rules (Dedman 2010: 176). EU leaders meeting in Berlin in March 2007 used the opportunity of the fiftieth anniversary of the Treaties of Rome to emphasize the symbolic aspects of European integration in a less controversial manner—the non-binding Berlin Declaration on the Union's aims and values—while also calling for a new treaty to be in place by 2009. A new IGC was called for the summer of that year.

On 19 June, the German presidency presented its 'draft mandate'. It proposed that instead of consolidating and replacing the existing treaties—the Treaty on European Union (TEU) and the Treaty establishing the European Community (TEC)—these should be amended to incorporate most of the provisions of the Constitutional Treaty. However, the more controversial aspects of the Constitutional Treaty would be dropped: the term 'constitution', an article referring to symbols of the Union (including the EU anthem and flag) and references to an 'EU Minister' for foreign affairs. The EU's legal instruments would remain as regulations, directives, and decisions and not be replaced by the terms 'law' and 'framework law'. In short, the text would be 'changed significantly in order to remove the kind of language that could be seen as an indication of statist aspirations' (Christiansen 2010: 25–6).

The mandate for the IGC to finalize a 'reform treaty' was soon agreed by the European Council and subsequently by the EP, the Commission, and the European Central Bank. The IGC was launched on 23 July 2007 and negotiations over the content of the new treaty continued into the autumn. Sticking points included the Polish government's position over various institutional changes (in particular relating to blocking minorities in the Council of Ministers) and UK and Irish opt-outs in justice and home affairs. The text of the new treaty was finally agreed in Lisbon in October

2007 and signed by heads of state and government in the same city in December. While some of the more controversial aspects of the Constitutional Treaty were removed, the vast majority of its provisions were retained in the Lisbon Treaty. Over sixty revisions were made to the TEU and nearly 300 changes were made to the TEC (or Treaty on the Functioning of the European Union (TFEU) as it would be renamed). The terms of the Treaty are reviewed in detail in Chapter 12. Dedman (2010: 177) commented that:

> Lisbon contained 95 per cent of what was in the Constitutional Treaty as its Chief Architect, Valéry Giscard d'Estaing was keen to announce in successive interviews, undermining governments' cases against referendums that they had originally promised but now insisted were not necessary.

Ultimately though, re-badging the treaty as a more technical 'reform treaty' allowed a number of governments—such as France, the Netherlands and the UK—to avoid ratification via referendum (Sedelmeier and Young 2008: 2). Only Ireland was committed to a popular vote.

Despite the revisions that the Treaty contained, on 12 June 2008 the Irish people rejected it with a vote of 53.4 per cent against (from a turn-out of 53.1 per cent). The vote shook EU leaders, while giving succour to those who had viewed the revised treaty as simply a cynical attempt to repackage a treaty once rejected. As Copsey and Haughton (2009: 2) noted:

> The very fact that Ireland was the only Member State to ask its citizens to pass judgement on the treaty only fuelled the fires of critics of the EU such as Czech President Vaclav Klaus, for example, who could not contain his glee when the result was announced, claiming he could write a better treaty from his hospital bed.

Opinions varied on the reasons for the vote against. Those disappointed by the outcome spoke of misinformation being spread about the purposes of the treaty in relation to issues such as abortion, euthanasia, and defence policy. Domestic politics also played a role, not least the unpopularity of Irish Prime Minister Bertie Ahern, who was in favour of a 'yes' vote. There was also wide recognition that the 'yes' campaign had been lacklustre. The Irish people were clearly not persuaded of the case for the Treaty, despite the fact that the EU remained broadly popular in Ireland: a Eurobarometer poll taken soon after the referendum showed that 87 per cent of Irish people thought Ireland benefited from EU membership, a higher percentage than for any other state (Dedman 2010: 178).

Despite the Irish vote, and the soul searching this caused, EU leaders urged other member states to continue with the ratification process: eighteen had already done so and these were joined by another five by the end of 2008. The four countries that had not ratified by this point were Ireland, the Czech Republic, Germany, and Poland.

At the European Council of December 2008, Ireland was given reassurances in relation to areas of concern raised in the referendum campaign, including taxation policy, family and social issues, and foreign policy. In exchange, the Irish government agreed to hold a new referendum by the end of 2009 (Carbone 2010: 224–5). The European Council also reversed its decision on reducing the number of Commissioners, so that all states retained one each. While some claimed this had been an issue in the Irish referendum—not least the Irish Commissioner Charlie McCreevy and former

Commissioner Ray MacSharry—there was general recognition among EU leaders that this move was neither necessary nor desirable, particularly for smaller states.

That there were not referendums in other member states did not mean the absence of controversy. In Germany, the Federal Constitutional Court had been asked to rule on the compatibility of the Lisbon Treaty with the German constitution (the Basic Law). Its 2009 judgment ruled that the Treaty was compatible, but placed domestic conditions on further transfers of power, conditions that have been interpreted as likely to contribute to a decline in Germany's support for integration in the future (Bulmer and Paterson 2010). The presidents of both the Czech Republic and Poland refused to sign the ratification instruments and there were splits between political elites in a number of member states.

However, the fate of the Treaty ultimately rested on a positive vote in the second Irish referendum. That this was secured in October 2009 with a clear majority in favour (67.13 per cent of a 59 per cent turn-out) was largely explained by deteriorating economic circumstances, although this time the 'yes' campaign was far more effective and the negative consequences for Ireland of a 'no' vote emphasized more (van der Veen 2010). The second Irish referendum cleared the way for the Treaty to come into effect on 1 December 2009.

CONCLUSION

Why did national governments keep proposing reforms to the treaties when national electorates were so reluctant to accept them? And why did national electorates reject the proposals?

One of the main reasons for the repeated efforts to revise the treaties was enlargement (see Chapter 27). Arrangements that had worked tolerably well for fifteen member states were less viable for twenty-seven or more. At the same time, the new members were predominantly medium-sized states, and the straight application of the existing rules on voting and allocation of seats in the central institutions would have significantly reduced the influence of the larger member states.

Intergovernmental bargaining made it difficult to get agreements on new arrangements that would suit everyone, which is why the first attempts to resolve the problems resulted in inadequate solutions in the Amsterdam and Nice Treaties.

There was also growing concern during the late 1990s and into the 2000s about the inability of the EU states to act in concert in matters of external security and defence. The inability of the European states to take effective concerted action in response to the tragedy in former Yugoslavia in the late 1990s (see Chapter 26, History) was compounded by the new sense of urgency to ensure security co-operation in the wake of the terrorist attacks on the United States in September 2001 (Chapter 26, CFSP and ESDP in Action).

Enlargement was also one of the factors in the rejection of the proposals by national electorates. Enlargement caused concern in existing member states about the dilution of the benefits that they derived from the budget of the EU, and following the successful admission of the new member states in 2004 there was growing concern about the employment implications of the free movement of workers from the new east European member states to the older member states. Although nearly all of the older member states imposed restrictions in the short term on free movement, these controls were limited to a maximum of five years, or seven if it could be proved that the free movement would seriously disrupt the economies of the old member states. The concerns for the future were compounded by the effects of the monetary union, which led to a weakening of economic performance in some participant states.

Our primary analytical theme here is that of legitimacy—a recurring theme since the Maastricht Treaty (see Chapter 9, Conclusion). Scholars have identified a gap between elites and public opinion in relation to integration, and domestic political audiences have become more difficult to ignore. In the words of Carbone (2010: 230), 'the "permissive consensus" that characterized the early years of the European Union has increasingly turned into a "constraining dissensus"'.

The warning signs were very evident when turn-out for the EP elections in 2004 reached a record low. As suggested in Chapter 3, low turn-outs can be read in more than one way. A low turn-out may be seen as tacit support by the public for the process of European integration—the notion of the permissive consensus (see Chapter 3, Democracy). Alternatively, it may be viewed as apathy or disenchantment with the political system. In most cases, the decline in participation in EP elections has been seen as the latter. Put together with the evidence from the ratification process for the Constitutional Treaty, this would seem to be the more persuasive argument.

The decision to create a Constitutional Convention to make proposals for a Constitutional Treaty was in part a response to existing concerns over the EU's legitimacy (see Chapter 3) and the Convention model itself was seen as a step in the direction of more open and inclusive decision making at the EU level. However, the operation of the Convention was subject to contrasting interpretations. Intergovernmentalists emphasized the dominance of national governments and the hard-bargaining approach to negotiations, while others emphasized the supranational dimension and a process characterized largely by problem-solving rationality (see Chapter 2), rather than bargaining.

The draft Treaty that emerged was viewed differently in different member states. For example, the right in Britain saw the Treaty as a major step towards a federal Europe and the loss of national sovereignty. By contrast, many on the left in France saw the Treaty as dominated by the Anglo-Saxon model of capitalism and a threat to French models of social welfare. The Constitutional Treaty was in large part an attempt to bring the EU closer to its citizens, but it was seen to have the opposite effect. At the same time, it did galvanize a widespread public debate on the EU in those states where a referendum took place.

The EU's action in re-packaging many of the proposals from the rejected Constitutional Treaty in the Lisbon Treaty, and then pushing it through as a 'reform treaty' without a popular vote in any of the member states except Ireland, was viewed as high-handed elitism by those who had voted against the earlier treaty. The demand of the EU for a second referendum in Ireland was also viewed with cynicism in many quarters. Dedman (2010: 175) claimed that the first vote was treated by EU leaders as a 'mistake' and that '...this contempt for popular opinion actually confirms Eurosceptics' charge that the EU is elitist and undemocratic'. The whole episode further undermined the legitimacy of the EU.

KEY POINTS

The Nice Treaty

- Nice became the longest European Council in the history of the EC/EU as leaders negotiated over institutional changes in preparation for enlargement. There was particular tension between large and small states over voting weights under QMV, and more widespread disagreement about the extension of QMV to new areas of policy.

- Reform of voting weights led to a complex 'triple majority' system, which seemed to advantage the larger member states against the smaller.

- QMV was extended into around thirty new areas, but the veto remained in others.

- In a parallel initiative, also confirmed at Nice in December 2000, the EU set out its commitment to citizens' rights in the Charter of Fundamental Rights of the European Union.

The Lisbon Strategy

- In March 2000 a special European Council in Lisbon agreed to pursue a new strategy to make the EU more competitive.
- The strategy was to be pursued through the OMC.
- In November 2004 the Kok report described progress as disappointing, despite some achievements.
- Commission President Barroso made the strategy a priority of his term in office.

European Security and Defence Policy

- Progress on the ESDP was stalled by the 2001 terrorist attacks on the United States, with splits emerging between key member states on how to respond to the subsequent US decision to take military action against Iraq.

The Constitutional Treaty

- The Constitutional Convention prepared the ground for a European Constitution. It was unique in its composition and purpose.
- The Convention's proposals were presented in June 2003 and, following some amendments, the Treaty establishing a Constitution for Europe was signed by the EU heads of government and their Foreign Ministers in October 2004.
- The worst fears of the Treaty's supporters were realized in May 2005 when the French referendum returned a 55 per cent vote against. The vote prompted arguably the biggest crisis in the EU's history.

Enlargement

- In 2004 ten states, mainly from central and eastern Europe, became members of the EU, and negotiations on membership were opened with Croatia.

The European Parliament and the New Commission

- Turn-out at EP elections fell to a record low in 2004, and national issues remained prominent in the election campaigns in most member states.
- Barroso's appointment was a compromise between federalists and Atlanticists, and also appeased smaller member states.
- The proposed Commission hit problems over a number of nominees, and the changes that were made were seen as a victory for the EP.

The Lisbon Treaty

- The rejection of the Constitutional Treaty in France and the Netherlands in 2005 increased uncertainty over the EU's legitimacy and future trajectory.
- After a period of reflection, some of the more controversial aspects of the Treaty were removed. References to 'constitution' and key symbols were dropped.
- The revised 'Lisbon Treaty' was signed in the Portuguese capital in December 2009.
- For some, the Lisbon Treaty was a serious dilution of the intentions of the Constitutional Treaty; for others the substance of the original remained and the revisions were seen as mainly cosmetic.
- In Ireland, the only state to hold a referendum, 53.4 per cent of the public voted against ratifying the Treaty in June 2008.

- Although there were no other referendums, ratification proved controversial in other member states, most notably Poland and the Czech Republic.

- Following assurances in relation to areas of concern, including taxation policy, family and social issues, and foreign policy, a second Irish referendum in October 2009 produced a vote of 67.13 per cent in favour of ratifying the Treaty.

FURTHER READING

On the Treaty of Nice see **M. Gray and A. Stubb**, 'Keynote Article: The Treaty of Nice—Negotiating a Poisoned Chalice?' in **G. Edwards and G. Wiessala (eds)**, *The European Union: Annual Review of the EU 2000/2001* (Oxford: Blackwell, 2001), 5–24; and **K. Feus (ed.)**, *The Treaty of Nice Explained* (London: Federal Trust for Education and Research, 2001).

Detailed analysis of the Constitutional Convention's process, and of the emergence of the resultant Treaty, is available in **P. Norman**, *The Accidental Constitution: The Making of Europe's Constitutional Treaty* (Brussels: EuroComment). For analyses of the European Constitution, see **C. Church and D. Phinnemore**, *Understanding the European Constitution: An Introduction to the EU Constitutional Treaty* (London: Routledge, 2006), and **G. Amato and J. Ziller (eds)**, *The European Constitution: Cases and Materials in EU Member States' Law* (Cheltenham: Edward Elgar, 2007).

Assessments of the 2004 European elections are contained in **J. Lodge (ed.)**, *The 2004 Elections to the European Parliament* (Basingstoke: Palgrave Macmillan, 2005).

M. Carbone (ed.), *National Politics and European Integration: From the Constitution to the Lisbon Treaty* (Cheltenham, UK; Northampton, MA: Edward Elgar, 2010) covers the domestic politics of treaty reform. The period before the second Irish referendum is covered by both **M. Dedman**, *The Origins and Development of the European Union, 2nd edition, 1945-2008,* (London: Routledge, 2010) and **R. McAllister**, *European Union: An Historical and Political Survey* (London: Routledge, 2nd edn, 2010). Further reflections on the Lisbon Treaty can be found in *EUSA Review*, 23, 1 (European Union Studies Association, USA) Winter 2010 (http://eustudies.org/publications_review_winter10.php).

 online resource centre **Visit the Online Resource Centre that accompanies this book for links to more information on the EU in the first decade of the twenty-first century: http://oxfordtextbooks.co.uk/orc/bache4e/**

Chapter 11

The EU in Crisis (2009–)

Chapter Overview

The period after the Lisbon Treaty was adopted in 2009 was dominated by the eurozone crisis. This crisis presented a range of challenges for the sometimes unwieldy European institutions, which were forced to act and implement reforms quickly in order to safeguard the viability of the single currency (this chapter should be read alongside the relevant sections of Chapter 21). The crisis affected member states in starkly different ways and acute disagreements emerged over the appropriate reform agenda, particularly between 'debtor' and 'creditor' countries. For students of integration the crisis brought to the fore long-standing questions about which actors are central to EU politics. Responses to crisis arguably marked a shift towards greater intergovernmentalism, with the European Council—heads of state and government—becoming the key actor. Within this context Franco-German leadership became a driver of reform, although German preferences most often prevailed. The reform agenda seemed initially to push the eurozone closer together in important ways, including with the ratification of the Treaty on Stability Co-ordination and Governance. However, both the direction and democratic legitimacy of this reform process were widely questioned and opposition movements resisted it via, inter alia, popular protest, legal challenge, and the ballot box. Furthermore, EU member states outside of the eurozone were not party to this deeper integration and in some cases—notably that of the UK—they actively sought greater detachment.

The Unfolding Eurozone Crisis

The euro at first appeared to be relatively unaffected by the financial crisis that hit the global economy in 2007, even as certain European economies felt its force (see Insight 11.1).

Then, in October 2009, a new Socialist government took office in Greece and revealed that the fiscal position of the state was far worse than the previous government had admitted. It soon became apparent that Greek government statistics had concealed the true extent of the national budget deficit, which was far in excess of the 3 per cent of GDP allowed under the rules of the eurozone. In December 2009, two of the leading agencies that rate national creditworthiness downgraded Greece, and financial markets became reluctant to buy Greek government debt. This was despite a show of intent by the Greek government to tighten government finances by cutting expenditure and increasing taxes, a move that provoked street demonstrations and strikes (for an overview, see Chakrabortty 2011).

> ### Insight 11.1 From 'sub-prime' to 'eurozone' crisis
>
> The causes of the global financial crisis which began in 2007 were widely debated, but the concept of 'systemic risk' was central to many accounts. This refers to the risks associated with an economy based on high levels of debt and the financialization of that debt. Of particular significance in many accounts is mortgage securitization in the US: the process whereby large volumes of 'sub-prime' mortgage debt—mortgages sold to individuals in the US with low levels of credit worthiness—were effectively sold on to domestic and international financial intermediaries such as investment banks, often with 'triple-A' credit ratings. This process spread the risks associated with highly risky loans to the global financial system, while reducing or eliminating the risk to the originator of the loan, who was thereby incentivized to issue further loans. When interest rates rose in many economies in the mid-2000s in response to, inter alia, inflation induced by rising oil prices, many individuals, including many with 'sub-prime' mortgages, defaulted on their loans and the waves were felt throughout the global economy. While the waves emanating from the US were particularly significant, it is important to note that this 'systemic risk' was also present within the EU itself at the outset of this crisis. For instance, countries such as the UK, Ireland, Spain, Hungary, and the Baltic states had particularly high and rapidly increasing levels of mortgage debt in the 2000s. In other words, as Hay and Wincott (2012) emphasized, the causes of the economic difficulties in the EU were endogenous as well as exogenous. These circumstances prompted government bailouts of various sorts, which, coupled with the perceived frailties of the euro as a currency area, led to the protracted crisis in the eurozone.

In February 2010, EU leaders met to consider whether Greece should be given assistance to allow it to cover its existing debts. As the cost of borrowing money on the international markets became steadily higher for the Greek government, there was a risk of it having to default on some of its debts, which could have led to a serious collapse in the value of the euro. Yet, there was strong resistance in Germany to what was seen as a bailout for a country that had been profligate in its fiscal management.

By April, though, it was apparent that the markets had decided Greece was incapable of rescuing itself, and belatedly the other members of the eurozone agreed a €30 billion rescue package. This turned out to be too little and too late, even after the International Monetary Fund (IMF) offered to put up another €15 billion. Spreads between the interest rates on Greek and German government bonds reached 4.69 per cent after the package was agreed, and one credit agency slashed Greece's rating even further.

At the beginning of May 2010, a €110 billion package was agreed by eurozone finance ministers, comprising €80 billion from the other fifteen euro states at 5 per cent interest, well below what Greece would have to pay on financial markets, with the rest being provided by the IMF. Greece had to accept a €30 billion package of spending cuts and tax increases to reduce its budget deficit by five percentage points in 2010 and a further four percentage points in 2011. As it became increasingly likely that the crisis would spread beyond Greece, agreement was also reached on a general facility of €750 billion (supported by the EU and IMF) available to all eurozone states that might find themselves under pressure (see also Chapter 21).

At the end of September 2010 the Irish government announced that the cost of rescuing its ailing banking sector would be much higher than anticipated, leading to a downgrading in Ireland's sovereign debt by credit ratings agencies. Following Ireland's request in November 2010, the EU/IMF granted the country an assistance package worth €85 billion. In accord with what was by now 'a drearily familiar script' (Cohen 2012), in April 2011 Portugal requested financial assistance following downgrades in its own sovereign debt, and in May a package worth €78 billion over three years was agreed.

Throughout the second half of 2011 the crisis continued and European leaders agreed in October on a second package of support for Greece, which faced continuing pressure from the financial markets despite the initial support packages. Notably, this package included 'private sector involvement'; in other words, private holders of Greek debt were required to take losses. Given the level of social upheaval in Greece—a consequence of the austerity being implemented in accordance with EU/IMF conditionality—Prime Minister George Papandreou announced a referendum on the new deal. But under significant pressure from European governments the referendum was called off, leading to Papandreou's resignation in November. His replacement as head of an interim coalition government was the economist and former vice president of the European Central Bank (ECB), Lucas Papademos.

During the same period, Spain and Italy were hit by a wave of ratings downgrades and the cost of borrowing was becoming particularly acute in Italy. This led to the resignation of Silvio Berlusconi as Prime Minister in November and his replacement by Mario Monti—an economist by training and a former EU Commissioner—who, until mid-2013, headed an interim government tasked with implementing a series of austerity measures and liberalizing the Italian economy. The appointment of two unelected and ostensibly 'market friendly technocrats' in Greece and Italy could be interpreted as evidence of the way in which the crisis had exacerbated a 'democratic deficit' in the EU (see Chapter 3, Democracy). That said, following drawn-out election processes in both countries—in 2012 in Greece and 2013 in Italy—new coalition governments were formed, headed by new prime ministers.

In late 2011 and 2012 the crisis continued, with the title feature of *The Economist* asking in November 2011: 'Is This Really the End?' A number of further downgrades of eurozone countries' sovereign debts occurred during this period, including that of France which was stripped of its triple-A status. Throughout 2012 the situation in Spain grew increasingly critical with further downgrades of sovereign debt, the consequence in large part of downgrades to a number of Spanish banks that had significant exposure to its severely ailing housing and construction sectors. In May 2012, Bankia, a conglomerate of several Spanish regional banks, was nationalized and in June Spain became the first country to request financial assistance in order to recapitalize its banking sector. This was the first assistance package to be managed via the European Stability Mechanism (ESM) (see discussion in this chapter and Chapter 21). It was accompanied by policy conditionality which focused in particular on reform and regulation of the banking sector.

In June 2012, Cyprus became the fifth eurozone member state formally to request financial assistance from the EU/IMF. It had previously been loaned €2.5 billion by Russia—with whom it had close relations due to the large number of Russians who reside and bank in Cyprus—but this had proved to be insufficient. Like the other cases discussed, Cyprus had faced a series of downgrades (and was downgraded to 'junk' status in March) and, like Ireland and Spain, its banking sector was under particular pressure due to its exposure to a burst property bubble, and in this case also its interdependence with the ailing Greek economy. Following prolonged wrangling over the conditions of the deal, in March 2013 a €10 billion loan was agreed that included the usual range of EU/IMF conditions, but also a controversial levy on all personal bank deposits over a certain amount. After protests and vociferous criticism from both within and beyond Cyprus—including a rejection of the deal by the Cypriot parliament—this latter condition was ultimately removed.

The bailout responses to the series of crises recounted above could be described as acts of 'firefighting'. Since at least 2011 concerted efforts were also being made to put in place long-term reforms aimed at prevention rather than just a short-term cure. Such efforts were primarily based on two pillars: the development of a permanent financial support facility and the implementation of stricter EU-level rules governing the economies and fiscal positions of eurozone member states. The first pillar centred on the establishment by treaty of the ESM, facilitated by an amendment to Article 136 of the Lisbon Treaty which allows for the establishment of a 'stability mechanism'. The second centred on the 'Fiscal Compact' contained in the Treaty on Stability Co-ordination and Governance (TSCG) (see Insight 11.2 and Chapter 21 for more details on various reform packages).

Insight 11.2 The Treaty on Stability Co-ordination and Governance (TSCG)

The push for a new treaty to ensure greater economic discipline within the eurozone came primarily from Germany. In particular, Germany was concerned that the Maastricht Treaty (and the later Stability and Growth Pact) and reforms to monetary and economic governance implemented during the crisis (the so-called 'six-pack' and 'two-pack'—see Chapter 21) had not gone far enough in terms of obliging eurozone member states to observe budgetary discipline or ensuring co-ordination of macroeconomic management between them. In particular, Germany was keen to ensure that eurozone governments would enshrine into national laws a credible commitment to such discipline, in particular via the principle of a balanced budget which would effectively require governments to balance income (tax revenue) and expenditure in the long term (see also Chapter 21). Obliging governments to enshrine such a rule would require a treaty change. The initial intention of Germany, and later the European Council President, Herman van Rompuy, was to incorporate these rules through treaty reform. However, the UK withdrew its support for treaty change when it was unable to extract concessions on financial services regulation (see this chapter, Other Developments). The TSCG is therefore not EU law, but an intergovernmental treaty which nevertheless uses EU institutions to ensure compliance. It was signed by twenty-five member states (not the UK nor the Czech Republic) on 2 March 2012. It was ratified using an expedited process requiring ratification by twelve eurozone member states and entered into force (for those states that had ratified it) on 1 January 2013. It would enter into force for other eurozone member states once ratification procedures were complete, and for non-eurozone contracting parties when they adopted the euro. For a discussion of the key policy features of the TSCG see Chapter 21.

The ECB was increasingly active throughout the crisis. In 2012 its president, Mario Draghi, declared that 'the ECB is ready to do whatever it takes to preserve the euro. And believe me, it will be enough' (Wilson 2012). With this declaration, backed up with the initiation of so-called Outright Monetary Transactions (OMTs)—a pledge to purchase member states' sovereign bonds if they committed themselves to the ESM conditions—the ECB was able to narrow bond-yield spreads within the eurozone. Some voices, particularly in Germany (see this chapter, Power in Crisis EU), argued that these interventions exceeded the ECB's mandate in the Lisbon Treaty. But such interventions were arguably fundamental to the survival of the euro.

Crisis Politics

Cutting through the considerable complexity of the politics of the crisis, it could be said that it was driven by two key debates. The first was an economic debate between advocates of budgetary discipline (and austerity) and advocates of economic growth (and employment), which had long been an important backdrop to discussions of economic and monetary union (see Chapter 21) but became particularly heated within the crisis context. The second—prominent throughout the history recounted in these chapters—was the perennial debate over the extent and nature of EU integration.

The Economic Debate

While they are not necessarily mutually exclusive concerns, a central debate during the crisis was whether economic discipline or economic growth should be prioritized by the EU.

Advocates of economic discipline (variously described as adopting an 'orthodox', 'neoliberal', or 'ordo-liberal' perspective) saw it as important in the short term in order to placate the markets and credit rating agencies and reduce the cost of borrowing for those member state most afflicted by the crisis. This approach was seen as particularly important for those member states in receipt of the financial support packages and this is why significant conditionalities were attached to these. In the long term, economic discipline and structural reforms were seen as crucial for 'rebalancing' the eurozone economy and restoring its global competitiveness.

By contrast, those emphasizing the importance of growth and employment (sometimes described as adopting a 'Keynesian' or 'neo-Keynesian' position) argued that, in the short term, economic discipline and austerity could undermine prospects for recovery through reducing consumption and aggregate demand (see Blyth 2013). Some also emphasized the potential for any detrimental social impacts to translate into domestic political crises that would have knock-on effects at the EU level.

While positions taken in this debate cannot be unambiguously mapped on to particular member states, it has tended to be the case that key actors in 'creditor' and 'debtor' member states aligned at its poles—the creditors at the 'discipline and austerity' end and the debtors at the 'growth and investment' end.

Popular support for these two positions was reinforced by a highly moralized narrative of blame that emerged in domestic public and media discussions of the crisis. In

Germany and some other 'creditor' European member states, a prominent discourse emphasized the ill-discipline, irresponsibility, and even moral decay in the 'debtor' south. As early as February 2010 the German news magazine *Focus* ran a story on Greece with the headline 'Cheats in the Euro Family'. Conversely, in a number of 'debtor' European countries the blame ran the other way, with an anti-German discourse prevailing in the media and public opinion. For instance, in a number of 'debtor' European countries, Germany's Nazi past was invoked in the tabloid media and by protestors (see, for instance, Heyer and Batzoglou 2012). Such narratives clearly have the potential to create disunity and undermine solidarity within the eurozone, and EU more generally.

More or Less EU?

Throughout the crisis, a debate about integration and national sovereignty operated alongside this economic debate. Numerous political actors on both sides of the economic debate, both within and outside the eurozone, claimed that a robust solution to the crisis would require moves towards some form of greater integration (at least within the eurozone). Depending on their position in the economic debate, the integration that they envisaged took different forms. For advocates of economic discipline, the priority was robust and enforceable EU-level rules ensuring balanced budgets at national level (reflected in some of the features of the reforms to date, including the TSCG—see Insight 11.2 and Chapter 21). For many advocates of economic growth, it would require such things as shared responsibility for debt obligations (for instance, 'eurobonds'—see Chapter 21) and perhaps even the creation of a federal fiscal union with tax-and-spend powers along the lines of the United States (Cohen 2012). But such moves could not be easily accomplished in the face of significant political and popular opposition to 'more EU'.

Indeed, opponents of such moves identified the cause of the crisis as too much rather than too little EU. They expressed concerns about moves towards greater integration and sought to oppose steps in that direction through the reassertion of national sovereignty and democracy. This anti-EU, pro-sovereignty narrative played out in different ways in different national contexts, again often depending on the position taken in the economic debate. Thus, in pro-discipline creditor countries, the EU was often portrayed as over-reaching its mandate with initiatives such as the ESM unfairly exposing Germany and other 'creditor' nations to the indebtedness of other member states (see this chapter, Power in Crisis EU). In 'debtor' countries, the Commission, the ECB, and the IMF—often called 'the troika' for shorthand—were blamed for the harsh conditions that accompanied financial assistance programmes. The importance of this opposition was reflected in survey data. The total percentage of people positively predisposed to the EU fell from 48 per cent in 2008 to 30 per cent in 2012 (Eurobarometer 2012). In most of those member states exposed to the harshest austerity measures, support for the EU had fallen below 50 per cent by 2013 (Pew Research Centre 2013). Politically, the crisis struck a significant blow to the EU's already fragile 'permissive consensus' (see Chapter 3, Democracy).

A blame game was also played out at the domestic level, where politicians in power were criticized for their handling of the economic crisis and their emasculation in the face of EU institutions (see Pew Research Centre 2013). Such dissatisfaction fuelled an increase in support for various populist, nationalist, and anti-EU political parties in several member states. A number of incumbent governments were voted out of office and the growing popularity of such parties was reflected in the European Parliament election results of 2014 (see this chapter, Other Developments, and Chapter 15). Popular dissatisfaction also manifested itself in widespread demonstrations and protests, particularly in those countries most acutely affected by spending cuts. Such protest is perhaps unsurprising given the socio-economic situation in those countries, where unemployment, poverty, and hardship increased dramatically. A particular concern was youth unemployment: in Spain and Greece in 2013 nearly 60 per cent of adults aged under twenty-five were unemployed.

Power in Crisis EU

The crisis raised interesting questions about which actors are dictating and driving the EU agenda and what kinds of reform agenda different actors support. In many respects the crisis led to the increased relevance of intergovernmentalism within the EU (see Chapter 1). As Herman van Rompuy, the European Council President, noted, this was perhaps unsurprising given that it required emergency responses that the supranational EU institutions with 'delegated responsibilities' were not practically or legitimately able to offer (cited in Closa 2012).

Within the auspices of the European Council, a system of ad hoc 'Euro summits'—regular meetings of the heads of governments of eurozone member states—emerged during the crisis and was institutionalized within the TSCG's provisions on governance (see also Chapter 21). These meetings granted a stronger role to heads of government, but some suggested that this came at the expense of the Council of Ministers (Closa 2012).

The importance of national-level leadership was also evident in the renewed significance of Franco-German or unilateral German leadership after 2010. Certainly, the alliance of German Chancellor Angela Merkel and French President Nicolas Sarkozy was an important driver of policy in 2010 and 2011, encapsulated by the European press in the sobriquet 'Merkozy' (see, for instance, Wolf 2011). While the two countries had generally aligned along different poles of the above-mentioned 'austerity-growth debate', these leaders reached agreement that some form of further fiscal co-ordination and integration was of central importance to resolving the crisis. For the most part Merkel managed to persuade Sarkozy of the importance of her economic discipline agenda, and it was agreement between these two leaders which seemed to pave the way to the TSCG (see Insight 11.2) and a number of other reforms geared towards greater fiscal discipline and co-ordination.

However, the election of François Hollande to the French Presidency in 2012 led to the emergence of more pronounced differences in the French and German positions. Hollande, a socialist and much more closely aligned with the pro-growth position (and thus with southern 'debtor' member states) than his predecessor, had been outspoken in his critique of the TSCG and called for greater measures to promote economic growth. He had also championed the notion of 'eurobonds', a policy vehemently opposed by Merkel. Eurobonds would amount to some form of collectivization of sovereign debt within the eurozone, reducing the costs of debt refinancing for 'debtor' member states but increasing it for 'creditor' states, including Germany. He had also sought to promote a European Banking Union (EBU), which Germany had not prioritized, partly because of concerns relating to its own local and regional banking sector but also to avoid the prospect of bailing out other states' banks. While Hollande found some support for his agenda in the European Commission, as of 2014 it had for the most part failed to materialize (for further discussion, see Chapter 21, The Eurozone Crisis). According to some analysts, the weakening of the Franco-German relationship, coupled with the steep decline in the French economy, reinforced unilateral German leadership (Closa 2012). Throughout the period a number of observers discussed the increasing significance of Germany—by far the EU's leading economic power—as an unrivalled 'hegemon' within the EU. A special report on Germany by *The Economist* (June 2013) claimed that, 'in Beijing or Washington DC, the question: "Where is Europe going?" has become synonymous with: "What do the Germans want?"'. To the extent that German preferences were reflected in various European Council positions and in the prevalent reform agenda—emphasizing rules and economic discipline—the concept of German hegemony was at least partially accurate.

That said, what might be regarded as a German 'orthodox' line on economic discipline did not always prevail and the German government itself demonstrated flexibility in this respect (as arguably it had to in order to safeguard the euro). For instance, Germany supported the ESM support facility and tacitly endorsed ECB activism of the sort highlighted above, despite domestic opposition to both of these initiatives. Such opposition was manifest in two cases brought before Germany's Federal Constitutional Court, the first of which focused on whether the ESM violated the German Parliament's sovereignty in budgetary matters and the second of which challenged the ECB's OMT policy (see this chapter, The Unfolding Eurozone Crisis). In the first case, in September 2012 the Constitutional Court gave its qualified endorsement for the ESM. However, its February 2014 ruling in the second case was highly critical of the ECB's Outright Monetary Transaction (OMT) policy, judging it to represent a significant threat to German fiscal sovereignty and democracy. According to some commentators, the decision made it very unlikely that the ECB would be able to deploy OMT (Münchau 2014). At the time of writing the full implications of this decision remained to be seen.

The German government had to navigate a difficult line between appeasing more 'orthodox' domestic interests—which were, among other things, calling for greater economic discipline from others and seeking to limit Germany's financial commitments—and the imperative of safeguarding the euro (and EU), which at times required discretionary, even 'emergency', crisis management that did not fit with the orthodoxy. Given the weight of these competing demands, it is perhaps appropriate to describe Germany as a 'reluctant' hegemon in the EU context (Bulmer and Paterson 2013). Despite some domestic opposition, Merkel was very successful in maintaining her domestic popularity, thanks in large part to the perception that she was responsible for Germany's relatively favourable economic environment. In the September 2013 elections—which held particular significance for the entire EU—her Christian Democrat (CDU/CSU) party secured their strongest result since 1990 and came very close to securing an outright majority for the first time since 1957. After over two months of negotiations the new coalition government was announced in December 2013, bringing together the CDU/CSU and the Social Democrats (SPD). The coalition agreement made little mention of the eurozone crisis, but it did rule out eurobonds. Still headed by Merkel, and with Finance Minister Wolfgang Schäuble retained in post, the coalition seemed set on continuity in dealing with the eurozone crisis.

This analysis of national government power in the crisis context is not to suggest that EU institutions were sidelined. The reforms put in place by governments delegated new responsibilities to such institutions, particularly the Commission in terms of its increasing oversight of national economies (as discussed in Chapter 21). And, as noted, the ECB became an active and arguably critical participant in crisis management.

Other Developments

Elections and Appointments

In the period under consideration two elections to the European Parliament took place, in June 2009 and May 2014.

Due to the delay with the ratification of the Lisbon Treaty, the 2009 elections took place under the existing rules, meaning that 736 MEPs were elected rather than the 750 provided for in the new Treaty. The main feature of these elections was that turnout was again down—from 45.6 per cent in 2004 to 43.2 per cent in 2009. This was the lowest turnout since direct elections began thirty years earlier and added further weight to concerns about the contribution of the EP to the Union's democratic legitimacy.

In 2010, José Manuel Barroso secured a second five-year term as President of the Commission. His reappointment had faced some opposition within the EP, most notably from the Greens and some MEPs on the left, but his case was helped by a strengthening of centre-right parties in the EP elections of June 2009. The new Commission as a whole was approved by a vote in the EP on 9 February 2010, but the process was not without incident.

The proposal of Michel Barnier, a former French Foreign Minister and ally of President Sarkozy, as Internal Market Commissioner was controversial in some circles because it promised stricter regulation of financial services. In particular, the UK government had concerns that this might undermine the City of London as a financial centre. The deal struck involved a British official becoming the leading civil servant in the Directorate (Traynor 2009). Another proposed Commissioner, the Bulgarian, Rumiana Jeleva (International Co-operation, Humanitarian Aid, and Crisis Response), performed poorly during the hearings and was subsequently replaced as the Bulgarian nominee.

In May 2014 751 MEPs were elected to the EP (750 plus a president) for the first time, in accordance with the Lisbon Treaty rules. Turnout was similar to the 2009 elections at around 43 per cent. Eurosceptic and non-mainstream political parties enjoyed electoral success in a number of member states. Of particular note, the right-wing Front National (FN) won the largest share of the vote in France (25 per cent), as did the UK Independence Party (UKIP) in the UK (27 per cent). Notwithstanding these significant advances for Eurosceptic parties, in terms of overall numbers of seats the large party groups remained the dominant forces in the EP (see Chapter 15 for further information on the EP's composition, and for details of the Commission appointed following the 2014 EP elections see online resources).

External relations and Enlargement

On 1 July 2013, Croatia became the twenty-eighth member of the EU (see Chapter 27). Twelve Croatian MEPs were elected in spring 2013 and joined the EP from July. Neven Mimica, a former deputy prime minister of Croatia, became Commissioner for Consumer Protection. Under the weighted voting system in the Council of Ministers, Croatia was allocated seven votes (see Chapter 14). The membership prospects of other Western Balkan states improved throughout the period, with Montenegro and Serbia beginning accession negotiations in 2010 and 2014 respectively and Albania applying for membership in 2009. Negotiations with Turkey, which had begun in 2005, slowed during the period, officially as a result of its continued non-recognition of Cyprus, but also because of some renewed scepticism within both the EU and Turkey with regard to its European vocation (see Chapter 27, Turkey).

Particularly notable with respect to Serbia's progress was the important role played by Catherine Ashton—the 'High Representative of the Union for Foreign Affairs and Security Policy'—in successfully brokering a deal over the Kosovo issue in 2013 (see Chapters 26 and 27). The EU was active in other areas of external relations, notably in response to a number of events that took place during this period. These included the series of revolutions that unfolded in the Middle East from 2010 in the context of the so-called 'Arab Spring'; the thawing of relations between Iran and the West after 2013; and the upheavals in the Ukraine prompted by its government's decision, domestically unpopular, to turn its back on an EU association agreement in 2013 and pursue closer ties with Russia. The EU's effectiveness as a foreign policy actor in these different contexts has varied, as discussed in greater detail in Chapter 26.

Europe 2020

In 2010, the EU launched its 'Europe 2020' strategy as the successor to the Lisbon Strategy/Agenda (see Chapter 10, The Lisbon Strategy). Like its predecessor, it focused on promoting jobs and growth. Framed in the context of the then-emerging crisis, the Europe 2020 strategy (European Commission 2010) claimed to provide the vision required for member states to 'exit from the exceptional support measures adopted to combat the crisis'. It supported the moves towards budgetary consolidation (austerity), while emphasizing that this should be 'growth-friendly'. The strategy referred to the EU as embodying a 'social market economy' and promoted such an economy in a similar fashion to the Lisbon Strategy.

The new strategy was not simply a response to the crisis, but an attempt to reform Europe's 'growth model'. In particular, it established specific targets for governments in the areas of employment, education, research and innovation, social inclusion, and poverty reduction; and put in place a series of programmes aimed at achieving these targets. In order to make EU-level governance of this process more robust than was the case in relation to the Lisbon Strategy, the EU developed what it termed 'the European semester'. This amounted to a timetable of action for governments based on regular oversight and recommendations from the European Commission and Council. It remains to be seen whether this strategy will prove more effective than the Lisbon Strategy, which was largely judged to be unsuccessful. The difficult economic climate for member states was certainly not favourable in terms of meeting the targets that were set.

Nobel Peace Prize

In 2012, the EU was the recipient of the Nobel Prize for Peace in recognition of its role in advancing peace, reconciliation, democracy, and human rights in Europe. This was a controversial decision for many, given the ongoing crisis and the diminishing public support for the EU. Indeed, the award prompted protests from an awkward coalition of anti-EU, left wing, and peace campaigners; a group of peace prize laureates wrote a letter criticizing the award of the prize to the EU; and a number of EU leaders opted to snub the award ceremony (Higgins 2012). For others it served as an important reminder of the EU's achievements in the service of peace in Europe, which, as Nobel Committee President, Thorbjørn Jagland, said, 'should not be taken for granted'. This was the line adopted by the European leaders who collected the award. For instance, Commission President Barroso stated in his acceptance speech that, 'our quest for European unity... is not an end in itself, but a means to higher ends. In many ways, it attests to the quest for a cosmopolitan order... in which abiding by common norms serves universal values'. And 'this federalist and cosmopolitan vision is one of the most important contributions that the European Union can bring to a global order in the making' (for more on cosmopolitan thinking in relation to the EU, see Chapter 4, Critical Social Theory).

The Budget

In December 2013, EU leaders reached an agreement on a €960 billion budget for the seven-year period 2014–20. In the context of austerity within the EU, discussions over the budget were heated. While a number of net-contributor member states, including the UK, argued for a reduction in the budget, EU institutions and some net-recipient member states opposed significant cuts. The budget that was eventually agreed represented a 3 per cent reduction on the previous multi-annual budget. It was the first time that the budget had been reduced. The most notable cuts were to cohesion policy and the common agricultural policy, while investment in research and competitiveness-related activities was increased (BBC 2013).

The United Kingdom and the EU

Relations between the United Kingdom and the EU became increasingly strained following the election of a coalition government in the UK in 2010, dominated by a Conservative party that contained many 'Eurosceptic' parliamentarians. Notwithstanding the presence of the generally pro-EU Liberal Democrats in this coalition government, the UK, following the election, reinforced further its status as 'a stranger' (Wall 2008) or 'awkward partner' (George 1998), placing itself in the EU 'slow lane' (Geddes 2013). This was due in part to an increased Euroscepticism in an already Eurosceptical UK that ran parallel to the rise of the UKIP. Attentiveness to UKIP for electoral reasons in turn strengthened the hand of the Eurosceptic wing of the Conservative party. The UK government's refusal to sign up to the TSCG in December 2011 (see Insight 11.2) was illustrative of an increased Euroscepticism. The government claimed that its decision was prompted by a failure to extract concessions in relation to the regulation of financial services (House of Commons 2012), but others saw the move by Prime Minister David Cameron primarily as an attempt to appease Eurosceptic elements in the party.

Even more significantly, in January 2013 Cameron pledged that, should the Conservatives be elected in 2015, there would be a referendum before the end of 2017 on whether the UK should remain in or withdraw from the EU. The referendum would follow an attempted renegotiation of terms with the EU, which would seek to return some delegated powers to the UK. In this context, an ongoing 'review of the balance of competences'—being conducted by the UK government since July 2012 in line with a commitment made in the coalition government agreement—took on new significance. This review was an audit of what the EU does and how it affects the UK. Whether the UK would be able to renegotiate its position successfully prompted significant debate. Many pro-Europeans in the UK and elsewhere argued that these moves would find little sympathy in the EU and other member states, raising the prospect of a British exit. On the other hand, the government in Berlin was keen for the UK to remain a member because it was an important ally in certain policy areas, despite not being inside the eurozone.

It is notable that, notwithstanding these attempts by the Conservative-led government to reassure the electorate of its circumspect approach to the EU, the unambiguously anti-EU UKIP enjoyed significant electoral gains in the 2014 EP elections, as highlighted earlier.

CONCLUSION

The period following the start of the economic crisis threw up major challenges and dilemmas for the EU. It sought to preserve the eurozone through a combination of 'firefighting' and long-term reform measures (see also Chapter 21). A long-term bailout mechanism was established and a number of reforms geared towards greater fiscal discipline and EU oversight were passed, including an agreement among the majority of member states on an intergovernmental treaty outside of EU law (see Insight 11.2). However, the effects of the crisis prompted widespread political and public dissatisfaction.

In this chapter the political fault lines of the crisis were considered in terms of two overlapping debates: one related to the economic reasoning on the causes of and solutions to the crisis, and one related to the extent of EU power vis-á-vis national governments. Various tensions emerged as a consequence of these debates: between 'creditor' and 'debtor' eurozone states, between populations and governments; and between eurozone and non-eurozone EU member states. The crisis brought to the fore long-standing questions—pertinent to the history described throughout these chapters and much debated among theorists of integration (see Chapter 1)—about which actors are most important in the EU. While member state governments led the way in terms of responses to the crisis, new powers were delegated to EU institutions throughout this period and the ECB sought to broaden its remit, albeit controversially. It remained unclear at the time of writing (early 2014) whether supranational institutions would be able to exercise their authority effectively in national contexts where the economic situation remained difficult.

While the crisis breathed new life into some old debates, it also illustrated the importance of questions emanating from beyond the mainstream EU literature (see Table I.1). It prompted the posing of fundamental questions about the nature of European political economy: what were the key ideas and agendas that dominated economic and monetary thinking prior to and during the crisis and who were the winners and losers from such agendas (see Chapter 4, Critical Political Economy)? It also raised questions in relation to democratic legitimacy: in particular, to what extent does the EU undermine national democracy and self-determination (see Chapter 3, Democracy)?

We should not understate the significance of the latest crisis or underestimate its potential consequences, which at the time of writing (early 2014) remained unclear (see Webber 2014). However, it should be clear to readers of these history chapters that 'crises' of various sorts have accompanied the process of integration from its inception, and EU institutions, and the interdependencies that they create, are not easily or quickly dismantled. Indeed, as discussed in this chapter, even during this crisis the EU engaged in much 'business as usual' in terms of its budget, foreign policy, and enlargement. Member states even continued to join the euro amidst the crisis (for instance, Latvia in 2014). It is this 'business as usual' which provides the focus for much of the rest of this book and certainly the following section on EU institutions.

KEY POINTS

The Unfolding Eurozone Crisis

- The eurozone crisis dominated EU business after 2010. Its effects were acutely felt in several 'debtor' member states in the eurozone. These states were the recipients of a series of bailouts from other EU member states and the IMF. The bailouts required 'debtor' states to make significant budgetary cuts and pursue policies of austerity.
- The ECB carved an important role for itself in crisis management, pledging to 'do whatever it takes to preserve the euro'.

Crisis Politics

- The crisis prompted two inter-related debates: an economic debate and a debate on further integration.
- The economic debate pitted those advocating an 'ordo-liberal' approach geared towards economic discipline—including 'creditor' states and, in particular, Germany—against those advocating a 'Keynesian' approach of economic growth and consumption—including most 'debtor' states.
- Those supporting further integration had different visions of what that should look like depending on their position within the economic debate. Advocates of economic discipline tended to emphasize the importance of harder supranational rules and oversight to underpin such discipline. Advocates of growth often argued for reforms that would require greater solidarity and amount to greater political union.
- At the same time, the crisis fuelled Euroscepticism throughout the EU and reduced popular support for further integration of any kind.

Power in crisis EU

- Member states played a central role in driving reforms, even as they delegated new powers to supranational actors such as the Commission. As the largest and economically strongest eurozone state, Germany played a particularly significant role, albeit at times reluctantly.

- While German preferences for economic discipline prevailed to a large extent in the reform agenda, Germany supported (both politically and financially) the bailout programmes and accepted ECB interventions (albeit with important conditions attached). That said, significant actors in Germany challenged the legality of these policies.

Other Developments

- Despite the crisis, other 'business as usual' continued in the period, with European Parliament elections in 2009 and 2014. The latter saw electoral success for a number of non-mainstream and Eurosceptic political parties.

- A further enlargement to include Croatia took place in 2013.

- In 2010, the EU launched its replacement to the Lisbon Strategy; 'Europe 2020', aimed, in particular, at reforming the European model of growth.

- In 2012, the EU was awarded the Nobel Peace Prize.

- The UK coalition government, led by an increasingly Eurosceptic Conservative Party, adopted a series of measures that raised doubts about the UK's future relationship with the EU.

FURTHER READING

We are dealing in this chapter with very recent history, meaning that academic material covering the period is still limited. For reading relating to the crisis, see also Chapter 21.

For a discussion of the possible trajectory of the EU following the eurozone crisis, see the debate on the future of the euro between **B. J. Cohen** and **H. Schwartz**, in *Review of International Political Economy*, 19, 4 (2012): 689–710. On the role of Germany in the context of the crisis, see, **S. Bulmer and W. Paterson**, 'Germany as the EU's Reluctant Hegemon? Of Economic Strength and Political Constraints', *Journal of European Public Policy*, 20, 10 (2013): 1387–405.

A recent contribution on the UK's relationship with the EU which covers some of the period discussed in this chapter is offered by **A. Geddes**, *Britain and the European Union* (Basingstoke, Palgrave Macmillan, 2013).

 online resource centre **Visit the Online Resource Centre that accompanies this book for links to more information: http://oxfordtextbooks.co.uk/orc/bache4e/**

Part Three
Institutions

Theories derived both from international relations (IR) and from the analysis of domestic policy making include positions that emphasize the importance of institutions. In the IR literature on international regimes, there is an emphasis on institutions as 'persistent and connected sets of rules (formal and informal) that prescribe behavioural roles, constrain states, and shape expectations' (Keohane 1989: 3). In the 'new institutionalist' approaches to the study of domestic policy making, there is a similar emphasis on the importance of institutions, broadly defined. In short, *institutions matter*, although not only institutions matter, nor is it only formal institutions that matter. However, to understand the politics of the European Union it is necessary to know something about the nature of the formal institutions and the relationships between them. The long-standing debate between intergovernmentalist and neofunctionalist accounts of integration is reflected in assessments concerning which of the institutions are most influential.

There are six chapters in this part of the book. The opening chapter on 'The Institutional Architecture' provides essential introductory information on the institutions, the treaties, the legislative and budgetary processes, and other broad features. It presents the context within which the institutions operate, and provides background to understanding the debates that are presented in later chapters.

For most of the rest of this part of the book, the choice of which subjects to include was straightforward. Traditionally, the EU has had four 'main' institutions: the Commission, the Council of Ministers, the European Parliament, and the European Court of Justice. The Lisbon Treaty gave the *European Council* separate status from the *Council of Ministers*. The European Council is now considered more fully, but, because of the similarities in its make-up, it is considered within the same chapter as the Council of Ministers. All five of the main institutions are therefore treated in detail. The final chapter in this part deals with 'Organized Interests', the interaction of which with the formal institutions is a central component of the EU's decision-making process.

Chapter 12
The Institutional Architecture

Chapter Overview

Up to now, this book has introduced the institutions of the European Union (EU) only as part of the history of European integration, and their powers have only been briefly outlined. To understand the debates that surround the institutions themselves, though, it is necessary to understand in more detail their powers and their roles in relationship to one another. The same material is needed to understand the debates around the various policies of the EU, which are the subject of Part Four of the book.

This chapter examines the pattern of institutions and the formal rules that govern them. It also gives information on the composition of the less-important institutions, although for the main ones—the Commission, the Council of Ministers (or 'Council') and the European Council, the European Parliament (EP), and the Court of Justice of the European Union (CJEU)—that information is provided in the separate chapters devoted to them.

The chapter starts with a review of the Treaties that form the founding 'constitutional' documents of the EU. The main institutions involved in the processes of decision making are then introduced. Decision making is examined, covering both the budgetary and legislative procedures. Brief consideration is also given to the different decision-making process on foreign and security policy. The chapter then looks at the implementation of decisions once they have been made. Finally, the chapter returns to some broader considerations relating to the post-Lisbon institutional architecture.

The Treaties

The EU is governed by Treaty. Specifically, since the implementation of the Lisbon Treaty in December 2009, it has been governed by two Treaties: the Treaty on European Union (TEU) and the Treaty on the Functioning of the European Union (TFEU). In order to understand the current arrangements, it is necessary to look at the evolution of Treaty provision.

There were three 'founding Treaties'—the Treaty of Paris (1951) and the two Treaties of Rome (1957) (see Chapter 6, The European Coal and Steel Community, and The Road to the Rome Treaties). They were supplemented in ways that affected the powers of the institutions by three further Treaties in the 1960s and early 1970s. One merged the Councils and the Commissions of the three Communities, while the other two were concerned with budgetary provisions. After the last of these, in 1975, there were no further major revisions of the Treaties for another decade, but then there were four new Treaties in the next fifteen years: the Single European Act (SEA); the Maastricht Treaty; the Amsterdam Treaty; and the Nice Treaty (see Box 12.1). Leaving aside the Treaty of Paris, which expired in 2002, and the Euratom Treaty, which maintains its separate status, by 1997 the Treaties had been consolidated into two: the TEU, and the Treaty establishing the European Community (TEC). The Constitutional Treaty, agreed at the Brussels European Council on 18 June 2004, was designed to consolidate the existing Treaties into one. However, following its abandonment in 2005, the somewhat more modest Lisbon Treaty made revisions to the existing Treaties (see Chapter 10, The Lisbon Treaty,). However, it also renamed the TEC the TFEU. Although more modest than the Constitutional Treaty that was originally planned, the Lisbon Treaty was very important. First of all, it changed the general organization (or architecture) of the EU in a way comparable with the earlier Maastricht Treaty. Second, it included many amendments to the existing Treaties.

The Maastricht Treaty had introduced a structure consisting of three 'pillars': the EC pillar, governed by the TEC; and two intergovernmental pillars, covering the Common Foreign and Security Policy (CFSP) and Justice and Home Affairs (JHA) (see Figure 12.1), governed by the TEU. Subsequent amendments, made by the Treaties of Amsterdam and Nice, scaled back the policies covered by the JHA pillar by moving some to the EC pillar. However, the CFSP remained distinctively intergovernmental. This three-pillar structure was an important part of the EU's functioning from 1993 to 2009. However, it was abolished as of December 2009. The CFSP remains distinctively intergovernmental, but all other policies are consolidated into a single order governed by the TFEU.

The staff of the EU institutions constantly refer to the Treaties. They are always careful to check the Treaty base of any action that they take. In the Preamble of any

---

Box 12.1 The Treaties

- The Treaty of Paris (signed 1951; took effect 1952) created the European Coal and Steel Community (ECSC)

- The two Treaties of Rome (signed 1957; took effect 1958): the first created the European Atomic Energy Community (Euratom); the second created the European Economic Community (EEC)

- The Treaty Establishing a Single Council and a Single Commission of the European Communities, also known as the Merger Treaty (signed 1965; took effect 1967)

- The Treaty Amending Certain Budgetary Provisions of the Treaties (1970)

- The Treaty Amending Certain Financial Provisions of the Treaty (1975)

- The Single European Act (signed 1986; took effect July 1987)

- The Maastricht Treaty (signed 1992; took effect November 1993), which introduced the Treaty on European Union (TEU)

- The Treaty of Amsterdam (signed 1997; took effect 1999)

- The Treaty of Nice (signed 2001; took effect 2003)

- The Lisbon Treaty (signed 2007; took effect December 2009)

- The Treaty on Stability, Co-ordination and Governance in EMU (signed 2012; took effect January 2013)

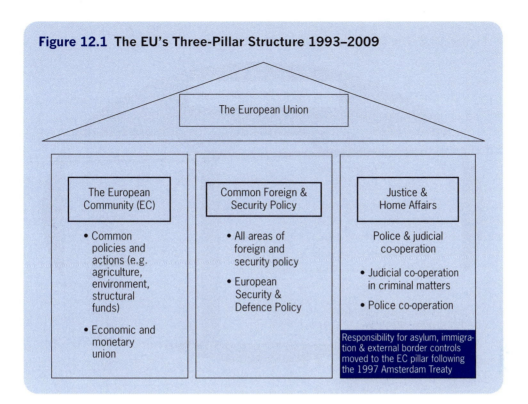

Figure 12.1 The EU's Three-Pillar Structure 1993–2009

The European Union

The European Community (EC)

- Common policies and actions (e.g. agriculture, environment, structural funds)
- Economic and monetary union

Common Foreign & Security Policy

- All areas of foreign and security policy
- European Security & Defence Policy

Justice & Home Affairs

- Police & judicial co-operation
- Judicial co-operation in criminal matters
- Police co-operation

Responsibility for asylum, immigration & external border controls moved to the EC pillar following the 1997 Amsterdam Treaty

legislative proposal, the Commission is formally obliged to state under which Article of the Treaties it is making the proposal. This incessant engagement with the text of the Treaties has led to the internal discourse of the institutions being peppered with references to Articles of the Treaties, usually just citing them by number.

However, as the founding Treaties were amended and added to by the later ones, the numbering grew more and more complex, with letters having to be used in addition to numbers. Finally, at Amsterdam in June 1997, the heads of government agreed to renumber the Articles and consolidate all revisions to the original Rome Treaty on the European Economic Community (EEC) in the TEC. The other Treaties, including the TEU, were kept separate. The Lisbon Treaty repeated this renumbering exercise. In the book we use the Treaty Article numbers following the Lisbon Treaty revisions, occasionally followed by the old one in brackets where it is relevant. Where the reference is purely historical, the numbering prevailing at the time is given first followed by the current, 'post-Lisbon' numbering in brackets. In all cases, the reference is to what is now called the TFEU (previously the TEC), unless it is indicated that it is to the TEU.

The key distinction between these two Treaties is as follows. The TEU sets out:

- the broad principles governing the EU, such as its commitment to democracy;
- the general role of the institutions;
- the principles governing who may apply to join the EU;
- how a member state may leave the EU (a provision that was introduced by the Lisbon Treaty).

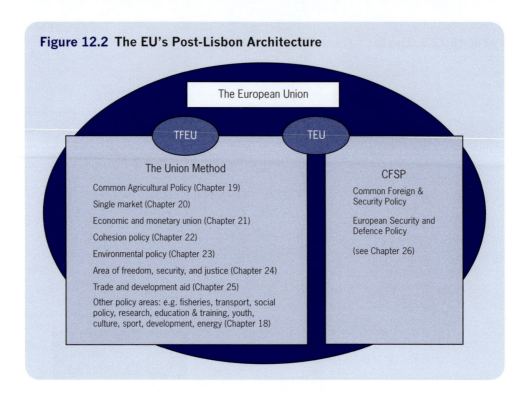

Figure 12.2 The EU's Post-Lisbon Architecture

It also sets out the details of the operation of the CFSP, making clear that its location in this Treaty designates it as not subject to the full authority of the Court of Justice. The TFEU, by contrast, sets out the detailed operation of the institutions and of all other policy areas. In what follows, the arrangements covered by the TFEU will be termed the **Union method**. As an indication of the scale of the revisions made by the Lisbon Treaty, over sixty revisions were made to the TEU and nearly 300 were made to the TEC in addition to renaming it the TFEU (see Figure 12.2).

The Decision-Making Institutions (the Union Method)

Following ratification of the Lisbon Treaty, the most logical way in which to understand the decision-making institutions is to consider first of all the Union method. Later in the chapter, we consider the arrangements for CFSP. With one exception, the main decision-making institutions of the EU central to the Union method are those that were set up in the Treaty of Rome (EEC):

- the Commission;
- the Council of Ministers;
- the European Parliament (EP).

The exception is the European Council. This body was set up in 1974 and has grown in importance, but the Treaties did not spell out its operation in detail until the Lisbon Treaty.

In addition to the main institutions there are also two consultative committees:

1. the Economic and Social Committee, which was in the original Treaty of Rome (EEC), and which in 2002 became the European Economic and Social Committee (EESC) following the incorporation within it of the formerly independent Consultative Committee of the European Coal and Steel Community (ECSC);

2. the Committee of the Regions (CoR), which was established in 1994 under provisions in the Maastricht Treaty.

Under the Union method, just as in CFSP, the European Council should be seen as the main agenda-setter of the EU. Either through overseeing Treaty reform or through identifying policy strategy, it steers the broad direction of integration and of individual policies. However, it does not legislate. In legislation, it is the European Commission that plays the initial role. It is the proposer of legislation, and the Council of Ministers and the EP are the joint legislative decision makers. The EESC and the CoR also have a right to be consulted on legislative proposals. Implementation of legislation once it has been passed is partly a responsibility of the Commission, but mostly it is the responsibility of the member states. The Commission and the Court of Justice act as watchdogs to ensure that the member states fulfil their obligations.

A similar division of functions exists for budgetary decision making. The European Council agrees the multi-annual financial perspectives, setting the EU's financial envelope for a seven-year period. The Commission proposes the annual budget; the Council of Ministers and EP jointly decide on the annual budget. The Court of Justice and the Court of Auditors perform the watchdog role.

The European Council

The important agenda-setting role of the European Council has already been identified, as well as its oversight of all EU activity including CFSP. Article 15 TEU states:

> The European Council shall provide the Union with the necessary impetus for its development and shall define the general political directions and priorities thereof. It shall not exercise legislative functions.

This latter sentence is important, since it makes a clear delineation of responsibilities between the European Council and the Council of Ministers. While this is a functional distinction—the European Council plays a political role while the Council of Ministers plays a legislative one—the other essential difference is of composition. The European Council comprises the EU's top political figures: the heads of state and government of the twenty-eight member states, the President of the European Council, the President of the European Commission, and the EU's High Representative for Foreign Affairs and Security Policy. By contrast, the Council of Ministers comprises regular ministers. Fuller discussion of the membership of both bodies is undertaken in Chapter 14, but the key point here is that the European Council represents the EU's summit of member-government power and has the political clout to drive forward the EU's agenda. The European Council has effectively positioned itself at the apex of the European Union, guiding the direction of all EU policies. In practical terms, this situation means that legislation and other decision making typically takes place in a context that the European Council may have already shaped.

The Commission

In the formal decision-making system of the EU, the Commission has two important roles (see Figure 12.3). It submits legislative proposals to the Council of Ministers, and it draws up the draft annual EU budget for agreement by the Council of Ministers and the EP.

The Commission is formally the sole institution with the right to propose legislation. In the view of the Commission, it is only its monopoly of the right of initiative that allows a coherent agenda to emerge for the EU as a whole. However, even leaving aside its limited authority in CFSP, there are several qualifications to its exclusive right to initiate proposals. First, as noted, the European Council—the EU summit meetings—sets out the EU's strategy and *may* therefore set the agenda that the Commission then follows in terms of specific legislation. Second, as a legacy of the situation relating to JHA under the three-pillar EU structure from 1993 to 2009, the Commission shares the right of initiative in measures relating to police and judicial co-operation (see Chapter 24).

The Commission's exclusive right to initiate legislation was also somewhat undermined by an amendment made under the Maastricht Treaty. Under Article 225 TFEU, the EP 'may, acting by a majority of its component Members, request the Commission to submit any appropriate proposal on matters on which it considers that a Union act is required for the purpose of implementing the Treaties'. Given that the democratic legitimacy of the EP has been increasingly emphasized, it would be difficult for the

Figure 12.3 Decision-Making Institutions of the EU (Post-Lisbon Powers)

EUROPEAN COMMISSION
Initiates legislation
Drafts annual budget

COUNCIL OF MINISTERS
Decision-making powers
Joint budgetary authority

EUROPEAN PARLIAMENT
Co-decision powers
Consent powers
Consultation
Joint budgetary authority

CoR & EESC
Consulted
Issue Opinions

Commission to ignore such a request. Mirroring this power, the 'Council acting by a simple majority may request the Commission to undertake any studies the Council considers desirable for the attainment of the common objectives, and to submit to it any appropriate proposals' (Article 241 TFEU). Finally, even in the areas in which it retains the full right of initiative, to say that the Commission is the sole proposer of legislation should not be taken to imply that it works on legislative proposals in isolation. In practice, it has always consulted widely with interest groups, committees of technical experts, and civil servants from the member states. Nevertheless, despite the qualifications to its right of initiative, the standard practice is that the Commission initiates legislation and this is a powerful role in the legislative process.

The Commission's legislative proposals can only be amended by the Council of Ministers if the latter acts unanimously, and the Commission may withdraw or amend its own proposals at any stage as long as the Council has not acted on them. However, where the EP has the right of co-decision with the Council, and where the Council and the EP cannot agree on the text presented by the Commission, they may agree an alternative in a Conciliation Committee that can be passed without unanimity in the Council (see this chapter, Decision-Making Procedures). The alternative does not have to be proposed by the Commission.

The Council of Ministers (the Council)

The Council of Ministers consists of representatives of the member states. Most meetings in the Council structure are not of Ministers themselves, but of various committees of member state officials (see Chapter 14, COREPER and other Preparatory Bodies). Nearly all business for the meetings of Ministers is filtered through such committees, and then through the Committee of Permanent Representatives (COREPER), which consists of the ambassadors from the member states to the EU (see Chapter 14, COREPER and other Preparatory Bodies).

The Council makes decisions on proposals from the Commission either unanimously or through **qualified majority voting (QMV)** depending on the Treaty provision. As was explained in Chapter 7, The 1965 Crisis, in 1965 de Gaulle blocked the formal transition to QMV, but the SEA introduced it for legislative acts related to the single-market programme, and it has been extended at every subsequent Treaty reform to cover a range of other policies. The TEU's Article 16(3), as revised by the Lisbon Treaty, presented QMV as the default provision for decision making: 'The Council shall act by a qualified majority except where the Treaties provide otherwise.' There were quite a large number of new provisions for QMV in the Lisbon Treaty but quite a lot of them are limited in scope. The key moves to QMV were on energy security, emergency humanitarian aid, intellectual property, social security for migrant workers, and judicial co-operation (the last after a five-year transition period that expired in 2014) (see Box 12.2). The key areas that remain subject to unanimity are: tax; social security; foreign policy; common defence; operational police co-operation; language rules; and the location of the EU's institutions.

Two additional points are worth noting about the extension of QMV in the Lisbon Treaty. First, the Treaty provided for some institutional matters to be decided by QMV in the European Council—for instance, when deciding its own President or in proposing to the EP a candidate for the President of the European Commission. These

> ### Box 12.2 Policy Areas Covered by Qualified Majority Voting
>
> **The Maastricht Treaty extended QMV to:**
>
> - environment
> - development co-operation
> - the free movement of workers
>
> **In the Treaty of Amsterdam, QMV was extended to:**
>
> - freedom of establishment
> - equal pay and treatment of men and women
> - mutual recognition of qualifications
> - the framework programmes for research and development
> - the internal market
> - public health
> - access to official documents
> - consumer protection
> - combating fraud
> - co-ordination of national provisions on the treatment of foreign nationals
> - customs co-operation
>
> **The Lisbon Treaty extended QMV to:**
>
> - energy security
> - emergency humanitarian aid
> - social security for migrant workers
> - intellectual property
> - specific areas of judicial and police co-operation (with effect from 2014)
>
> QMV also applies to the implementation of a range of policy areas.

changes were an important innovation for the summit meetings, which had traditionally reached decisions by unanimous consent. Second, the Lisbon Treaty introduced potentially significant provisions for further moves to QMV without the need for treaty revision. By including so-called *passerelle* **clauses**, it is possible to move some policy areas to QMV, notably on CFSP (but not defence-related matters), the multi-annual financial framework, employment law, environmental taxation, and judicial co-operation on family law. In each case the European Council has to agree to the step by unanimity, and then in most cases has to get agreement from all national parliaments (Dougan 2008: 642). By early 2014 these clauses had not been used. Among those issues regarding which unanimity remains with no prospect of change under a *passerelle* clause are taxation, social security, citizens' rights, the location of the EU institutions, and languages.

The voting arrangements in the Council have been disputed over the history of European integration. The scheduled move to QMV was one of the triggers of the

1965 'empty chair' crisis (see Chapter 7, The 1965 Crisis). At each round of treaty reform from the Single European Act onwards there have been disagreements over which policy issues should be moved from unanimous voting to QMV. Thus, it might come as something of a surprise that despite widespread provision for QMV, the Council tends to practice consensual decision-making. According to research by Mattila (2008: 27), approximately 90 per cent of votes in the Council are uncontested. Hence the heated Treaty-reform debates related only to the principle and not necessarily to the practice of QMV.

A new voting system was provided for in the Lisbon Treaty under Article 16 (TEU) but only for introduction from November 2014. Although one of the thorniest issues in negotiations leading to the Lisbon Treaty, on the face of it the provisions under Article 16 are very straightforward. Under the new rules, a double qualified majority is introduced that requires:

- support from 55 per cent of the members of the Council comprising at least fifteen member states where voting on proposals tabled by the Commission;
- support from at least 65 per cent of the population of the EU.

A blocking minority has to include at least four member states, thereby limiting the ability of the biggest states to block measures. The figures are different for votes on proposals that were not tabled by the Commission. In that case, the qualified majority must be 72 per cent of the member states representing at least 65 per cent of the population of the EU.

This relatively simple system is rendered more complex for the period between 1 November 2014 and 31 March 2017 because the Polish government, in particular, did not want to give up its relatively influential position under the previous system that can be traced back to the Nice Treaty. In consequence, it is possible during this period for a member state that feels disadvantaged by the new system to insist on a vote also being taken under the old weighted majority system that applied up to the end of October 2014. It is difficult to anticipate at the time of writing whether this provision will be called upon, but details of the previous system are now discussed for completeness, not least because of their applicability when formal votes were called in the period up to the end of October 2014.

The weighting of votes is indicated in Table 12.1, giving the details following Croatia's accession in July 2013. These weightings were agreed at the Nice European Council in December 2000, and incorporated into the Nice Treaty to anticipate the enlargement of the EU later in that decade. This system of weighted votes can be traced back to the 1957 Treaty of Rome. However, as indicated earlier, there is a strong preference on the part of the member governments to use consensus wherever possible in order to avoid isolating states.

The European Parliament (EP)

In the original blueprint for the ECSC, Jean Monnet did not include any parliamentary body—but in an attempt to make the new community more democratic, a European Parliamentary Assembly was added to the Treaty of Paris (Diebold 1959: 62). This body was carried over into the Treaties of Rome.

Table 12.1 Weighting of National Votes under Qualified Majority Voting (until 2014)

Austria	10	Greece	12	Romania	14
Belgium	12	Hungary	12	Slovakia	7
Bulgaria	10	Ireland	7	Slovenia	4
Croatia	7	Italy	29	Spain	27
Cyprus	4	Latvia	4	Sweden	10
Czech Republic	12	Lithuania	7	United Kingdom	29
Denmark	7	Luxembourg	4		
Estonia	4	Malta	3		
Finland	7	Netherlands	13		
France	29	Poland	27		
Germany	29	Portugal	12	**TOTAL**	352

Note: When a vote was called, a qualified majority came about in the Council of Ministers under the following circumstances:

- a minimum of 260 votes was cast in favour—which was 73.9 per cent of the total; and
- a two-thirds majority of member states approved.

In addition, a member state could insist on confirmation that the votes in favour represented at least 62 per cent of the total population of the Union.

The EP has consistently tried to insert itself more effectively into the decision-making process of the EU, especially since 1979 when it became a directly elected body. Under the original process, the Council of Ministers was obliged to consult the EP before deciding on legislative proposals made by the Commission, but it could ignore the EP's opinion if it wished. This remains the case in only a very few policy areas following a series of reforms from the Single European Act to the Lisbon Treaty. In most policy areas the so-called **ordinary legislative procedure** (OLP) applies. Under the OLP, the EP, taking its decision by simple majority, co-legislates with the Council, which may decide by QMV. Under the OLP, the EP is able to block legislation altogether, an ultimate power that makes it difficult for the Council to ignore amendments proposed by the EP lest the legislation as a whole be lost. These powers are outlined under the heading 'Decision-Making Procedures' below.

The EP is formally a co-decision maker with the Council on the annual budget, and its approval is necessary for the budget to be given effect (see this chapter, Decision-Making Procedures). The other areas in which the EP has gained influence are in holding the Commission and the Council of Ministers to account, and these powers are examined in Chapter 15, Composition and Functions.

The European Economic and Social Committee (EESC)

The EESC consists of representatives of producers, farmers, workers, professionals, and of the general public. It is divided into three groups representing employers, workers, and 'various interests', although members are not obliged to join any of the groups. The 'various interests' group includes farmers, the professions, the self-employed, consumers, and environmental groups. Its 353 members are proposed by national governments and formally appointed by the Council of Ministers. They sit on the EESC in a personal capacity and formally may not be bound by any mandate or instructions from their organizations.

The main work of the EESC is carried out by its six sections, which are the equivalent of the committees in the EP. They are:

1. Agriculture, Rural Development, and the Environment;
2. Economic and Monetary Union and Economic and Social Cohesion;
3. Employment, Social Affairs, and Citizenship;
4. External Relations;
5. Single Market, Production, and Consumption;
6. Transport, Energy, Infrastructure, and the Information Society.

A secretariat-general is responsible for the EESC's administration.

The EESC is consulted on a range of issues including agricultural matters, freedom of movement for workers, the right of establishment of companies, social policy, internal market issues, measures of economic and social cohesion, and environmental policy. In addition, the Commission may consult it on any matter that it thinks appropriate; the EESC has the right to issue opinions on any matter on its own initiative.

In practice, the EESC is not particularly influential. It has become overshadowed by the EP, which has increased its legitimacy and powers significantly over the last decades as a result of direct elections and, more recently, with the growth of co-decision powers. By contrast, the EESC's powers have remained consultative and its influence has declined in comparative terms. Under the Lisbon Treaty, the EESC's term of office was extended from four to five years.

The Committee of the Regions (CoR)

The CoR was created by the Maastricht Treaty, and was given the right to be consulted on proposals that affected regional and local interests, and the right to issue opinions on its own initiative. Its members are chosen by the member states and officially appointed by the Council of Ministers. As with the EESC, they moved to a five-year, renewable term with implementation of the Lisbon Treaty. Like the EESC, it has 353 members following Croatian accession and in the same breakdown of membership (see Table 12.2).

The members, collectively known as the Assembly, participate in the work of seven specialized commissions that are responsible for drafting the CoR's opinions. The Bureau, which organizes the work of the Committee and its commissions, includes the chair, a first vice-chair, plus one vice-chair from each of the member states, elected by the members of the Assembly. They also include the chairs of the political groups. A secretariat-general is responsible for the Committee's administration.

At first sight, the CoR appears to be another incarnation of the EESC, with which it originally shared a meeting chamber and support staff. However, there is an important difference: the CoR is strongly backed by political actors of considerable influence. The CoR was created at the insistence of the German Federal government under pressure from the Länder, the regional states that make up the German federation. With the political weight

Table 12.2 Membership of the Committee of the Regions

Austria	12	Latvia	7
Belgium	12	Lithuania	9
Bulgaria	12	Luxembourg	6
Croatia	9	Malta	5
Cyprus	6	Netherlands	12
Czech Republic	12	Poland	21
Denmark	9	Portugal	12
Estonia	7	Romania	15
Finland	9	Slovakia	9
France	24	Slovenia	7
Germany	24	Spain	21
Greece	12	Sweden	12
Hungary	12	United Kingdom	24
Ireland	9		
Italy	24	**TOTAL**	**353**

and the resources of these significant political actors behind it, the CoR acquired influence on those policies of the EU that have a regional focus. The Commission therefore has every incentive to work closely with the Committee, particularly because the Commission itself has tended to favour the emergence of a 'Europe of the regions' that would break down the domination of all decision making by the central governments of the member states. So, as well as being another constraint on the freedom of action of the Commission, the CoR provides it with a potential ally against national governments.

In 2009, and linked to the momentum associated with the Lisbon Treaty, the Committee proposed a political project to 'build Europe in partnership' through its White Paper on multi-level governance (MLG) (Committee of the Regions 2009). The Committee explicitly took on the role of advocate of MLG and undertook consultation on how to embed it more strongly in its programme of work. This step bears some resemblance to the way in which the European Commission has been seen to encourage more integration through cultivated spillover (see Chapter 1, International Relations Theories of European Integration). In this case, the CoR has explicitly embraced and sought to promote the body of academic work on MLG (see Chapter 2, Multi-Level Governance).

Decision-Making Procedures

There are two types of decision-making procedure within the Union method: that for adopting the annual budget of the EU—the budgetary procedure—and the various legislative procedures. The precise workings of both procedures are usually facilitated by inter-institutional agreements.

The Budgetary Procedure

The budget demonstrates the importance of the European Council as agenda-setter. This is because the annual budget negotiations take place within a multi-annual financial framework (MFF). Proposed by the Commission, the focus of the political bargaining is in the European Council. Under the Lisbon Treaty, the MFF must also then be formally signed off by the Council of Ministers, deciding—like the European Council—by unanimity. The EP's involvement is limited to giving its consent to the Council's agreement. The current financial framework runs from 2014–20 and was agreed in 2013. Within the European Council, the United Kingdom, with support from the Netherlands and Sweden, wanted to scale back the budget proposed by the Commission and a settlement that showed real spending cuts compared to the previous period. Discussed at several European Council summits, agreement was reached in June 2013, with German Chancellor Angela Merkel acting as a broker between budget 'hawks' and those governments that were concerned about cuts to support for agricultural policy and the structural funds (see Chapters 19 and 22, respectively). The proposals still needed the consent of the EP, however, and it was keen to deploy its new powers under the Lisbon Treaty. In bargaining with the Council of Ministers, it managed to secure some detailed changes under different budget headings, some concessions on flexibility within the budget, as well as a top-up to the 2013 annual budget in order to ensure it remained in balance. The MFF for the period 2014–20 amounts to some €960 billion (in 2011 prices (and €1,083 billion in current prices)), which budget 'hawks' could present as a reduction in real terms, compared to the previous financial framework.

The annual budgetary negotiations thus take place within limits strongly influenced by the European Council, which plays no formal role in the annual process. The annual budgetary procedure was amended by the Lisbon Treaty and is now set down in Article 314 TFEU. Happily, this is a change arising from the Lisbon Treaty that brings simplification, abolishing a previous distinction between different categories of spending (see Bache and George 2006: 238–40 for the pre-Lisbon process).

The budgetary procedure begins with the Commission drawing up a preliminary draft budget, which it has to do under the Treaty by 1 September of each year, but which it normally completes by June (see Figure 12.4). The work is performed by the Budget Directorate-General in consultation with the other services of the Commission and under the supervision of the Budget Commissioner. In preparing this document, the Commission is constrained by the multi-annual budgetary framework agreements.

Once the preliminary draft budget is prepared, and agreed by the Commissioners as a whole, it is sent to the Council of Ministers, which formally has until 1 October to adopt a draft budget. Often, however, the draft budget has been adopted earlier than this. Most of the detailed work at this stage is done by the Budget Committee, a specialist body responsible to the Council. The Budget Committee is 'composed of senior officials (the "tough guys") from the national finance ministries' (Hayes-Renshaw and Wallace 2006: 43). The Council acts by QMV to adopt its position.

The draft budget is then sent to the EP, which has forty-two days either to approve the Council's position (or to take no decision), in which case the budget is approved, or to amend the Council's position, for which an absolute majority of members of the European Parliament (MEPs) is required. The Budgetary Committee of the EP takes

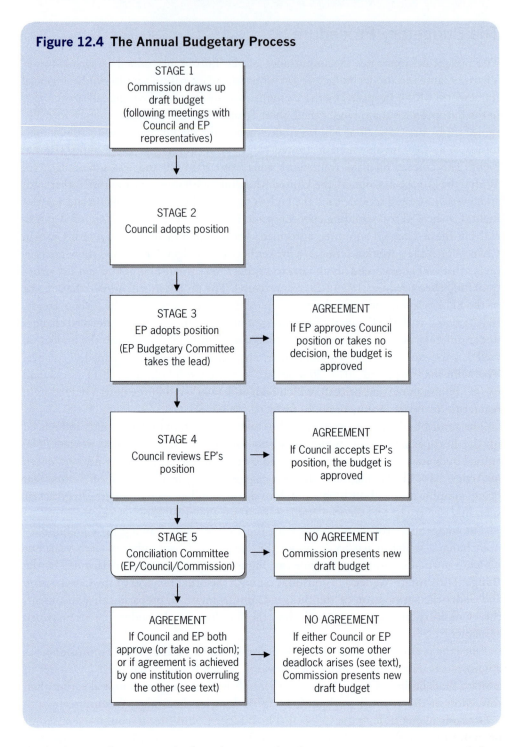

Figure 12.4 The Annual Budgetary Process

the lead, co-ordinating with the other specialized committees as necessary, and then reports to the plenary for the vote. Typically in the past, the EP has proposed a lot of amendments to the preliminary draft budget, most of which increase expenditure to the maximum permissible level. If this occurs, the draft budget goes back to the Council. The Council then has ten days to consider its response to the amendments proposed by the EP. It either then accepts the EP's amendments (by QMV), thereby adopting the budget, or rejects them, which would lead to the convening of the Conciliation Committee.

The Conciliation Committee comprises an equal number of representatives of the Council and of the EP. The Commission is also present and attempts to broker an agreement. An agreed position at this stage requires both a qualified majority on the part of the Council representatives and a majority on the part of the EP representatives. If no agreement is reached, the Commission has to present a new budget. However, if agreement is reached in the Conciliation Committee, the draft budget as amended is set for the final stage of the process.

This stage is arguably the most complex and should be read in conjunction with Figure 12.4. There are fourteen days for the EP and Council to act. If they both approve (or fail to act), the budget law is approved. If the EP adopts the budget but the Council rejects it (by QMV), the EP may decide to restore some or all of its amendments. If it can secure an absolute majority and three-fifths of the votes, the amendments are restored and the budget law is approved. If the three-fifths threshold is not met, the amendments fall and the 'conciliated' budget is passed. Symbolically, the President of the EP declares the budget to be adopted when that stage is reached. In all other circumstances, which includes the Council adopting the budget by QMV but the EP rejecting by absolute majority, the budget falls and the Commission has to present a new proposal.

If no budget has been agreed by the 1 January start of the financial year, the EU has to operate on a system known as 'provisional twelfths'. This means that, each month, one-twelfth of the previous year's budget total is released to cover expenditure. This will obviously prove cumulatively more restrictive as the year progresses, and in particular it will mean that new programmes, which had no budget line the previous year, will not be able to begin operation. Although there was the possibility of the 'provisional twelfths' regime being used for the 2011 budget, agreement was eventually reached after brinksmanship over the first use of new Lisbon Treaty provisions.

As revised in the Lisbon Treaty, the budget process has given more powers to the EP. In addition, detailed parts of the process were revised, including the functioning of the Conciliation Committee. The new arrangements draw on experience with the co-decision process for legislation (see below). The annual process has also depended on some ground rules. These have taken the form of an inter-institutional agreement. A new such agreement was under discussion in 2010 following the implementation of the Lisbon Treaty. These agreements govern how the three institutions (Commission, Council, and EP) work together as well as a wide range of technical issues. They are designed to help decision making in the process, such as the agreement in November 2013 at Stage 4 of Figure 12.4 on the 2014 budget.

The pattern of EU budgetary expenditure can be seen in Figure 12.5, which shows the budget for 2013.

There is one other part to the budgetary process. Every year, the Commission is required to submit to the Council and the EP the accounts of the previous financial year. These are considered by both institutions in the light of the annual report from the Court of Auditors. The EP receives a recommendation from the Council, and in the light of this and its own deliberations, gives discharge to the Commission in respect

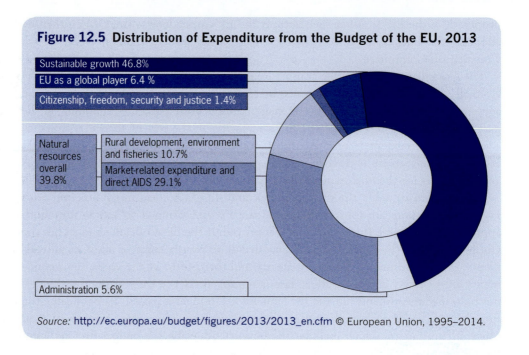

Figure 12.5 Distribution of Expenditure from the Budget of the EU, 2013

Sustainable growth 46.8%

EU as a global player 6.4 %

Citizenship, freedom, security and justice 1.4%

Natural resources overall 39.8%

Rural development, environment and fisheries 10.7%

Market-related expenditure and direct AIDS 29.1%

Administration 5.6%

Source: http://ec.europa.eu/budget/figures/2013/2013_en.cfm © European Union, 1995–2014.

to implementation of the budget. This means that the EP formally acknowledges that the Commission has implemented the budget properly and efficiently.

Legislative Procedures

The Lisbon Treaty provided some significant simplification of previous legislative procedures. It reduced the number from four to three. It also created the OLP as a default pattern. All other arrangements are termed 'special legislative procedures' but there is quite some variation between them, so the term is not of much use in this outline. The process becomes 'special' if the Council decides by unanimity and/or the EP uses the consultation or consent procedures.

The three main procedures are:

1. the ordinary legislative procedure (or co-decision) (see Figure 12.6);
2. consultation (see Figure 12.7);
3. consent.

The Ordinary Legislative Procedure (Co-decision)

Until the reforms introduced by the 1986 SEA, the EP had not really functioned as a legislative body. In other words, it had not gone through a process of scrutinizing legislation and then tabling amendments, which the Council in turn had to consider and take into account. Previously, the EP's role was restricted to giving Opinions, which the Council could simply ignore (see below). The first step away from this, introduced in the SEA, was the co-operation procedure. It entailed two readings of legislation, each followed by the Council taking a decision. The second step, one of the key changes introduced by the Maastricht Treaty into the EU's legislative process, was the co-decision procedure. Unlike the co-operation procedure, co-decision

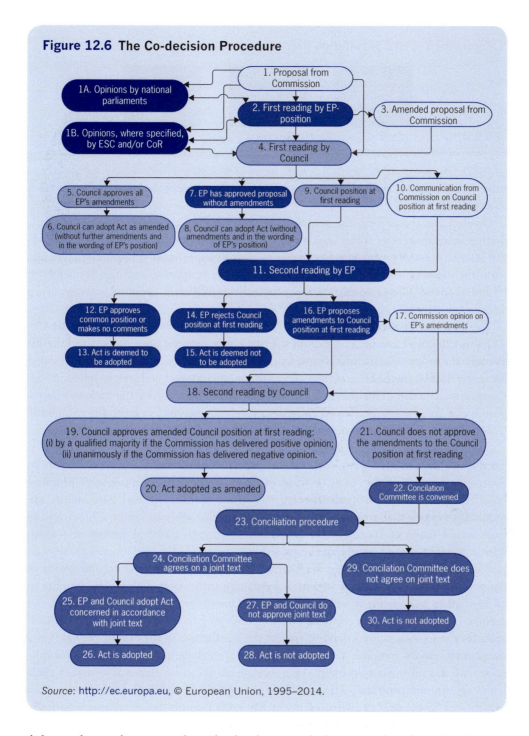

Figure 12.6 The Co-decision Procedure

1. Proposal from Commission

1A. Opinions by national parliaments

2. First reading by EP-position

3. Amended proposal from Commission

1B. Opinions, where specified, by ESC and/or CoR

4. First reading by Council

5. Council approves all EP's amendments

7. EP has approved proposal without amendments

9. Council position at first reading

10. Communication from Commission on Council position at first reading

6. Council can adopt Act as amended (without further amendments and in the wording of EP's position)

8. Council can adopt Act (without amendments and in the wording of EP's position)

11. Second reading by EP

12. EP approves common position or makes no comments

14. EP rejects Council position at first reading

16. EP proposes amendments to Council position at first reading

17. Commission opinion on EP's amendments

13. Act is deemed to be adopted

15. Act is deemed not to be adopted

18. Second reading by Council

19. Council approves amended Council position at first reading:
(i) by a qualified majority if the Commission has delivered positive opinion;
(ii) unanimously if the Commission has delivered negative opinion.

21. Council does not approve the amendments to the Council position at first reading

20. Act adopted as amended

22. Conciliation Committee is convened

23. Conciliation procedure

24. Conciliation Committee agrees on a joint text

29. Conciliation Committee does not agree on joint text

25. EP and Council adopt Act concerned in accordance with joint text

27. EP and Council do not approve joint text

30. Act is not adopted

26. Act is adopted

28. Act is not adopted

Source: http://ec.europa.eu, © European Union, 1995–2014.

did not leave the Council with the last word, but introduced a Conciliation Committee to try to reconcile differences at the end of the process. The co-operation procedure had more or less disappeared as a result of amendments in the Amsterdam Treaty, but was formally abandoned by the Lisbon Treaty, and so is not considered in detail here. However, the Lisbon Treaty made a further change by using the terminology of the OLP to designate what is now the norm in EU law making: namely, the

Figure 12.7 The Consultation Procedure

1. Commission submits proposal to Council → 2. Council seeks opinion of EP (& ESC, where required) → 3. Council makes final decision (by unanimity)

provision for QMV in the Council combined with co-decision between the Council and the EP.

Co-decision is based on the principle of parity between the EP and the Council: neither institution may adopt legislation without the other's agreement. The procedure starts informally with the Commission consulting interest groups, civil servants from the member states, and MEPs in order to gather expertise and gain feedback on its initial ideas. The Commission then formally publishes a proposal after securing internal agreement.

This step commences the first stage of the formal process as provided for in Article 294 TFEU (see Figure 12.6: boxes 1–10). In the first phase, national governments and the EP examine the proposal in their respective working groups and committees. Where provided for in the TFEU, the EESC and the CoR examine the proposal and seek to influence the Council and the EP. This role is also played through lobbying by the various interest groups that are potentially affected. Indeed, interest groups typically lobby the EP and the Council (or the individual member governments) throughout all stages of this process.

Also participating at this stage, and formalized for the first time by the Lisbon Treaty, are the national parliaments. Their specific role, under a process set out in Protocols 1 and 2 of the TEU, is to scrutinize whether the Commission's proposal breaches the principle of **subsidiarity**. In other words, national parliaments are required to check that action at EU level is appropriate and can better achieve results than action taken at the member-state level. If enough national parliaments deem within an eight-week period that the subsidiarity principle is being breached, they can play the 'yellow card' and oblige the Commission to review the proposal and decide to maintain, amend, or withdraw it, with supporting justification. This practice applies to all legislation and means in effect that the parliamentary chambers of a third of the member states must issue a 'reasoned opinion' objecting to the infringement of subsidiarity for the Commission to have to review the legislation. In the case of the OLP, if a simple majority of national parliaments continues to challenge the proposal's compliance with the subsidiarity principle, the 'orange card' can be played as a further challenge against the proposal. Their challenge is upheld if either the Council (with a majority of 55 per cent of the votes) or the EP (with a simple majority) agrees with the breach of subsidiarity, and the proposed legislation falls. In May 2012 a sufficient number of national parliaments were able, with just hours to spare, to make the first use of the yellow card on a piece of legislation that was seen as impacting on the right to strike, which the parliaments regarded as unnecessary interference from the EU (Cooper 2013). Later that year the Commission decided to withdraw the legislation. In November 2013 proposals for a European Public Prosecutor's Office were subject to a yellow card. The rules in fact require a lower threshold of only a quarter of member states' parliaments in relation to matters of freedom, security, and justice. On this occasion, parliaments in eleven states issued a reasoned opinion on the grounds of interference in their judicial systems. The orange card procedure has not been utilized hitherto and it seems difficult to envisage the circumstances where it would have to be used.

Leaving aside the (very rare) intervention of the national parliaments through the 'card' procedures, the first stage is characterized by the EP holding its first reading, and deciding to approve the proposal or suggest amendments. In the latter case, the Commission may amend its proposal if it considers the EP amendments to have improved it. If the Commission reissues the proposal, the Council may decide by QMV when it holds its first reading. If the Commission has not revised its proposal, the EP's amendments are only passed if unanimity is secured in the Council. If the EP and Council are of the same view, the legislation is adopted, and this has become the predominant pattern. Where no agreement has been reached, the Commission is given the opportunity to offer its opinion, including whether it supports the Council's common position.

This opinion commences the second phase (see Figure 12.6: boxes 11–20) comprising scrutiny by first the EP and then the Council, working on the basis of the Council's common position. Once again, it is quite likely that legislation will be agreed at this stage. However, if the EP rejects the common position, or the Council does not approve the EP's amendments, then a Conciliation Committee is set up: the third phase (Figure 12.6: boxes 22–28). The Committee consists of representatives of the twenty-eight members of the Council, and an equal number of representatives of the EP. With the help of the Commission, which acts in the role of a facilitator, the Conciliation Committee tries to negotiate a mutually acceptable compromise text, which can then be recommended to both institutions. The Committee has six weeks in which to do so, operating on the basis of QMV for the Council members and simple majority voting for the EP members. Provided that they can agree a joint text, the legislation goes back to the Council and EP for final adoption, for which a six-week period is available. The Council is likely to adopt since its delegation will have comprised a representative of each member state. However, it is more difficult to ensure that the EP delegation to the Conciliation Committee represents the whole of the EP. Hence a very small number of instances have arisen in which the EP has not approved the Committee's joint text. Along with a different scenario—namely, the failure on the part of the Committee to reach an agreement—these two sets of circumstance result in no legislation being adopted.

The Lisbon Treaty brought in three changes, which are worth reiterating here. First, national parliaments have been given powers in the early stages of the process. Second, co-decision between the Council and the EP (the OLP) has become the predominant pattern of work between the two institutions. Third, it is important to note the very close alignment of co-decision with the provision for QMV in the Council as the new normal pattern of the OLP. The second and third changes suggest a more supranational legislative process, while the first change offers the opportunity for national parliaments to intervene in the process and in rare cases (in which the requirements of the orange card can be met) to stop more legislation at EU level.

The Consultation Procedure

The original 'consultation procedure' for deciding on EU legislation involved the Commission submitting a proposal to the Council of Ministers, which was then obliged to seek the opinion of the EP, and, where required by the Treaty, of the EESC.

In the *Isoglucose* case (1980), the European Court of Justice (ECJ) ruled that the Council could not act legally in deciding on a proposal from the Commission without receiving the opinion of the EP. However, having received that opinion, the Council could, if it so wished, simply ignore it and agree to the proposal, or reject it. Amendments could only be made by unanimity in the Council. This procedure still exists, but the Lisbon Treaty has further reduced the circumstances under which it can be used to about twenty (see Figure 12.7). For example, agricultural policy, transport, the structural funds, and asylum and immigration were among the prominent policy areas in which consultation was replaced by co-decision through the revisions, thereby strengthening the EP's powers.

Consent

Prior to the Lisbon Treaty, the EP was able to block decisions under what was then known as the assent procedure. This was originally introduced for agreements with non-member states, but was extended to other policy areas through different Treaty reforms. Some policy areas assigned to the assent procedure were subsequently re-allocated to co-decision; for instance, the structural funds (as a result of the Lisbon Treaty), and citizens' rights (as a result of the Amsterdam Treaty).

The Lisbon Treaty introduced the renamed consent procedure. Its main area of application is agreements with non-member states (including to accession of new members). New areas added include some aspects of judicial co-operation as well as the multi-annual financial framework for the EU budget. Consent requires the EP's agreement for a measure to be adopted. There is no provision for the EP to amend proposals. However, the fact that its consent is required does give it considerable influence at the stage when proposals are being prepared.

Implementation

The policy process does not end once agreement has been reached on a legislative proposal. The agreement still has to be implemented before the policy has any real existence. In other words, implementation is an integral part of the policy process. For many types of legislation, the primary implementers are the governments and administrations of the member states. The Commission itself has a central role in the case of other types of legislation, and is charged by Article 17 TEU to 'ensure the application of the Treaties, and of measures adopted by the institutions pursuant to them'. In performing this latter task, the Commission has recourse to judicial authority through the referral of cases to the ECJ. Finally, the implementation of all financial instruments is subject to scrutiny by the Court of Auditors.

National Authorities and Implementation

There are three main types of EU instrument that are legally binding: decisions, directives, and regulations. Alongside these are recommendations and Opinions. They do not have legal status; they are of political significance only. The legal instruments may be legislative or non-legislative: a new distinction introduced by the Lisbon Treaty.

Hitherto, attention has focused on legislative instruments as part of an exploration of the role of the institutions in law making through the ordinary and special legislative procedures. However, non-legislative instruments (that is, those that do not go through the whole legislative process) such as European Commission rulings on competition policy do have legal force, perhaps requiring a company to pay a large fine for anti-competitive behaviour.

Much of this chapter is concerned with decision making in relation to legislative instruments, notably via the OLP (see this chapter, The Decision-Making Institutions (the Union Method)). However, before examining the specific instruments, it is important to note three areas where the work is political in nature rather than legislative and underpinned by legal instruments. First, the work of the European Council is concerned with reaching political agreements (or failing to do so) and not with legislating. Second, in CFSP (see this chapter, The Decision-Making Institutions (the Union Method)), political decisions are predominantly declaratory, making diplomatic pronouncements such as condemning states for breaching democratic principles or for aggression against other states. Legislation is unusual in CFSP, so political decisions are the norm. Finally, on some policy issues where the EU lacks clear authority (see this chapter, The Post-Lisbon Architecture of the EU), the member states may meet to exchange good practice with a view to learning from each other but without any commitment to legislate. This pattern of EU member state co-operation is known as the Open Method of Co-ordination. It has been practised particularly in the period from 2000 on a range of issues, such as combating social exclusion, raising female participation in the workforce, and, in particular, in the context of enhancing the EU's global competitiveness (the Europe 2020 initiative, see Chapter 18). The EU is thus a very political animal, although much—but by no means all—of its work is underpinned by law. Where its work is political in nature, implementation is normally a matter of 'political will' at the domestic level.

Where its work has legal underpinning, the EU system has clearer rules about implementation, depending on the legal instrument utilized. Decisions are addressed to particular individual legal actors such as companies or individual states. Directives are the most common form of general legislation agreed in the Council of Ministers; it is left to individual member states to decide *how* they are incorporated into national law. Regulations are directly applicable in all member states.

Where directives are concerned, there are two stages to implementation by national authorities. First, the directives have to be transposed into national law through appropriate national legal instruments. Second, they have to be implemented on the ground—that is, they have to be applied by national administrative authorities. Regulations do not need the extra stage of being transposed into national law through national legal instruments since they are directly applicable. However, it is still the responsibility of national administrative authorities to ensure that they are applied.

In the case of both aspects of implementation, the record of member states in actually doing what they have agreed to do varies considerably. This means that the outcomes of EU decisions are not always the same as the intention. The Commission monitors the record of member states in implementing EU law in specific areas. For example, the varying record of member states in implementing single-market legislation was recorded in the successive reports on the implementation of the Internal Market Strategy (European Commission 2004*a*, 2005*a*).

The Commission and Implementation

Formally, the Commission has overall responsibility for the implementation of EU decisions. There are several processes of implementation in the EU, in each of which the Commission has a role. First, there is the implementation of common policies that are centrally administered by the Commission itself. These are few, but some of the powers of the Commission—notably competition policy, including the control of large-scale mergers—fall under this heading. A slightly different area is the administration of international policies such as the provision of food aid, where again the Commission is the sole responsible EU body, although it has to work in conjunction with other organizations. Second, there is the implementation of common policies, which takes place partly at the European level and partly at the national level: the administration of the Common Agricultural Policy (CAP) and the structural funds come under this heading. Third, there is the implementation of Council directives, where the Commission has a dual role as guardian of the Treaties: to ensure that directives are promptly and accurately incorporated into national law in the member states, and to ensure that they are actually implemented on the ground.

Under Article 258 TFEU, if the Commission considers that a member state has failed to fulfil its obligations, it is required to deliver a reasoned Opinion on the matter after giving the government of the member state concerned the opportunity to submit its own observations. If the state does not comply with the reasoned Opinion, the matter may be brought before the ECJ. Another member state may also bring an alleged infringement of obligations to the attention of the Commission, which is required to act on the matter within three months, or the case automatically goes to the ECJ.

The European Court of Justice (ECJ)

Article 19 TEU charges the ECJ to ensure that European law is observed. It is the final arbiter on the interpretation of the Treaties and the application of EU law. As such, it is a referee in disputes between institutions and member states.

Where the ECJ is asked to rule on whether a member state has fulfilled its obligations under EU law, its decision is final. Originally there was no penalty other than moral pressure if a member state still failed to fulfil its obligations after an adverse ruling by the Court. However, the Maastricht Treaty amended Article 171 EEC (now Article 260 TFEU), to allow the Commission to return to the ECJ if it felt that a state was not complying with a ruling, and to request that a financial penalty be levied against the state.

The Court of Auditors

In 1975, the Treaty Amending Certain Financial Provisions of the EEC created a new institution: the European Court of Auditors. The Treaty confers upon the Court of Auditors the main task of auditing the accounts and the implementation of the budget of the European Union with the dual aim of improving financial management and the reporting to the citizens of Europe on the use made of public funds by the authorities responsible for their management.

The Court of Auditors is based in Luxembourg, and consists of one member from each member state appointed for a renewable six-year period. Members must have belonged to national audit offices, or be especially qualified for the office, and their independence must be beyond doubt. The members of the Court themselves elect a President from among their number for a period of three years. The court has some 850 staff, of whom about one-third are auditors.

This Court examines the accounts of all revenue and expenditure of the EU to determine whether the revenue has been received and the expenditure incurred in a lawful and regular manner. It provides the EP and the Council with a statement on the reliability of the accounts, and publishes an annual report. It also prepares special reports on aspects of the audit, either on its own initiative or at the request of another institution; it also delivers opinions on request from the other institutions concerning the financial implications of proposed legislation.

The Decision-Making Institutions (CFSP)

The 1992 Maastricht Treaty introduced a three-pillar structure. As already noted, this structure was abolished as a result of the Lisbon Treaty and the 'Union method' became the predominant character. Nevertheless, some EU activity remains subject to different arrangements: namely, the CFSP, which used to be the second pillar of the EU. Reflecting this situation, the CFSP is governed by the TEU, whereas the TFEU addresses those policy areas governed by the Union method.

The CFSP is concerned with a range of activities, such as (see also Chapter 26):

- safeguarding the common values, fundamental interests, independence, and integrity of the Union in conformity with the principles of the United Nations Charter;

- strengthening the security of the Union;

- preserving peace and strengthening international security;

- promoting international co-operation;

- developing and consolidating democracy and the rule of law, and respect for human rights and fundamental freedoms.

With the passage of the Lisbon Treaty, these objectives are now absorbed into a wider set of goals relating to the EU's external action, including trade and aid policy, which are governed by the Union method.

The Lisbon Treaty introduced the new position of High Representative of the Union for Foreign Affairs and Security Policy, a position to which (Baroness) Catherine Ashton was appointed in January 2010. The post is combined with that of Vice-President of the European Commission. The High Representative thus pulls together two strands of external action that are subject to different decision-making rules. Here, the concern is with the rules concerning foreign and security policy, but not trade, aid, enlargement, or other provisions covered by the TFEU.

CFSP is almost exclusively intergovernmental in character. In consequence, the ECJ, the Commission, and the EP are either absent or have very limited powers.

The principal actors are the European Council, the Council of Ministers (meeting as the Foreign Affairs Council), and the High Representative.

The key characteristics of decision making on the CFSP are as follows:

- The European Council is responsible for the strategic interests and objectives of the Union.
- The European Council acts unanimously on the basis of recommendations from the Council of Ministers.
- The High Representative may submit proposals to the Foreign Affairs Council on CFSP matters (and chairs this formation of the Council as well).
- The decisions under CFSP are non-legislative in nature. This makes clear that the legislative procedures considered above under the Union method are not applicable.

The CFSP is put into effect by the High Representative, who acts as an international envoy and negotiator, and by the member governments, using national and Union resources. These resources refer to the diplomatic networks of the member states, the Commission, and the Council. These networks were brought together following the passage of the Lisbon Treaty to form the European External Action Service (EEAS).

- The work of the Foreign Affairs Council is prepared by a committee of diplomats known as the Political and Security Committee.
- The High Representative consults regularly with the EP on policies under the CFSP and shall 'ensure that the views of the European Parliament are duly taken into consideration' (Article 36 TEU).

The character of the CFSP is overwhelmingly intergovernmental, requiring unanimous decisions. Because the member states were not ready to risk any surrender of control over foreign and security policy, CFSP is not subject to the Union method. Nevertheless, there are some departures from this intergovernmental pattern. First, the already-accepted practice of 'constructive abstention' may be utilized. Under this arrangement, a member government may abstain from a decision—as opposed to voting against it—and is consequently not bound by it. However, it is expected that any government in this situation will act in a spirit of solidarity and not work against the interests of the majority (Article 31 TEU). Further, there are some specific circumstances in which decision-making may be by QMV. Essentially, these circumstances relate to the operationalization of decisions already reached by unanimity, or to the appointment of special representatives. If this provision sounds like a shift towards supranationalism, it is worth bearing in mind the following safeguard clause:

> If a member of the Council declares that, for vital and stated reasons of national policy, it intends to oppose the adoption of a decision to be taken by qualified majority, a vote shall not be taken. The High Representative will, in close consultation with the Member State involved, search for a solution acceptable to it. If he [sic] does not succeed, the Council may, acting by a qualified majority, request that the matter be referred to the European Council for a decision by unanimity.

(Article 31(2) TEU)

This provision bears some relationship to the Luxembourg Compromise of 1966 (see Chapter 7, The Luxembourg Compromise), except that it only applies to the CFSP. Where QMV *is* used, the voting rules are the same as those outlined for the Union method earlier in the chapter.

Decision making under CFSP remains largely intergovernmental in character, as national governments are concerned to retain their full authority. However, the creation of the EEAS raised the possibility that diplomats across the EU and the EU institutions would, by virtue of their networked relations, develop shared understandings that may transcend the purely national perspectives that have predominated hitherto.

The Post-Lisbon Architecture of the EU

Hitherto, this chapter has been concerned with the decision-making arrangements and the key institutional players under the Union method and for CFSP. There are some other architectural considerations that need to be taken into account. These address four features that have an overarching character and impact on the EU. The first is the creation of a catalogue of competencies that sets out the balance of authority between the EU and the member states. The second relates to differentiated integration: the situation whereby not all member states participate in all of the EU's activities, such as the single currency. The third concerns the somewhat haphazard emergence of a set of 'emergency brake' procedures. The fourth is slightly different, but also relates to scattered provisions across the Lisbon Treaty, known as *passerelle* clauses, which permit future procedural changes to take place on specific matters without the need to go through the whole process of Treaty reform (see this chapter, The Decision-Making Institutions (the Union Method)). Taken together, they comprise an important set of considerations, which can bear upon the decision-making process.

Catalogue of Competencies

Behind this legal terminology is a rather simple matter: what the EU can or cannot do. This issue was shaped by the debate at the time of the Maastricht Treaty concerning subsidiarity (see this chapter, Decision-Making Procedures). The basic principle of subsidiarity is that decisions should be taken as closely as possible to citizens. Or put another way, the EU should demonstrate that it can deliver policy more effectively than the member governments (or even sub-national governments). This concern has chimed with British governments, which have consistently revealed a concern about the loss of national sovereignty. However, it has also been supported by sub-national governments, notably the German Länder, which became concerned in the run-up to the Maastricht Treaty that their national government was giving up sub-national law-making powers to the EU, thus reshaping the balance of domestic power in the German federation. This concern has never really gone away, and a catalogue of competencies was a German demand in the constitutional debate so that there could be some demarcation of what the EU can or cannot do (Bulmer 2010). Accordingly, the Lisbon Treaty spells out four types of EU competence: exclusive; shared; co-ordination; and supporting, co-ordinating, and supplementary action (see Insight 12.1). The CFSP

Insight 12.1 The EU's Catalogue of Competencies

Areas of exclusive competence

Customs union

Competition rules for the internal market

Monetary policy for those states in the eurozone

Conservation of marine biological resources under the Common Fisheries Policy

Common commercial policy

Where an international agreement is necessary to enable the Union to exercise its internal competence

Areas of shared competence

Internal market

Aspects of social policy

Economic, social, and territorial cohesion

Agriculture and fisheries (except marine conservation)

Environment

Consumer protection

Transport

Trans-European networks

Energy

Area of freedom, security, and justice

Aspects of public health safety

Research, technological development, and space

Development and humanitarian aid

Areas of policy co-ordination

Member states' economic policies

Member states' employment policies

Member states' social policies

Areas of supporting, co-ordinating, or supplementary action

Protection and improvement of human health

Industry

Culture

Tourism

Education, vocational training, youth, and sport

Civil protection

Administrative co-operation

The Common Foreign and Security Policy

The Union shall have competence ... to define and implement a common foreign and security policy, including the progressive framing of a common defence policy.

Source: Summarized from Articles 3–6 TFEU. The CFSP provisions derive from Article 2 TEU.

provisions are not included in the detailed catalogue of competencies in the TFEU because they are outside the Union method and therefore contained in the TEU.

Exclusive competencies represent the core business of the EU or what Duff (2009: 32) terms the 'lynch-pins of the *acquis communautaire*'. Most of these powers are long-standing. Two innovations were embodied in the Lisbon Treaty. First, marine conservation was made an exclusive competence of the EU, on the basis that preservation of fishing stocks would only be effective if responsibility were to lie at Union level. Second, the Lisbon Treaty slightly strengthened the competencies of the EU in external relations. The wording relating to the external authority of the EU that derives from its internal competencies was strengthened, and intellectual property and foreign direct investment were added to powers in commercial policy.

As regards areas of shared competencies, the list again mainly codifies the existing balance of authority. The main exceptions were the addition of space policy and some shifts within the environmental and energy provisions to include climate change and energy security, respectively. In areas of supporting action, there were some small additions: namely, administrative co-operation, civil protection, tourism, and sport. The catalogue of competencies forms an important component of the EU's post-Lisbon architecture. However, there are possibilities for the EU to promote co-operation between its member states even where it lacks clear authority according to the catalogue of competencies. In these areas the European Commission may simply facilitate exchanges of views between the member states through the open method of co-ordination. If a member state decides to change its policy following such exchanges, it acts within the domestic context, since there is no basis in the treaties for EU legislation.

Differentiated Integration

Differentiated integration allows for permanent or temporary arrangements whereby not all member states proceed at the same pace in all policy areas. Differentiated integration has been practised within the EU since the 1970s, notably in monetary policy. As noted already, the Maastricht Treaty provided opt-outs for the UK regarding monetary union and the social chapter, although the Labour government of Tony Blair opted into the latter in 1997 at the time of the Amsterdam Treaty. Under the Amsterdam Treaty, the UK and Ireland exercised opt-outs thereby retaining passport controls and not participating in the practices of the Schengen area (see Chapter 24). By early 2014, only eighteen of the twenty-eight member states had joined the single currency. These examples of differentiated integration developed in an ad hoc manner. However, from the Amsterdam Treaty onwards, member governments started to make general provision for core groups to proceed more quickly with integration, should they wish to do so. The official terminology for this practice is 'enhanced co-operation'.

Enhanced co-operation was introduced in the Amsterdam Treaty largely as a response to the obstructionist European diplomacy of the British Conservative government of John Major, which had a small parliamentary majority during the period 1992–97. German Chancellor Helmut Kohl was concerned at integration having to proceed at the pace of the slowest ship in the convoy. The provisions of the Amsterdam Treaty were designed to circumvent such a situation, but were quite tightly drawn and had negligible practical impact on the EU. Their basic principles were that enhanced co-operation could be used only as a last resort, needed a majority of the member states as participants, and had to allow other member states to join at a later stage. The safeguards were so tightly drawn that, according to David Phinnemore (2010: 39), it was not until 2008 that the first formal proposal was made to use these provisions.

The Lisbon Treaty has relaxed the requirements for enhanced co-operation in a number of ways. They are now governed by Article 20 TEU and Articles 326–34 TFEU. The basic principles are set out in Insight 12.2. The conditions are less onerous than before, so resort to them can be expected to be greater. In particular, it is possible for the core group to decide that it wishes to take decisions by QMV within enhanced co-operation even in a policy area in which the Treaties provide for unanimous voting for the twenty-eight states. Potentially, such a decision could then bypass provisions for an emergency brake (see below).

Had they been in existence at the time, these provisions for enhanced co-operation might well have been used in the mid-1990s to bypass the obstructionism of the then British government; it is perhaps worth bearing in mind that a **Eurosceptic** government—from whichever member state—might in future find itself marginalized, rather than being able to hold up policy making. Among recent resort to enhanced

---

Insight 12.2 Enhanced Co-operation in the EU

- Enhanced co-operation may only be practised in the EU's non-exclusive competencies (see Insight 12.1) and must follow detailed provisions in Articles 326–34 TFEU.
- Enhanced co-operation shall aim to advance the EU's objectives, protect its interests, and reinforce its integration process.
- A minimum of nine member states is needed to launch enhanced co-operation.
- Enhanced co-operation shall be open at any time to all member states.
- 'The decision authorising enhanced co-operation shall be adopted by the Council as a last resort, when it has established that the objectives of such co-operation cannot be attained within a reasonable period by the Union as a whole, and provided that at least nine Member States participate in it' (Article 20(1) TEU).
- All members of the Council may participate in its deliberations, but voting is confined to those member states participating in enhanced co-operation following rules set out in Article 330 TFEU.
- Only participating member states are bound by the resultant acts in the framework of enhanced co-operation. These acts do not form part of the *acquis communautaire*, which accession states must accept prior to membership.
- Enhanced co-operation must not undermine the internal market or economic, social, and territorial cohesion.
- Requests to move to enhanced co-operation are addressed to the Commission in the case of the Union method, and to the High Representative of the Union for Foreign Affairs and Security Policy in the case of CFSP. The Commission and High Representative give their opinion. The decision to proceed is taken by the Council of Ministers acting unanimously.
- Procedures are spelt out in the TFEU for any state wishing to join an existing group of states undertaking enhanced co-operation. In the Union method, the Commission takes a decision within four months. In CFSP, unanimous agreement is needed by the Council of Foreign Affairs, but with only the core group voting.

co-operation was the financial transaction tax—often known as the Tobin tax—which eleven member states plan to proceed to introduce, with agreement of the EP. The UK was among the opponents of the original proposal for an EU-wide tax because of concerns about its impact on the City of London. The British government has challenged the legality of the tax before the Court of Justice and, at the time of writing, it had not been introduced. Another case related to judicial co-operation in relation to divorce proceedings, approved in 2012 by fourteen member states, with Lithuania subsequently joining. The EU patent is subject to a similar process. Twenty-five member states (excluding Italy and Spain) approved the legislation in 2012 so that, once all the ratification processes were completed, a patent can be obtained with validity across all the twenty-five states. The EU patent therefore simplifies the protection of inventions compared to a system where separate approval was needed in each state.

A slightly different manifestation of differentiated integration that emerged from the eurozone crisis is the Treaty on Stability, Co-ordination and Governance in the Economic and Monetary Union, usually termed the Fiscal Compact. This treaty was signed in March 2012 and is designed to bring in stricter, EU-monitored control of public expenditure in the member states. However, it was only signed by twenty-five states, as Britain and the Czech Republic did not wish to be bound by its rules. This is a treaty version of differentiated integration, although it is not formally part of the EU's legal framework. The Fiscal Compact came into effect in January 2013 for the sixteen states that had ratified it by that stage. Other states were still ratifying the treaty that did not—unlike the EU treaties—require all states to ratify before it could take effect. Finally, Croatia is eligible to join the Compact but had not done so at the time of writing. In short, the Fiscal Compact is a further manifestation of the increasing differentiation that is perhaps an inevitable outcome of the size of the EU and the diversity of interests among the member states.

Emergency Brakes

In a very small number of policy areas, the Lisbon Treaty introduces an emergency brake. The principle is that a member government can suspend the OLP (in which it could be overruled by a QMV decision) and appeal to the European Council (Dougan 2008: 643–4). The details differ between the policy areas, but apply to the co-ordination of social security systems and judicial co-operation. An emergency brake may also be invoked in the CFSP to stop an operational decision being taken by QMV. In short, the emergency brake has emerged as a device that was built into the Lisbon Treaty where one or a small number of governments had concerns about sovereignty, but were prepared to recognize that QMV was likely to make decision making more effective in principle.

Passerelle Clauses

The idea behind a *passerelle* clause is that it provides the possibility of changing at a later stage the procedure applicable to decision making, without the need for Treaty reform. For example, in a range of policy areas, it is possible to move to the OLP from one of the special legislative procedures, thereby adding either QMV in the Council or co-decision with the EP, or both, to what the current rules specify. In all cases, the shift would be towards a more supranational set of decision-making rules. However, the *passerelle* clause requires approval by a 'super-majority': namely, the agreement of all member states in the European Council, and approval by the EP under the consent procedure. In addition, in most cases, national parliaments have six months in which to lodge an objection, otherwise the change to QMV is deemed to be approved. There are also some special cases in which a move to QMV in the Council could occur, but not to the OLP because the EP's powers remain under the consent procedure, for instance in connection with the EU's multi-annual financial framework (see Dougan 2008: 642).

The basic principle of these clauses is to enable a more efficient decision-making method to be introduced if this is an uncontroversial step, and provided that the super-majority can be achieved. The need for Treaty reform in order to make such changes is side-stepped, although the super-majority offers some comparison to the requirements of Treaty ratification. By early 2014 no use had been made of the clauses.

CONCLUSION

The Lisbon Treaty made some fundamental changes to the EU's architecture. The abolition of the three-pillar system introduced in the Maastricht Treaty provided some simplification. The creation of the default pattern of the OLP under the Union method should also help students to find their way out of what had become a procedural maze. Alas, the (very limited) use of enhanced co-operation or the possibility of deploying *passerelle* clauses does risk restoring some complexity.

So, the decision-making procedures of the EU are complex, but have generally been tidied up somewhat by the Lisbon Treaty. In theory, this tidying should lead to greater clarity over the legislative procedures to be followed on particular policy issues. In the past, the procedure to be followed was by no means immediately apparent. In such cases, the Commission could exercise some discretion in deciding under which Articles of the Treaties it would bring forward its proposals. Sometimes this was challenged. For example, in 1990, the Commission brought forward proposals on maternity rights under what was then the new Article 118A of the EEC Treaty (now Article 153 TFEU), which the SEA had introduced. This meant that the measure was subject to QMV in the Council, rather than unanimity. The British government objected to the Treaty base, and threatened to refer the matter to the ECJ, before eventually accepting a compromise solution. Nowadays, the predominance of the OLP provides a fair measure of consistency across the legislative process, with the Commission, the Council of Ministers, and the EP the dominant institutional actors. Behind the scenes of the formal constitutional arrangements, interest groups always exercise a considerable influence on both the content of proposals and the outcome of the decision-making process. At the implementation stage, the Commission and the ECJ are particularly important in the Union method, but national governments are often the key to how policies are implemented.

The formal relationships outlined in this chapter are only one part, although an important part, of the analysis of the role of the EU institutions. The informal relationships between the institutions themselves, and between the institutions and the member states, are the part not covered here. In the chapters that follow, these informal relationships enter the discussion, and attention focuses on the academic debates that have been generated about these relationships and their implications.

KEY POINTS

The Treaties

- The EU was founded by the Treaty of Paris (1951) and the two Treaties of Rome (1957), which were amended and supplemented by later Treaties.
- The Maastricht Treaty (1992) created the three-pillar EU.
- In 1997 the various Treaties were codified into two: the Treaty on the European Community (TEC) and the Treaty on European Union (TEU).
- The Lisbon Treaty, implemented in December 2009, abolished the EU's 'pillar' architecture dating from 1993 and created the 'Union method', which applies to all policy areas except the CFSP. The TEC was renamed the Treaty on the Functioning of the EU (TFEU).

The Decision-Making Institutions (the Union Method)

- The European Council sets the EU's broad policy agenda and the general direction of integration.
- The Commission has the sole formal right to initiate legislation, although this has been undermined in practice.
- The Council of Ministers has to agree to proposals for them to become law. Originally, it had to agree unanimously, but there has been a steady move towards the adoption of QMV.
- Since it became directly elected in 1979, the powers of the EP have grown, particularly in relation to the legislative process, until today it is effectively the co-legislator with the Council of Ministers in most policy areas.
- The EP is co-equal decision maker with the Council on the annual budget.
- The EESC consists of representatives of producer and consumer groups, and has to be consulted before certain categories of legislation can be adopted, but its opinions are not often influential.
- The CoR consists of representatives of regional and local authorities, and represents an advocate for MLG in the EU's territorially organized policies.

Decision-Making Procedures

- There are two main types of decision-making procedure in the Union method: budgetary and legislative.
- The EU annual budget passes through a complex process, which involves the Commission, the Council, and the EP.
- The Lisbon Treaty creates the OLP as the norm: QMV in the Council and co-decision with the EP. Consultation and consent remain for a reduced set of circumstances.

Implementation

- Implementation is an integral part of the policy-making process.
- Three main types of EU legislative instrument are legally binding: decisions, directives, and regulations.
- While the Commission has formal responsibility for implementation, in practice national authorities play an important role.
- The ECJ has the power to interpret EU law, and its decisions are final.
- The Court of Auditors checks the legality and regularity of EU expenditure.

The Decision-Making Institutions (CFSP)

- In CFSP, which is predominantly intergovernmental in character, the Commission, the EP, and the ECJ have less authority than under the EU pillar.

- The High Representative of the Union for Foreign Affairs and Security Policy plays a key role in CFSP decisions and in co-ordinating a new External Action Service.

The Post-Lisbon Architecture of the EU

- The EU's powers are set out in a catalogue of competencies.

- In a small range of policies, the Lisbon Treaty built in a number of 'emergency brakes' to ensure that the member states can appeal if supranationalism threatens their sovereign interests.

- The Lisbon Treaty has increased the prospects for the emergence of further core groups in specific policy areas or 'pioneer' groups on individual items of legislation. It also introduced possibilities to move to more supranational decision making on specific policies under *passerelle* clauses.

FURTHER READING

In view of the continuing influence of the changes brought about by the Lisbon Treaty, an important reference is **J.-C. Piris**, *The Lisbon Treaty: A Legal and Political Analysis* (Cambridge: Cambridge University Press, 2010). Shorter accounts on the Lisbon Treaty are offered by **A. Duff**, *Saving the European Union: The Logic of the Lisbon Treaty* (London: Shoehorn Books, 2009) and, from a more legal perspective, by **M. Dougan**, 'The Treaty of Lisbon 2007: Winning Minds not Hearts', *Common Market Law Review*, 45 (2008): 617–701. For more detail on decision-making and implementation, see chapters 4 and 11, respectively, of **H. Lelieveldt and S. Princen,** *The Politics of the European Union* (Cambridge: Cambridge University Press, 2011).

 online resource centre   **Visit the Online Resource Centre that accompanies this book for links to more information on the institutional architecture, including the text of the Treaties: http://oxfordtextbooks.co.uk/orc/bache4e/**

Chapter 13

The European Commission

Chapter Overview

When the European Economic Community (EEC) was established, the European Commission was expected to be the motor of European integration. Because of this, it attracted considerable academic attention, becoming a focal point for the theoretical disputes between intergovernmentalists and supranationalists (see Chapter 1). This chapter sets out the Commission's functions and its structure, before detailing its role in policy making. It reviews the debate on the extent to which the Commission is an autonomous political actor or simply an agent of the member states. It then turns to the increasing challenges faced by the Commission in securing effective implementation of European Union (EU) policies and its response to concerns over its financial management of EU programmes.

Functions

The Commission has several key functions in the political system of the EU. It is the formal initiator of legislative drafts and of the budget (see Chapter 12). It may act as a mediator during the legislative process, for instance in helping to find agreement between the member governments, or between the Council of Ministers and the European Parliament (EP). It has an important role in managing certain Commission policies, such as competition policy, where executive powers are at the EU level. It is the 'guardian of the Treaties', in that it is entrusted with ensuring, in those areas in which policy is implemented by member states' authorities, that they are correctly putting EU legislation into effect. It has traditionally held an important role in external economic relations, such as trade negotiations. Finally, it is the 'conscience of the European Union'. Traditionally seen as *the* supranational voice of the collective interest in EU legislation, the Commission has found competitors for this role in recent decades: notably the EP, in which the EU's elected representatives develop their own positions. The European Council, as the institution in which heads of government set the EU's strategic direction, has become the intergovernmental voice of the collective interest. As noted in Chapter 12, these Commission functions relate to the **Union method** and not to the Common Foreign and Security Policy (CFSP), in relation to which its functions are very limited.

Composition and Appointment

In an echo of debates between intergovernmentalists and supranationalists, the Commission has been pilloried by **Eurosceptics** as a bureaucratic monster that is out of control and usurping the rights of the member states. In fact, it is a relatively small organization in comparison not just with national civil services, but even with individual departments of state in national governments.

The European Commission consists of a College of Commissioners and a permanent civil service. On 1 January 2013 the Commission employed precisely 32,666 staff in total according to its own figures (European Commission 2013a). However, a more typical figure of about 24,000 is quoted when a host of auxiliary staff, contract agents, and service providers are excluded. Of this smaller figure, around 19,000 are permanent or temporary administrators, the rest being employed either in scientific research, as translators and interpreters, or in the Commission delegations around the world. This is the 'Brussels bureaucracy' that is frequently attacked or ridiculed by critics of the EU. 'The Commission' in fact refers both to the Services of the Commission and to the College of Commissioners. However, these should be clearly distinguished, not least because, as Cram (2001: 776) pointed out, 'the members of each may have very different perspectives and, most importantly, very different interests or preferences'.

The Services are divided into twenty-nine Directorates-General (DGs), plus a number of special services. They are listed in Table 13.1. The DGs are the equivalent of national civil service departments of state. Originally, they were known by their number only (for example, DG IV for the Competition Directorate-General), but this system was abolished under Romano Prodi's presidency of the Commission (1999–2004) as part of a reform designed to bring the structure of the DGs more into line with the designation of portfolios within the College. Instead, a set of acronyms is now utilized (see Table 13.1).

The permanent senior administrators (in the so-called AD category) number about 12,500; additionally, about 1,000 'Detached National Experts' are seconded from the member states. Recruitment to the permanent posts is on the basis of merit, although a loose quota system is utilized to ensure an approximate balance of nationalities.

Political direction is given by the College of Commissioners. Since the Maastricht Treaty, Commissioners have been appointed for five-year terms (previously four-year) in order to achieve an alignment with the five-year terms of the EP. The pattern of the appointment process was adjusted in the Lisbon Treaty. Starting with the 2010–14 Commission, the process was as follows.

'Taking into account the elections to the European Parliament', as Article 17 TEU puts what is now recognized to be a politicized process, the European Council proposes a candidate for President of the Commission. He or she must be approved by a majority of members of the European Parliament (MEPs); if not, the European Council must propose a new candidate.

The member states put forward candidates for the post of Commissioners. The President-Elect of the Commission then selects a team and assigns portfolios before submitting the line-up to the Council of Ministers for approval by qualified majority vote (QMV). One of the Commissioners is the High Representative of the Union for

Table 13.1 **The Directorates-General and Services of the Commission (January 2014)**

Policies	External Relations	General	Key Services
DG Agriculture and Rural Development (AGRI)	DG Development and Co-operation—EuropeAid (DEVCO)	DG Budget (BUDG)	Secretariat General (SG)
DG Climate Action (CLIMA)	DG Enlargement (ELARG)	DG Communication (COMM)	Legal Service (SJ)
DG Communications Networks, Content and Technology (CNECT)	DG Humanitarian Aid and Civil Protection (ECHO)	DG Human Resources and Security (HR)	Bureau of European Policy Advisers (BEPA)
DG Competition (COMP)	DG Trade (TRADE)	DG Informatics (DIGIT)	European Anti-Fraud Office (OLAF)
DG Economic and Financial Affairs (ECFIN)		DG Interpretation (SCIC)	European Personnel Selection Office (EPSO)
DG Education and Culture (EAC)		DG Translation (DGT)	Eurostat (ESTAT)
DG Employment, Social Affairs and Inclusion (EMPL)			Infrastructures and Logistics—Brussels (OIB)
DG Energy (ENER)			Infrastructures and Logistics—Luxembourg (OIL)
DG Enterprise and Industry (ENTR)			Internal Audit Service (IAS)
DG Environment (ENV)			Joint Research Centre (JRC)
DG Health and Consumers (SANCO)			Office for Administration and Payment of Individual Entitlements (PMO)
DG Home Affairs (HOME)			Publications Office (OP)
DG Internal Market and Services (MARKT)			Service for Foreign Policy Instruments
DG Justice (JUST)			
DG Maritime Affairs and Fisheries (MARE)			

(Continued)

Policies	External Relations	General	Key Services
Table 13.1 (Continued)			
DG Mobility and Transport (MOVE)			
DG Regional and Urban Policy (REGIO)			
DG Research and Innovation (RTD)			
DG Taxation and Customs Union (TAXUD)			

In parentheses are the acronyms utilized within the European Commission and elsewhere. Directorates-General are denoted DG; others are Services.

Foreign Affairs and Security Policy (HRUFASP; see Chapter 14, The Council Presidency).

The EP, acting by the consent procedure (see Chapter 12, Decision-Making Procedures), must then approve the Commission team, following individual hearings of the candidates.

Finally, after this investiture by the EP, the Council of Ministers formally appoints the Commissioners (again with QMV available).

The number of Commissioners has increased over the years as a result of enlargements. Until 2005, each state had one Commissioner, and the larger member states (France, Germany, Italy, Britain, and Spain) had two each. In the Treaty of Nice (see Chapter 10, The Nice Treaty), it was agreed that, starting with the Commission that took office on 1 January 2005, the number of Commissioners would be limited to one per member state. The Lisbon Treaty (Article 17 TEU) made provision for the number of Commissioners to be reduced further with effect from the College to be nominated in November 2014. Its size would correspond to two-thirds of the number of member states, and be selected on a basis of equal rotation between the member states. When the Irish people rejected the Lisbon Treaty in the June 2008 referendum, the possibility of there not being an Irish Commissioner after 2014 was an issue that came to the fore. Consequently it was decided that one Commissioner would continue to be appointed for each member state, and this was confirmed by the European Council in May 2013. This arrangement satisfied Irish concerns, but means that it is increasingly difficult to find meaningful responsibilities for each Commissioner, especially in the event of future enlargement.

The 2010–14 College comprised twenty-eight Commissioners following Croatia's accession (see the list with their portfolios in Table 13.2). Commissioners are sworn to abandon all national allegiances during their tenure of office, and they are bound by the principle of collegiality, so all actions are the responsibility of the Commission as a whole.

The term of the Commission President is renewable and José Manuel Barroso's term was renewed in 2009 for five more years (see Chapter 15, The Struggle for Power). A new College will be appointed to commence its term at the start of

Table 13.2 Commissioners and their Portfolios (2010–14)

José Manuel Barroso	**President**	**Portuguese**
Catherine Ashton	Vice-President; High Representative of the Union for Foreign Affairs and Security Policy	British
Viviane Reding	Vice-President; Justice, Fundamental Rights, and Citizenship	Luxembourgish
Joaquín Almunia	Vice-President; Competition	Spanish
Siim Kallas	Vice-President; Transport	Estonian
Neelie Kroes	Vice-President; Digital Agenda	Dutch
Antonio Tajani	Vice-President; Industry and Entrepreneurship	Italian
Maroš Šefovi	Vice-President; Inter-Institutional Relations and Administration	Slovakian
Olli Rehn	Vice-President; Economic and Monetary Affairs	Finnish
Janez Potonik	Environment	Slovenian
Andris Piebalgs	Development	Latvian
Michel Barnier	Internal Market and Services	French
Androulla Vassiliou	Education, Culture, Multilingualism, and Youth	Cypriot
Algirdas Šemeta	Taxation, Customs, Statistics, Audit, and Anti-Fraud	Lithuanian
Karel De Gucht	Trade	Belgian
Tonio Borg	Health	Maltese
Máire Geoghegan-Quinn	Research, Innovation, and Science	Irish
Janusz Lewandowski	Financial Programming and Budget	Polish
Maria Damanaki	Maritime Affairs and Fisheries	Greek
Kristalina Georgieva	International Co-operation, Humanitarian Aid, and Crisis Response	Bulgarian
Günther Oettinger	Energy	German
Johannes Hahn	Regional Policy	Austrian
Connie Hedegaard	Climate Action	Danish
Štefan Füle	Enlargement and European Neighbourhood Policy	Czech
László Andor	Employment, Social Affairs, and Equal Opportunities	Hungarian
Cecilia Malmström	Home Affairs	Swedish
Dacian Cioloş	Agriculture and Rural Development	Romanian
Neven Mimica	Consumer Policy	Croatian

Table 13.3 Presidents of the European Commission

Walter Hallstein (West Germany)	1958–67
Jean Rey (Belgium)	1967–70
Franco Maria Malfatti (Italy)	1970–72
Sicco Mansholt (Netherlands)	1972
François-Xavier Ortoli (France)	1973–76
Roy Jenkins (UK)	1977–80
Gaston Thorn (Luxembourg)	1981–84
Jacques Delors (France)	1985–94
Jacques Santer (Luxembourg)	1995–99
Romano Prodi (Italy)	1999–2004
José Manuel Barroso (Portugal)	2004–14

2015 (see online resources for its composition). Perhaps the most prominent President of recent decades, Jacques Delors, held the office for two full terms (then of four years each), plus an interim two-year period to bring the period of office of the Commission into line with that of the EP under provisions in the Maastricht Treaty. A list of Presidents of the Commission is given in Table 13.3. There are also seven vice-presidents, one of whom—as High Representative for Foreign Affairs (HRUFASP), a joint appointment with the Council of Ministers—represents the EU on the world stage.

Each Commissioner has a team of policy advisers, typically six or seven. Collectively, the advisers are known by the French word *cabinet* (pronounced 'cab-ee-nay'). The President's *cabinet* is larger, approximately double the size of the others. The members of the *cabinet* act as the eyes and ears of the Commissioner within the organization, and perform a valuable co-ordination function—particularly valuable because the structure of the Commission tends to produce fragmentation of the policy-making process between the DGs. It is widely accepted that the dynamism of Jacques Delors' presidencies would not have been possible without the sheer energy and effectiveness of the President's *cabinet* under the leadership of Pascal Lamy, who later went on to become a Commissioner himself.

Each member of the *cabinet* will have responsibility for monitoring one or more areas of policy, and there are weekly meetings of these specialists, chaired by the relevant member of the President's *cabinet*, to discuss issues that are current and to monitor the progress of draft legislation. The heads of the units—*chefs de cabinet*—also meet weekly, two days prior to the weekly meetings of the College of Commissioners. All draft legislation that has been prepared within the DGs has to go to the College for final approval, in keeping with the principle of collegiality. Before it gets there, it is considered by the *chefs*, and if difficulties that can be resolved are spotted at that stage, the draft will be referred back for amendment or further consideration. Where differences are highly politicized, the matter will be allowed to go through to the College for discussion.

The Commission in the Policy-Making Process

There is considerable academic debate around the role of the European Commission in the policy-making process. There is no doubt about its formal role: it has the sole right to initiate proposals for legislation in all policy areas under the Union method, with the exception of the area of freedom, security, and justice (AFSJ), for which this power is shared (see Chapter 24). Thus, without a proposal from the Commission, neither the Council of Ministers nor the EP can legislate. However, the debate centres on whether the Commission actually determines the direction in which the EU moves, particularly given the European Council's similar aspirations (see Chapter 14, The European Council) as well as those of the EP.

In reality, the Commission has come to be seen as the body that puts together the detailed proposals that operationalize the political programme and strategy defined by the government heads in the European Council. That is not to say that the Commission is a mere secretariat 'following orders', because it retains autonomy on drafting proposals within the broad direction offered by the European Council. In addition, the European Council cannot, given the infrequency of its meetings, offer direction in all policy areas, so has to concentrate on what it sees as its priorities. Finally, as the Commission President is a participant in the European Council, there is scope for the Commission to play a part in shaping the European Council's agenda.

The Commission and the Member States

The changing fortunes of the Commission have been outlined in Chapters 7, 8, 9, 10, 11. For instance, its status declined after the empty chair crisis of 1965. Theorizations of the role of the Commission moved from the neofunctionalist view of it as the 'motor of integration' to the intergovernmental view of it as no more than the servant of the member states. This balance of opinion swung back under Jacques Delors' presidency (1985–94) after the launch of the single-market programme in the mid-1980s. After this development, it rapidly became a widely accepted view that:

> **The renewed drive for market unification can be explained only if theory takes into account the policy leadership of the Commission.**
>
> (Sandholtz and Zysman 1989: 96)

This view did not go unchallenged, though (see Chapter 20, Explaining the Single Market). The disagreements over the role of the Commission in the single-market programme represented fundamental disagreements about the nature of the Commission in more general terms. Is it simply an agent of the member states, acting at their behest and under their control, or is it an autonomous actor in its own right, capable of playing a leadership role in the EU? Echoes of this debate can be found amidst the eurozone crisis (see Chapter 11). On the one hand, the European Council has been the key institution for agreeing bail-outs for the debtor states, new fiscal arrangements, and a changed banking regime in the EU. Equally, however, the fiscal arrangements, under the Fiscal Compact, have empowered the Commission to enforce the new rules.

If the argument that the EU is an intergovernmental organization is to hold, then those who defend the position have to confront the assertion that the Commission is the prime mover of the process of European integration. This assertion was made from the early days of the EEC by Lindberg (1963) and other neofunctionalists (see Chapter 1). The counter-argument is that the Commission is simply an international secretariat like many others that help the member states of international organizations to achieve their collective aims. It simply acts on behalf of the member states and in accordance with their will. This view has been strongly argued by intergovernmentalists, notably Andrew Moravcsik (see Chapter 1). Each argument is now examined in turn.

The Commission as an Agent of the Member States

The intergovernmentalist view of the Commission is that it is only an agent of the member states. Its function is to make it easier for governments to find agreement on the details of co-operation with each other. Where there is agreement on the broad agenda for co-operation, it is convenient for member states to delegate some control over the detailed agenda to the Commission. They see it as a reliable source of independent proposals because it has technical information, and is a neutral arbiter between conflicting national interests. Delegating the making of proposals to the Commission in this way reduces the costs of co-operation by reducing the risk that 'decisions will be delayed by an inconclusive struggle among competing proposals, or that the final decision will be grossly unfair' (Moravcsik 1993: 512). Where there are alternative proposals that might win majority support, the choice is often decided by which proposal is backed by the Commission. Although this delegation of the right to make detailed proposals gives the Commission a certain formal power to set the agenda, in the intergovernmentalist view, the Commission does not determine the direction in which the EU moves. It is only helping the member states to agree on the details of what they have decided that they want to do anyway.

This intergovernmental interpretation also coincides with a principal–agent interpretation of delegation to the Commission that draws on work from comparative politics rather than integration theory (see Chapter 2). Majone (2001) argued that there are two reasons for delegating to agencies such as the Commission: for reasons of efficiency and credibility. The efficiency argument is that the agency—in this case, the European Commission—is endowed with better information and expertise than the individual member governments or the EP. The credibility argument is that it may be less exposed to being captured by powerful groups, such as the corporate lobby or, indeed, a powerful member state. The Commission's function of 'guardian of the treaties' is an important aspect of this credibility argument, since member states seeking to undermine EU legislation can ultimately be brought before the Court. These interpretations have generated significant debate and empirical testing (see, for instance, Franchino 2007).

The concern of Eurosceptic politicians and the critique offered from neofunctionalists is that the Commission may use the margin of discretion that the member states have delegated to it to try to manoeuvre the member states towards objectives that they had not anticipated. It is difficult for the states to keep a check on exactly what the Commission is doing because it is in possession of more information than they are. Nevertheless, there are ways in which the member states can keep a check on the Commission (Pollack 1997, 2003). First, they have set up a whole complex of implementation committees of national experts to monitor the actions of the Commission. There are approximately 250 of these committees—collectively known as comitology—but grouped into three categories. Advisory Committees give the Commission the greatest discretion; Management Committees make their decisions subject to being overruled by a QMV decision in the Council of Ministers; Regulatory Committees are a potential veto point for the Commission's decisions or the proposed measure is referred to the Council of Ministers for review. The Lisbon Treaty sought to tidy up this comitology system, which had developed in a rather ad hoc manner, as well as to ensure that the EP has proper oversight of it (Article 291 TFEU). Second, Article 263 TFEU allows challenges through the European Court of Justice (ECJ) to the actions of the Commission should any individual member state, or any directly affected individual or company, believe that it has overstepped its mandate. Other EU institutions, such as the EP and the Court of Auditors, also monitor the activities of the Commission, providing member states with the information that they need to keep a check on it.

The Commission as an Autonomous Actor

The alternative to the view that the Commission is no more than an agent of the member states is that it can and does act autonomously to provide policy leadership to the EU. Defenders of this view point to key resources that allow it to do so: its sole right of initiative in the legislative process of the EC; its ability to locate allies among influential interest groups; and its powers under the competition clauses of the Treaties to act against monopolies. (For a fuller list, see Nugent 1995: 605–13; also see Beach 2005.)

The Commission does not have to wait passively for the member states to ask it to bring forward proposals. It can identify a problem that has already started to concern governments, and propose a European solution. It can use its sole right of initiative to package issues in the form least likely to engender opposition in the Council of Ministers or the EP. Where there is opposition from member states to the full-blown development of a policy, the Commission may propose instead a limited small-scale programme; where there is resistance to a directive or regulation, the Commission may propose a less threatening recommendation or Opinion. In each case, the limited step establishes a precedent for action in the policy sector and can be followed up later with further steps if and when the environment in the Council of Ministers is more conducive (Cram 1997: 162–3).

The Commission can also act to put the Europeanization of a policy sector onto the agenda (cultivated spillover—see Chapter 1). By involving domestic interests at the EU level, through instruments such as advisory committees, the Commission seeks to win converts to the idea that an issue can best be handled at the European level. In the aftermath of the 2007 financial crisis, it actively advocated the strengthening of EU regulation of hedge funds and other financial instruments, aware that it had support in the EP and that the member governments were on relatively weak ground since the failure of domestic regulation was part of the explanation for the crisis.

Similarly, the Commission can utilize, and, if necessary, create, **transnational networks** of producers who will be its allies in the private sector and bring pressure to bear on governments to transfer competence in a sector to the EU level. It was most successful at this approach in the 1980s and 1990s: in the cases of technology policy (Sharp and Shearman 1987; Sharp 1989; Peterson 1991), telecommunications

(Dang-Nguyen et al. 1993; Fuchs 1994), and energy (Matlary 1993). In each of these last two sectors, it encouraged industrial users to press governments to move away from national monopolies to create a European market under European regulation. More recently it has supported civil society groups to ensure their voice is heard in policy making in line with its 2001 White Paper on governance (European Commission 2001*a*).

Once governments have become aware of a problem, and faced up to the possibility of a European solution, the Commission can use technical experts to increase the pressure on governments, as it did with the Cecchini report of economists for the single market (see Chapter 20, Explaining the Single Market), or for monetary union, the Delors Committee, which consisted mainly of central bankers (see Chapter 21, Origins of EMU).

Nevertheless, any move to develop a European competence in a policy sector will produce counter-pressures from groups that benefit from the status quo. The Commission can break down this opposition by threatening the use of its existing powers if actors in the sector will not co-operate to find a negotiated way forward. Again, it did this to achieve the opening up of national monopolies in telecommunications and energy supply and liberalizing the air-transport sector (Bulmer et al. 2007). In each case, the Directorate-General for Competition threatened to use its powers under what was then Article 90 of the Treaty (now Article 106 TFEU). This Article specifically said that national public monopolies were subject to the rules prohibiting the prevention of competition within the **common market**. The vested interests against change were therefore faced with the alternative of either reaching an agreement with the Commission to allow phased and regulated competition, or of facing legal proceedings. In many cases, these Article 90 challenges were linked to proposed legislation on liberalization going through the Council of Ministers. In all three cases cited, the alternative of having some say in *how* the transition from national monopoly to European market was carried out proved more attractive than the uncertainty of the alternative of legal proceedings, and the resistance to the Commission's proposals was seriously weakened as a result.

This pattern of Commission activism became less evident from the mid-1990s. Greater concern for **subsidiarity**, checks on the regulatory burden of Commission action, enlargement to twenty-eight states, and the changed EU agenda have been major contributors. A key emphasis of the Commission from 2005 to 2009 was the competitiveness of the European economy, but the Lisbon Strategy was much more one of policy co-ordination via the Open Method of Co-ordination (see Chapter 18) and therefore not amenable to Commission activism. The Commission has not been the driver of reforms during the eurozone crisis. The pace of reform has been set by the European Council. However, the Commission has been given important new oversight powers to monitor states' fiscal policy to ensure states do not run up unsustainable public debt (see Chapter 11).

The Commission and the European Parliament

While most attention has been paid to the relationship between the Commission and the member states, sympathetic practitioners have recently expressed concern about the erosion of the autonomy of the Commission resulting from the extension of the powers of the EP (De Gucht 2003). Similarly, some academic observers have identified an erosion of the Commission's powers and independence within the decision-making process (Tsebelis and Garrett 2000, 2001; Majone 2002; Burns 2004). Four main ways in which this has happened are identified.

(1) Although the Commission and the EP have traditionally been allies in attempting to wrest powers away from the member states, the Commission resisted suggestions that the EP be given an equal right of legislative initiative. The Commission argued that sharing the right of initiative would weaken its ability to give coherence and strategy to European legislation. Formally, the Commission has maintained its monopoly of initiative. Yet, since Maastricht, the EP has the right to request that the Commission 'submit any appropriate proposal on matters on which it considers that a Community act is required for the purpose of implementing this Treaty' (Article 225 TFEU). Majone (2002: 376) considered that this 'comes close to a true right of legislative initiative'.

(2) The introduction of co-decision (see Chapter 12, Decision-Making Procedures) has made it more difficult for the Commission to play the role of motor of integration because its proposals have to satisfy a larger number of actors. Specifically, co-decision requires the Commission to satisfy a majority in the EP as well as in the Council of Ministers (hereafter abbreviated to the Council). The more actors that have to be brought into agreement, the more the proposals are likely to become compromises rather than reflect the autonomous preferences of the Commission.

(3) Co-decision also opens the possibility of the Council and the EP agreeing an entirely different legislative text from that put forward by the Commission. If the Council and the EP cannot reach agreement on an amended version of the original Commission proposal, a Conciliation Committee is convened, in which the representatives of the two legislative institutions seek to reach agreement directly with one another. This may mean agreement on an entirely different text. The compromise text then has to be agreed in the Council by QMV, and by the EP by a simple majority. Thus, the original centrality of the Commission's proposal, which could only be amended by unanimity in the Council, is circumvented, thereby eroding the Commission's autonomy.

(4) The changes made to co-decision in the Treaty of Amsterdam further eroded the Commission's influence. Because the Council and the EP could reach agreement at first reading under the revised procedure, there was an incentive for them to open direct informal contacts at a much earlier stage than under the original co-decision procedure. This could reduce the Commission's pivotal role in the negotiations around the legislation. However, claims that it rendered the Commission irrelevant were rebutted by Burns (2004: 6), who pointed out that the Commission can still affect the chances of the EP's amendments being accepted by the Council. It should be pointed out that agreement between Council and EP at first-reading stage had become the predominant pattern by the 2004–09 EP legislative period (Duff 2009: 52).

The Commission and Managing Implementation

Up to this point we have focused on the role of the Commission in policy making. However, the Commission also has to be an effective manager of EU business if it is to play its part in putting policy into practice. Concern at its effectiveness initially emerged at the start of the 1990s. In 1991, the then Secretary General of the Commission, David Williamson, admitted to the failings of the Commission when it came to implementing the growing body of EC legislation. This analysis was echoed by Metcalfe (1992) and other academic observers. They had noted that the Commission was better adapted to proposing policies and legislation than to implementing them once they were agreed. Metcalfe went so far as to argue (1992: 118) that: 'The EC has a management deficit at least as significant for its future effectiveness as its more widely recognised democratic deficit.'

It had long been argued that the two functions of initiation and implementation required different types of organizational structure, which Coombes (1970) identified as *organic* and *mechanistic* organizations. He described the Commission as an organic organization, well equipped to generate proposals, but lacking sufficient of the qualities of a classical mechanistic bureaucracy to implement them effectively. Others have seen this bias against implementation as embodied in the culture of the Commission.

During the 1990s, the implementation problems of the Commission increased as a result of several factors.

(1) The success of the 1992 Programme and other policy initiatives taken under Delors' presidency left the Commission with a much larger body of legislation to implement.

(2) The extension of EU competences into new policy sectors, such as social and environmental policy, raised different problems of implementation (Peters 1997: 191).

(3) The question of consistent implementation of single-market rules became an issue because of the wide disparities between member states that were shown up by Commission monitoring reports. The states with the better records felt that they were being placed at a competitive disadvantage in comparison with states that were less meticulous about applying the rules.

(4) The crisis over the ratification of the Maastricht Treaty (see Chapter 9, After Maastricht), and the subsequent renewed emphasis on the principle of subsidiarity, further complicated the relationship between the Commission and the member states (Laffan 1997b: 425).

(5) The internal Commission crisis that culminated in the resignation of the Santer Commission in 1999 (see this chapter, Financial Management) revealed poor management and accountability structures within the Commission.

In consequence, the incoming Commission of Romano Prodi initiated a major programme of reform, for which the British Vice-President of the Commission, Neil Kinnock, took responsibility (Metcalfe 2000). It entailed changes to the structure, organization, and management of the Commission, designed not only to improve its implementation capacity but also to make its operations more efficient. Changes were introduced to terms of appointment of both Commissioners and personnel in the Services. Codes of conduct were introduced relating to their practices. As Metcalfe wrote at the time (2000: 819): 'The management deficit is not just about the inadequacies within the Commission—it is a structural problem that threatens the performance of the whole system.' A decade later, it became possible to evaluate the reforms. Hussein Kassim (2008: 548) offered the following verdict: 'When crisis forced member governments to intervene, the Commission in a case of self-reform under delegation seized the "once-in-a-generation" opportunity to implement an internal reform agenda.'

The Commission as Implementer

The Commission operates in two modes as implementer. First, there are a very few policy sectors in which the Commission has direct implementation powers. The most notable is competition policy, which has been called 'the first supranational policy' (McGowan and Wilks 1995). Others are fisheries and some of the programmes involved in the external relations of the EU, such as the Humanitarian Aid Programme. Second, for most internal policies, the Commission sits at the apex of a multi-level system of implementation that extends down to the central authorities of the member states, then below them to sub-national authorities and agencies. Morten Egeberg has argued that this multi-level EU administration represents a 'transformation of executive politics in Europe' (Egeberg 2006). In this second mode, the Commission acts as the agent of the member states; national and sub-national actors are the agents of the Commission. The problem for the Commission is ensuring that these agents do not pursue their own agendas.

This problem is compounded by two circumstances. First, the Commission has scarce personnel resources and lacks independent information. Second, the number of agents that it has to monitor has been increased by the fragmentation of public administration that has taken place in many member states under the banner of the 'New Public Management' (Peters 1997: 198). In consequence, the Commission has had to operate as the manager of European networks of member-state administrators. The latter may take on a 'double-hatted' role as both domestic policy managers and as part of an EU-centred administration co-ordinated by the Commission (see Egeberg 2006 for illustrations). The creation of the European External Action Service following the Lisbon Treaty added further complexity because it brought together administrative capacity from both the Commission and the Council of Ministers. Unsurprisingly, it experienced 'growing pains' in the immediate aftermath of its launch in 2011 (Allen and Smith 2012: 162–4).

Majone (2002) argued that the transfer of new competences to the EU had not involved increasing the exclusive competences of the EU, but had involved the extension of the number of areas in which the EU and the member states shared competence, or in which competences were dispersed to new institutional actors, such as the European Central Bank (Majone 2002: 376). The reluctance of member states to transfer further exclusive competences to EU institutions reflected their concern about the loss of control that earlier transfers had involved. However, it also reflected a realization that the implementation role of the Commission could not be increased further without an increase in its size and resources that the member states were unwilling to sanction (Majone 2002: 382). In the view of Majone (2002: 382–3), this situation obliged the Commission to share responsibility with national administrative authorities, even though it was difficult to do so because of differing national regulatory philosophies and differing levels of national administrative competence.

At the same time, the Commission faced the prospect of becoming increasingly subject to political interference with performance of its implementation function because of the reform measures taken to deal with the democratic deficit. The Lisbon Treaty reinforced this trend by stating in Article 17 TEU that the nomination of the Commission President must take into account the elections to the EP. The danger of such politicization is that it risks adversely affecting the credibility principle that lies behind delegation to the Commission in the first place.

Majone (2002: 387) argued that there was a case for a 'fourth branch of government' on the model of US federal regulatory agencies. In fact, further independent agencies were created in connection with the transfer of new competences. They were mainly charged to collect and collate information but some have regulatory powers. These agencies have grown incrementally over the years and by 2012 had a collective budget of some €750 million and employed some 7,000 staff, many of them temporary. A problem emerged in that they had inconsistent sets of management rules and standards, making them more exposed to criticism over conflicts of interest and potential scandals. Consequently, an effort was made to provide standardized arrangements (*European Voice*, 20 December 2012). This momentum was driven by provisions in the Lisbon Treaty to bring agencies under more systematic control, including their accountability to the Court and the EP. A list of these agencies is given in Box 13.1. Three agencies are concerned with CFSP activity. As an illustration of their continued

---

Box 13.1 Independent Agencies

EU Agencies

Agency for the Co-operation of Energy Regulators (ACER)

Body of European Regulators for Electronic Communications (BEREC)

Translation Centre for the Bodies of the European Union (CdT)

European Centre for the Development of Vocational Training (Cedefop)

European Fisheries Control Agency (EFCA)

Community Plant Variety Office (CPVO)

European Aviation Safety Agency (EASA)

European Asylum Support Office (EASO)

European Centre for Disease Prevention and Control (ECDC)

European Chemicals Agency (ECHA)

European Environment Agency (EEA)

European Food Safety Authority (EFSA)

European Institute for Gender Equality (EIGE)

European Monitoring Centre for Drugs and Drug Addiction (EMCDDA)

European Medicines Agency (EMEA)

European Maritime Safety Agency (EMSA)

European Network and Information Security Agency (ENISA)

European Railway Agency (ERA)

European Training Foundation (ETF)

European Agency for Safety and Health at Work (EU-OSHA)

Euratom Supply Agency (ESA)

European Foundation for the Improvement of Living and Working Conditions (EUROFOUND)

European Union Agency for Fundamental Rights (FRA)

European Agency for the Management of Operational Co-operation at the External Borders (FRONTEX)

European Global Navigation Satellite Systems Supervisory Authority (GSA)

Office for Harmonization in the Internal Market (OHIM)

European Police College (CEPOL)

The European Union's Judicial Co-operation Unit (EUROJUST)

European Police Office (EUROPOL)

European Agency for the operational management of large-scale IT systems in the area of freedom, security and justice (eu-LISA)

European Banking Authority (EBA)

European Insurance and Occupational Pensions Authority (EIOPA)

European Securities and Markets Authority (ESMA)

CFSP Agencies

European Defence Agency (EDA)

European Union Institute for Security Studies (ISS)

European Union Satellite Centre (EUSC)

Note: Excludes Euratom agencies as well as executive agencies established to administer individual EU programmes.

Source: **http://europa.eu/about-eu/agencies/index_en.htm**, January 2014.

growth, the European Banking Authority was created in 2011 to oversee national banking regulation in the aftermath of the financial and eurozone crises.

Financial Management

Alongside the Commission's burgeoning implementation problems, concern also grew about effective financial management of EU programmes. As Laffan (1997*b*: 427) noted, for many years, the annual reports of the Court of Auditors highlighted weaknesses in the Commission's financial management. As one response, the Maastricht Treaty upgraded the status of the Court of Auditors to that of a full EC institution, and raised the status of budgetary discipline and sound financial management to central principles (Laffan 1997*b*: 429).

The resignation of the Santer Commission in 1999 was partly due to problems of financial mismanagement, so it came as no surprise that the Commission's reform White Paper of 2000 included, as one of four key components, reform of the system of financial control and management (Kassim 2008: 659). Internal accountability was overhauled, with financial responsibility de-centralized to Director-Generals, and the creation of an Internal Audit Service (see Table 13.1). More broadly, the Commission has to make sure that fraud is not taking place using EU funds, but in this case including through malpractice at member state level. The main weapon to this end is the European Anti-Fraud Office, known by its French acronym, OLAF (see Table 13.1).

CONCLUSION

The debate over the role of the Commission remains central to explanations about the nature and pace of European integration. It is clearly central to one of the themes of this book: the debate about the nature of the EU itself. If the Commission can be shown to be an autonomous actor, the argument that the EU is an intergovernmental organization is severely weakened. The supranational challenge was greatest under the Delors Commissions (1985–94) and has fallen away in more recent years, although this is not to say that the Commission lacks autonomy.

The Commission has been fiercely criticized in its role as manager of EU policies and finances. It was forced to put its house in order following the crisis in 1998–99. Oversight of policy implementation remains a concern. While implementation is never straightforward for domestic legislation within member states, it becomes even more difficult in a union of twenty-eight member states, in which the Commission is dependent on national and sub-national tiers of government for effective compliance. Added to this, the proliferation of actors involved in the policy process and the increased role of 'agency government', has made the Commission's task even more difficult, since it is now managing complex networks of implementing bodies. Such developments have been central to the increased interest in the application of the concepts of governance and policy networks to the EU and of multi-level administration (see Chapter 2). While governance in the EU has become increasingly complex as the integration process has developed over the decades, the Commission has proved to be very resilient in maintaining a central role in administering EU policy, as well as in its formulation.

KEY POINTS

Functions

- The Commission initiates legislation, may act as a mediator, manages some policy areas, is guardian of the Treaties, is a key actor in international relations, and the 'conscience of the EU'.

Composition and Appointment

- The Commission consists of a College of Commissioners and the Services.
- The Services are the permanent civil service of the EU.
- The Commission President is a particularly influential figure, and is nominated by the European Council and then approved by the EP.
- The Commissioners are appointed by the European Council, subject to approval by the EP.
- There is one Commissioner per member state. They are sworn to abandon national allegiances.

The Commission in the Policy-Making Process

- Formally, the Commission has the sole right to propose EU legislation.
- There is debate about how much autonomy it actually has.
- The intergovernmentalist view is that the Commission is merely the agent of the member states; the supranationalist view is that the Commission can and does achieve a degree of autonomy from the member states to pursue its own agenda.
- Treaty changes designed to deal with the democratic deficit have reduced the autonomy of the Commission by increasing the control over it by the EP.

The Commission and Implementation

- The Commission was originally more active as a proposer than as an implementer of legislation, although the balance has shifted in more recent times.
- In most areas, the Commission has to work alongside the national administrations of the member states, leading to suggestions that it should evolve as a manager of European networks of implementation agents.
- Increasing politicization of the Commission because of its subjection to closer control by the EP threatens its perceived independence, and also points to the need for the emergence of transnational regulatory networks.

Financial Management

- The 1999 Commission crisis triggered a root-and-branch reform of the Commission's financial management.

FURTHER READING

Three recent publications cover the Commission comprehensively, and fill something of a void in recent such analyses. The first is by **H. Kassim et al.**, *The European Commission of the Twenty-First Century* (Oxford: Oxford University Press, 2013). It relies on extensive survey and interview data within the institution. The second is by **Anchrit Wille**, *The Normalization of the European Commission* (Oxford: Oxford University Press, 2013). The third is **A. Ellinas and E. Suleiman**, *the European Commission and Bureaucratic Autonomy* (Cambridge: Cambridge University Press, 2012). **D. Dimitrakopoulos (ed.)**, *The Changing European Commission* (Manchester: Manchester University Press, 2004) offers a useful collection of chapters on the European Commission, as does a special edition of the *Journal of European Public Policy*, 15(8) (2008). Still useful, although now dated, is **N. Nugent**, *The European Commission* (Basingstoke: Palgrave Macmillan,

2000). For the European Commission as a bureaucracy, see **A. Stevens and H. Stevens**, *Brussels Bureaucrats? The Administration of the European Union* (Basingstoke: Palgrave Macmillan, 2001).

online resource centre

Visit the Online Resource Centre that accompanies this book for links to more information on the European Commission, including the European Commission's own website: http://oxfordtextbooks.co.uk/orc/bache4e/

Chapter 14

The European Council and the Council of Ministers

Chapter Overview

This chapter examines those institutions principally composed of government representatives. Prior to the Lisbon Treaty coming into effect, these institutions could all be seen as part of a single 'Council' system. With its entry into force, the European Council became an institution in its own right, and the chapter title reflects this change. Even so, by virtue of their composition of government representatives (government heads, ministers, and civil servants), the two institutions remain part of a hierarchy of institutions (see Insight 14.1). The European Council is the name for the periodic summit meetings of heads of state and government that are largely responsible for determining the direction of the integration process. The Council of Ministers (officially known as the 'Council of the European Union' and in shorthand as the 'Council') is a multi-faceted and multi-tiered institution that does not have a constant membership, but involves different ministers depending on the policy under consideration. Even that, though, is not the full extent of the complexity of the Council. The work of the meetings of ministers is prepared by a myriad of committees, consisting primarily of national officials, that are brought together by the Committee of Permanent Representatives (COREPER) and a large number of preparatory committees at technical level. Each of these is considered in what follows.

Definitions and Distinctions

It is important at the outset of this chapter to be clear about terminology. The subject matter of the chapter is those European Union (EU) institutions composed of representatives of national governments. Both are important, but in different ways. The European Council is at the top of this hierarchy and is the institution that brings together the EU's heads of government (or, in the French case, the head of state). As will be seen, it is a relatively recent body, having been set up in 1974, and since implementation of the Lisbon Treaty (in December 2009) is a formal EU institution. It is not to be confused with the Council of Europe (see Chapter 6, Insight 6.1)—as it sometimes is in student essays—as this is a completely separate international

The European Council

Summit meetings of the heads of government (France sends the head of state), held four times per year, with provision for additional meetings. Since 2010 approximately six meetings per annum with further sessions for the eurozone states.

The Council of Ministers

Consists of a representative of each member state 'at ministerial level', authorized to commit the government of the member state. It meets in ten different formations depending on the subject matter under consideration.

The Committee of Permanent Representatives (COREPER)

The Permanent Representatives are the ambassadors of the member states to the EU. Their deputies meet as COREPER I and the Representatives themselves as COREPER II. They prepare business for the meetings of ministers.

High-Level Preparatory Bodies and the Working Parties

COREPER itself is prepared by a small number of specialized committees, such as on agriculture or trade policy. At the lowest level are Council working parties, which deal with most specialist policy issues. There are more than 150 such committees and working groups.

The Presidency

Prior to the Lisbon Treaty, the presidency was held for six months by one member state as determined by a rota. A representative of this state chaired all meetings of the Council and, indeed, of meetings in the Council hierarchy. The Lisbon Treaty ended the simplicity of this set-up by turning the presidency into a 'trio' of three states playing the above role across an eighteen-month period. Separate arrangements were introduced for the Presidency of the European Council, the Presidency of the Council of Foreign Affairs, and the Presidency of the Euro Group.

The Secretariat

The state holding the presidency is assisted by a Council Secretariat of over 3,000 staff, about a tenth of whom are senior administrators.

organization from the EU. The other institution to be considered in this chapter is the Council of the European Union or, as it is usually termed the Council of Ministers. It is the Council of Ministers that is referred to with the shorthand term 'the Council'. The so-called Council hierarchy comprises the Council of Ministers, as well as other preparatory bodies arranged beneath it (see Insight 14.1). It is attended by ambassadors and civil servants of the member states.

The Council of Ministers was first set up as part of the European Coal and Steel Community (see Chapter 7, The Schuman Plan for Coal and Steel). Over six decades later, its activities span the full range of public policy. Two things have remained constant, however. First, it is the institution that enshrines the importance of member governments in the EU. Second, it remains the focal point of the making of EU legislation, but has been joined increasingly over recent years by the European Parliament as a co-legislator. Its principal functions are decision making and legislating. The European Council was created in 1974 as part of an effort to re-energize the integration process in a more intergovernmental way, given the setback suffered by the supranational method in the aftermath of the 1965 crisis (see Chapter 7, The 1965 Crisis). The European Council has become the motor of European integration in the subsequent period. These two institutions may grab the headlines, but a large majority of decisions are made before they reach them: at the level of COREPER or the preparatory technical committees.

Intergovernmental and Supranational Interpretations

As with the previous chapter, a key theme in this one is the relationship between the intergovernmental and supranational interpretations. On the face of it, both the European Council and the Council of Ministers, comprised as they are of member governments and their officials, represent intergovernmentalism 'writ large'. The top layers of the hierarchy bring together 'the core executive' of the EU member states: the Prime Ministers, Foreign Ministers, and other departmental ministers, together with their officials. However, in their comprehensive study of the Council of Ministers, Hayes-Renshaw and Wallace (2006: 321) put paid to this simplistic analysis:

> to view the importance of the Council as the victory of intergovernmentalism over supranationalism, or to expect the Council to be able to 'run' the EU, is to misunderstand the institutional constellation of the EU. The Council shares and diffuses power between countries, between different kinds of interests and constituencies, and between national and EU levels of governance. The Council cannot act alone, but is dependent on intricate relationships with other EU institutions.

The supranational argument is less easy to present, but revolves around several points of departure from intergovernmentalism:

- that ministers and officials from the member states are partners who may work together frequently and will have regard to collective solutions as well as the national interest;
- that the provision for **qualified majority voting (QMV)** changes the calculation of ministers away from 'hard bargaining' based exclusively on the national interest, even if they prefer not to vote but to decide by consensus;
- that the Council increasingly needs to work with the European Parliament (EP) in the 'ordinary legislative procedure' (co-decision);
- that there is some evidence of socialization into shared values among participants at all levels in the hierarchy of intergovernmental institutions.

The European Council

Over the years, the European Council has held meetings at least twice a year and generally three or four times. The Lisbon Treaty states that it shall meet 'twice every six months' (Article 15(3), TEU). Additional informal meetings are also called in response to urgent matters. The origins of the European Council were in the summit meetings that started with the 'relaunching of Europe' at The Hague in 1969 (see Chapter 7, The Hague Summit). The first formal meeting of the European Council was in Dublin in March 1975.

The Rationale for the European Council

After de Gaulle's resignation in 1969, there was a wish by the national governments to re-start the development of the European Community (EC), but in the direction that they, not the Commission, decided; hence The Hague Summit of that year. The 1965 crisis had led to a loss of confidence inside the Commission. If the Commission was not going to drive the EC forward, another motor would be needed. The agreement to formalize summits in the form of the European Council was an indication that the governments were determined to play a continuing role. Despite the European Council taking on a fundamental role in steering the course of integration from the mid-1970s, its elusive and under-institutionalized nature led to a lamentable neglect in the academic literature.

The origins of the European Council stemmed from the French President, Valéry Giscard d'Estaing, and the German Chancellor, Helmut Schmidt, who both came to office in 1974. Both had been Finance Ministers and had participated in numerous meetings on the international monetary system. They both strongly valued the opportunity to sit with their counterparts and hold informal discussions in confidence without the requirement to take formal decisions (Bulmer and Wessels 1987: 76). This 'Library Group' approach, which was quite informal, was important at the outset, but the Lisbon Treaty can be seen as its abandonment. Characteristic of the earlier 'Library Group' approach was a strong effort to keep the European Council outside of the Treaties in order to allow it as much flexibility as possible in its political actions. This informality eventually became unsustainable, not least with twenty-eight participating states.

The existence of the European Council was first acknowledged in the 1986 Single European Act (SEA), albeit in just three sentences. The Maastricht Treaty formalized the European Council but did not cite it as being one of the EU's institutions. It gave the European Council a very small number of specific tasks: notably in economic and monetary policy, and in setting the direction of the Common Foreign and Security Policy (CFSP). However, the Lisbon Treaty set out much more explicitly the role of the European Council and unambiguously refers to it as an institution of the EU (see Insight 14.2).

A further explanation for the establishment of the European Council was to 'orchestrate' the EC. The 1969 Hague Summit had demonstrated that the heads of government could set the direction of integration: both broadly through authorizing enlargement negotiations and specifically through triggering particular policy

Insight 14.2 The European Council's Post-Lisbon Functions

(1) **General political guidance and momentum**

- 'The European Council shall provide the Union with the necessary impetus for its development and shall define the general political directions and priorities thereof. It shall not exercise legislative functions' (Article 15 TEU).

(2) **Oversight of Treaty reform and enlargement**

- Any proposals to revise the Treaties through the 'ordinary revision procedure' will be decided on by the European Council, which will consult the EP and the Commission and may decide by a simple majority to either convene a Convention or an intergovernmental conference (IGC) to consider the proposals (Article 48 TEU).

- Under 'simplified revision procedures', the European Council can agree less significant changes that nevertheless affect the character of the EU: for instance, to change decision-making rules to the ordinary legislative procedure (QMV in the Council and co-decision with the EP)—see Chapter 18 on the ***passerelle* clauses**.

- The European Council sets the eligibility conditions for accession states (Article 49 TEU).

- The European Council sets the guidelines for the process should a member state wish to withdraw from the EU (Article 50 TEU).

(3) **Foreign policy making**

- The 'European Council shall identify the strategic interests and objectives of the Union...[in relation]...to the common foreign and security policy and to other areas of the external action of the Union' (Article 22 TEU).

- 'If international developments so require, the President of the European Council shall convene an extraordinary meeting of the European Council in order to define the strategic lines of the Union's policy in the face of such developments' (Article 26 TEU).

(4) **Decision maker of last resort**

- Nominates the Commission President and appoints the Commission after the EP's consent (Article 17 TEU).

- Appoints the High Representative (HRUFASP) (Article 18 TEU).

- Decides on Council formations and presidency rota (Article 236 TFEU).

- Decides on number of Commissioners (Article 127 TEU and 244 TFEU).

- Decides on size of the EP (Article 14 TEU).

- Acts as court of appeal if a member state invokes the 'emergency brake' arrangements (scattered across the TFEU, but see Articles 48, 82, and 83 as examples).

(5) **Policy monitoring**

- 'The European Council shall define the strategic guidelines for legislative and operational planning within the area of freedom, security and justice' (Article 68 TFEU).

- The European Council 'shall, acting on the basis of the report from the Council, discuss a conclusion on the broad guidelines of the economic policies of the Member States and of the Union' (Article 121 TFEU).

initiatives, such as foreign policy co-operation. The European Council could also overcome the risk of policy segmentation, which arose because no single body could take an overview of policy. The General Affairs Council (see this chapter, The Council of Ministers) was supposed to act as policy co-ordinator, but the heads of government had more authority to play that role. Finally, the European Council was also an attempt to present a united front to the outside world and its role in this respect has expanded, to some extent usurping the role of the Council of Foreign Ministers.

Composition and Organization

Although the European Council comprises the heads of government, they are not the only participants. Traditionally, the Foreign Ministers of the member states have also participated, as has the Commission President and one Vice President. Membership was redefined under the Lisbon Treaty as follows (Article 15 TEU):

- the heads of state (France) or government of the member states, together with the President of the European Council and the President of the Commission;
- the High Representative of the Union for Foreign Affairs and Security Policy (HRUFASP);
- as necessitated by its agenda, heads of government may each be assisted by a minister and, in the case of the President of the Commission, by a member of the Commission.

As noted in Insight 14.1, the Presidency of the European Council became a separate appointment for two-and-a-half years (from January 2010, Herman Van Rompuy, the former Belgian Prime Minister, whose appointment was renewed for a second and last term in March 2012). The presidency no longer follows the previous system whereby meetings were chaired by the head of government from the presidency country. This change was introduced to ensure continuity in the European Council's work and to give an external face to the institution, for instance in reporting to the EP on its work. The second change is the close involvement of the High Representative: a step that reflects the importance of foreign and security policy to the European Council's work. Third, the previous default situation whereby heads of government were accompanied by their Foreign Ministers was amended. In reality, some changes had already occurred, notably with Economic or Finance Ministers attending the annual spring European Council meeting on the European economy.

The European Council's organization was undefined until the Lisbon Treaty. The Treaty provides for qualified or simple majority voting in the European Council, for instance in appointing its President, although the standard practice is decision making by consensus. In any event, neither the President nor the Commission President may vote. Having studiously avoided any internal regulation of its activities under the 'Library Group' model, the European Council took the radical step of agreeing rules of procedure, something already well established for the other institutions (European Council 2009). Herman Van Rompuy's selection as the first President of the European Council was widely interpreted as an attempt to ensure the office did not have too high a profile and did not challenge the authority of national leaders in the way that a better-known politician might. Another candidate had been Tony Blair, the former British Prime Minister, which would likely have given the position a higher profile.

The President's functions are to: convene meetings; prepare sessions; maintain continuity of work; represent the European Council in inter-institutional discussions (for instance, reporting to the EP); and draw up conclusions from its meetings.

One consequence of the new position was a possible confusion of roles with those of the Commission President, the High Representative, not to mention the country holding the presidency of the sectoral Councils of Ministers. Another consequence of the new position was an anticipated expansion of the European Council's activities. Kietz and von Ondarza (2010: 4) reported Van Rompuy as planning smaller, more frequent (six to eight per annum), and thematically organized sessions of the European Council, building on the pattern established by the annual spring session on the European economy. Another development worthy of note was that the government heads from the eurozone states have held meetings during the financial and eurozone crises from 2008. Meetings of the European Council over the period 2010–13 have numbered approximately six per annum, but some of these have been informal and some have doubled up as meetings of the eurozone states, of which there were an average of three per annum during the period 2010–13.

Functions and Dysfunctions

The European Council has five main functions (see also Insight 14.2), as follows.

- *General political guidance and momentum*   To this end, the European Council is like a 'board of directors' giving general guidance to the EU on its future direction. Although the details have to be filled out by interaction between the Commission, the Council of Ministers, and the EP, if the European Council gives a lead, the presumption is that the Commission will make proposals and the Council and EP will try to reach agreement on policy.

- *Oversight of Treaty reform and enlargement*   The European Council has been closely involved in authorizing and then finalizing all Treaty reforms from the 1986 SEA through to the 2012 Fiscal Compact. Of course, the European Council does not tie up twenty-eight government heads in detailed negotiations; those are conducted by officials and ministers. But without its initial agreement to start the process, and its consent at the end of it, Treaty reform would not be possible. Ever since The Hague Summit in 1969, summit meetings have taken key decisions on enlargement. For instance, the Copenhagen criteria of 1993 specified the requirements expected of all accession states and were defined at a European Council meeting in the Danish capital.

- *Foreign policy making*   Over the years, the European Council has issued many foreign policy declarations. These range from the 1980 Venice Declaration, in which it set out key principles on the Middle East, such as recognizing the Palestinian right to self-determination and to a homeland, to its December 2003 approval of a European Security Strategy. These powers were further developed by the Lisbon Treaty.

- *Decision maker of last resort*   From its very first meeting, the European Council has been called on to tackle problems that could not be resolved lower down the system. For many sessions from 1979 to 1984, the British Conservative government's efforts to secure a rebate on its budgetary contributions were on the European Council's agenda. However, it is not just a court of appeal, but is also brought in where decisions require its authority. It has had to thrash out agreement on the multi-annual financial perspective (see Chapter 12, Decision-Making Procedures). The Lisbon Treaty added specific provisions for the European Council to act as court of appeal if a member state wishes to use the 'emergency brake' because an exceptionally important interest is at risk of being overruled in the Council by a QMV decision (see Dougan 2008: 643–4). Finally, the European Council makes a number of key appointments as well as being able to take decisions on the size of some of the institutions (see Insight 14.2).

- *Policy monitoring*   Increasingly, the heads of government have sought to monitor the subsequent development of their own policy initiatives, in part to ensure policy delivery. For instance, the 2000–10 Lisbon Strategy on enhancing European competitiveness and the successor programme, known as Europe 2020, resulted in monitoring at the annual spring session of the European Council. Starting with the Tampere Programme of 2000, the European Council agreed a series of five-year programmes for developing the area of freedom, security, and justice (AFSJ). This role has become firmly established through five-yearly programmes, typically with the Commission providing a mid-term review on progress (see Chapter 24).

The European Council can still function as a forum for personal contact between heads of government. While the meetings have become more formal as the number of member states has increased, opportunities for informal conversations still exist—for instance, during meals.

In carrying out these functions, the European Council faces some serious problems. These can be considered the *dysfunctions* of the European Council. They can be summarized as problems of overload, over-optimism, over-cautiousness, and over-expectation.

- *Overload*   During the late 1970s and into the 1980s, there was a tendency for more and more problems to be referred up from the Council of Ministers to the European Council, so that it often found itself considering quite detailed and technical issues. However, since the introduction in the SEA and the Treaty on European Union (TEU) of QMV into the work of the Council of Ministers, the tendency for matters not to be resolved at lower levels has receded. European Council business can still be considerable for meetings lasting only five or six working days in a year.

- *Over-optimism*   Sometimes, the atmosphere of mutual co-operation that can be generated, together with the expectation that something will come out of every European Council, can lead to commitments being made that subsequently prove difficult to honour. When they go home after the meeting, heads of government may not be able to get the agreement of their own political parties or their cabinets/councils of ministers to carry through the commitment.

- *Over-cautiousness*   The publicity can make it more difficult for heads of government to make concessions that might be made in a less exposed bargaining context.

- *Over-expectation*   If the meetings do not produce dramatic results, this can cause disillusionment among the European public because the media has built up expectations.

Intergovernmentalism and Informality in the European Council

Although the European Council 'is the body universally recognized as the ultimate intergovernmental protectorate in the EU', it is also 'one which has paradoxically increased the supranational character of the EU over its three decades of operation' (Lewis 2003*a*: 1006). It has increased the supranational character of the EU because it provides the political framework for supranational legislation and other agreements. Although the heads of government do not themselves formally agree legislation, if they say that something should happen, it will be acted upon by the Commission and the Council of Ministers. Thus, the European Council gives legitimacy to supranational actions that might otherwise be contested at the level of the Council of Ministers.

Although its functions are now more specified, the European Council is still a forum for informal contact between heads of government, and this can increase the degree of collegiality of the institution. In the past, it was particularly important where French and German leaders had a close relationship—Giscard d'Estaing and Schmidt in the second half of the 1970s; Kohl and Mitterrand in the 1980s—since the Franco-German relationship had in some senses become the motor of integration. If leading members of the European Council remain in post for several years, they can become socialized into more co-operative working with the other heads of government. This effect is never likely to work as strongly for the heads of government as it does for other levels of the Council hierarchy, because the frequency of interaction is lower and the level of politicization of the heads of government is higher—but in reading the analyses that follow of the Council and its committees as supranational phenomena, it should be borne in mind that some of the same effects may operate even at the highest level of the European Council.

The Council of Ministers

The Council of Ministers is not an institution with a constant membership. It meets in a variety of formations depending on the subject under discussion (see Box 14.1). It should be noted that all formations act in the name of 'the Council of Ministers' and may decide on any business. Formally, there is no hierarchy between different Councils. However, the General Affairs Council (GAC), normally attended by Foreign Ministers, has a co-ordination function between the various technical councils and a relationship to the European Council, which implies that it has additional authority over the technical expertise possessed by the other formations.

The GAC was re-established as a separate formation after passage of the Lisbon Treaty, having previously been known as the General Affairs and External Relations Council (GAERC). GAERC was by far the busiest Council formation and a very

> ## Box 14.1 Formations of the Council of Ministers
>
> (Includes areas of responsibility where these are not clear from the title.)
>
> - **General Affairs:** cross-cutting issues such as enlargement and multi-annual financing, plus preparation for, and follow-up of, European Council meetings
> - **Foreign Affairs:** CFSP and ESDP, trade policy, development co-operation
> - **Economic and Financial Affairs:** economic policy co-ordination, monitoring of member states' budgetary policy and public finances, financial markets and capital movements, and economic relations with third countries
> - **Justice and Home Affairs:** the area of freedom, security, and justice (AFSJ)
> - **Employment, Social Policy, Health, and Consumer Affairs:** also includes equal opportunities
> - **Competitiveness:** internal market, industry, and research

important one as well, meeting on twenty-two occasions in 2006. However, following the Lisbon Treaty, the GAERC was split into the GAC and the Foreign Affairs Council. The latter is chaired by the High Representative.

Apart from the GAC and the Foreign Affairs Council, the other key formations are: the Council of Economic and Finance Ministers (ECOFIN), which normally meets every month, and the Agriculture and Fisheries Council (Agfish), which also normally meets monthly. In the past, other formations have been important: for instance, the then Council of Internal Market Ministers (now the Competitiveness Council) during the single-market programme in the late 1980s and early 1990s (see Chapter 20, Project 1992: Freeing the Internal Market).

ECOFIN meetings are important in the Council's informal 'pecking order' because of the importance and centrality of their subject matter. This position was enhanced in the late 1990s because the issue of monetary union dominated the agenda of the EU. The start of the single currency (the euro) on 1 January 1999 complicated the institutional position because, since then, the Finance Ministers from those member states that are also members of the eurozone have met prior to the full meetings of ECOFIN to discuss single currency matters (see Chapter 21). The existence of this Euro Group was formally recognized in a Protocol attached to the Lisbon Treaty. It is chaired by its own President, elected for a two-and-a-half year term from among the national Economic and Finance Ministers. Meetings of ECOFIN are prepared by three specialist groups—the Economic and Financial Committee; the Economic Policy Committee; and the Budget Committee—depending on the agenda issues.

The Agfish Council also has a privileged status because of the importance of agriculture to the EU, although this position has been scaled back in relative terms due to the rise of other policy areas. Agfish business is prepared by the Special Committee on Agriculture (SCA), the work of which becomes especially intensive at the time of the annual fixing of agricultural prices in the first half of each year.

The importance of the other Councils can be regarded as a function of two factors: first, the extent of EU competence (see Insight 12.1); and, second, the intensity of policy activity. Thus, a Council formation such as Education, Youth, and Culture, in which the EU has only supporting competences, does not carry the 'clout' of the Competitiveness Council, which covers important economic issues over which the EU has greater authority. The frequency of meetings varies considerably, although most of the sectoral councils meet between twice and four or five times a year (Hayes-Renshaw and Wallace 2006: 38–9; Bulmer and Burch 2009: 55–6).

The functions of the Council are characterized by Hayes-Renshaw and Wallace (2006: 323–7) as being legislature, executive, setter of guidelines, and forum. The Council's role as legislature was set out in Chapter 12. The Council meets in public when voting on a legislative act (Article 15 TFEU). The executive function relates to where the Council takes decisions that are not legislative in character. This is most obviously the case in CFSP, but is also applicable, for instance, in some of the work of ECOFIN and the Euro Group. Although the European Council has tended to set policy guidelines, there are some policy areas in which the Council steers the course of policy, such as overseeing the details of enlargement negotiations. This function is particularly associated with the GAC. Finally, the Council serves as a forum in those policy areas in which member state policy is being co-ordinated. The growth of this pattern of governance—known as the Open Method of Co-ordination (OMC)—in the last decade or so has increased this 'forum' function for the Council (on the OMC, see Chapter 18, The EU Policy Process).

Voting rules were discussed in Chapter 12, The Council of Ministers (the Council). As noted there, the practice of QMV is much less than the formal provision for it. VoteWatch Europe (2012) examined Council voting over the period July 2009–June 2012. Its data revealed that over that period 90 per cent of decisions were subject to QMV provision, while unanimity applied in the rest of the cases. In those instances where the QMV rules applied, 65 per cent of votes were taken unanimously. In the remaining 35 per cent of cases, some disagreement or abstention was noted. This does not mean that formal votes were called in all such cases. For instance, in a situation where only one state makes its opposition known, the chair is able to decide that a formal vote is unnecessary. In addition, individual states may also make a formal statement registering reservations—typically for the benefit of domestic public opinion—but again without a formal vote being called. Over this period it was the United Kingdom that was most often found to be in the minority through either abstaining or voting against a measure (Chapter 11, Other Developments). It was also the state most likely to be issuing formal statements or entering reservations (VoteWatch 2012: 12–13).

A Purely Intergovernmental Institution?

Fritz Scharpf (1989) contrasted 'problem solving' and 'bargaining' as modes of negotiation within the EC. His distinction at least partly corresponds to the differences between theorists about how to understand the operation of the Council. For intergovernmentalists, the Council is simply 'a forum for hard bargaining' (Lewis 1998: 479, 2000: 261). For those who adopt a more supranational perspective, combined with a social constructivist theoretical position (see Chapter 4, Social Constructivism), bargaining takes place between actors whose positions are influenced, at least partially, by their social interaction with their ministerial colleagues from other member states; 'communicative rationality' is at least as important as 'instrumental rationality', which means that the discussion is about how to find a solution to common problems rather than just about playing a negotiating game to win, and there is an instinct to proceed consensually (Lewis 1998: 480–81).

The hypotheses that these theories generate are fairly clear. If the supranational theorists are correct, one would expect to find more collegiality, and a discourse more oriented to joint problem solving, in Councils that meet more frequently than in those that meet less frequently, and also in the more technical Councils rather than in the more political Councils (although deciding what is technical and what is political is notoriously difficult).

The extent to which ministers meeting in the different Councils engage in hard-headed intergovernmental bargaining, or adopt a more supranational approach, is difficult to research. Perhaps the requirement for legislative decisions to be taken in public will enable observation of ministers' behaviour, but much of the Council's work—not to mention the work of its preparatory bodies—continues to be held in private.

One particularly interesting research finding in this respect is that very few issues are actually decided by the ministers themselves. Taking data from 2004, Hayes-Renshaw and Wallace (2006: 53) calculated that 78 per cent of all Council decisions were A-points: that is, where ministers rubber-stamp decisions taken lower down the Council hierarchy. (B-points are those in which ministers themselves need to reach political agreement, but which issue may then be referred back to the preparatory bodies for the details to be negotiated.)

COREPER and other Preparatory Bodies

There are three levels of committee considered in this section: COREPER, which is the formal filter beneath the Council; a group of high-level preparatory bodies, such as the Political and Security Committee (PSC), which is responsible for CFSP and European Security and Defence Policy (ESDP) co-ordination; and, beneath them, over 150 Council working parties, some with sub-committees (see Council of the EU 2009*a*).

Although it formally only prepares the agenda and meetings of the Council, COREPER has a great deal of discretion about what it classifies as A-points or B-points on the agenda. So although COREPER and the working groups formally prepare the meetings of the ministers, in one sense the ministers can be said to set the agenda for the meetings of the committees. This is the case where an issue has been discussed at ministerial level, and broad consensus has been reached, but the issue is then referred back down the hierarchy for the detail to be filled in.

COREPER

The Permanent Representatives are the ambassadors from the member states to the EU. Each heads up what is officially an embassy to the EU. They perform some formal functions in Brussels, but their main task is to co-ordinate the work of the various committees that meet under the banner of the Council of Ministers. Where possible, they negotiate an agreement arising from the work undertaken by the committees ahead of a meeting of the Council of Ministers. This they do in the context of COREPER.

COREPER meets at least weekly at ambassador level as COREPER II, and at deputy level as COREPER I. Both prepare the agendas of meetings of the Councils of Ministers. COREPER II is responsible for the agendas for meetings of the GAC, the Foreign Affairs Council, and ECOFIN. COREPER I is responsible for the agendas of all other Councils. It is worth noting that two bodies, the SCA and the PSC, more or less substitute for the role of COREPER in the specific domains of agriculture and CFSP/ESDP respectively. The Antici Group of officials, named after the Italian official who was the chair of the first such group, assists COREPER and the GAC in preparing the European Council.

All studies of COREPER indicate that its members consider themselves to have a dual role. According to Hayes-Renshaw et al. (1989: 136), while the Permanent Representatives 'are the trustworthy executors of the instructions from their respective capitals', they also have strong ties of solidarity with their colleagues in COREPER. These ties are developed as a result of intensive social interaction in Brussels. Committee members eat, drink, and breathe EU issues seven days a week. Lewis (1998: 487) argued that this constant interaction between the same individuals built up a considerable legacy of 'social capital', meaning that the individuals concerned trust one another, and understand and have sympathy for each other's points of view.

The ties are also the result of all of the Permanent Representatives being in the same position vis-à-vis their national governments. All of them will have sympathy with one of their number who is bound by a tight mandate on a particular issue, because they are sometimes placed in that position themselves. In such a situation, they will try to help each other out, perhaps by persuading their own government to make concessions if they feel that the issue is not so important for them. The attitude of the Permanent Representatives to a negotiation is ambivalent: they all want their government's position to prevail; they also want to reach agreement even at the cost of not achieving all of their own government's objectives in the negotiation (Hayes-Renshaw et al. 1989: 136).

One explanation of this approach is based on rational choice and game theory. It is also compatible with an intergovernmental bargaining image of the committee. On this view, when Permanent Representatives make concessions, or urge their governments to make concessions, it is not just because they feel a sense of social solidarity with their counterparts from other member states. It is also indicative of the strong sense that they have of being involved in a continuous process of bargaining with the same partners. In the language of game theory, they are involved in *iterated* games (that is, the same game is repeated several times with the same participants). This changes the calculation of what is rational as compared with isolated games. In a one-off game, it is rational to take any step to damage your opponent's position and to further your own, even so far as cheating on the rules if you can get away with it. In iterated games, the use of such tactics is likely to backfire during a subsequent round. If you have reneged on a deal in one round of negotiations, it will be difficult to get anyone to conclude a deal with you in subsequent rounds.

This logic of iterated games in EU bargaining is more apparent to Permanent Representatives than it sometimes is to ministers, who have many other concerns, such as accounting for their Brussels diplomacy to their national parliaments and cabinet colleagues, and are less intensively socialized into the **Union method** of bargaining. It means that Permanent Representatives are often involved in trying to educate their governments about the nature of the EU bargaining process. The German Permanent Representative is sometimes jokingly referred to in the national capital as the *ständiger Verräter* (permanent traitor) rather than the official designation as *ständiger Vertreter* (Permanent Representative) (see Barber 1995: I; Lewis 1998: 483). Although this sort of suspicion may occasionally exist in national capitals, it would be a foolish government that did not listen seriously to the advice of the Permanent Representative when deciding on its national negotiating position. This could be taken as evidence that the intergovernmentalist view, that national preferences are formulated independently of influence from the EU level, is false.

Another explanation of the approach of COREPER, which also challenges the intergovernmentalist view, is based on social constructivism. Lewis (2000) identified five main features of the operation of COREPER that resulted from the circumstances and socialization processes identified above. He labelled these: diffuse reciprocity; thick trust; mutual responsiveness; a consensus-reflex; and a culture of compromise.

- *Diffuse reciprocity* means that the Permanent Representatives will support one of their number on an issue that is important to that individual's member state but less important to their own, and in return will expect to receive such support when they themselves have a problem. This is not the same as the sort of formal agreement that is allowed for in rational-choice bargains, in which deals are done that A will support B on issue C in return for the support of B on issue D. The reciprocity is diffuse, not specific. It relates to the collectivity of COREPER across the whole range of issues.

- *Thick trust*—as opposed to 'thin trust'—means that the Permanent Representatives feel that they can be honest and open with one another without anything that they say being reported back to other governments. In restricted sessions, they feel that they speak freely, knowing that what they say will not come out.

- *Mutual responsiveness* means that the Permanent Representatives, because they work together so closely, come to understand one another's perspectives and problems, and will try not to approach an issue in a way that they know will cause problems for other members of COREPER.

- The *consensus-reflex* is deeply embedded in the culture of COREPER. Although there is provision for QMV where the Treaty specifies, it is not used extensively, and is always the last resort. COREPER will continue to seek a consensus long after it is apparent that a qualified majority could be mustered if a vote were called.

- The *culture of compromise* arises from a spirit of accommodation that brings together the previous features. Lewis (2000: 271) refers to the Permanent Representatives spending extra time to 'bring everyone on board' even if one member state is being inflexible in its position.

High-Level Preparatory Bodies

There are several of these high-level preparatory bodies. Some have been mentioned already: the three that prepare ECOFIN; the SCA in agricultural policy; and the

PSC as one of the preparatory bodies for the Foreign Affairs Council. Two other bodies prepare the Foreign Affairs Council: the Trade Policy Committee, which deals with the common commercial policy, and the EU Military Committee, which is responsible for ESDP and which may be attended by the chiefs of military staff of the member states, but is more likely to be attended by Brussels-based military attachés.

Lewis (2000) went on to ask whether the pattern of socialization applied to these bodies as with COREPER. He surveyed six of these preparatory bodies, which correspond to the present-day SCA, the Trade Policy Committee, the Budget Committee, the Economic and Finance Committee (EFC), the PSC, and the K-4 Committee (a co-ordinating body for Justice and Home Affairs that was later split up). The conclusion of this investigation (Lewis 2000: 282) was that only the EFC came close to exhibiting the five features to anything like the same extent as COREPER. This weakened somewhat the thrust of the supranationalist argument, but not the validity of the social constructivist approach, because the empirical findings underlined the need to investigate the 'sociality and normative environment in which interests are defined and defended' (Lewis 2003b: 262). Lewis's research was pioneering in highlighting the socialization effects, but the data are now well over a decade old and a re-examination of these findings is overdue.

The Working Parties

Moving further down the hierarchy, the working parties that prepare recommendations for the Permanent Representatives involve intensive interaction between national and Commission officials. The processes of socialization that Lewis and others argued apply to COREPER also apply here. Although the people who sit on these committees are national representatives, research by Beyers and Dierickx (1998: 307–8) showed that members of working groups soon started to judge other members on the basis of the level of expertise that they showed in the committee rather than on nationality. Ludlow (1991: 103) went further to argue that 'Commission officials act as thirteenth members of the Council machinery', implying that the distinction between national and Commission representatives was almost meaningless in the work of these groups.

The thrust of all of these arguments is that the members of the working parties develop a sense of collegiality and engagement in a joint enterprise that makes it more sensible to see them as individuals participating in a team effort than as representatives of individual states. They are operating very much at the 'problem-solving' end of Scharpf's spectrum of types of negotiation. Agreements are reached largely on the basis of convincing arguments, not political weight or bargaining skill.

The Council Presidency

Under the original Treaty provisions, a different member state assumed the presidency of the Council every six months. During its period of office, that member state had responsibility for preparing and chairing meetings of the European Council, the Council of Ministers and its various committees, as well as for some functions of representing the EU externally. In the course of its six months in charge, the presidency arranged and chaired from seventy to ninety meetings of ministers, and many more times that of committees. In addition, at least one European Council meeting fell during the six months' presidency. Although assisted in this considerable task by the Council Secretariat (see Insight 14.3), the civil service of the state holding the presidency carried much of the burden of this work. Some authors, for instance Tallberg (2003), argued that states holding the presidency were able to advance their interests during their term in charge of the EU's agenda.

This system was subject to two main criticisms: that six months was too brief a period for the tenure of the presidency; and that the scale of demands on the country holding the presidency had outstripped the capacity of all but the largest member states to cope (for analysis of the old system, see Hayes-Renshaw and Wallace 2006: 154–7). The increasing range of policy areas from the 1980s simply added additional activities for the presidency to prepare. Moreover, with twenty-eight member states, holding the presidency is infrequent: once every fourteen years.

Insight 14.3 The Council General Secretariat

- According to Lewis (2010), the Council Secretariat employs about 3,300 people. A tenth of these are at the senior A grade. It is the 'institutional memory' of the Council of Ministers and assists with the organization of meetings, and can help with mediating between national delegations. It is based in Brussels in the Justus Lipsius building.

- The two most senior positions were, until the Lisbon Treaty, the post of Secretary-General and High Representative and the Deputy Secretary-General. The former position was held by Javier Solana from 1999 to 2009. The appointment of Catherine Ashton to an enhanced position that straddles both the Commission and the Council resulted in change at the top of the Council Secretariat.

- The Council Secretariat has a Legal Service as well as over 1,000 translators. Interpreters are drawn from the European Commission's staff. There are currently eight Directorates-General (DGs). The DG for External and Political-Military Affairs will become integrated into the new European External Action Service, which will also encompass staff from DG RELEX in the Commission.

- Also situated under the auspices of the Council Secretariat is the EU's Military Staff (EUMS), which oversees ESDP activities, and is headed by a three-star general. Within the EUMS, there are several Directorates responsible for such functions as intelligence, operations, and logistics. The operations function includes provision of a Council facility, the EU Operations Centre, which can command small operations of up to 2,000 troops anywhere in the world. Twenty-four military or civilian operations had been conducted (or were under way) under the auspices of the ESDP by February 2010, so the role of the EUMS is very important.

The Lisbon Treaty aimed to tackle these issues. The new system comprises four different presidencies:

- the European Council—an appointment for two-and-a-half years, this arrangement is consistent with the European Council being designated a separate institution;
- the Council of Foreign Affairs, chaired by the High Representative for Foreign Affairs and Security Policy (a five-year appointment) (see Chapter 26);
- the Euro Group, which comprises only states in the eurozone, elects its own president to a two-and-a-half-year term (see Chapter 21);
- a 'trio presidency' of three member states, which spans an eighteen-month period, and is responsible for other sectoral Councils and their preparatory bodies.

The trio system had, in fact, commenced in 2007 after reform to the Council's rules of procedure. The Lisbon Treaty merely formalized this change. The basic principle is that the state holding the presidency for six months has an agreed programme with the states preceding and succeeding its term in office. Thus, at the start of 2014, Greece (January–June) held the six-month presidency, and the trio presidency consisted of its predecessor, Lithuania (July–December 2013), and its successor, Italy (July–December 2014). Their trio programme had been presented in the Council in December 2012 (Council of the EU 2012). The current sequence of presidencies, agreed in 2007, is set out in Table 14.1.

Council presidencies, even in their scaled-back role after the Lisbon Treaty reforms, continue to entail a lot of organizational responsibilities. For instance, the Irish presidency (January–July 2013) was reported to have entailed 2,000 meetings at all levels

Table 14.1 List of Council Presidencies, 2014–20

Member State	Time Period
Greece	January–June 2014
Italy	July–December 2014
Latvia	January–June 2015
Luxembourg	July–December 2015
Netherlands	January–June 2016
Slovakia	July–December 2016
Malta	January–June 2017
United Kingdom	July–December 2017
Estonia	January–June 2018
Bulgaria	July–December 2018
Austria	January–June 2019
Romania	July–December 2019
Finland	January–June 2020

of the Council hierarchy, 349 three-way meetings of the EP and Council as part of inter-institutional decision making, and fifty-four ministerial Councils (*European Voice*, 4 July 2013: 10). The preceding presidency had been held by Cyprus and the number of meetings placed a significant burden on a state with a small diplomatic service.

CONCLUSION

The European Council and the Council of Ministers are quite different institutions and with different paths of development. The European Council is of central importance to the 'high politics' of the EU, while the Council of Ministers is central to decision making and legislation. The European Council has moved from the informality of the 'Library Group' to an institution in its own right. The Council of Ministers has gradually become more of a co-legislator as the powers of the EP have increased (see Chapter 15, The Struggle for Power). Like the Council of Ministers, the European Council holds occasional informal sessions to try to attain some of the advantages of the less-structured organization of the past. Formal sessions of the Council of Ministers have to take place with camera and screen facilities so that the speakers can be identified in a chamber comprising twenty-eight delegations (plus the presidency, the Commission, the Council Secretariat, and interpreters), each being permitted a minister and at least one official. In other words, meetings are typically attended by over a hundred participants. The increased size of the Council may reduce the socialization effects reported in earlier research. It may also be that the Lisbon Treaty's strengthened provisions for enhanced co-operation will lead to greater use of pioneer groups of like-minded states (see Chapter 12, The Post-Lisbon Architecture of the EU).

At first sight, it would appear obvious that the Council of Ministers is an intergovernmental organization. However, this is a simplification of a complex situation. First, it is clear that the Council of Ministers as a collective entity may also be regarded as a **supranational institution**, because it can and does agree to legislation that is then binding on all of the member states. Second, it is not clear that the Council of Ministers, in all of its manifestations, operates simply as an intergovernmental bargaining forum. Wessels (1991: 136) insisted that 'the Council is not an "interstate body"... but a body at the supranational level'. Hayes-Renshaw and Wallace (1997: 278) were less sure of that, but were clear that it was 'not a wholly "intergovernmental" institution'. As they put it:

> For the analyst the Council and its processes embody the recurrent tension in the construction of the EC between the 'supranationalists' and the 'intergovernmentalists'.
>
> (Hayes-Renshaw and Wallace 2006: 2–3)

To try to analyse the role of the Council of Ministers as a whole would be a mistake. It is important to disaggregate its component parts in order to understand at exactly which point in the machinery issues are dealt with. Only with this knowledge can an informed judgement be made concerning the key actors involved and their motivations. Even then, the task is complicated by the secrecy that surrounds the activity of the Council in virtually all of its manifestations. The holding of open sessions when passing legislative acts—as formalized in the Lisbon Treaty—may simply transfer the secrecy to other venues or to other parts of Council sessions. Here it is worth noting the provisions in Article 16 TEU, that 'each Council meeting shall be divided into two parts, dealing respectively with deliberations on Union legislative acts and non-legislative activities'.

The most informed research suggests that a high proportion of Council of Ministers' decisions are taken relatively low down in the decisional hierarchy. It is here, within COREPER and the preparatory bodies, that observers have found the greatest departure from intergovernmentalism in Council activities. At the ministerial level, decisions tend to be more politicized and national positions less open to negotiation. However, to complicate matters further, anecdotal evidence suggests that, even at the ministerial level, some formations of the Council are more collegial than others. Lewis (2000) also concluded that there is considerable variation in the degree of collegiality exhibited by the senior preparatory committees. The conclusion must be, therefore, that the argument between intergovernmental and supranational theorists cannot be settled finally so far as the Council is concerned, but that there are some grounds for not assuming too readily that because the Council is the institution in which the governments of member states are most directly represented, it is necessarily an intergovernmental body. The increasing provision for decision making in the Council of Ministers by QMV is a further dimension to any departure from pure intergovernmentalism, since even the provision—if not the practice—can result in a shift in the calculation of national interests.

The other theoretical debate around the Council of Ministers concerns whether to approach it using the techniques of rational choice institutionalism and game theory, or whether to understand it as a case study in social constructivism. To some extent, this division corresponds with the division between intergovernmental and supranational theories of the nature of the Council of Ministers. Intergovernmentalists tend to favour rationalist approaches to understanding its workings because they see it as a forum for hard bargaining around national interests, and it is in understanding the operation of such forums that rational choice and game theory have made some of their biggest contributions. Supranationalists tend to rest their arguments on evidence that the representatives of the member states on the various committees and Council of Ministers formations become socialized into a different construction of what they are trying to achieve from a simple defence of national interests, and into informally institutionalized procedures that emphasize consensus and co-operation rather than instrumental bargaining. However, it is possible to accept a social constructivist **epistemology** and still come to the conclusion on the basis of empirical evidence that the socialization process does not operate very effectively in some of the committees and some of the manifestations of the Council.

KEY POINTS

Definitions and Distinctions

- There is a hierarchy of EU institutions that comprise representatives of national governments.
- At the top of the hierarchy is the European Council, which consists of regular summit meetings of the heads of government of the EU member states.
- Below the European Council is the Council of Ministers, which consists of several Councils of national Ministers for different areas of policy together with their preparatory bodies of officials.

Intergovernmental and Supranational Interpretations

- At first sight the Council is a purely intergovernmental body.
- A deeper analysis reveals a more complex picture, with elements of supranationalism.

The European Council

- The European Council was established in the 1970s to provide a collective response to the challenges of economic interdependence, to allow national governments collectively to control the direction of the EC, to avoid policy segmentation, and to present a united front to the outside world.

- The functions of the European Council now include: to provide general direction to the EU; to oversee Treaty reform and enlargement; to make key foreign policy decisions; to act as policy maker of last resort; and to monitor the development of certain policies.

- The European Council faces problems of overload, over-optimism, over-cautiousness, and over-expectation.

- The European Council's work has arguably resulted in it increasing the supranational character of the EU.

The Council of Ministers

- The Council of Ministers meets in a variety of formations depending on the subject under consideration.

- Although there is no formal hierarchy of Council meetings, informally the GAC and those sectoral Councils concerning foreign affairs, finance, and agriculture have the highest status.

- The frequency with which ministers meet in sectoral Councils can lead to the emergence of a sense of collective enterprise, marked by communicative rationality rather than instrumental rationality.

- Because of the large measure of secrecy in which the Council of Ministers meets, it is difficult to research the degree to which individual Councils engage in problem solving rather than bargaining around national interests.

COREPER and other Preparatory Bodies

- A large proportion of 'Council' decisions are actually taken lower down the decisional hierarchy. Arguments that the Council is a supranational entity are strongest at this level.

- The Permanent Representatives of member governments interact regularly and develop trust and solidarity, which makes agreement between them easier than between politicians who are less regularly engaged and who have broader concerns.

- The operation of COREPER can be explained either from a rational choice bargaining perspective as the behaviour appropriate to actors involved in iterated games, or from a social constructivist perspective as the building of a new sense of identity among the Permanent Representatives.

- Other senior preparatory bodies have not achieved the same degree of trust and solidarity as COREPER, with the exception of the Economic and Financial Committee.

- National representatives on working parties also undergo a process of socialization that produces a problem-solving approach in which decisions are taken more on the strength of evidence than of political considerations.

The Council Presidency

- Originally, the Council presidency applied to all levels of the hierarchy and rotated between member states every six months. This system was criticized on the grounds of brevity of tenure and for the scale of the demands that it placed on smaller member states.

- Following the Lisbon Treaty's implementation, the European Council has its own President, as does the Council of Foreign Affairs and the Euro Group. All other business is run by 'trio presidencies' comprising three states over a period of eighteen months.

FURTHER READING

The most recent detailed interpretation of both institutions is by **U. Puetter**, *The European Council and the Council. New Intergovernmentalism and Institutional Change* (Oxford: Oxford University Press, 2014). **Puetter** has also authored an interpretive article on the European Council: 'Europe's Deliberative Intergovernmentalism: The Role of the Council and European Council in EU economic Governance', *Journal of European Public Policy*, 19 (2012): 161–78. Other post-Lisbon studies of the Council are currently lacking. An extremely comprehensive treatment of the functioning of the Council, which remains a standard work on the subject despite pre-dating the Lisbon Treaty, is **F. Hayes-Renshaw and H. Wallace**, *The Council of Ministers*, 2nd edn (Basingstoke: Palgrave Macmillan, 2006). **M. Westlake and D. Galloway (eds)**, *The Council of the European Union*, 3rd edn (London: John Harper Publishing, 2006) pre-dates the Lisbon Treaty changes, offers a comprehensive profile, and is written by knowledgeable Brussels insiders. For analysis of decision making in the Council, see **D. Naurin and H. Wallace (eds)**, *Unveiling the Council of the European Union* (Basingstoke: Palgrave Macmillan, 2008) as well as the VoteWatch Europe website: **http://votewatch.eu**.

Apart from Puetter's study, contemporary studies of the European Council are limited. An edited collection by **F. Foret and Y-S Rittelmeyer**, *The European Council and European Governance: The Commanding Heights of the EU* (Abingdon: Routledge, 2013) covers aspects of the institution. Also still of use is **J. Werts**, *The European Council* (London: John Harper, 2008). An early assessment of the strengths and weaknesses of the institutionalized summit meetings, which remains relevant, is provided in **S. Bulmer and W. Wessels**, *The European Council: Decision-Making in European Politics* (Basingstoke and London: Macmillan, 1987).

Finally, the European Council (by **de Schoutheete**) and the Council of Ministers (by **Hayes-Renshaw**) are each given chapter-length consideration in **J. Peterson and M. Shackleton (eds)**, *The Institutions of the European Union*, 3rd edn (Oxford: Oxford University Press, 2012).

 online resource centre **Visit the Online Resource Centre that accompanies this book for links to more information on the Council: http://oxfordtextbooks.co.uk/orc/bache4e/**

Chapter 15

The European Parliament

Chapter Overview

The European Parliament (EP) is the one directly elected institution of the European Union (EU). The members of the EP (MEPs) are elected once every five years, and since the first direct elections, in 1979, the EP has campaigned for more power and influence. Over the subsequent period, there has been a considerable increase in its powers, including through the Lisbon Treaty. The struggle for increased powers is discussed in more detail below, after the basic structure and functions of the EP have been summarized. The chapter then turns to look at debates and research on the EP. One theme of the academic debate is the extent to which the EP has become an effective independent actor in the affairs of the EU, and how far it will continue to move in that direction in the future. This clearly parallels the discussion in the previous two chapters, on the Commission and the Council.

Composition and Functions

The EP, as elected in 2014, consists of 751 MEPs, divided between the member states on a basis that is approximately proportionate to size of population, although the small countries are somewhat over-represented to strengthen their voice. The distribution of the 751 seats following the 2014 elections is shown in Table 15.1.

The EP meets in plenary session in Strasbourg for three or four days every month, except August, and additional plenaries are held in Brussels. However, most of its work is channelled through standing committees, which may change designation following elections (see Box 15.1 for those in the 2009–14 Parliament). It can also establish temporary committees (a special committee on the Financial, Economic, and Social Crisis was meeting in 2009–11) and committees of enquiry. Committee meetings are normally held in Brussels.

The EP has a President, a Bureau, a Conference of Presidents, and a Secretariat. The President is elected by the MEPs from among their number for a two-and-a-half-year renewable term. The President represents the EP on official occasions and in relations with other institutions, presides over debates during plenary sessions, and chairs meetings of the Bureau and the Conference of Presidents. The Bureau consists of the President, the fourteen Vice-Presidents, and five 'quaestors' who deal with administrative and financial matters relating to MEPs. The members are elected by the MEPs for

Table 15.1 Distribution of Seats in the European Parliament (2014)

Austria	18	Germany	96	Poland	51
Belgium	21	Greece	21	Portugal	21
Bulgaria	17	Hungary	21	Romania	32
Croatia	11	Ireland	11	Slovakia	13
Cyprus	6	Italy	73	Slovenia	8
Czech Republic	21	Latvia	8	Spain	54
Denmark	13	Lithuania	11	Sweden	20
Estonia	6	Luxembourg	6	United Kingdom	73
Finland	13	Malta	6		
France	74	Netherlands	26	**TOTAL**	**751**

Box 15.1 Committees of the European Parliament (as of February 2014)

- Agriculture and Rural Development Committee
- Budgets Committee
- Budgetary Control Committee
- Civil Liberties, Justice, and Home Affairs Committee
- Constitutional Affairs Committee
- Culture and Education Committee
- Development Committee
- Economic and Monetary Affairs Committee
- Employment and Social Affairs Committee
- Environment, Public Health, and Food Safety Committee
- Fisheries Committee
- Foreign Affairs Committee
  — Security and Defence Sub-Committee
  — Human Rights Sub-Committee
- Industry, Research, and Energy Committee
- Internal Market and Consumer Protection Committee
- International Trade Committee
- Legal Affairs Committee
- Petitions Committee
- Regional Development Committee
- Transport and Tourism Committee
- Women's Rights and Gender Equality Committee

a term of two-and-a-half years. The Conference of Presidents consists of the President and the Chairs of the Political Groups. It draws up the agenda for plenary sessions, fixes the timetable for the work of parliamentary bodies, and establishes the terms of reference and size of parliamentary committees and delegations. The Secretariat consists of over 5,000 administrative and clerical staff, headed by the Secretary-General (Judge and Earnshaw 2008: 166). Around one-third of the staff are in the language service, concerned with translation and interpretation. In addition to the Secretariat, the political groups have their own administrative support.

The political composition of the EP is determined by the elections, which are held every five years. Historically, the three largest political blocs in the EP have been the European People's Party (largely Christian democrats), social democrats (currently called the Progressive Alliance of Socialists and Democrats) and the Alliance of Liberals and Democrats for Europe. The Parliament elected in 2014 (see also Table 15.2) was distinctive because it witnessed a major increase in electoral support for Eurosceptic parties, some on the political extremes (see Table 15.2). Indeed, approximately a third of the MEPs challenge the mainstream pro-EU agenda. This Euroscepticism includes the European Conservatives and Reformists, dominated by the British Conservatives and Polish counterparts in the Law and Justice Party; the Europe of Freedom and Direct Democracy group, dominated by the UK Independence Party and the Italian 5 Star Movement; and the Non-Attached. This last 'non-group' comprises MEPs who could not form, or were not accepted into, a group. By far the biggest national delegation is the *Front National*, which secured the most votes in the French election. This outcome is likely to have an impact on parliamentary business, with opposition to immigration and further EU integration. Nevertheless, the other side of the coin is that two-thirds of MEPs remain in the mainstream. Given that the Eurosceptic forces, especially those in the non-attached category, will likely be characterized by intense rivalries, it is possible that the impact might not be so great on the pattern of EP politics outlined throughout this chapter.

The powers of the EP are summarized in Insight 15.1. It has legislative, budgetary, and supervisory functions. In the legislative field, it has emerged as a co-legislator with the Council of Ministers in most areas of EU legislation primarily via the ordinary legislative procedure (co-decision), which applies to over eighty specific provisions in the Treaty on the Functioning of the European Union (TFEU). The various legislative procedures, and the powers of the EP in each of them, are discussed in Chapter 12, Decision-Making Procedures. The EP and the Council of Ministers are the joint budgetary authorities of the EU. The budgetary procedure, and the role of the EP in it, is described in Chapter 12, Decision-Making Procedures.

The supervisory functions of the EP relate to both the Commission and the Council. Under the Maastricht Treaty, the EP was given the right to approve appointment of the President and members of the Commission. The Treaty of Amsterdam strengthened the power relating to the President, who needed specific approval by the EP. Under the Lisbon Treaty, the candidate for the presidency has to be chosen taking into account the results of the most recent EP elections: a provision that led to parties entering the 2014 elections with candidates nominated to become Commission President. The EP has the power to dismiss the whole of the Commission on a vote of censure—but in neither case can it target individual Commissioners. A motion of censure requires a positive vote from an absolute majority of MEPs and

> ### Insight 15.1 The Powers of the European Parliament
>
> **Legislative**
>
> - Under the ordinary legislative procedure, the EP shares the final decision on most proposals with the Council (co-decision procedure).
> - Consent is required for the enlargement of the EU, agreements with third countries, and a range of other decisions.
> - It delivers opinions on Commission proposals under the consultation procedure in a limited number of policy areas.
>
> **Budgetary**
>
> - Its approval is required for the annual budget.
> - Its Budgetary Control Committee checks expenditure (together with the Court of Auditors).
>
> **Supervisory**
>
> - It approves the appointment of Commission President.
> - It approves the appointment of the Commission after public hearings.
> - It questions the Council and Commission.
> - It can censure and dismiss the whole Commission.

two-thirds of the votes cast. The EP also has the right to ask the Commission written and oral questions.

In respect to the European Council and the Council of Ministers, the powers of the EP are more limited. It can table written and oral questions about the activities of the Council of Ministers, and the Foreign Minister of the state holding the presidency of the Council reports to the EP at the beginning and end of the presidency. For the European Council, the Lisbon Treaty (Article 15 TEU) formalized the practice whereby the EP is given a report following each European Council meeting. The President of the EP is invited to the start of European Council sessions 'to be heard' (Article 235 TFEU) but does not participate in its meetings after this opening opportunity to make a contribution.

Outside the '**Union method**', the EP is to be kept informed of developments relating to the Common Foreign and Security Policy (CFSP) and the Parliament's views are to be taken into consideration. The High Representative of the Union for Foreign Affairs and Security Policy (HRUFASP) is responsible for maintaining relations with the EP.

The Struggle for Power

In the original Treaties, the forerunner of the present EP was neither directly elected nor endowed with significant powers. Members of the European Parliamentary Assembly

(EPA) were members of national parliaments who were seconded to the EPA. The EPA had the right to be consulted by the Council of Ministers before legislation was agreed, but its opinion could be, and frequently was, ignored; it could dismiss the Commission as a whole on a vote of censure, but only if it could achieve the difficult degree of unity needed to reach the double majority requirement (two-thirds of those voting, constituting an absolute majority of members). From the outset, though, the EPA set about trying to extract the right to be directly elected, and to have stronger powers.

The main steps in the transformation of the weak EPA into the much stronger EP were listed by Corbett et al (2003: 354) as:

> the budget Treaties of 1970 and 1975; the introduction of direct elections by universal suffrage in 1979; the 1980 *Isoglucose* ruling of the European Court of Justice, giving Parliament a *de facto* delaying power; the Single European Act in 1987, introducing the co-operation procedure and the assent procedure; the Treaty of Maastricht in 1993, bringing in the co-decision procedure, and giving Parliament the right to allow (or not) the Commission as a whole to take office through a vote of confidence; and the Treaty of Amsterdam, which greatly extended the scope of co-decision, modified it to Parliament's advantage, and gave Parliament the right to confirm or reject a designated President of the Commission.

Subsequently, the Lisbon Treaty greatly extended the scope of co-decision, while renaming assent as the consent procedure (see Chapter 12, Decision-Making Procedures).

In achieving these gains, the EP has used a number of tactical devices. First, most of its members have lobbied for increased powers for the EP within their national parties. Here, the most significant step forward was the introduction of direct elections. Direct elections 'created a new class of elected representatives in Europe ... whose career depended on making something of the European dimension' (Corbett et al. 2003: 356). Second, the argument that the powers of the EP needed to be increased in order to close the 'democratic deficit' has been consistently used by the EP. The academic debate about the democratic and legitimacy deficits is reviewed in Chapter 3 (Democracy). Third, it has made the most extensive use possible of its existing powers, and tried to stretch the definition of those powers. In this, the EP sometimes found an ally in the European Court of Justice (ECJ). A number of judgments of the ECJ, on cases brought to it by the EP, increased the powers of the EP in the 1980s and 1990s, starting with the 1980 *Isoglucose* judgment. These judgments are examined in Chapter 16 (ECJ Rulings on the Powers of Institutions). Alongside this 'minimalist' approach, the EP has also pursued a 'maximalist' approach. In 1984, the EP, under the leadership of the Italian federalist MEP, Altiero Spinelli, produced its draft Treaty Establishing the European Union. It had little influence on the shape of the EU at the time, but set out the EP's ambition and provided inspiration for some of the changes introduced by the member states in later Treaty reforms. During the Constitutional Convention of 2002–03, sixteen MEPs participated in the drafting of what became the Constitutional Treaty (see Chapter 10, The Constitutional Treaty).

In what follows, the powers of EP and how they were gained are discussed in more or less the order that they were granted. The granting of additional budgetary powers came before direct elections, but so fundamental were direct elections that they are discussed before the budgetary powers. Then the increased legislative and scrutiny powers are considered.

Direct Elections

Agreement to replace the EPA with a directly elected body was reached at the Rome meeting of the European Council in December 1975. Why was this decision taken—and what were its consequences?

The decision took place in a less-than-transparent deal among the heads of government in the European Council. Germany, Italy, and the **Benelux** countries had long favoured a directly elected EP. The governments of these states were convinced by the argument that transferring competences to the EC would lead to a democratic deficit unless there were a directly elected parliament at that level that could take over the role of scrutiny that would be lost to national parliaments. The crucial shift was on the part of France under the presidency of Valéry Giscard d'Estaing.

This shift in position placed Britain, which was even more reluctant, in a more isolated position. Having agreed to the elections, the Labour government, which was contending with divisions in its own party and was reliant on support from the Liberal Party to stay in office, delayed the implementation arrangements. Consequently, the first elections were put back a year, until June 1979. The first directly elected Parliament sought to exploit its new democratic credentials by several routes. It challenged the Council of Ministers over the annual budget. It was also emboldened to demand more powers of decision making and control over the Commission.

Budgetary Powers

The first granting of additional powers to the EP came in the Treaty of Luxembourg in 1970, when it was given the right to amend 'non-compulsory' items of expenditure in the budget. This agreement was the outcome of an intergovernmental negotiation about the settlement of the long-running budgetary dispute that had led to the 1965 crisis (see Chapter 7, The 1965 Crisis). France continued to be reluctant to grant any budgetary powers to the still indirectly elected EPA at that time, but President Pompidou was anxious to get the system of 'own resources' agreed prior to the opening of entry negotiations with Britain. For France, the goal was to set up a budgetary system to fund the Common Agricultural Policy (CAP) in a way that would leave France a large net beneficiary from the system. As Britain would inevitably lose out from such a system, agreement could not be left until after British entry because the British government would block any such settlement. However, the other five member states insisted that the loss of parliamentary control over national budgetary contributions must be redressed by an increase in the control of the EPA. As with all such intergovernmental negotiations, the outcome was a compromise.

> A distinction introduced by the French between expenditure items that followed directly from Community legal acts (compulsory expenditure) and expenditure that did not, such as administrative expenses (non-compulsory expenditure), was accepted, albeit grudgingly by some delegations (the Dutch delegation most notably) as it gave the EP a final say over only about 4–5 per cent of the entire Community expenditure (that is, non-compulsory expenditure).

(Rittberger 2003: 217)

Subsequently, in the 1975 Budget Treaty, the EP was granted the formal right to reject the budget as a whole. Working with these limited powers, the EP pushed its budgetary role to the maximum, especially after the first direct elections in 1979, so that '[i]n the early 1980s the annual budgetary cycle was punctuated with unending disputes between the institutions on what were relatively small amounts of money' (Laffan 1997a: 77).

In December 1979, the first directly elected EP blocked the passing of the budget for 1980 in a test of strength against the Council. For several months, the EC had to survive on the system of 'provisional twelfths', whereby it is allowed to spend each month an amount equivalent to one-twelfth of the previous year's budget. Eventually, the MEPs came under tremendous pressure from their national parties to lift their veto, which they did without winning any further concessions on the substance of the budget from the Council—but a marker had been put down that the Council should not treat the directly elected EP with disdain. An informal agreement was reached on resolving such disputes should they arise in the future, although this did not prevent another crisis the following year, when the EP passed a budget that exceeded the maximum rate of increase. The EP was taken to the Court of Justice by the Council, but an out-of-court agreement was reached in June 1982. Again, the EP gave way on the substance of the dispute, but in return got agreement on a joint declaration on the definitions of compulsory and non-compulsory expenditure, and on the respective roles of the two institutions in the budgetary process (Laffan 1997a: 82).

After further acrimonious exchanges in each of the next two years, in 1985 another serious crisis erupted. The EP was becoming increasingly agitated at the failure of the member states to provide adequate funds for new common policies that had been agreed. The main reason for this failure was an inability to bring under control expenditure on the CAP, over which the EP did not have the power of amendment. At first reading on the 1986 budget, the EP inserted amendments to reduce agricultural expenditure, which it had no right to do. The Council removed the amendments, but the EP restored them, and declared the budget passed. The case went to the Court again, where the budget was declared illegal, but the ECJ also banged heads together, telling the Council and the EP that they were joint budgetary authorities, that neither could act unilaterally, and that they had to find means of reaching agreement (Laffan 1997a: 82; Corbett et al. 2003: 360–2).

It was clear that the disputes and delays in agreeing the annual budgets could not go on indefinitely. Out of this awareness arose the 1988 Inter-Institutional Agreement on Budgetary Discipline. After this, the budget ceased to be at the forefront of the EP's struggle for power. Finally, as a result of reforms in the Lisbon Treaty, the distinction between compulsory and non-compulsory expenditure was abolished. The EP also secured the right to approve the seven-year multi-annual budget. Consequently, the EP and the Council are co-equal budgetary authorities and follow procedures set out in Chapter 12 (The Budgetary Procedure).

Influence in the Legislative Process

The EP from the outset argued the case for it to be an effective co-legislator with the Council of Ministers. This was gradually introduced, first through the now-abolished co-operation procedure, and then through the co-decision procedure (see Chapter 12,

Decision-Making Procedures). The crucial breakthrough was the introduction of the co-operation procedure in the Single European Act (SEA). This was insisted upon by the governments of those states—especially Germany and Italy—that were most convinced by the federalist arguments and concerns regarding the democratic deficit (Rittberger 2003: 220). Consensus gradually emerged between the governments that, for the single market to be created, they would have to accept **qualified majority voting (QMV)**, otherwise every individual measure would be vetoed by the government of the state that stood to be most adversely affected. This implied, though, that national parliaments would no longer be able to reject a proposed measure by instructing their government's representative to veto it in the Council. The democratic deficit argument implied that the loss of control by the national parliaments should be made up by an increase in the role of the EP.

Once the principle of a larger role for the EP in the legislative process had been established, the extension of that role followed; as experience of operating the new system made it clear that co-operation was a clumsy procedure, and that the EP would use its powers to improve legislation, not just to be obstructive. Subsequent Treaty reform increased the number of policy issues on which co-decision applies and the co-operation procedure was abolished by the Lisbon Treaty. The move to the co-decision process provoked an academic debate as to how far that increased the effective influence of the EP in the legislative process.

The EP and the Commission

There are two main aspects of the ability of the EP to exercise control over the Commission. The first is in its powers over the appointment of the College of Commissioners. The second is in its power to dismiss the College if it disapproves of their conduct.

The power of the EP in the appointment of a new Commission was originally zero. This is an area, however, in which the maximalist strategy produced results: Treaty amendments gave the EP limited powers that were then exploited fully under the minimalist strategy. The interaction between the maximalist strategy (formal rule change) and the minimalist one (informal rule changes) has been charted well in an institutionalist analysis undertaken by Adrienne Héritier (2007: 139–59). At Maastricht, the heads of government agreed to consult the EP on the choice of the President of the Commission and to give it the right to consent (or not consent) to the appointment of the College of Commissioners as a whole. They also agreed to bring the term of office of the Commissioners into line with that of the EP, so that the newly elected Parliament would be asked, as one of its first acts, to approve the proposed new Commission. In 1994, the EP introduced hearings of Commissioners-Designate. In the Amsterdam Treaty, there was a further extension of powers, when the EP was given a formal right of approval of the European Council's nominee for President. These changes were made with an eye on the need to address the democratic deficit. It was hoped that the new powers would persuade voters that the EP was an institution that had the characteristics of a real parliament, and thereby contribute to increased interest in the European parliamentary elections (Smith 1999: 68).

Having gained the right to approve the appointment of the President, and separately of the other Commissioners as a whole, the EP reverted to its minimalist strategy of making the most extensive use possible of its powers. It adapted its internal rules of procedure so that the approval or rejection of the Commission President required only a simple majority, and if the nomination was rejected, the member states would be asked to make a new nomination. It also adopted a rule of procedure that the approval of the Commission as a whole would follow parliamentary hearings in which each of the Commissioners would be subjected to cross-examination *in public* by the members of the relevant specialist committee of the EP (Judge and Earnshaw 2002: 355). These procedural adaptations increased the leverage of the modest extra powers granted in the Maastricht Treaty in ways that will be explored below.

The other aspect of parliamentary control over the Commission is in its power to dismiss Commissioners. Here, the Treaty gives the EP what at first sight is a powerful weapon. If a motion of censure on the Commission is passed by a two-thirds majority of the votes cast, representing a majority of MEPs, then the Commission must resign as a body (Article 234 TFEU). However, this right is less powerful than it seems for at least two reasons. First, the majority required is very difficult to attain. Second, the most likely reason for a censure is because of the behaviour of an individual Commissioner or a small number of Commissioners, yet the censure motion can only target the College as a whole.

Despite these problems, at the end of the 1990s, the EP managed to use the blunt instrument given it by the Treaty to effect a shift in its influence. In 1998, its Budgetary Affairs Committee postponed a decision on whether to discharge the 1996 budget because it was unhappy with the response of the Commission to certain charges of lax financial administration. Although the Committee subsequently decided by one vote to recommend the grant of discharge, the EP meeting in plenary rejected the recommendation. Jacques Santer, the President of the Commission, then made the issue one of confidence by challenging the EP either to give discharge to the budget or to lay down a motion of censure on the whole Commission. This the EP did, although when it was voted on in January 1999, it failed to get even a majority, let alone the two-thirds majority that was required. However, the vote of 232 for and 293 against was the biggest vote ever for a motion of censure, and prompted the Commission to agree to set up a committee of independent experts to report to the EP on fraud, mismanagement, and nepotism in the Commission. When the report appeared in March 1999, it was so damning of the level of mismanagement by some Commissioners that the whole Commission resigned. Although the EP had not managed to summon the substantial majority needed to censure the Commission formally, by adept use of its limited powers, it achieved a considerable 'informal' victory.

At this point, the powers of the EP to approve the new Commission President and College of Commissioners took centre stage. The new nominee for President was Romano Prodi. He anticipated that the EP would want to seek some assurance that, in future, it would not need to attack the whole Commission if, as had been the case with the Santer Commission, the problem lay with certain individuals. In fact, the Santer Commission probably could have survived had one individual Commissioner (Edith Cresson) agreed to resign, but her refusal to do so left the Commission with no option but to resign as a whole. Prodi therefore told the EP at his own confirmation hearing that he would require every individual Commissioner to promise to resign if asked by the President to do so. The promise was repeated by Prodi's successor, José Manuel Barroso. Although it did not give the EP the right to dismiss individual Commissioners, it did mark a further advance towards that goal. The EP then underlined the importance that it set on this development by requiring each of the proposed new Commissioners to make a public declaration at their confirmation hearing that they would resign if asked by the President to do so. In July 2000, a new Framework Agreement on Relations between the European Parliament and the Commission was adopted by the EP. In it, the commitment of Prodi to hold Commissioners individually responsible was strengthened by a commitment that, if the EP were to express a lack of confidence in an individual Commissioner, the President would consider whether to ask that individual to resign.

Five years later, the EP again flexed its muscles during the confirmation hearings for the incoming Barroso Commission, when the EP expressed an unwillingness to confirm the new Commission in office if the Italian nominee, Rocco Buttiglione, was a member of the team, and expressed doubts about the competence of other nominees. After something of a stand-off, Barroso agreed to rethink the position. Buttiglione's nomination was withdrawn, the Italian government put forward another Italian nominee, and two other changes were made to national nominations. This outcome was achieved because of the impressive degree of independence demonstrated by MEPs in the Socialist and Liberal groups, in the face of intense pressure from national governments to allow the contested nominations.

Ratification of the Lisbon Treaty did not evidently bring about major changes. The Treaty itself mainly introduced nuances into the provisions for approval of the Commission President. As noted already, the nomination—once again of Barroso—had to take into account the elections to the EP, as newly provided for under Article 17 TEU. He was then 'elected', as the new terminology terms this process. During the hearings, Bulgarian Commissioner-Designate Rumiana Jeleva (International Co-operation, Humanitarian Aid, and Crisis Response), a former MEP, performed poorly and failed to allay concerns that she had conflicts of interest. She resigned as Commissioner-Designate on 19 January 2010. The Bulgarian Prime Minister then nominated Kristalina Georgieva, and she 'passed' her hearing in early February. Following this change of line-up, the Commission was approved on 9 February 2010 by a 'vote of consent' (as it is now termed) under Article 17 TEU. With the new post of High Representative overseeing the EU's emerging External Action Service, a joint Commission/Council appointment, the EP attempted to extend its powers to the right to a hearing on the appointment of EU ambassadors (Kietz and von Ondarza 2010: 7). This attempt was resisted, but it indicates that the EP is likely to seek to develop its checks on the Commission still further.

The Lisbon Treaty's requirement that election of the Commission President should take account of the election outcome led to proposals, including from the Commission, for each transnational party group in the EP to nominate a candidate ahead of the 2014 elections. For instance, in February 2014 the Alliance of Liberals and Democrats for Europe selected the former Belgian Prime Minister, Guy Verhofstadt, as candidate for the Commission presidency with Olli Rehn, the Commissioner for Economic and Monetary Affairs, as co-leader of the election campaign. It remains to be seen how this politicization of the Commission President and other posts impacts on the nomination of the Commission in 2015 and on its subsequent work programme. However, it meant that there was a new dimension to the election campaign in 2014, and one that has been proposed as a way to bring voters closer to the EP. One other development is worth recording. In January 2013, the (Maltese) Commissioner for Health and Consumer Protection was forced to resign after allegations of corruption in relation to funding from the tobacco industry (*European Voice*, 10 January 2013: 7). The allegations remained contested, and lawsuits ensued. However, this first resignation by an individual Commissioner was facilitated by the EP's attempts to strengthen its controls during the scandal that occurred under the Santer Commission.

Debates and Research

Debate and research on the EP have been far-reaching and diverse. In a very useful summary, Hix, Raunio, and Scully (2003: 193–6) classified contemporary research on the EP into four areas:

- work on the general development and functioning of the EP;
- research on political behaviour and EP elections;
- research on the internal politics and organization of the EP;
- examinations of inter-institutional bargaining between the EP, the Council, and the Commission.

The first of these has been dealt with already in this chapter. In this section of the chapter, each of the other three categories of research will be briefly reviewed to indicate the main academic concerns. Related debates on the EU's democracy and legitimacy are considered in Chapter 3.

Political Behaviour and EP Elections

The strongest argument for the direct election of the EP was that it would increase the legitimacy of the institution and thereby of the EU as a whole—yet turnout in European elections has gradually fallen. Overall turnout declined from 63 per cent (1979) to 49 per cent (1999), to 46 per cent (2004), and 43 per cent (2009). In 2014 the turnout again reached 43 per cent. Turnout has varied between member states, but the more significant fact is that, in every state, the turnout is much lower than for national elections.

Successive European elections studies have examined this phenomenon (Reif and Schmitt 1980; van der Eijk and Franklin 1996; Schmitt and Thomasen 1999). The thrust of the argument of these studies is that European elections are treated by the electorate as 'second-order national elections', which means that they are seen as secondary to national elections, while being conducted as national rather than European contests. The electorate behaves in this way as it considers European elections not to affect which party or coalition governs the EU. The outcome is perceived to affect neither the composition of the Commission, nor that of the Council of Ministers, the two most powerful institutions in the system. So, the campaigns are fought predominantly on domestic issues rather than European ones. Most of the actual campaigning centres on the record of the national government rather than on the differences between the parties on European issues. This held true in 2014.

There are two different competing interpretations of the pattern of results in EP elections, which typically result in setbacks for the incumbent governments. These are the 'punishment' and 'protest' explanations, and they have been examined by Simon Hix and Michael Marsh (2007). The punishment thesis is that EP elections function as mid-term elections in which incumbent national governments are punished by their voters. The competing thesis holds that the support for protest parties, such as the United Kingdom Independence Party (UKIP), together with the falling turnout at European elections, reflect specific protest against the EU. Of these two explanations, the punishment thesis is more closely in line with the 'second-order national elections' interpretation. By contrast, the protest thesis assumes that the EU does matter in voters' thinking, and that it is the source of the protest. Hix and Marsh (2007) examined the results for all EP elections from 1979–2004. Their findings showed that the punishment thesis better explains the results. They argued that protest against the EU remained 'at best a minor element in these elections in most cases' (Hix and Marsh 2007: 506). Held against the background of the eurozone crisis, the 2014 elections brought about a rise in support for Eurosceptic and other protest parties. Doubtless, these results offer valuable new data for revisiting the punishment versus protest argument.

Internal Politics and Organization of the EP

Hix, Raunio, and Scully (2003: 194–5) divided research under this heading into three categories: analysis of the committee work in the EP; analysis of party groups; and 'other aspects of political behaviour inside the EP', by which is meant the issue of the independence of MEPs as demonstrated by their behaviour in the EP.

Committee Work in the EP

For many years, this was a neglected area of research, although one early piece of research found that, beyond the requirements that proportionality was respected in the composition of committees (in terms of both nationality and party group), scope had emerged for 'specialized membership and recruitment' (Bowler and Farrell 1995: 254). This line of research area developed strongly in the 2000s, building upon research questions and methods that have been applied to committee work in the US Congress. Other analysts have explored the mechanisms through which party groups, while respecting the requirements of proportionality, have tried to influence the allocation of committee chairs, membership, and the important task of selecting a rapporteur, the MEP charged with producing a committee report on a piece of legislation and with speaking on the committee's behalf when full debate takes place in the EP. Mamadouh and Raunio (2003) showed that the allocation of all of these positions tended to be influenced by national delegations within the EP's transnational party groups. A burgeoning literature emerged on the politics of EP committee work (for a fuller review, see Judge and Earnshaw 2008: 167–78).

The Party Groups

Just as the EP cannot expect to extend its power and influence unless MEPs show themselves to be competent, so it cannot do so by definition if it lacks independence and autonomy. The main constraint on MEPs acting autonomously is the influence of

Table 15.2 Membership Numbers of Political Groups in the European Parliament (as at July 2014)

Group	MEPs
European People's Party	220
Progressive Alliance of Socialists and Democrats	191
European Conservatives and Reformists	70
Alliance of Liberals and Democrats for Europe	68
European United Left/Nordic Green Left	52
Greens/European Free Alliance	50
Europe of Freedom and Direct Democracy	48
Non-attached	52
Total	**751**

Source: European Parliament website, July 2014.

national political parties. Unless the party groups in the EP can establish their autonomy from national parties, the EP will be constrained.

MEPs do not sit in the EP in national delegations, but in transnational party groups. A party group may be established by twenty-five MEPs from at least seven member states. These rules have fluctuated over time in line with the accession of new member states and changes to the size of the EP. The aim has remained constant: to promote groupings that have a truly transnational character. Each party group has its own administrative and support staff, paid for out of the central budget of the EP. Groups are co-ordinated by a Bureau, consisting of a Chair, a Vice-Chair, and a Treasurer as a minimum. The groups play an important role: for instance, in setting the agenda of the EP and allocating speaking time in plenary sessions. A full list of the groups, and their level of representation in the 2014–19 Parliament, is given in Table 15.2.

There are definite advantages to being a member of one of the party groups. The groups receive funding from the EP to cover their administrative costs. Memberships of committees, and their chairs and rapporteurs, are allocated to groups in proportion to their size. (For a list of EP committees, see Box 15.1). It is not surprising, therefore, that there are strong incentives for national parties and individual MEPs to form a group. For instance, the Rainbow Group in the 1984–89 Parliament consisted of members of environmentalist parties, regionalist parties, and anti-EC Danish MEPs; the only thing that they had in common was a wish to draw down the funding and other advantages that would be denied them if they did not join a group. As Table 15.2 indicates, in the summer of 2014, a number of MEPs were not located within a political group.

Even the longer-established groups may be subject to change, highlighting the way in which the EP's party system is weak even if its committees are quite powerful: a characteristic that makes it comparable to the US Congress. Following the 2009 election to the EP, the British Conservative Party formed the cornerstone of a new group, the European Conservatives and Reformists. Previously, it had been in a grouping known as the European People's Party and European Democrats (EPP-ED). However, when David Cameron campaigned for the leadership of the Conservative Party, he made a commitment to withdraw from this grouping on the grounds that it was too pro-European, thus tapping into the Euroscepticism of his party's backbenchers in the national parliament. The EPP-ED thus became the EPP from 2009. On the centre left of the political spectrum, the Socialist Group adopted a broader title after the 2009 elections—the Progressive Alliance of Socialists and Democrats—to accommodate the Italian Democratic Party, which had only been established in 2007 as an amalgamation of several parties. (For a short profile of each parliamentary group in the 2014 parliament, see the online resources: **http://oxfordtextbooks.co.uk/orc/bache4e/**.)

These shifting formations also hint at the fact that cohesion of transnational parties is less than the norm in national parliaments. Not only can genuine differences of national perspective lead to divergence in voting behaviour in the EP, but the MEPs in the party groups are also subject to pressure from their national parties. In many, although not all member states, the proportional representation (PR) electoral systems that operate make it easier for national party leaders to put pressure on their MEPs, because European elections are held on the basis of closed party lists—that is, the voter is presented with a list of the candidates for that party in the order of preference decided by the party, and is unable to change the order. The chances for an individual of being elected on any particular level of vote for the party depend on where he or she is placed on the list. As the lists are drawn up by the national party organizations, the MEPs face the prospect of being dropped down the list, and of their seats being jeopardized, if they offend the national party leadership too much.

Despite the relative weakness of the transnational party groups, research indicates that their internal cohesion has generally increased over time. For instance, Hix, Kreppel, and Noury (2003; see also Hix et al. 2005) undertook an analysis of **roll-call voting** over the period from 1979 and concluded that the party system in the EP had become more consolidated over time. Kreppel (2002, 2003) correlated the increasing group cohesion with the increased power of the EP. As the powers of the EP were increased under successive revisions of the Treaties, so the party groups tended to become more cohesive in order to be more effective.

> Where the parties have similar policies (on EU integration and external trade) they tend to vote together, and where they have differing positions (on environmental, agriculture, economic and social issues) they tend to vote on opposite sides.
>
> (Hix et al. 2003: 327)

One important point provides context to this pattern of growing cohesion: namely, the striking number of near unanimous votes in the EP. For instance, Hix et al. (2003: 318) reviewed roll-call votes over the period 1979–2001 and found that the two largest party groupings, the socialists and the European People's Party (Christian Democrats), voted together in a minimum of 61–71 per cent of cases depending on the parliamentary term. In national parliaments, party cohesion and competition arise because of the government's wish to secure its legislative programme and the opposition's wish either to obstruct or to modify the legislation. This situation finds no parallel in the EP because there is no EU government based on a majority of MEPs. Instead, co-operation between the two parties is incentivized by the rules of the Ordinary

Legislative Procedure (Hix and Høyland 2011: 144). Specifically, amendments at the second reading in the EP require an absolute majority of MEPs, and that is most easily achieved if the two largest parties can find common ground. Equally, this requirement for an absolute majority may contribute to the fact that agreement is increasingly found between the EP and the Council at the first reading. In some circumstances, inter-institutional dynamics can encourage the EP to line up in opposition to the Council. Both groups may sometimes share a common interest in increasing the powers of the EP, resulting in a strategic calculation in favour of voting together in the later stages of the legislative process (see Kreppel 2000).

The wider point, however, is that the party politics of the EP has become a major area of research, strengthened by the growing importance of the EP in the legislative process. In a survey of twenty years of co-decision (now the OLP), VoteWatch's headline findings were: that the participation rate of MEPs in roll-call votes had gone up over the period; that party cohesion had increased in the transnational party groups; that legislation was increasingly adopted at the first reading; and it was being adopted by larger majorities (VoteWatch 2013). Research on the party groups has opened up a debate about whether behaviour in the EP reflects 'party politics as usual' or whether the distinctive character of the EU's institutions prevents the patterns of behaviour that we would recognize from national parliaments (Lindberg et al. 2008). As most commentators agree, the terrain of party politics in the EP has begun to change markedly over the past decade or so (on this, see Hix 2008). Alongside this, the debate concerning the behaviour of party groups in the EP has advanced considerably and attention has now begun to explore partisan voting in other institutions: notably, the Council of Ministers and the European Council, in which the focus has traditionally been upon governments voting along national lines (Hagemann and Hoyland 2008; Tallberg and Johansson 2008).

The Independence of MEPs

One of the peculiarities of the relationship between voters and the EP is that the electorate may be completely unfamiliar with the political group for which they are effectively voting in the European elections. Moreover, the party groups in the EP add to the allegiances that MEPs already have to their home party, their constituents, and their nation.

As suggested above, one of the factors that affects the ability of the EP to extend its power and influence further is the independence of MEPs from national party influence. Because candidate selection is undertaken by political parties at member-state level, independence from this level is seen as being the appropriate measure of MEPs adopting a role defined by the EP. In the early years of the EP, few MEPs had any real incentive to assert their independence from their national parties. Some MEPs were senior politicians who served out the latter years of their political career at EU level, while younger members often saw the EP as the first step prior to taking up a career in national politics.

What was less evident was an obvious career route at the European level. National MPs can aspire to enter government, or at least to become an official spokesperson for their party if it is in opposition. At the European level, the executive has not been drawn from the EP, although the 2014 elections marked a slight departure in light of choices being available among party groups with different candidates for the Commission presidency. Thus, although it has not been unusual to find some former

MEPs among the European Commissioners, no obvious career trajectory has been evident in a manner comparable to politics in the member states.

Comparison with the United States is of some help in explaining what has developed over the years, since the executive in Washington is also not chosen from members of the legislature. Nevertheless, that has not prevented the emergence of professional members of Congress who aspire to occupy senior committee chairs. As the powers and influence of the EP have grown, so a similar career route has come to be followed by some MEPs, as suggested by Bowler and Farrell (1995) (see also Westlake 1994). These findings were supported in a later study by Scarrow (1997), who saw the proportion of European career politicians steadily increasing, and similarly predicted that MEPs would become increasingly independent of national parties.

A number of studies have explored the relationship between MEPs and their national parties in the subsequent period. Tapio Raunio (2007: 255) stated that 'national party delegations are the cornerstones upon which the EP groups are based'. Yet, while most national party delegations have their own staff and hold meetings before participating in the transnational parliamentary groups, the scope for national parties to 'control' their MEPs is limited (see Scully 2001). Indeed, 'MEPs often perceive themselves to be rather peripheral actors in their parties, complaining that their work is not taken seriously enough' (Raunio 2007: 257). And yet, as Raunio also notes (2007: 256), another slightly contradictory finding has been that national political parties are increasingly paying attention to their MEPs.

The EP and Inter-Institutional Bargaining

This is an area that has attracted a lot of academic attention, which has centred on the extent to which the effective influence of the EP over the legislative process has really increased. The general view of the progression from consultation through the now-abolished co-operation procedure to co-decision was that 'the consecutive institutional reforms are moving the EU towards a genuinely bicameral system' (Crombez 2000: 366). On the face of it, each step represented an increase in both the power and influence of the EP. However, some analysts have challenged this automatic growth of power.

Under its original power—the *consultation* procedure—its opinion could be ignored whether the voting rule was unanimity or QMV. However, the SEA also introduced the *co-operation* procedure. Under this procedure, the Commission and the EP shared the power to determine the final form of the legislation. If the EP and the Commission could agree on a proposal that was acceptable to a coalition in the Council that constituted a qualified majority, they together had the decisive influence on the form of the legislation. The co-operation procedure was largely replaced by the Amsterdam Treaty and finally abolished by the Lisbon Treaty.

The *co-decision* procedure, introduced by the Maastricht Treaty, changed the inter-institutional balance again. As introduced at that stage (termed Co-decision 1), it gave the EP:

- three readings of legislation;
- the right to negotiate directly with the Council via a Conciliation Committee on any amendments for which there was an absolute majority in the EP, but with which the Council did not agree;
- an absolute right of veto.

While academics—largely using rational choice or game-theoretical interpreta-tions—argued over the impact of this change, in particular regarding the Commission's powers (see Garrett and Tsebelis 1996; Tsebelis and Garrett 1996; and the counter-arguments by Crombez 1996, 1997, 2000; Moser 1996, 1997; Scully 1997a, 1997b), others observed that this debate missed the informal aspects of the inter-institutional bargaining process. This failing is perhaps related to the rational choice framework of analysis that they adopted, which risks over-emphasis on rules and rational behaviour. Scholars whose approach involved intensive research 'in the field' were clear that 'the informal dimensions of inter-institutional relations are of major significance in under-standing policy-making in the EC' (Judge et al. 1994: 45).

Initially, the Council attempted to minimize the impact of the changes on the way in which legislation was dealt with. However, the determination of the EP to make the maximum use of its new powers soon convinced the Council that it could not carry on as before. The EP showed itself willing to take even relatively uncontroversial legislation to conciliation unless its positions were taken seriously. As a backlog of leg-islation began to mount, the Council agreed to institute informal 'trialogues' with the Commission and EP in an attempt to ease the passage of important measures.

Subsequently, the experience of trying to make the system introduced at Maastricht operate effectively led to further changes to the formal rules at Amsterdam: the creation of what is called Co-decision 2. These changes allowed the Council and EP to conclude the process at first reading if they could reach agreement, and changed the rules of con-ciliation so that there was no longer the possibility of legislation that had been rejected by the EP being passed if the Conciliation Committee failed to reach agreement. The decision to allow agreement after the first reading reflected the concern of the Council Secretariat that, with the transfer of even more areas to co-decision, the system needed to be streamlined. However, the new rule implied a further extension of informal dis-cussion, effectively involving the EP in the formulation of legislative proposals at the same early stage as the Commission consulted with the Council.

The change of rule on what happened after an unsuccessful conciliation simply reflected acceptance that the EP would never accept the reinstatement of a Council common position, as it had demonstrated in 1994. According to Shackleton and Raunio (2003: 173), in an assessment that is given authority by the fact that Shackleton was the Head of the Conciliations Secretariat of the EP at the time:

> Co-decision is now seen as an interlinked, continuous procedure where it is essential and normal that there be intensive contacts throughout the procedure from before first reading onwards. Such contacts offer the opportunity of coming to agreements without having recourse to the time-consuming procedure of conciliation.

Accordingly, empirical analysis of Co-decision 2, now known as the Ordinary Legislative Procedure, has revealed a growing trend towards early agreements, thereby rendering the formal rules at the conciliation stage of less practical relevance (VoteWatch Europe 2013). In the 2004–09 Parliament, Judge and Earnshaw (2008: 233) noted that two-thirds of legislative dossiers were agreed in the first reading. In addition, as they also noted, informal agreements at the start of the second reading accounted for a further 15 per cent of measures. In this way, norms of early agree-ment, along with 'trialogues' between the three institutions, were being practised in order to minimize resort to the conciliation stage.

What emerges from practice on the ground and academic analysis is that, through Treaty reform and informal agreements, the EP has become a co-legislator with the Council. Moreover, the analysis of the EP's power cannot simply rely on interpretation of formal rules, because informal rules and conventions are also important factors.

CONCLUSION

The themes of the book that are brought out in this chapter reflect the way EU studies have developed. Originally, the debate was about whether the EP was a 'toothless tiger' with the Council acting as the main legislative body. After a long struggle the EP has emerged as a full co-legislator with the Council in almost all areas of EU business; CFSP being the main exception. Academic attention has shifted from the trajectory of the EP's development, reflecting an integrationist frame (Chapter 1), to research agendas that characterize legislative studies in comparative politics (Chapter 2). Rational choice institutionalists investigate the way MEPs individually, and the EP collectively, respond to the formal institutional rules, especially under the Ordinary Legislative Procedure. By contrast, sociological institutionalists or social constructivists focus on the role of norms and culture as an important part of the everyday politics of the EP. Finally, available roll-call voting databases, notably via VoteWatch Europe, have facilitated the analysis of the evolving party politics within the EP.

Understanding the character of the EU as an organization is clearly affected by the view that is taken of the effective influence of the EP. If it is accepted that the successive changes in the EP's formal role have made it a co-legislator with the Council of Ministers, then the view that the EU is no more than an intergovernmental organization cannot be sustained. There is no other such organization internationally in which the member governments have to share decision making with a directly elected institution. With the further extension of its powers that occurred under the Lisbon Treaty, it is no longer tenable to regard the EP as a 'toothless tiger'; it is in fact a very powerful legislature.

The main reason why the powers of the EP were extended is attributable to the argument that this would help to close the democratic deficit, and therefore the legitimacy deficit of the EU. The evidence does not indicate that much has been achieved in that direction, in particular because there are limits to the legitimacy of the EP's democratic mandate that may only be eased with the development of a stronger sense of European identity among EU citizens. The Lisbon Treaty arguably recognized this situation by giving new powers to the national parliaments (see Chapter 12, Decision-Making Procedures). Nevertheless, the austere economic circumstances in the aftermath of the financial and eurozone crises have led some commentators to emphasize a 'new intergovernmentalism', in which the member governments have sought to assert their position in the face of the supranational institutions like the EP (Bickerton et al. forthcoming). Moreover, the election of an increased number of Eurosceptic MEPs in the 2014 election suggests that fundamental problems remain in relation to voter identification with the EP.

KEY POINTS

Composition and Functions

- The EP elected in June 2014 had 751 seats, which were distributed between the member states approximately in proportion to population.

- It meets monthly in plenary sessions in Strasbourg, but most of its work is done in Committee in Brussels.
- Organizationally, it has a President, a Bureau, a Conference of Presidents, and a Secretariat.

The Struggle for Power

- The forerunner of the EP (the EPA) was not directly elected and had limited powers.
- The EP has steadily increased its powers by putting pressure on national parties and governments, arguing that it needed increased powers to close the EU's democratic deficit.
- The first direct elections to the EP took place in June 1979. Direct election emboldened MEPs to challenge the member states over the budget and to demand more powers.
- In 1970, the power of the EP over the budget was increased when it was given the power to amend 'non-compulsory expenditure', which excluded the CAP. In 1975, it was given the power to reject the budget as a whole. As a result of the Lisbon Treaty, the EP and the Council of Ministers are co-equal budgetary authorities.
- The EP can force the Commission as a whole to resign by a motion of censure, but to do so requires a positive vote from an absolute majority of MEPs and two-thirds of the votes cast. It cannot dismiss individual Commissioners.
- Originally, the EP had no say in the appointment of the Commission. Under successive Treaty amendments, it gained the right to elect the governments' nomination for President and subsequently hold a vote of consent for the new College of Commissioners.
- The 2014 election signalled a shift towards choosing competing candidates for the post of Commission President, even though national politics remained the key focus of election campaigns.

Debates and Research

- The electorate in all member states treats European elections as less important than national elections. They are fought primarily on domestic issues, and turnout is lower than for national elections.
- MEPs sit in transnational party groups, which can contain within them a wide variety of ideological positions, but research indicates that the degree of group cohesion has increased as the powers of the EP have increased.
- In the early years, no obvious career path existed, but research has indicated that being an MEP is increasingly attractive to ambitious politicians.
- The role of the EP in the legislative process has moved from the weak position in the consultation procedure, through successively stronger positions under co-operation and co-decision.
- Academic debate over the power of the EP in the legislative process has been contested from different perspectives. A concentration on formal rules by some analysts has been criticized by others who hold that informal rules can be as important.

FURTHER READING

A very good review of the emergence of the EP, although not covering the most recent developments, is offered by **B. Rittberger**, *Building Europe's Parliament: Democratic Representation Beyond the Nation State* (Oxford: Oxford University Press, 2005). For general guides to the EP, see

R. Corbett, F. Jacobs, and M. Shackleton, *The European Parliament*, 8th edn (London: John Harper Publishing, 2011) and **D. Judge and D. Earnshaw**, *The European Parliament*, 2nd edn (London: Palgrave Macmillan, 2008). For a study of the politics within the EP from a comparative-politics standpoint, see **S. Hix, A. Noury, and G. Roland**, *Democratic Politics in the European Parliament* (Cambridge: Cambridge University Press, 2007). Another detailed analysis is offered by **N. Ringe**, *Who Decides, and How? Preferences, Uncertainty, and Policy Choice in the European Parliament* (Oxford: Oxford University Press, 2009).

For an analysis that argues that the EP's representative role is being undermined by the electoral systems utilized at member-state level, see **D. Farrell and R. Scully**, *Representing Europe's Citizens? Electoral Institutions and the Failure of Parliamentary Representation* (Oxford: Oxford University Press, 2007). **Juliet Lodge** has edited several books on European elections, including *The 2009 Elections to the European Parliament* (Basingstoke and New York: Palgrave Macmillan, 2010). On the party system in the EP, see **A. Kreppel**, *The European Parliament and Supranational Party System: A Study in Institutional Development* (Cambridge: Cambridge University Press, 2002). Also recommended is the website of VoteWatch Europe: **http://votewatch.eu**.

online resource centre

Visit the Online Resource Centre that accompanies this book for links to more information on the European Parliament, including the EP's own website: http://oxfordtextbooks.co.uk/orc/bache4e/

Chapter 16

The European Court of Justice

Chapter Overview

Unlike international organizations more broadly, much of the work of the European Union (EU) is undertaken through legislation and other legal acts. It therefore follows that its legal system is an important feature. At the apex of that system sits what is formally known as the 'Court of Justice of the European Union' (CJEU). It in fact comprises three courts: the Court of Justice; the General Court; and the EU Civil Service Tribunal. The first of these, commonly referred to as the European Court of Justice (ECJ), is the most important one. It makes binding decisions on disputes over Treaty provisions or secondary legislation. It therefore plays an essential role in the developing EU.

This chapter looks first at the structure and functions of the Courts, and then at some of the ECJ's main rulings and their significance. It considers rulings on the powers of the institutions, some key legal judgments made in response to questions referred to the ECJ by national courts, and some illustrations of the impact of ECJ rulings on EU policy. The chapter then turns to look first at the evolving political reactions towards the judgments of the Court, and at the debate over whether the member states have lost control of the process of European integration because of the radical jurisprudence of the ECJ.

Context

There is consensus on the need for a European judicial order to exist with an authoritative interpreter of both the Treaties and the secondary legislation (directives, regulations) put in place by member states. This task falls to the ECJ. As sometimes occurs with courts more generally, especially constitutional courts such as the US Supreme Court or the German Federal Constitutional Court, the ECJ has been criticized for stepping beyond its legal role into the realm of politics. However, unlike controversies in other political systems, the ECJ not only has to tread the line between law and politics, but it also polices the boundary between EU and national law and politics. This is important because 'there is joint responsibility between national courts and the Union courts for the interpretation and maintenance of EU law' (Chalmers et al. 2010: 142). The ECJ has been accused in the past of ruling in favour of integration-ist solutions to disputes. This has provoked hostility from member states that see their powers or sovereignty being undermined by Court rulings. In the period after the Maastricht ratification crisis, the ECJ was subjected to increased criticism from member states for its radical jurisprudence, known as judicial activism. However, while the 1990s witnessed questions concerning the ECJ's growing influence, 'in recent years ... its level of activism has fallen' (Kapsis 2010: 187). Cardwell and Hervey (forthcoming) have argued further that EU law has become 'decentred'.

Structure and Functions
Structure

The Court of Justice of the EU comprises three courts:

the European Court of Justice (ECJ);

the General Court;

the European Union Civil Service Tribunal.

It is the ECJ that is of greatest interest in this chapter, but it is worth briefly discussing the other two courts beforehand.

The EU Civil Service Tribunal, established in 2005, is a very specialized court the responsibility of which is for hearing disputes between employees of the EU institutions and the institutions themselves, and not of political significance. The General Court has a rather wider remit. It was established in 1989 as the Court of First Instance, but was renamed with implementation of the Lisbon Treaty in 2009. It was created to help the ECJ with the sheer volume of business that it had to get through. It comprises twenty-eight judges, with one from each member state. The General Court is effectively the central administrative court of the EU. The General Court can act in a range of circumstances, but it plays a particularly important role in hearing 'challenges by private parties adversely affected by EU measures': notably, in competition law or external trade law (Chalmers et al. 2010: 147). The most important cases, including those of political significance, are the responsibility of the ECJ.

Like the General Court, the ECJ meets in Luxembourg, which is a legacy of its origins dating from its creation as part of the European Coal and Steel Community, the institutions of which were all located in the Grand Duchy. It comprises twenty-eight judges and eight advocates-general, who are appointed by common accord of the governments of the member states and hold office for a renewable term of six years (Article 19 TEU). The judges are chosen from persons whose independence is beyond doubt and who are of recognized competence. Approximately half of the judges and advocates-general are replaced every three years. Candidates for the positions of judge or advocate-general are scrutinized by a panel of seven people, comprising former EU judges, national Supreme Court judges, and a nominee of the European Parliament (EP). The panel's Opinion is offered to the Council on candidates' suitability, although it is not binding in its effect.

The judges select one of their number to be President of the Court for a renewable term of three years. The President directs the work of the Court and presides at hearings and deliberations. The advocates-general assist the Court in its task. They deliver legal opinions on cases before the Court at a stage before the ECJ issues its own judgment.

The ECJ's work is primarily conducted in chambers of three or five judges; important matters can, upon request, come before a Grand Chamber of fifteen judges and exceptionally important ones come before the Court as a whole (Chalmers et al. 2010: 145). Like the General Court, the ECJ has problems keeping up with the volume of cases referred to it. The ECJ's authority is confined to 'Union business'. It therefore has no jurisdiction on Common Foreign and Security Policy. The ECJ's remit was expanded at the end of 2014 as a result of provisions in the Lisbon Treaty. This arose from the transfer of remaining areas of Justice and Home Affairs co-operation to the '**Union method**' as part of the Area of Freedom, Security and Justice, taking effect after a five-year transition period from the Lisbon Treaty coming into effect (see Chapter 24).

Functions

It is the responsibility of the ECJ to ensure that the law is observed in the interpretation and application of the EU Treaties with the exception of the provisions relating to foreign and security policy. To enable it to carry out that task, the Court has wide jurisdiction to hear various types of action and to give preliminary rulings.

The Court may hear several different categories of proceeding, as follows.

(1) Failure to fulfil an obligation (TFEU Articles 258, 259, and 260)

A member state may be taken to the Court by the Commission or by another member state for failing to act to meet its obligations under the Treaties or EU secondary legislation. If the Court finds against the state so charged, it must comply without delay. If it fails to do so, the Commission may go back to the Court and ask, under Article 260 TFEU, for a fine to be imposed on the state.

(2) Application for annulment (TFEU Articles 263 and 264)

This judicial review power allows a member state, the Council, the Commission, the EP, the Court of Auditors, the European Central Bank, and the Committee of the Regions to apply to the ECJ as plaintiffs for the annulment of EU acts or legislative acts. Individuals may, via the national court system, seek the annulment of a legal measure that is of direct concern to them. The annulment may be sought and granted on grounds of lack of competence, infringement of an essential procedural requirement, infringement of the Treaty, or misuse of powers. Expansion of the scope of Article 263 under the Lisbon Treaty has extended judicial review beyond acts of the Commission, the Council, and the EP to include such acts of the European Council, the European Central Bank, and EU agencies as have legal effects (Dougan 2008: 676).

(3) Failure to act (TFEU Articles 265 and 266)

The Court may review the legality of a failure to act by a Community institution (the EP, the European Council, the Council, the Commission, or the European Central Bank), and penalize silence or inaction.

(4) Actions to establish liability (TFEU Article 268)

In an action for damages, the Court rules on the liability of the EU for damage caused by its institutions or servants in the performance of their duties.

(5) Appeals (TFEU Article 256)

The Court may hear appeals, on points of law only, against judgments given by the General Court in cases within its jurisdiction.

(6) Reference for a preliminary ruling (TFEU Article 267)

Preliminary rulings are judgments by the Court on the interpretation of the Treaties or secondary legislation arising under the Treaties. Under Article 267, national courts that are hearing cases involving EU law may request a ruling from the ECJ on the interpretation of the law, and where the issue is raised before a national court against the judgment of which there is no appeal in domestic law, that court must seek a preliminary ruling from the ECJ. The ECJ cannot deliver a preliminary ruling unless it is asked to do so by a national court.

Although judges are usually thought of as conservative, that cannot be said of the ECJ judges. It has been argued in the past that the ECJ has done more than any other institution to advance European integration (Freestone 1983: 43). Its approach has been heavily criticized by some commentators as stepping beyond the bounds of legal interpretation to become political (Rasmussen 1986). Perhaps this lack of conservatism is because some of the members of the ECJ are not judges by profession. Many of the appointees have been academics rather than professional lawyers. Whatever the reasons, the ECJ pursued a form of judicial activism that created a supranational legal order in the mid-1960s. This development came at the time when The Empty Chair Crisis brought political integration to a halt and entrenched an intergovernmental political order, thus demonstrating why the legal dimension of integration must be kept in view. The Court's judicial activism was to be found both in judgments on the powers of the institutions arising from actions brought under the Articles listed above, and in Article 267 referrals from national courts seeking clarification of points of EU law.

ECJ Rulings on the Powers of the Institutions

The biggest beneficiary of the ECJ's distinctive approach to institutional relations was the EP. In a series of judgments, the ECJ interpreted the powers of the EP in an expansive manner. Key cases, which are considered here, were:

Roquette v. *Council* (1980) (the *Isoglucose* case) Case 138/79;

Parti Écologiste, '*Les Verts*' v. *Parliament* (1986) Case 294/83;

European Parliament v. *Council* (1988) (the *Comitology* case) Case 302/87;

European Parliament v. *Council* (1990) (the *Chernobyl* case) Case C-70/88.

The *Isoglucose* Case (1980)

In March 1979, the Commission submitted to the EP a draft regulation on fixing quotas for the production of isoglucose—a food sweetener produced from cereals—to take effect from the beginning of July. The draft regulation went to the EP's Committee on Agriculture, which reported to the May plenary session of the EP. However, the plenary rejected the report of the Committee containing an Opinion on the regulation. This effectively meant that the quotas could not be introduced at the beginning of July (1979 was an election year for the EP, so there was no June plenary). In the meantime, the Council had considered the draft regulation and agreed to adopt it. Faced with a possible delay of four months or more, the Commission acted on the approval of the Council and published the directive in the Official Journal.

Subsequently, an individual who was directly affected by the directive brought a case to the ECJ under Article 173 of the EEC Treaty (now Article 263 TFEU), claiming that the Council and Commission had acted beyond their powers by adopting the directive without having received the Opinion of the EP. The Court could have decided that the EP had been consulted, and had failed to deliver an Opinion in time. Instead, it upheld the complaint, choosing to interpret 'consult' to mean that the formal Opinion of the EP had to be delivered before the Council could act.

In its judgment, the Court insisted that the EP had a duty to give an Opinion within a reasonable length of time, without defining what would be considered reasonable. Thus, the judgment did not give the EP an effective power to veto legislation under the consultation procedure, but it did give it a significant power to delay legislation by holding back on formally delivering its Opinion.

Les Verts v. European Parliament (1986)

In 1984, the French Green Party (*Les Verts*) stood candidates for election to the EP for the first time. In doing so, it discovered that those of its opponents that had been represented in the previous Parliament had been funded by the EP to defray their election expenses. Subsequently the Greens brought a case to the ECJ under Article 173 EEC (now Article 263 TFEU) claiming that the EP had acted beyond its powers in effectively supporting the election of existing parties at the expense of new parties.

The immediate issue here was whether any such case could be brought to the Court. Article 173 explicitly said: 'The Court of Justice shall review the legality of acts of the Council and the Commission.' There was no mention of the ECJ reviewing the legality of acts of the EP. The Court nevertheless accepted the case on the grounds that, although the Treaty did not explicitly make the actions of the EP subject to judicial review, this omission was not in keeping with the spirit of the Treaty.

The Court argued that the EP must have been omitted from Article 173, because when the Treaty was signed, the EP had no real powers. Subsequently, it had acquired powers that would normally be subject to judicial review. These included the powers that were contested in this case, and as these *should* be subject to judicial review, the Court would review them.

In this judgment, the ECJ increased its own powers by a unilateral reinterpretation of the Treaty. Although apparently acting in a way that would restrict the powers of the EP, the judgment also took the first step towards giving the EP a legal personality that it had not been granted by the member states when they signed the Treaty. Once it had been decided that the EP could be a defendant in such a hearing, it seemed logical that it should also be accorded the right to be a plaintiff—that is, that it be allowed to bring cases to the Court under the same Article. The Court was given the opportunity to take this step in the next case reviewed below.

European Parliament v. Council (the Comitology Case) (1988)

This case was brought by the EP under Article 175 EEC (now revised as TFEU Article 265), which said:

> Should the Council or the Commission, in infringement of this Treaty, fail to act, the Member States, and the other institutions of the Community may bring an action before the Court of Justice to have the infringement established.

The EP argued successfully that it was allowed to bring a case under this Article because it was one of the 'other institutions of the Community'. But it also argued that it should be allowed to bring a case under Article 173 if the issue was one of another institution acting beyond its powers, rather than of not acting at all. The EP argued that it was illogical for it to be allowed to bring a case under Article 175, but not under Article 173. It also quoted the Court's judgment in *Les Verts* that the EP could be a defendant under Article 173, and argued that if it could be a defendant, it was illogical that it should not be allowed to be a plaintiff.

The Court rejected the EP's arguments. It said that: there was no logical link between the circumstances outlined; the EP could normally rely on the Commission to take up a case under Article 173 on its behalf; and the member states had recently had the specific opportunity to grant this right explicitly to the EP in the Single European Act and had declined to do so. However, within a short period of time, the Court appeared to have a change of heart on the issue.

European Parliament v. Council (the Chernobyl Case) (1990)

In this case, the EP applied to the Court for a review of the procedure adopted for agreeing a public health regulation on the permissible radioactive contamination of food that could be sold for public consumption following the Chernobyl disaster (see Insight 16.1). The Commission proposed the regulation under Article 31 of the Euratom Treaty, which dealt with basic standards for the protection of the health of the general public arising from radiation. Proposed legislation under this Article was subject to the consultation procedure. The EP maintained that the matter was a single-market issue, and therefore should have been introduced under (the then) Article 100A

Insight 16.1 Chernobyl

On 26 April 1986, a major accident occurred at the Chernobyl nuclear power station in Ukraine. Radioactive pollution extended over a vast geographical area. Contamination was detected in the food chain as far west as Ireland. The EU introduced standardized rules on the permissible levels of radioactive contamination, and provided financial support for the farmers worst affected.

of the EEC Treaty (now TFEU Article 114). This would have brought it under the co-operation procedure, and given the EP a second reading. The EP wished to challenge the treaty base under which the regulation was adopted, but first had to establish that its case was admissible because it was invoking Article 173 EEC (now Article 263 TFEU).

Despite the Court's decision in the *Comitology* case, its decision in this one, coming soon after, was even more surprising. Here, the Court decided that the EP could bring the case after all, despite its reasoning in the *Comitology* judgment, because the ECJ's role was to preserve the institutional balance. In the *Comitology* judgment, the Court had asserted that the Commission could normally be relied upon to protect the prerogatives of the EP where Parliament required an Article 173 case to be brought. However, in this instance, the dispute over the treaty base pitted the Commission against the EP. Therefore in these and similarly limited circumstances, the EP had to be granted the right to be a plaintiff in an Article 173 case. The other argument that had appeared in the *Comitology* judgment, that the member states had only recently declined to grant this power explicitly to the EP, now disappeared from view.

ECJ Rulings on the Nature of EU Law

If the jurisprudence of the ECJ has pushed back the limits of the Treaty in judgments based on judicial review cases, it has been even more radical in its judgments on references for preliminary rulings. In a number of judgments, the Court laid out principles that expanded the EU's legal order. The following cases were particularly important:

> *Van Gend en Loos* (1963) Case 26/62;
>
> *Costa* v. *ENEL* (1964) Case 6/64;
>
> *Van Duyn* v. *Home Office* (1974) Case 41/74;
>
> *R.* v. *Secretary of State for Transport, ex parte Factortame* (1990) Case 213/89;
>
> *R.* v. *Secretary of State for Transport, ex parte Factortame* (1991) Case C-221/89;
>
> *Francovich* v. *Italy* (1991) Cases C-6 and 9/90.

Van Gend en Loos (1963)

In this early case, the Court first asserted the principle that EU law confers rights on individuals as well as on member states. This was the principle of 'direct effect', which had no explicit authority in the Treaties, and represented a dramatic departure from international law. Under international law, treaties are held to impose obligations on the states that sign and ratify them, but neither to confer rights nor impose obligations directly on individual citizens.

A Dutch company claimed that its rights had been breached by the Dutch government, which had levied a higher rate of duty on formaldehyde—a chemical used as a disinfectant and preservative, and in the manufacture of synthetic resins—after the date on which it was agreed in the EEC Treaty that there would be no increase in internal tariffs. The Dutch government maintained that the company had no power to claim a right deriving from an international treaty. The Court disagreed. It maintained that a new legal order had come into existence with the signing of the Treaty, in which citizens could claim rights against their governments. The ruling of the Court contained the following famous phrase:

> the Community constitutes a new legal order of international law for the benefit of which the states have limited their sovereign rights, albeit within limited fields, and the subjects of which comprise not only member states but also their nationals. Community law therefore not only imposes obligations on individuals but is also intended to confer upon them rights that become part of their legal heritage.

(Quoted in Kuper 1998: 5)

As a result of this judgment, 'in individuals and in the national courts, the ECJ found two powerful allies in efforts to force national governments to comply with European law' (Kapsis 2010: 183).

Costa v. ENEL (1964)

In this case, the Court first asserted the supremacy of EU law over national law. Again, there was no explicit authority for this in the Treaty. An Italian court referred the case to the ECJ, asking whether an Act of the Italian Parliament, passed later in time than the Act that embodied an EU directive into Italian law, took precedence. The Court said that it did not, making clear that national law cannot take precedence over EU law. This was a perfectly logical position, but it had particular consequences for those states—in this case Italy, but after its accession in 1973, also the UK—in which Parliament holds sovereignty. In such systems, the principle that prevails is *lex posterior priori derogat*: 'the later law overrides the earlier'. The *Costa* v. *ENEL* judgment struck at the heart of this principle of parliamentary sovereignty.

Van Duyn v. Home Office (1974)

A Dutch national who had been debarred from entering Britain because she was a member of the Church of Scientology, which the British Home Office considered to be a socially undesirable organization, brought a case in the English courts challenging the ruling. This case was brought on the grounds that Article 48 of the EEC Treaty (now TFEU Article 45) committed the member states to allow free movement of workers, and that the British government had accepted Directive 64/221 which implemented this Treaty provision as part of the **acquis communautaire** when it joined the EC. The Court was asked to decide whether rights could be acquired directly in this way from a directive that had not yet been incorporated into national law.

The Court decided that the directive did, in fact, have direct effect. Although the relevant directive had not yet been explicitly incorporated into English law, the Court maintained that the defendant could still quote it as grounds for her opposition to the British government's position. This ruling had wide implications since a member state's failure to transpose a directive could not prevent citizens from invoking it in the national courts.

The *Factortame* Cases (1990, 1991)

These cases arose because Spanish fishermen had been purchasing British fishing vessels, and with them the quotas that the boats had been allocated to catch fish under the EU's Common Fisheries Policy. In effect, the Spanish fishermen had been catching fish on the British quota and landing it in Spain. The British government had responded by passing the Merchant Shipping Act 1988, which required 75 per cent of the shareholders and directors of a company to be British in order for the company to be able to register as British. The Spanish fishermen claimed that this was a breach of their rights under European law.

In its 1990 judgment, the ECJ underlined the supremacy of European law, but also empowered the House of Lords to overturn British legislation: the first time that British courts had been allowed to set aside an Act of Parliament. (At the time the House of Lords was the highest court in the UK: a function now played by the Supreme Court, which was established in 2009.) The ruling had major constitutional implications in Britain. In its 1991 ruling, the ECJ subsequently agreed with the Spanish fishermen that the Merchant Shipping Act was in breach of European law because of its discriminatory nationality rules on ownership. Each of these steps caused a furore in the British Parliament, both because of what was seen as the manifest unfairness of allowing Spanish fishermen to take fish on the British quota, but also because of the domestic constitutional implications. The full impact of the ECJ's judicial activism only really came home to many British parliamentarians with these cases.

Francovich v. *Italy* (1991)

Before this case arose, the Italian government had already been taken to the ECJ by the Commission and charged with not incorporating into Italian law a directive that gave redundant workers the right to compensation, and made such compensation the first claim against the assets of a bankrupt employer. It had still not been incorporated when workers for a bankrupt Italian company took a case to court in Italy because they had received no compensation for redundancy. The Court's ruling established the principle of state liability—that is, that any government that did not properly implement European law was liable to damages claims by its own citizens.

Subsequently, the Court used the same principle, that a government that did not properly implement EC law was liable to damages claims, to decide that the Spanish fishermen in the *Factortame* case were eligible for compensation from the British government for loss of earnings during the period when they were prevented from catching fish on the British quota. It also decided, in another case—*Brasserie du Pêcheur* (1996)—that a French brewery could claim damages from the German government for the period when the German government enforced its beer purity laws, which the Court had subsequently ruled to be an illegal barrier to trade. So in these two cases, the liability of a government that had not properly applied a directive to be sued for damages was extended beyond its own citizens to cover other citizens of the EU.

ECJ Rulings and Policy Impact

The ECJ has made many important rulings that have not only defined the shape of the legal order (see this chapter, ECJ Rulings on the Nature of EU Law) or, as discussed earlier, by clarifying the powers of the institutions, its rulings have also been influential for EU policies. The single market will serve as illustration.

The original route to creating a **common market** was based upon agreeing harmonized regulations. This method proved unwieldy, since it could be highly contentious as to what should be the ingredients of, say, beer. As unanimity was needed in the Council, progress was going to be very slow. However, in 1979, the ECJ made a ruling known as *Cassis de Dijon* (Case 120/78), which centred on Germany's discriminatory alcohol legislation. The ECJ ruled that if cassis (a French blackcurrant liqueur) was acceptable under French legislation, then it should be acceptable in Germany as well unless some pressing public health argument could be mounted. The *Cassis de Dijon* ruling, which identified no pressing public health argument, set an important principle: namely, that of mutual recognition. In other words, if goods lawfully met the standards of one member state, they should be accepted for sale in another member state. This principle was fundamental to the achievement of the single market, since it made clear that it was not necessary to harmonize legislation for every product. Instead, mutual recognition combined with a much more limited legislative package would accomplish the single market (see Chapter 20).

A second example relates to air transport liberalization. Prior to the 1990s, air transport was highly regulated and dominated by national flag carriers (British Airways, Air France, Lufthansa, and others), which were typically state-owned. Routes across Europe were regulated between pairs of governments and pairs of airlines. Intra-EU competition was very limited, because all routes were duopolies between flag carriers, which shared revenues on individual routes. The European Commission, with support from the British and Dutch governments, was trying to liberalize the market, but progress was slow because of the vested interests of the airlines, the other governments, and other actors. In 1986, the ECJ issued its *Nouvelles Frontières* judgment (Joined Cases 209–213/84). The ruling effectively declared the current bilateral air transport regime to be contrary to the EU's competition rules. With the authority of this ruling behind it, the Commission could apply more pressure to secure the passage of its liberalization legislation, which was later to usher in the era of low-cost air travel associated with easyJet and Ryanair (Armstrong and Bulmer 1998: 177–8).

It is important to point out that many of the ECJ's rulings are not as significant as these cases. Nevertheless, a proper understanding of the dynamics of those policy areas falling under the 'Union method' is usually facilitated by grasping a set of court judgments. Since the EU is distinctively characterized by its legislation and its supranational body of law, these features tend to be integral to policy dynamics. It is also worth underlining that the Commission has an important role in ensuring that agreed legislation is put into effect. Under Articles 258–260 TFEU, it proceeds through a set of stages that may ultimately lead to the ECJ. The ultimate sanction, introduced by the Maastricht Treaty, is for the ECJ to impose a penalty where a state has not complied with an earlier judgment. This power was first used as a result of a ruling by the ECJ in 2000 (*Commission* v. *Greece*, Case C-387/97), when the Greek government was fined for failure to comply with a 1992 ECJ ruling concerning the closure of a toxic waste tip on the island of Crete. The fine was €20,000 for each day of delay beyond the original 1992 ruling. Although a lengthy process, this case showed that a member state could receive a substantial fine for flouting an ECJ ruling.

Post-Maastricht Trends in the ECJ and EU Law

After a long period during which the pro-integration stance of the ECJ was tolerated by the governments of the member states, there was something of a backlash against the process of European integration generally, and against the ECJ more particularly, in the 1990s. The difficulties that were encountered in several member states in getting ratification of the Maastricht Treaty reinforced a tendency that had already been apparent in the inclusion in that Treaty of clauses on **subsidiarity** (see Insight 16.2). The desire to limit the transfer of competences from member states to the EU institutions came from different quarters: John Major's government in Britain; some subnational governments (notably the German *Länder*); and the French government, which pressed for the *acquis communautaire* to be reviewed in the light of subsidiarity.

> The formal introduction by the Maastricht Treaty (TEU) of subsidiarity as a general principle into EC ... law both symbolized and contributed to a gradual change in the political and legal culture of the European Community. If much of the Community's legal activity before the 1990s reflected a self-conscious teleology of integration, the teleology of subsidiarity suggests a rather different future.
>
> (De Búrca 1998: 218)

In more recent years, the ECJ's judicial activism has arguably declined, although intense debates continue among legal scholars. Several factors may be seen as explanations. The first is the greater attentiveness to subsidiarity in the post-Maastricht period.

Insight 16.2 Subsidiarity Articles of the TEU and TFEU

Article 1 of the TEU

This Treaty marks a new stage in the process of creating an ever closer union among the peoples of Europe, in which decisions are taken as openly as possible and *as closely as possible to the citizen*. [Our italics]

Article 5 of the TFEU

In areas which do not fall within its exclusive competence, the Community shall take action, in accordance with the principle of subsidiarity, only if and insofar as the objectives of the proposed action cannot be sufficiently achieved by the Member States and can therefore, by reason of the scale or effects of the proposed action, be better achieved by the Community.

Equally, the EU's character has diversified from the more 'classical' forms of top-down governance associated most closely with the original form of the CAP. The growth of regulation via EU agencies (rather than 'command-and-control' by law) in the aftermath of the single market is one form of diversity. The Open Method of Co-ordination's rise in the 2000s is another, since it entailed member state co-operation where the role of law, and thus the ECJ, was minimal. Another explanation is the maturing of the EU such that the ECJ is less of a player in the transformation of Europe and more of a kind of constitutional court within the EU. The scope for the ECJ to be transformative has become limited because it is shaped by its own prior rulings. Thus the era of the major rulings on the nature of EU law (see this chapter, ECJ Rulings on the Nature of EU Law) has declined. In addition, with the exception of the transfer of fiscal authority to the supranational level as part of rectifying design faults of the eurozone, the willingness of states to pursue deeper integration reached a plateau with the Lisbon Treaty. Moreover, the recent Treaty on Stability Co-ordination and Governance, TSCG (see Insight 11.2), often known in shorthand as the Fiscal Compact, was not signed by all member states and is not part of EU law. This development highlights another development: the emergence of a more diverse legal order. Differentiated integration creates its own challenges for the ECJ and the legal order of the EU, since there is no longer one legal system for all member states. Cardwell and Hervey (forthcoming) have argued that the accumulation of these developments has amounted to a 'decentring' of EU law. As the ECJ is at the apex of the legal system, there are clear implications for its role.

Is the ECJ out of the Control of the Member States?

The evidence that the ECJ was instrumental in considerably advancing the cause of European integration was quite convincing. However, the question arose of how the Court was able to get away with its radical jurisprudence. In the 1990s, an academic debate emerged on this question that paralleled the intergovernmental vs neofunctionalist debate of the 1960s (see Chapter 1). The intergovernmental case is considered first, and then the 'legal neofunctionalist' argument.

The Intergovernmental Case

Geoffrey Garrett and his collaborators (Garrett 1992, 1995; Garrett and Weingast 1993; Garrett et al. 1998) put the intergovernmental case. Their argument was summarized by another contributor to the debate (Carrubba 2003: 78), that 'the ECJ helped to facilitate integration, but only to the degree that member state governments desired it'. Although governments did sometimes contest cases brought to the ECJ, they often accepted and applied the judgment after it was handed down. This reflected the fact that governments were under pressure from domestic interests that would be adversely affected by a particular interpretation of EC law, and so argued against it. However, member states all accepted that they would be better off in the long term if the rules of the single market were implemented by everyone, and for that to happen required an independent and impartial referee to adjudicate on disputed interpretations of the rules, which is the role of the ECJ. To refuse to accept an adverse ruling would weaken the legitimacy of the impartial referee, and that was a cost that member states would be loath to pay.

In some cases, Garrett (1995) argued, the strength of a domestic interest that was adversely affected by a ruling of the ECJ would be sufficiently great that the government of a member state would attempt to placate it by unilaterally, but covertly, not implementing the ruling. In that way, it could avoid weakening the legitimacy of the independent arbitrator, while possibly avoiding the political costs of not doing so. Whether this course was followed would depend on the relative gains to the member state from the existence of an efficiently functioning internal market when set against the political cost of upsetting a powerful interest group. The states that stood to gain the most from the single market—generally the more northern member states—would be most reluctant to risk damaging the legitimacy of the ECJ even by covert non-compliance. Those that stood to gain less—mainly the southern member states—might be more inclined to engage in unilateral non-compliance to try to evade the political costs of displeasing a powerful domestic vested interest. Even then, the government would try to conceal evasion, and would plead implementation problems if caught.

For its part, the ECJ was very aware that its legitimacy was dependent on the behaviour of the member states. If governments were openly to flout its decisions, its legitimacy would be seriously damaged, and pressure might build for its powers to be weakened by revision of the Treaties. As a result, according to this intergovernmentalist interpretation, the ECJ avoided making decisions that would place powerful governments in a difficult position. It was able to do this because, although the Treaty prohibited restrictions on internal trade, exceptions were allowed if 'justified on grounds of public morality, public policy or public security; the protection of health and life of humans, animals or plants; the protection of national treasures possessing artistic, historic or archaeological value; or the protection of industrial and commercial property' (Article 36 TFEU). According to Garrett (1995: 178), this gave the ECJ plenty of scope to find a reason for allowing an exception if it would be politically uncomfortable not to do so.

The Neofunctionalist Case

Burley and Mattli (1993) and Mattli and Slaughter (1995) argued that the ECJ had been the prime mover in European integration, and that the governments of the member states had passively accepted this lead. The ECJ had used European law as a 'mask' to cover its integrationist agenda, wrapping its promotion of integration in the discourse of legal logic and necessity. It had also used the law as a 'shield' to protect itself from political attack. If the governments of the member states did not like the activism of the ECJ, they had the means available to counter it, either by non-compliance with the rulings or by amendment of the Treaties. Yet, the first had not been done to any significant degree, and the second had not been done at all. Burley and Mattli (1993) used the example of the famous *Cassis de Dijon* case to illustrate their argument, and were subsequently challenged specifically on their interpretation of this case by Garrett (1995).

The 'mask and shield' part of the argument was frequently quoted in later contributions to the debate (Garrett 1995: 171–2; Garrett et al. 1998: 149–50). However, it was never a particularly strong element in the neofunctionalist argument. As Carrubba (2003: 78) pointed out:

First, to assume that law 'masks' the political ramifications of a decision is to suggest that governments are incapable of evaluating what outcome would serve their purposes best. Since governments make observations on ECJ cases on a regular basis, it seems demonstrably implausible that the governments do not have well-formed preferences over outcomes. Further, to say that the legal venue 'shields' decisions from political interference, owing to the domestic norms of the rule of law, is to assume that governments will obey court rulings because governments have been observed doing so in the past. There are a number of reasons why governments may obey court rulings in one situation and not in another.

The threat of Treaty revisions could also 'be dismissed fairly easily' (Carrubba 2003: 76) because it required the unanimous consent of all member states' governments, which was unlikely to be achievable given the commitment of some states to the enforcement of the single market, and of others to the enhancement of integration.

The second part of the legal neofunctionalist argument was stronger. It started with the observation that, for the legal doctrines of the ECJ to be effective, they had to be accepted by national courts. This seemed to have happened. By making Article 267 references for a preliminary ruling, national courts had been the main accomplices of the ECJ in its 'constitutionalization' of the Treaties. Why had this collaboration taken place? Burley and Mattli (1993) suggested that a legal version of neofunctionalism was at work. Spillover was implicit in the concept of EC law itself, but it was cultivated by the ECJ to give the most integrationist interpretation possible to the existing laws. Other actors—national courts, private individuals—fed the process simply by pursuing their own self-interest in a rational manner within the changed context: for example, individuals did so by bringing cases against their own governments under European law when they felt that their rights had been breached.

Alter (1996, 1998, 2001) went further, arguing that the Article 267 procedure (previously the Article 177 procedure) actually empowered lower national courts. They were used to having their judgments overturned on appeal by higher national courts, but by making Article 267 references, they could directly influence the evolution of national legal principles. Higher courts might be able to overturn the substance of their judgments, but they were unable to challenge the points of European law on which they were based.

The ECJ has also been careful always to get the national courts on its side by proceeding in what another advocate of this theory, Mancini (1991: 185), described as a 'courteously didactic' manner. The judges:

developed a style that may be drab and repetitive but explains as well as declares the law, and they showed unlimited patience vis-à-vis the national judges, reformulating questions couched in imprecise terms or extracting from the documents concerning the main proceedings the elements of Community law that needed to be interpreted with regard to the subject matter of the dispute.

(Mancini 1991: 185)

In this way, the European judges won the confidence of their national colleagues. Those who presided over even the lowest courts knew that they would receive sympathetic treatment if they were to make an Article 267 referral, and were therefore more inclined to do so.

This co-opting of national courts raised the stakes for national governments that might be inclined to defy the jurisprudence of the ECJ, for it would also be defying the jurisprudence of its own domestic courts. The indirect political costs of undermining the legitimacy of the rule of law in the domestic arena were considerably higher than the costs of undermining the ECJ. Research reported by Carrubba (2003: 95) indicated that European publics would be inclined to support their own government if it were in dispute with the ECJ, but not if it were in dispute with national courts.

A criticism of this analysis is that the alliance forged between the ECJ and lower national courts is not the whole story. The reception of the jurisprudence of the ECJ by national supreme courts has been less enthusiastic. Problems have arisen with the reception of the judgments of the ECJ by the Italian, French, British, and German supreme courts (Kuper 1998: 19–27). In no case has a national Supreme Court attempted to negate a decision of the ECJ: were one to do so, it would cause a constitutional crisis. In several cases, though, the national Supreme Court has disagreed with the reasoning of the ECJ, while finding alternative lines of legal reasoning to arrive at the same substantive decision. In particular, the doctrine of the supremacy of EU law over national law has not been universally accepted by member states. However, this is compatible with the argument that lower courts were prepared to collaborate with the ECJ on preliminary rulings because that increased their influence within their national legal hierarchies. The corollary of that argument is that higher courts would see their influence weakened, and so would be expected to resist the jurisprudence of the ECJ.

CONCLUSION

This review of the role of the ECJ particularly raises two of the themes that run through the book. The first is the theme that has been most prominent in the chapters on the institutions: the intergovernmental–supranational debate about the nature of the EU. A second theme is that of legitimacy.

If the role of the ECJ is approached in the same way as was the discussion about the role of the Commission in Chapter13 (The Commission in the Policy-Making Process)—that is, whether it is an agent of the member states or an autonomous actor in its own right—there is little doubt that the judgments of the Court have gone beyond what the governments of the member states were expecting. The radical jurisprudence of the Court may represent the logical consequences of the actions of the member states, but it is not a logic that was thought through by their governments, nor was it always welcome to them. In this sense, the ECJ has proved itself to be an autonomous, supranational actor in the process of European integration.

As intergovernmentalists would point out, the member states can rescind those powers that they have given to the Court—but this is not easy, because, without an independent and authoritative interpreter of the law, all of the rules put in place by the Treaties and by EU secondary legislation would be subject to different interpretation by different parties. There has to be an authoritative source of interpretation, and it has to be unquestionably independent.

Some parties to any dispute will not like some of the decisions of the independent arbitrator, but they will abide by them rather than see the collapse of the system from which they benefit generally. The result is to make it difficult to recall powers once delegated. Treaty changes require unanimity, and if even one member state is happy with the thrust of the ECJ's decisions, it will not be possible to reduce its powers because its one supporter has a veto on any attempt to do so.

There is no doubt that the ECJ has the formal right to reach the decisions that it does. Whether those decisions are accepted as legitimate is another matter. Most decisions of the Court have not impinged on the consciousness of national politicians or members of the public. They have received legitimacy through being accepted by national courts, especially those lower down the legal hierarchy. When ECJ judgments have come to the attention of national politicians, there has sometimes been a strong negative reaction, suggesting that the legitimacy of the Court's doctrines does not extend beyond the national courts and professional judges. The strength of reaction in Britain to the *Factortame* judgment is indicative of this. As Carrubba (2003: 96–7) noted, 'public perceptions of institutional legitimacy are critical to the EU legal system being able to act as an effective democratic check', but 'the ECJ remains woefully short on public legitimacy today'.

The highest courts in the member states have been less comfortable than have lower courts with the judgments of the ECJ. In consequence, difficult domestic constitutional issues have been raised intermittently. Essentially the ECJ has, in effect, 'constitutionalized' the EU from the raw material of the Treaties (Weiler 1999: 19–29). It has had plenty of scope to impose its own interpretation of what that constitution should look like because Treaties are not carefully crafted legal documents; rather, they are the outcome of diplomatic negotiations and compromises. These far-from-watertight documents leave judges plenty of space to fill in the gaps. In doing so, the ECJ has enunciated principles that conflict with some fundamental national constitutional principles. The legal conflict shows the impossibility of taking several different national constitutions and reconciling them with one overarching European constitution. The political reaction raises again the issue of identity, which appears in the discussion of the legitimacy of the EP in Chapter 3. National politicians and publics find it difficult to accept that decisions made by their democratically elected national institutions can be overruled by an organization that has far less legitimacy in their eyes.

While this debate about the role of the ECJ in European integration has subsided somewhat, attention has shifted to the role of EU law in a more diversified EU in the post-Maastricht period. As the ECJ has matured towards a constitutional court for the EU, attention has shifted from its role in integration to its role in EU governance. This development reflects the 'turn' in EU studies more generally towards governance approaches.

While this chapter has necessarily been selective in the material covered, it should be clear that the ECJ's impact through its rulings has been felt widely: across the EU institutions; across the EU's policies; and across the member states. Integration has not only been economic and political, as charted elsewhere in this book, but it has also had an important legal dimension. Moreover, the legal and political dimensions are often closely intertwined.

KEY POINTS

Context

- The ECJ is the authoritative interpreter of the Treaties and EU secondary legislation.
- It is sometimes accused of making political decisions that favour European integration at the expense of the powers of member states.

Structure and Functions

- The Court consists of twenty-seven judges and eight advocates-general.
- It is charged to ensure that EU law is observed.
- It has wide-ranging powers to hear various types of action and to give preliminary rulings.

ECJ Rulings on the Powers of the Institutions

- The EP has been a major beneficiary of the Court's radical jurisprudence.
- Although on occasions the Court has found against an extension of the EP's legal position, it also reversed this in subsequent judgments.

ECJ Rulings on the Nature of EU law

- The ECJ has been most radical in cases referred by national courts under Article 267.
- In early rulings, the Court stated the principles of 'direct effect'—that EU law confers rights on individuals—and the supremacy of EU over national law. Subsequent rulings confirmed these principles.
- A series of later cases also produced rulings that surprised the governments of the member states, because they placed upon them obligations to which they did not think that they had agreed.

ECJ Rulings and Policy Impact

- The ECJ's rulings have had significant impact on policy areas such as the single market.

Post-Maastricht Trends in the ECJ and EU Law

- The ECJ has been criticized for stepping beyond its legal role and behaving politically in favouring judgments that advance European integration.
- The ECJ's judicial activism has declined in more recent years.
- Subsidiarity and differentiated integration, along with a maturing of the system, have encouraged diversity in the EU legal system, while the ECJ has matured towards the role of an EU constitutional court.

Is the ECJ out of the Control of the Member States?

- Both intergovernmental and neofunctionalist explanations have been offered of why member states have accepted the radical jurisprudence of the ECJ.
- The intergovernmental argument is that member states have tolerated the rulings of the ECJ because it is important to them to have an independent arbitrator that can enforce the single-market contract between them, and they do not want to undermine the legitimacy of the arbitrator by defying its rulings.
- The neofunctionalist case is that the ECJ had used the legal system as a 'mask' and a 'shield' to advance integration further than the member states have wanted, and that it has recruited national courts to assist it in this process.

FURTHER READING

For a useful review of scholarship on the EU's judicial system, see **A. Arnull**, 'European Union Law: A Tale of Microscopes and Telescopes', in **M. Egan**, **N. Nugent**, **and W. Paterson (eds)**,

Research Agendas in European Union Studies: Stalking the Elephant (Basingstoke: Palgrave Macmillan, 2010), 168–88. A very good non-technical introduction to the role of the ECJ, but no longer up to date on detail is **R. Dehousse**, *The European Court of Justice: The Politics of Judicial Integration* (Basingstoke and London: Macmillan, 1998). It is therefore important to check the details with an authoritative textbook on EU law, such as **D. Chalmers**, **G. Davies**, **and G. Monti**, *European Union Law*, 3rd edn (Cambridge: Cambridge University Press, 2014), **P. Craig and G. De Búrca**, *EU Law: Text, Cases and Materials* (Oxford University Press, 5th edition, 2011), **S. Weatherill**, *Cases and Materials on EU Law* (Oxford University Press, 2012), or **R Schütze**, *European Constitutional Law* (Cambridge University Press, 2012). Specifically recommended on the ECJ is **A. Arnull**, *The European Union and its Court of Justice* (Oxford University Press, 2nd edition, 2006).

A view of the relationship between the ECJ and both national courts and national governments that is in line with what has here been described as the 'legal neofunctionalism' perspective is presented in **K. J. Alter**, *Establishing the Supremacy of European Law: The Making of an International Rule of Law in Europe* (Oxford: Oxford University Press, 2001). A collection of very good essays on legal integration is available in **J. Weiler**, *The Constitution of Europe: 'Do the New Clothes Have an Emperor?' and Other Essays on European Integration* (Cambridge: Cambridge University Press, 1999).

 online resource centre **Visit the Online Resource Centre that accompanies this book for links to more information on the European Court of Justice, including the ECJ's own website: http://oxfordtextbooks.co.uk/orc/bache4e/.**

Chapter 17

Organized Interests

Chapter Overview

The term 'interest group' is used to describe a range of organizations outside of the formal institutions that seek to influence decision making. They provide a link between state actors and the rest of society, sometimes termed 'civil society'. Within the political systems of member states, interest-group activity is long established and it has increased considerably in the European Union (EU) arena since the launch of the single-market programme in the mid-1980s.

This chapter looks first at the general growth of interest-group activity at the European level, before analyzing the types of group that try to influence EU policy making and the forms of representation open to interests. The resources that interest groups bring to the task are considered, as is how these resources gain the groups access to institutional actors. The chapter then looks at the strategies and tactics that groups use to try to influence the different institutions. Lastly, it looks at the issue of regulating interest-group access to the institutions.

The Growth of Interest-Group Activity at the EU Level

Interest-group activity aimed at EU decision makers has grown spectacularly, particularly from the launch of the single-market programme in the mid-1980s. By the end of the 1990s, Mazey and Richardson (1999: 105) could speak of 'a dense European lobbying system ... which now exhibits many of the features of interest group intermediation systems long familiar in Western Europe'. Finding precise statistics on this growth is more difficult, as is identifying the current scale of activity. A first problem is ensuring that the definition of interest groups is clear. If an encompassing approach is to be adopted, corporate lobbying by individual firms should be included, as should the offices of regional and local governments, as well as law firms and public affairs consultants that lobby the EU on behalf of clients. Another important distinction is between these different types of groups and lobbyists; the latter being larger because it includes the number of individuals working for the former. Commission figures suggested that, in the mid-1990s, there were around 3,000 interest groups active in Brussels, with around 10,000 individuals involved in the lobbying industry (Greenwood 1997: 3). More recent figures related to the number of groups and lobbyists need to be treated with some caution (Greenwood 2011: 8–12). For instance, in 2005, the then Commissioner for Administrative Affairs, Siim Kallas, who was seeking to regulate lobbyists, quoted figures of 2,600 groups and 15,000 lobbyists; Graziano (2012: 1) asserted that there are 15,000–20,000 lobbyists working in Brussels; while Corporate Europe Observatory (2011: 7) puts the figure between 15,000 and 30,000.

An alternative approach is to rely on the data Joint Transparency Register that was set up by the Commission and European Parliament (EP) in 2011 as part of an Inter-Institutional Agreement. Unlike the previous register from 2008 (which covered the Commission only and comprised 4,000 registered organizations), the current one went beyond 'traditional lobbyists' and included law firms, NGOs, think-tanks, and other organizations. The EP had had a separate register, but this recorded lobbyists rather than organizations and, by April 2006, had issued 4,435 passes, but not all lobbyists were registered (Greenwood 2007: 11). As of 31 October 2013 there were 5,952 registrants in the new Joint Transparency Register (Joint Transparency Register 2013: 14). This register entails organizations signing up to a code of practice, and the growth of numbers since 2011 reflects the growing acceptance of this registration system. The register includes think-tanks and churches, so has an inclusive approach to the definition of interest groups. It should be noted that the register is not without its flaws, as Greenwood and Dreger (2013) note, but has been seen in comparative terms as in the vanguard of the 'new wave' of lobbying regulation. It is not a mandatory system, so it is still not a comprehensive register of lobbying organizations.

For many organized interests, the development of direct representation at the EU level is in addition to their continuing attempts to influence national governments as part of their overall strategy to shape EU policy. However, the Brussels end of the strategy is increasingly important. Factors that contribute to this include:

the growing policy competence of the EU;

changes in the formal rules of decision making;

the receptiveness of EU officials to interest-group representations;

the 'snowballing' effect of groups following the lead of others, so as not to risk being disadvantaged;

the Commission's support for a wider engagement of European civil society, particularly in the period following its 2001 White Paper on Governance, in which it committed itself to trying to ensure that the policy process was not biased towards certain interests (European Commission 2001a).

In line with the maxim that 'where power goes, interest groups follow', the increasing powers of EU institutions is an important reason for the rapid growth in interest-group activity at the European level. Whereas, in the early years, the coal and steel industries and agriculture were the sectors most affected by the setting up of the European Communities (EC), there are now very few policy sectors that do not have an EU dimension (see Chapter 18).

Increased competences have been accompanied by changes in the rules of decision making (see Chapter 12, Decision-Making Procedures). The move within the Council of Ministers to **qualified majority voting (QMV)** for most policy sectors makes it less sensible to lobby only at the national level, because a single state no longer has a veto over legislative proposals where QMV applies. There has also been a shift of power within the policy-making process to the EP, while the Commission's key role as initiator of legislation remains.

The EU provides relatively easy access for those seeking to influence decision making, which provides 'part of the explanation for the intensity of participation in the process by so wide a range of political and economic actors' (Wallace and Young 1997: 250). There are several advantages for policy makers of good relations with interest groups:

> Put simply, it is very difficult to make effective public policy without the *specialized expertise* that interest groups possess. Moreover, their cooperation in the *implementation* of public policy is often a prime condition for implementation success. Finally, from the bureaucratic perspective, the mobilization of a constituency of *support* is vital to the long-term survival of bureaucracies.

(Mazey and Richardson 1999: 106)

The importance of organized interests to policy makers, particularly in the complex emerging system of the EU, means that many groups find themselves greeted by an open door when they seek discussions in Brussels. Justin Greenwood (2011: 5) has spelt out the need for interest groups and other lobby organizations from the perspective of the EU institutions:

> Apart from the need for policymaking expertise, and implementation and monitoring capacity, the potential for consolidated collective viewpoint, and the potential to enhance legitimacy, EU institutions also work with organized civil society because the latter has the ability to convey political messages.

Equally, the freedom of access to interest groups has led to pressure to regulate lobbying in order to ensure that groups do not 'capture' a policy area to the detriment of the collective interest. Given that industrial and professional groups predominate, with public interest groups representing a minority, the danger of capture is not insignificant. Indeed, the Commission has funded some non-governmental organizations in order to promote balance.

Although no one can be sure of the benefits of lobbying activities in Brussels, the fear of missing out has become a motivating factor for EU-level activity. Once some groups start to shift their activity to Brussels, a momentum builds up that carries other groups along with it. Mazey and Richardson (1999: 107) suggested that 'rather like bees around a honey pot, interest groups are attached to regulatory institutions in swarms. Once one set of groups begins to exploit incentives and opportunity structures at the European level, others are bound to follow; they cannot afford to be left out, whatever the cost'. Brussels has acquired the reputation of being 'an insider's town' (Greenwood 1997: 55, 2003: 2), in which those who do not have an established presence operate at a disadvantage. Corporate Europe Observatory (2011) offers a tour of the lobbying quarters, both in publication form and for those wishing to undertake a guided tour 'on the ground'.

Types of Interest Group

There are different ways of classifying interest groups. We have followed the categories used in the EU Transparency Register and offer some illustrations of each type (and their number) from the 5,952 total registered on 31 October 2013 (Joint Transparency Register 2013).

(1) *Professional consultancies, law firms, self-employed consultants* (N = 715). Hill & Knowlton and Burson-Marsteller are major players in the first category; Freshfields Bruckhaus Deringer is one of the large law firms. Note that law firms, many of which have not registered, may help their clients by drafting legislative amendments that they hope members of the European Parliament (MEPs) will be able to utilize during the ordinary legislative procedure.

(2) *In-house lobbyists, trade and professional associations* (N = 2,972). This category includes trade associations like the Chemical Industries Association as well as big corporations like Microsoft or Shell.

(3) *Non-governmental organizations* (N = 1,536). An example here would be the European Women's Lobby.

(4) *Think-tanks, research and academic institutions* (N = 422). There are numerous think-tanks in Brussels, most of which are undertaking analysis rather than directly lobbying, but sometimes the distinction can break down, especially if the funding is from big corporate players. The Centre for European Policy Studies and Bruegel are major think-tanks. Individual universities may act as lobbyists because they often receive sizeable amounts of research funding from the EU, although they tend to be represented collectively.

(5) *Organizations representing churches and religious communities* (N = 32). Churches may act in connection with welfare issues and therefore deem it appropriate to register, as in the case of the Churches' Commission for Migrants in Europe.

(6) *Organizations representing local and regional authorities or other public bodies* (N = 275). Reflecting the EU's multi-level governance and its source of funding via the Cohesion Funds, many authorities act as lobbyists, for instance, the German federal states (Länder), Scotland Europa, or the City of Malmö.

The breakdown of the 5,952 members is set out in Figure 17.1.

Different types of organization can represent any given set of interests at the same time. Business interests provide a good example. Business representation in Brussels takes the form of individual companies, collective national organizations (such as the Confederation of British Industry), and collective European organizations. The last category includes BUSINESSEUROPE, which brings together national business associations (and was known until January 2007 as the Union of Industrial and Employers' Confederations, or UNICE), and the European Round Table of Industrialists (ERT), which is made up of chief executives of major firms. The ERT was particularly active in moves to launch the single-market programme in the mid-1980s (see Chapter 20, Explaining the Single Market). In addition, firms individually or collectively might employ lobbying consultancy firms to advance their case.

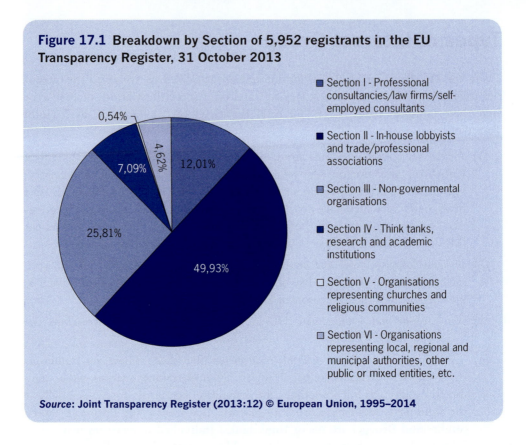

Figure 17.1 Breakdown by Section of 5,952 registrants in the EU Transparency Register, 31 October 2013

■ Section I - Professional consultancies/law firms/self-employed consultants

■ Section II - In-house lobbyists and trade/professional associations

■ Section III - Non-governmental organisations

■ Section IV - Think tanks, research and academic institutions

□ Section V - Organisations representing churches and religious communities

□ Section VI - Organisations representing local, regional and municipal authorities, other public or mixed entities, etc.

0,54%
4,62%
7,09%
12,01%
25,81%
49,93%

Source: Joint Transparency Register (2013:12) © European Union, 1995–2014

Business interests were represented in Brussels from the establishment of the European Economic Community in 1958. The creation of the Common Agricultural Policy (CAP) stimulated a growth of interest groups from that sector in the 1960s. Following the logic that activity by one set of interests stimulates competing interests into similar activity, there is now a wide range of groups that act as countervailing forces to business lobbying in Brussels. Trade unions, consumer groups, and environmentalists are examples of countervailing forces to business interests, although these groups were late to the game and only really became prominent in the 1990s. (For brief portraits of five European interest organizations, see Insight 17.1.) The other type of group that has exploded in numbers in Brussels is the lobbying consultancy firm, which sells its expertise and contacts to a range of clients.

Forms of Interest Representation

Several forms of interest representation coexist in the EU:

- the full institutionalization of representation through the European Economic and Social Committee (EESC);
- the semi-institutionalized 'social dialogue';

Insight 17.1 Illustrations of EU-Level Interest Groups

BUSINESSEUROPE can trace its origins back to the establishment in 1958 of the Union of Industrial and Employers' Confederations of the European Community (UNICE). It changed its name in 2007. BUSINESSEUROPE is a 'horizontal' body reflecting industrialists' and employers' groups. Specific industries have their own organizations. It has forty-one member federations from thirty-five countries, including Turkey and Iceland. It has around forty-five staff in Brussels, and its member organizations, such as the British Confederation of British Industry, have offices nearby. Website: **http://businesseurope.eu/**.

The **European Round Table of Industrialists** was established in April 1983 when a group of leading European business leaders from companies such as Fiat, Philips, and Volvo met to form an organization to promote Europe's industrial competitiveness. It now comprises almost fifty chief executives and chairmen of major European multinational companies from eighteen countries. It 'advocates policies, at both national and European levels, which help create conditions necessary to improve European growth and jobs'. It has a small secretariat in Brussels. Website: **http://ert.eu/**.

The **European Trade Union Confederation (ETUC)** styles itself as 'the voice of European workers'. The ETUC can trace its origins back to the 1950s, but only took on its current title in 1973. Owing to competing trade union organizations in some member states (Christian, socialist, communist), it was only by the 1990s that the ETUC took on its broad representative character of today. It comprises eighty-five national trade union confederations from thirty-six European countries and ten industry federations (such as the European Metalworkers' Federation). It works for a European social model comprising sustainable economic growth, full employment, and social protection. Its secretariat is in Brussels and has approximately fifty staff. Website: **http://etuc.org/**.

The **Committee of Professional Agricultural Organizations (COPA)** and the **General Confederation of Agricultural Co-operatives (COGECA)** are the key interest groups relating to the farming sector. Set up in 1958 and 1959, respectively, they have a shared secretariat of over fifty staff, based in Brussels. COPA comprises farmers' unions from the member states, while COGECA's membership is of member states' agricultural co-operative associations. COPA-COGECA has a large number of working parties on different agricultural products: from eggs and poultry to wine. Website: **http://copa-cogeca.be/**.

The **European Women's Lobby** was created in 1990. It aims to promote women's rights and equality between women and men in the European Union. It has member organizations in all twenty-eight member states. It has a small secretariat in Brussels. Website: **http://womenlobby.org/**.

Source: All information sourced from the respective websites.

- a **pluralist** system based on competitive lobbying;
- informally institutionalized policy networks;
- legal representation.

The EESC has its origins in the '**corporatist**' institutions that were set up between the wars in Germany (the Economic Council) and France (the *Conseil Economique et Social*), and which were created or recreated in five of the six original member states after the war, Germany being the exception. The EESC has not proven to be a particularly effective institution (see Chapter 12, The Decision-Making Institutions (the Union Method)), and when new forms of institutionalized relations between government, business, and trade unions were tried in several member states during the 1970s, attempts to replicate them at the EU level did not involve this institution. Instead, the Ministers of Social Affairs and Economic and Financial Affairs organized a series of tripartite conferences bringing together European business and trade union organizations in an arrangement that is often referred to as **neo-corporatism**. The tripartite conferences met six times in 1978 to discuss issues such as employment, inflation, wage restraint, fiscal policy, vocational training, and measures to increase productivity. The business groups were reluctant participants, though, and by the end of 1978, the European Trade Union Confederation (ETUC) had withdrawn from the process because of lack of progress.

The idea was revived by Jacques Delors when he became President of the Commission. In 1985, an approach was made to both ETUC and UNICE to open a 'social dialogue' to flank the momentum towards the single market. Delors suggested that, if the idea were accepted, the Commission would refrain from introducing further social legislation and would instead let it emerge out of the dialogue. Initially, two working parties were set up: on employment policies and on new technology and work. They met at the chateau of Val Duchesse outside Brussels, and the dialogue therefore became known as the 'Val Duchesse process'.

From the outset, there were difficulties about the status and functioning of the social dialogue, which was incorporated into the Social Protocol of the Maastricht Treaty. It was agreed that, where the social partners could negotiate agreement on any aspect of social legislation, that agreement would automatically be accepted by the Commission and formulated as a proposal to the Council of Ministers, with the expectation that it would become part of the social legislation of the EC—although it would not apply to Britain, which at that time had an opt-out from the Social Protocol. The first piece of legislation to be agreed in this way, in 1995, concerned paid parental leave. However, subsequent progress was limited. The lack of enthusiasm of UNICE and its member organizations for EU-level neo-corporatism reflected the fact that business interests are in a stronger position to get their views heard under the alternative, pluralist system of interest representation.

Separate from this 'social dialogue' approach, many specialized interest groups are able to secure membership of EU advisory committees, assuring themselves of 'semi-institutionalized' status via this route.

A pluralist approach to lobbying suggests that interest groups operate in a more open and competitive political process. This pluralist approach is generally associated with lobbying in the United States. However, there are clear differences between lobbying in the EU and in the United States. As Cornelia Woll puts it (2006: 461): 'According to most studies, lobbying in the US is much more direct and aggressive than in the EU, where lobbyists take a more subtle and consensus-oriented approach.' Pluralism tends to be characterized by the dominance of large firms, putting them in an advantageous position to become core members of any emerging policy networks. In theory, this pluralist system could be just a temporary stage in the evolution of interest representation. Once the EU system settles down, it could move to a greater informal institutionalization based on policy networks (see Chapter 2, Governance and Networks), which has already occurred in some of the more established policy sectors, such as agriculture.

Overall, the relationship between organized interests and the EU wavers between pluralism and informal institutionalization. As evidence of the latter, the Commission maintains partnership arrangements with interest groups, as Greenwood points out (2007: 5). Accordingly, several Commission Directorates-General (DGs) have contact groups for 'civil dialogue', including the DGs responsible for Development, Trade, the Environment, and Employment and Social Affairs. The Commission has encouraged the establishment of some interest groups, such as, in 1990, the European Women's Lobby (Greenwood 2003: 223). It also has financial resources to promote the work of civil society groups, helping to ensure that 'asymmetries between different types of interests are less extreme than might otherwise be the case' (Greenwood 2011: 16–17).

Finally, although it constitutes a very different activity from lobbying, for certain categories of interest group, targeting the European Court of Justice (ECJ) has been a particularly fruitful activity. Mazey and Richardson (1999: 115) noted that '[w]omen's and environmental groups (and also trade unions) have been adept in securing favourable ECJ decisions which have been just as, if not more, effective than bringing about change in EU policy via other means'. Here, 'whistleblowing' activity of groups in highlighting non-compliance with EU decisions by member states has been prominent.

Resources

The extent to which groups command resources of varying types is crucial to understanding their relative influence. The control of key resources is an important factor in deciding whether a group will secure 'insider status' with policy makers or remain outside the core process.

Greenwood (1997: 18–20) identified eight types of resource as important to interest groups (see Insight 17.2). When it comes to such resources, size matters: larger organizations are generally better resourced than smaller ones. At the level of individual firms, big-business interests possess far more of the resources that are needed to operate effectively than do small-business interests. For example, large firms will often have their own public relations departments, which means that they are better equipped to present their views than smaller firms. Also, the complexity and multi-level nature of EU decision making puts a premium on being able to deploy sufficient personnel to cover all possible access points.

> The diffuse character of the Brussels process within and between institutions means that to be a participant often requires covering several access points in order to find the most useful one. Small groups, and small firms, thus find it much harder to engage than the better resourced organizations or firms.
>
> (Wallace and Young 1997: 244)

Only large individual firms or other particularly well-resourced interest groups are able to pursue their own information gathering and lobbying without joining forces with other actors. To become more effective, smaller organizations have to pool resources. Kohler-Koch (1997: 58) made the point with reference to business: 'Large

> ## Insight 17.2 Resources Available to Interest Groups
>
> information and expertise;
>
> economic muscle;
>
> status;
>
> power in implementation;
>
> the organization of the interest into a non-competitive format;
>
> coherent organization with representative outlets able to make decisions with ease and alacrity;
>
> the ability to help the overloaded Commission with carrying out policies;
>
> the ability of a group to influence its members.

firms find it easy to become privileged interlocutors of the political-administrative system, thanks to their economic importance, while small and medium-sized firms rely more heavily on their collective force.' However, while there are resource advantages in separate interests coming together, such combinations of interests increase the risk that they will encounter problems of collective action: the interests aggregated within a combined group may find it difficult to agree among themselves about priorities and tactics.

This disparity in material resources does not necessarily mean that large individual firms have the best access to the policy-making process. Bouwen (2002, 2004*a*, 2004*b*) argued that the degree of access that an interest group can achieve to any of the EU's institutions depends on its ability to offer each institution the type of information that it most needs to perform efficiently its functions within the decision-making system. He identified three types of information that are important in differing degrees to the various EU institutions:

(1) expert knowledge;

(2) knowledge of the needs and concerns of actors in the relevant sector across Europe;

(3) knowledge of the specific concerns of national actors in the relevant sector.

Expert knowledge is essential for the institution to understand the technical working of the context into which the legislation is an intervention. It results in legislation that is better adapted to its purpose, and is therefore likely to work better. Information about the needs and concerns of actors in the relevant sector, both across Europe as a whole and in specific national contexts, enhances the legitimacy of the decision-making process, because a wide range of affected actors will feel that they have been listened to, and this ought to contribute to their compliance with the legislation and therefore to the chances of successful implementation.

Different types of interest group possess these different types of information in varying degrees. Interests that pursue their own lobbying—which will most often be large firms, because they have the resources to do so—are very good at providing expert information. European and national associations are less efficient at providing expert information, but they are very good at providing information on the concerns of actors across Europe in the case of European organizations, and on the concerns of national actors in the case of national associations. On the basis of this theoretical analysis, Bouwen (2002) drew up a number of hypotheses about the degree of access that different types of group would have to the different institutions of the EU. These are reviewed in the next section.

Organized Interests and the Institutional Actors

The Commission

For a number of reasons, the Commission is an important target for interest groups:

- it has a central role in setting the agenda;
- all proposals have to pass through it;
- it is within the Commission that the detail of proposals is decided;
- it is receptive to approaches from interest groups.

The Commission's agenda-setting role is of particular importance to interest groups. If they want to get particular issues placed on the agenda of the EU, the Commission is a good place to start lobbying. Alternatively, if they want to prevent measures from coming onto or rising up the agenda, influence in the Commission is vital. All policy proposals 'have to pass through the Commission gateway and are subject to detailed *processing* at that institutional site' (Mazey and Richardson 1999: 112). This means that the Commission is an important channel to monitor. It also means that it is the primary place for influencing the detail of proposals, which is often what concerns interest groups.

The Commission is widely recognized as being receptive to interest-group representations. This is not least because the Commission's limited human resources make it more dependent than other institutions on the information and expertise that interest groups can offer. Bouwen (2002: 379) argued that, in terms of the three types of knowledge that he had identified, the Commission needed expert knowledge most, to allow it to construct viable legislation that successfully addressed the problem and was most likely to be implemented successfully. Second, it required information on the concerns of actors across Europe in order to boost both its own legitimacy and that of the specific piece of legislation. It needed information on the concerns of specific groups of national actors only in so far as it proved necessary for it to broker a deal within the Council of Ministers between differing national preferences.

Mapping the Commission's demand for each type of information against the supply from different types of actor, Bouwen (2002: 382) hypothesized that large individual firms, which could provide good-quality expert knowledge efficiently, would have the best access to the Commission, followed by European associations, which could

317

provide reliable information on the concerns of the sector across Europe. While national associations would enjoy the lowest level of access during the crucial drafting stage of legislation, at the later stages of the passage of the legislation through the Council of Ministers, they might well find that their particular expertise on the concerns of national actors was sought by the Commission. However, subsequent research indicated that European associations actually had the best access to the Commission, despite the fact that they were 'often considered to be internally divided, poorly resourced and unable to respond quickly to Commission requests for information' (Bouwen 2004a: 355). Large firms were close behind in second place, while national associations were far behind.

This finding was not predicted in Bouwen's original model of access to the Commission, but it was consistent with the observation of Greenwood (1997: 4) that the Commission preferred interaction with Euro groups where possible:

> **Places on its advisory committees are handed out to Euro groups first. Drafts of directives and other policy initiatives are often given to European business sector associations to comment on. Although single-firm representations to the Commission are heard, the firm concerned is usually told that the Commission would wish to explore the issue further by talking to the interest group concerned in order to ensure that it gets a more representative opinion.**

Kohler-Koch (1997: 53) noted further that the Commission 'has actively promoted the organization of the less represented social interests in order to achieve more balanced participation'. It has also sought alliances with influential groups to strengthen its position vis-à-vis the Council in the EU system. Authoritative and representative interest groups can provide the unelected Commission with legitimacy in its arguments with the Council. As noted earlier, it has justified this position in connection with its 2001 White Paper on Governance, and the wish to avoid large groups becoming overly dominant in lobbying.

The Council of Ministers

The authority of the Council makes it an important target for interest groups. Yet in reality there is little opportunity for them to lobby either the European Council or the Council of Ministers directly. These institutions meet behind closed doors and, generally, groups do not have direct access. This doubtless explains why the Council is not party to the EU Transparency Register. Because its members are supported by national administrations and permanent officials in Brussels, the Council has less need for the information resources of interest groups than does the Commission, and is thus less receptive to approaches. The consequence is that most lobbying of the Council is indirect rather than direct.

To influence the Council indirectly, groups seek contact with individual national governments. Initially, of course, they will try to influence their own national government—but as understanding of the EU policy process has grown, interest groups' lobbying techniques have become more sophisticated, and interest groups in one member state may now seek to influence governments in other member states. Which governments matter will vary with the issue. For obvious reasons, the member state holding the Council presidency will be a particular target.

Although lobbying national governments is only an indirect way of influencing EU affairs, it is a process that is familiar to most interest groups. It is, as Greenwood (2003: 39) argued, an arena 'where established policy networks and dependency relationships operate which can equally well be used for the purposes of EU representation as for the governance of domestic affairs'. Moreover, for those groups that do not have the necessary resources to lobby EU institutions, the national route may remain the only real option. However, the value of lobbying individual governments has declined with the extension of QMV in the Council. Even where a group has successfully persuaded a government of its case, under QMV, it is far from certain that the government will be able to assist, assuming it is persuaded of the lobbyists' case in the first place.

Bouwen (2002: 381) noted that, at the ministerial level, the Council is the most intergovernmental of the institutions—but at the level of the officials involved in the preparation of the ministerial meetings, there is also a considerable degree of supranationalism. In terms of his model, the governments of member states primarily need information on the needs and concerns of their own state's actors in the policy sector, so that they can formulate their national preferences on any legislation. However, at the level of officials, there is considerable concern for the impact of legislation on the European market as a whole, as well as the narrower focus on national interests, so the expert committees might well be open to representations from European associations. Expert knowledge is less needed from outside sources, as there is plenty available from national officials who staff the committees that consider the proposed legislation.

On this basis, Bouwen (2002: 382) expected national associations, together with large national firms that constituted 'national champions', to have the best access to the Council of Ministers via the national route. European associations were expected to have some access via the European route, with large individual firms (except 'national champions' who gained access through the national route) having the least access. These hypotheses were largely supported by subsequent research (Bouwen 2004a). The best access was for national associations, closely followed by large firms that were national champions. Other large firms and European associations had very much less access.

The European Parliament

Despite the fact that the EP traditionally had less influence over decision making than either the Council or the Commission, it has always attracted considerable attention from interest groups. This is largely because of its long-standing advisory role, which has been viewed as an indirect route to influencing the other institutions. Moreover, MEPs are relatively accessible. In particular, those with a constituency interest in an issue will be the focus of attention. Its post-Lisbon status as co-legislator makes it a very important focus of lobbying.

The EP is seen as a 'natural ally' for groups lobbying on behalf of consumers, the environment, and a range of human rights including women's and children's rights. This is 'not because MEPs necessarily favour their demands, but because their interests match. MEPs are eager to take up those issues which attract a broad public interest and are grateful for any external support which mobilizes public attention, because this will increase their political weight in the decision-making process' (Kohler-Koch 1997: 55–6). In addition to representations to individual MEPs, they can also be targeted collectively through the numerous inter-groups that bring together MEPs with similar interests in a relatively formal arena.

As the logic of interest-group activity suggests, lobbying around EP plenary sessions and committee meetings increased with the enhancement of Parliament's powers in the various Treaty reforms from the Single European Act (SEA) to the Lisbon Treaty. For example, in 2010, the EU's draft Capital Requirements Directive 3 was going through the legislative process under the co-decision process. With a range of controversial issues including bankers' remuneration in the draft legislation, it was no surprise that the full firepower of the banking lobby was directed at the EP and members of its Economic and Monetary Affairs Committee (see Corporate Europe Observatory 2011's section on the financial lobby for an indication of the lobby groups in this sector: 37–90).

Like the Commission, the EP lacks the national administrative support that is available to the members of the Council. Bouwen (2002) argued that while the EP does rely on interest groups for expert knowledge to some extent, it initially has a much greater need for information on the concerns of the relevant actors in the sector across Europe, to alert it to impending legislation that might not meet the needs and interests of the European market as a whole. If it seeks to amend legislation in detail, it will also need expert knowledge. This is where lobbyists, perhaps assisted by lawyers, will suggest legislative amendments: perhaps by drafting them as part of their lobbying. On the other hand, individual MEPs need information on the concerns of their own national actors in the relevant sector to alert them to legislation that might be damaging to their own constituents.

On this basis, Bouwen (2002: 382) expected European associations to have the best access to the EP as an institution, because they could provide the initial and crucial information on the likely impact of impending legislation on the sector at the European level. National associations were expected to have a lower level of access, but might well be able to gain access via the national route, through the offices of MEPs. Large firms were expected to have the lowest level of access. These hypotheses were again supported by subsequent research: European associations had the best access to the EP, closely followed by national associations, with individual large firms a long way behind (Bouwen 2004b: 492).

Strategies and Tactics

The strategies and tactics of interest groups will vary depending on the targeted decision maker and/or the issue concerned. There is no magic formula for success in lobbying. There are, however, tried-and-tested practices that suggest that some approaches are better than others. Greenwood (1997: 8) offered some advice for lobbying Brussels (see Insight 17.3), much of which amounts to good common sense. Policy makers are often under great pressure, and even those who respond to interest-group approaches need to feel this is a good investment of their time. Those interests that are professional in their approach, that keep to the point and do not waste time, and that have realistic expectations of the policy process are likely to develop the best relationships with decision makers.

> **Insight 17.3 How to Lobby in Brussels**
>
> Have a clear strategy.
>
> Develop long-term relations with authorities. Establish a track record as a provider of useful, accurate, well-researched information.
>
> Find out who is drafting an item and make your representations early.
>
> Prepare well for meetings. Beware of using hired hands to present cases where their knowledge of your issue will inevitably be limited.
>
> Present with brevity and clarity.
>
> Be aware of all sides of the argument. Keep it low-key; do not over-lobby. Appreciate the limits of what can be achieved.
>
> Keep all viable channels of communication open.
>
> Know the system, and get to know the points of entry to the decision-making process.
>
> Remain vigilant.
>
> *Source:* Greenwood (1997: 8)

This advice also indicates clearly the importance of timing in the lobbying process. For many groups, making representations early is vital, particularly in relation to policy formation. Related to this is the need to maintain ongoing relationships with Brussels policy makers to ensure that there is a good flow of information so that issues can be identified quickly. Ongoing relations are also important in responding to issues, in that '[i]f you need to start forming a relationship when there is a problem it is probably too late' (Greenwood 1997: 8).

Moreover, the impact of lobbying is affected by the extent to which the views of an interest group 'chime with the emerging prevailing wisdoms of policy and with the quest of European policy makers (including those from national governments) for a form of legitimation for their proposed actions' (Wallace and Young 1997: 245–6). Even interests that are effective in every way advocated by Greenwood may well find that their efforts are without success if they advocate views that are out of line with the views of key decision makers.

As any card player knows, skill in playing the hand that you have been dealt can allow you to win even when your opponents have better cards. There are limits, though, to how far effective strategy and tactics can equalize the disparity of resources. As argued above, attempts by other interests to combine resources may reduce the effectiveness with which they can be deployed, because of tensions within the coalition about priorities. Also, big business has the financial resource to buy the expertise that it needs to take the maximum advantage of its already strong hand. Perhaps it is in order to gain some insight into how to play their hand more effectively that smaller players turn to Brussels-based consultancy firms, despite their apparently poor record in gaining access to the institutional actors.

There is one other strategic approach open to interests that fail to achieve insider status: they can, in effect, turn over the gaming table by politicizing the issue. Pluralist lobbying usually is most effective when it takes place out of the view of the public, and well away from the political debate. Similarly, policy communities are cosy relationships between organized interests and officials. Politicians are sometimes included in these relationships, but are usually peripheral to them. The policy community can get on with the business of making public policy without interference so long as the issues do not attract the notice of the politicians or the public. In either case, if the profile of the issue is raised above the political threshold, then the nature of the process changes. The strategy of excluded groups with interests in the field is therefore to seek access by politicizing issues. As issues become politicized, they disrupt the exclusive relationships between public agencies and insider interests (Greenwood 1997: 23).

The adoption of such disruptive techniques may be more common in the EU context than is sometimes supposed. Research by Jan Beyers (2004) rejected the idea that the technocratic nature of decision-making processes in the EU meant that interest groups would avoid public activism. Beyers (2004: 211) found that, although the institutional supply of access favoured specific interests, the EU contained important institutional opportunities for other ('diffuse') interests that aimed to expand the scope of political conflict or signal policy concerns by using 'public political strategies'. Finally, those interest groups that normally have insider status may 'go nuclear' on an issue as a matter of last resort. Farmers' interest groups have assumed the highest profile with this tactic. For instance, in May 2009, in a protest against milk quotas, farmers blocked streets in the European quarter of Brussels with their tractors during a meeting of the Council of Agriculture Ministers.

Regulating Lobbying

Concerns about the transparency of the lobbying process have raised questions as to whether access to policy makers should be regulated. This issue was already debated in the 1990s (Bache and George 2006: 345–6). More recently, in 2005, Commissioner Siim Kallas launched the European Transparency Initiative as a way of trying to raise trust in the lobbying process (Eising and Lehringer 2010: 195–6). This approach was consistent with the Commission's 2001 White Paper on Governance. It culminated in the Commission establishing a register for lobbyists. The EP, by contrast, is sceptical of having 'accredited organizations' on the grounds that this could be bureaucratic (Greenwood 2007: 4). The breakthrough was achieved in 2011 with the Transparency Register shared between the Commission and the EP, and the source of data already discussed. The system continues to have its critics because it is not mandatory. Moreover, a range of other non-transparent practices remain. Examples include the move of Commissioners or Commission officials to work for lobby groups and occasional media attention to what is perceived as improper behaviour. One example of the latter was the 'cash for laws' scandal, when *Sunday Times* journalists exposed that MEPs were willing to submit amendments to EU legislation in return for cash (*European Voice*, 24 March 2011). Another instance was the allegation that the Maltese Commissioner for Health and Consumer Protection, John Dalli, had been involved in improper lobbying relations by the tobacco industry: a charge that he disputed at the time that he resigned in January 2013, (*European Voice*, 10 January 2013). An organization known as ALTER-EU (**http://alter-eu.org**)

campaigns for lobbying transparency and seeks to limit the predominance of business interests.

CONCLUSION

This chapter raises issues connected with two of the themes identified in the opening section of the book. The first is the theme of supranational versus intergovernmental interpretations of the nature of the EU. The second is the theme of how best to ensure the EU's legitimacy and combat the democratic deficit.

Interest-group activity may provide a litmus test for the degree to which the **supranational institutions** of the EU exercise independent influence over the policy process. If interest groups transfer their lobbying activities away from national governments to Brussels, this may be taken as an indication that the EU is a supranational organization. However, such a conclusion has to be modified in the light of arguments and evidence presented in this chapter. First, the increased level of interest-group activity in Brussels has not replaced activity at the national level, but has generally supplemented it: lobbying tends to follow a multi-level approach. Second, although groups must have some reason to expend financial resources on establishing a presence in Brussels, this does not mean that the reasons are well founded: they may simply be afraid of missing out on something. There is a point at which the sight of other groups swarming to Brussels will lead groups to follow on the assumption that there must be something worth pursuing, even if there is not.

Once located in Brussels, groups will not all be equally effective in influencing the supranational institutions (the EP and the Commission; the intergovernmental Council of Ministers being less amenable to lobbying). Most studies suggest that business interests are more influential than other interests, such as organized labour, consumers, or environmental groups. Within the category of business interests, large firms are more influential than small firms. Whether this relative influence matters, of course, depends on the answer to the question of how much independent influence the supranational institutions have over policy outcomes. If they do have some influence, and if it is true that big-business interests have the most influence over the supranational institutions, then this could provide one explanation for the observation that the policies that emanate from Brussels tend to be pro-business and in line with an Anglo-Saxon model of capitalism. For their parts, and in different ways, the Commission and the EP seek to ensure that a wide range of interests are heard in the policy process.

On the other hand, the domination of the process by big-business interests may not be as clear as several writers suggest. Beyers (2004) showed that interests that feel themselves excluded can make their voice heard by politicizing the process, while the research undertaken by Bowen (2002, 2004a, 2004b) indicated that business interests do not have the privileged access to the institutions that is often asserted. It should also be noted, though, that formal access is not the same as effective influence: from a critical political economy perspective (see Chapter 4, Critical Political Economy), it could be argued that big business can exercise a structural power over decisions by influencing what Wallace and Young (1997: 245–6) called the 'prevailing wisdoms of policy'.

The second theme highlighted by the chapter is that engagement with interest groups is an important way for the EU institutions to obtain legitimacy at the input stage of policy making. It is particularly clear that the Commission is dependent on the expertise of interest groups, thereby legitimating its work. There have been attempts to advance this type of interaction as a new form of governance, characterized by the Commission's engagement with civil society (see Smismans 2007 for a justification based on 'reflexive deliberative polyarchy'). However, it is questionable whether this interaction offers a solution to the EU's democratic deficit. Moreover, if lobbying lacks transparency, its legitimacy is called into question. Attempts to regulate lobbyists' access to the institutions have been the response to this concern.

KEY POINTS

The Growth of Interest-Group Activity at the EU Level

- Interest-group activity in Brussels has increased greatly since the mid-1980s.
- Factors in this growth are: the growing policy competence of the EU; the perception of a shifting balance of institutional power in Brussels, most notably in favour of the EP; the receptiveness of EU officials to interest-group representations; and the 'snowballing' effect of groups following the lead of others so as not to risk being disadvantaged.

Types of Interest Group

- There are several different types of interest organization active in Brussels.
- Business interests were the first to locate in Brussels, and still account for the largest number of groups.
- Interest groups representing workers, consumers, environmental interests, and other parts of civil society have become increasingly active.

Forms of Interest Representation

- Five forms of interest representation coexist in the EU: 'corporatist'; 'neo-corporatist'; pluralist; informally institutionalized policy networks; and legal representation.
- Of these five, pluralism and informal institutionalization predominate.

Resources

- The most effective interest groups in a pluralist system are generally those that control key resources such as information and expertise, economic muscle, and status.
- Small organizations can pool resources, but they may then find problems in agreeing on priorities and tactics.
- The three types of information sought by the institutions are expert knowledge, information on the needs and concerns of actors in the relevant sector across Europe, and information on the needs and concerns of national actors in the sector.

Organized Interests and the Institutional Actors

- For some EU actors, interest groups are an important source of information and legitimation and, as such, are enthusiastically consulted.
- The Commission is in need of the expert knowledge that big-business interests can often provide most effectively, but it has also sought to cultivate links with European-level associations and to promote less-represented social interests.
- The Council is less reliant on organized interests than other institutions and, as such, is less open to approaches. Much lobbying of the Council is indirect, through individual national governments.
- The EP is a key target for organized interests, particularly following the growth of its powers since the mid-1990s. MEPs are thought to be particularly sympathetic to representations on issues of broad public interest.

Strategies and Tactics

- Effective strategies and tactics can increase the influence even of interest groups with limited resources at their disposal.

- It is possible to identify good practice in lobbying. Developing good ongoing relationships with policy makers and careful timing of interventions are important.

- To be influential, groups generally need to be in tune with the prevailing thinking of policy makers.

- Groups that find it difficult to gain access to the institutions often seek to politicize issues.

Regulating Lobbying

- Both the Commission and the EP have sought to regulate lobbyists' access.

FURTHER READING

For a thorough and comprehensive review of organized interests in the EU, see **J. Greenwood**, *Interest Representation in the European Union*, 3rd edn (Basingstoke: Palgrave Macmillan, 2011). In addition to considering interest group strategies, resources, and channels of influence, this book includes separate chapters on some of the major interests, including business, labour, and territorial interests. For an accessible (though non-academic) guide to 'lobby planet Brussels', see Corporate Europe Observatory (2011).

Two valuable collections of essays on interest groups are **D. Coen and J. Richardson (eds)**, *Lobbying the European Union: Institutions, Actors, and Issues* (Oxford: Oxford University Press, 2009), and **J. Beyers, R. Eising, and W. Maloney (eds)**, *Interest Group Politics in Europe: Lessons from EU Studies and Comparative Politics* (Abingdon: Routledge, 2009). The latter volume comprises articles published in a special issue of *West European Politics,* 31 (2008): 1103–302. A useful analysis of how some interests are privileged over others in their relations with the EU is offered in **R. Balme and D. Chabanet**, *European Governance and Democracy: Power and Protest in the European Union* (New York: Rowman and Littlefield, 2008). For a study that has a more normative position, suggesting that deliberative democracy in the EU can compensate for the democratic deficit, see **J. Steffek, C. Kissling, and P. Nanz (eds)**, *Civil Society Participation in European and Global Governance: A Cure for the Democratic Deficit?* (Basingstoke: Palgrave Macmillan, 2008). Also concerned with civil society is the study by **B. Kohler-Koch and C. Quittkat**, *De-Mystification of Participatory Democracy: EU-Governance and Civil Society* (Oxford: Oxford University Press, 2013).

 online resource centre **Visit the Online Resource Centre that accompanies this book for links to more information on organized interests: http://oxfordtextbooks.co.uk/orc/bache4e/**

Part Four
Policies

So many policy sectors now have a European Union (EU) dimension that it is difficult to provide comprehensive coverage, especially within the confines of a general textbook in which the policies are just one part of the overall book. Essentially, the choice that we had to make was between coverage in breadth or in depth. We settled for depth.

With one exception, each of the ten chapters in Part Four of the book provides a detailed account and analysis of the development of one of the major areas of EU policy. They are 'major' both in the sense that these policy sectors have been central to the development of the EU, and that they have attracted a good deal of scholarly attention and generated academic debate. The exception is Chapter 18, which outlines the main patterns of policy making, and gives an overview of those policies that do not receive separate chapters to themselves.

Agriculture and *cohesion policy* between them account for over three-quarters of EU spending. In addition, agriculture was the first common policy of the EC and therefore has a central place in the history of what is now the EU. Early theories of European integration were built around the agricultural policy on the assumption that it would form the model for future common policies. When it did not, the explanations of why the predicted developments had not happened helped to advance theory further. Cohesion policies (such as regional development) have taken an increasing share of the budget of the EU, now around one-third of all spending. This policy sector has been at the forefront of experiments with innovative programmes and modes of governance. It was here that the partnership principle was first developed for EU policies, and here that there has been the clearest evidence of multi-level governance in operation. Inevitably, therefore, the study of the policy sector has become an important arena of theoretical endeavour.

Creating a common market has been a central objective of the process of European integration since the signing of the Treaty of Rome (EEC) in 1957. Moreover, the project to complete the *single market* in the mid-1980s revived the faltering process of European integration, and attempts to understand the success of the single market programme, and the spillover from it to other common policies, generated a parallel revival of theoretical endeavour.

The most significant spillover was from the single market to the creation of a single currency. *Economic and monetary union* has been around as an objective since The Hague Summit in 1969 (see Chapter 7, The Hague Summit). It had proved both controversial and elusive, so there was inevitably a degree of scepticism when attempts were made to use the momentum from the single market programme to move to a single currency. This time, though, the effort succeeded, albeit without the participation of all member states. As with the single market, the explanation for monetary union generated heated academic debates. At the same time, many of the economic and political issues that the sceptics had believed would prevent the creation of the single currency were not resolved once it was created. This became apparent to even the most optimistic of observers with the eurozone crisis which began in the late 2000s (see Chapter 11). Unsurprisingly, critics of the design of economic and monetary union became increasingly vocal in this context.

In the twenty-first century, the physical safety and security of its citizens has become of greater concern to the EU in line with a greater emphasis on these aspects of policy in the domestic politics of the member states, and in the light of the greater uncertainty of an international context marked by threats from pollution and climate change and from organized crime. Protecting citizens from these threats is increasingly difficult for individual national governments acting alone. Pooling sovereignty at the level of the EU offers the possibility of more effective action. As a result, both *environmental policy* and the creation of an *area of freedom, security, and justice* have become more important EU policy areas in the past decade or so.

While all EU policies have an external dimension, the two policy sectors mentioned in the previous paragraph operate very close to the interface between the internal and external aspects of policy. External relations proper have two aspects: economic and political. Although not constituting the totality of the EU's external economic relations, *trade and development aid* together form the most important part of that aspect of external relations, and have also been the subject of academic analysis from a wide variety of different theoretical perspectives. Each involves a political aspect as well as an economic, but external political relations in the traditional sense of foreign and (military) security policy come under the general heading of the *Common Foreign and Security Policy* of the EU.

Finally, the process of *enlargement* is one whereby external relations are transformed into internal relations. In addition, this process has profound implications for the operation and nature of the EU as a whole, while the promise of accession is an important incentive allowing the EU to bring about changes in the politics and governance of neighbouring states.

Chapter 18

Policies and Policy Making in the European Union

Chapter Overview

Starting in 1958, with policies on internal tariffs, agriculture, and overseas development, the EC/EU has gradually acquired competence in more and more areas of policy. A complex system of policy making has emerged to deal with these responsibilities. This chapter reviews the main patterns of policy making, and looks at those policies that have not been given separate chapters to themselves in the rest of this section of the book.

In July 1988, in a speech to the European Parliament (EP), Jacques Delors predicted that, 'In ten years, 80 per cent of economic legislation—and perhaps tax and social legislation—will be directed from the Community' (European Parliament 1988: 140). The prediction infuriated the British Prime Minister of the day, Margaret Thatcher, yet twenty years later the range of EU activity had increased to such an extent that the Europa website listed an EU competence in some thirty-one policy areas (see Table 18.1). The Lisbon Treaty provided additional competence in the areas of space, tourism, sport, civil protection, and administrative co-operation; it re-cast others in areas such as energy and environment; it also spelt out the balance of different competence between the Union and the member states (see Box 18.1).

These policy areas vary in significance, which means that they have received very different levels of attention in academic studies. Several of the most significant policy areas, both from a practical and from an academic viewpoint, are considered in separate chapters in this section of the book. Others are considered in more cursory form in this chapter. They in turn are divided into policy areas that are relatively minor or derivative and others that could have justified separate chapters had space been unlimited.

Before turning to the policies, though, the chapter looks at how the European policy agenda is formed, and at the main patterns of policy making that have emerged to handle that agenda. Much of this material recaps what has already been said in the section on the institutions, so it will be briefly covered here with cross-references to the relevant sections of Part III where appropriate.

The European Policy Agenda

What is meant by 'the policy agenda'? The domestic policy agenda for governments comprises issues that pose problems demanding solutions. Some of these issues arise from domestic political pressures, either from interest groups or from public opinion,

Table 18.1 Policy Competence of the European Union

Agriculture	Employment and Social Affairs	Humanitarian Aid
Audiovisual and Media	Energy	Human Rights
Budget	Enlargement	Information Society
Competition	Enterprise	Internal Market
Consumers	Environment	Justice and Home Affairs
Culture	External Relations	Public Health
Customs	External Trade	Regional Policy
Development	Fight against Fraud	Research and Innovation
Economic and Monetary	Fisheries & Maritime Affairs	Taxation
Affairs	Food Safety	Transport
Education, Training, Youth	Foreign & Security Policy	

Source: http://ec.europa.eu © European Union, 1995–2014.

Box 18.1 The EU member state balance of policy competence

Areas of exclusive competence

customs union;

competition rules for the internal market;

monetary policy for those states in the eurozone;

conservation of marine biological resources under the common fisheries policy;

common commercial policy.

Where an international agreement is necessary to enable the Union to exercise its internal competence.

Areas of shared competence

internal market;

aspects of social policy;

economic, social, and territorial cohesion;

agriculture and fisheries (except marine conservation);

environment;

consumer protection;

transport;

trans-European networks;

energy;

area of freedom, security, and justice;

aspects of public health safety;

technological development and space;

development and humanitarian aid.

Areas of policy co-ordination

member states' economic policies;

member states' employment policies;

member states' social policies.

Areas of supporting, co-ordinating, or supplementary action

protection and improvement of human health;

industry;

culture;

tourism;

education, vocational training, youth and sport;

civil protection;

administrative co-operation.

The Common Foreign and Security Policy

The Union shall have competence ... to define and implement a common foreign and security policy, including the progressive framing of a common defence policy.

Summarized from Articles 2A and 2B of the Treaty establishing the European Community as revised by the Lisbon Treaty (*Official Journal of the European Union C* 306, 17 December 2007: 46–8)

or both. Others arise from the international environment, such as security concerns or the effects of the globalization of production on economic interests. These two sources of inputs can interact. International events can raise an issue up the domestic political agenda, which is what happened with environmental policy in the 1970s (see Chapter 23). Disasters such as oil tankers polluting seas and shores, and accidents at nuclear power stations elsewhere in the world, increased public awareness in Europe of the potential environmental consequences of industrialization in the 1970s, and made it easier for domestic environmental pressure groups to recruit new members and to draw attention to long-term environmental damage, such as the effects of acid rain on the Scandinavian and German forests.

In some instances the policy agenda can be quite diffuse and wide-ranging rather than confined to a single policy. An important illustration of this is the so-called Lisbon Strategy, launched in 2000, and seeking to increase the EU's global competitiveness over a ten-year period. It gave momentum to major policy areas, such as cohesion policy and the single market, while also adding a new focus to research and innovation policy, labour-market reform, anti-poverty policy, and a host of less prominent EU policies. In 2010 the Lisbon Strategy was re-cast as 'Europe 2020', a similar agenda seeking to give focus to developments in a range of different policy areas.

How do such issues find their way onto the EU agenda, rather than remaining domestic issues? Sometimes it is because there is an obvious functional logic to trying to solve the problem collectively. Even the British government, often hostile to the adoption of European solutions, recognized in the 1980s that the economic problems of Europe could only be effectively tackled by joint action to create a genuine single European market (see Chapter 20). Sometimes it is because the problem itself arises from *spillover* from other EU policies (see Chapter 1, International Relations Theories of European Integration), and therefore demands a European solution. The single European market led to a spate of cross-border mergers, some of which threatened to create monopolistic enterprises that would prevent the achievement of greater competition, which was the purpose of the single market initiative. This put pressure on national governments to agree to regulation of mergers at European level (see this chapter, Major Policy Areas). Sometimes the pressure on governments from domestic interest groups is specifically for the transfer of regulation to the European level, as it was for the deregulation of national telecommunications (see Chapter 20, Insight 20.2). Sometimes governments are receptive to a European approach to problems because it allows them to escape political unpopularity for the measures that are necessary. There was a strong element of this in the commitment of most EU member states to the creation of a single currency (see Chapter 21).

Within this complex picture there are plenty of opportunities for an actor with a commitment to increased European integration to exploit the various pressures on governments. The usual suspect here is the European Commission, an institutional actor that owes its existence and importance to the process of European integration and therefore has every incentive to try to maximize the extent to which governments are prepared to transfer policies to the European level (see Chapter 13, The Commission in the Policy-Making Process). However, the actor that is responsible for definitively putting items on the EU policy agenda is the European Council. Indeed, all of the examples cited above arose from declarations by the European Council. While the Commission may exploit the circumstances to influence agenda setting, it does not set the agenda in terms of strategy and large-scale initiatives. Also, much of the shift of activity to the EU level is voluntary on the part of national governments, in search of collective solutions to problems that are increasingly difficult to resolve to the satisfaction of organized interests and public opinion domestically.

The EU Policy Process

Once an issue is accepted as a legitimate item on the policy agenda of the EU, a complex political and bureaucratic process is set in motion, which involves a plethora of actors. This used almost always to be based around the formal institutional procedures that are described in Chapter 12 (Decision-Making Procedures), and it often still is, although other options have been used more frequently in recent years.

Although the details of the involvement of different institutional actors vary according to the procedure that is relevant to a particular policy area, all the formal procedures begin with the Commission formulating a proposal for legislation. In doing this, the Commission normally consults widely. It will usually discuss the range of options with the most obviously relevant interest groups at an early stage. There is no point in coming up with proposals that stand no chance of being accepted by governments due to strong lobbying against them by interest groups at national level.

The Commission will also consult widely with technical experts in the field, either on an ad hoc basis or through its own complex of committees of experts. Just as there is no point in formulating proposals that interest groups will work hard to block, there is no benefit in pushing through legislation that will prove to be impossible to implement, a possibility that can be avoided by consulting experts. Finally, the Commission will sound out national government officials to discover the parameters within which it might prove possible to get an agreement in the Council of Ministers.

Of course, the Commission will receive conflicting opinions and advice when formulating its proposals, and will have to make judgments of its own between these viewpoints. There is sometimes an element here of the Commission being forced to go for the lowest common denominator in order to ensure that it can get some legislation through. This is most often likely to be the case where the policy area is a new one for the EU, when the premium for the Commission is to make a start on building an *acquis communautaire* that can form the basis for further advance at a later date. Often, though, the Commission will take risks in order to push a certain position. This can backfire, but in many cases the Commission has already ensured that it has allies, either among powerful interest groups or within the bureaucracies of national governments, who will back its proposals against opposition from elsewhere.

In preparing its proposals, the Commission will also often consult those MEPs who have a particular interest in a policy area, especially those who are members of the relevant specialist committee of the EP. It is sometimes assumed that the EP is inevitably an ally of the Commission, because it too is considered to be an institution with a vested interest in further European integration (Garrett and Tsebelis 1996; Tsebelis and Garrett 1996). However, the relationship between the EP and the Commission is much more complicated than that. MEPs have to respond to democratic pressure from their constituents, they face party-political pressures, and they are subject to lobbying from a wide variety of interest groups. Also, the EP has a vested interest in standing up to the Commission to prove its independence and importance.

Adding to the difficulties facing the Commission, other procedures have appeared for governments to pursue European solutions to their policy problems without delegating as much responsibility to the Commission. Less formal and more intergovernmental procedures were introduced in the form of what is known as the 'open method of co-ordination' (OMC) (see Chapter 10, The Lisbon Strategy). Also, in the Treaty on European Union (TEU) two new 'pillars' were created alongside the EC pillar (see Chapter 12). These covered Justice and Home Affairs (JHA; see Chapter 24), and the Common Foreign and Security Policy (see Chapter 26). In neither of these pillars did the formal rules of the EC apply. They were explicitly 'intergovernmental' pillars, and although the Commission had a role to play, it did not have the sole right of initiative, as it did in the EC pillar. The Lisbon Treaty abolished this three-pillar structure, bringing what had been JHA—and was now known as the Area of Freedom, Security, and Justice—largely under the ordinary legislative procedure (OLP) (see Chapter 12, Decision-Making procedures), although the CFSP remained subject to a different balance of institutional power.

Minor Policy Areas

To classify any areas of EU competence as 'minor' is likely to be controversial. Certainly they are not minor for the actors directly affected; and some of the areas so classified here actually have quite a high profile with the general public. However, the extension of EU competence to these policy areas did not have major implications for the development of European integration, and consequently they did not attract a great deal of academic attention or analysis.

These minor policy areas can be roughly divided into four groups: those that have some independent functional justification of their own; those that arise largely as a result of functional spillover from the single market programme; those that are really about building a sense of European identity among the citizens; and those that arise from the commitment made at the Lisbon European Council in 2000 to make the EU into 'the most competitive knowledge-based economy in the world' by 2010. However, several of these policy areas show aspects of more than one of these types.

Those policies that arise from independent functional logics include: fisheries, fraud, and some aspects of both public health and food safety. Those that arise largely as a result of spillover from the single European market include: consumers, taxation, and some aspects of both food safety and the information society. Those that arise from efforts to build a sense of European identity include: culture and education. Those that arise directly from the Lisbon commitment include: enterprise and many aspects of policy on the information society.

The Common Fisheries Policy (CFP)

The CFP arose from the need to regulate the exploitation of the EU's fish stocks. It originally also had the objective of encouraging the modernization of the less efficient national fishing fleets; but as depletion of fish stocks reached critical levels, the policy was reformulated in a comprehensive review in 2003, after which grants were available only to improve the safety and comfort of boats, not to provide them with the most modern equipment for taking as many fish out of the sea as possible.

Although the allocation of strict quotas to national fleets is invariably unpopular with the fishing industry, and every new allocation produces new predictions of the demise of fishing in one region or another, there is a clear functional logic to regulating fishing in EU waters. The alternative is either a new 'tragedy of the commons', where every national fleet insists on taking as much as it can from the common pool until fish stocks collapse to unsustainable levels, or the emergence of national protectionism for coastal waters. The latter option is not feasible because of the overlap of coastal waters; and even if the boundaries could be sorted out, fish would be unlikely to recognize them, so that one state's efforts to conserve stocks could be easily undermined by a neighbouring state's persistence in over-fishing.

Despite the obvious logic of setting quotas, the 2003 reform adopted a crude system of 'total allowable catches', which produced the unintended result of fishermen throwing large quantities of dead fish back into the sea because the species were not commercially valuable, and the fishermen understandably wanted to reserve their limited catch-quota for species that they could sell profitably. This perverse unintended consequence of the policy led to the serious depletion of several species and a public outcry in some member states, including Britain.

In 2013 further reform was agreed—for the period from 2014 to 2020—which would stop penalizing fishermen for landing less-commercial species, and would require them to land 95 per cent of whatever they caught, with scientific monitoring of catches to collect information on the quantities of each species. The allocation of quotas was decentralized to the national level, and national governments were allowed to take measures to support small-scale and artisanal fishing fleets. Conservation measures, which had been made an exclusive competence of the EU in the Lisbon Treaty, were to be agreed between the governments of states that bordered a maritime basin, and only if agreement could not be reached would it be imposed by the EU, and even then not by the Commission acting unilaterally, but through the OLP.

Fraud

Fraud against the EU started almost as soon as the first common policies emerged. The first positive common policy, agriculture, was the victim of some very elaborate schemes to obtain payments outside of the rules. Some farmers mis-stated the amount of land that they had under cultivation, and claimed subsidies for non-existent herds. Middlemen returned fraudulent figures for the quantities of produce that they held in storage. Export subsidies were claimed for grain that had never left the EU.

When the structural funds were expanded following the Mediterranean enlargement in the 1980s (see Chapter 22, History), many figures for the costs of projects were artificially inflated, and some money simply disappeared. The existence of different rates of indirect taxes on goods such as cigarettes and alcohol within a frontier-free EU has led to big increases in the smuggling of such goods from countries with low tax rates for sale in countries with higher rates.

So, once the EU existed, fraud against it existed; and this clearly needed to be investigated centrally given that the perpetrators of the fraud often operated in several different states. Today, there is a European Anti-Fraud Office (OLAF) that operates within the Commission, but with a special status to ensure its independence.

Public Health and Food Safety

Public health policy has several aspects, one of which is the control of communicable diseases. In a world where people travel extensively, diseases quickly cross national boundaries. This is especially true in an area without frontiers, such as the EU. Although the outbreak of severe acute respiratory syndrome (SARS) in 2003 did not affect Europe as badly as it did other parts of the world, it did show up the inadequacy of the EU's existing system of exchange of information between national public health authorities. As a direct result it was agreed to set up a European Centre for Disease Prevention and Control, based in Sweden, which would take the leading role in co-ordinating efforts to combat the spread of disease and responding to threats of bio-terrorism.

This aspect of public health policy is a function that is more efficiently performed at a European level than at the national level, and is therefore directly justified by func-tional logic, as are harmonized regulations on the use, storage, and distribution of blood products, and on ensuring access to health care for citizens of one member state while they are resident in another member state. Much the same arguments about the appropriate functional scale of policy making apply to food safety, especially where trade in food products crosses national boundaries, as it does in the single European market.

The creation of a single European market (see Chapter 20) gave the biggest boost to European integration since the creation of the EEC, not only because of what it meant for producers and consumers directly, but also because of the spillover effects. These included strengthening the independent functional logic of regulating food safety at a European level, which already existed but was enhanced by the need to ensure that consumers were not wary of buying food from other member states because they were worried about whether it was safe to eat. Similarly, the need to remove the real or imagined concerns of consumers about the safety of manufactured products, and about their ability to claim their rights in the event of the failure of a product bought from another member state, created a spillover to the need for an EU-wide policy on consumer protection and consumer rights.

The Information Society

For producers, the need to ensure a level playing-field of opportunity led to moves to open up cross-national competition in telecommunications (see Chapter 20, Insight 20.2), which was the beginning of an EU policy on the information society. Once national regulation of telecommunications had been swept away, it became nec-essary to re-regulate the industry at the European level. Mostly, though, this policy arose in pursuit of the Lisbon Strategy to transform the EU into 'the most competitive knowledge-based economy in the world by 2010'. This led directly to the '*e*Europe' programme, which set ambitious targets such as ensuring that all businesses, schools, and universities of EU members had broadband access to the Internet by 2005, with further targets for enabling new members to catch up. Facilitating broadband access for remote and rural areas also became a major priority of the Regional and Social Funds.

Building a European Identity

A few of the minor policy areas date back to an earlier commitment to try to build a stronger sense of European identity among the members of the EC/EU. Although the cultural dimension to European integration was only formally recognized in the TEU in 1992, attempts to build a stronger European cultural profile date back at least to 1985 when the practice began of naming one or more cities annually as the 'European capital of culture'. The funding of the capital of culture and of other initiatives to develop artistic and literary creation, to develop heritage sites, and to stimulate inter-cultural dialogue come under a budget head known as 'Culture 2000'.

The Executive Agency for Education, Training, and Youth oversees the administration of one of the main programmes that had its origins as part of the programme for building a European identity, but has now outgrown those origins to become an important part of education policy throughout the EU. The Lifelong Learning Programme (LLP) is the successor to programmes such as Socrates, an umbrella programme that supported exchanges of university students and staff, the development of teaching materials, and the building of trans-European educational networks. The main elements of the LLP are:

- Gruntvig for adult learners and their teachers;
- Comenius for schools;
- Erasmus for higher education;
- Leonardo da Vinci for vocational training.

While formal EU competence over education policies generally has been strictly limited by national governments, the Commission has been an active participant in pan-European initiatives on higher education that fall under the heading of the 'Bologna process' (see Corbett 2005; Bache 2006). Initiated by the Bologna Declaration, which was signed by Ministers of Education from twenty-nine European states in 1999, the process aims to create a European higher education area by making degree standards more comparable throughout Europe. It has achieved a considerable modification of national degree programmes and quality standards, and has done so through the use of the OMC, despite scepticism in some quarters of the capacity of the OMC to bring about such fundamental changes.

Major Policy Areas

As well as these minor policy areas, there are several major policy areas for which it is not possible to include full chapters in this book. These are policies that have considerable practical significance in their own right, and that have attracted a certain amount of academic attention as well. They are: competition, employment and social policy, energy, research, and transport. Like the minor policy areas, most of these can be justified either through independent functional arguments, as spillover from the single European market, or as part of efforts to build a sense of European identity. The academic analyses also allow us to say more about the political logic behind these policies.

Competition

Competition policy has been called the 'first common policy' of the EC/EU (McGowan and Wilks 1995). Yet, though some elements of competition policy did exist prior to the adoption of the single market programme, it was considerably enhanced as a direct spillover from the single market. As McGowan and Cini (1999: 177) pointed out, competition policy is a necessary adjunct to the single European market because, if large firms reacted to the opening of national markets by adopting anti-competitive practices, such as collusion through cartels, or mergers to create effective European monopolies, the aim of the single market—to increase efficiency and benefit consumers by enhancing competition—would be frustrated. To counter such anti-competitive practices, EU competition policy has four main aspects: anti-trust and cartels, merger control, state aids, and liberalization.

Antitrust activity is aimed at preventing cartels. The Commission investigates reports of collusion between producers, for example to fix prices, and penalizes through fines those companies found guilty of acting in restraint of competition. This is necessary to prevent large producers from colluding to stop new producers from breaking into the market, or to maintain profits at artificially high levels by not passing on cost-savings to consumers.

Merger control is a centralized system for approving mergers that have Europe-wide implications. The Treaty of Rome contained no provisions for merger control. Various attempts by the Commission to persuade the member states to redress this omission failed, until the single market programme led to a big increase in the number of cross-border mergers (McGowan and Cini 1999: 178–9). Concern about the possible emergence of monopolistic market conditions put the issue firmly on the agenda.

It was pushed to the top of the agenda by the ruling of the European Court of Justice (ECJ) in the Philip Morris case (1987) that the power to prevent market domination through mergers could be inferred from other Articles of the Treaty. This introduced a major element of uncertainty into the calculations of industry about how extensive the inferred powers of the Commission might be, and this uncertainty led in turn to demands from big companies for the member states to adopt clear and explicit legislation defining those limits. The Council of Ministers responded by indicating to the Commission in November 1987 that, despite having rejected four previous proposals, it would now welcome a draft merger regulation. The proposal led to protracted debates and negotiations, but the regulation was eventually adopted in December 1989 and became effective in September 1990 (McGowan and Cini 1999: 180). Under the regulation originally adopted, a proposed merger had to be cleared by the Commission if the merged company would have a turnover within the EU in excess of 250 million euros, and a world-wide turnover of more than 5 billion euros, unless more than 2/3 of the turnover would be within one country, in which case the merger is subject to national scrutiny.

The Commission has considerable autonomy in merger control. Proposed mergers are considered by a merger task force within the Directorate-General for Competition. Merger control is very political because it raises issues such as whether large European companies should be allowed to emerge to act as 'European champions' in global competition with companies from the United States and Japan. This is the position particularly of French governments, and contrasts with the position of the British, Dutch, and other governments that the most important issue is the preservation of competition in the European market. Under the guidance of a series of Commissioners who have shown a strong commitment to the free-market interpretation (Leon Brittan, Karel van Miert, Mario Monti, Neelie Kroes), the Directorate-General has moved in that direction, but all rulings have to be approved by the full College of

Commissioners, and here the outcome is not always certain as political considerations can intervene.

Politics is even more at the forefront of policy on state aids, which involves the Commission investigating instances where the government of a member state grants any of its own companies subsidies, loans, tax breaks, loan guarantees, or preferential purchase deals on goods and services, to ensure that this is not giving those companies an unfair competitive advantage. As Michael P. Smith (1998: 58) pointed out, the difference between merger control and state aids is that in the latter the Commission is confronting governments directly. Autonomous powers were granted to the Commission at an early stage in the history of the EEC, because there was a widespread wish among governments to remove distortions to competition in the common market, and it was obvious that an impartial arbitrator was needed. The powers granted, though, proved to give the Commission more autonomy than envisaged.

> Were Member States given the choice today, they would probably not delegate the same powers to the Commission as they did 40 years ago.

(Smith 1998: 76)

However, rolling back those powers would require a revision of the Treaty, and could jeopardize the success of the single market.

Pursuing competition cases has always been a time-consuming process, and the Directorate-General for Competition has long felt under-resourced and under pressure. With the prospect of further enlargement of the EU, the DG moved to involve national competition authorities more in the enforcement of EU competition law. This move was formally implemented in 2003 through a Council Regulation known as 'the Modernization Regulation' (1/2003). Since then the Commission has become more of a co-ordinator within a formally-constituted European Competition Network of national competition authorities, leaving its own expert staff to concentrate on particularly complex cases, especially those that have extensive cross-national implications and those that are most politically sensitive.

Employment and Social Policy

From a focus on workers' rights in the early years of the EEC, employment and social policy has come to emphasize the liberalization of labour markets in the context of the Lisbon Strategy to improve the global competitiveness of the EU.

At first, social policy was about the protection of workers' rights. The Treaty of Rome, generally a laissez-faire document, contained mention of the need to achieve social cohesion, to improve health and safety at work, to facilitate the free movement of labour, to promote equality between men and women in the workplace, to harmonize social security provision, and to promote a social dialogue between management and workers. The political reason for this focus was to create a level playing-field of competition by imposing on all producers the same levels of protection for employees as applied in the most regulated markets. An example of this is gender equality, which was given its own Article of the Treaty of Rome (originally Article 119, now Article 157 TFEU) because France had extensive domestic legislation on equal pay between men and women before the EEC was set up, and wanted to ensure that the competitiveness of French companies was not damaged by this in comparison with other member states.

After the common market had been established, some of the first pieces of social legislation to be passed concerned the equal rights of women and men in work-related matters. The Equal Pay Directive of 1975 imposed a legal requirement of equal pay for equal work; the Equal Treatment Directive of 1976 made discrimination illegal in access to employment and training and in respect to rights concerning dismissal; and the Social Security Directive of 1978 required equal treatment in access to state benefits. All of these were rights that were already embodied in French domestic legislation, and the other member states came under intense pressure from trade unions and women's groups to adopt them at European level. That pressure was increased by the ECJ with its rulings in equality cases such as Defrenne (1978), in which it stated that although Article 119 (EEC) dealt explicitly with equal pay between men and women, the Article clearly established the principle of elimination of discrimination between men and women in the workplace as a fundamental principle of Community law.

Other than in legislation on gender equality, social policy had made little progress by the mid-1980s. Jacques Delors tried to revive it by arguing that the single market needed a social dimension if it were to be acceptable to those who would initially lose out. Yet, the member states were prepared to make only health and safety in the workplace subject to qualified majority voting (QMV) in the Single European Act (SEA). Not only were there financial limits to what the richer member states would pay as compensation for the single market programme, governments generally remain sensitive to the transfer of policy competence in this domain. In addition, the variety of national types of welfare provision among the member states has made harmonization of policy impossibly complicated (Majone 1993: 160–1).

In one area, though, Delors did lay the foundations for what at one stage began to look like a promising approach to extending the social dimension. Soon after becoming President of the Commission he instituted a 'social dialogue' with representatives of employers and employees at the European level, mainly involving the Union of Industries in the European Community (UNICE) and the European Trade Union Confederation (ETUC). Fundamental disagreements between the two sides meant that little progress was made in the early rounds of talks, but Delors managed to get the dialogue incorporated into the Social Protocol of the TEU, and it became part of the Social Chapter of the Treaty after the British Labour government signed up to the Protocol at Amsterdam in 1997.

Under the terms of this 'social agreement', the Commission is obliged to consult the 'social partners' on proposed legislation under the Social Chapter twice, first on the principle and then on the content of the draft legislation. At either stage, the social partners may inform the Commission that they wish to initiate discussions to reach a collective agreement. This effectively stops the formal procedure for at least nine months. If a collective agreement is reached in that time, the partners can ask the Commission to present it to the Council of Ministers for formal approval, which is normally expected to be given, so that their agreement then becomes law.

This institutionalization of the social dialogue appeared for a time to offer what Wendon (1998: 343) called 'alternative venues' for the Commission to pursue integrative measures. Strøby Jensen (2000: 86), using neofunctionalist concepts, talked about 'institutional-legalistic' spillover, a similar idea whereby once the institutional basis for the social dialogue was established, it provided a forum for Commission activism. In practice, though, the legislative achievements of the social agreement were very limited.

The first item that was taken under the new procedure, on European Works Councils, could not be agreed, although legislation was subsequently adopted under the normal procedures in September 1994 (Falkner 2000: 707–8). Subsequently, directives were adopted through the new procedure on parental leave (December 1995, adopted by Council in June 1996), and two on 'atypical work' in 1999—one on the rights of part-time workers and one on the rights of workers on fixed-term contracts (Falkner 2000: 709–11). By 1999, though, this method had already been overtaken by a change of emphasis away from protecting the rights of workers towards providing opportunities for work for the unemployed, and by the introduction of the OMC into employment and social policy.

Persistent unemployment throughout the EU led to the introduction in the Amsterdam Treaty of a new title on Employment, which called for a 'co-ordinated strategy for employment'. A special 'jobs summit' was held in Luxembourg in November 1997 at which a strategy was agreed that became the model for what the later (2000) Lisbon European Council was to entitle the OMC. The Luxembourg process involves agreement on a common set of European targets, with member states drawing up what were originally called National Action Plans for Employment (NAPs), and subsequently became National Reform Programmes (NRPs). The NRPs are then submitted to the Commission and Council for scrutiny, and recommendations may be made. The Commission then produces an annual report on the performance of member states and of the EU as a whole in achieving its objectives, and targets may be adjusted accordingly (Adnett 2001: 353–9). This annual review process was part of the Lisbon Strategy and the emphasis was placed upon labour-market liberalization. The Commission's review powers were strengthened in the Lisbon Strategy's successor—Europe 2020—because of the connection between improving the competitiveness of labour with the need to boost economic growth in the context of the eurozone crisis.

Although no member state is obliged to adopt a particular approach to achieving its objectives, the emphasis on emulating best practice has led to moves to free labour markets of restrictions and provide training for the unemployed, an approach more in line with the Anglo-Saxon model of capitalism than with the various continental models that have traditionally put more emphasis on protecting the rights of those in work. On the other hand, Adnett (2001: 360) reported that there was little evidence of a convergence of national policies, and that indeed in some areas there was evidence of increasing diversity.

Following the Lisbon European Council (2000), the OMC was also applied to social policy as more traditionally understood in the EU. At Lisbon, member states committed themselves to draw up national action plans to combat poverty and social exclusion, to devise indicators for assessing progress, and to develop mechanisms for ensuring the achievement of objectives in these fields (Hodson and Maher 2001: 726, Table 1). This commitment underlines the argument of Borras and Jacobsson (2004: 190) that the Lisbon Strategy addresses *both* competitiveness and social cohesion. As they went on to emphasize, though, the outcome of adopting the OMC would change the nature of the social dimension, which 'had arrived at a stalemate' because 'more EU rights would have invariably undermined the socio-economic agreements and social contracts upon which each national welfare arrangement has been historically built ... There was simply no political support for the further transfer of legal competencies to the EU in these areas' (Borras and Jacobsson 2004: 190).

In the area of employment and social policy, the OMC produced progress where the traditional method of European legislation was severely hindered by the lack of any consensus over priorities, and where the prospect of more such legislation risked further damaging the legitimacy of the EU. The result was to change the nature of the policy sector, both the content of policy outputs and the process. The influence of the EP and the ECJ was weakened by their effective and formal exclusion from the OMC. Although the OMC did not similarly weaken the Commission (Borras and Jacobsson 2004: 198), it did change the nature of the game, and sidelined the institutional forum centred on the social dialogue that was identified by Wendon (1998) and Strøby Jensen (2000). This in turn led to the suggestion that the adoption of the OMC put the states in control of the design and implementation of EU social policies, marginalizing both the Commission and the social partners (Edquist 2006; Gold et al. 2007).

Energy

Energy is an area where policy objectives have changed as a result of changing circumstances. Prompted by the experience of the single market, from the 1990s the main objective of energy policy for the Commission was the liberalization of national markets, which were dominated by monopolistic national suppliers. This resulted in high energy costs, which damaged the global competitiveness of European manufacturers. The situation came to the fore in the aftermath of the single market programme, with the Commission acting as a **policy entrepreneur** to cultivate spillover. This story is told in a later chapter (see Chapter 20, Insight 20.3)

Once the principle had been established that national energy markets would be opened up to competition from other member states, the potential existed to shift other aspects of energy policy to the EU level. In 2004, the Commission identified problems concerning the high level of dependence of the EU on fossil fuels and on imported sources of energy, such as Russian gas. Fossil fuels are finite, and burning them contributes to global warming. The supply of imported energy is liable to disruption from international crises, which can also increase prices quite dramatically. From these problems arises the need to develop co-ordinated programmes to save energy, to use it more efficiently, and to develop alternative sources.

In 2005, the European Council approved the development of a comprehensive European energy strategy, and, in 2006, the Commission produced a Green Paper outlining such a strategy (European Commission 2006a). The first Commission proposals to implement this strategy were brought forward in January 2007, including the introduction of binding targets for each member state to switch to the use of renewable energy sources—biomass, hydro, wind, and solar—by 2020. These proposals were also accepted by the Council.

The Commission used concerns raised by wider global developments, particularly concern about the security implications of an over-reliance on energy from unstable parts of the world and about climate change, to expand its competence beyond those concerned with opening the market to cover these other issues. Spillover from energy policy into transport and into research policy was also recognized by the Commission. Thus, the transfer of energy supply from a national to a European market brought in its train the prospect of whole new areas of competence for the EU. The Lisbon Treaty, Article 147, amended the wording of Title XXI of the TEU on energy policy to reflect these revised policy objectives, emphasizing security of supply and the need to achieve energy efficiency and energy saving in the context of environmental concerns.

Transport

A common transport policy was one of the Titles of the original Treaty. There is an obvious functional necessity for efficient cross-border transport, to make a reality of the ideal of a common market, and a functional logic to organizing it at the European level. Arising from this, the European Commission has responsibility for the planning and part-financing of trans-European networks (TENs) for different modes of transport. Despite several statements of support for the TENs, though, the member states have never been prepared to provide adequate funding, so that the programme is always lagging behind the aspirations.

Spillover from the single market programme allowed the Commission to push through measures to open national transport markets to competition. The liberalization of air transport contributed to a reduction in fares and a consequent increase in passengers; and the liberalization of rail transport, which began with the implementation of a first package of measures in March 2003, held out the prospect of opening 70 to 80 percent of rail freight traffic over main lines to competition. In the road-haulage industry, internationally competitive firms had long argued against the principle of cabotage with respect to loads, a principle that had reserved to national transport firms the right to transport national goods. This had meant that lorries carrying goods from their own state to another member state had to return home empty, which was obviously uneconomical. It was possible to get agreement on the abolition of this principle once the single market was in operation.

As with other policy sectors, different problems were exacerbated by the opening of the markets, and these provided a continuing agenda for action by the Commission. Problems with road congestion, pollution, and the continuing fragmentation of some transport infrastructure were highlighted in a 2001 White Paper on Transport, which also set ambitious targets:

- to reduce road deaths;
- to improve the speed of freight trains by eliminating the causes of delay;
- to reduce flight delays by developing an integrated air-traffic control system;
- to regulate the allocation of airline landing slots;
- to promote investment in inland waterways;
- to improve maritime safety standards;
- to improve port services;
- to introduce integrated ticketing and baggage handling for mixed-mode journeys.

Through a combination of these measures it was hoped to move the EU away from its heavy dependence on road transport, to eliminate some of the consequent congestion, and to reduce the consequent pollution. These objectives were explicitly linked by the Commission to the Lisbon agenda for creating economic growth and jobs, and to the increasing concern for protection of the environment and reduction of carbon emissions.

A mid-term review in 2006 said the plan should now concentrate on making railways more competitive, introducing a ports policy, developing transport systems making use of the latest technology, charging for infrastructure use, producing more biofuels, and finding ways to make towns and cities less congested.

Research

Although a European technological community had been part of the original vision of Jean Monnet, technological research was not included in the Treaty of Rome. The main reason was that the idea of developing 'national industrial champions' held strong sway in the 1950s, as it continued to do through until the 1980s. Despite several periods of concern about the technological lead of the United States over Europe—for example, the furore sparked by Jean-Jacques Servan-Schreiber's book *The American Challenge* (Servan-Schreiber 1968)—attempts by the Commission to persuade member states to institute collaborative research programmes had little effect until the 1980s, when a major breakthrough occurred with the approval by the Council of Ministers in 1982 of the European Strategic Programme in Information Technology (ESPRIT).

The reasons for this breakthrough were similar to those that brought about the even bigger breakthrough of the single market programme (see Chapter 20, Explaining the Single Market). The weak recovery of Europe from the 1979 oil-price shock, in comparison with the vigorous recovery of the United States and Japan, led to much talk of 'Eurosclerosis'. The policy of supporting national champions was clearly not working. In particular, the crucial electronics sectors in Europe were 'showing a poor performance in both capital and consumer goods' (Sharp 1991: 63). At the same time, national research budgets were under pressure because national budgets were being pushed into deficit by high unemployment, and the cost of research was increasing. It was increasingly apparent that the United States and Japan had a range and scale of research and technological development programmes that no individual European state could afford to match (Peterson 1992: 231).

Those were the structural factors that made the 1982 breakthrough feasible. Agency was provided by Étienne Davignon, the EC's Commissioner for Industry from 1977 to 1985. Davignon responded to the concern about Europe's technological performance in electronics by convening the 'Big 12 Round Table' of leading European electrical and electronics firms. This organization provided the model for the later, more extensive, European Round Table of Industrialists. The consensus among the Big 12 was that EC-level support for research and development was essential if the European electronics industry were not to slip even further behind its competitors. This consensus was then pressed on national governments by the powerful large corporations (Sharp and Shearman 1987: 49). What made their lobbying even more effective was that Davignon had used his own network of contacts to ensure that the Round Table met not only at a technical level, but also at the level of chief executives:

> Until then the Commission had tended to work with research directors or their equivalents and initiatives had come unstuck because they had been unable to carry them higher up the hierarchy.

(Sharp 1991: 64)

Here, then, was a prime example of the Commission, in the form of Davignon, playing the role of a policy entrepreneur: identifying a problem, suggesting a solution at the European level, and creating then mobilizing a transnational network of producers to act as its allies in the private sector and to bring pressure to bear on governments to adopt the European solution.

Once the principle of centrally-funded research was established in the field of electronics and information technology, other industries soon began to demand that they get similar support. There followed a whole series of 'Framework Programmes' that served to put the policy into practice. In the 2000s these programmes became closely linked to the Lisbon Strategy to boost the EU's competitiveness. The EU's Seventh Framework Programme, covering 2007–13, had a budget of €50.5 billion and covered a wide range of research areas, including:

- health;
- food, agriculture, and biotechnology;
- information and communication technologies;
- nanosciences and nanotechnologies;
- environment (including climate change);
- fusion energy—ITER;
- nuclear fission;
- transport (including aeronautics);
- security;
- space.

The Eighth Framework Programme, covering the period 2014 to 2020, was given the title *Horizon 2020* (echoing the EU's updated 'Europe 2020' programme for economic competitiveness) and allocated a budget of approximately €70 billion, a big percentage increase over the allocation to FP7. It is divided into three pillars:

- Pillar 1: Excellent Science, which supports cutting-edge scientific projects.
- Pillar 2: Industrial Leadership, which aims to improve Europe's industrial competitiveness.
- Pillar 3: Societal Challenges, which covers health and other societal issues.

Instead of funding specific topics, as in the past, *Horizon 2020* aims to fund horizontal research on tackling challenges such as climate change or demographic change.

CONCLUSION

One of the first conclusions that leaps out from this brief review of the policy process and of various policy sectors is that there is no one consistent pattern of policy making. As suggested by governance and networks approaches (see Chapter 2), different elements are important in different sectors and, as such, there is a need to disaggregate analysis of the policy process to understand these different patterns. At the same time, however, some patterns emerge.

The extent to which policies have either originated or, more often, have accelerated because of spillover from the single European market is clear. This emphasizes the central importance of the single market programme, but also the continuing theoretical relevance of neofunctionalism (see Chapter 1). The validity of neofunctionalism is also clear in the role played by the Commission in exploiting the spillover pressures to engineer transfers of competence to the EU, often through forming alliances with interest groups. It fits well, too, with the way in which the deregulation of national markets in energy and transport led to the involvement of the EU in finding solutions to other problems in these sectors.

Yet, introduction of the OMC into an increasing number of policy areas indicates the resilience of national sovereignty. It allows the governments to keep a tighter control over developments. It also adds weight to governance approaches that emphasize the increasing importance of informal modes of co-ordination rather than formal legislative initiatives.

KEY POINTS

The European Policy Agenda

- Policy agendas are composed of problems that governments face as a result of domestic political pressure and/or international developments.

- Issues on domestic policy agendas are pushed up to the EU level because of functional logic, because they arise from spillover from other EU policies, because domestic interest groups seek action at the EU level, or so a government can escape domestic unpopularity for a necessary reform.

- The Commission is often able to exploit these circumstances to promote a European solution.

- The European Council is ultimately responsible for adding issues to the European agenda.

The EU Policy Process

- The formal process begins with the Commission drawing up proposals for legislation, at which stage it will consult widely with interest groups, technical experts, and national government officials. It will also consult MEPs.

- The TEU introduced two intergovernmental 'pillars' of the EU—CFSP and JHA—where EC rules did not apply. The three-pillars structure was abolished by the Lisbon Treaty, although CFSP still has its own largely intergovernmental rules of procedure.

- OMC has been introduced into what was the EC pillar, giving the member states stronger control and excluding the EP and ECJ.

Minor Policy Areas

- Of the more minor policy areas, fisheries, fraud, and some aspects of both public health and food safety arise mainly from the functional logic of handling problems at the EU level.

- Policies on consumers, taxation, and some aspects of both food safety and the information society arise predominantly from spillover from the single European market.
- Policies on culture and education look back to an earlier commitment to strengthen a sense of European identity.
- Policies on enterprise, labour-market reform, research and innovation, and many aspects of policy on the information society are closely linked to the Lisbon commitment to make the EU the world's most competitive knowledge-based economy, now known as 'Europe 2020'.

Major Policy Areas

- Competition policy developed largely through spillover from the common market and single market. It is an area in which the Commission has considerable autonomy, but in exercising its powers it is often brought into conflict with individual national governments.
- Social policy was included in the original Treaty, but made little progress before the 1980s, and was boosted in the 1990s by a new emphasis on combating unemployment and the introduction of OMC into both employment and social policy.
- In the energy sector, spillover from the single market allowed the Commission to mobilize a coalition of industrial users of energy in favour of liberalization of national energy markets. Once an EU-wide energy market had been established in principle, it became logical to handle other problems, such as security of supply and environmental effects, at the EU level.
- A similar process operated for transport: spillover from the single market allowed the Commission to push through liberalization of national markets, and then other issues needed to be handled at the European level.
- Research policy started with the ESPRIT programme in the electronics and information technology sectors. The Commission exploited European concerns about US and Japanese advances in these sectors to pressurize governments to adopt an EC-wide programme of support for research. Policy was subsequently re-cast in the context of the EU's competitiveness agenda (the Lisbon Strategy/Europe 2020).

FURTHER READING

The standard text on policy making in the EU is **H. Wallace, M. Pollack, and A. Young (eds)**, *Policy-Making in the European Union* (Oxford: Oxford University Press, 6th edn, 2010). Students should especially read the introductory chapters, written by the editors, but also the individual chapters on specific policies are the best possible starting point for following up on the other policies included in this chapter—competition, energy, research, social, and transport policy.

Other studies of policy making and the policy process are: **L. Buonanno and N. Nugent**, *Policies and Policy Processes of the European Union* (Basingstoke: Palgrave Macmillan, 2013); and **E. Versluis, M. van Keulen, and P. Stephenson**, *Analyzing the European Union Policy Process* (Basingstoke: Palgrave Macmillan, 2011).

Because of its influence on later analysis of policy making, it is important to read **J. Peterson**, 'Decision-making in the European Union: Towards a Framework for Analysis', *Journal of European Public Policy*, 2 (1995): 69–93.

On the OMC, there are two articles that, read consecutively, will give a good overall picture of the method and of its strengths and weaknesses. They are **D. Hodson and I. Maher**, 'The Open Method as a New Mode of Governance: The Case of Soft Economic Policy Co-ordination', *Journal of Common Market Studies*, 39 (2001): 719–46; and **S. Borras and K. Jacobsson**, 'The Open

Method of Co-ordination and New Governance Patterns in the EU', *Journal of European Public Policy*, 11 (2004): 185–208.

A useful review of the EU's Lisbon Strategy, its constituent policy measures, and its evolution into Europe 2020 is contained in **P. Copeland and D. Papadimitriou (eds)**, *The EU's Lisbon Strategy: Evaluating Success, Understanding Failure* (Basingstoke: Palgrave Macmillan, 2012).

online resource centre

Visit the Online Resource Centre that accompanies this book for links to more information on European Union policy-making processes.
http://oxfordtextbooks.co.uk/orc/bache4e/

Chapter 19

Agriculture

Chapter Overview

The Common Agricultural Policy (CAP) was the first redistributive policy of the EC, and for many years the only one. The success of agriculture sustained the hopes of the advocates of integration during the 1960s, when it was seen as the start of a process that would lead to other common policies; but for a long time the other common policies did not appear. As a result, agriculture dominated payments from the common budget. Developed to ensure security of food supplies in the Community, the CAP proved highly expensive, with overproduction by farmers keen to maximize subsidies. Despite widespread criticism, the policy proved notoriously difficult to reform. Farmers' groups fiercely resisted change and their importance in the domestic politics of key member states ensured that reform was slow and piecemeal. Only in the context of new internal and external pressures from the 1990s was significant change secured.

History

Agriculture was one of only four common policies that had its own Title in the Treaty of Rome. The importance given to the sector owed a great deal to food shortages at the end of the Second World War. Governments agreed that it was important to ensure adequate supplies of food at reasonable prices. To achieve this it was necessary to provide an adequate income to farmers, while taking measures to increase their productivity. All of the states involved in the original EEC were in agreement on these objectives.

France had a particular interest in agriculture. Small French farmers were politically important because they had the sympathy of the French people. On the other hand, France also had a lot of large and efficient farms. Part of the price that the French insisted on for their participation in the **common market** in industrial goods was the subsidization of the cost of maintaining their small farmers, plus the guarantee of a protected market for French agricultural exports.

Had the EC simply abolished restrictions on free trade in foodstuffs, the effect would have been to produce competition between member states to subsidize their own farmers. So free trade was not viable. Yet, it was also recognized that the equalization of food prices was important for fair competition in industrial products. Higher food prices meant that workers demanded higher wages, thus raising industry's costs. To have a level playing field of competition in industrial goods, cost differences arising from the effect of food prices needed to be limited.

Before reform in the 1980s, the CAP was a price support system. Every year national Ministers of Agriculture decided the level of prices for agricultural products that were covered by the CAP. These prices were ensured by the intervention of the Commission in the market to buy up enough of each product to maintain the agreed price. If prices subsequently rose above the agreed level, the produce that the Commission had purchased and placed into storage would be released onto the market to bring the price back down. In practice, though, this did not occur.

Prices were set at the level that would ensure the least efficient farmers in the EC an adequate income, which encouraged the more efficient, large-scale farmers to maximize their output, because the price was more than adequate to guarantee them a return on their investment. Thus surpluses in most products became permanent. The Commission's interventions in the market were all in one direction: to keep up prices by intervention buying. The amounts of produce in storage constantly grew and became an embarrassment, prompting press reports of 'food mountains' and 'wine lakes'. The cost of storage in itself became a significant burden on the Community budget.

The problems stemmed from the failure of agricultural policy itself to develop. What was commonly known as the CAP was in effect only a policy on agricultural price support. Sicco Mansholt, the Commissioner in charge of agriculture during Hallstein's presidency, saw a clear line of spillover from price support to the restructuring of European agriculture to create fewer, larger, more efficient farms. This would have allowed guaranteed prices to be reduced.

At the request of the Council of Ministers, Mansholt introduced proposals for such a restructuring in the late 1960s, but an economic recession in the 1970s led to resistance to the restructuring measures from those governments that had considerable agricultural populations.

Price settlements tended to remain high because of the political influence of farmers, which was everywhere considerable. At the same time, the high prices acted as a burden on the Community budget, and put a particular burden on the national budgets of West Germany and Britain, the two largest net contributors to the Community budget.

Failure to reform the CAP led to ever-larger surpluses of produce being kept in storage, and the cost of storage itself added to the budgetary burden. In an attempt to address at least this part of the cost, a decision was made in the course of the 1970s to encourage the export of the surpluses instead of storing them. As world market prices for all products covered by the CAP were consistently lower than the guaranteed internal prices, it was necessary for the EC to pay farmers the difference between the price they received for the exports and the guaranteed price. Such export subsidies technically constitute what is known as the 'dumping' of products on world markets. It had the adverse effect of lowering world prices by adding to supply; but it also encouraged other agricultural producers to subsidize their own farmers so that they could compete with the EC farmers. This move from storage to export of surpluses was eventually to produce irresistible external pressure for reform of the CAP, although these pressures did not hit home until the 1980s.

Agriculture in the 1980s and 1990s

In the course of the 1980s and 1990s the pressures built up for reform of the CAP (see Insight 19.1). Together these pressures did produce some reforms in 1984 and 1988, and a more radical reform in 1992.

In 1984 a system of quotas for dairy products was agreed. In 1988 agreement was reached on a complex package that put a legal limit on agricultural price support for 1988 and fixed future increases above that level at an annual maximum of 74 per cent of the increase in Community GDP. If this limit were breached there would be automatic price cuts for the relevant products in subsequent years until the ceilings ceased to be breached. Also, money was made available to encourage farmers to set aside arable land and to let it lie fallow (Butler 1993: 116–17).

Commissioner MacSharry introduced a further package of reform proposals in July 1991, and they were agreed with some modifications, and side-payments to sweeten the pill, in a very rapid ten months, by May 1992. Although known as the 'MacSharry reforms', they nevertheless bore the imprint also of President Delors and his *cabinet*. The package involved a sharp decrease in the prices for cereals and beef, to bring them more into line with world prices, linked to a move from supporting farmers through subsidies on production to direct support for rural incomes. More land was to be taken out of production altogether, with the farmers being compensated by direct payments; an early retirement scheme was introduced to encourage older

---

Insight 19.1 Pressures for CAP Reform in the 1990s

- Budget pressures, which had abated in the 1980s, again became significant as the USA allowed the value of the dollar to decline and reintroduced agricultural export subsidies of its own. This forced down world prices, and so increased the cost of export subsidies.

- The reunification of Germany brought into immediate membership of the EC considerable grain-producing areas, as well as extra dairy and beef livestock, adding to the problems of overproduction.

- The need to stabilize democracy and capitalism in the states of central and eastern Europe demanded that the West buy exports from them to allow them to obtain the hard currency necessary to buy from the West to re-equip their industries. These countries had few products in which they had any comparative advantage. Agricultural products were among the few. If the CAP had not prevented it, several of the states could have exported their agricultural goods to the EC.

- By 1992 the Uruguay Round of the GATT had reached a critical stage. In previous rounds of the GATT, agriculture had been raised as an issue, but had always been eventually left on one side because the participants did not want the overall package to collapse. This time the fate of farmers was so serious that both the USA and the Cairns Group appeared to be prepared to collapse the deal unless it was included. Eventually in 1992, with the original deadlines for agreement already well past, the Cairns Group agreed to allow the United States to negotiate directly with the EC on agriculture.

farmers to cease production; and more environmentally friendly farming was encouraged, with the implication that this would lower yields (Ross 1995: 200).

Sceptics claimed that the reforms would not solve the budget problem, and in the short term would even increase the cost of the CAP. However, at the end of November 1993 MacSharry's successor, René Steichen, claimed that cereal production for 1993 was 16 million tons lower than it would have been without the reforms (*The Week in Europe*, 2 December 1993). More significantly, the reforms accepted for the first time that support for farmers could be separated from production.

To understand why it proved possible to agree these reforms, it is necessary to understand the pressures on policy makers. The main sources of pressure were the escalating cost of the CAP, enlargement, increasing concern about the environmental effects of intensive farming, and external pressures, particularly in the context of world trade negotiations.

The Cost of the CAP

Between 1974 and 1979 the cost of the CAP rose by 23 per cent, twice the rate of increase of incomes. It then stabilized between 1980 and 1982, but in 1983 the cost soared by 30 per cent, and the EC reached the ceiling of expenditure that could be covered from its own resources. Agreement to lift the limit had to be unanimous, and the British government would not agree to any increase without firm measures to curb the cost of the CAP. This led to the 1984 agreement on dairy quotas, and on a system of budgetary discipline whereby a maximum limit would be set to the size of the budget each year before the annual round of negotiations on agricultural prices. Ministers of Agriculture would therefore be negotiating within fixed parameters. Any budgetary overshoot would be clawed back in the following years.

In the event, this system did not work because there was no automatic mechanism for making the necessary adjustments to costs in the years following an overrun. Between 1985 and 1987 the cost of the CAP increased by 18 per cent per annum. Although the EC did not appear to face the immediate exhaustion of its financial resources as it had in 1984, by 1987 there was an estimated budgetary shortfall of 4 to 5 million European currency units (ecus), which was covered by creative accountancy that simply pushed the problem forward in time.

So, although some of the reforms in the 1980s marked significant departures from earlier policies, they 'failed to halt the relentless rise in the budget required for the CAP, and the reforms of 1992 became inevitable' (Colman 2007: 81).

Enlargement

The Southern enlargement (see Chapter 27, History) brought new demands on the budget that could only be met by either diverting money away from existing beneficiaries or expanding the size of the budget. This situation was compounded by the insistence of the Spanish, Portuguese, and Greek governments that they would not be able to participate in the freeing of the internal market of the EC by the end of 1992 unless the structural funds were substantially increased. At the London meeting of the European Council in December 1986 agreement was reached in principle on the doubling of the structural funds by 1993 (see Chapter 22, History), thus requiring an increase in the resources of the EC. The first enlargement therefore added to the pressure for reform of the CAP to make room within the existing budget for these new items of expenditure.

With the collapse of communism at the end of the 1980s, Germany moved rapidly to reunification. In effect this constituted an enlargement of the EC. The former east German territories included areas that were considerable agricultural producers, so threatening a big increase in the cost of the CAP.

Pressure on the EU to continue the process of reform of the CAP became greater as the former communist states of east-central Europe began to press ever more strongly for full membership of the EU in the 1990s. After some initial reluctance, most member states came round to the realization that it would be necessary to grant membership to most of these states. Germany in particular became a strong advocate of eastern enlargement. However, reports prepared by the Commission indicated that the existing CAP could not simply be applied to the applicant states without dramatic consequences for the budget of the EU.

Extension of the CAP in its present form to the acceding countries would create difficulties. Given existing price gaps between candidate countries and generally substantially higher CAP prices, and despite prospects for some narrowing of these gaps by the dates of accession, even gradual introduction of CAP prices would tend to stimulate surplus production, in particular in the livestock sector, thus adding to projected surpluses. World Trade Organization (WTO) constraints on subsidized exports would prevent the enlarged Union from selling its surpluses on third markets (Avery and Cameron 1998: 153).

Environmental Pressures

In the 1980s there was growing concern about the environment in general, and about the effect of the CAP in particular (Lynggaard 2007: 300). The main beneficiaries of the CAP were large farmers who responded to the high prices by maximizing output. To do this they pumped more and more fertilizer into the land, and hormones into animals, to improve yields. The rise of environmentalism provided a counter-weight to the general sympathy of European public opinion for farmers, and made it politically easier for governments to respond to the financial pressures with reform measures.

Sympathy for modern farming methods was further reduced in the late 1980s and early 1990s by the outbreak of a number of scares about the safety of food. Of these, the most serious was the epidemic of 'mad cow disease', or bovine spongiform encephalopathy (BSE) in the United Kingdom, which reached its height in 1992. Blame for this was put on intensive farming methods that ignored the welfare of animals. The issue of food safety is not strictly an environmental concern, but it is closely related and was associated with concerns about damage to the environment in the minds of the European public.

These problems became linked with the pressing issue of surpluses to produce a change in the perception of the CAP even among those institutions and groups most closely associated with it, so that 'by 1992, the conception that intensive farming is the source of both problems of agricultural surplus production and environmental depletion was institutionalized among all the central agents within the CAP' (Lynggaard 2007: 302).

External Pressures

External pressures proved a strong incentive for change in the CAP. The United States made the phasing out of agricultural subsidies a central part of its negotiating position for the trade talks under the **General Agreement on Tariffs and Trade (GATT)**, which began in 1986 and were known as the Uruguay Round. It was joined by the Cairns Group of fourteen agricultural-producing states, including Australia, Canada, New Zealand, and several Latin American states. All felt that they suffered from the dumping of the EC's agricultural exports onto world markets, which drove down prices and prevented them selling some of their own production.

The 'MacSharry reforms' of 1992 allowed Ray MacSharry, the Commissioner for Agriculture, to negotiate a deal on agricultural trade that temporarily satisfied the United States and the Cairns Group, and meant that it was possible to conclude the Uruguay Round. That was not the end of the story, though. At the conclusion of the Uruguay Round it was agreed to open a further round of trade talks at the end of 1999. It was clear that the compromises on agricultural trade reached in the Uruguay Round were provisional, and that agriculture would be a central element of the new round.

In June 1996 the British National Farmers' Union (NFU) produced a paper explaining why the EU would come under great pressure in these trade talks to reform the CAP further. At the end of the Uruguay Round, agreement had been reached to allow both the EU and the USA to continue to subsidize cereal and livestock farmers. These measures had, in the terminology of the agreement, been placed in a 'blue box'. This meant that the subsidies did distort production, but could be continued without legal challenge until 2003 provided that they were not increased. Another 'green box' was created, consisting of support for farmers that did not distort production. These included measures such as those that had already been introduced into the CAP by the MacSharry reforms: measures to take land out of production, or to encourage environmental protection. Since the agreement, the USA had unilaterally moved almost all of its support measures out of the blue box into the green box, leaving the EU alone in the blue box. Although the blue box measures could be sustained until 2003, the EU would now be under tremendous pressure to reciprocate the unilateral US gesture (NFU 1996).

It was in this context that Franz Fischler, Agriculture Commissioner in the Santer Commission, produced a package of proposals for further reform in November 1995. These continued the pattern of the 1992 reforms, decoupling support for farmers from production and linking it to social and environmental objectives (European Commission 1995). They were subsequently incorporated into the Commission document *Agenda 2000: For a Stronger and Wider Europe* (European Commission 1999).

Agenda 2000 and the 2003 Reform

Agenda 2000 'consisted essentially of the Commission's recommendations for the Union's financial framework for the period 2000–6; the future development of the Union's policies, and in particular its two most important spending policies—the cohesion and structural funds, and the Common Agricultural Policy; and the strategy for enlargement of the Union' (Avery and Cameron 1998: 101). On CAP it proposed large reductions in support prices and giving compensation to farmers in the form of direct payments, with a ceiling on the level of aid that any one individual could receive. Although explicitly linked to the eastern enlargement in *Agenda 2000*, these reforms were in line with shifting support from the GATT 'blue box' to the 'green box'.

When negotiations began on the CAP proposals of *Agenda 2000* in February 1999, the French government predictably pressed for more limited reform. This position was supported by 30,000 farmers—mainly from France, Germany, and Belgium—protesting on the streets of Brussels, the biggest demonstration since those against the Mansholt reforms in 1971. After a temporary suspension of the negotiations, the Agriculture Ministers agreed, on 11 March, to cut cereal prices by 20 per cent, as proposed by the Commission, but to do so in two stages—a half in 2000–01 and the other half in 2001–02. They agreed to lower milk prices by 15 per cent in line with the Commission's proposals, but only over three years starting in 2003, and dairy production quotas were actually raised slightly. They also agreed that beef prices should be cut by 20 per cent, but this was only two-thirds of the cut proposed by the Commission.

Fischler hailed the agreement as the most far-reaching reform of the CAP for forty years; but the states that had most strongly supported reform—Britain, Italy, Sweden, and Denmark—expressed their disappointment. They did not like the delays in implementing the cuts that had been forced through by France and Germany (which held the presidency of the Council). They were to be even more disappointed following the Berlin European Council in March 1999, which was intended to approve the reform.

In Berlin, President Chirac of France simply refused to accept what the French Minister of Agriculture had negotiated. This reflected the fact that Chirac was a conservative President who was forced to work with a socialist government. He was blatantly playing domestic politics. However, so important was it to the German government to get an agreement during its presidency, and not to break publicly with France, that Chancellor Schröder eventually agreed to support a significant further dilution of the reform package. The dairy reforms were further delayed, and the cuts in cereal prices were scaled back from the compromise level reached by the Ministers of Agriculture. The other member states went along in return for side-payments: Spain and Greece got agreement to continuation of the Cohesion Fund (see Chapter 22, The 1999 Reform); Britain got agreement to the continuation of the British budgetary rebate with only minor concessions.

> The Agenda 2000 outcome was thus deeply compromised and must be judged a missed opportunity to reform the CAP.

(Lowe et al. 2002: 4)

But Commissioner Fischler did not give up. The 1999 reforms, although not as far-reaching as the Commission had wanted, did continue with the principle, first conceded in the MacSharry reforms, that the reduced production subsidies would be compensated by direct payments that were decoupled from production. In June 2001 a further reform in this direction was agreed as a way of helping small farmers who found the complexities of operating the multiple strands of the revised CAP just too burdensome. Under the Small Farmers' Scheme, farmers who received less than

€1,250 in total from the CAP could opt to convert their payments into a single decoupled flat-rate payment based on a historical reference point (Daugbjerg 2009: 403). This reinforced the precedent of flat-rate decoupled payments that had been established as part of the 1999 reforms.

The shift to direct payments was also used to provide a solution to the problem of how to accommodate the very large farming sectors in the states of Central Europe that were negotiating for membership of the EU. It was clear that these farmers could not be offered production incentives equal to those available to farmers in the existing member states. Both the budgetary implications and the implications for agricultural surpluses would have been unbearable for the EU. Also, the administrative structures that needed to be put in place to implement the complex system of different payments would have stretched the capacities of the states and their farmers. Instead, in January 2002, the Commission proposed what it called the 'Simplified Approach' to calculating agricultural support in the new member states. The new member states would receive a flat-rate decoupled payment based on farm size, starting at 25 per cent of the average rate for the existing EU member states. This would be distributed to farmers by the state itself, using whatever criteria it deemed most relevant, so long as production subsidies were not involved.

Having established, and then reinforced, the principle of flat-rate decoupled payments, in July 2002 Fischler put forward a revised proposal for the full decoupling of agricultural subsidies from production in the existing EU by the end of 2004. He was helped by difficulties in the new Doha Round of WTO negotiations, which became bogged down at an early stage by disputes over agricultural subsidies.

Under these proposals, the amounts of money that each member state would receive would be the same as under the system that had been agreed at Berlin, but the money would be paid in a lump sum to the governments, which could then distribute between their farmers as they saw fit, so long as it was not paid in the form of a production subsidy. So, governments that did not wish to enter into a confrontation with their larger farmers, who received the bulk of the subsidies under the existing system, could simply pay the money out according to historic distributions; whereas those that were keen to bring about a domestic restructuring of agricultural holdings could divide the money up differently. In either case, the payment would be linked to requirements for farmers to comply with EU-wide standards on environmental protection, food safety, and animal welfare. Fischler argued that the reforms would help the EU to meet the requirements of the Doha Round, and would at the same time integrate the new member states with the system of agricultural support operating in the rest of the EU. They also implied a degree of re-nationalization of the CAP.

After almost a year of debate, the Council of Agriculture Ministers reached a compromise at the end of June 2003. The essence of the Commission's proposals was adopted, although the shift to direct payments was deferred until 2005, and individual member states could apply for exceptions until 2007 to continue to subsidize production where there was a risk of farmers withdrawing from production altogether.

In 2008 there was an interim review of the state of the CAP, which went by the name of a 'health check'. Completed under the French presidency in the second half of 2008, the review agreed to shift money to rural development from 2009 and progressively to liberalize the dairy sector before the expiry of existing milk production quotas in 2015.

The 2013 Reform

With the arrival of the new Commission came a new Commissioner for Agriculture. Taking up post at the start of 2010, Dacian Cioloş soon after announced a wide-ranging public debate on the future of the CAP. This was in the context of warnings from the Budget DG that big cuts in the allocations to agriculture were inevitable in the context of a demand from national governments for overall budgetary constraint in the face of the gathering crisis in the eurozone.

Further reform of the CAP seemed inevitable, but the whole process soon became messy. First, the Lisbon Treaty had transferred agriculture to co-decision, so agreement had to be reached not just within the Council of Ministers, as previously, but also with the EP. Although the change had been made in the name of increasing democratic control, the main effect was to provide the farm lobby with another channel for resisting further reform. Second, the negotiations on the future of agriculture were taking place at the same time as those on the next multi-annual financial framework. The financial framework talks dragged on into the start of 2013, and neither the Council of Agricultural Ministers nor the EP's Agriculture Committee was prepared to adopt a position to take into negotiations with the other institutions until the overall amount of money available was known.

Despite not knowing the exact figure, all the actors involved knew that there would be a cut in funding in real terms, even if agriculture kept its share of the budget, because the overall figure would be smaller. Thus, the debate was about where savings would be made. Cioloş made it clear that he favoured making savings by imposing a cap on the amount of payments for which larger farms were eligible. This position reflected his nationality, Romania having many small farms and few large. It was a position, though, that was bound to run into opposition from the member states that normally supported reform of the CAP, particularly Britain and Germany, which themselves had many large farms; and from the formidable lobby of large farmers.

The position of the farmers' organizations as a whole was that as much money as possible should be saved from Pillar 2, which supported environmental measures and rural development, rather than from the direct payments that constituted Pillar 1. Their hand in this was strengthened by a decline in the level of public concern about environmental issues since the negotiation of the 2003 reforms, reflecting the more difficult economic situation faced by consumers across the EU. Accepting the inevitability of some savings being made in Pillar 2, the Commission tried to keep the environmental groups happy by strengthening the requirements on farmers receiving direct support under Pillar 1 to adopt measures of environmental protection, such as leaving uncultivated strips of land for the benefit of wildlife. The farmers considered these requirements to be a financial burden that they could do without.

As well as a decline in the pressure on farmers from public concern over the environment, the pressure from world trade talks for changes to the CAP, which had been prominent in the preceding rounds of agricultural negotiations, no longer figured. The Doha Round of the WTO had become bogged down, and as the EU agricultural talks got under way it became increasingly obvious that a rapid conclusion of the WTO talks was unlikely, not least because the Obama Administration, which took office in the United States in January 2009, soon showed itself to be keener on bi-lateral than multi-lateral deals (see Chapter 25).

At the start of 2013 it looked as though there was little prospect of agreement being reached on reform of the CAP in time for the new rules to start in January 2014, as they were supposed to do. The multi-lateral financial framework negotiations were only concluded at the start of February, and they imposed a CAP budget that was nearly €16 billion below what the Commission wanted, a 10 per cent cut. This obviously made agreement on CAP reform even more difficult to achieve. Nevertheless, the Irish government made concluding an agreement a priority for its presidency of the Council in the first half of 2013, perhaps encouraged by the importance of agriculture to the Irish economy, but also by the inexperience of the Lithuanian government that would take over for the second half of the year.

Against the expectations of most commentators, the Irish presidency did reach an agreement in co-decision with only days of its term left. It was only agreed, though, by leaving decisions on some of the most controversial issues to be taken by the heads of government, including the capping of direct payments, the pace of convergence of payments to the older and newer member states, and the transfer of resources from Pillar 2 into Pillar 1. Although agreement was reached to tie 30 per cent of direct payments to the adoption of measures to protect and enhance the environment, each of the three environmental criteria was weakened and made easier and less expensive to meet, much to the fury of environmental groups, who were scathing about the outcome. Some MEPs were also unhappy at the way that they felt they had been railroaded into reaching an unsatisfactory agreement by the tight deadlines that the Council presidency imposed and pressure from national governments.

The Effect of Reform

Although it had been a long and sometimes frustrating series of negotiations, the cumulative effect on the CAP of the reform process that started in 1992 was to bring about a considerable shift in the pattern of support for farmers away from price support to direct support. By 2002–03, direct payments, or 'compensatory payments', accounted for 65 per cent of CAP support, and the June 2003 agreement meant that by 2007 all support would be in this form. This, when combined with 'set aside' requirements, did have the effect of reducing the production surpluses that had plagued the system since it was set up, but it did nothing to redress the problem that the bulk of receipts from the CAP went to a small number of large farmers. In 2003 the Organization for Economic Co-operation and Development (OECD) estimated that 70 per cent of CAP support still went to the richest 25 per cent of farms.

Large farmers had always benefited more than small farmers from the CAP because they were able to achieve higher yields. Thus, when payments were related to output, the larger and more efficient farmers pocketed the largest share. Direct payments were introduced under MacSharry to compensate farmers for the reduction in guaranteed prices towards world market prices. In order to minimize opposition to the changes, the direct payments were based on the size of farms. Farmers received payments linked to the number of hectares that they farmed. This reduced the incentive to maximize yields, which was the primary aim of the exercise. Production was further curtailed by making it a requirement of receiving the direct payments that 15 per cent of arable land be set aside and not used to produce crops. Similarly, meat producers were required to reduce the density of livestock per hectare in order to qualify for the direct payments. *Agenda 2000* extended the same principle further. It did nothing, though, to redirect subsidies from rich farmers to poor farmers. This political hot potato was effectively dropped into the laps of national governments by the June 2003 agreement to move to a 'single farm payment' that governments could distribute between different categories of farms as they chose. The 2013 reform was driven primarily by overall budgetary concerns, and the desire of the governments of the member states to save money over the period of the next multi-annual financial framework. As the CAP, despite previous reforms, still accounted for 40 per cent of the EU's overall budget, it was obvious from the outset that it would have to take its share of the austerity in public spending that set in with recession and the crisis in the eurozone. Although the hand of the big farmers had been strengthened by developments since the 2003 negotiations, they were only able to play this hand within the actual agricultural negotiations, whereas the financial decisions were being taken in a different forum. The result was an agreement that reversed some of the previous gains in environmental protection and rural development, and did nothing to resolve the imbalance in payments to large and small farmers. It did, though, mean that CAP expenditure would decline to below 40 per cent of the overall budget for the first time ever, and this is a remarkable difference from the 70 per cent that it took immediately before the series of reforms began in the 1980s.

Explaining the CAP

Hardly surprisingly, intergovernmentalism (see Chapter 1, International Relations Theories of European Integration) explains well the setting up of the CAP. Until the signing of the treaties there were no European institutional actors to take into account. The importance of agriculture has to be understood in terms of the perceived national interests of the six states that came together to form the EEC. It is often told as the story of how French agricultural interests made a deal with German industrial interests to produce an EEC founded on the twin pillars of the industrial common market and the guided price support system of the CAP. This, though, is an oversimplification, and liberal intergovernmentalism, which looks at the domestic politics that produce the positions taken up by national governments in international negotiations, directs our attention to the importance of agriculture and of farmers in all the member states.

Neofunctionalism (see Chapter 1, International Relations Theories of European Integration) could only come into play once the EEC and the CAP existed, with institutional actors being formed at the European level, but several elements of neofunctionalism can be seen in the history of the CAP. Setting up a system of support for agriculture that was based on fixing the prices of commodities, in a context of mixed farming sizes, inevitably caused problems. The price level that was needed to keep inefficient small farmers in business was so high that it encouraged more efficient farmers to increase output to the maximum level. When combined with technological advances, this led to the food surpluses that became one of the biggest headaches of the EC. This outcome was not an unanticipated consequence of the CAP, though. It was foreseen by the Commission, and Sicco Mansholt tried to use it as a lever to get member states to take the next step, of rationalizing farm sizes. So this was a potential example of cultivated spillover. However, it did not work because the governments of the member states retreated from radical reform in the face of domestic political pressures, thus providing some support for the liberal intergovernmental critique of neofunctionalism (see Chapter 1, International Relations Theories of European Integration).

Neofunctionalism predicted also that the creation of a single common policy would set up spillover pressures for the adoption of other common policies. This did appear to be working in the 1970s, when frequent changes in the exchange rates of the currencies of the member states threatened to render the CAP unworkable. Again, though, the governments of the member states avoided the apparent implication that they would either have to fix their exchange rates or abandon the CAP, by improvising a solution based on 'green currencies', regulated by levies and rebates when produce crossed national boundaries. The spillover pressures certainly existed, but the governments proved able to resist them until they felt that they wanted to take the next step. Again this seemed to vindicate intergovernmental analyses.

Ultimately, though, these ad hoc solutions were unstable. Neofunctionalism might be thought to have been vindicated when agreement between governments on the single market programme, and the consequent removal of customs checks between states, forced the abandonment of the 'green currency' system. On the other hand, this was only made necessary by the intergovernmental decision to proceed with the removal of customs checks, and it was only made feasible by the adoption of the single currency, which again was the result of an independent decision by governments.

Turning to the theories of governance (see Chapter 2), the CAP appears at first sight to be a prime example of a sector where supranational governance applies. Support for agriculture had been transferred from the national to the EC/EU level. Policy communities of national farmers' organizations and bureaucrats in national ministries of agriculture were apparently replaced by a European policy community of EU farmers' organizations and Commission officials in the Directorate-General for Agriculture. However, decisions both on fixing annual price levels and on the regulation and reform of the system remained firmly with national ministers of agriculture meeting in the Council of Ministers. The extent to which these ministers became identified with the interests of their sector rather than with the interests of their governments is a question for empirical research, but examples of ministers having to be overruled by the heads of government suggest that this particular Council may have developed a supranational tinge. More significantly, perhaps, the national bureaucrats in agriculture ministries remained involved, if for no other reason than that the actual implementation and administration of the policy remained at national level. The CAP may always, then, have been more accurately analysed as a system of multi-level governance rather than an example of supranational governance, and the reform process that was concluded in June 2003 enhanced the multi-level nature of the sector by restoring considerable discretion over the expenditure of CAP receipts to the national level.

That reform of the CAP became possible at all in the 1980s and 1990s has been explained through a variety of different theoretical perspectives.

Fouilleux (2007: 345), without using the term 'epistemic community' (see Chapter 2, Governance and Networks), adopted an explanation that invoked the importance of academic experts. She emphasized a learning process within the international agricultural policy community, a process that was sparked off by an exercise that the OECD initiated to review the agricultural policies of its member states. The responsible officials asked academics, mainly agricultural economists, to undertake a critique of existing policies, and, '[t]his process engendered a learning process within the international agricultural policy community, and induced a profound change in the way agricultural policy issues were defined'.

Moyer and Josling (1990) emphasized the weakening of the European agricultural policy community. The 1984 reforms were ineffective in restraining the growing cost of the CAP, because they were both too modest in their aims, and lacked effective enforcement mechanisms. This reflected two aspects of the reforms. First, that they were drawn up by an EC agricultural policy community that consisted of the Agriculture Directorate-General of the Commission, the European Agriculture Commissioner, and the representatives of farmers in the Committee of Professional Agricultural Organizations of the European Community (COPA). These groups had developed close working relationships, and were unlikely to produce proposals that would seriously damage the interests of farmers, or reduce the importance of agriculture as an EC policy sector. Second, the proposals had to be agreed by the Council of Agriculture Ministers, most of whom were strongly influenced by national farmers' representatives.

By the time of the 1988 reforms, according to Moyer and Josling (1990: 86–7), the coalition against change had been weakened by the formation within the Commission of an inner circle. This inner circle consisted of the President, Jacques Delors, the Agriculture Commissioner between 1985 and 1989, Frans Andriessen, and the Budget Commissioner, Hening Christophersen. Delors's reason for supporting reform was the damage that failure to achieve it might do to the single market programme. 'Delors had made the single European market something of a personal crusade and could not easily see this goal frustrated by agricultural stalemate' (Moyer and Josling 1990: 86). Under pressure from the Commission, which was prepared to take the Council of Ministers to the European Court of Justice if it did not agree a budget for 1988, a system of price stabilizers for agricultural produce was accepted in February 1988. That did not resolve the problems, though, and further reform was planned within the Commission during 1990.

The MacSharry reforms were the result of the same combination of internal and external pressures that had produced the 1988 reforms, but there is a vigorous academic debate about how important the different pressures were in producing the reforms. Rieger (2000: 193–6) argued that it was the mounting cost of the CAP that forced reform. Swinbank and Daugbjerg (2006; and Daugbjerg and Swinbank 2008) dismissed this argument and sided with Grant (1997: 196) in emphasizing the central importance of the international trade negotiations; indeed, according to Daugbjerg and Swinbank (2008: 637), this pressure 'had a decisive impact on the EU's decision to embark on CAP reform'.

In contrast, the 2013 reforms were undertaken against the background of faltering negotiations on world trade, which considerably reduced the pressure for change in the CAP. Global economic conditions deteriorated rapidly after 2008, and governments faced a tide of public opinion against further liberalization of trade in a context of rising domestic unemployment. At the same time, the need to reduce government debt put a premium on reining-in public expenditure, especially in the eurozone (see Chapter 21, The Eurozone Crisis), which meant that finance ministers and heads of government insisted on a tight overall budgetary settlement for the EU. It was this budgetary squeeze, rather than the pressure from international trade negotiations, that drove the 2013 reforms. The difference from 2003 was that then the requirements of the WTO talks implied a particular direction of reform for the CAP, whereas the budgetary constraint in 2013 required only that CAP expenditure be reduced. In this context, and with a relaxation of the level of public concern about the environment, the strength of the traditional agricultural lobbies came to the fore once more to produce an agreement that did little to restructure agriculture or promote rural development, and left crucial questions about issues such as the balance of payments between large and small farms to national governments, further contributing to the fragmentation and re-nationalization of the CAP. Intergovernmental theories of the EU seem most relevant here.

CONCLUSION

For three decades, from the late 1950s to the late 1980s, agricultural policy was absolutely central to both European integration and to academic attempts to understand the process. Then, at the end of the 1980s, a programme of reform began that rapidly moved the policy sector to the periphery of the EU. After many unsuccessful attempts to bring about reform, the CAP was beginning to look entrenched and immutable. Yet, when reform began, it moved remarkably quickly. Within a few years, one of the pillars of European integration had been effectively dismantled, and the policy had been effectively re-nationalized.

Today, the CAP is no longer central to the politics of the EU. The extent to which successive reforms dismantled the supranational elements of the policy is indicated by the fact that within the United Kingdom agriculture is one of the policies that has been devolved from Westminster, and different spending priorities are pursued in England, Scotland, Wales, and Northern Ireland. This would have been inconceivable under the old CAP.

Although new policy areas have pushed agriculture out of its central role within the EU, the explanation for the evolution of the CAP remains an interesting historical and theoretical case study. The variety of explanations offered for the CAP's movement from pillar to peripheral policy covers a wide range of the theoretical perspectives identified in Part One of this book, and fully justifies the continued study of the sector.

KEY POINTS

History

- France made it a condition of its participation in the EEC that agricultural policy be a joint pillar alongside the common market in industrial goods.
- The policy that was set up was based on supporting the price of agricultural products so as to maintain the incomes of farmers.
- Prices were set through political bargaining, and tended to be high so as to give an adequate income to small, inefficient farmers, who were politically influential.

- The high prices encouraged large, efficient farmers to produce large surpluses.
- Storing the surpluses put a huge strain on the budget of the EC, and disposing of them through export subsidies attracted hostility from other agricultural-producing states.

Agriculture in the 1980s and 1990s

- Reforms were made in 1984, 1988, and 1992.
- The reforms were forced by the increasing budgetary cost of the CAP, enlargement, environmental pressures, and demands from other states in the context of world trade negotiations.

Agenda 2000 and the 2003 Reform

- Further reforms to the CAP were proposed in the context of the *Agenda 2000* budget negotiations, but they were watered down in intergovernmental bargaining between France and Germany.
- The principle of decoupling payments from production was accepted in the 1999 reforms, and was fully applied to the new member states of central and eastern Europe.
- Reforms were finally agreed in 2003 that continued the processes begun in 1992 of decoupling from production subsidies to farmers in the rest of the EU, and re-nationalizing the CAP.

The 2013 Reform

- Reform of the CAP was undertaken against a background of tight budgetary constraint. Talks on the multi-annual financial framework were taking place at the same time as those on the future of agriculture.
- Negotiations were complicated because agriculture now came under the co-decision procedure, which meant more actors were involved in more forums.
- The Commission wanted to cap direct payments to large farms, against opposition from the large farmers.
- Farmers wanted to see savings made on environmental and rural development rather than direct payments.
- The final agreement reduced environmental protection and left other key decisions to national governments.

The Effect of Reform

- Decoupling subsidies from production allowed for better budgetary control and put the EU in a stronger position in world trade negotiations.
- The subsidies were only gradually extended to new member states in central and eastern Europe, thus preventing the feared sudden hike in budgetary costs.
- As a result of the 2013 reform, agricultural expenditure would decline below 40 per cent of the overall EU budget for the first time, but several decisions were left to heads of government, and some, such as the balance in payments to large and small farmers, were decentralized to national level.

Explaining the CAP

- Intergovernmentalism and liberal intergovernmentalism explain the setting up of the CAP.
- Neofunctionalists expected spillover from the initial CAP both to lead to the reform of agriculture and to produce other common policies, but governments managed to resist these pressures for a long time.

- Arguments can be made for both supranational governance and multi-level governance as the best description of the CAP prior to the 1992 and 2003 reforms. After the 2003 and 2013 reforms the case for describing it as an example of multi-level governance is stronger.

- Various explanations have been given of the reform of the CAP, emphasizing the role of ideas, of policy communities, of internal pressures, and of external pressures.

FURTHER READING

On the difficulties and emerging prospects of reform of the CAP, in chronological order see: **H. W. Moyer and T. E. Josling**, *Agricultural Policy Reform: Policy and Process in the EC and the USA* (Ames: Iowa University Press, 1990); **A. Swinbank**, 'CAP Reform in 1992', *Journal of Common Market Studies*, 31 (1993): 359–72; **W. Grant**, 'The Limits of Common Agricultural Policy Reform and the Option of Renationalization', *Journal of European Public Policy*, 2 (1995): 1–18; **W. D. Coleman**, 'From Protected Development to Market Liberalism: Paradigm Change in Agriculture', *Journal of European Public Policy*, 5 (1998): 632–51; **P. Lowe, H. Buller, and N. Ward**, 'Setting the Next Agenda? British and French Approaches to the Second Pillar of the Common Agricultural Policy', *Journal of Rural Studies*, 18 (2002): 1–17; **C. Daugbjerg**, 'Sequencing in Public Policy: The Evolution of the CAP over a Decade', *Journal of European Public Policy*, 16 (2009): 395–411. For a more encompassing study, see **I. Garzon**, *Reforming the Common Agricultural Policy* (Basingstoke: Palgrave Macmillan, 2006). A comprehensive analysis of the main reforms, drawing on the evidence of some of those involved in making the decisions (including Ray MacSharry and Franz Fischler) is presented in **A. Cunha with A. Swinbank**, *An Inside View of the CAP Reform Process: Explaining the MacSharry, Agenda 2000, and Fischler Reforms* (Oxford: Oxford University Press, 2011).

The organization **Bird Life International** provided a critique of the environmental effects of the CAP after 2005, when cross compliance was introduced, setting rules for farmers who received subsidies, in *Through the Green Smokescreen: How is CAP Cross Compliance Delivering for Biodivesity?* (Birdlife International, Brussels, 2009).

Wyn Grant for many years ran an invaluable website on the CAP, which is still available in an archived version, and is now continued as a blog. Both are accessible via the Online Resource Centre to this book.

online resource centre

Visit the Online Resource Centre that accompanies this book for links to more information on agriculture and the CAP: http://oxfordtextbooks.co.uk/orc/bache4e/

Chapter 20
The Single Market

Chapter Overview

Although the European Union (EU) is much more than just a **common market**, the economic ideal of a common or single European market lies at its core. The aspiration to create a common market was fundamental in the decision in the mid-1950s to set up the European Economic Community (EEC). Thirty years later, the decision to institute a drive to achieve a single internal market by the end of 1992 was fundamental to the revival of European integration.

This chapter looks at the original decision to create a common market, the patchy record of progress from the 1960s through to the 1980s, then at the moves to complete the internal market—what became known as the single market programme—in the 1980s. It reviews the development of internal-market policy, the record of implementation beyond 1992, and it outlines recent policy developments in relation to the single market in the context of the eurozone crisis which began in 2009. Finally, it considers the academic literature on the single market, outlining the main explanations for its development and exploring some key ideological or normative perspectives on its consequences.

History

Article 9 of the Treaty of Rome (EEC) stated, 'The Community shall be based upon a **customs union**'. Also, a substantial section of the Treaty was devoted to the free movement of persons, services, and capital (now Articles 45–66 TFEU). Together, these objectives constitute the construction of a single European market (SEM). Progress in achieving them has varied over time.

The decision to create a common market reflects two of the main motivations for setting up the EEC: to avoid any return to the national protectionism that had been economically disastrous for Europe between the world wars, and to promote economic expansion by creating a large internal market for European producers that would rival the large US market. The history of the decision is recounted in Chapter 6.

It was clear that the creation of a customs union would result in an uneven distribution of benefits and losses between the member states; although the precise distribution of those benefits and losses could not be predicted in advance, there were reasonable grounds for believing that West German industry might gain more than

French industry would. That is why French negotiators were anxious to ensure that other commitments were made in the Treaty of Rome, to develop policies in areas in which their country could be expected to benefit more than West Germany, particularly agriculture. But the reason why the plunge was taken to create the EEC was that all six states expected their economies to be better off as a result of creating the internal market, even if some benefited more than others.

In 1960, the Council of Ministers took the decision to accelerate the original timetable for removing internal tariffs and quotas, and erect a common external tariff, so that the common market would be completed by 1968 instead of 1970.

All seemed to be progressing smoothly, until, in July 1965, President de Gaulle withdrew France from all participation in the work of the Council of Ministers, plunging the European Community (EC) into crisis (see Chapter 7, The 1965 Crisis). This 1965 crisis was to blame for taking much of the momentum out of the EC. However, de Gaulle did not stop the completion of the customs union, which was complete by July 1968. He did cause a delay, though, in the implementation of the rest of the Treaty. The wait turned out to be much longer than just for the retirement of de Gaulle. By the time that Pompidou became President of France, and adopted a more accommodative attitude to the EC, world economic circumstances had begun to shift away from the high growth of the 1950s and 1960s. By the time that the negotiation of the entry of Britain, Ireland, and Denmark had been completed at the start of 1972, clearing the way for a further deepening of the level of economic integration, the capitalist world was teetering on the brink of recession, and was soon to be pushed over the edge by the **Organization of Petroleum Exporting Countries (OPEC)** (see Chapter 7, Into the 1970s).

Throughout the '**stagflation**' years of the 1970s, further progress on the creation of a genuinely free internal market became almost impossible (Hodges and Wallace 1981; Hu 1981). Given the economic problems that they were experiencing, and the political problems that resulted, governments became particularly prone to short-termism, and sensitive to the protectionist impulses of domestic interest groups and public opinion. This was not a favourable environment for strengthening the internal market. Indeed, throughout the 1970s, there was a marked retreat from the common market by the member states. Unable to raise tariffs or quotas against imports from other members of the EC, governments became adept at finding different ways of reserving domestic markets for domestic producers. Non-tariff barriers (NTBs) proliferated.

These NTBs took a wide variety of forms. Some, such as state aids to industry, were against the competition clauses of the EEC Treaty, and the Commission frequently took member states to the European Court of Justice (ECJ). However, the compliance of guilty states with the rulings of the ECJ was often tardy, and only effected once an alternative system for supplying the aid had been devised. The long process of investigation by the Commission, issuing of warnings, reporting to the ECJ, and waiting for the case to make its way to the top of the Court's increasingly long agenda, then had to begin all over again.

Other NTBs were more subtle. Particularly prevalent were national specifications on the safety of products, some of which were so restrictive that only nationally produced goods could meet them without modification to their basic design. Differing regulations could prevent a single manufacturer from producing on the same production line for the whole EC market; in effect, the market was fragmented into a series of national markets again. Governments also used border customs formalities to make importing difficult, and only placed public contracts with national companies (Pelkmans and Winters 1988: 16–53).

Project 1992: Freeing the Internal Market

In the mid-1980s, the situation in the EC began to change rapidly, again in response to the changing international economic environment. In June 1984, at the Fontainebleau meeting of the European Council, two major steps were taken in breaking out of the *immobilisme* that had been afflicting the EC. First, agreement was reached on the long-running dispute over British contributions to the Community's budget; second, a committee was set up to look into the need for reform of the institutional structure and decision-making system of the EC.

At the beginning of 1985, a new Commission took office under the presidency of Jacques Delors, and in June 1985 Lord Cockfield, the British Commissioner for Trade and Industry, produced a White Paper on the freeing of the internal market from NTBs to trade in goods, services, people, and capital (European Commission 1985). This listed some 300 separate measures, later reduced to 279, covering the harmonization of technical standards, opening up **public procurement** to intra-EC competition, freeing capital movements, removing barriers to free trade in services, harmonizing rates of indirect taxation and excise duties, and removing physical frontier controls between member states (see Insight 20.1). The list was accompanied by a timetable for completion.

At the Milan European Council in June 1985, the heads of government accepted the objectives of the White Paper and the timetable for its completion by the end of 1992. It was also agreed, against the protests of the British Prime Minister, Margaret Thatcher, to set up an intergovernmental conference (IGC) to consider what reforms of the decision-making process should accompany the initiative to free the market. The outcome of this IGC was the Single European Act (SEA), which was agreed by the heads of government at the Luxembourg European Council in December 1985, and eventually came into force, after ratification by national parliaments, in July 1987. It introduced **qualified majority voting (QMV)** into the Council of Ministers, but only for measures related to the freeing of the internal market, and even here certain areas—including the harmonization of indirect taxes and the removal of physical controls at borders—were excluded at British insistence.

Beyond 1992

The deadline of the end of 1992 was the target date for the Council of Ministers to agree all the 279 measures in the White Paper. To facilitate meeting the deadline, the Commission drew up a timetable for proposals to be made and to be agreed. As a result of this, over 95 per cent of the measures mentioned in the White Paper had been

369

The White Paper provided no simple definition of what 'freeing the internal market' constituted, but it dealt with four 'freedoms':
*   the free movement of goods;
*   the free movement of services;
*   the free movement of labour;
*   the free movement of capital.

The aim of the White Paper was to remove physical barriers, fiscal barriers, and technical barriers to these four freedoms of movement.

The removal of physical barriers was dealt with by a series of proposed directives to end elaborate border checks on goods crossing from one EC member state to another, which were costly in themselves and caused long delays.

The removal of fiscal barriers was dealt with in a series of proposals to harmonize rates of VAT and excise duties.

'Technical barriers' was a portmanteau term covering a range of different things, including national standards for products, barriers to the free movement of capital, the free movement of labour, and public procurement rules.

National standards were dealt with by the adoption of the so-called 'new approach'. This was based on the principle enunciated by the ECJ in its judgment in the *Cassis de Dijon* case (Case 120/78, 1979). Ruling that the German government had acted illegally in preventing the sale of a French liqueur in Germany because its alcohol content was lower than specified in German law, the ECJ stated that any product that could legally be offered for sale in one member state should also be allowed to be offered for sale in every other member state. The only exceptions permitted to the principle were those imposed on health and safety grounds. In order to overcome this potential barrier, the Commission proposed that minimum health and safety standards for all products should be laid down by two European standards authorities, each of which is known by the initial letters of its name in French: CEN (the European Committee for Standardization), and CENELEC (the European Committee for Standardization of Electrical Products). If products met these minimum standards, they would be awarded a 'c.e.' mark, and could not legally be prevented from being put on sale in any member state.

Barriers to the free movement of capital had already started to disappear within the EC, and the White Paper simply proposed to complete this process through three directives covering cross-border securities transactions, commercial loans, and access to stock exchanges in other countries.

Barriers to the free movement of labour were to be tackled by directives covering the extension of rights of residence that already existed for workers, to citizens who were not active members of the labour force (students, retired people, the unemployed), and guaranteeing non-discrimination in access to social and welfare benefits. The Commission also undertook to prepare guidance and draft directives on the mutual recognition of professional and educational qualifications.

Public procurement referred to the purchasing policies of public authorities, which in most member states discriminated in favour of national suppliers and contractors. The aim was to open the largest contracts to competitive bidding by firms from across the EC.

agreed by the end of 1992 (Calingaert 1999: 157). This remarkable record of success, however, needs to be set against three further considerations, as follows:

- Council agreements have to be implemented; thus, agreement in the Council did not in itself mean that the single market was working. Before that stage would be reached, there were two further requirements: transposition and enforcement.
- The 5 per cent of the measures that had not been agreed included some of the most intractable and controversial in the White Paper.
- The White Paper did not cover some areas in which businesses wanted to see liberalization, because they were considered too controversial.

These difficulties post-1992 are reviewed below. It must be noted, though, that the single market programme has, overall, been a considerable success, and that the momentum has been maintained despite the problems.

Transposition and Enforcement

Once a directive has been agreed by the Council of Ministers, it has to be transposed into the national laws of the member states. This process was slower in some states than in others, which meant that there were transposition problems ongoing more than a decade after the 1992 agreement. The Commission kept a running tally of the record of member states on transposition, and published the results annually as a league table. Concern about the low level of transposition overall, and particularly in certain member states, led to agreement in 2003 on an Internal Market Strategy that set the target for every state of keeping its 'implementation deficit' below 1.5 per cent. This meant that, at any one time, no state should have failed to transpose more than 1.5 per cent of all single market directives that had been agreed at EU level. Some member states responded vigorously to the target. For example, Ireland more than halved its implementation deficit between May 2003 and January 2004 to get below 1.5 per cent. Other member states, however, responded less to the target. Although there was variation in the performance of member states, a small group of persistent offenders emerged, consisting of France, Germany, Greece, Italy, and Luxembourg. At the other end of the spectrum, Denmark, Spain, Finland, and Britain (in approximate order of merit) consistently kept within the target (European Commission 2004a).

Even when the member states have transposed internal market legislation, it still has to be enforced, and the record of national governments on this is very variable. The Commission has had to deal with a constant flow of complaints from member states about infringements of the rules by other member states, although the records of different states vary considerably. Two areas in which the record on enforcement is particularly bad are those products for which there are no harmonized EU standards, and public procurement.

Where there is no uniform EU standard for a product, internal market regulations require national authorities to accept the standards of other member states. However, companies have often found their products being subjected to a battery of national test and certification requirements, especially in France and Germany.

Similar problems of non-recognition in the absence of harmonized standards have arisen in the services field, in which there has been a marked reluctance to recognize the qualifications of individual workers, thus putting limits on the free movement of labour. Barriers have also been placed in the way of service companies operating across frontiers.

On public procurement, despite EU directives obliging public authorities to advertise tenders for large contracts, very few contracts have been awarded to non-national firms and concerns related to corruption persist.

Problem Areas

Some issues that were included in the White Paper proved particularly difficult for member states to agree on, and this is why only 95 per cent of the programme had been agreed by the end of 1992. Two that stand out are tax harmonization and company law. Arguably, agreement on both is necessary if there is to be a genuine single market in which companies can operate without regard to national boundaries. Without harmonization of taxes and a common company statute, companies that operate in several different states face a complex of regulations and paperwork. Others have argued from a broadly neofunctionalist perspective that the spillover pressures (see Chapter 1) of a single market have even more significant implications, creating a logical impetus for integration in a range of politically sensitive areas, including public services of various kinds and monetary policy (see Chapter 21).

While the areas of tax and company law were included in the White Paper but did not lead to integration, other areas were not mentioned, but some integration did take place. Two notable examples were telecommunications and energy. These were identified by businesses in the EU as two of the areas that most raised their costs of production in comparison with the United States. They were omitted from the 1992 Programme because they were sectors that had traditionally been in public ownership in the member states, and they had a public service aspect to them. However, the Corfu European Council in June 1994 recognized that the extension of the internal market to telecommunications and energy was a priority action to raise European competitiveness. The Commission then tried, and to a certain extent succeeded, to liberalize these market sectors (see Insights 20.2 and 20.3), although it was considerably more successful in the case of telecommunications than in the energy sectors, largely because energy was more highly politicized within member states and the pressure for change was not so great. With increased concern in the early twenty-first century about energy supplies and about the need to reduce carbon emissions, though, it became possible to build on the loose agreements reached earlier and a new package was agreed in late 2009.

The Services Directive

Telecommunications and energy supply are specific examples of service industries, which as a whole proved to be much more difficult to liberalize than did trade in goods. By 2005, only 20 per cent of sales of services in the EU were traded across frontiers. This slow progress led the Lisbon European Council in March 2000 to request that the Commission produce an action plan to remove barriers. Liberalizing services was part of the 'Lisbon Agenda' (see Chapter 10, The Lisbon Strategy, and Chapter 18). Following widespread consultations, in July 2002, the Commission published its *Report on the State of the Internal Market for Services*. This was followed in January 2004 by a proposed Services Directive (see Insight 20.4).

Insight 20.2 The Liberalization of Telecommunications

Telecommunications in Europe was traditionally dominated by national monopoly suppliers—the post, telegraph, and telephone (PTT) public utilities. Attempts by the Commission to involve itself in the sector prior to 1982 proved fruitless. It was a sector dominated by national policy communities, which collaborated with each other at the international level to preserve the status quo.

An opportunity was opened for the Commission by the implications of deregulation of the telecommunications market in the United States in the early 1980s. This led to pressure from the government of the United States for the EC to open its markets for telecommunications equipment. AT&T, which had been forced to open up its domestic operations, was anxious to recoup lost revenue by moving into Europe, and IBM was looking to diversify into what promised to be an increasingly profitable market (Dang-Nguyen et al. 1993: 103).

The Commission responded by commissioning a number of reports on how Europe was losing out to the United States following US deregulation. It used these to build a momentum in the same way that Delors and Cockfield used the Cecchini Report on the 'Costs of Non-Europe' (Cecchini 1988) to build up momentum for the internal market. It also mobilized producer groups that had an interest in seeing an increase in the efficiency and a decrease in the cost of telecommunication services: the Union of Industrial and Employers' Confederations of Europe (UNICE), and the Information Technology User Group (INTUG).

Another element in the strategy was that the Commission tried to ride its project on the back of the single market programme. Its discourse on telecommunications drew heavily on the 1992 Programme. Its approach assumed that a single market required a common infrastructure, of which telecommunications would be a part. Thus, the creation of a European policy for telecommunications gathered momentum by association with the 1992 Programme (Fuchs 1994: 181).

Having established the legitimacy of a European policy for the sector, in 1987 the Commission produced a Green Paper on the *Development of the Common Market for Telecommunications, Services and Equipment*. This discussion document became the basis for the development of a policy in the sector much as the White Paper on the internal market had been the basis for the 1992 Programme. It advocated deregulation and increased competition, proposals that were consistent with developments in those member states that had begun to respond to the problem at national level, of which Britain was the leader.

The Green Paper advocated the separation of regulation of the sector from operation of the system, a reform that had already been introduced in Britain, France, and Germany; and the introduction of Open Network Provision (ONP), so that rival operators could compete using a common infrastructure. A concession to the PTTs was that they would remain in control of the provision of network services.

In 1988, the year after the publication of the Green Paper, the Directorate-General for Competition issued an administrative directive on the liberalization of the terminal-equipment market. The Commission argued that it had the right to act without specific approval by the Council of Ministers because it was acting in pursuance of Article 90(3) of the Treaty of Rome (EEC) (now Article 106(3) TFEU), under which the Commission is charged to ensure that special rights conferred on national companies by their governments do not prevent the completion of the common market. Although the Council of Ministers had approved the Green Paper—which listed liberalization of the market among its objectives—France, Belgium, Germany, and Italy took the Commission to the ECJ, alleging that it had exceeded its powers by not seeking the approval of the Council for the directive. In March 1991, the Court found in favour of the Commission.

With backing from the ECJ, and assisted by strong pressure on national governments from the users of telecommunications, the Commission managed to secure the passage of a series of directives between 1992 and 2002, when a telecommunications regulatory package was agreed that came into effect in 2003. This set up a framework for national regulation. In late 2009, agreement was reached on further reform that would create EU-wide regulation of the sector.

The Services Directive ran into vocal political opposition because it proposed to apply to services the 'country-of-origin principle' that had applied to trade in goods since the *Cassis de Dijon* judgment of the ECJ in 1979 (see Chapter 16, ECJ Rulings and Policy Impact). Under the *Cassis* judgment, if a good could be sold legally in one member state, it could be sold legally in any member state. This meant that where there were no EU-level standards for a product, it had only to meet the national standards of the state in which it was produced, and could then be legally exported to any other member state. Although it had caused some protest at the time, this principle had come to be accepted for trade in goods. The application of the same principle to trade in services, though, was not readily accepted.

Insight 20.3 The Liberalization of Energy Supply

According to Matlary (1997), a similar approach to that used in the case of telecommunications was used to push forward a common energy policy. Like telecommunications, the energy sectors were dominated by national monopolists, which most commonly were publicly owned. An open market in energy was originally part of the White Paper on the single market, but the opposition of national monopoly suppliers led to it being excluded. However, the Commission returned to the issue in 1989, making proposals for a phased dismantling of national monopolies over the electricity grids and gas supply networks. The linking of energy policy to the single market programme was explicit. In April 1991, Sir Leon Brittan, the Commissioner for Competition Policy, said that there were two sectors that were vital to the internal market: telecommunications and energy.

It was unlikely that the national monopolists themselves would support liberalization moves, but the Commission was able to mobilize the support of large industrial users of energy, working through the existing institutionalized networks of UNICE and the ERT.

Negotiations in the Council of Ministers were protracted. The French government in particular was reluctant to end the monopoly of Electricité de France (EdF) over the distribution of electricity in France. It claimed that its primary concern was to protect the access of rural French domestic consumers to electricity at the same price as was available everywhere else in France. This was known as 'the public service argument'. However, it was also bowing to intense pressure from the Confédération *Générale du Travail* (CGT) trade union, which feared that liberalization would mean job losses.

Eventually, in June 1996, agreement was reached on a phased liberalization of electricity supply over six years, but it would only apply to large industrial users. The whole process of negotiation then had to be repeated to secure an agreement on liberalization of the market in gas supply, with the French government fighting as hard to protect the position of Gaz de France as it had to protect EdF. Eventually another compromise deal was reached in December 1997.

Insight 20.4 What is the Scope of the Services Directive?

The Services Directive applies to the provision of a **wide range of services**—to private individuals and businesses—barring a few specific exceptions. For example, it covers:

- **distributive trades** (including retail and wholesale of goods and services);
- the activities of most **regulated professions** (such as legal and tax advisers, architects, engineers, accountants, surveyors);
- **construction** services and **crafts**;
- **business-related services** (such as office maintenance, management consultancy, event organization, debt recovery, advertising, and recruitment services);
- **tourism** services (e.g. travel agents);
- **leisure** services (e.g. sports centres and amusement parks);
- **installation** and **maintenance** of equipment;
- **information society** services (e.g. publishing—print and web, news agencies, computer programming);
- **accommodation** and **food** services (hotels, restaurants, and caterers);
- **training** and **education** services;
- **rentals** and **leasing** services (including car rental);
- **real estate** services;
- **household support** services (e.g. cleaning, gardening, and private nannies).

The Services Directive does not apply to the following services, which are explicitly excluded:

- **financial** services;
- **electronic communications** services with respect to matters covered by other Community instruments;
- **transport** services falling into Title V of the EC Treaty;
- **healthcare** services provided by health professionals to patients to assess, maintain, or restore their state of health where those activities are reserved to a regulated health profession;
- **temporary work** agencies' services;
- **private security** services;
- **audiovisual** services;
- **gambling**;
- certain **social services** provided by the state, by providers mandated by the state, or by charities recognized as such by the state;
- services provided by **notaries** and **bailiffs** (appointed by an official act of government).

In any event, national rules and regulations relating to these excluded services have to comply with other rules of Community law, in particular with the freedom of establishment and the freedom to provide services as guaranteed in the Treaty on the Functioning of the European Union.

Source: Commission website: **http://ec.europa.eu/internal_market/services/services-dir/guides_en.htm#What_is_the_scope_of_the_Services_Directive_** (accessed March 2014); **http://ec.europa.eu**, © European Union, 1995–2014.

For services, the country-of-origin principle meant that if the company that provided a service met the legal requirements of the member state in which it was based, it could offer the service in other member states. This implied, for example, that a British building firm could build a house in Germany using British workers whose terms and conditions of employment complied with British law, even if they did not comply with German law. From the outset, this alarmed both employers and trade unions in those member states that had the highest wages and conditions of service. The concern really became focused, though, in the aftermath of the 2004 enlargement. Whereas there might be a small difference in employment standards between Britain and Germany, the differences between the established member states and the new entrants were considerable. Fierce opposition was mounted to the directive in the run-up to the 2004 European Parliament (EP) elections, especially in Germany, France, and Sweden. In France, the directive was given the name 'the Frankenstein directive', a rather poor pun on the name of the Commissioner who introduced it, Frits Bolkestein, suggesting that the directive was a monstrous creation that would destroy jobs and social consensus.

When the new Commission took office in late 2004, the Services Directive became the responsibility of the new Irish Commissioner for the Internal Market, Charlie McCreevy. He quickly indicated that he would listen to the criticisms that had been voiced, and consider amending the directive. Some such action was considered prudent because the directive had become one of the issues around which discontent had crystallized in the French debate on the EU Constitution (see Chapter 10, The Constitutional Treaty). President Chirac had called a referendum on whether to ratify the Constitution for 29 May 2005, but as polling day approached, opinion polls were showing a majority in favour of a 'no' vote. Those member states the governments of which favoured the Services Directive agreed to re-examine its provisions in an attempt to help Chirac to win his referendum. This did not mean that there were no underlying tensions: the new member states in particular were extremely keen to see the directive adopted in something like its existing form, as they expected to benefit considerably from it.

The directive was finally adopted on 12 December 2006, with a deadline for transposition into national legislation of 28 December 2009. At first reading, the EP removed the Commission's proposed country-of-origin principle. In its final form, the directive explicitly stated that its provisions did not affect national labour laws. The EP also excluded from the directive some of the most controversial services: broadcasting; postal services; audiovisual services; public transport; gambling; health care. The EP also successfully provided member states with a series of legally valid excuses for restricting activity by non-national companies, including national security, public health, and environmental protection. Notwithstanding these apparent safeguards, it is notable that recent ECJ rulings on freedom of establishment and services have, according to some commentators, challenged national social and collective labour rights (Scharpf 2010).

The Single Market and the Eurozone Crisis

The post-2009 eurozone crisis (see Chapter 11) had important repercussions for the functioning of the single market. It led to a substantial decline in intra-EU trade and, as with previous economic crises, raised concern among supporters of the single market that this downturn would prompt a significant upsurge in economic nationalism and protectionism.

It was against this crisis backdrop that Commission President Barroso asked former Commissioner Mario Monti (who was also briefly interim Italian Prime Minister during the crisis – see Chapter 11, The Unfolding Eurozone Crisis) to write a report on the future of the single market. Entitled 'A New Strategy for the Single Market' (Monti 2010), the report amounted to a plea to populations and national governments to avoid economic nationalism and adopt further specific measures to promote market integration.

Monti's report served as the basis for the two Commission communications, the Single Market Act (2011) and Single Market Act II (2012). These communications established a set of priorities for single market reforms in a range of areas where further economic benefits might be had, including energy and transport networks, intellectual property, the digital economy, and services. However, Commission calls for a renewed political commitment to the single market, both in these communications and in its 'Europe 2020' strategy (see Chapter 11, Other Developments), did not meet with the sustained engagement of member states. In the context of a general preoccupation with crisis management, progress was always likely to be slow.

Explaining the Single Market

There are four episodes in the story of the single market that have attracted attempts at explanation using theoretical perspectives: the original decision; the 1960 acceleration agreement; the successful initiative to complete the internal market by 1992; and the pattern of successes and failures in pursuit of this objective.

The Original Decision

The original commitment to create a common market is best explained using an intergovernmentalist framework. There might, though, be the possibility of constructing an explanation based on neofunctionalism (see Chapter 1), stressing spillover from the European Coal and Steel Community (ECSC) (see Chapter 6, The European Coal and Steel Community). According to neofunctionalism, the success of the ECSC ought to have led other groups of producers to put pressure on their governments to extend the common market to their products so that they too could benefit. Yet there is no evidence that any national group of producers lobbied for the extension of the ECSC. So the experience of the creation of the EEC does not lend support to the neofunctionalist concept of political spillover.

There is also little evidence of supranational actors playing a key role in the original decision. The proposal for the EEC originated with the Dutch government supported by the Belgian government, and was a revival of a scheme that they had long favoured and had implemented on a more limited scale between themselves in the form of the **Benelux economic union**. The initiative was taken by the political and administrative elites in small states, in pursuit of what they perceived as their national interest in being part of a larger economic grouping.

377

The Acceleration Agreement

Although the original decision to create a common market did not lend support to the neofunctionalist idea of spillover, the surprisingly rapid progress that was made in the 1960s towards achieving the common market did seem to do so. In particular, a decision taken by the Council of Ministers in 1960 to accelerate the original timetable for removing internal tariffs and quotas, and erecting a common external tariff, was celebrated by Leon Lindberg (1963: 167–205) as a graphic illustration of political spillover at work.

The EEC Treaty (Article 14) specified a precise timetable for the progressive reduction of internal tariffs. On the original schedule, it would have taken between eight and twelve years to get rid of all internal tariffs. This rather leisurely timetable reflected the concerns of some industrial groups about the problems of adjustment involved in ending national protection. However, once the Treaty was signed and it became obvious that the common market would become a reality, those same industrial interests responded to the changed situation facing them. Even before the Treaty came into operation on 1 January 1958, companies had begun to conclude cross-border agreements on co-operation, or to acquire franchized retail outlets for their products in other member states.

Corporate behaviour adjusted so rapidly to the prospect of the common market that companies became impatient to see the benefits of the deals concluded and of the new investments made. This led to pressure on national governments to accelerate the timetable. Remarkably, the strongest pressure came from French industrial interests, which had opposed the original scheme for a common market.

On 12 May 1960, the Council of Ministers agreed to a proposal from the Commission to accelerate progress on the removal of internal barriers to trade and the erection of a common external tariff, linked to the creation of the Common Agricultural Policy (CAP). Interest groups had only pressed for the common market to be accelerated. Progress was slow on agriculture; the negotiations had been dogged by disagreements over the level of support that ought to be given to farmers for different commodities. But the issues were clearly linked: progress on the CAP to accompany progress on the industrial common market had been part of the original deal embodied in the EEC Treaty.

In keeping the linkage between the two issues at the forefront of all of their proposals to the Council of Ministers, the Commission played a manipulative role that coincided with the view of neofunctionalism about the importance of central leadership and 'cultivated' spillover (see Chapter 1). As described by Lindberg (1963: 167–205), the progress of the EEC between 1958 and 1965 involved the Commission utilizing a favourable situation to promote integration. Governments found themselves trapped between the growing demand from national interest groups that they carry through as rapidly as possible their commitment to create a common market, and the insistence of the Commission that this could only happen if the same governments were prepared to overrule the conflicting pressures on them from other groups and reach agreement on the setting of common minimum prices for agricultural products. It should be noted, though, that this interpretation was contested from a liberal intergovernmentalist perspective (see Chapter 1) by Andrew Moravcsik (1998: 159–237).

The 1992 Programme

The decision to adopt the 1992 Programme provoked a fierce academic debate about the explanation. All voices in this debate agreed that structural factors favoured the single market. The differences concerned the role of supranational versus national actors.

The structural context was the sluggish recovery of the European economies from the post-1979 recession in comparison with the vigorous growth of the US and Japanese economies. In particular, the tide of direct foreign investment turned, so that, by the mid-1980s, there was a net flow of investment funds from western Europe to the United States. This augured badly both for the employment situation in Europe in the future, and for the ability of European industry to keep abreast of the technological developments that were revolutionizing production processes. European industrialists indicated that what would be most likely to encourage them to invest in Europe would be the creation of a genuine continental market such as that which they experienced in the United States. It was therefore in an attempt to revive investment and economic growth that governments embraced the single market programme.

While there was scholarly agreement on this part of the explanation, disagreement arose over which institutions were responsible for turning the concern with the competitiveness of the EC into a positive programme for action. From a position that was close to neofunctionalism, although missing the commitment to the key neofunctionalist concept of spillover, various analysts emphasized the role of the Commission, ECJ, and of supranational business interests. This analysis, though, was comprehensively contested by Andrew Moravcsik (1991).

According to Sandholtz and Zysman (1989: 96): 'The renewed drive for market unification can be explained only if theory takes into account the policy leadership of the Commission.' In their explanation, the Commission manipulated a conjunction of international events and domestic circumstances to push forward the process of European integration much as neofunctionalists had expected it would back in the 1960s. It was seen as providing the essential leadership to exploit the prevailing international and domestic circumstances. In one of the earliest assessments of the single market programme, Stanley Hoffmann (1989), who had been the main advocate of intergovernmentalism in the 1960s, emphasized the importance of Jacques Delors.

Before assuming office in January 1985, Delors spent much of the autumn of 1984 casting around for a 'big idea' that would provide a focus and an impetus for the incoming Commission (Grant 1994: 70). Institutional reform, monetary union, and defence co-operation were all considered, but eventually the completion of the single market was chosen. There were two main reasons for this decision. First, extensive consultations indicated that each of the other possibilities would be strongly resisted by the governments of some member states, but the opening up of the European market would command general support. Second, Delors believed that market integration would inevitably bring other important issues onto the agenda. For example, it would only be possible to pass all of the laws necessary to complete the single market if there were a reform of the decision-making process; in addition, movement towards a more integrated market would raise the question of monetary integration.

So, Delors was instrumental in giving the single market objective a high priority, and he encouraged the members of the European Round Table of Industrialists (ERT) to bring pressure to bear on governments to support the single market programme, so utilizing a **transnational network** to push forward the issue. He commissioned the Cecchini Report (Cecchini 1988) of leading European economists to put the weight of technical experts behind the project. The issue was already on the agenda, but Delors singled it out and pushed it to the top of that agenda. He acted as a policy entrepreneur, recognizing an opportunity to promote a policy that went with the grain of existing thinking, that would increase the level of integration between the member states, and that would put other integrative measures onto the agenda in its wake.

Sandholtz and Zysman (1989) also emphasized the role of supranational business interests in pushing the single market, mentioning particularly the role of the ERT. This, too, became almost accepted wisdom, with Cowles (1995) making the strongest statement of the importance of the role of the ERT (see also, for a critical perspective, van Apeldoorn 2002).

Moravcsik (1991) contested these neofunctionalist or supranational accounts. He considered two broad explanations for developments that furthered European integration: supranational institutionalism and intergovernmental institutionalism. His first category, supranational institutionalism, covered explanatory factors such as pressure from the EC institutions (primarily the EP and the ECJ), lobbying by transnational business interests, and political entrepreneurship by the Commission; it was therefore a model consistent with neofunctionalist theory. Moravcsik tested it against the empirical evidence relating to the SEA and found it wanting. He argued that the EP was largely ignored in the negotiation of the SEA; the transnational business groups came late to the single market, when the process was already well under way as a result of a consensus between governments on the need for reform; and the Commission's White Paper on the single market was 'a response to a mandate from the member states' rather than an independent initiative from a policy entrepreneur (Moravcsik 1991: 45–8).

His second category, intergovernmental institutionalism, stressed bargains between states, marked by lowest-common-denominator bargaining and the protection of sovereignty. It was an example of what Keohane (1984) had described as the 'modified structural realist' explanation of the formation and maintenance of international regimes, but it took more account of domestic politics. Indeed, in his application of the model to the SEA, Moravcsik put a good deal of emphasis on domestic politics, and he ended his article with a plea for more work on this aspect of EC bargaining.

Bulmer (1998), summarizing the insights from research conducted and published by Armstrong and Bulmer (1998), argued that both neofunctionalist and intergovernmentalist accounts oversimplified the relationship between the actors. While Moravcsik was formally correct to stress that the Cockfield White Paper was a response to a request from the heads of government, the request came from the European Council. Although the Commission is not a formal member of the European Council, it has 'insider status' at these meetings, and Delors was able to use his position at the table to press the case for the SEM.

For Bulmer, this privileged access, and the use made of it by Delors, illustrated the importance of institutional arrangements: an important aspect of the historical institutionalist approach (see Chapter 2, New Institutionalism).

The Success of the Programme

Bulmer (1998) also provided an historical institutionalist explanation for the success of the 1992 Programme. Once it was launched, the single market framework changed the context within which the EC operated. A new logic operated on governments holding the presidency; the ECJ became very important in interpreting the new commitments; and new norms were spread throughout the EC.

Once the single market programme was accepted and publicized, governments holding the presidency found themselves under pressure to record a high rate of success on both the passage of directives and the transposition of directives into national legislation. A successful presidency was now judged partly on that record.

In every one of the six case studies looked at by Armstrong and Bulmer (1998), the role of the ECJ in handing down judgments on contested interpretations of the rules was significant. Given the clear and explicit commitment of the member states to the single market programme, these judgments favoured free-market interpretations. For example:

> In air transport, the EC had played next to no regulatory role until the 1980s. The ECJ's ruling that existing bilateral regulatory arrangements were illegal, combined with the QMV introduced by the SEA, made liberalization inevitable and thus skewed things in favour of states advocating, and with expertise on, such a policy (the UK and the Netherlands).

(Bulmer 1998: 380)

Alongside the intervention of the ECJ, applying the new norms that had been incorporated into interpretation of existing EC law by the adoption of the single market programme, the above quotation makes clear that the move to QMV in the Council of Ministers on single market measures was also important to the success of liberalization in this sector.

From the perspective of historical institutionalism, the success of the single market programme can be explained by the way in which the SEA changed the formal rules, and the adoption of the single market programme changed the normative context within which those rules were operated.

Evaluating the Single Market

Not all scholarly engagement with the single market has been primarily explanatory in nature. As suggested above, both its character and its impact have been politically contested. Normative or ideological contestation of this sort is also present within the academic literature, particularly among political economists (see Table I.1).

Majone (1996) is among the advocates of the SEM. For him the single market project has allowed the EU to emerge as a regulatory centre which ensures a credible and efficient European market place. His account connects developments in Europe with more general moves towards regulatory modes of governance globally since the 1970s, particularly in the US. He understands the willingness of member states to delegate regulatory competences to the EU in terms of their desire to overcome the above-mentioned issues of regulatory competition and the strategic use of regulation (for example, to gain a competitive advantage in a particular area).

This delegation involves a transfer of policy-making responsibilities from the domain of what Majone terms a 'majoritarian' politics to 'non-majoritarian' institutions such as regulatory agencies and judiciaries. 'Majoritarian' politics is the domain of national party and parliamentary politics and interest-group lobbying, which may be suitable for making policy with 'redistributive' implications, but for Majone can have a negative impact on market efficiency. From this perspective a 'non-majoritarian' technocracy associated with the EU and particularly the Commission is best equipped to maximize market efficiency, which in turn has widespread 'welfare' benefits for Europeans. In this sense, Majone does not recognize arguments which claim that the EU suffers from a democratic deficit because it is legitimated in terms of its 'output' (see Chapter 3, Democracy).

A number of critics are less sanguine about the effects of the SEM. Indeed, they note that a regulatory governance has the capacity to undermine the 'redistributive' schemes to which Majone refers. While it is acknowledged by some such critics that processes of market integration might in the early period of integration have generated positive economic outcomes in a way that facilitated the creation of welfare states (Milward 1992), it is claimed that more recent policy has had the opposite effect. In particular, the 1992 project is regarded by many as opening the way for the EU to regulate not only the anti-competitive practices of non-state actors but increasingly the ostensibly anti-competitive activities of states themselves (Scharpf 1998). From this perspective the EU becomes a promoter of 'neoliberal' policies such as privatization and perhaps even certain forms of welfare retrenchment. The shift to new domains such as services can be regarded as a continuation of such a logic. For instance, Scharpf (2010) has highlighted the ways in which, notwithstanding the above-mentioned 'social safeguards' introduced to the Services Directive, ECJ rulings have prioritized liberalization of services over national social and collective labour rights. More generally he has suggested that the SEM has been a key factor in constituting a structural asymmetry which prioritizes economic over social and democratic priorities, or 'negative' over 'positive' integration at different governance levels within the EU (Scharpf 1998). As discussed in Chapter 21 (Explaining and Critiquing EMU), a range of critical perspectives have perceived policies associated with EMU as yet further steps in this erosion of member state autonomy and democracy (see also Chapter 3, Democracy).

However, from a broadly constructivist position (see Chapter 4), it can be argued that both these advocates and critics tend to overstate the structural imperatives associated with the SEM. In short, the single market may not be an entirely 'depoliticized' domain: its scope is contestable by a variety of agents and, indeed, it has been politically contested. This was manifest in the above-mentioned debacle over the Services Directive and in a number of ECJ decisions which have, contrary to a generally liberal market bias, protected the social prerogatives of nation states (Hay and Wincott 2012: 144). More generally, such contestation is apparent in the continued distinctiveness of welfare capitalism among EU member states, which have not undertaken wholesale neoliberal reforms (Hay and Wincott 2012).

CONCLUSION

Whether called the 'common market' or the 'single market', the concept of a geographical area free of barriers to economic and commercial activity has always been central to the process of European integration. It has also been central to attempts to theorize the process. Some of the fiercest arguments have raged over the theoretical implications of developments in this policy sector. Such debates have concerned the key explanatory factors for market integration, with intergovernmental and supranational accounts identifying and prioritizing different actors and drivers.

They have also concerned the normative status of different aspects of market integration: whether, for various reasons, they ought to be regarded as a good thing or a bad thing. Despite the apparent victory of pro-market ideas, these normative or ideological debates have been present in Europe since the ECSC and have never been entirely settled. The series of economic, social, and political crises that hit the EU after 2009 once again prompted such debate (see also Chapter 11). This was reflected in the concerns of single market advocates, including the European Commission, who cautioned against a return to national economic protectionism in Europe.

While established regulatory structures may render a reversal in single market policies difficult, significant popular dissatisfaction with the EU may, at the very least, act as a brake on further market integration in the short term. Moreover, a full or partial break-up of the euro (see Chapter 21) would have significant repercussions for the single market (Dullien 2012).

KEY POINTS

History

- The original decision to create a common market was one of the pillars on which the EEC was constructed.

- Progress towards this goal varied over time, with agreement to accelerate the timetable in the 1960s. By the 1980s, progress had stalled and was even going backwards with the proliferation of NTBs.

Project 1992: Freeing the Internal Market

- In the mid-1980s, the governments of the member states adopted proposals from the Commission for the freeing of the internal market from NTBs by 1992, and this was linked to changes in the institutional rules.

Beyond 1992

- Despite a good record on passing directives to implement the 1992 Programme, both transposition of directives into national legislation and enforcement of the new rules were uneven between member states.

- Some policy sectors that were included in the 1992 Programme proved particularly difficult on which to get agreement, especially tax harmonization and company law.

- Other policy sectors were so controversial that they were not included in the original programme at all, especially telecommunications, energy, postal services, and railways.

- The liberalization of services generally proved difficult.

Explaining the Single Market

- Liberal intergovernmentalism effectively explains the original commitment to the common market.

- Agreement to accelerate progress on the common market in the mid-1960s was interpreted by Lindberg (1963) as support for neofunctionalism because of the role of the Commission and industrial interests, but this was later contested by Moravcsik (1998).

- Academic explanations of the acceptance of the 1992 Programme in the mid-1980s agreed on the importance of the global economic environment, but disagreed on the respective role of national governments, the Commission, and supranational interests.

- Historical institutionalism provides an explanation for the continued momentum of the single market, based on the institutionalization of new rules and norms.

Evaluating the Single Market

- The creation of an ever more integrated single market has been accompanied by a normative debate among political economists, with some highlighting its positive economic and social benefits and others pointing to its negative consequences.

FURTHER READING

The great debate between theorists about the single market began with **W. Sandholtz and J. Zysman**, '1992: Recasting the European Bargain', *World Politics*, 42 (1989): 95–128; and continued with **A. Moravcsik**, 'Negotiating the Single European Act', *International Organization*, 45 (1991): 19–56. **P. Budden** responded to Moravcsik's arguments from a **pluralist** perspective in his article, 'Observations on the Single European Act and the "Relaunch of Europe": A Less "Intergovernmental" Reading of the 1985 Intergovernmental Conference', *Journal of European Public Policy*, 9 (2002): 76–97. Another contribution worth reading is that by **M.G. Cowles**, 'Setting the Agenda for a New Europe: The ERT and EC 1992', *Journal of Common Market Studies*, 33 (1995): 501–26. For a new institutionalist account, see **K. Armstrong and S. Bulmer**, *The Governance of the Single European Market* (Manchester: Manchester University Press, 1998).

On the case studies of telecommunications and energy, see **P. Humphreys and S. Padgett**, 'Globalization, the European Union, and Domestic Governance in Telecoms and Electricity', *Governance: An International Journal of Policy, Administration, and Institutions*, 19 (2006): 383–406.

 online resource centre

Visit the Online Resource Centre that accompanies this book for links to more information on the single market: http://oxfordtextbooks.co.uk/orc/bache4e/

Chapter 21

Economic and Monetary Union

Chapter Overview

Economic and monetary union (EMU) first became an official objective of the European Community (EC) in 1969, but it was not achieved until thirty years later. This chapter examines the various attempts at EMU between 1969 and 1992, the launch of the single currency, the euro, and its subsequent progress up to and including the crisis that engulfed the eurozone in the late 2000s. It then looks at some of the explanations for and critiques of EMU that have been offered by various academic commentators.

History

Economic and monetary union first came to the fore as an objective of the EC in 1969 when the Commission produced the Barre Report. In December of the same year, The Hague Summit meeting of the EC heads of government made a commitment to the achievement of EMU 'by 1980'.

To make the commitment to EMU was one thing, but to agree how to do it was another. There were two broad approaches that were represented most clearly by the positions of the French and West German governments. The French government wanted a system for the mutual support of fixed exchange rates between national currencies. It argued that this in itself would produce economic convergence (Dyson 1994: 79–80). The West German government rejected that approach because it believed that it would involve using up West Germany's considerable foreign currency reserves to support the currencies of states that were following what the Germans saw as irresponsibly lax and inflationary economic policies. For West Germany, common economic policies had to come first—and they wanted their preference for monetary stability, rather than the growth-orientated policies of France, to be the basis of the common policies. At the time, the French position was described as 'monetarist', because it advocated monetary union ahead of economic union, while the German position was described as 'economist', because it advocated economic union ahead of monetary union (Tsoukalis 1977; Dyson 1994: 79–80).

The 'Snake'

This fundamental disagreement produced the compromise proposals of the Werner Committee in November 1970 (see Chapter 7, The Hague Summit). Werner proposed that the co-ordination of economic policy and the narrowing of exchange rate fluctuations should proceed in parallel. This arrangement for approximating the exchange rates of member currencies one to another became known as the 'snake in the tunnel' because each currency could move up and down ('snake' up and down) between a minimum and maximum value against other currencies in the system, which formed a floor and a ceiling of fluctuation (the tunnel).

Although the original 'snake' collapsed following the ending of the convertibility of the dollar in August 1971, it was reconstituted in April 1972, only to run into the same problems as its predecessor. Essentially, the problem was that some of the economies of the member states were very much weaker than that of the strongest, West Germany, and the Germans were not prepared to support the value of the currencies of the weaker economies. For example, in 1972, the German Federal Bank (Bundesbank) refused to intervene in the foreign exchanges to support the pound, with the consequence that speculation forced sterling out of the system.

By 1974, economic divergence was glaringly apparent in the EC, indicating that there were definite structural weaknesses in the economies of the peripheral states, including Britain. France sat delicately balanced on the edge between centre and periphery. These strains caused the complete collapse of the original EMU experiment after 1973.

The European Monetary System (EMS)

In October 1977, the Commission President Roy Jenkins took the initiative to revive EMU (see Chapter 8). It was taken up by West German Chancellor Helmut Schmidt and French President Valéry Giscard d'Estaing.

By this time, one of the main factors that had been a barrier to German enthusiasm for the original snake had been removed. Gradually, the governments of the other member states were coming round to accepting the West German economic priority of controlling inflation. Mainly this reassessment of policy was because of the acceleration of inflation following the 1973 oil-price rises. It was obvious that the economies that were having the least success in controlling inflation were also those with the highest rates of unemployment, and the poorest record on growth.

In December 1978, the Bremen European Council created the EMS. The central element was the exchange rate mechanism (ERM) for holding fluctuations in exchange rates within narrow bands. Accounting within the system was in a notional currency called the 'ecu', the value of which was an average of the values of the member currencies (Britain remained outside of the ERM, but sterling was included in the calculation of the value of the ecu). This system limited fluctuations in the values of the participating currencies for a number of years.

Origins of EMU

Moves to strengthen and extend the EMS were part of the programme of the Delors Commission from the outset. However, the issue really came into the forefront of

> **Insight 21.1 The Delors Report**
>
> The 'Delors Report' proposed a three-stage progression to monetary union.
>
> (1) The EC currencies that remained outside the ERM of the EMS (those of Britain, Greece, Portugal, and Spain) would join, and the wider band of fluctuation would disappear.
>
> (2) Economic policy would be closely co-ordinated, the band of fluctuation of currencies within the EMS would be narrowed, and the governors of central banks would meet as a committee to prepare the ground for the institution of a European Monetary Co-operation Fund (EMCF).
>
> (3) National currencies would be irrevocably locked together, and the ecu would become a real currency in its own right, administered by the EMCF.

debate in the aftermath of the decision to free the internal market by the end of 1992.

At the end of 1985, the Luxembourg European Council agreed on the terms of the Single European Act (SEA), including a commitment to monetary union. Further progress had to wait until the June 1988 Hanover European Council, which agreed to set up a committee of central bankers and technical experts, under the chairmanship of the President of the Commission, to prepare a report on the steps that needed to be taken to strengthen monetary co-operation. The report of this committee (see Insight 21.1) was accepted by the June 1989 European Council meeting in Madrid. The momentum was sustained when the December 1989 European Council in Strasbourg agreed to set up an intergovernmental conference (IGC) to consider the institutional changes that would be necessary in order to move towards monetary union.

Monetary Union in the 1990s

The IGC on monetary union took as its negotiating text the report of the Delors Committee, which recommended that movement to monetary union should be to a timetable. This starting point still left plenty of significant details to be negotiated. Before the IGC began to meet in 1991, West Germany was reunified with East Germany in October 1990. Germany entered the negotiations as clearly the largest state as well as the largest economy in the EC, putting it in a particularly strong negotiating position. Also in 1990, Britain joined the ERM.

Early in the IGC, there was a consensus that a monetary union would only be sustainable if it were underpinned by a considerable degree of economic convergence. The Treaty on European Union (TEU) provided five convergence criteria that would have to be met by any state before it could take part in the monetary union. Prospective members would have to have:

- a budget deficit of not more than 3 per cent of gross domestic product (GDP);
- a public debt of not more than 60 per cent of GDP;
- a level of inflation no more than 1.5 percentage points above the average level achieved by the three states with the lowest levels of inflation;

- interest rates that were no more than 2 per cent above the average level of the three states with the lowest levels;
- a record of respecting the normal fluctuation margins of the ERM for two years.

These criteria reflected the policy priorities of the German government in that they were all concerned with monetary stability.

Although the criteria were stringent, the Treaty did appear to leave room for some relaxation if states were moving in the right direction on all of the relevant indicators. At the same time, it was written into the Treaty that any state that did qualify would join the monetary union when it was set up, which would be in 1997 if possible, and not later than 1999. Only Britain was initially allowed to opt out of signing up for the monetary union in advance, although following the rejection of the Maastricht Treaty in the Danish referendum in June 1992, Denmark was granted a similar opt-out clause in a Protocol to the Treaty.

Putting Maastricht into Operation (1992–2002)

On 16 September 1992, Britain was forced out of the ERM by intensive speculation against the pound. The next day, the Italian lira also had to leave the mechanism. Then, in August 1993, the system came under so much pressure that it only survived by allowing the value of each national currency to fluctuate by 15 per cent either side of its notional value within the system. This was a very large margin of fluctuation for a system that was supposed to approximate to fixed rates of exchange.

One interpretation of these developments was that the member states were not ready for a single currency if they could not hold their exchange rates. Another interpretation was that the episode showed how important it was to move to a single currency so that speculators could not push the economies of the members apart. Certainly the problems deflected neither French President François Mitterrand nor German Chancellor Helmut Kohl from their commitment to monetary union.

It was not entirely clear, though, how much support the President and the Chancellor had in their own countries. In France, high unemployment made the policy of tying the franc closely to the Deutschmark increasingly unpopular, and the country was paralyzed by strikes in the later months of 1995, as the government tried to introduce policies that would allow it to meet the convergence criteria. In Germany, public opinion polls showed growing opposition to abandoning the Deutschmark, despite a consensus among the political elite to insist that the monetary union was the only course for the country. In November 1995, a poll published in *Die Woche* indicated that 61 per cent of the German people were opposed to the single currency (*Financial Times*, 11–12 November 1995).

Public scepticism about the single currency put the German government in an even stronger position in the bargaining about the detail of the arrangements. It could always argue that unless the German public was confident in the arrangements made, there would be no German participation, and therefore no single currency. In this way, Germany won all of the main arguments.

It was agreed that the European Central Bank (ECB) (see Insight 21.2) would be located in Frankfurt; then, that the name of the new currency would not be the 'ecu', which the French preferred because it was the name of an old French coin, but the 'euro', because the German people did not have confidence in the existing ecu.

France put up a stronger fight on three other issues:

(1) the level of political control that would be exerted over the ECB;

(2) the rules that would govern budgetary policy after the start of the single currency;

(3) the identity of the first president of the ECB.

On the level of political control, the German government insisted that the ECB should be as independent as it was possible to make it. This was the only way that the German people would have confidence that the single currency would be run on a sound basis. The French government never accepted this: it wanted the ECB to be answerable to national governments.

This fundamental philosophical clash also underlay the differences between the two governments on the terms of the budgetary rules that would apply after the start of the single currency. The German government wanted the Maastricht convergence criterion for budget deficits—that budget deficits should not exceed 3 per cent of GDP—to become permanent. It also wanted a system to penalize states that overshot this target, and proposed a fine that would be automatic. The French government argued that the fine should be discretionary, and that the finance ministers should decide the issue in the light of prevailing economic circumstances. The clash between the German preference for 'rules-based' economic governance and the French preference for discretionary governance has long had an impact upon the politics of the single currency, including in the context of the post-2008 crisis (see this chapter, The Eurozone Crisis).

At the Dublin European Council in December 1996, it was agreed that states that ran a deficit in excess of 3 per cent of GDP would be fined, but the fine would be automatically waived if GDP had fallen by more than 2 per cent in the previous year. If GDP had fallen by less than 2 per cent, but by more than 0.75 per cent, the finance ministers would have discretion to decide whether a fine should be imposed. This compromise allowed everyone to claim that they had won, but the rules-based system was generally in accord with the preferences of the German government.

When a new Socialist government was elected in France in June 1997, it made clear that it was unhappy with the stability and growth pact (SGP) that had been agreed at Dublin. At the Amsterdam European Council in June 1997, it was agreed that the SGP would be supplemented by an employment pact, and this was written into the Treaty. Nevertheless, as with Dublin, the outcome at Amsterdam on monetary union has to be seen primarily as a success for the German government. The French government accepted the SGP in return for much less than the employment chapter that it had originally wanted to be written into the Treaty.

Having lost the major arguments on EMU to Germany, the French government made an issue of the identity of the first president of the ECB. In May 1998, at a special European Council meeting in Brussels that had been called to launch the single currency, the French President, Jacques Chirac, refused to accept the nomination of the Dutchman, Wim Duisenberg, as the first president of the ECB. Duisenberg had been President of the forerunner of the ECB, the European Monetary Institute, and was the first choice of the clear majority of member states, including Germany. Eventually, in order to satisfy the French President, Duisenberg reportedly agreed to step down halfway through his term of office to allow the Governor of the Banque de France, Jean-Claude Trichet, to take his place (although this was publically denied by all parties) (Kaltenthaler 2006: 94–5). Trichet would eventually replace Duisenberg in 2003.

The launch of the single currency was only slightly marred by this political controversy, and the financial markets reacted calmly to the shenanigans. The euro formally came into existence on 1 January 1999 with eleven members. Only Greece, in the end, was excluded by the convergence criteria. Britain, Denmark, and Sweden met the criteria, but excluded themselves. Britain and Denmark were allowed to do this under the terms of their 'opt-outs'. Sweden was able to claim on a technicality that it had not fulfilled the conditions because it had not been a member of the ERM for two years prior to the launch of the euro. Denmark and Greece joined a revised ERM-2 that was set up at the same time as the launch of the single currency, but which retained the wide 15 per cent fluctuation band. Britain and Sweden chose not to join ERM-2.

The ERM-2 continues to operate as, in effect, a training area for future members of the single currency, in which they are obliged to adopt good habits of economic management. The 2004 enlargement committed all of the new member states to becoming members of the single currency, but they were required to fulfil the convergence criteria before being allowed in, and had to be members of the ERM-2 for two years. Slovenia, Cyprus, Malta, Slovakia, Estonia, and Latvia have since joined the euro (see Box 21.1).

The Single Currency in Operation

The Euro Group

Because decisions on matters relating to the monetary union needed to be taken by the governments of the participating states, in 1998 an informal 'Euro Group' was set up

> ### Box 21.1 Membership of the EMS and the Single Currency
>
> | | |
> |---|---|
> | 1979 | Start of EMS. Joined by Belgium, Denmark, France, Germany, Ireland, Italy, Luxembourg, and the Netherlands (all of the then member states of the EC except Britain) |
> | 1986 | Portugal and Spain joined the EC and the EMS |
> | 1989 | Spain joined the ERM |
> | 1990 | Britain and Portugal joined the ERM |
> | 1992 | Britain and Italy forced out of the ERM |
> | 1996 | Italy re-entered the ERM and Finland joined |
> | 1998 | Greece joined EMS and the ERM |
> | 1999 | Austria, Belgium, Finland, France, Germany, Ireland, Italy, Luxembourg, the Netherlands, Portugal, and Spain formed the eurozone. Denmark and Greece joined a revised ERM-2 |
> | 2001 | Greece joined the euro |
> | 2002 | Introduction of euro notes and coins |
> | 2004 | Estonia, Lithuania, and Slovenia joined ERM-2 |
> | 2005 | Cyprus, Latvia, and Malta joined ERM-2; rules of eurozone SGP revised |
> | 2007 | Slovenia joined the euro |
> | 2008 | Cyprus and Malta joined the euro |
> | 2009 | Slovakia joined the euro |
> | 2011 | Estonia joined the euro |
> | 2014 | Latvia joined the euro |

consisting of the eurozone finance ministers, each accompanied by one economic official, together with representatives of the ECB and the Economic and Financial Committee of EU officials. It meets ten to twelve times a year, usually on the evening before the formal sessions of the Economic and Financial Affairs Council (ECOFIN) meeting of the Council of Ministers. It elects a president for two years—since 2013 the Dutch finance minister, Jeroen Dijsselbloem—and it is the presidency that issues the invitations, prepares the agenda, and afterwards circulates an informal memorandum of the most important points discussed and agreed.

A system of 'Euro summits'—regular meetings of the heads of government of eurozone member states—has emerged alongside Euro Group meetings since 2010 and was institutionalized in the Treaty on Stability Co-ordination and Governance which entered into force in 2013 (see Chapter 11).

Problems of Monetary Union

Although the single currency came into existence more smoothly than many economists predicted, it soon ran into difficulties. The external value of the euro fell steadily against the US dollar, and the eurozone itself began to exhibit some of the problems of having a single interest rate for such a diverse economic area. In particular macroeconomic imbalances became apparent, with Spain and Ireland experiencing the symptoms of repressed inflation, including rapidly rising property prices and shortages of labour, while the core economies of Germany and France were experiencing sluggish growth. A majority of states within the eurozone experienced lower rates of growth and higher unemployment than the economies of those EU member states—Britain, Denmark, and Sweden—that remained outside the single currency.

Against this background, it was perhaps unsurprising that the Danish people rejected membership of the euro in a referendum in September 2000, that the British government concluded in June 2003 that the time was not right to make an application to join, and that the Swedish people followed the Danish example in September 2003.

Redefining the Stability and Growth Pact

While Britain and Sweden were in the process of deciding that they did not want to be part of the eurozone, serious disputes broke out among the member states that were in the single currency over the application of the SGP. The pact effectively made the Maastricht convergence criteria permanent requirements for the participating states. In particular, they were expected to keep their budget deficits below 3 per cent of GDP. This proved very difficult to achieve in the context of low growth, teetering on the brink of recession. Although agreement was reached on making both Portugal and Ireland come into line when they breached the spending limits, by 2003, the states in the dock were the two giants of the eurozone: France and Germany. In November 2003, the eurozone finance ministers discussed a formal proposal from the Commission that sanctions be applied against both France and Germany unless they took steps to reduce their budget deficit for 2004 below the 3 per cent limit. Once it became obvious that there was no majority for the Commission's proposal, the Italian presidency proposed a suspension of the sanctions, and this was accepted by a majority vote. With this decision, the SGP in effect became no more than a set of guidelines on policy to national governments.

Yet, neither Germany nor France ever challenged the principle of the pact, and in an attempt to minimize the damage that their action might cause, both agreed voluntarily to try to reduce spending for 2004. This seemed to make it clear that the principle at stake was not the need for fiscal discipline, but who was in charge: national governments or the European Commission.

That principle was also the reason for the decision of the European Commission, in January 2004, to take the Council to the European Court of Justice (ECJ) under Article 230 (previously 173) of the Treaty. The decision was taken by a majority vote in a badly divided College—but the view prevailed that it was the duty of the Commission in its role as guardian of the Treaty to test the legality of the pact. In July 2004, the ECJ ruled that the Council had acted illegally in suspending the pact's mechanism for sanctioning member states, but affirmed that responsibility for making the member states observe budgetary discipline lay with the Council, not the Commission (*Financial Times*, 14 July 2004).

In March 2005, the SGP was revised to relax the conditions under which a 3 per cent deficit would not be considered 'excessive', and the timetable for correcting an excessive deficit was stretched. A member state exceeding the 3 per cent deficit could argue that it was doing so legitimately if it was trying through its excess expenditure to achieve European goals or to 'foster international solidarity', both of which are very broad objectives. Conditions for the correction of an excessive deficit were also considerably eased. These reforms to the pact were made possible by an apparent convergence in French and German interests, with the latter accepting (at least temporarily) greater flexibility and discretion in economic governance.

Euro Notes and Coins

The other main development in monetary union after 1999 was the introduction of euro notes and coins on 1 January 2002. Between 1999 and 2002, the euro officially existed as an international currency, but national currencies continued to be used for domestic purposes. The replacement of the national currencies with the euro notes and coins was a significant development because it gave physical form to the new currency for ordinary citizens of the eurozone, and made it a part of their daily lives. The creation of a single currency in physical form provided an important symbol of European integration and for some signalled an important step towards the development of a European identity (Risse 2003).

The Eurozone Crisis

The various causes of the eurozone crisis, which began in 2009, are debatable. It has been connected to the broader financial crisis of the capitalist world which began in 2008, itself the consequence of excessive risk-taking and indebtedness by banks, other financial institutions, and publics in Europe and beyond (see Insight 11.1). It has been connected to the more specific weaknesses in the governance of the single currency: the failure of states to follow rules or of European institutions to enforce them, and the weakness of the rules themselves to address macro-economic imbalances in the eurozone. More generally, it has been connected to a perceived lack of political and economic (particularly fiscal) integration in Europe, which for many is a necessary but missing counterpart to monetary integration.

A flurry of activity from EU institutions and actors in response to the crisis sought to address each of these issues. This was done through a combination of crisis management aimed at bringing short-term respite and substantive reforms aimed at establishing a more robust system of monetary and economic governance (see also Chapter 11, The Unfolding Eurozone Crisis). It also entailed—albeit to a much lesser and arguably insufficient extent—ensuring proper regulation of banks and financial institutions.

Crisis Management

The EU was largely reactive in its response to the unfolding crisis in the eurozone (see also Chapter 11, The Unfolding Eurozone Crisis). When the crisis first became manifest in Greece in 2009—following its sovereign debt downgrade and the realization that its budget deficit was far worse than it had reported—EU leaders were relatively slow to appreciate and react to the wider implications. After some procrastination, a €110 billion bailout for Greece was agreed as part of a bilateral agreement with other eurozone member states and the International Monetary Fund (IMF). But as the bond markets and credit rating agencies turned their attention to other eurozone states, and it became clear that Greece would not be a stand-alone case, the EU and IMF put together a larger financial support mechanism worth €750 billion. This had three components: the European Financial Stability Facility (EFSF), backed by member states, was authorized to raise €440 billion; the European Financial Stabilization Mechanism (EFSM), backed by the EU budget, was able to raise €60 billion; and the IMF was to provide a further €250 billion. In 2010 and 2011, support packages were put in place via these mechanisms for Ireland, Portugal, and Greece (its second 'bailout'). In each case, these packages were operationalized following negotiation with the European Commission and the IMF of domestic-reform programmes which required unanimous approval by the Euro Group and the signature of a memorandum of understanding (MoU) by the relevant state. The implementation of these programmes was to be assessed by the European Commission, IMF, and the ECB (known collectively as 'the troika'). As noted below, these financial support mechanisms were subsequently superseded by a permanent mechanism, meaning that, after 2012, support was no longer channelled from EFSF/EFSM.

In addition to these various support mechanisms, the ECB played an active role in crisis management. In particular, at the end of 2011 it injected money into Europe's struggling banks through so-called Long-Term Refinancing Operations (LTRO). This provided temporary liquidity to a banking sector in which banks were nervous even to lend to each other. The ECB intensified this interventionism in 2012 with its commitment to so-called Outright Monetary Transactions (OMTs): a pledge to purchase member states' sovereign debt if required. With this move, the ECB was able to calm markets, radically narrow bond–yield spreads within the eurozone, and ease the burden of debt refinancing on struggling member states (for a discussion of its controversial nature, see Chapter 11, Power in Crisis EU).

In addition to these acts of 'fire-fighting', the EU developed long-term reforms aimed at both solving the crisis and preventing its recurrence. Despite clear differences within the EU on both the major causes and potential solutions to the crisis (see also Chapter 11, Crisis Politics), a programme of substantive reform did emerge, which, as with the initial design of EMU, was generally in line with German preferences (see also Chapter 11, Power in Crisis EU).

As the crisis unfolded, EU leaders recognized, in December 2010, that a more permanent financial assistance mechanism than EFSF/EFSM (due to expire in 2013) would be required for dealing with crisis situations in eurozone member states. This permanent institution, the European Stability Mechanism (ESM) was agreed by treaty and established on 27 September 2012 with a lending capacity of up to €500 billion. To receive assistance from this mechanism ESM member states must—as with previous mechanisms—sign a MoU and must have ratified the 'fiscal compact'. In other words, assistance would once again come with significant conditionality, particularly in terms of so-called fiscal consolidation. In 2012 and 2013, respectively, Spain and Cyprus first received funds through this new mechanism, while Greece, Portugal, and Ireland continued to receive funds from the temporary mechanisms.

The major reforms to economic governance sought to render meaningful and substantially 'harden' the previously-flouted rules associated with the SGP. The 2011 'six-pack' of legislation was aimed at reinforcing both fiscal surveillance mechanisms and enforcement mechanisms of the SGP, while also increasing EU oversight of member states' budgetary and economic policies in order to avoid large macro-economic imbalances. Such oversight was facilitated by reforms to the economic co-ordination timetable, particularly the introduction of the so-called 'European semester' after 2011, which allowed for closer monitoring of national budgets by the Commission. The 2013 'two-pack' of legislative reforms built on the 'six-pack', reinforcing oversight with respect to eurozone member states and particularly those in receipt of financial assistance.

The 'fiscal compact' within the Treaty on Stability Co-ordination and Governance (TSCG) (on the Treaty see Chapter 11, Insight 11.2) referred to and built upon these reforms and significantly contributed to this reinforcement of economic governance. It was signed by twenty-five member states (all excluding the UK and Czech Republic) and called for balanced-budget rules to be written into national laws or constitutions. At its heart was the so-called 'golden rule' which limits structural deficits to no more than 0.5 per cent of GDP over the full economic cycle. Along with the above-mentioned legislation, the TSCG also referred to monitoring by the European Commission of national economic and budgetary policies and foresaw costly sanctions for governments that breached the SGP deficit limit of 3 per cent. This can only be blocked by a 'reversed qualified majority' in the Council: in other words, a qualified majority (see Chapter 12) is needed to reject (rather than approve) the Commission decision. The accent of these reforms was, in accord with German preferences, on greater fiscal discipline and increased powers of oversight from the EU centre. For Germany, such discipline is regarded as the quid pro quo for the collective commitment to bailout mechanisms such as the ESM, which might otherwise create a situation of so-called 'moral hazard', whereby states in receipt of financial assistance are able to continue in their profligate ways. However, a number of academics were highly critical of these disciplinary measures and, as discussed in Chapter 11 (Crisis Politics), such opposition manifested itself in various forms of political opposition to these moves.

German concerns about moral hazard are perhaps the key reason why certain other proposed collective-action initiatives were not pursued. Chief among these is the idea of 'eurobonds', which would involve collectivizing debt obligations within the eurozone. The maximalist version of this idea would entail replacing all sovereign bonds within the eurozone with a single 'eurobond', meaning that eurozone member states take collective responsibility for overall debt. The effect would be to reduce the cost of borrowing for those member states under pressure from the bond markets, although it would perhaps increase these costs in the short term for Germany. The Commission proposed moves in this direction (albeit emphasizing the need for even greater discipline as its counterpart) and France, particularly after the election of President Hollande in 2012, backed the initiative. Germany was resolutely opposed, however, because of the moral hazard concern.

In terms of regulatory reforms of the finance sector, a proposal for a European Banking Union (EBU) received strong support from the European Commission. The EBU would centrally regulate European banks and contribute in particular to the breaking of a negative feedback loop between private and sovereign debt (whereby banking debt becomes sovereign debt when the sector is bailed out by national governments). While such a proposal appeared to have the backing of most member states, the progress that had been made up to 2014 reflected a compromise deal that left many dissatisfied (Barker and Fleming 2014). And some commentators doubted whether the reforms had in fact broken the aforementioned 'feedback loop' which was so important in the context of various crises (Smaghi 2013).

More generally, the Commission proposed a number of policies aimed at closer and more co-ordinated regulation of the banking and finance sectors, including a controversial financial transactions tax. The tax did not have the backing of all member states, but as of 2014 a sub-group of member states was in discussions about implementing such a tax (under so-called 'enhanced co-operation' procedures—see Chapter 12, The Post-Lisbon Architecture of the EU). While the EU has successfully implemented certain rules aimed at clamping down on forms of speculative activity in the financial markets which were perceived to have exacerbated the crisis, many critics argued that reforms did not go nearly far enough (see, for instance, Patomaki 2013).

Explaining and Critiquing EMU

Academics have vigorously debated both why the decision to adopt a single currency was finally made, and why the particular form of monetary union was agreed. Supranationalist and intergovernmentalist explanations have both been offered in the literature, while international factors form the background to both sets of explanation. Moreover, both before and particularly during the crisis, a range of voices, emerging in particular from a critical political economy literature (see Chapter 4, Critical Political Economy), offered an important critique of EMU.

Spillover

It could be argued, as it was argued by the Commission, that pressure for monetary union came as spillover from the decision to free the internal market. Making a reality of the single market implied eliminating the fluctuations in exchange rates that were a source of interference with trade across national boundaries. However, Sandholtz (1993: 20–2) rejected the argument that there was a clear functional spillover from the single market to a single currency. The reasoning behind it was contentious:

> Among economists, there is no consensus on the desirability of monetary integration, much less on its functional necessity.

(Sandholtz 1993: 21)

However, he argued that there was clearly what others have called 'cultivated spillover'. This occurs when the Commission 'cultivates' pressure on the governments of member states to adopt further measures of integration (see Chapter 1, International Relations Theories of European Integration).

Others have emphasized the role of central bankers in designing EMU. Verdun (1999: 317), for instance, identified the central bankers as an epistemic community in this process (see Chapter 2, New Institutionalism). Central bankers were certainly involved early on, notably through their participation in the Delors Committee, which produced the report on EMU. Later, they played an active role in the drafting of the relevant articles of the Treaty. Central bankers agreed that the aim of monetary policy was to achieve price stability. Verdun (1999) argued that they tended to agree that, to achieve this, monetary policies had to be freed from political influence. They all supported a supranational regulatory agent in the form of the European System of Central Banks (ESCB). However, Kaelberer (2003) argued that there was a lack of consensus between the central bankers on how to approach monetary union, with the divisions between the French monetarist and the German economist positions apparent. Contrary to the definition of an epistemic community, there was, for Kaelberer, a clear hierarchy within the Committee because of the strong bargaining position held by the Germans. Both Verdun and Kaelberer had some sympathy with intergovernmental arguments to the extent that they viewed EMU as a political decision made by governments. Central bankers—whether or not they agreed with the concept of EMU—were 'trapped' into engaging with its implementation. That said, whether it was primarily the Delors Commission or member states that mobilized central bankers in this process is debatable.

Irrespective of whether the initial moves to EMU can be regarded in terms of functional spillover, some commentators read the subsequent crisis itself as providing the functional spillover pressures that would lead to further economic and political integration. For instance, German journalist, Gabor Steingart, interpreted the crisis as 'the birth pangs of a new country... the United States of Europe' (*The New York Times*, 22 May 2010). It is certainly too early to adjudicate on such predictions. However, at the time of writing, the direction of reform did not support them (Cohen 2012: 698), and for other commentators some kind of 'dis-integration' remained a possible consequence of the crisis (see, for instance, Webber 2013).

Intergovernmentalist Explanations

Intergovernmentalists have often argued that a government might welcome having its hands tied by commitments to the EC/EU and this argument can be applied to EMU in particular:

> monetary union would provide price stability for governments that would be unable, for domestic political reasons, to achieve it on their own.

(Sandholtz 1993: 35)

This hypothesis might explain why German preferences prevailed on the issues of the independence of the ECB and the constitutional commitment that the ECB should aim for price stability above other goals. Whatever other governments' public protestations that they found the German preferences too restrictive, in private they perhaps welcomed the opportunity to be tied into policies that they believed to be right, but did not believe that they could persuade their electorates to support. In states in which the general value of the EU was never in doubt, this technique was used without undermining the legitimacy of EU membership itself. Arguably this was due to the concept of 'output legitimation': the notion that the EU can, despite removing certain policy areas from national democratic oversight, maintain its legitimacy—and a 'permissive consensus'—as long as it delivers a set of positive outcomes, particularly economic (see Chapter 3, Democracy). In the context of the post-2008 crisis such output legitimacy was significantly undermined (see Chapter 11, Crisis Politics).

Another explanation for EMU starts from the experience that member states had of the EMS. Sandholtz (1993: 27–30) noted that the EMS was working well, but that there was growing discontent in France and elsewhere with the way in which decisions on interest rates were made by the Bundesbank in the light of conditions only in West Germany, and these were then transmitted throughout the EMS member states because of the need to keep all currencies aligned. Furthermore, Cameron (1997) identified the way in which adjustment costs within the EMS fell particularly heavily on the weak-currency states. If the exchange rate of a weak-currency country threatened to fall below the range of its parity, it was expected to take the necessary action to support its currency. Failure to maintain the parity could lead to a devaluation, which would again place adjustment costs on the weak-currency state by feeding inflationary tendencies. Relatedly, states that had higher levels of inflation would find that their exports were relatively less competitive while states with lower rates of inflation would find their exports becoming steadily more competitive. This is how West Germany came to run large surpluses with all of its main EC trading partners (although, as noted above, such imbalances were not overcome in the context of EMU). To these factors, Loedel (1998) added a further motivation for France: international monetary influence. It was with West Germany that the United States conducted such dialogue as it held with Europe on international monetary matters, while other members of the EMS had no say in such monetary diplomacy.

It is clear, though, that the asymmetries in the EMS do not explain why West Germany supported the single currency. After all, the EMS was a system that favoured German interests. Here, Sandholtz (1993: 31–4) invoked West German foreign policy aims. EMU can be seen from this perspective as a means of balancing West German policy to the east with a strengthening of its interdependence with the EC. In particular, the issue became linked to German reunification. In late 1989, Kohl produced a ten-point plan for German unification. Shortly afterwards, the EC states agreed to convene the IGC on EMU in 1990. Sandholtz suggested that this decision was precipitated by the concern of France and other neighbours of Germany that the reunified German state would lose interest in the EC, and might even become nationalist again. Such a danger became a theme of speeches given by Helmut Kohl in defence of the single currency. He repeatedly associated the single currency with European integration, and European integration with the avoidance of war in Europe. The single currency was an essential step on the way to political union, which in turn was essential to peace and stability.

In contrast, Moravcsik (1998: 381) was dismissive of the explanation based on German reunification because, he maintained, the timing was wrong. Firm commitments by France and West Germany to move decisively forward with EMU—and opposition by Britain to that goal—predated the fall of the Berlin Wall and remained unchanged after unification was completed in August 1990. He argued that there was a German economic interest in monetary integration. The steady appreciation of the Deutschmark against other currencies was reducing the competitiveness of German exports, and merging it into a wider European currency offered the opportunity to dampen down this trend. Concerns about currency appreciation intensified in the 1990s in the face of the large costs of reunification and the collapse of the ERM in 1992 (Moravcsik 1998: 392).

Kaltenthaler (2002) attempted to cut through the dichotomy between explanations of German policy that stressed geo-political factors and those that stressed economic interests by distinguishing three distinct groups of actors who influenced German policy on monetary union whenever it was proposed. The first group was a 'foreign policy coalition', consisting of the Foreign Ministry and the Chancellor's office. The second group was a 'monetary stability coalition' of state actors with responsibility for financial and monetary policy, consisting primarily of the Finance Ministry and the Bundesbank. The third group consisted of societal actors, predominantly bankers and industrialists operating through organizations such as the Federation of German Banks (BDB), the Federation of German Industry (BDI), and the German Chambers of Commerce (DIHT). There was always a tension between these actors. The foreign policy coalition had the primary aim of 'embedding Germany in western institutions' (Kaltenthaler 2002: 70), and was particularly concerned to maintain the key diplomatic relationship with France. The monetary stability coalition, as the name implies, was concerned to ensure that domestic monetary stability was maintained. Which of these coalitions had the greater success in influencing policy was largely determined by their ability to attract the support of the third group, the societal actors (Kaltenthaler 2002: 72–3).

When the French government, dissatisfied with the asymmetrical operation of the EMS, first proposed moving to full monetary union in early 1988, the immediate reaction of the West German government was cool. This reaction reflected the combined opposition of the monetary stability coalition and the societal interests, which saw the French proposal as a device to gain control of German monetary policy and move it away from its emphasis on price stability. Chancellor Kohl and Foreign Minister Genscher both supported the proposal for geo-strategic reasons, to shore up the alliance with France. The balance of power shifted, though, with the fall of the Berlin Wall and the prospect of reunification. The banking and industrial interests saw tremendous prospects for expansion into East Germany, and therefore very much favoured reunification. France, though, held a veto over reunification, because it was one of the four powers that had occupied Germany after the war (together with Britain, the United States, and the Soviet Union), and the agreement of all four was needed for reunification to proceed.

Kaltenthaler (2002: 80) disagreed with Moravcsik (1998) that reunification was unimportant in explaining the commitment to monetary union, but whereas Sandholtz (1993) emphasized the strategic thinking behind the decision—that Kohl and Genscher wanted to reassure France and the other EU member states that it was still committed to the EU—Kaltenthaler emphasized the politics behind the decision. The foreign policy coalition won the support of the societal interests when it seemed as though monetary union was the price that would have to be paid to get France to agree to reunification. However, in the IGC, the monetary stability coalition was able to dictate the terms of monetary union because, on the principle of monetary stability, it still had the backing of the societal interests.

International Pressures

Pressures for monetary union from the global system were present at several stages in the story. From at least the early 1980s on, there was continuing and growing concern about the extent to which the United States was prepared to use the still-dominant position of the dollar in the international monetary system to benefit the US domestic economy. Large fluctuations in the value of the dollar threw off course the economic and budgetary plans of the EC, and gave it a strong incentive to develop a single European currency that could displace the dollar from its position of pre-eminence in the international system, which it continued to hold more by default than because of the strength of the currency. While the euro did become an important competitor currency, it did not in its first decade displace the dollar as the major global reserve currency.

Critical voices

It is not surprising that the crisis in the eurozone—a crisis of EMU and potentially of the EU more generally (see Chapter 11)—provoked a range of critical commentary from both within and beyond academia. It should be noted, however, that a number of scholars, particularly those adopting a critical political economy perspective (see Chapter 4, Critical Political Economy), were long-standing critics of the single currency and its design. Many such scholars critically expounded on the neoliberal (see Gill 1998; Cafruny and Ryner 2007) or German **ordo-liberal** (see Berghahn and Young 2013; Bonefeld 2012) bias inherent in EMU.

For instance, in the late 1990s Gill (1998) argued from a neo-Gramscian perspective that EMU's rule-based juridical regime (part of what he termed a neoliberal 'new constitutionalism') would significantly circumscribe the possibilities and flexibility available to the governments of member state in terms of economic-policy making. Such policies were portrayed as detrimental to distinct varieties of capitalism and welfare and also national democracy. The persistent breaching of the SGP in the first decade of the single currency brought into question Gill's assertions (Parker 2008). But the moves described above, to harden economic governance during the crisis, particularly for those countries in receipt of financial assistance, might amount to the realization of Gill's thesis. The crisis certainly served to reinforce claims of a democratic deficit in the EU (see also Chapters 11 and 3).

Many commentators and academics argued, from a 'neo-Keynesian' perspective, that the official reforms, geared towards policies of austerity, would undermine aggregate demand (consumption) and therefore economic growth in the European economy, and potentially extend and prolong the crisis (see, for instance, Patomaki 2013). Such 'neo-Keynesian' views were echoed in political debate during the crisis, as described in Chapter 11 (Crisis Politics).

For many of these critics, the roots of the crisis lay, above all, in the financial sector. Any policy reforms should therefore involve radical reforms to finance at various levels of governance. However, given the important entanglements between certain national economic growth models and such sectors—and the interconnectedness of populations and these sectors (through, for instance, mortgages and pensions)—such reform seemed likely to remain elusive.

CONCLUSION

Economic and monetary union raises many of the issues that are consistent themes of this book. The debate between supranational and intergovernmental interpretations of the nature of

European integration rages as fiercely here as it does for the single market programme; and the creation of another independent **supranational institution**, the ECB, feeds the argument between the same positions about the nature of the EU and its institutions. The form of monetary union that was adopted gave rise to a chorus of critiques of EMU, that became all the louder in the context of the post-2008 crisis.

The previous history of attempts to achieve EMU clearly indicated that the attempt at the end of the 1980s would have to face up to the difficult issue of the form that the monetary union would take. French and German views on the matter had long differed. France favoured institutional arrangements that would put the ECB directly under the guidance and ultimate control of the governments of the member states. West Germany favoured an independent central bank, not because the West German government wanted to increase the degree of supranationalism inherent in the EC's institutional architecture, but because the West German post-war tradition was that the value of the currency should not be subject to political interference, but should be determined by an independent bank. The Bundesbank had always been fiercely independent of the federal government in West Germany, and the confidence of the West German people in the new currency would be vitally dependent on similar arrangements applying to the ECB.

In terms of economic governance, a divide between these two countries has also long existed. Germany favoured a strict rules-based system which would promote economic discipline (and convergence) among member states within the eurozone, while France favoured greater flexibility and discretion in national economic management. Ultimately German preferences prevailed on both the ECB and economic governance. However, persistent breaching of the SGP (including by Germany) created doubts about the effectiveness of economic governance. Such concerns intensified during the eurozone crisis.

In the context of the crisis, the German-inspired rules-based system was significantly hardened. At the same time, however, the crisis precipitated various forms of 'fire-fighting'—notably the deployment of financial assistance to struggling states and an increasingly activist and politicized ECB—which created anxiety in Germany. The conditions attached to financial support served at the same time to exacerbate the sense in heavily-affected 'debtor' member states that monetary union (and the EU more generally) had emasculated the ability of member states' governments to manage their domestic economies and thereby effectively undermined national democracy (see also Chapters 11 and 3).

For many observers, the underlying issue—long recognized but still apparently insoluble—is that monetary union does not amount to political and economic union, but might ultimately require such union (Cohen 2012). The post-2008 crisis, and assaults by the financial markets on the sovereign debt of certain member states, revealed—indeed, it may to some extent have been *caused by*—the weakness of a system which has a single centralized monetary policy but no common fiscal or transfer policy. However, radical reforms in that direction will not be easily achieved. Member states within the eurozone have very different views on what form any deeper integration should take and those outside are unlikely to want to become involved in the project in the near future (see also Chapter 11).

KEY POINTS

History

- In 1969, The Hague Summit committed the EC to achieve 'EMU by 1980'.
- There was tension over EMU between Germany and France. Germany made anti-inflationary policies the priority; France made economic growth the priority, even at the risk of higher inflation.

- This disagreement led to the compromise proposals of the Werner Committee for closer co-ordination of economic policy accompanied by tying together the exchange rates of member states within narrow margins of fluctuations (the 'snake in the tunnel').

- The snake was ultimately broken by a combination of divergence in the economic performance of the members and the US policy of allowing the dollar to devalue.

- In the period following the 1973 oil crisis, other member states began to follow Germany's lead in supporting a low-inflation policy. This removed a major barrier to greater currency co-operation.

- In October 1977, the Commission President, Roy Jenkins, called for a new attempt at EMU. This initiative was supported by German Chancellor Schmidt and French President Giscard d'Estaing.

- In December 1978, the Bremen European Council created the EMS.

Origins of EMU

- In 1988, the Hanover European Council set up the Delors Committee to report on the steps needed to strengthen monetary co-operation in the light of the single market.

- An IGC in 1991 set a timetable for completion of monetary union, which would be not later than January 1999.

- The Maastricht Treaty (1992) set stringent criteria to ensure the convergence of member state economies prior to participation in monetary union.

- Only Britain was initially allowed to opt out of signing up for the monetary union in advance. Following the rejection of the Maastricht Treaty in the Danish referendum in June 1992, Denmark was granted a similar opt-out.

Putting Maastricht into Operation (1992–2002)

- Germany won all of the main arguments over the details of the monetary union, including the name of the single currency, the criteria that would guide its operation, the location of the ECB, and the identity of its first governor.

- The euro was launched in January 1999. Only Britain, Denmark, and Sweden declined to take part, while Greece failed to meet the qualifying criteria.

- Denmark and Greece joined a revised ERM-2. Later members of the EU were required to be members of this system for two years before being allowed into the euro.

The Single Currency in Operation

- A Euro Group was set up by the members of the single currency, and it assumed considerable importance, weakening the main ECOFIN.

- Soon after it started, the euro ran into problems. Its value fell against the dollar, and the outlying economies experienced inflation at the same time as the core economies experienced recession.

- The economies that remained outside of the eurozone experienced high levels of growth. Between September 2000 and September 2003, Britain, Denmark, and Sweden all decided not to apply for entry. On the other hand, the new member states of the EU all wanted to join EMU as soon as possible.

- Euro notes and coins were introduced at the start of 2002.

- When France and Germany breached the rules of the SGP in 2002–03, they refused to accept censure from the Commission. In March 2005, the mandatory system for enforcing budgetary discipline was replaced by a more flexible set of guidelines.

The Eurozone Crisis

- The eurozone crisis began in 2009 when it was revealed that Greece had concealed the true state of its public finances and it became increasingly difficult for the Greek government to finance its debt. The crisis soon spread to other eurozone states.
- The EU responded with a series of crisis management 'fire-fighting' exercises, including a 'bailout' mechanism for struggling member states and a series of interventions by the ECB in support of both banks and governments.
- Bailouts came with tough conditions attached, which effectively imposed deflationary austerity programmes on governments in receipt of assistance.
- Germany and other northern 'creditor' member states emphasized lax rules of economic governance in explaining the crisis and their reform preferences were geared towards toughening such rules.
- France and southern 'debtor' member states emphasized the need for greater political management of EMU, and increased solidarity, particularly from Germany.
- The social, political, and economic effects of the crisis led to a sharp decline in the popular legitimacy of the EU.

Explaining and Critiquing EMU

- Supranationalist explanations have included spillover, the role of the Commission, and the role of central bankers as an epistemic community.
- Intergovernmental explanations have stressed geo-political factors and domestic economic factors.
- International factors form the background to both supranational and intergovernmental explanations.
- Critical perspectives on EMU argue that both its original design and recent 'crisis' reforms contain a neoliberal bias which privileges particular groups and is inherently anti-democratic.

FURTHER READING

The essential starting point for further reading is **D. R. Cameron**, 'Economic and Monetary Union: Underlying Imperatives and Third-Stage Dilemmas', *Journal of European Public Policy*, 4 (1997): 455–85, which examines why the member states perceived EMU to be in their national interest, and considers some of the practical problems involved in operating a single currency. **W. Sandholtz**, 'Choosing Union: Monetary Politics and Maastricht', *International Organization*, 47 (1993): 1–39, reviews the history of the decision on monetary union, and analyses it in the light of theoretical perspectives, including neofunctionalism and intergovernmentalism. Unsurprisingly, the intergovernmental viewpoint is best represented by **A. Moravcsik**, *The Choice for Europe: Social Purpose and State Power from Messina to Maastricht* (London: UCL Press, 1998), 379–471. An excellent, detailed history is provided by **K. Dyson and K. Featherstone**, *The Road to Maastricht: Negotiating Economic and Monetary Union* (Oxford: Oxford University Press, 1999). More recent books that provide valuable insights are **M. Chang**, *Monetary Integration in the European Union* (Basingstoke: Palgrave Macmillan, 2009), and **D. Marsh**, *The Euro: The Politics of the New Global Currency* (New Haven, CT, and London: Yale University Press, 2009). Books dealing specifically with the post-2008 crisis include **D. Marsh**, *Europe's Deadlock: How the Euro Crisis*

Could be Solved - and Why it Won't Happen (New Haven, CT, and London: Yale University Press, 2013), and **H. Patomaki**, *The Great Eurozone Disaster: From Crisis to Global New Deal* (London and New York: Zed Books, 2013).

 online resource centre

Visit the Online Resource Centre that accompanies this book for links to more information on economic and monetary union, including the website of the European Central Bank: http://oxfordtextbooks.co.uk/orc/bache4e/

Chapter 22

Cohesion Policy

Chapter Overview

In its narrow sense, cohesion policy can be understood as the governing principles of various funding instruments aimed at addressing social and economic inequalities in the European Union (EU). More broadly, it can be seen to have political goals connected to the development of a just society. What is today known as EU cohesion policy had its origins in EC regional policy (see Insight 22.1). Yet, despite evidence of wide disparities between Europe's regions, the Treaty of Rome made no specific commitment to the creation of a Community regional policy. It was not until 1975 that a European regional fund was created, and 1988 before a coherent supranational policy emerged. Up to this point, national governments prevented a more effective supranational approach and the regional policy process was viewed as a 'virtual paragon of intergovernmentalism' (McAleavey 1992: 3). From 1988, control of the policy fluctuated between the Commission and member governments over time, issue, and policy stages. As a result, academic study of the field has been dominated by the intergovernmental–supranational debate (see Chapter 1). This chapter traces key developments and highlights shifts in the intergovernmental–supranational nature of policy control in the sector that first gave rise to the notion of multi-level governance (MLG).

History

While the Treaty of Rome made no specific commitment to the creation of a Community regional policy, it did provide a more general objective of promoting throughout the Community 'a harmonious development of economic activities, a continuous and balanced expansion' (Article 2). The Preamble to the Treaty also made reference to 'reducing the differences between the various regions and the backwardness of the less favoured regions' (Swift 1978: 10). At this stage, it was not clear whether these disparities would be addressed through member state or Community regional policies, or a combination of both. For almost two decades, the responsibility for regional policy remained with the member states, but wide disparities between EC regions persisted.

The Creation of a European Regional Policy

Agreement to create the European Regional Development Fund (ERDF) at the Paris Summit of 1972 reflected the increased salience of the issue of regional disparities in the context of the impending enlargement to include Britain, Denmark, and Ireland. The British government in particular pushed for the fund, being in need of something tangible to persuade a reluctant public and Parliament of the benefits of European Economic Community (EEC) membership. The other influential factors in the creation for the ERDF were a push towards economic and monetary union (EMU) provided by the Werner Report of 1970, and Commission plans to control member states' aid to industries (Bache 1998: 36–7).

From the decision in principle to create the ERDF, taken in 1972, it was a difficult journey to final agreement two years later, which came only when the Irish and Italian governments threatened to boycott the Paris Summit of 1974 unless they were promised progress on the matter. The size of the initial fund—1.3 billion European units of account (EUAs)—disappointed the *demandeur* member states, but was nonetheless seen as an important breakthrough. It would provide up to half of the cost of development projects in eligible regions, with the remaining cost met from domestic sources. This principle of co-financing was to ensure domestic commitment to projects and has remained a fixture of the regional policy (and cohesion policy).

The new ERDF was distributed according to national quotas thrashed out by governments, rather than according to objective Community criteria. Each government demanded a quota, even though this meant that relatively prosperous regions in wealthier member states received funding at the expense of poorer regions elsewhere (see Table 22.1).

Governments also dominated policy implementation. In particular, they were reluctant to accept the additionality requirement that 'the Fund's assistance should not lead member states to reduce their own regional development efforts but should complement these efforts' (European Commission 1975). On this issue, the British government was particularly difficult (Wallace 1977; Bache 1998). Resistance to this rare supranational principle of regional policy continued even when the Commission

Table 22.1 ERDF National Quotas (1975)

	Percentage (%)
Belgium	1.5
Denmark	1.3
France	15.0
Germany	6.4
Ireland	6.0
Italy	40.0
Luxembourg	0.1
Netherlands	1.7
United Kingdom	28.0
Total	100.0

Note: Ireland was also to receive a further six Monetary Units of Account (MUA) taken proportionally from the other countries, with the exception of Italy.

Source: Preston (1984: 75).

became more powerful to act after 1988, and the struggle over this issue became an important barometer in the intergovernmental–supranational debate.

The additionality requirement apart, there was little supranational influence over the principles of regional policy before the 1988 reform. There were some experiments with non-quota programmes after the review of 1979, and experiments with multi-annual programmes after 1984, which proved to be important forerunners of later policies. Generally, though, national governments shaped the broad contours of the policy and managed its effects, while supranational actors had only marginal influence. Moreover, there were no significant cross-sectoral or multi-level policy networks that were important to the later development of MLG.

The Emergence of Cohesion Policy

Two important developments provided the political and economic context for the major reform of EU regional funding that came into effect on 1 January 1989: the enlargement of the Community to include Portugal and Spain in 1985; and the push towards greater economic and social cohesion given expression in the Single European Act (SEA) of 1986.

The accession of Spain and Portugal meant a considerable widening of regional disparities in the EU, leading to a doubling of the population of regions with a per capita gross domestic product (GDP) of less than 50 per cent of the Community average (European Commission 1989: 9). This in itself required an increase in regional allocations. Southern enlargement (Greece, Spain, and Portugal) was also important in prompting the introduction of a new type of regional development programme in 1985, the Integrated Mediterranean Programmes (IMPs). The IMPs experimented with principles of multi-annual programming and partnership that proved important to later reforms.

Moves to complete the internal market in the mid-1980s led to talk of a 'Golden Triangle' connecting the prosperous parts of the Community that would benefit most from the single market. In response to the concerns of the poorer regions, Article 130A of the SEA (now Article 187 TFEU) set out the need to strengthen 'economic and social cohesion' within the EC, in particular through 'reducing disparities between the various regions and the backwardness of the least-favoured regions' (European Commission 1989: 11).

The term *cohesion*, developed within the Commission as the counterpart of the moves to completing the internal market, had a dual meaning:

> It summarized a novel policy rationale to deal more effectively with the old problem of regional economic disparities, but it also held a political promise to involve subnational actors more openly in European decision-making ... subnational mobilization was crucial to its success.

(Hooghe 1996*b*: 89)

The 1988 Reform

The ERDF, the European Social Fund (ESF), and the European Agricultural Guarantee and Guidance Fund (EAGGF), referred to collectively as the 'structural funds', were central to cohesion policy. Article 130D of the SEA (now Article 161 TEC) called for a reform of these three funds through a Framework Regulation on their tasks, their effectiveness, 'and on co-ordination of their activities between themselves and with the operations of the **European Investment Bank (EIB)** and other financial instruments' (European Commission 1989: 11). The Brussels European Council of February 1988 agreed the draft Regulations in principle and also agreed to a doubling of structural fund allocations by 1993. Approximately 9 per cent of the structural fund budget would be allocated through Community Initiative (CI) programmes, for which the Commission had greatest influence over both design and implementation. The final details were agreed in three main regulations that came into effect on 1 January 1989.

The operation of the funds would be guided by four complementary principles—concentration, partnership, programming, and additionality (see Insight 22.2)—which were essentially those that the Commission had advocated throughout the development of regional policy. The share of funding received by each member state is detailed in Table 22.3.

Following the principle of *concentration*, several 'Objectives' were defined on the basis of which eligibility for funds would be determined (see Insight 22.3). Despite the creation of new Objectives with detailed criteria for eligibility, the decisions on which regions (and thus which member states) received assistance under both Objectives 1 and 2 were either taken by or heavily influenced by member states.

Programming: After more than a decade of trying, the Commission finally secured Council support for multi-annual programmes for all structural funding. This switch promised more coherence in formulating strategies for regional development and brought greater certainty to the spending process. Objective 1 regions received programme funding for five years and Objective 2 regions for three years.

Insight 22.2 Principles Guiding the Operation of the Structural Funds

- **Concentration:** of the funds on the areas of greatest need as defined by the accompanying objectives (see Insight 22.3).
- **Programming**: multi-annual programmes would be the norm for all funding, to ease the Commission's administrative burden and promote a more coherent approach.
- **Partnership**: partnerships would be established to oversee the administration of the funds and would require the formal involvement of local and regional actors for the first time.
- **Additionality**: the additionality requirement would be strengthened by a new regulation and by the greater involvement of the Commission and local and regional actors in the new partnership arrangements.

Insight 22.3 Priority Objectives of the 1988 Reform

Following the principle of concentration, structural fund expenditure was focused on five objectives, three with an explicit regional dimension (Objectives 1, 2, and 5a). The bulk of spending was focused on the most disadvantaged regions eligible under Objective 1 (approximately 65 per cent of total structural fund allocations).

- **Objective 1:** promoting the development of 'less developed regions', i.e. those with per capita GDP of less than, or close to, 75 per cent of the Community average under 'special circumstances' (ERDF, ESF, and EAGGF—Guidance Section).
- **Objective 2:** converting the regions seriously affected by industrial decline (ERDF, ESF).
- **Objective 3:** combating long-term unemployment—assisting people aged over 25, unemployed for over a year (ESF).
- **Objective 4:** assisting the occupational integration of young people, i.e. people below the age of 25 (ESF).
- **Objective 5:** (a) accelerating the adjustment of agricultural structures (EAGGF—Guidance Section); (b) promoting the development of rural areas (EAGGF—Guidance Section, ESF, ERDF).

Programming followed a three-stage process. First, after full consultation with the sub-national implementers, national governments submitted regional development plans to the Commission. Each of these identified regional problems, set out a strategy indicating priorities, and provided an estimate of required funding. Second, the Commission incorporated member states' views in Community Support Frameworks (CSFs) that prioritized spending, outlined the forms of assistance, and provided a financial plan. Third, detailed operational programmes were agreed by the partners to provide the basis on which they would implement the objectives of the CSFs. These would identify appropriate measures, beneficiaries, and costings. Beyond this, each programme was monitored and assessed to ascertain whether money had been spent appropriately (European Commission 1989).

Partnership: The principle of partnership formed part of the Commission's view of regional policy from the 1970s (McAleavey 1995: 167). However, early Commission attempts to involve sub-national authorities in the making of regional policy received a mixed response. In Britain, for example, the 1984 reform agreement on this had little impact on a government, 'reluctant to allow local authorities much say in the preparation of the non-quota programmes …' (Mawson et al. 1985: 49). The partnership principle of the 1988 reform made the consultation of appropriate local and regional authorities a formal requirement for the first time. In addition to addressing the broader goal of cohesion, it was an attempt to make regional policy more effective by engaging in policy making those actors closest to the problems and priorities of targeted regions.

In addition to the 'mainstream' structural funds allocated according to the five Objectives, approximately 9 per cent of the ERDF budget was retained for CIs. These were programmes devised by the Commission to meet outstanding regional needs. As with the non-quota and Community programmes, such as RESIDER (steel areas) and RENAVAL (shipping and shipbuilding areas), CI programmes would primarily address the needs of particular categories of regions, such as those suffering from the decline of a dominant industry.

The 1993 Reform

The funding agreements reached in 1988 ran until 1993, when a further review of the policy took place. The general thrust of the 1993 reform was towards continuity rather than radical change, with the principles and structures of the 1988 reform remaining largely intact. Yet, the political and economic context in which the 1993 reform took place was very different from that of 1988, and so, consequently, was the scope for advancing Commission preferences.

While enlargement again formed part of the context, negotiations to include Austria, Finland, and Sweden were relatively straightforward. The new members posed no major sectoral problems for the EU. In terms of regional policy, this enlargement involved three concessions: part of Austria gained Objective 1 status; a new Objective 6 status was created for sparsely populated areas; and EC competition rules were adapted to accommodate the subsidy practices of the Nordic states (Wishlade 1996: 57). However, the crucial factor in shaping the context of the 1993 reform was the signing of the Treaty on European Union (TEU) at Maastricht in December 1991.

The TEU upgraded the importance of regional policy in the context of further moves towards closer economic and political union. Yet, the period between the Maastricht European Council and the 1993 reform of the structural funds was marked by a change in the political and economic climate. In particular, 'growing unemployment and other economic difficulties within some northern member states heightened concerns about the costs and the cost-effectiveness of Community policies' (Wishlade 1996: 48).

By the time of the Edinburgh European Council in December 1992, 'agreement on the future Community budget (providing funding for the commitments entered into at Maastricht) was the most critical item requiring decision' (Bachtler and Michie 1994: 790). The compromise that was reached included an increase in the structural funds' budget to 27.4 billion European currency units (ecus) by 1999, virtually doubling the amount previously allocated. The context of monetary union was crucial in securing this increase, with the loss of national control of exchange rates increasing pressure for additional compensatory funds.

Following the budgetary envelope agreed at Edinburgh, the Commission's proposals for the 1993 reform were framed within the principles of concentration, partnership, programming, and additionality set out in the 1988 reform. The main proposals related to eligibility criteria, programming periods, and administrative arrangements.

Provisions of the 1993 Reform

The Commission's initial proposals for the 1993 reform were intended to address member states' concerns over the operation of the funds after 1988. Despite this, the member governments 'proceeded to change the substance of the Commission's proposals in several nontrivial ways to respond to concerns about the distribution of funds, efficiency, and member state control of the funds' operation' (Pollack 1995: 381). Thus, while the major principles adopted in the 1988 reform were maintained, governments secured important modifications to some of these principles.

The principle of concentration continued attempts to focus aid on the areas of greatest need. To do this, some amendments were made to the existing priority objectives (see Insight 22.4). More controversial was the designation of eligible areas. A

Insight 22.4 Priority Objectives of the 1993 Reform

Objectives 1 and 2 were not changed from 1988. Objectives 3 and 4 were merged to create a new Objective 3. This aimed at 'facilitating the integration ... of those threatened with exclusion from the labour market' (European Commission 1993: 11). The new Objective 4 was designed to give effect to new tasks laid down in the Maastricht Treaty to 'facilitate workers' adaptation to industrial changes and to changes in production systems' (European Commission 1993: 11). Objective 5a maintained its initial goal of accelerating the adjustment of agricultural structures as part of the CAP reform, but a new fund was added to assist the fisheries: the FIFG. Problems arising from the decline in fishing and fish-processing activities would also be addressed through Objectives 1, 2, and 5b. Objective 5b changed slightly from the 'development of rural areas' to the 'development and structural adjustment of rural areas' (European Commission 1993: 11). Objective 6 status was added to the list.

- **Objective 1:** promoting the development of 'less developed regions' (ERDF, ESF, and EAGGF—Guidance Section).
- **Objective 2:** converting the regions seriously affected by industrial decline (ERDF, ESF).
- **Objective 3:** combating long-term unemployment and promoting entry into the labour market (ESF).
- **Objective 4:** facilitating the adaptation of workers to industrial change (ESF).
- **Objective 5:** (*a*) accelerating the adjustment of agricultural and fisheries structures (EAGGF—Guidance Section, FIFG); (*b*) promoting rural development and structural adjustment (EAGGF—Guidance Section, ESF, ERDF).
- **Objective 6:** developing sparsely populated Nordic areas (ERDF, ESF, EAGGF—Guidance Section).

number of governments pressed for, and secured the inclusion of, regions that did not meet the objective Community criteria. More generally, governments pressed their claims for a share of the total fund allocations. In particular, the Irish government claimed to have been promised a 13.5 per cent share of allocations at the Edinburgh European Council of December 1992 in return for concessions on allocations to the new Cohesion Fund. The Irish government threatened to veto the 1993 reform agreement if this promise was not honoured, which ultimately it was (Pollack 1995: 381–2).

In addition to conflicts over redistributive matters, the Council also amended the Commission's proposed administrative arrangements. Four issues were important (Pollack 1995: 382–3):

(1) Provisions for the monitoring and assessment of structural fund operations were strengthened, largely at the insistence of the British government.

(2) Member states were given a more important role in the designation of Objective 2 and 5b regions. Here, the governments of France, Germany, and Britain were most influential.

(3) The Council made amendments to the Commission's proposed wording on additionality, adding that it should take account of 'a number of specific economic circumstances, namely privatizations, an unusual level of public structural expenditure undertaken in the previous programming period and business cycles in the national economy'. This allowed member states to reduce spending on domestic structural measures without contravening the additionality requirement.

(4) The Council insisted on the creation of a Management Committee to facilitate greater national government control over CI programmes.

The Cohesion Fund

During the negotiations over the Maastricht Treaty, the Spanish government argued for a new compensatory mechanism additional to the structural funds. Spain was worried that otherwise it would be a net contributor to the Community budget by 1993. While the Spanish government did not get a compensatory financial instrument, it did secure the support of other poorer member states—Portugal, Greece, and Ireland—in arguing for additional resources to compensate for regional disparities. Ultimately, faced with the threat of veto from the Spanish government, the Council agreed to establish a new Cohesion Fund (Morata and Munoz 1996: 215), with allocations of approximately 16 billion ecus for the period 1993–99 (European Commission 1996a: 147).

The Cohesion Fund provided broadly equal amounts for environmental improvements and transport infrastructure. It was targeted at member states with a GDP of less than 90 per cent of the Community average, not at specific regions. It would support up to 85 per cent of the costs of projects, a higher intervention rate than with any of the structural funds. As with the structural funds, the Cohesion Fund—and the interim instrument established before the Fund came into operation—was subject to indicative allocations: Greece, 16–20 per cent; Spain, 52–58 per cent; Portugal, 16–20 per cent; and Ireland, 7–10 per cent (Scott 1995: 38) (see Tables 22.2 and 22.3).

Table 22.2 Cohesion Fund Allocations 1994–99 (estimated)

	%	ECU m (1994 prices)
Spain	55	7950
Greece	18	2602
Portugal	18	2601
Ireland	9	1301
	100	14454

Source: European Commission (1996*a*: 147); **http://ec.europa.eu**, © European Union, 1995–2014.

Table 22.3 Scale of Structural Intervention (including Cohesion Fund and Community Initiatives) 1994–99 (Allocations for 1989–93 in Parentheses)

	% Share of EU aid	EU aid as % of national GDP
Austria	1.13 (0)	0.19 (0)
Belgium	1.25 (1.18)	0.18 (0.11)
Denmark	0.50 (0.59)	0.11 (0.08)
Germany	12.97 (11.46)	0.21 (0.13)
Greece	10.58 (12.51)	3.67 (2.65)
Finland	1.19 (0)	0.40 (0)
France	8.92 (9.46)	0.22 (0.14)
Ireland	4.42 (6.68)	2.82 (2.66)
Italy	12.92 (16.0)	0.42 (0.27)
Luxembourg	0.06 (0.10)	0.15 (0.17)
Netherlands	1.56 (1.11)	0.15 (0.07)
Portugal	10.53 (12.9)	3.98 (3.07)
Spain	25.30 (20.57)	1.74 (0.75)
Sweden	0.93 (0)	0.37 (0)
United Kingdom	7.75 (7.27)	0.25 (0.13)

Source: Calculated from figures in Commission (1996*a*: 144); **http://ec.europa.eu**, © European Union, 1995–2014.

Key principles guiding the structural funds did not apply to the operation of the Cohesion Fund. As Scott (1995: 39) noted: 'In the first instance, nowhere in the interim instrument or in the European Council guidelines regarding the main elements of the forthcoming Cohesion Fund Regulation is there any reference to the concept of partnership.' Instead, decisions on the projects (*not* programmes) to be funded would be made by the Commission in agreement with the 'member state' concerned. In terms of additionality, the Preamble to the Interim Regulation stipulated that member states should not 'decrease their investment efforts in the field of environmental protection and transport infrastructure', but the more tightly defined principle of additionality included in the Structural Fund Regulations did not apply.

While the relaxed requirements on additionality and partnership for the Cohesion Fund left the implementation of these principles to the discretion of member states, this had to be understood in the context of moves towards monetary union that required severe constraints on public expenditure. In this context, governments were left with considerable discretion over how Cohesion Fund allocations would be spent. In particular, insistence on additionality would have created serious tension with the objective of reducing public expenditure in the 'Cohesion Four' countries.

The 1999 Reform

Negotiations over policy reforms for the post-2000 period took place in the context of negotiations to enlarge the EU to include central and eastern European (CEE) countries, and of a majority of member states joining the single currency.

Enlargement to include up to ten CEE countries, with an average GDP per capita typically at around one-third of the existing EU average, required a change to the existing structural fund criteria. Under the Structural Fund Regulations for 1994–99, the entire territories of the CEE countries would have qualified for Objective 1 and Cohesion Fund assistance. Applying the existing funding criteria to only Poland, Hungary, the Czech Republic, and Slovakia would have increased the total cost of the funds from 27.4 billion ecus to approximately 48 billion ecus.

Somehow, the Commission's proposals for reform had to strike a balance between the demands of existing member states and the need to facilitate enlargement. The context did not favour Commission advances on the principles of regional policy. In addition to the challenges of proposed enlargement, EMU was framing a mood of uncertainty within member states, creating a political atmosphere against further integration.

Commission Proposals

In March 1998, the Commission presented its proposed regulations for governing the structural funds for the period 2000–06. The proposed reform was centred on three priorities: greater concentration; decentralized and simplified implementation; and a strengthening of efficiency and control set against a background of budgetary discipline (European Commission 1998a: 2).

The Commission proposed to maintain the four governing principles of the structural funds—partnership, concentration, additionality, and programming. The partnership principle would be reformed so that the responsibilities of each of the partners would be defined more clearly to improve implementation, and a fifth principle—'efficiency'—was proposed to reassure people that public money allocated to the structural funds was well used. These proposals were relatively modest and in some areas hinted at a further re-nationalization of the funds.

The Commission signalled its intention to take a lesser role in the day-to-day management of the funds. This meant withdrawing its officials from involvement in partnership activities below the level of programme monitoring committees. Commission officials emphasized, though, that that programme monitoring committees would take on a more strategic role than previously. In addition, the Commission proposed retaining 10 per cent of the structural funds as a 'performance reserve' for it to allocate during the programme period to those regions spending funds most effectively.

The proposed enlargement of the EU focused the Commission's efforts on concentrating the funds on a smaller proportion of the existing EU population. While existing member states accepted the need for concentration in principle, agreeing which areas would be affected by greater concentration in 1999 was difficult in practice. Moreover, the proposed Regulations suggested that, in addition to determining Objective 1 areas, the Council would have more control over the designation of Objective 2 areas.

The convergence criteria for monetary union established at Maastricht had provided a loose interpretation of the additionality requirement after the 1993 reform. While the Commission's proposal for 'negotiated additionality', if accepted, appeared to be an improvement on this, its success would depend in large part on what the Commission would be able to negotiate with member states, most of which were about to experience the first challenges of monetary union to their national budgetary policies. The Commission proposed taking a specific indicator of additionality for each objective to facilitate more effective monitoring.

Programming remained a relatively uncontroversial principle of structural funding. One proposal for improvement was to reduce the three-stage programming process to two stages, except for very large allocations.

Partnership remained at the core of Commission thinking and its proposals for 1999 strengthened the principle by increasing the emphasis on involving the social partners, environmental agencies, and other non-governmental organizations that had a role in social and economic development.

The need to reduce the number of CIs to simplify procedures and reduce duplicative structures was accepted by the Commission. While CIs were to be reduced to three in number, this would mean more resources for each remaining CI.

Provisions of the 1999 Reform

The General Affairs Council formally adopted the new Structural Fund and Cohesion Fund Regulations in June 1999, following political agreement at the Berlin European Council in March and approval by the European Parliament in May. Financial allocations to the structural funds were €195 billion over the period 2000–06, with a further €18 billion provided for the Cohesion Fund. In addition, €7.28 billion was set aside for pre-accession structural assistance to applicant states. Total funding under these measures remained at 0.46 per cent of the EU's gross national product (GNP) over the period. Allocations by member state and by Objective are outlined in Table 22.4.

The guiding principles proposed by the Commission were accepted. On *concentration*, this meant that the number of structural fund Objectives was reduced from six to

Table 22.4 Structural Funds: Breakdown by Member State for the Period 2000–06 (in €m at 1999 Prices)

Member state	Obj. 1	Transitional support for former Obj. 1 areas	Obj. 2 for former Obj. 2 and 5(b) areas	Transitional instrument (outside Obj. 1 areas)	Obj. 3	Fisheries	Total
Austria	261	0	587	102	528	4	1473
Belgium	0	625	368	65	737	34	1829
Denmark	0	0	156	27	365	197	745
Finland	913	0	459	30	403	31	1836
France	3254	551	5437	613	4540	225	14620
Germany	19229	729	2984	526	4581	107	28156
Greece	20961	0	0	0	0	0	0
Ireland[a]	1315	1773	0	0	0	0	3088
Italy	21935	187	2145	377	3744	96	28484
Luxembourg	0	0	34	6	38	0	78
Netherlands	0	123	676	119	1686	31	2635
Portugal	16124	2905	0	0	0	0	19029
Spain	37744	352	2553	98	2140	200	43087
Sweden[b]	722	0	354	52	720	60	1908
UK[a]	5805	1166	3989	706	4568	121	15635
EU15[c]	127543	8411	19733	2721	24050	1106	183564

Note: [a] Including Peace (2000–04). [b] Including the special programme for Swedish coastal zones. [c] EU totals for all fifteen member states.

Source: Inforegio Newsletter No. 65, June 1999, pp. 3–4; **http://ec.europa.eu**, © European Union, 1995–2014.

> **Insight 22.5 Priority Objectives of the 1999 Reform**
>
> • **Objective 1:** would continue to assist the least-developed regions, defined as those with a GDP per capita at 75 per cent or less of the EU average over the previous three years. Henceforth, this criterion would be strictly enforced. In addition, the new Objective 1 included the regions that previously qualified under Objective 6, which were the sparsely populated regions of Finland and Sweden.
>
> • **Objective 2:** the changes to designation here were more significant. The existing Objectives 2 and 5b were merged into the new Objective 2, which thus covered 'areas undergoing socioeconomic change in the industrial and service sectors, declining rural areas, urban areas in difficulty and depressed areas dependent on fisheries' (Wishlade 1996: 39). Also significant was that Objective 2 would be concentrated on no more than 18 per cent of the EU population, with the safety-net mechanism ensuring that no member state's Objective 2 population would be less than two-thirds of its coverage under the 1994–99 programme period.
>
> • **Objective 3:** would apply across the EU, except for Objective 1 regions, and would assist in modernizing systems of education, training, and employment.

three (see Insight 22.5). Also, as proposed by the Commission, the number of CIs was substantially reduced from the existing thirteen. The Commission had proposed retaining three Initiatives:

- Interreg (cross-border, transnational, and inter-regional co-operation);
- Leader (rural development);
- Equal (tackling discrimination in the labour market).

However, at the insistence of the European Parliament, a fourth programme was retained:

- Urban (to regenerate inner cities).

The *programming* process was retained, with the Commission adopting a more strategic role and delegating greater responsibility to domestic actors for the day-to-day implementation and monitoring of programmes. The reworded *partnership* principle required the involvement of organizations that reflected the 'need to promote equality between men and women and sustainable development through the integration of environmental protection and improvement requirements' (OJ L161, 26/6/99: 12). The principle of *additionality* was maintained, although its verification would depend on baseline figures of domestic spending that member states would play a key role in determining. Finally, in line with the principle of *efficiency*, a performance reserve was agreed by member states. However, this was limited to 4 per cent of each member state's share of funding, rather than the 10 per cent that the Commission had proposed.

The 1999 reform signalled a general acceptance that, after the 2004 enlargement, the bulk of funding would have to be redirected towards the new CEE member states. To help them to prepare for accession, a number of pre-accession instruments were put in place. The Instrument for Structural Policies Pre-Accession (ISPA) provided funding for transport and environmental projects, the Special Accession Programme for Agricultural and Rural Development (Sapard) provided assistance for agriculture and rural development, while the Poland and Hungary: Aid for Economic Restructuring programme (Phare) aimed to strengthen economic and social cohesion and administrative and institutional capacity. These three programmes would be worth €3 billion a year in the pre-accession period, and Phare alone would continue for the period 2004–06 at the rate of €1.6 billion. In this period, Bulgaria and Romania (which would join in 2007) would also be eligible for this funding. In addition, the new member states would be eligible to claim up to €21.8 billion of structural funding in the period 2004–06 (European Commission 2004*b*: xxii–xxiii).

The 2006 Reform

The context of this reform was shaped by the effects of the 2004 enlargement and by the Lisbon Agenda (see Chapter 10, The Lisbon Strategy), which accorded cohesion policy an important role.

The 2004 enlargement led to a doubling of socio-economic disparities in the EU and a decrease in the average GDP of the EU by 12.5 per cent, emphasizing the need for significant financial transfers between member states. The Lisbon Agenda prioritized growth, jobs, and competitiveness, which threatened to compromise the previous emphasis on decentralization and partnership (Andreou 2007). However, it was clear that the MLG dimension of cohesion policy was linked positively to this agenda by the Commissioner for Regional Policy:

> Cohesion policy's very specific system of governance, involving all relevant partners in the region, is as important as the financial contribution. The emphasis we have on partnership in fact allows us to do two things: First of all, it allows us to increase understanding of what the Lisbon ... agenda is all about. Secondly it ensures that all the stakeholders involved realise that there is an enormous synergy between their interest in regional development and the EU interest in competitiveness.

(Hübner 2004: 1)

The Commission set out its proposals for the structural funds for the period 2006–13 in its Third Report on Economic and Social Cohesion (European Commission 2004*b*). It argued that the three existing Objectives (1, 2, and 3) should be replaced by three new priorities:

- convergence—supporting growth and job creation in the least-developed member states and regions (Cohesion Fund; ERDF; ESF);
- regional competitiveness and employment—anticipating and promoting change (ERDF; ESF);
- European territorial co-operation—promoting the harmonious and balanced development of the Union territory (ERDF).

The *convergence* priority would cover those regions with a per capita GDP of less than 75 per cent of the Community average (previously covered by Objective 1) and would account for approximately 78 per cent of the structural fund budget. The *competitiveness* priority, effectively replacing Objectives 2 and 3, would have two strands: regional programmes to promote the attractiveness and competitiveness of industrial, urban, and rural areas; and national programmes to promote full employment, quality, productivity at work, and social inclusion. The *co-operation* priority would build on experience of Interreg, to promote co-operation on issues at cross-border, transnational, and inter-regional level. Interreg, along with the other CI programmes (Equal, Leader, and Urban) would no longer exist separately, but their strengths would be incorporated into the new mainstream programmes. For example, in relation to Urban, the Commission proposed that there be a sub-delegation of responsibilities to city authorities (European Commission 2004*b*: xxxii). Finally, the Commission proposed that the EAGGF and Financial Instrument for Fisheries Guidance (FIFG) be removed from the structural fund programmes and be incorporated into mainstream policies for agriculture and fisheries.

In terms of the long-standing principles, it suggested that while the *programming* approach had increased planning capabilities, there had also been increasing concerns over the complexity of the programming process. *Partnership* was seen as a success that was increasingly inclusive and leading to more effective policies. *Concentration* was seen to have increased, but there was still concern that resources were being spread too thinly. Finally, the Commission suggested that *additionality* had been 'largely respected' in Objective 1 regions, but that verifying it for Objective 2 and 3 programmes had proved more difficult (European Commission 2004*b*: xxii). In response, the Commission proposed a simplification of the programming approach, offered member states greater responsibility for ensuring additionality, sought to strengthen the partnership requirement, argued for increased concentration of resources on the less prosperous member states, and placed a greater emphasis on performance.

As with previous reforms, the Commission proposals signalled the beginning of a bargaining process. A number of states, led by Britain, argued that there should be an end to the financial transfers to the richest member states. This would reduce the gross contributions to the EU budget of the richer states, which would then use the savings for their own regional policy purposes: a partial re-nationalization of EU regional policy. This proposal was eventually resisted by the Commission with support from an alliance of the southern member states. However, the Commission's concession was to repackage Objectives 2 and 3 as the 'regional competitiveness and employment' objective, which was linked to the goals of the Lisbon Agenda and which gave member states more discretion on how it could be used. This concession, while giving member states responsibility over area designation, also allowed the Commission to retain its influence over cohesion policy in the new member states (Bachtler and Mendez 2007: 545).

Provisions of the Reform

The 2006 reform led to a simplification in the architecture of cohesion policy for the 2007–13 period (see Insight 22.6).

Insight 22.6 Objectives and General Rules of the 2006 Reform

The Cohesion Policy Architecture

2000–06		→	2007–13	
Objectives Community Initiatives Cohesion Fund	**Financial Instruments**	→	**Objectives**	**Financial Instruments**
Objective 1 Regions lagging behind in development terms	ERDF ESF EAGGF— Guarantee EAGGF— Guidance FIFG	→	Convergence	ERDF ESF Cohesion Fund
Cohesion Fund	Cohesion Fund			
Objective 2 Economic and social conversion zones	ERDF ESF	→	Regional competitiveness and employment	ERDF ESF
Objective 3 Training systems and employment policies	ESF			
Interreg III	ERDF	→	European territorial co-operation	ERDF
URBAN II (*)	ERDF			
EQUAL (*)	ESF			
Leader +	EAGGF— Guidance			
Rural development and restructuring of the fishing sector beyond Objective 1	EAGGF— Guarantee FIFG			
Four Objectives Four Community initiatives Cohesion Fund	**Six instruments**		**Three objectives**	**Three instruments**

(*) In 2007–13, Urban II and Equal were part of the convergence objective, as well as of the regional competitiveness and employment objective.

Source: European Commission 2007*a*: 10; **http://ec.europa.eu**, © The European Communities, 2007.

The three new objectives—convergence, regional competitiveness and employment, and European territorial co-operation—incorporated the previous Objectives 1 and 2, and also the CIs Interreg, Equal, and Urban. The Cohesion Fund became part of cohesion policy proper through being included in the convergence objective. The EAGGF and the Leader programme were replaced by the European Agricultural Fund for Rural Development (EAFRD) and the FIFG became the European Fisheries Fund (EFF). Both the EAFRD and EFF were given their own legal basis and were no longer part of cohesion policy (European Commission 2007a: 11). The overall cohesion policy budget for the 2007–13 period was €347 billion, 81.5 per cent of which would be spent in the 'convergence' regions.

The key principles again remained intact, with some amendments. A new corrective mechanism was introduced for instances in which the additionality principle might not be respected, and the principle of partnership was widened to say that 'any appropriate organization' can participate in negotiations relating to the use of the structural funds (see Table 22.5). The principle of *proportionality* was introduced to modulate the obligations attributed to member states contingent on the total amount of expenditure of an operational programme (European Commission 2007a: 27).

A new strategic approach was adopted that introduced the national strategic reference framework (NSRF) as a new programming instrument that would provide a single overall vision of strategy at the level of each member state. This would be prepared by national governments in consultation with domestic partners and in dialogue with the Commission. The CSFs relating to Objective 1 and the single programming documents related to Objectives 2 and 3 would be cancelled so that operational programmes would be the only programming and management tool. These would be more strategic than in the past, with priorities rather than actions being detailed, thus giving member states greater autonomy over the details of implementation (European Commission 2007a: 33). This rationalization of the programming process was a response to the demands of member states, particularly those receiving relatively small amounts of structural funding, the complaints of which about bureaucracy had led to tension with the Commission in the 2000–06 period (Bachtler and Mendez 2007: 554).

Outside of the framework of cohesion policy, a new Instrument for Pre-Accession (IPA) was introduced in January 2007. IPA brought together all of the existing pre-accession instruments (including ISPA, Phare, and Sapard) into a single framework. This new instrument covered the candidate states (Croatia, the Former Yugoslav Republic of Macedonia, and Turkey) and the potential candidate states (Albania, Bosnia and Herzegovina, Montenegro, and Serbia—including Kosovo). IPA has five components; (1) transition assistance and institution building; (2) cross-border co-operation; (3) regional development; (4) human resources development; and (5) rural development (European Commission 2007c: 1). The latter three components are precursors to structural funding and involve preparing candidate countries for developing the necessary institutional capacity to be able to manage them effectively post-accession. This was seen as a weakness of the previous pre-accession instruments. Under IPA, the relevant components ((3) and (4)) would thus be administered along the same lines as the structural funds, with programming activities involving the relevant stakeholders.

Table 22.5 Indicative Allocation by Member State, 2007–13 (2007 Prices, in €m)

	Convergence			Regional competitiveness and employment		European territorial co-operation	Total
	Cohesion Fund	Convergence	Phasing-out	Phasing-in	Regional competitiveness and employment		
Austria			177		1027	257	1461
Belgium			638		1425	194	2258
Bulgaria	2283	4391				179	6853
Cyprus	213			399		28	640
Czech Republic	8819	17064			419	389	26692
Denmark					510	103	613
Estonia	1152	2252				52	3456
Finland				545	1051	120	1716
France		3191			10257	872	14319
Germany		11864	4215		9409	851	26340
Greece	3697	9420	6458	635		210	20420
Hungary	8642	14248		2031		386	25307
Ireland				458	293	151	901
Italy		21211	430	972	5353	846	28812
Latvia	1540	2991				90	4620
Lithuania	2305	4470				109	6885

Table 22.5 *(continued)*

	Convergence			Regional competitiveness and employment		European territorial co-operation	Total
	Cohesion Fund	Convergence	Phasing-out	Phasing-in	Regional competitiveness and employment		
Luxembourg					50	15	65
Malta	284	556				15	855
Netherlands					1660	247	1907
Poland	22176	44377				731	67284
Portugal	3060	17133	280	448	490	99	21511
Romania	6552	12661				455	19668
Slovakia	3899	7013			449	227	11588
Slovenia	1412	2689				104	4205
Spain	3543	21054	1583	4955	3522	559	35217
Sweden					1626	265	1891
United Kingdom		2738	174	965	6014	722	10613
Inter-regional/Network co-operation						455	455
Technical Assistance							868
Total	**69578**	**199322**	**13955**	**11409**	**43556**	**8723**	**347410**

Source: European Commission (2007a: 25); **http://ec.europa.eu**, © European Union, 1995–2014.

The 2013 Reform

The reform of cohesion policy that came into effect in January 2014 took place in the context of economic crisis. In this context, the Commission had instigated hearings on the future of cohesion policy, led by the economist Fabrizio Barca, of the Italian Ministry of Economy and Finance. The resulting 'Barca Report' criticized a number of aspects of cohesion policy and called for a 'comprehensive reform', including changes to governance and a greater concentration of priorities and for 'greater coherence with the place-based or territorial concept' (Barca 2009: viii). It argued for a clearer distinction between policies aimed at efficiency objectives (increasing income and growth) and those aimed at social inclusion, and suggested that concentrating on fewer priorities would 'attract political and public attention to the measures implemented and enable the Commission better to focus its human resources and play a more strategic role' (Barca 2009: viii).

The Commission's proposal for the post-2014 period subsequently aimed to revive some core purposes of cohesion policy along the lines suggested by Barca, including a stronger contractual relationship between the Commission and member states through partnership contracts; an increased focus on core priorities, including a 'territorialized' social agenda and more rigorous programming and evaluation; and the institutionalization of high-level reporting on policy effectiveness to the Council and Parliament (Mendez 2013: 646). However, the proposals fell short of the coherent place-based approach Barca called for as they tied cohesion policy more closely to the goals of the Europe 2020 Strategy (see Chapter 11, Other Developments), which succeeded the Lisbon Agenda. The proposals did, though, suggest that there would be more EU-wide accountability in exchange for greater member-state control over implementation.

The Multi-annual Financial Framework agreed by the European Council in February 2014 (see Chapter 11, Other Developments) identified two broad goals for cohesion policy: 'investment for jobs and growth', to be supported by all funds; and 'European territorial cooperation', to be funded by ERDF specifically. Overall funding for cohesion policy for the financial period 2014–20 would not exceed €325.1 billion, which represented an overall cut from the previous period. Of this funding, 'investment for growth of jobs' would take the lion's share (see Box 22.1).

Box 22.1 Cohesion Policy Funding 2014–20

Total of upto €325.1 billion:

- 'Investment for growth and jobs': €313.2 billion—€164.3 billion for less developed regions; €31.7 billion for transition regions; €49.5 billion for more developed regions; €66.4 billion for member states supported by the Cohesion Fund

- 'European territorial co-operation': €8.9 billion

- 'Top-up for youth employment initiative': €3.0 billion

Explaining Cohesion Policy

Two of the theoretical debates that have been identified in this book as central to the development of the study of the EU have been particularly relevant in this policy sector: first, the intergovernmental–supranational debate about the nature of the EU (see Chapter 1) and, second, the debate about whether European integration has produced MLG (see Chapter 2, Multi-Level Governance).

The Intergovernmentalist–Supranationalist Debate

There is academic consensus that the major decisions on the creation of regional policy were taken by the heads of government, in particular at the summits in Paris in 1972 and 1974 and in Copenhagen in 1973. The Commission's influence over initial allocations and policy guidelines was at first limited, although the Commission was important in keeping the issue of regional policy alive in the difficult circumstances of the 1960s and early 1970s. Yet, while the eventual establishment of the ERDF in 1975 owed a great deal to the Commission's persistence, intergovernmental politics ensured that it fell some way short of the redistributive policy instrument that the Commission sought.

While some member states sought to limit the increase in the fund allocations in the 1988 reform, the doubling of allocations owed much to the commitment of larger member states to the single market programme. Although the funds did continue to benefit regions in the more prosperous member states, the main impact of the doubling of the funds was to transfer resources from Belgium, Denmark, Germany, France, and the Netherlands to Greece, Spain, Ireland, Italy, and Portugal, with the impact on Britain largely neutral (Marks 1992: 194).

Pollack (1995) argued that agreement to major reform in 1988 could be explained by changes in the preferences of the various member states—in particular net contributors such as Britain, France, and Germany—and as a result of the accession of Greece, Spain, and Portugal. The preferences of the net contributors changed in three ways. First, with the Iberian enlargement, the proportion of structural funds received by the 'big three' member states decreased significantly. This meant that, for these governments, 'the idea of greater Commission oversight seemed less like an intrusion into the internal affairs of one's own state, where EC spending was minimal, and more like a necessary oversight of the poor member states where the bulk of EC money was being spent' (Pollack 1995: 372). Second, the Iberian enlargement made France, like Britain and Germany, a net contributor to the EC budget, thus giving the 'big three' governments a common interest in the efficient use of the structural funds. Third, the spiralling costs of both the Common Agricultural Policy (CAP) and the structural funds made the level and efficiency of EC spending a 'political issue' of increasing concern to the governments of France, Germany, and Britain in the 1980s (Pollack 1995: 372).

In terms of the budgetary envelope agreed in 1988, an intergovernmentalist interpretation found favour among most commentators. The more prosperous member states strongly supported the completion of the single market and wanted this market extended to include Spain and Portugal. In this context, the doubling of the structural funds was accepted by the likely paymaster governments as a 'side-payment to Ireland

and the Southern nations' in exchange for their political support on other issues (Moravcsik 1991: 62). Although not contesting this fundamental argument, Marks (1992: 198) conceptualized the side-payment argument as an illustration of *forced spillover*, 'in which the prospect of a breakthrough in one arena created intense pressure for innovation in others', thereby linking it to neofunctionalist analysis, and giving it a more supranationalist spin.

Consensus between scholars over other aspects of the 1988 reform is harder to find. For example, Hooghe (1996*b*: 100) argued that the Commission emerged 'as the pivotal actor in designing the regulations' through its 'monopoly of initiative'. An example was the inclusion of the partnership principle in the regulations, which was the major innovation of the 1988 reform. In contrast, Pollack (1995) suggested that this shift was a response to pressure from national governments to secure 'value for money' in the funds' administration.

While the context of the 1988 reform gave the Commission considerable scope for advancing its policy preferences, the 1993 reform represented a reassertion of control by the member governments in key areas. A good example was additionality. The tenacity with which the Commission had sought the implementation of additionality after 1988 was met by governments effectively diluting the requirement in 1993. Indeed, given the convergence criteria for monetary union agreed at Maastricht, for the Commission to pursue genuine additionality at this time would have been difficult: while additionality required member states to demonstrate additional public expenditure, the Maastricht convergence criteria limited domestic public spending.

Other changes in 1993 also reflected the reassertion of government preferences. While the partnership principle was confirmed, governments remained in control of the designation of 'appropriate partners'. The creation of a Management Committee to oversee CIs curtailed Commission discretion. In a high-profile conflict over the implementation of additionality after 1988, the Commission had used its control over the content, coverage, and timing of CIs to undermine the British government's arguments in defence of its approach to implementation (Bache 1999). The 1993 changes meant that this would be more difficult for the Commission to do in future.

In summary, the 1993 reform provided a measure of how the relative influence of actors fluctuated over a short period of time. The context had changed dramatically in the five years after the 1988 reform, leading to a shift in the balance of political resources away from the Commission towards the Council, which was reflected in the 1993 outcome.

As previously, the budgetary envelope for the 1999 reform of the structural funds was decided at Council level. In addition to limiting total allocations, member states secured safety-net mechanisms and transitional arrangements to protect their assisted regions from a sudden and dramatic reduction of funding. Moreover, the reduction of the proposed performance reserve from 10 per cent to 4 per cent was accompanied by provisions for member states' involvement with the Commission in determining the allocation of this reserve to regions that were performing well.

While the partnership principle was maintained, and its requirements made more precise, the selection of partners remained with governments. The additionality principle was also retained, but the new regulations did not suggest that member states' compliance would be any easier for the Commission to ensure. The reduction in the number of CIs, and of financial allocations to them, limited the Commission's scope for autonomy and innovation somewhat, although in its proposals the Commission had acknowledged the need for such a reduction. Institutional politics aside, CIs had been subject to criticism from a broad range of actors who deemed some programmes to be unnecessarily bureaucratic.

If the 1999 reform was not simply a re-nationalization of the structural funds, a number of changes from the Commission's initial proposals reflected the preferences of governments. Perhaps more significantly, in the context of proposed enlargement, the Commission's initial proposals were themselves relatively modest. Yet the Commission retained a key role in the process: for example, over issues of eligibility, programming, allocating the performance reserve, and in the design and implementation of CIs. Moreover, the key principles guiding the operation of the funds essentially remained those developed by the Commission.

In relation to the 2006 reform, Andreou (2007: 26) suggested that 'the compromise achieved by member states…bears much more resemblance to the financially restrictive approach of the net payers, than to the original Commission proposal supported by the less prosperous member states'. Bruszt (2008: 616) argued that:

> the new EU regulations for the 2007–13 planning period did not alter the 'renationalizing' tendencies of the SF [Structural Funds] policies significantly. For the time being, the Commission does not seem to be interested in re-kindling its pro-regional activism of the 1990s.

Instead, the priority was on ensuring the effective absorption of the funds, which often meant the development of central capacity.

Yet, while aiming to promote effectiveness, the 'Lisbonization' process was also seen to promote goal congestion and policy confusion (Begg 2010). In this light, a sub-text of the 2013 reform was the re-legitimization of cohesion policy, leading to the most fundamental review since 1988 (Mendez 2013).

While the intergovernmental-supranational debate has led theorizing on cohesion policy negotiations, it is important not to see these negotiations purely in terms of the Commission versus the member states: while negotiations on some issues have been adversarial, on others there has been more collaboration and consensus (Bachtler and Mendez 2007: 551). Related to this point, power relations between the Commission and member states should not necessarily be conceived in zero-sum terms, in which for one party to gain the other must lose. Instead, there is evidence of positive-sum outcomes, in which both parties achieve more of their goals. Moreover, Bachtler and Mendez (2007) suggested that claims over the re-nationalization of cohesion policy, while valid in some respects, were less convincing when applied to the development of the principles of concentration and programming, where the Commission's influence has been greater than acknowledged in much of the literature.

Multi-Level Governance

Much of the conceptual debate around cohesion policy has focused on the domestic effects of implementation and in particular the implementation of the partnership principle, which has been at the forefront of research on MLG (see Chapter 2, Multi-Level Governance).

Hooghe (1996*a*) co-ordinated an early cross-national study on the effects of the 1988 reform principles on 'territorial restructuring' within eight member states. The study found that the implementation of the partnership principle varied considerably across member states. Actors at different levels—national, sub-national, and supranational—controlled different resources in different member states, influencing their ability to shape policy implementation within the framework set by EU-level agreements. In centralized member states, where central government actively sought to play a gatekeeper role over the political impact of the new arrangements, such as in Britain, it met with considerable success. Here, sub-national actors were mobilized, but not necessarily empowered. In more decentralized member states, sub-national authorities—normally regional governments—were better placed to take advantage of the opportunities provided by the partnership requirement. Later research (Kelleher et al. 1999) confirmed this pattern of differentiated MLG emerging through EU cohesion policy.

As funding shifted towards CEE states, so did much of the academic research. Moreover, while research continues to discuss features of MLG, it often does so within the framework of Europeanization (see Chapter 4). The role of the Commission in advancing MLG has been brought under particular scrutiny in this literature.

While the Commission initially sought to advance regionalization in CEE states, inspired by ideals of MLG, as accession grew closer, its position shifted to ensuring that the funds were absorbed on time, even if this meant that they were managed centrally through national ministries (Leonardi 2005: 164; Marcou 2002: 25). A study of the Czech Republic, Estonia, Hungary, Poland, and Slovenia identified national government 'gatekeepers' as generally 'firmly in control' of sub-national actors, who were able to participate in, but not significantly influence, the policy process (Bailey and De Propris 2002). Research on Estonia, Hungary, Poland, and Slovenia emphasized the importance of institutional traditions in each state in shaping the degree of regionalization emerging (Hughes et al. 2004, 2005), echoing the findings of earlier research on the EU15 (Hooghe 1996*a*).

Two studies provided a mixed picture of the impact of cohesion policy on regionalization in the CEE states. Bachtler and McMaster (2008: 420–1) identified 'several points to support the contention that the role of regions has increased in terms of their legitimacy, institutional capacity and stability', but also suggested that 'the limitations and barriers to regional participation in the funds currently outweighs the opportunities'. Their bottom line was to challenge the idea that structural funds necessarily lead to stronger regions. Bruszt (2008) explained how the Commission's turn to (re)centralization for administering funds in the pre-accession period was resisted in some states, and thus features of MLG emerged. Here, the governance changes were explained in historical institutionalist terms as 'layering': 'the emergence of change on the margins, implying local rule transformation within a basically unchanged institution that does not challenge the dominant characteristics of the mode of governance' (Bruszt 2008: 620).

The study by Bache (2008) of the EU25 considered the impact of cohesion policy on Type I and Type II MLG (see Chapter 2, Multi-Level Governance). It identified a trend towards MLG across Europe, although this remained uneven. Moreover, the study indicated that while this trend was generally not due to states' engagement with the EU, it was not possible to understand the nature and pace of the changes taking place without reference to the EU and its cohesion policy. However, the effects of EU cohesion policy seemed more pronounced on Type II MLG than on Type I, with ad hoc functionally specific governance arrangements emerging at various territorial levels as a direct response. For the most part, this Europeanization effect was driven by rational responses to EU financial incentives, although there was also evidence that deeper learning could take place in the longer term, characterized by the voluntary adoption of EU practices in the domestic sphere.

More recently, research has begun on the impact of cohesion policy and the related pre-accession instruments—and particularly the relevant components of IPA—on governance in the candidate states of south-east Europe. Here, the prospects for EU-induced cohesion policy are enhanced by the increased alignment of pre-accession funding with structural fund requirements, but are reduced by the problems of limited governance capacities at both national and sub-national levels, leading to the Commission again emphasizing centralized implementation of funding, at least in the first phase (Bache 2010).

CONCLUSION

Judgements of the economic impact of EU cohesion policy often cast doubt on its effectiveness in addressing disparities between territories and social groups. However, it is arguably the political impact of the funds that has been of most significance. While the degree to which cohesion policy has reshaped governance and politics in recipient states should not be overstated, there has been increasing participation and dialogue between actors located in different sectors and at different territorial levels.

Yet, the legitimacy of the policy has been placed under increasing scrutiny and has led to calls for fundamental changes. The Barca Report made the case for a territorialized social agenda as part of cohesion policy and, more radically, the Committee of the Regions (2011) proposed that more weight should be given to social and environmental indicators in the allocation of funds. In a similar vein, others have argued for a more rounded concept of cohesion, supported by a wider set of indicators of success that might demonstrate a broader range of ways in which cohesion policy 'works' (Bache 2014): in short, a new direction for new times.

KEY POINTS

History

- EC regional policy first emerged in the 1970s.
- Member states' governments dominated the policy process and there was no major movement towards the creation of a supranational policy.

The 1988 Reform

- Enlargement and the single market programme provided the context for a major reform of the structural funds in 1988, which doubled financial allocations, strengthened the additionality principle, and introduced the principle of partnership.

429

The 1993 Reform

- The 1993 reform maintained the guiding principles established in 1988, although aspects of the reform reflected a reassertion of member states' control.
- The Cohesion Fund was established as an additional compensatory instrument for the poorer member states.

The 1999 Reform

- Proposed enlargement and completion of monetary union provided the context for the 1999 reform, which retained the principles of additionality, concentration, partnership, and programming while adding the principle of efficiency.
- A number of pre-accession instruments were introduced to prepare candidate states for membership.

The 2006 Reform

- The context of the 2006 reform was the 2004 enlargement and the Lisbon Agenda.
- The reform led to a simplification of the architecture of cohesion policy.
- IPA replaced previous pre-accession instruments, and components of this instrument mirrored administrative arrangements for the structural funds to prepare candidates states more effectively for accession.

The 2013 Reform

- The Barca Report of 2009 called for comprehensive reform of cohesion policy and an emphasis on closer territorial co-operation to achieve social objectives.
- The Commission's subsequent proposals linked cohesion policy to the goals of the Europe 2020 growth strategy.
- The Multi-annual Financial Framework agreed in February 2014 incorporated both the objectives of closer territorial co-operation and job creation, but allocated more resources to the latter.

Explaining Cohesion Policy

- The intergovernmental–supranational debate has been central to theorizing EU-level decision making over cohesion policy.
- The respective influence of key actors has fluctuated over time and across issues, and there is debate over the extent to which there has been a reassertion of government control over EU-level decision making since the 1988 reform.
- The concept of MLG is closely related to cohesion policy, particularly in understanding developments at the implementation stage, although there is significant variation in the degree of MLG evident across the EU.

FURTHER READING

Two books provide an overview of key developments in cohesion policy, while also contributing original case studies and analysis. **I. Bache**, *Europeanization and Multilevel Governance: Cohesion Policy in Britain and the European Union and Britain* (Lanham, MD: Rowman and Littlefield, 2008) brings together two of the main conceptual concerns in the field, with a detailed case study of the domestic effects of cohesion policy in Britain, and summary case studies of seven other states of the EU fifteen, and three from central and eastern Europe. **R. Leonardi**, *Cohesion Policy in the European Union* (Basingstoke: Palgrave Macmillan, 2005) takes an interdisciplinary approach to highlight the socio-economic as well as political impact of cohesion policy, drawing on a case study of Italy and of the ten new member states of the 2004 enlargement.

A number of articles and chapters have contributed to the conceptual debates around inter-governmentalism, supranationalism, and MLG. **G. Marks** developed his arguments about MLG from his analysis of the 1988 reform of the structural funds and subsequent disputes over implementation in 'Structural Policy and Multi-Level Governance in the EC', in **A. Cafruny and G. Rosenthal (eds)**, *The State of the European Community, vol. 2: The Maastricht Debates and Beyond* (Boulder, CO, and Harlow: Lynne Rienner and Longman, 1993), 391–410. **M. Pollack**, 'Regional Actors in an Intergovernmental Play: The Making and Implementation of EC Structural Policy', in **C. Rhodes and S. Mazey (eds)**, *The State of the European Union, vol. 3: Building a European Polity?* (Boulder, CO, and Harlow: Lynne Rienner and Longman, 1995), 361–90, reflects on both the 1988 and 1993 reforms and provides an essentially intergovernmental response to the arguments of Marks. **I. Bache**, 'The Extended Gatekeeper: Central Government and the Implementation of EC Regional Policy in the UK', *Journal of European Public Policy*, 6 (1999): 28–45, emphasizes the important contribution of policy implementation in shaping outcomes and informing conceptual debate.

More recently, **J. Bachtler and C. Mendez** critique the re-nationalization thesis applied to cohesion policy in 'Who Governs EU Cohesion Policy? Deconstructing the Reforms of the Structural Funds', *Journal of Common Market Studies*, 24 (2007): 535–64; **J. Bachtler and I. McMaster** look at regionalization effects in central and eastern Europe in 'EU Cohesion Policy and the Role of the Regions: Investigating the Influence of Structural Funds in the New Member States', *Environment and Planning C*, 28 (2008): 398–427, as does **L. Bruszt**, 'Multi-Level Governance: The Eastern Versions—Emerging Patterns of Developmental Governance in the New Member States', *Regional and Federal Studies*, 18 (2008): 607–27. Finally, the special issue of the *Journal of Southeast European and Black Sea Studies* (2010) 10(1) is dedicated to the subject of 'Cohesion Policy and Multi-Level Governance in South East Europe', drawing on case studies of established, new, and prospective member states.

 online resource centre **Visit the Online Resource Centre that accompanies this book for links to more information on European regional and structural policies, including the website of the Commission's Directorate-General for Regional Policy: http://oxfordtextbooks.co.uk/orc/bache4e/**

Chapter 23

Environmental Policy

Vasilis Leontitsis

Chapter Overview

The environment is a relatively new policy area of the European Union. It was not officially created until 1973, and it did not acquire a sound legal basis in the Treaties until the Single European Act in 1987.

When the European Communities were established, environmental issues were low on the political agenda. However, they increasingly became more prominent at both national and European levels, and there is now a comprehensive environmental policy at the EU level. Nowadays, environmental considerations are supposed to inform all aspects of EU policies, and notions such as sustainability have become increasingly important within EU discourse. The EU has experimented with new environmental policy instruments and has attempted to become a major player at the global level. However, implementation deficits have raised concerns over its ability to resolve environmental problems, whereas, at the international level, its leading role has been compromised by its inability to speak with one voice.

This chapter gives a brief historical account of the policy, examines recent developments, and discusses some of the major issues of current concern. Finally, the policy's evolution is discussed drawing on the theories presented in Part One of this book.

History

In the founding treaties there was no reference to the environment. The European Communities were established on economic grounds, and economic logic dictated the direction of European integration. Even at the national level, there were no coherent environmental policies in most member states during that period, so there was no pressure to co-ordinate policy measures at the Community level, other than to avoid trade distortions.

The situation changed drastically in the 1960s, when a series of environmental disasters and a better understanding of the consequences of unchecked economic development led to increased public consciousness of environmental issues. Environmental values found their way into the radicalized politics of the late 1960s and the green movement gained in salience in western European countries, especially in Germany.

> **Table 23.1** Environmental Measures Taken Prior to 1973
>
> Directive 59/221 on ionizing radiation (amended with directives 62/1633 and 66/45);
>
> Directive 67/548 on the classification, packaging and labelling of dangerous substances (amended with directive 71/144);
>
> Directive 70/157 on noise from vehicle exhaust systems;
>
> Directive 70/220 on carbon monoxide and hydrocarbon emissions from road vehicles;
>
> Directive 72/306 on emissions from diesel-engined vehicles.

Source: (Based on McCormick 2001: 45).

The 1972 United Nations Conference on the Human Environment, held in Stockholm, further increased awareness of environmental issues. As a response, several European countries tightened environmental regulation within their own territories. However, though environmental concerns had started to influence the domestic politics of some member states, there was not much activity in the EEC. Until 1973, environmental measures taken at the Community level were few and far between (see Table 23.1).

Prior to the Single European Act

Increased environmental measures at the national level posed a serious threat to the Common Market. There was always a danger that some of the member states would use environmental regulation to discriminate against products imported from other member states. Additionally, countries with high environmental standards were afraid of losing competitiveness to others with laxer environmental regulations. Finally, politicians acknowledged that pollution knows no boundaries and some environmental issues would be better tackled at the supranational level. Hence, the conditions were ripe for co-ordinated action to be taken at Community level.

At the Paris European summit in 1972, the leaders of the member states stressed the importance of protecting the environment and urged the Community institutions to draw up an environmental action programme. The Commission took up the challenge and drafted the first European Environmental Action Programme (EAP) in 1973. Additionally, a small unit was created in the Commission responsible for the environment, and a dedicated committee was established in the European Parliament (EP). If the years prior to that date represent the pre-history of the EU environmental policy, 1973 marks the beginning of its history proper.

The First EAP covered the years from 1973 until 1976. It was followed by the Second (1977–81) and Third (1982–86) EAPs. These environmental programmes did not contain any binding legal provisions. However, they did put in place a number of general principles that continue to guide environmental action in the EU.

Among others, they stated that prevention is better than cure (the 'preventative principle'), that polluters should pay for the environmental damage they cause (the 'polluter pays principle'), and that environmental damage should be combated at its source (McCormick 2001: 48–9; Lenschow 2005: 306–7). More importantly, they made increasingly obvious that any environmental policy at Community level was to be firmly based on the overarching principle of ecological modernization, namely the perception that both economic growth and environmental protection are attainable with the help of technology and the use of more efficient ways of production (for an overview of the debates surrounding ecological modernization see Mol and Sonnenfeld 2000).

However, the Commission still lacked explicit treaty provisions on which to base its environmental initiatives. Throughout this period, it had to rely either on Article 100 (now Article 115 TFEU) on the approximation of laws affecting the Common Market, or the so-called 'catch all' Article 235 (now Article 352 TFEU), which allowed for some action to be taken in areas that were not mentioned in the Treaties but where it was deemed necessary for the achievement of the main Community objectives. In both cases unanimity was required in the Council of Ministers.

Irrespective of those legal complications, environmental legislation continued to accumulate during this period. According to Burchell and Lightfoot (2001: 36), 120 directives, twenty-seven decisions, and fourteen regulations were adopted between 1973 and 1985. This was mainly due to the leadership exhibited by the European Commission, supported by the rulings of the European Court of Justice (ECJ). Additionally, the role of member states with high environmental standards was pivotal in pushing for the adoption of some of their policies at the EU level. Nevertheless, the lack of specific environmental provisions in the initial Treaties hindered the Commission in its efforts to promote environmental legislation and resulted in a 'piecemeal and reactive' environmental policy at the Community level (McCormick 2001: 55).

From the Single European Act (SEA) to the Treaty of Maastricht

The SEA gave environmental policy the treaty base it had previously lacked. The SEA inserted a new Environment Title into the Treaties (Article 130 r-t; now Articles 191-3 TFEU). Hence, environmental protection formally became part of the competences of the Community. The fundamental environmental principles adopted in the EAPs were confirmed. Furthermore, it was stated that '[e]nvironmental protection requirements shall be a component of the Community's other policies' (Article 130r; now Article 191). This sought to promote a more integrated approach when dealing with the environment at the Community level. Additionally, the right of individual member states to put in place environmental legislation stricter than that in other member states was recognized (Article 130t; now Article 193 TFEU). One more article related to the environment was inserted in the Treaties. Article 100a (now Article 114 TFEU) explicitly provided for the adoption of environmental legislation at the Community level when the creation of the Single Market was otherwise affected.

When Article 130 r-t was utilized, unanimity was required in the Council, together with consultation with the EP. On the other hand, when Article 100a was used, the new co-operation procedure was followed together with Qualified Majority Voting (QMV) in the Council. Hence, there were two different procedures that could be followed depending on whether a piece of environmental legislation was connected to the Single Market. This caused some confusion, and led to treaty-based games between actors.

The Commission attempted to use Article 100a in most of its dealings, in order to bypass the hurdle of unanimity in the Council of Ministers, but it was legally challenged on a number of occasions (Burchell and Lightfoot 2001: 38). All in all, the new provisions did clarify the right of the Community to act in the sphere of the environment, but the two different policy-making procedures caused complications.

Nevertheless, EC environmental policy continued growing, boosted by its formal recognition in the SEA. The Fourth EAP was adopted for the years 1987–92 and a European Environment Agency (EEA) was established. The EEA was founded in 1990, but disagreements about its location meant that its official opening was delayed until 1993. It was eventually located in Copenhagen, with a remit to collect and disseminate information.

At the global level, the publication of the Brundtland report in 1987, with its gloomy observations on the effects of current patterns of economic development and its prompting towards sustainability, increased awareness of environmental issues. This gave a further push towards a more proactive environmental policy at the EC level, where the role of certain actors in promoting environmental regulation was critical.

In the early 1980s, the Commission unit on the environment was upgraded into a Directorate-General (DG), which, although small compared to other DGs, pursued environmental issues with great determination. The partial application of QMV in the Council of Ministers gave the Commission more leeway in its efforts to increase EC-wide environmental standards. During that period, the Commission acted as a successful policy entrepreneur, promoting ambitious and far-reaching legislation, such as the directive on environmental information and the habitats directive. However, it continued to be torn between an economic and an environmental logic that were to some extent incompatible.

The Danish bottle case (Case 302/86) was a characteristic example. The Danish government had introduced legislation that required all soft-drink and beer bottles to be recyclable. This would have caused increased costs for the producers and would particularly have affected exporters to the Danish market. The Commission reacted by taking the Danish government to the ECJ, arguing that such a measure constituted a trade barrier. In the end, the ECJ ruled in favour of Denmark, insisting that environmental protection was of such importance for the Community that under certain circumstances it could even justify measures that distorted trade. The significance of the decision was that, for the first time, the environment was put on an equal footing with the Common Market. The decision also showed the limits of the Commission's role as a promoter of environmental legislation and the continuing important role of the ECJ in solidifying the EC's environmental policy. The Court was willing 'to adjust a simple integrationist approach to the specific requirements of a common environmental policy' (Koppen 1993, quoted in Jordan 1999a: 9).

Finally, some member states continued pushing for more European-wide environmental regulation. Leading states on environmental issues attempted to upload environmental measures to the European level. In the case of acid rain, for example, the role of Germany was critical. Alarmed at the damage caused to its forests by acid rain, and responding to national pressures, Germany adopted laws on the reduction of sulphur dioxide (SO_2) at the national level in 1983. However, the fear of loss of competitiveness, alongside the understanding that acidification was a trans-boundary issue, led to pressures for action to be taken at the EU level. As a result, the Large Combustion Plant Directive was adopted, mirroring the relevant German legislation (Sbragia 1996).

From the Treaty of Maastricht to the Treaty of Lisbon

The 1993 Maastricht Treaty increased further the visibility of environmental policy in the Treaties. The environment was now listed in the opening articles as a major goal of the EU, alongside the other major goals of an economic nature. In terms of processes, QMV was extended to almost all areas of environmental policy, but unanimity was retained in sensitive areas such as town and country planning, taxation, and energy choices (Article 130s; now Article 192 TFEU). The new co-decision policy-making procedure was adopted for all measures related to the Common Market, increasing the powers of the EP. On the other hand, co-operation was reserved for most, but not all, matters related to Article 130s. Hence, albeit to a lesser extent, the complicated and confusing policy-making procedures persisted.

The Amsterdam Treaty confirmed the mainstreaming of environmental policy by inserting the goals of sustainable development and environmental protection into the preamble of the Treaties. Additionally, it provided for the integration of environmental policies into all other policies of the EU. The co-decision procedure became the norm regardless of whether a piece of legislation was concerned with the Internal Market. Thus, the duality in policy processes that had persisted for more than a decade was finally eliminated and the role of the EP increased. However, unanimity was kept for the most controversial issues.

The Fifth EAP (1993–2000) was a major step towards a more coherent EU environmental policy. First, it continued the marked shift towards a more integrated approach when dealing with environmental issues. Unlike its predecessors, it focused on the sources of pollution rather than the elements being polluted. Hence, it dealt with different economic sectors, such as agriculture, energy, and transportation. Second, it put an emphasis on so-called new environmental policy instruments (NEPIs), such as eco-taxes and eco-labels. NEPIs offered the possibility of more flexibility in the instrument used (for a more detailed analysis see this chapter, Recent Developments). Third, the Fifth EAP set concrete environmental objectives to be achieved in the medium-term and in the long-term. Finally, it introduced the principle of 'shared responsibility', aimed at involving an increased number of actors in the policy-making and implementation processes (European Commission 1992). All in all, the Fifth EAP continued the trend towards more sophisticated environmental governance at EU level.

Fears that the accession of Greece, Spain, and Portugal in the 1980s would affect negatively the level of environmental regulation in the Community failed to materialize in practice. Environmental legislation in those countries was strengthened alongside the general level of environmental regulation at the European level (Schreurs 2004). Moreover, the accession in the 1990s of Austria, Sweden, and Finland, countries with very high environmental standards, helped to solidify further the EU environmental policy and strengthened the pro-environment camp within the Council of Ministers (Liefferink and Andersen 1998). Those countries took the initiative on several occasions when they held the presidency of the Council of Ministers and helped to increase environmental standards within the EU. The Lisbon Treaty reaffirmed the trend to greater consolidation. Although it mentioned the issue of climate change for the first time, it left most environmental provisions unchanged (Benson and Jordan 2008). The environment was explicitly mentioned as a policy area where both the member states and the European Union shared competence, whereas the list of sensitive matters requiring unanimity in the Council remained intact.

Within thirty years, the EU's environmental policy had 'moved from silence to salience' (Weale 1999*b*: 40). However, there had been a change in emphasis about when it was right to act at the EU level. The introduction of the principle of subsidiarity into the Treaties meant that the Union had to justify to what extent it could deal with environmental issues better than the member states and sub-national authorities. More emphasis was now put on better implementation and the integration of environmental considerations into other EU policies (Haigh 1999). The role of the member states, the Commission, and the ECJ remained important; but a growing role was now reserved for the EP and environmental lobbying groups in Brussels. The policy landscape had become more complex.

Recent Developments

EU environmental policy has now reached a mature stage. Since the core of EU environmental legislation has already been put in place, producing new legislation has decreased in importance. Instead, four major issues have gained prominence: environmental policy integration, addressing the implementation deficit of EU environmental legislation, the possible use of NEPIs, and the role of the EU as an actor in the global arena. Those issues were to some extent addressed in the Sixth EAP (2002–12) and further highlighted in the Seventh EAP that was adopted in 2013 for the period 2013–20. Each will now be reviewed in turn, the background filled in, and post-Lisbon developments outlined.

Environmental Policy Integration

Starting in the 1970s, the environment progressively moved from the periphery to the centre of EU policy making. Nevertheless, awareness grew that, regardless of the progress that had been achieved, for EU environmental policy to be successful, all other policies had to support its aims. Although during the 1990s there were some efforts to 'green' the structural and agricultural policies (Lenschow 1999), a more general strategy for environmental policy integration (EPI) was deemed necessary (Jordan et al. 2008).

At the Cardiff European Council in June 1998 it was decided that the different sectoral Councils would present specific strategies aimed at incorporating environmental considerations into their respective policy areas. This became known as the 'Cardiff Process'. At the summit three sectoral Councils were invited to submit their strategy plans: Agriculture, Transport, and Energy. Six months later, the Development, Industry, and Single Market Councils were asked to participate in the process, followed by the General Affairs, Economic and Finance, and Fisheries Councils.

However, the Cardiff Process soon faltered. A Commission report in 2004 admitted that '[i]t may be concluded that the Cardiff process has produced mixed results' (European Commission 2004*c*: 31). The same report identified several weaknesses in the process, such as lack of priority areas, implementation deficiencies, a great variation in quality among the different strategies, and lack of commitment on behalf of the sectoral Councils (European Commission 2004c: 31). Even more importantly, the Commission's attention had moved towards the adoption of a new Sustainable Development Strategy. According to Jordan and Schout (2006: 73):

> By late 2002, the production of new strategies and/or updating of existing ones had all but ceased, and the entire process began to move into the shadow of the newly emerging Lisbon process on social and economic reform.

In the late 1990s, stagnant economic conditions and high unemployment in Europe forced the EU governments to pay more attention to the economy. Hence, at the Lisbon European Council in March 2000, the Lisbon Agenda was put in place promising to make Europe the most dynamic and competitive knowledge-based economy in the world (see Chapter 10, The Lisbon Strategy).

The Lisbon Agenda initially contained two pillars: an economic and a social. However, under the influence of the Swedish presidency, a third, environmental, pillar was added at the Gothenburg European Council in June 2001. In Gothenburg, the leaders of the member states decided on a European Sustainable Development Strategy (SDS), in order to 'green' the Lisbon Agenda. An external dimension was added to the existing SDS in the following year. Finally, the whole strategy was reviewed and revised during 2005–06, in order to improve its outcomes.

In June 2010, the Europe 2020 strategy replaced the Lisbon Agenda. Europe 2020 adopted a number of principal targets related to important climate and energy indicators. More precisely, the EU committed to acquiring 20 per cent of its energy consumption from renewable sources by 2020, to increasing its energy efficiency by 20 per cent, and to reducing greenhouse gas emissions by 20 per cent (European Commission 2010). These are the so-called '20-20-20 targets'. Hence, the EU has now moved towards a more coherent climate and energy policy (see Wettestad et al. 2012). These headline policy targets are to inform all EU policies, aimed at 'greening' the EU. Moreover, the EU's recent 'GDP and Beyond' initiative, which provides a roadmap of five key actions to improve the EU's indicators of progress (see Table 23.2), promises a more rounded way of conceptualizing and measuring the EU's progress that foregrounds environmental concerns (see Bache 2013).

Nevertheless, the truth is that the multiplicity of strategies that have been used in the recent past, and the confusion they have caused, have hampered the goal of EPI. The new century has brought with it a more determined commitment towards EPI,

---

Table 23.2 GDP and Beyond

The five actions that the Commission proposes to implement are:

- complementing GDP with environmental and social indicators;
- near real-time information for decision making;
- more accurate reporting on distribution and inequalities;
- developing a European Sustainable Development Scoreboard;
- extending national accounts to environmental and social issues.

Source: (Bache 2013: 27).

but at the same time the EU seems to lack an overarching plan on how to achieve it. As a result, tensions remain between the two fundamental policy goals: economic growth and environmental protection.

Implementation Deficit

Although EU environmental policy has evolved over the years, there are huge implementation deficits making the environment one of the worst-performing policy areas in the EU. From the 1980s onwards it became clear that implementation in the environmental field was a serious problem that could potentially lead to policy under-achievement. The Fourth EAP devoted a whole section to implementation and the issue has retained a high profile ever since.

Implementation can be understood either in legal or in practical terms. The former refers to the extent that there has been transposition of EU legislation into national laws, whereas the latter refers to whether a law has been implemented in practice (Weale et al. 2000: 297–8). Since the Commission is chronically understaffed and under-resourced it has found it easier to focus more on the legal than on the practical implementation deficit.

Problems with the legal aspect of implementation are exacerbated because most EU environmental legislation comes in the form of directives (for the main types of EU legislation see Chapter 12, Decision-Making Procedures). Since directives are not directly applicable in the member states, national governments are responsible for translating them into national laws. Hence, problems arise when a member state does not take the appropriate action. Additionally, the member states and sub-national authorities are responsible for the practical implementation of those laws inside their territory. Consequently, the EU institutions, as in many other policy areas, are in the peculiar position of adopting environmental measures that are to be applied and enforced by national and sub-national authorities.

The Commission is formally responsible for overseeing the implementation of EU legislation, commensurate with its role as 'the guardian of the Treaties'. Since the Environment DG lacks the necessary resources to perform this role effectively, it depends to a great extent on the complaints procedure to be notified of infringements of the law. Non-governmental organizations (NGOs), the general public, governments, parliaments, and corporations can all file a complaint with the Commission when there is incomplete implementation of an environmental law by a member state. The role of the Commission is to investigate the complaint and, if the complaint holds, to begin infringement proceedings against the member state. This can ultimately lead to a referral to the ECJ.

Until recently, the ECJ lacked the 'teeth' to enforce its verdicts on the member states. However, since the Treaty of Maastricht, the Commission can request the ECJ to fine member states that have failed to comply with previous Court decisions (Article 171; now Article 260 TFEU). The Commission was quick to threaten the use of the amended article in a number of cases. Greece was the first member state to be convicted to pay a fine because of non-compliance with a previous Court decision (see Chapter 16, ECJ Rulings and Policy Impact).

Greece had already been found guilty of the maintenance of an illegal landfill site at Kouroupitos in the prefecture of Chania, Crete. However, the government failed to close the site as requested and so was referred back to the Court by the Commission. The ECJ, in a seminal decision, obliged Greece to pay €20,000 daily until it stopped the operation of the landfill (Case C-387/97). Since then, the Article has been used several times, albeit cautiously, and has helped the enforcement of EU environmental legislation.

The Commission has adopted a number of strategies to increase the efficiency of environmental law and subsequently reduce the implementation deficit. Hence, it has opted for a simplification and codification of the existing regulations (European Commission 2007b: 14). Additionally, it has adopted a bottom-up approach when dealing with implementation issues. It has thus opted for wider consultation with a number of environmental-policy actors during the early stages of policy making, in order to enhance legitimacy and acquire the highest level of agreement with its proposals. In the Sixth EAP, for example, one reads that:

> The thematic strategies [adopted in the Sixth EAP] should be developed and implemented in close consultation with the relevant parties, such as NGOs, industry, other social partners and public authorities, while ensuring, as appropriate, consultation of Candidate Countries in the process.
>
> (European Commission 2001b: Article 4.3)

The importance of improving the implementation record has been similarly picked up by the Seventh EAP (European Commission 2012). Better policy implementation has been clearly defined as one of the priority objectives for the years to come. The document suggests, among other measures, more stringent surveillance and inspections, improved access to court for EU citizens, and the use of scoreboards for the member states (European Commission 2012: 24–5).

Despite efforts to improve EU environmental policy implementation, problems remain. In 2009, there were 451 infringement cases in the area of EU environmental policy alone (European Commission 2012). One way to decrease the burden of implementation, at least in principle, is by using more flexible policy instruments. The next section analyses the attempts that have been made to turn away from command-and-control measures and towards more market-oriented approaches.

From Regulation to New Environmental Policy Instruments

The discussion on NEPIs is not new. They have been used in the past by several member states experimenting with new ideas. Even at the EU level, with the Fifth EAP, there was a clear turn towards NEPIs. Until then, the old command-and-control approach was prevalent. According to Golub (1998: 2):

> [Command-and-control] is characterised by direct regulation: the government prescribes uniform environmental standards across large regions, mandates the abatement methods required to meet such standards, licenses production sites which adopt the required methods, and assures compliance through monitoring and sanctions.

Although the command-and-control approach has been widely used since the early years of environmental policy in both the EU and the member states, it has been criticized as economically inefficient, as inherently undemocratic, and above all as inflexible and ineffective (Golub 1998; Jordan et al. 2003). Instead, the NEPIs have been pro-posed as a better way of achieving environmental policy goals. They consist of market-based tools such as eco-taxes, subsidies, and tradeable permits, and non-market-based instruments such as voluntary agreements, eco-labels, and eco-audits (for a full presen-tation of the different kinds of NEPIs see Golub 1998 and Jordan et al. 2003).

The Commission has been willing to experiment with some NEPIs, but not always with great success. For example, in the early 1990s it attempted to introduce a carbon tax, but its efforts were successfully resisted by the UK and other member states. The unanimity hurdle in the Council, which still applies for taxation measures, was too difficult to overcome. In the end, in 2003 a rather minimal outcome was achieved: a modest directive allowing for the harmonization of energy taxes across the EU.

Another ambitious market-based measure, the EU carbon emissions trading scheme (ETS) (see Insight 23.1), has met with more success. The scheme was initiated in 2005, in order to reduce carbon dioxide (CO_2) emissions and help combat climate change. Its first phase lasted for two years and was severely criticized for the over-allocation of carbon permits (Ellerman and Buchner 2007: 78). This issue continued casting a shadow on the scheme in the following years. Making things worse, demand weak-ened as a result of the sluggish economic performance of the EU countries. This led to the collapse of carbon prices, which fell below €5 per tonne. The European

---

Insight 23.1 The EU carbon emissions trading scheme (ETS)

The EU carbon ETS is the main tool used by the EU to combat climate change. It covers the 28 EU member states, alongside Norway, Iceland, and Liechtenstein. It is a 'cap and trade' scheme, which means that it sets an overall emissions cap, but it also allows trade to take place among the companies within the system.

Each company that participates in the scheme receives or buys a certain number of allowances. An allowance is equal to a tonne of CO_2 emissions. The companies that pollute less than anticipated can keep their spare allowances for future use or sell them to other companies that exceed their emission permits. Thus a carbon market is created that in theory rewards the companies that make efforts to reduce emissions and penalizes com-panies that do not. The overall cap is progressively lowered, in order to reduce greenhouse gas emissions according to the EU international obligations. In particular, the cap will be reduced by 1.74 per cent annually until 2020, allowing for 21 per cent less greenhouse gas emissions in 2020 compared to 2005.

During the first (2005–2007) and second (2008–2012) phases of the EU's ETS, each member state was obliged to draft a National Allocation Plan (NAP). This determined not only the total number of allowances each country was permitted to allocate, but also con-tained a detailed plan on how many allowances each company that participated in the scheme received.

The third phase of the ETS was launched in January 2013, covering the years from 2013 until 2020, and has brought about considerable change. NAPs have now been abolished and the system is managed centrally at the EU level. Additionally, in 2013 more than 40 per cent of allowances were auctioned rather than allocated freely, as was the case in the past. This proportion will be increased progressively. Finally, more industry sectors and more greenhouse gases are to be added to the scheme in the years leading up to 2020.

Commission has attempted to address the problem proposing a number of corrective measures, although at the time of writing (2014) it remained to be seen whether these would ameliorate the carbon market imbalances. Despite the challenges the EU's ETS has faced, it remains the first, and up to 2014, the only such trading programme to operate on a large, supranational scale.

The philosophy underpinning the use of NEPIs has received severe criticism from radical ecologists, who disagree with green consumerism measures, such as the endorsement of eco-labels, on the grounds that such measures justify and promote consumption instead of reducing it (Dobson 2007: 120–1). Similarly, a considerable number of radical ecologists and academics remain sceptical about market-based measures, since they see capitalism as part of the problem rather than the solution (Eckersley 1993). The most important criticism remains that their increased use has not always led to the positive results initially anticipated.

Despite this, the Commission remains enthusiastic about NEPIs. In several reports it has praised market-based instruments and their positive effects (European Commission 2005b; European Commission 2005c; European Commission 2007b). Hence, it has made it a priority to promote the use of market-based instruments 'for the flexibility they offer in meeting sustainable development objectives' (European Commission 2005c: 16).

It is important to remember, though, that despite the recent popularity of NEPIs, the old command-and-control measures still constitute the bulk of EU environmental legislation (Holzinger et al. 2006). Jordan (1999a: 15) claimed that, at the time of writing, 'Regulation shows no sign of being totally eclipsed by alternative tools'. The same observation holds today. A mixed bag of both traditional and new policy instruments are in use and this is likely to continue well into the future.

The EU as a Global Actor

The environmental role of the EU has recently increased at the global level. The EU has managed to play a leading part in international environmental conferences and to broker global agreements on crucial environmental issues, such as climate change. Nevertheless, this new role has not come about easily. The EU had to develop the institutional capacity to perform such a task and also acquire the legitimacy, both at home and in the international arena, to operate as an international actor.

Sbragia and Damro (1999: 55) traced the origins of the EU's international presence in the early 1970s. In this period, the member states started signing a series of international environmental agreements that threatened to derail the Common Market. Hence, the Commission felt the need to expand its competence in the field, in order to protect the goal of economic integration in Europe. Additionally, the ECJ's European Road Transport Agreement (ERTA) ruling of 1971 acknowledged that when the EEC is given the right to legislate in a policy area it is automatically given external competence in that area, and thus paved the way for an EU international environmental pursuit.

With the acquisition in the SEA of formal environmental powers within the EC, the European Commission became more assertive on the world scene. Hence, when the 1985 Vienna Convention and the 1987 Montreal Protocol on the ozone layer were signed, the EC succeeded in becoming a signatory. The USA and other countries initially reacted badly to that, but the dispute was finally resolved when both the member states and the EC were accepted as contracting parties (Sbragia and Damro 1999: 57). From then onwards, the joint participation of both the EC/EU and the member states in world environmental conferences became the norm. In the following years, the EC/EU emerged as an important global player in international environmental negotiations, such as the world summits on sustainable development in 1992 in Rio de Janeiro and in 2002 in Johannesburg (Lightfoot and Burchell 2005).

However, the single most important issue where the EU has shown a leadership role has been that of climate change. Starting in the early 1990s, it became accepted that action should be taken to reduce emissions of greenhouse gases in order to combat climate change. As the debate on the greenhouse effect was gradually pushed higher up the environmental agenda, the EU managed to solidify its position as a world leader due to its ability to strike a burden-sharing agreement among its member states, and the unwillingness of the USA to commit to binding reductions in emissions.

The Council initially agreed in 1997 that, although the EU as a whole was committed to reduce the emission of greenhouse gases, the poorest member states should be allowed to increase their emissions, with the increase being offset by higher decreases in the most developed countries. In the 1997 Kyoto Protocol, the EU agreed to reduce its emissions of greenhouse gases by 8 per cent from their 1990 levels by 2008–12. The final, post-negotiation burden-sharing agreement saw Greece, Portugal, Spain, and Ireland being allocated an increase of more than 10 per cent and countries such as Germany, Denmark, and Luxembourg accept reductions higher than 20 per cent. Because of the great success of this initial burden-sharing agreement, the member states have decided to adopt a similar strategy for the second Kyoto commitment period up to 2020 (see Table 23.3). The ability of the member states to distribute the burden of the Kyoto Protocol between themselves showed the degree of solidarity within the EU. Alongside the reluctance of the USA to ratify the agreement, this gave the EU the necessary credibility to lead the talks on climate change and, despite occasional setbacks, it has remained a leading international actor on that issue ever since.

Regardless of those successes in making an impact in the international environmental arena, the external dimension of the EU remains precarious. There is still great confusion regarding 'who speaks on behalf of the EU'. A rule of thumb is that the Commission speaks for the EU in all areas where it has exclusive competence, and the Council when there is mixed competence (Sbragia and Damro 1999: 55). In practice, the situation is much more complicated. First, there is rivalry within the Commission about who is to take the lead in global negotiations, especially when complicated issues are discussed that relate to a number of different DGs (Lightfoot and Burchell 2005). Second, there are grey areas about when the Commission or the Council is to take the lead, although co-ordination processes have been improved. Finally, questions arise about the stance of the member states in the negotiations and to what extent they follow the line adopted by the EU.

Nevertheless, an 'informal division of labour' has emerged (Delreux and Van den Brande 2013). The rotating Council Presidency is officially responsible for leading negotiations, but in many instances assigns responsibilities to the Commission and/or member states. This allows burden sharing and the exploitation of different sources of expertise, thus increasing EU efficiency in international negotiations (Delreux and Van den Brande 2013: 125–6).

Table 23.3 Member State Greenhouse Gas Emission Limits in 2020 Compared to 2005 Greenhouse Gas Emissions Levels

Country	Emissions reductions (Base year: 2005)
Belgium	−15%
Bulgaria	+20%
Czech Republic	+9%
Denmark	−20%
Germany	−14%
Estonia	+11%
Ireland	−20%
Greece	−4%
Spain	−10%
France	−14%
Italy	−13%
Cyprus	−5%
Latvia	+17%
Lithuania	+15%
Luxembourg	−20%
Hungary	+10%
Malta	+5%
Netherlands	−16%
Austria	−16%
Poland	+14%
Portugal	+1%
Romania	+19%
Slovenia	+4%
Slovakia	+13%
Finland	−16%
Sweden	−17%
United Kingdom	−16%

Source: Decision No 406/2009/EC © European Union, 1995–2014.

Explaining EU Environmental Policy

The rapid expansion and increasing importance of EU environmental policy make it an interesting test case for theorizing. Why was the policy created in the first place and what has been the motor behind its apparently impressive expansion? This section discusses the contrasting explanations of the policy's creation and evolution offered by different theoretical perspectives.

There are not many pure intergovernmentalist analyses (see Chapter 1, International Relations Theories of European Integration) of EU environmental policy (Lenschow 2007). This is not surprising taking into account the strong role the EU institutions have played. Intergovernmentalist accounts put emphasis on the role of the member states in advancing or containing environmental policy. They explain its emergence as a rational decision made by the member states aimed at decreasing the possible negative consequences of environmental competition. Thus, the member states initially delegated power to the EC institutions in the environmental field in order to protect the goal of the Common Market, which was beneficial to all of them.

One should expect lowest-common-denominator (LCD) outcomes to have prevailed, at least during the initial period when unanimity applied in the Council of Ministers. However, as Lenschow (2007: 415) points out, 'the rather remarkable expansion of the field did not usually come at the price of LCD decisions'. If LCD had been the case, the poor countries of the south would have dictated the pace of environmental policy evolution. Rather, these countries had to increase their environmental standards considerably, converging upwards with the other member states.

Intergovernmentalists would also stress that, even after the SEA, unanimity has been retained for the most important issues, such as energy use and taxation. Although QMV was progressively expanded, a cluster of these core issues has remained untouched. Long negotiations prior to the Amsterdam and Nice Treaties did not succeed in expanding QMV to those areas. The member states have retained the initiative where it matters. The case of the failed carbon tax proposal is a good example. As noted above, the Commission did try in the 1990s to advance the idea of an EU-wide energy tax, but was defeated in the Council of Ministers. So, while the member states have chosen to concede some powers on environmental issues, they have kept control in the most important cases.

Although intergovernmentalism has been used only rarely in its pure form, state-centric explanations have been widely used by scholars (Sbragia 1996; Liefferink and Andersen 1998). According to such analyses, there are two major camps of countries within the EU on environmental policy: the leaders and the laggards. Denmark, the Netherlands, Germany, Austria, Sweden, and Finland are generally considered as leading countries in promoting legislation, whereas Greece, Portugal, Ireland, and Spain—together with the new member states—are considered to put obstacles in the way of the adoption of tougher environmental measures. It is the pull and push between these two camps that has contributed the most towards the evolution of EU environmental policy.

However, a model that crudely divides the member states into opposing camps is far too simplistic. Börzel (2000) demonstrated that there is no clear-cut divide between the rich north and the poor south in promoting and implementing environmental legislation. Hence, although the state-centric, pull-push model is parsimonious and gives a robust explanation of the policy, it could lead to oversimplifications.

A member state might resist a policy measure not because it is an environmental laggard, but rather because this measure does not relate to either its regulatory policy tradition or to the relevant policy measures it has adopted at home. It has thus been proposed that what primarily matters is the extent of 'fit' or 'misfit' between the domestic environmental policies of a member state and environmental policies at the EU level (Risse et al. 2001). In order to minimize the costs of EU environmental policy, the member states attempt to upload their own environmental policies to the EU level (Börzel 2002). This has often caused regulatory competition among them (Héritier et al. 1996; Sbragia 2000).

The UK, for example, has recently managed to increase its influence over the policy-making process (Héritier et al. 1996; Sbragia 2000). This state has traditionally conceived environmental policy in a different way from the leading states of central and northern Europe, Germany in particular (Sbragia 1996: 250–3). So long as Germany had the lead in influencing EU legislation, Britain was perceived as a laggard. However, since the 1990s, the UK has shown a more proactive role, uploading elements of its own regulatory model (Jordan 2002, 2006). As a result, the initial role of the two countries has been reversed, with Germany having difficulties in transposing a number of environmental directives into national laws (Sbragia 2000).

The literature has also looked at the role the new member states have played in EU environmental policy and the impact of accession. Schreurs (2004), for example, attempted to offer a broad account on how past accessions affected the EU environmental policy-making process. Liefferink and Andersen (1998) looked at the way Finland, Sweden, and Austria influenced environmental policy after they became full members. Finally, there have been several publications focusing on the member states of central and eastern Europe (Jehlicka and Tickle 2004; Carmin and VanDeveer 2004).

Neofunctionalist analyses (see Chapter 1, International Relations Theories of European Integration) stress the importance of spillover effects following the creation of the Common Market to explain the emergence and evolution of environmental policy. The argument here is that the environmental measures that several member states took from the late 1960s onwards threatened to derail the goal of economic integration (Zito 1999). The environmental issues that affected the smooth functioning of the Common Market had to be tackled at the EC level. Once a distinct environmental policy was created, it could not be contained by national governments. Unanimity was progressively replaced by QMV, and the role of the EP increased, whereas environmental issues not relevant to the Common Market were finally brought within the EU policy-making remit. Weale (1999b: 40) described the expansion of environmental policy as integration by stealth and argued that it could 'be regarded as a textbook illustration of the [Monnet] method at work' (on the Monnet method see Chapter 1, The Intellectual Background).

The strength of this theoretical perspective lies in its ability to accommodate more fully the role of the EU institutions. According to neofunctionalism, the European Commission was quick to respond to the European Council's calls for environmental measures. It thus exploited the window of opportunity that opened at the beginning of the 1970s to promote the idea of an EC environmental policy. Throughout the following years, the Commission showed policy entrepreneurship in advancing important legislation. This could explain some far-reaching directives, such as the drinking water and bathing water directives. Neither drinking water nor bathing water is directly relevant to the Common Market, nor do they have any obvious supranational justification. Indeed, one could argue that both are sub-national goods. In that sense, there was cultivated spillover promoted by the Commission that advanced European integration in this policy area.

The ECJ's role has also been pivotal (Koppen 1993). It supported the Commission throughout the years in its struggles with the Council of Ministers. In some cases, such as the Danish bottle and the 'Kouroupitos' cases (see this chapter, Recent Developments), it showed clear signs of environmental leadership. Finally, the EP, which many observers consider to be the 'greenest' of the EU institutions, has increased in importance, especially since the SEA. In most instances, the co-decision procedure (see Chapter 12, Decision-Making Procedures) has given the EP increased powers, which it has used to advance a green agenda.

However, while the Commission has been of paramount importance in promoting EU environmental policy, closer scrutiny reveals that, as a result of its inherent internal divisions, it has not always been in favour of unconditional policy expansion. There is great competition between the economic DGs (Trade, Competition) and the much smaller Environment DG in particular, and DG Environment does not always gain sufficient support for green legislation within the college of Commissioners. The Danish bottle case reveals that the Commission has sometimes adopted points of view that are less environmentally friendly. Its role has not always been expansionist. Finally, even when the Commission has attempted to increase the level of environmental legislation, the member states have in some cases managed to contain its ambitions.

Neofunctionalism has been strongly criticized for adopting a linear view of progress (Zito 1999: 21; Lenschow 2007: 416). It seems to assume a progressive strengthening of EU environmental policy and expects a decreasing input from the member states as the policy advances. Reality does not support these predictions. For example, the Nice and Lisbon Treaties hardly changed anything in their provisions concerning the environment. In addition, although the Cardiff Process promised to integrate the environment into other EU policies within a few years, it faltered. The Lisbon Agenda showed that the perennial clash between the environment and the economy had not been resolved and that there was always a possibility of a setback in environmental policy if other, more pressing matters demanded the attention of the EU leaders.

Governance theories (see Chapter 2, Governance and Networks) have difficulty explaining the origins of the policy, since their main focus is on day-to-day politics. Nevertheless, they provide a detailed account of the present situation and the complexity surrounding it. They can accommodate a whole range of new actors that play an increasing role in EU environmental affairs, such as NGOs or epistemic communities (see Chapter 2, Governance and Networks), without denying the continuing importance of both the member states and the EU institutions. According to governance theories, the evolution of EU environmental policy cannot be explained unless we take into consideration the fact that the EU has evolved to become a polity in its own right. New tools, borrowed from domestic and comparative politics, are thus necessary, since thinking in the traditional terms derived from international relations cannot adequately capture this fundamental change.

The policy networks approach (see Chapter 2, Governance and Networks) attempts to trace and analyse networks that are created by a cluster of actors participating in the development and execution of EU environmental policy. This perspective pays particular attention to pooled resources, alliances formed, and bargaining within networks. It also assumes that the hierarchical model of government has given way to a more fluid and complex model of governance. One could observe the increasing reliance of the EU on the creation and stirring of policy networks. Jordan and Schout (2006: 21) argued that 'the EU has decided to rely more heavily on networked governance to tackle wicked policy issues such as environmental coordination'. The increasing use of the open method of co-ordination and the Cardiff Process are two good examples of that turn (see Chapter 18, Major Policy Areas).

New Institutionalism (see Chapter 2, New Institutionalism) puts emphasis on institutions and their ability to restrict and/or shape actors' preferences. Rational choice institutionalism, in particular, focuses on the inter-institutional and intra-institutional power games developed during the policy-making process. It deals with the way institutional reforms have changed the rules of the game and have restricted or enabled actors. Unlike neofunctionalism, it does not subscribe to the irreversibility of European integration, nor does it expect the EU institutions to be pro-integration and policy expansionist in all instances. It rather focuses on the fragmentation within the Commission and the Council, the fight for more power among the EU institutions, and the power games between the member states and the institutions at the EU level (Jordan 1999*b*). Strategic thinking by rational actors is at the heart of its explanatory framework.

The environment is a policy area where practitioners are faced with a great level of uncertainty. Hence, the epistemic communities approach (see Chapter 2, Governance and Networks) could be used to explain some of the policy shifts that have been observed during recent years. Acid rain, ozone depletion, and climate change are complicated phenomena that the politicians have had difficulty in grasping. Practitioners have turned to environmental experts to increase their information on the causes of these phenomena and how to combat them. Thus, through the channel of epistemic communities, ideas have been diffused and environmental policies reshaped.

A very good example of the influence of epistemic communities is the issue of climate change. The broad agreement among environment experts that there is a strong causal relationship between climate change and the level of greenhouse gases was decisive in pushing measures to reduce CO_2 onto the policy agenda. Moreover, not only did policy experts dictate what gases had to be reduced, but they also helped shape the policy schemes for this to happen, namely the creation of the carbon emission trading scheme. Their influence was fundamental in providing technical expertise and changing the broader framework within which EU environmental policy functioned.

There is no one theory that can completely explain the origins and evolution of EU environmental policy in its entirety. Different perspectives shed light on different aspects. Intergovernmentalism, and state-centred theories generally, give an insightful account of the way member states influence policy. Neofunctionalism accommodates the importance of the EU institutions in advancing the policy, whereas governance theories account for day-to-day politics, the multiplicity of actors, and their interconnections.

One way to deal with this issue is by combining theoretical perspectives, aiming at a more holistic theoretical explanation. Weale et al. (2000: 45), for example, claimed that both a neofunctionalist and an intergovernmentalist logic can be traced in the way the EU's environmental policy system was created. As Zito (1999: 33) pointed out: '[Combining theoretical perspectives] lacks parsimony, but it does provide the means for explaining task expansion in the absence of a single theory of task expansion.'

CONCLUSION

The environment is a good example of how a once peripheral policy area can transform in importance within a few years. However, although the policy has expanded greatly, the future remains unclear. Despite the progress the EU has made in dealing with environmental problems, it has found it difficult to reconcile the policy goals of economic development and environmental protection. In that sense, the foundations on which its environmental policy lies, namely the principle of ecological modernization, have yet to prove their solidity. The notions of sustainable development and EPI could provide the links to bridge the gap between these two competing policy goals, but the full incorporation of environmental principles into the core of EU decision making remains to be seen. Additionally, further attention needs to be paid to a number of important matters that have been discussed in this chapter, such as making use of the appropriate policy tools, addressing the perennial implementation deficit, and acquiring a leading role in world environmental politics. Addressing these issues, in order to tackle global and regional environmental problems, will determine the future success or failure of EU environmental policy,

KEY POINTS

History

- The initial Treaties did not contain any environmental provisions.
- 1973 marked the beginnings of environmental policy at Community level.
- The SEA formalized EC environmental policy.
- The Treaty of Maastricht increased the visibility of the environment in the Treaties.
- The Amsterdam Treaty provided for the integration of environmental objectives into all other EU policies and eliminated the previous duality of decision-making procedures.
- The Lisbon Treaty mentioned climate change for the first time, and explicitly identified environmental policy as a shared competence.

Recent Developments

- Recently the area of focus has moved from producing new legislation to greening all other EU policies, improving implementation records, using new, more flexible policy instruments, and increasing the ability of the EU to perform as an international environmental actor.
- Although EPI has improved, there are problems deriving from the multiplicity of actions and the lack of an overarching strategy.
- The implementation record for environmental policy is one of the worst in the EU. Although efforts have been made to address the implementation deficit, success has been limited.
- The EU has started experimenting with NEPIs, although the old command-and-control instruments remain important.
- The EU has attempted to increase its international role on environmental issues, although issues remain concerning who is to speak on behalf of the EU and to what extent the EU can achieve the environmental goals it has set for itself.

Explaining Environmental Policy

- No individual theory or approach can adequately explain the origins and evolution of EU environmental policy.

- Intergovernmentalism captures best the influence of certain member states in advancing the case for EU policy.

- Neofunctionalism explains the active role that the Commission, the ECJ, and the EP have played in shaping the content of environmental policy.

- Governance theories are better equipped to explain the multiplicity of actors currently taking part in EU environmental policy and the fluidity of the current policy environment.

FURTHER READING

For excellent overviews of EU environmental policy see **J. McCormick**, *Environmental Policy in the European Union* (Basingstoke: Palgrave Macmillan, 2001), and **J. Burchell and S. Lightfoot**, *The Greening of the European Union? Examining the EU's Environmental Credentials* (London and New York: Sheffield Academic Press, 2001). A review of the use of NEPIs at both the national and EU levels is provided in **R. K. W. Wurzel, A. R. Zito, and A. J. Jordan**, *Environmental Governance in Europe* (Cheltenham, UK, and Northampton, MA: Edward Elgar, 2013). On EPI see **A. Jordan et al.**, 'The European Union' in *Innovation in Environmental Policy? Integrating the Environment for Sustainability* (Cheltenham, UK: Edward Elgar: 2008), pp. 159–79. Additionally, the collection of seven articles published in the special themed issue of *Environment and Planning C: Government and Policy* (Volume 17: 1), entitled 'European Union Environmental Policy at 25', shed light on all major issues of the EU environmental policy ranging from theory to issues related to the use of NEPIs, implementation concerns, and the rise of the EU as a global actor in this policy area.

online resource centre **Visit the Online Resource Centre that accompanies this book for links to more information on Environmental policies: http://oxfordtextbooks.co.uk/ orc/bache4e/**

Chapter 24

Freedom, Security, and Justice

Chapter Overview

The policy activity of the European Union (EU) in Justice and Home Affairs (JHA) was given formal recognition in the 1992 Treaty on European Union (TEU). Through subsequent reforms, latterly the implementation of the Lisbon Treaty, the policy has been recast around creating an area of freedom, security, and justice (AFSJ). This chapter initially explores the emergence and growth of JHA policy in the EU, and the Treaty reforms that led to the emphasis on creating an AFSJ. It looks at the policies related to the AFSJ, as well as the associated political struggles. Finally, it explores the debates and interpretations that have been offered for the policy area's dynamics. A key feature of this policy area's evolution has been the use of 'laboratories' outside the EU and of EU measures that have not involved all of the member states.

Context

Freedom, security, and justice are areas that have traditionally been understood as the core responsibilities of the nation state. It is an indication of the wide-ranging nature of the integration process that these policy areas have come under the EU's umbrella. Introduced principally by the Maastricht Treaty of 1992, the policy area initially was termed JHA and was located in its own 'third' pillar of the EU (on pillars, see Figure 12.1). However, the Amsterdam Treaty moved immigration and asylum policy to pillar one as part of an aim to create an AFSJ. The AFSJ was greatly enhanced by the Lisbon Treaty, which ended the separate existence of the third pillar and also consolidated police and judicial co-operation into the AFSJ. Reflecting this move, this chapter is entitled 'Freedom, Security, and Justice', although the early part is framed in terms of JHA. The policy area has matured over time, even though it remains contested because of the way in which it strikes at national sovereignty. The AFSJ has developed its own governance arrangements, including a range of agencies. A key characteristic of JHA and AFSJ has been the use of differentiated integration, whereby not all member states participate in all of the arrangements.

The chapter explores the history, culminating in the AFSJ becoming the overarching policy framework under the Lisbon Treaty. It considers the AFSJ's institutional character and policy content. Finally, it explores the key explanations and debates relating to this policy area.

History

Early Co-operation: Before the Treaty on European Union

The founding Treaties of the 1950s made few provisions relating to what has emerged since the 1990s. The commitment to the free movement of persons, and specifically of workers, was notable (Article 48 EEC Treaty). However, this provision only became significant with the developing momentum in the mid-1980s to create the single market (see Chapter 20). Other very limited rights bestowed on individuals in the early decades of integration were economic- and market-related. Even with the fragmented policy initiatives of the 1980s, there was no indication of the scope that the AFSJ would take in the EU of today, where two Commission directorates-general oversee a range of policy issues (see Insight 24.1).

Until the 1990s, the driving forces behind co-operation lacked real salience. In consequence, the policy responses resembled a patchwork. Accordingly, one of the key characteristics in this early period, and still relevant today, was the use of a 'laboratory' approach to the policy area (Monar 2001: 748–52). Co-operation thus took place in different forums and was not confined to the European Community (EC)/EU. Three particular 'laboratories' undertook experiments that prepared the ground for the rapid policy advances of the 1990s. These were the Council of Europe, 'Trevi', and the Schengen group.

The Council of Europe's texts on extradition, mutual legal assistance in criminal matters, the international validity of criminal judgments, and the transfer of sentenced persons—some dating back to the late 1950s—were to become central to JHA

Insight 24.1 The Scope of the Area of Freedom Security and Justice

Home Affairs	Justice
Immigration	Fundamental rights
Common European Asylum System	EU citizenship and free movement
Schengen, borders and visas	Civil justice, criminal justice, effective justice
Internal security	Data protection
Organized crime and human trafficking	Gender equality
Crisis management and terrorism	Tackling discrimination
Police co-operation	Drug control policy
The international dimension of the above	External relations on the above

Full details of the policy measures in force are obtainable at the webpages of the Commission's directorate-generals for justice and home affairs, respectively:

http://ec.europa.eu/justice/index_en.htm#newsroom-tab;

http://ec.europa.eu/dgs/home-affairs/what-we-do/policies/index_en.htm;

http://ec.europa.eu, © European Union, 1995–2014.

co-operation between EU member states. Indeed, they have become part of the *acquis* that applicant states are required to adopt before they can become new members (Monar 2001: 749). Perhaps more importantly, though, through co-operation in the Council of Europe, the traditionally parochial outlook of interior ministries began to be broken down. National officials gained experience of working co-operatively with European counterparts. Awareness was raised of national sensitivities and peculiarities, and of the problems involved in co-operation. 'Trevi' was a loose form of co-operation within the European political co-operation (EPC) machinery (see Chapter 26). It was an intergovernmental process comprising EC member governments, set up in 1975 as a response to increasing terrorist activity in Europe. It was later extended to the fight against drugs trafficking and organized crime. It paved the way for more structured co-operation once the TEU was put into effect in 1993. The work of Trevi was particularly influential for the development within JHA of Europol (the European Police Office) (see this chapter, The Area of Freedom, Security, and Justice).

The third 'laboratory' comprises the 'Schengen group' of member states that agreed to eliminate internal border controls. This initiative can be traced back to Franco-German efforts in 1984 to include some components of JHA activity in what became the Single European Act (SEA). It became clear that one of the core components—the lifting of passport controls to accompany the opening of the single market—was not acceptable to Britain, Ireland, and Denmark. In consequence, the Schengen group emerged outside the EC as a laboratory for developing a passport-free zone (see Insight 24.2). The implications of removing passport controls proved to be more far-reaching than envisaged and the scope of JHA co-operation widened to include compensatory control measures.

The Schengen 'laboratory' undertook valuable work that paved the way for JHA agreements on asylum and policies, extradition, and police co-operation. It also created a 'culture of co-operation' (Monar 2001: 752) and laid the basis for the **transnational networks** of police and judicial authorities that are essential to the successful implementation of JHA measures. The EU's Amsterdam Treaty (1997) incorporated policy agreed under the Schengen provisions into the EU Treaties, giving it a new legal personality.

One consequence of the Schengen arrangements was the need to start work on complementary external measures. The Dublin Convention, signed in 1990 and coming into force in 1997, was designed to stop asylum seekers making more than one application to enter the EU, trying to find the easiest point of access: a tactic known as

Insight 24.2 The Schengen Area

The name 'Schengen' comes from a small town in Luxembourg located at the border with both Germany and France. The signing of the Schengen Agreement on 14 June 1985 took place on board the pleasure boat, *Princesse Marie-Astrid*, moored on the river Moselle, which, at Schengen, forms the boundary between Luxembourg and Germany. Initial members were France, Germany, Belgium, Luxembourg, and the Netherlands. The Agreement's implementing arrangements were agreed in 1990 through the Schengen Convention. The term Schengen is still utilized to denote the area comprising those states that have given up border controls with each other (see Figure 24.1).

'asylum shopping'. Unlike with the Schengen arrangements, however, Britain, Ireland, and Denmark chose to participate. In 2003, the Convention was revised and subsequently became known as the Dublin Regulation.

Policy Dynamics and JHA Structures under the Treaty on European Union

How did the policy co-operation in these laboratories culminate in the creation of the JHA 'pillar' within the EU, as agreed at Maastricht in 1991? A number of overlapping dynamics were at play and became irresistible during the negotiation of the TEU. First, the Treaty was negotiated when European integration had attained a new level of dynamism from the SEA and creation of the single market. Giving JHA prominence in the new Treaty was part of this dynamic and was championed by the German Chancellor, Helmut Kohl. At the same time, specific consequences of the single market, with its removal of border controls, gave new urgency to intensified co-operation in order to provide alternative means of control over illegal immigration and cross-border criminality. Free movement of goods could facilitate smuggling, especially of goods such as cigarettes that attracted very different levels of tax in different parts of the EU. Free movement of people could allow criminals to commit a crime in one member state and retreat to another to evade detection and capture. Free movement of capital could facilitate financial crime, including the 'laundering' of money obtained from criminal activities. Also, individuals and businesses that took advantage of the single market to buy or sell in other member states found it difficult and prohibitively expensive to gain access to another state's system of justice if things went wrong. These potential threats necessitated a collective policy response.

A third dynamic arose from the interaction between globalization and the redefinition of notions of security. While the single market raised the scope for cross-border criminality, this was part of a larger-scale phenomenon. The end of the Cold War dramatically increased the opportunity for international crime and cross-border migration from the former communist states, although the scale of the threat was not as great as some of the predictions (Geddes 2006: 453). Economic migrants and asylum seekers were drawn to EU states. The civil wars in former Yugoslavia led to increases in asylum applications. Subsequently, the threat from terrorism took on particular salience with the Al-Qaeda '9/11' terrorist attacks in the United States in September 2001 and subsequent bombings in Madrid (March 2004) and London (July 2005). These actions produced further rapid escalation in JHA policy making within the EU. Alongside these developments, the growth of the Internet has introduced new challenges associated with 'cyber crime'.

The new global challenges were intrinsically linked to a redefined security agenda. Traditionally, security was seen as how states guaranteed their defence in military terms: as part of foreign policy in a state-centred system of international relations. However, this understanding has been challenged on two fronts. First, security has come to be understood in different ways: for instance, as societal security. Issues such as cross-border criminality or illegal immigration have taken on greater importance on the political agenda. Second, the international concern with terrorism after 9/11 has emphasized the role of non-state actors, such as Al-Qaeda and its affiliates, in internal security. Thus, security has established itself as a key theme in *home* affairs policy—or to use the academic terminology, home affairs policies have become 'securitized'.

A final dynamic for JHA policy came from a small number of states that, recognizing such dynamics, advocated the development of the EU's capacity to address the new internal security agenda. Foremost among these was Germany, the member state with the largest number of borders with different states: a situation exacerbated by the opening up of frontiers to its east with end of the Cold War. At the same time, its relatively liberal asylum policy was attracting increasing numbers of applicants. The Kohl government sought to utilize the EU as an argument for making its asylum rules more restrictive and thus justifying the necessary domestic reforms.

These stimuli were making the case for EU responsibility stronger. The laboratories discussed earlier and a growing number of other intergovernmental agreements were creating multiple (and messy) institutional arrangements. According to Jörg Monar, the interior and justice ministry officials, the police, and the customs authorities gradually came to realize that they were 'increasingly sitting in "the same boat" as regards a broad range of issues' (2001: 754). There was therefore a strong logic to providing a common EU framework for the policy responses.

The agreement reached in the Maastricht Treaty was to create a separate intergovernmental 'third pillar' within which JHA co-operation could be developed. The Treaty identified many of the main areas detailed in Insight 24.1. However, the institutional arrangements proved far from satisfactory. During the Maastricht negotiations, a majority of states had unsuccessfully favoured integrating JHA policy into EC business, but failed to agree on how to achieve this. At the same time, a few states, but primarily Britain, were insistent on not giving authority to the European Commission and other supranational bodies, notably the Court of Justice. Consequently, the institutional arrangements in the third pillar were a compromise.

The JHA Council and the Commission shared the right to initiate policy. Much of the detailed work was undertaken under the auspices of three steering groups, which reflected sub-areas of JHA work: asylum and immigration; police and customs co-operation (the busiest); and judicial co-operation in civil and judicial matters (den Boer and Wallace 2000: 502–3). Officials from different national agencies, including customs and the police, as well as the judicial authorities, worked more intensively than in the past, leading to changes in their working practices as well as those of interior and justice ministries. Some non-governmental organizations concerned with human rights and asylum issues began to emerge at EU level in response to the EU's new powers.

The main policy-making difficulty, however, was that JHA showed the pitfalls of an intergovernmental system. Decision making was slow and unwieldy; decisions, if taken, tended towards the lowest common denominator. In addition, the visibility of JHA decision making was low and parliamentary control virtually non-existent. Dissatisfaction led to pressure for institutional reform, which came about with the 1997 Amsterdam Treaty.

The Reforms of the Amsterdam Treaty

The Amsterdam Treaty brought about a number of significant changes to JHA policy. Of central importance was the new overarching mission to create an AFSJ (see Insight 24.3). This terminology was used in order to present the reforms as a major new programme in integration that, according to the Amsterdam Treaty, 'would provide citizens with a high degree of safety'. The AFSJ therefore sought to engage with the European public on the emerging new security agenda. Once again, the new arrangements represented a compromise between the different member governments in the Treaty negotiations (for details, see den Boer and Wallace 2000: 513). The **Benelux** states were among the most supportive of communitarization of JHA policy into the first pillar. Britain, by contrast, was opposed.

The most important institutional change was the transfer of visa, asylum, and immigration policies to the first pillar. The policy provisions went hand in hand with new decision-making rules: namely, **qualified majority voting (QMV)** in the Council. These rules in fact only came into operation from January 2005, by which time much legislation was agreed, but on the basis of unanimity. Pillar three remained, but with a narrower set of JHA responsibilities: namely, police and judicial co-operation in criminal matters (PJCCM).

At a relatively late stage in the negotiations leading to the Amsterdam Treaty, several states proposed the incorporation of the Schengen system into the EU. The Dutch government, which held the presidency of the Council in the first half of 1997, was extremely influential in securing this outcome. However, the exact 'outcome' was not entirely clear for some time because 'there was indeed no definitive or agreed text of the Schengen *acquis*' (den Boer and Wallace 2000: 514). Hence, a major immediate task in JHA policy making, once the Amsterdam Treaty came into force in May 1999, was to actually catalogue the accumulated decisions taken within the Schengen 'laboratory'. This task was made complex by the fact that some of the decisions and associated policy instruments were matters for the first pillar and others for the third pillar.

What was at first clearer about the incorporation of the Schengen provisions into the EU was that the British and Irish governments had negotiated opt-outs in view of their non-participation in the Schengen system. These opt-outs, it should be noted, stemmed primarily from UK governments' preference to maintain passport controls, a position usually justified by reference to the country's island status. In order to maintain its common travel area with the UK, Ireland maintained a similar opt-out. Denmark's participation in the Schengen zone had by this time increased, since the 1995 enlargement had brought in other states within the Nordic passport area. In effect, the Nordic passport area became part of the Schengen zone, the rules of which consequently were extended to Iceland and Norway.

The Area of Freedom Security and Justice (AFSJ): From Amsterdam to Nice

The ambition to develop the AFSJ as a new 'project' for the EU bore fruit. The European Commission began to build up its policy capacity, reflecting its enhanced powers of initiative arising from the Amsterdam Treaty. It reorganized its existing task force, creating in October 1999 a fully fledged Directorate-General (Directorate-General for Justice, Freedom, and Security). The European Parliament (EP) was given consultation rights on first pillar JHA decision making during the transition period. It increased its policy engagement and strengthened its committee, eventually called the Civil Liberties, Justice, and Home Affairs Committee. The European Court of Justice for the first time obtained some very restricted powers in relation to first-pillar JHA policy. Finally, the Council of Ministers also underwent some reorganization. Since JHA policy was located in two separate pillars of the EU, two separate committee structures were established under the authority of the Justice and Home Affairs Council. A final key institutional development arose from the engagement of the heads of government. In October 1999, the European Council, meeting in Tampere (Finland), was devoted to the development of the AFSJ. It agreed on a substantial programme of work for the period ahead and set in train a pattern of five-yearly programmes underpinned by scorecards and other mechanisms to ensure that momentum would be maintained. The Hague Programme (2004) and the Stockholm Programme (2009) were agreed subsequently by the European Council to maintain the policy momentum.

The Treaty of Nice made less fundamental changes to JHA. QMV was extended to limited parts of judicial co-operation as well as to anti-discrimination measures and matters relating to refugees. The first two of these were also to be covered by the co-decision process, thus making small inroads into a policy area in which the EP had historically lacked real powers. With one exception, the other main JHA-related changes arising from the Treaty of Nice were general institutional reforms, prepared for the forthcoming enlargement. The exception was the Charter of Fundamental Rights of the European Union. The Charter comprised six chapters spelling out a set of principles. They covered dignity (for example, the right to life and the prohibition of the death penalty); freedoms; equality; solidarity; citizens' rights; and justice. The British government was opposed to the Charter of Fundamental Rights being given legal status as part of the Treaty of Nice. Consequently, the Charter was 'solemnly proclaimed' at Nice in December 2000. For the time being, its status was to be political, but it was then subject to discussion as part of the subsequent constitutional debate.

The Lisbon Treaty

The Lisbon Treaty brought about some fundamental institutional reforms to JHA policy (Duff 2009: 95–102; Kietz and Parkes 2008) (see Insight 24.4). The first point to note is the new, upgraded commitment that:

> The Union shall offer its citizens an area of freedom, security and justice without
> internal frontiers, in which the free movement of persons is ensured in conjunction

with appropriate measures with respect to external border controls, asylum, immigration and the prevention and combating of crime.

(Article 3 TEU)

Symbolically, this objective was located ahead of such priorities as the single market and the single currency. In addition, the abolition of the three-pillar system meant that those parts of JHA that remained in the third pillar—namely PJCCM—were brought into the '**Union method**' (see Chapter 12, The Decision-Making Institutions (the Union Method)). The 'third pillar' was abolished and incorporated in a single part (or 'Title') of the Treaty on the Functioning of the European Union (TFEU) on the AFSJ. Thus, the whole of JHA policy in principle moved back to a single pattern of policy making: one in which the Treaty provides for QMV in the Council, co-decision rights for the EP, and, with some restrictions, the jurisdiction of the European Court of Justice (ECJ). The work of agencies was brought under closer parliamentary scrutiny.

At first glance, it appears as if the whole of JHA policy, including PJCCM, is now conducted within a supranational framework. However, a number of exceptional arrangements are written into the Treaties and reflect the fact that the member governments were unwilling to give up their powers quite so easily:

- the Commission continues to be denied the exclusive right of initiative on some AFSJ matters, notably PJCCM, since a quarter of the member states may also launch initiatives;

- the European Council is given the powers to set the strategic guidelines of policy (such as it has done with the five-yearly programmes, latterly the 2009 Stockholm Programme);

- an 'emergency brake' procedure has been introduced into PJCCM whereby a member state can declare a matter to be of national interest through appeal to the European Council;

- PJCCM is only fully subject to the Union method after a five-year transition period and there are some special exceptions because member states wished to limit the possible impacts on their systems of criminal justice;

- Britain, Ireland, and Denmark have secured new opt-outs from PJCCM.

Insight 24.4 The Key Changes to the AFSJ in the Lisbon Treaty

Abolition of the third pillar and transfer of police and judicial co-operation (PJCCM) into a new chapter within the TFEU's provisions on the AFSJ;

All proposals in the AFSJ to be adopted by the 'Union method', but with five-year transitional rules for PJCCM as well as various other exceptional policy-making rules;

EU Charter on Fundamental Rights becomes legally binding, but with special provisions weakening its application in the UK, Poland, and the Czech Republic;

New opt-out provisions for the UK, Ireland, and Denmark.

The Area of Freedom, Security, and Justice

In exploring the post-Lisbon AFSJ we review first the range of policies covered and then the institutions delivering them and the political struggles that they reflect.

AFSJ Policy Measures

Many of the policy activities entailed by the AFSJ can be identified from the evolution of JHA co-operation and are reflected in the work of the EU's executive agencies. Table 24.1 summarizes the policy work as well as indicating the relevant agencies.

Free movement of persons enshrines the right of all EU citizens to travel freely around the member states of the EU and to settle anywhere within the EU. This provision means that no special requirements are needed other than a valid travel document to enter the member state concerned. The same principle is extended to Norway, Iceland, and Liechtenstein (as member states of the European Economic Area; see Insight 27.2) and to Switzerland on the basis of a bilateral accord. For the Schengen zone

Table 24.1 An Overview of the AFSJ

Policy area	EU-level Agencies or Other Bodies Involved	'Pioneer Groupings'
Free movement	None directly	Schengen zone, including Schengen Information System
Immigration and asylum	Frontex, European Asylum Support Office	Prüm Convention
Judicial co-operation in civil and criminal matters	Eurojust, European Judicial Network	
Police and customs co-operation	Europol, European Police Chiefs' Task Force, European Police College (CEPOL)	Schengen provisions, Prüm Convention
Combating organized crime	Europol, Eurojust	
Combating terrorism	Europol, Eurojust, European Police Chiefs' Task Force	
Combating the drugs trade	Europol, Eurojust	
Combating human trafficking	Europol, Eurojust, Frontex	
Fundamental rights and anti-discrimination	Fundamental Rights Agency, European Institute for Gender Equality	

states (see Figure 24.1), internal border checks have been abolished. Their abolition has been accompanied by harmonized controls at the external frontiers of the Schengen zone, supported by the Schengen Information System (see later in this section).

The EU member states have committed themselves to a common *immigration and asylum* policy. Large numbers of legal and illegal migrants, as well as asylum seekers, have sought to come to the EU. Asylum is granted to a person who fears persecution for reasons of race, religion, nationality, membership of a particular social group, or

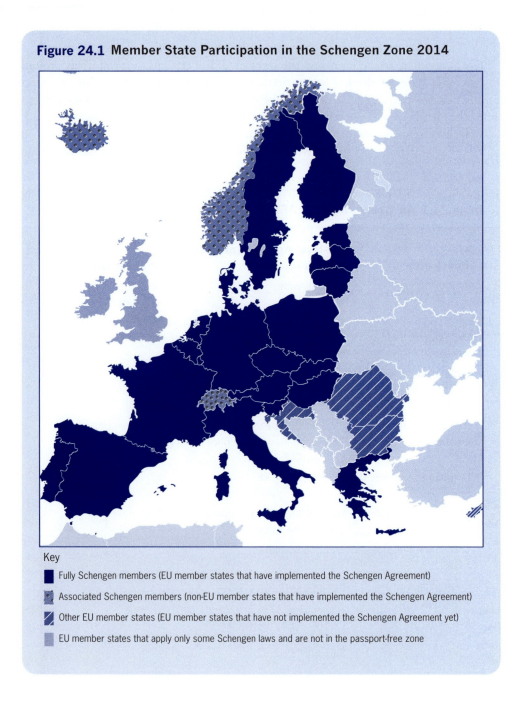

Figure 24.1 Member State Participation in the Schengen Zone 2014

Key

■ Fully Schengen members (EU member states that have implemented the Schengen Agreement)

▨ Associated Schengen members (non-EU member states that have implemented the Schengen Agreement)

▨ Other EU member states (EU member states that have not implemented the Schengen Agreement yet)

▨ EU member states that apply only some Schengen laws and are not in the passport-free zone political opinion and should be in conformity with the international standards set by the **Geneva Convention**. The EU aims to have a fully harmonized system in which applicants for asylum would receive equivalent treatment across member states. Work continues on creating this common system under the 2009–14 Stockholm Programme, as the 2012 deadline was missed. At the end of 2009, it was agreed to set up a European Asylum Support Office in 2010, based in Malta, with the role of facilitating member states' co-operation in implementing the EU's common asylum system.

The work on immigration entails: spelling out who may legally enter the EU, for example as an economic migrant; monitoring 'illegal' immigration and developing an action plan against it; and encouraging policies to enable integration of legitimate immigrants within member states. In May 2009, the EU adopted a so-called 'blue card' visa system to attract young, highly skilled workers to Europe in areas in which their skills are needed. The scheme drew on the US green card system, but the colour was changed to reflect the EU flag. The card gives recipients a specified set of rights. Danish, British, and Irish opt-outs apply. However, the member states control a key component: determining the numbers of economic migrants who will be allowed to enter their country.

Judicial co-operation in civil and criminal matters has not proceeded as rapidly as with asylum and immigration, although a priority of the Stockholm Programme. Member governments have taken longer to recognize the EU's role in justice matters: hence the intergovernmental processes of the third pillar until implementation of the Lisbon Treaty. Member states have agreed to 'approximate' the definition of, and the level of sanctions for, specific types of offence, in particular those with transnational aspects. Second, mutual recognition of decisions taken by judges in other member states is set to become the cornerstone of judicial co-operation in criminal matters. Finally, the EU is starting to be perceived as an international actor in judicial co-operation.

It was particularly in this part of policy that new momentum was gained following the 11 September 2001 bombings in the United States. This culminated in the best-known development, the European Arrest Warrant (EAW), which has replaced conventional extradition between member states with a judicial procedure (Baker 2009: 842). The challenge faced by the EU was that in areas in which cross-border crime takes place it is possible for criminals to exploit differences in criminal justice systems to their advantage. Areas in which the EU has identified this problem as requiring action extend beyond terrorism to include human trafficking, child pornography, financial crime (for example, money laundering), cyber crime, environmental crime, and racism and xenophobia. The transfer of judicial co-operation to the Union method under the Lisbon Treaty was designed to enable a better EU response.

Similar principles underpin action in civil law, except that it is usually in recognition of the rights of citizens and companies. For instance, greater mobility has increased the number of international marriages/partnerships and these may result in the need for access to another member state's system of justice, such as over child custody when a relationship breaks down. Similarly, the increase in cross-border commerce results in the need for access to justice beyond the 'home' member state. As with co-operation on criminal matters, policy making has taken on a new legislative character following implementation of the Lisbon Treaty. The European Judicial Network, which has set up national contact points in each of the member states, is a means of facilitating judicial co-operation and access to justice in other member states. Eurojust is the agency enabling co-operation between prosecuting authorities in the member states.

Police and customs co-operation has become increasingly necessary as a result of European integration itself but also because of globalization and the securitization of home affairs. Police co-operation concentrates on crime prevention, as well as specific tasks on terrorism and combating cross-border hooliganism at international sport events. Operational co-operation of police forces is the task of Europol, while the European Police Chiefs' Task Force provides a top-level arena for discussion between police forces. CEPOL (the European Police College) was set up as an EU agency in 2005. Its task is to bring together senior police officers from across the EU in a network enabling cross-border co-operation in the fight against crime, and promoting public security and law and order. It does so specifically by organizing training activities and presenting research findings.

More intensive police co-operation can take place under the auspices of Schengen, including the 'hot pursuit' by police authorities of suspected criminals into the territory of a neighbouring Schengen state. Such measures are a logical consequence of removing border controls, otherwise escape across borders would obstruct criminal justice. Nevertheless, 'hot pursuit' is a clear departure from traditional notions of national sovereignty. It also necessitates a strong degree of trust between police forces, possibly including joint patrols or investigation teams in border regions, as well as a likely need for language training. Customs administrations of the member states also contribute to the fight against cross-border crime through the prevention, detection, investigation, and prosecution of illegal movement of goods, the trafficking of prohibited goods, money laundering, and so on.

Combating organized crime, terrorism, drugs, and human trafficking represent four areas of intensive co-operation in which member state police and customs authorities play a key role. In each area, a strategy and programme/action plan has been agreed. For instance, the fight against terrorism has numerous component parts, focused around prevention, protection, prosecution, and response. Detailed measures include: analysis of radicalization and disrupting terrorist-related flows of money (prevention); countering chemical and biological threats (protection); information exchange between law-enforcement agencies and retention of telecommunications data (prosecution); and improving 'consequence management' (response).

As can be seen from the above, internal security looms large in many of the EU's policy measures. However, there is more to the 'freedom' component of the AFSJ than free movement. A key contribution comes in the form of the protection of *fundamental rights*, which is closely linked with action taken to *combat discrimination*, such as racism and xenophobia. These components of AFSJ complement the more security-focused policy activities.

The EU's role in assuring fundamental rights has been far from straightforward. On the one hand, a core of fundamental rights is associated with the 1950 European Convention on Human Rights. The Convention, which all member states have signed, is attached to the Council of Europe (the quite separate European organization, based in Strasbourg; see Insight 5.2). Principles of non-discrimination were agreed in the

Amsterdam Treaty enabling the EU to 'combat discrimination based on sex, racial or ethnic origin, religion or belief, disability, age or sexual orientation' (now in Article 19 TFEU). On the other hand, as Joseph Weiler (1999: 102) notes, 'the definition of fundamental human rights often differs from polity to polity'. Consequently, a few member states have been concerned about the development of the EU's profile on fundamental rights, while there have also been substantive issues arising from the jurisprudence of the ECJ. Under Article 6 TEU, the EU is committed to adhere to the Convention's principles; indeed, the EU has committed to accede to the Convention in its own right (see Insight 24.5). A draft accession agreement was reached in April 2013.

The most obvious example of the different member state attitudes is the UK's unwillingness to allow the Charter of Fundamental Rights of the EU to be given legal status in the Nice Treaty. This issue became contentious again during the protracted negotiations leading to ratification of the Lisbon Treaty. Consequently, while the Charter of Fundamental Rights now has the same legal status as the Treaties, its text is still not included in them. Further, the UK, Poland, and the Czech Republic have obtained assurances in Protocols to the Lisbon Treaty that make exceptions to the 'justiciability' of the Charter (in other words, the ability to invoke the Charter in domestic courts). Historically, the German Constitutional Court challenged the primacy of European law until it embodied a set of fundamental rights.

The granting of legal status to the EU Charter of Fundamental Rights, as well as the EU's eventual accession to the European Convention of Human Rights, should place its commitments on these matters beyond doubt. In March 2007, the EU's

---

Insight 24.5 The EU and Fundamental Rights

(1) The Union recognizes the rights, freedoms, and principles set out in the Charter of Fundamental Rights of the European Union of 7 December 2000, as adapted at Strasbourg, on 12 December 2007, which shall have the same legal value as the Treaties.

The provisions of the Charter shall not extend in any way the competences of the Union as defined in the Treaties.

The rights, freedoms, and principles in the Charter shall be interpreted in accordance with the general provisions in Title VII of the Charter governing its interpretation and application and with due regard to the explanations referred to in the Charter, that set out the sources of those provisions.

(2) The Union shall accede to the European Convention for the Protection of Human Rights and Fundamental Freedoms. Such accession shall not affect the Union's competences as defined in the Treaties.

(3) Fundamental rights, as guaranteed by the European Convention for the Protection of Human Rights and Fundamental Freedoms and as they result from the constitutional traditions common to the Member States, shall constitute general principles of the Union's law.

Source: Article 6 TEU.

Fundamental Rights Agency was established to: collect information and data; provide advice to the European Union and its member states; and promote dialogue with civil society to raise public awareness of fundamental rights. It built on the work of the European Monitoring Centre on Racism and Xenophobia, but the remit was widened to reflect the EU's explicit concern with fundamental rights after 2000.

Further related areas of work include children's rights and data protection.

Citizenship is the final area of rights-related policy on the part of the EU. The Maastricht Treaty initiated the notion of EU citizenship, which supplements rather than replaces national citizenship of a member state. By developing fundamental rights in EU law and in political declarations, as outlined above, the objective is to flesh out what it means to be an EU citizen. The four specific citizenship rights provided for in the Maastricht Treaty are set out in Insight 24.6.

All of the above have an *enlargement-related* dimension. Accession states have to meet the EU's human rights requirements to secure entry. Equally, they need to demonstrate that they can meet EU standards on such matters as secure external frontiers, standards of justice, and policing systems. Financial assistance and training programmes have been available to accession states to help them to adapt to the *acquis communautaire* in JHA/AFSJ policy.

Finally, many of the security measures outlined above have an *external dimension* beyond enlargement (Lavenex 2010: 474–5). In this sense, the AFSJ has given a new dimension to the EU's foreign policy. Some of these external activities have already been outlined: the liaison of Europol and Eurojust with US authorities in combating terrorism, for example, and of Frontex with states from which there are significant flows of illegal immigrants. Initially developed in a somewhat ad hoc manner, the Hague Programme called for the development of a strategic approach covering all external aspects of the AFSJ. The document—*A Strategy for the External Dimension of JHA: Global Freedom, Security and Justice*—was adopted by the Council in

---

Insight 24.6 Citizenship of the EU

Citizens of the Union shall enjoy the rights and be subject to the duties provided for in the Treaties. They shall have, inter alia:

(a) the right to move and reside freely within the territory of the Member States;

(b) the right to vote and to stand as candidates in elections to the European Parliament and in municipal elections in their Member State of residence, under the same conditions as nationals of that State;

(c) the right to enjoy, in the territory of a third country in which the Member State of which they are nationals is not represented, the protection of the diplomatic and consular authorities of any Member State on the same conditions as the nationals of that State;

(d) the right to petition the European Parliament, to apply to the European Ombudsman, and to address the institutions and advisory bodies of the Union in any of the Treaty languages and to obtain a reply in the same language.

Source: Article 20 TFEU.

December 2005 (Council of the EU 2005). Themes addressed include combating corruption, organized crime, terrorism, illegal immigration, drug production, and trafficking. In geographical terms, the immediate focus is on stability in the western Balkans and preparing candidate states to meet EU standards; freedom, security, and justice work in relation to the European Neighbourhood Policy (see Chapter 25, The European Neighbourhood Policy); co-operation with strategic partners such as the USA or Russia; and working with international organizations, such as the United Nations.

Andrew Geddes (2008: 170–85) outlined the evolution of the external dimension of immigration and asylum policy and highlighted two phases of development. Its initial concern was with enlargement (ahead of the 2004 and 2007 expansions). In a second phase, policy attention shifted to the European 'neighbourhood': an arc of states bounding the EU from Belarus on the north-eastern flank to Morocco on the southern one. In order to try to discourage illegal immigration, various measures have been taken: information campaigns in the sending states; financial aid to try to improve economic conditions in the sending states; the creation of a 'return fund' to repatriate illegal immigrants; and financial support for the integration of third-country nationals in the EU. As Geddes (2008: 184) notes, while it was straightforward to obtain the co-operation of accession states, since the incentive of membership was clear enough, the EU's leverage on other countries addressed by the external dimension of asylum and immigration policy is both reduced and very variable between states. The Arab Spring revealed the limitations of the attempts to prevent immigration from the EU's southern flank when that area was suffering political turmoil (see Insight 24.7).

AFSJ Institutions and Politics

The AFSJ is a policy area comparable to others of the EU in that it shares a common problem of balancing member state sovereignty with a competing functional logic that suggest many problems can be better tackled by collective action. Even following the Lisbon Treaty the member governments maintain strong powers because, distinctively, the Commission does not have the exclusive right of initiative. In addition, the European Council signs off on the overall strategy, such as the Stockholm Programme. Insight 24.7 gives a flavour of the continuing importance of national interests in the AFSJ policy area. Like a number of other policy areas, AFSJ has seen less formal methods of governance consistent with the Open Method of Co-ordination introduced (see Chapter 12, Implementation) alongside rule by law (Cardwell 2013).

The AFSJ is also characterized by strong traits of differentiated integration: the UK, Ireland, and—to a lesser degree—Denmark do not apply the full set of rules. In 2013, the UK government was considering withdrawing from further AFSJ measures—as provided for in a Protocol to the Lisbon Treaty—but in the process exposed disagreements between coalition partners and with authorities like the police. Romania, Bulgaria, and Croatia are not deemed to have high enough standards to be admitted to the Schengen border control system. In 2010, enhanced co-operation was used in this policy area for the first time when fourteen states agreed to legislation in judicial co-operation on matters relating to divorce and separation. This use of enhanced co-operation or pioneer groupings—see Table 24.1—is a variation within the EU of the

Insight 24.7 The Arab Spring's challenge to the AFSJ

(1) The Arab Spring posed major challenges for the AFSJ because of an acceleration of migratory flows to the EU to flee turmoil in North Africa and the Middle East. Italy was particularly exposed to the former via the island of Lampedusa, where 14,000 Tunisians were reported to have arrived in March 2011 alone. Italy felt exposed because of weak burden-sharing measures offered by EU partners and its government proposed to grant temporary visas that would be valid throughout the Schengen area. The French government became alarmed that those visa holders might want to join a large Tunisian immigrant community in France. It introduced border controls at a major frontier post with Italy, thus challenging the principles of the Schengen travel area. Denmark also toughened border controls. Eventually, the issue was dampened down even though migratory flows accelerated again after the civil war in Libya. However, the broader issue of solidarity remains, since northern European states are not immediately affected by the migratory flows and therefore have different interests from states such as Italy and Malta that have to contend with the immediate problem of arriving migrants.

(2) The European Commission subsequently proposed legislation whereby it would be the institution to decide on the implementation of emergency measures and the deployment of border guards in such circumstances. The proposal was blocked because of resistance from many member state governments. Subsidiarity concerns that such proposals intervened in member state powers led to threats by national parliaments to invoke the 'yellow card' procedure (see Chapter 12, Decision-Making Procedures). In 2012, the Danish Council presidency took an initiative on emergency measures with a view to breaking the deadlock. It chose a different legal base under which the EP only needed to be informed. The EP was hostile to this step as it challenged the democratic control measures introduced by the Lisbon Treaty. A fundamental breakdown of relations occurred between the EP and Council, affecting other AFSJ legislation as well. National sovereignty and inter-institutional politics were at stake.

(3) The Arab Spring thus increased mistrust among Schengen states, fuelled by populist sentiment in some member states. It revealed the persistence of different national interests despite the progress made by AFSJ, as well as the nature of inter-institutional politics in the post-Lisbon era.

laboratory approach that the Schengen Convention initially offered outside the EU. It also found expression in the work of the 'G5/G6' (an inner group of France, Germany, Italy, Spain, the UK, and, later, Poland) that played an agenda-setting role within JHA/AFSJ policy. A further example, more along the lines of Schengen, was the Prüm Convention. Initiated by the German government, the convention was to facilitate the exchange of data (including access to other signatories' DNA databases) for crime prevention and prosecution purposes. Signed by seven EU states on 27 May 2005, it seemed designed to circumvent possible obstruction by some states and avoid the scrutiny anticipated by the EP after treaty reform. However, it included explicit provision for later adoption by the EU, which duly occurred, albeit with some controversial provisions excluded, in the 2007 German presidency. In short, differentiated integration is more embedded in AFSJ policy than any other.

A further distinctive feature is the plethora of agencies and networks that have been developed in order to operationalize the AFSJ on the basis of co-operation between member-state administrations, as discussed in the next sections.

As for the supranational institutions, the Commission divided its AFSJ responsibilities across two directorates-general following the implementation of the Lisbon Treaty: DG Justice and DG Home Affairs. The constraints on its powers were highlighted in 2010, when its efforts to shape the Stockholm Programme into an action plan were met with criticism from ministers, who refused to endorse the plan for having departed too far from their own programme. The EP has become a more important player, flexing its muscles in February 2010, when it made first use of new powers under the Lisbon Treaty to reject, on civil liberties grounds, a counter-terrorist agreement between the EU and the United States to exchange data on bank transfer payments. The EP has emerged as an important defender of privacy, including in relation to the 2013 revelations by Edward Snowden about the work of the American National Security Agency and others in data-gathering, including allegations of spying on the Commission (*European Voice*, 25 July 2013: 4). The full effects of the Lisbon Treaty changes will only become apparent in 2015, when the transitional arrangements end for PJCCM. Thereafter the ECJ's role might become significant.

Much of the operation of the AFSJ is underpinned by data systems, agencies, and networks. As illustrations, we explore the role of the Schengen Information System, Europol, Eurojust, and Frontex.

Schengen Information System

The Schengen Convention provided for a multinational database for use by immigration, border control, police, and judicial authorities in any of the Schengen member states. This database is called the Schengen Information System (SIS). It is a key policy instrument put in place to accompany removal of border and passport controls. Another policy instrument is the 'Schengen visa', which allows the holder to visit—in the absence of border controls—any of twenty-five states (see Figure 24.1). The SIS is therefore an important instrument linking together participants' databases in order to facilitate JHA co-operation. A second-generation of the system—SIS II—came into operation in 2013 and incorporated enhanced functionality, such as biometric data.

The SIS can be used to pursue AFSJ policies in a range of situations. Someone taken into custody in one member state might be found to be the subject of an extradition request or EAW, listed in the SIS. A Schengen visa might be refused because of a ban from another member state emerging from SIS. A suspicious vehicle might turn out via SIS to have been reported stolen in another member state.

A separate database exists in relation to the asylum regime under the Dublin Regulation. Known as EURODAC, this Commission-run database is designed to identify whether an asylum applicant or a foreign national found illegally present within a member state has previously claimed asylum in another member state, or whether an asylum applicant entered the Union territory unlawfully. All twenty-eight member states plus Norway, Iceland, and Switzerland—the signatories to the Dublin Regulation—participate in EURODAC.

Europol, Eurojust, and Frontex

Europol, Eurojust, and Frontex (see Table 24.2) are three key agencies in charge of particular aspects of the AFSJ (on agencies more generally, see Lavenex 2010: 467–70; see also Table 24.1). They aim to facilitate co-operation between member-state agencies in different areas of policy that are all of centrality to achieving the AFSJ. Each has

Table 24.2 Europol, Eurojust, and Frontex

Agency	Europol	Eurojust	Frontex
Responsibility	European law enforcement agency	EU's judicial co-operation unit	Securing the external borders of the EU
Date of establishment (decision; operational)	1992; 1999	1999; 2002	2004; 2005
Location	The Hague, Netherlands	The Hague, Netherlands	Warsaw, Poland
Mode of operation	Facilitates bilateral exchange of information between all member state police forces	Facilitates co-operation between investigating and prosecuting authorities in the member states; exchange of personal data and judicial information	Exchange of information and co-operation between member states' border guards, customs, and police
Policy remit	Combating international crime: motor vehicle crime; organized crime; drug trafficking; illicit immigration networks; terrorism; forgery of money (counterfeiting of the euro); trafficking in human beings; and money laundering	Largely as for Europol	Integration of member states' national border security systems to deal with threats at the EU's external frontier. Tasks include immigration, repatriation, surveillance, border checks, and risk analysis
Staffing/ structure	Almost 800 staff, including 145 police liaison officers from the member states	Twenty-eight 'national members', typically senior judges or public prosecutors (one per member state)	Approximately 310 central staff, plus member states' border guards ready for deployment to a 'hot spot'

grown in size and been allocated new tasks as policy has developed in the face of new threats and as confidence has developed between domestic agencies, such as the police.

All three agencies have developed an 'external face' as part of their work, reflecting the way in which thinking about policy has evolved. Europol and Eurojust work closely with European neighbours, such as Norway and Switzerland, but also with counterparts elsewhere, such as in the United States. Frontex's co-operation with third countries tends to focus on states that are major transit points for illegal immigrants or are the ultimate sources of the migration flows. An examination of one of Frontex's work programmes gives an indication of the focal points of its operations (Frontex 2009). These are the perceived weak spots in the EU's frontiers: the EU's external land borders in south-eastern Europe and the Western Balkans and with Ukraine; the sea borders in the Atlantic and the Western Mediterranean; and air borders at major international gateways. All of these are recognized routes for illegal immigration and, in the case of land and sea routes, for people-smuggling.

One distinctive feature of Frontex is that it can mount operations by providing short-notice assistance where a security threat emerges, for example through its 'Rapid Border Intervention Teams' (known in Frontex jargon as 'RABITs'). Frontex also has aircraft, helicopters, and patrol vessels at its disposal. For example, from 2007, Frontex sea patrols have monitored areas in which large numbers of illegal immigrants were arriving by sea: notably, the Canary Islands, Malta, and Italy. RABITs are deployed when sudden influxes of illegal migrants challenge the capacity of a particular state. For instance, in 2013 some 175 border guards were deployed to the Turkish-Greek border. In 2011, Frontex was tasked with establishing a border surveillance system, known as EUROSUR.

Explaining the AFSJ

Neofunctionalist accounts of AFSJ related policy emphasize a functional spillover from the lifting of border controls as part of the single-market project (see Boswell 2010: 281–2; Geddes 2006: 455–6). However, there do seem to be some limits to this explanation. Important early developments took place in the Schengen Agreement and not the EU. The murky procedures gave little scope for interest groups to pursue 'political spillover', never mind 'cultivated spillover' from central institutions, since they were absent from Schengen arrangements until communitarization in the late-1990s. A more plausible interpretation in terms of 'institutionalizing European space' is offered by Turnbull and Sandholtz (2001), emphasizing the early (functional) spillover but linking it to external factors (the end of the Cold War) and the advocacy role of Helmut Kohl. However, this analysis only covers the period to mid-1995.

An alternative account of policy dynamics is offered by Virginie Guiraudon (2000). It draws on the public policy literature on 'venue-shopping' and applies it to immigration policy. It is argued that interior and justice ministries sought to escape control from their respective domestic justice and rights regimes. Anticipating further migratory flows arising from greater openness of borders, they sought increased control through developing new policy arenas within an international institutional setting in which their interests would be strengthened. This explanation looks plausible both for the EU and for the 'laboratories' such as Schengen. However, it does not sit well with the way in which it was German Chancellor Kohl and French President Mitterrand who advocated lifting passport controls. They had to put pressure on their interior ministries, who dragged their feet in the early period (Bulmer 2010). Venue-shopping becomes a much more persuasive argument for subsequent developments. The venue-shopping account acknowledges the spillover effects of neofunctionalism but places national actors in a prominent role. However, it does not correspond to intergovernmentalism because the venue-shopping account is about particular ministries trying to escape domestic control, and is thus more differentiated. It aligns better with the broader EU policy pattern identified by Helen Wallace (2005: 87), and termed 'intensive transgovernmentalism'.

A more orthodox intergovernmentalist account of policy appears to have some importance, given that member governments retained the key decisional powers for a significant period (see Insight 24.7; also Lavenex 2010: 466–7). Moreover, the continued insistence by the UK on retaining border checks is consistent with an emphasis on national government gatekeeping. However, this position has become less persuasive than was originally the case due to the communitarization of immigration and asylum policy after Amsterdam and of PJCCM after Lisbon. Multi-level governance has some limited application, but only in those states where policies relating to freedom, security, and justice straddle different levels of governance: notably, in a federal system such as Germany or devolved systems such as Spain or the UK.

Finally, a persuasive interpretation has been offered by Stephan Stetter (2000). While he acknowledged that spillover effects from the single market and from migratory pressures had some explanatory value, he suggested that 'they do not explain the specific institutions and methods which have been established at the EU level to deal with this policy area' (Stetter 2000: 81). Instead, his explanation builds on regulation and **principal–agent theories**. His argument, which is applied to immigration policy, is that the early efforts at international intergovernmental co-operation were not effective. Putting the Schengen and Dublin Conventions *into effect* was protracted. Consequently, the EU's third pillar offered a potential escape from this problem but the member governments constantly had to balance the potentially more efficient nature of delegated policy against the possible loss of domestic control. For most member states, the third pillar was ineffective as a solution to migration policy problems owing to the lack of clear objectives, timetable, and the weak legal instruments. This failure therefore led to the member states communitarizing the policy subject to a five-year transition period in which the Commission was effectively 'on probation' to ensure that control of policy was not being lost. It had become clear, as Stetter (2000: 96) puts it, that 'only Community instruments and methods could provide a guarantee that [the Amsterdam Treaty's AFSJ] objectives could be achieved'. Hence key regulatory authority has been delegated to EU institutions—in line with principal–agent theory—to tackle the shortcomings of the original, intergovernmental policy framework.

Following the Lisbon Treaty, this pattern of communitarization was repeated for the remainder of the third pillar. Furthermore, the delegation of authority moved beyond the Commission to the array of agencies described above (see Table 24.2). These developments appear to strengthen Stetter's interpretation.

Critiquing the AFSJ

A number of critical voices have engaged with the evolving area of AFSJ. Such critique has often involved the assertion that the EU promotes a 'fortress Europe' that permits free movement for 'insiders'—EU citizens—while making it increasingly difficult for 'outsiders'—migrants of various categories—to enter, reside in, and work in the EU. Such concerns have only been exacerbated by a number of tragic cases where those seeking to reach EU territory have lost their lives, such as an incident in 2013 when over 350 migrants drowned near the Italian island of Lampedusa.

Such critiques are often made via the concept of 'securitization'—a much-debated term emanating from critical security studies within international relations (Waever 1996; Bigo 2000). In its simplest form, the term refers to the way in which certain issues, such as migration, become conceived primarily through the lens of security and often at the expense of a consideration of human rights and justice. In the aftermath of 11 September 2001, and in the context of growing concerns about terrorism, scholars debated whether AFSJ policies had become securitized in this way (Boswell 2010). Exponents of this claim emphasized the ways in which experts in home affairs played upon popular insecurity to extend new controls, such as over immigration (see, for instance, Huysmans 2006; van Munster 2009; Guild et al. 2008). Other critics have claimed that when it comes to anti-terrorism measures which have encroached on the rights and freedoms of EU citizens (as well as non-citizens) the EU is 'world leader rather than reluctant follower' of the US (de Goede 2008: 162).

It has been argued that the term 'fortress Europe'—and the associated concept of 'securitization'—may be somewhat misleading when applied to the EU, since large numbers of visitors are permitted to enter legally, as do many migrants, especially for reasons of family reunification or work (Boswell and Geddes 2011: 42–3; Boswell 2007). Indeed, if the EU is a fortress, it is one that selectively opens its gates to certain 'outsiders' (for instance, note the 'blue card' scheme discussed above in this chapter) and works according to a variety of rationales which go beyond classic security concerns.

While the gates are not closed to all 'outsiders', it has conversely been highlighted that not all EU citizens as 'insiders' may be able to take advantage of the freedoms of movement and residence associated with that status. With reference to the high-profile expulsions of Roma EU citizens from France in 2010, Parker (2012*b*) noted that such freedoms are granted conditionally by member states—often in accordance with an economic logic—and this may be in conformity with an EU law which permits such conditions.

CONCLUSION

The development of the AFSJ has been a very significant development in European integration. Starting from modest beginnings and in large part outside the EC itself, the policy area was established as an intergovernmental pillar and then communitarized over a staged process. The development is striking given that JHA policy areas—not least the issue of border control—have traditionally been seen as key powers of the nation state. It is not surprising that these areas of policy did not reach the EU agenda until after many others. However, it is also clear that there was some linkage arising from the dismantling of barriers to trade as part of the single market.

The analysis of AFSJ policy has not generally been oriented around the integrationist theoretical debates examined in Chapter 2. Nevertheless, it is clear that these debates are relevant, since policy dynamics have tended to be either functional or political. Member governments have been extremely reluctant to delegate their sovereign powers unless there is a clear demonstration that an issue cannot be addressed without co-operation among the EU states. Despite these concerns, the delegation of tasks to the EU has been rapid, often for functional reasons.

A number of scholars researching AFSJ focus less on its evolution as an EU competence and are more concerned with emphasizing the ways in which the EU has increasingly contributed to the establishment of a 'fortress Europe', preoccupied with security concerns often to the detriment of professed EU ideals of freedom and justice. Whatever one's view on such assertions, it is unlikely that the political and normative debates over the issues falling within the AFSJ are going to diminish in the context of the economic crisis and its aftermath.

KEY POINTS

Context

- The Maastricht Treaty brought JHA into the EU, where it had its own intergovernmental 'pillar' (the third pillar).
- In the Amsterdam Treaty, this policy area became part of an ambition to create an AFSJ, and entered the first pillar.
- The policy area has been marked by the use of differentiated integration.

History

- JHA was not envisaged in the founding Treaties.
- The initial steps in co-operation were taken in diverse forums ('laboratories'), such as the Council of Europe, Trevi, and Schengen.
- The free movement of goods and people under the SEA increased the number of problems that demanded a collective policy response.
- Globalization and changes in the international system posed new security threats. Security became more widely defined and more politically salient.
- In the TEU, JHA was made a 'third pillar' of the EU. The institutional arrangements were a compromise between those who wanted closer co-operation and those who wanted to retain more national control.
- The Amsterdam Treaty committed the EU to creating an area of freedom, security, and justice. Visa, asylum, and immigration policies were transferred to the first pillar and came under QMV. Pillar 3 became PJCCM. Schengen was incorporated into the EU.
- At Nice in 2000, the heads of government solemnly declared their commitment to a Charter of Fundamental Rights.

The Lisbon Treaty

- Lisbon abolished the third pillar and incorporated PJCCM into a Title on the Area of Freedom, Security, and Justice.

- In line with broader trends in public administration, new policy tasks have been delegated to expert bodies and new technology has been deployed.
- Important institutional developments include the SIS, Europol, Eurojust, and Frontex.

The Area of Freedom, Security, and Justice

- Creating an AFSJ is now a central objective of the EU.
- The AFSJ involves: free movement of persons; common immigration and asylum policies; judicial co-operation in civil and criminal matters; police and customs co-operation; combating organized crime, terrorism, drugs, and human trafficking; the protection of fundamental rights; action to avoid unjust discrimination; and citizenship.
- Many of these activities have implications for the enlargement process and have a wider international dimension.
- Differentiated integration is a striking characteristic of the politics of the AFSJ.
- The EP and the Commission have sought to assert their new, post-Lisbon authority but with variable results.

Explaining the AFSJ

- Neofunctionalist explanations of JHA stress spillover, but its explanatory value is limited.
- Related analyses invoke the concepts of 'institutionalizing European space' and 'venue-shopping'.
- Intergovernmental explanations were plausible for early developments, but less so with the communitarization of key JHA policies.
- Regulatory analysis and principal–agent theory have also been used to explain aspects of JHA.
- JHA is very broad in scope and has been studied independently by scholars from different disciplines, leading to fragmentation.
- More critical debates have emerged around the themes of 'fortress Europe' and 'securitization'.

Critiquing the AFSJ

- The AFSJ has been critiqued on different grounds. First it has been seen as a fortress privileging insiders over migrants from outside. Against this, it is pointed out that a significant number of outsiders are still allowed in.
- A second criticism is that, since 11 September 2001, the AFSJ has become 'securitized', that is that it has come to be dominated by security concerns, emphasizing controls of various kinds at the cost of human rights and liberties of EU and other migrants.

FURTHER READING

Useful analysis of the early evolution of this policy area is offered by: **J. Monar**, 'The Dynamics of Justice and Home Affairs: Laboratories, Driving Factors and Costs', *Journal of Common Market Studies*, 39 (2001): 747–64. More recent analysis is to be found in: **S. Lavenex**, 'Justice and Home Affairs: Communitarization with Hesitation', in **H. Wallace, M. Pollack, and A. Young (eds)**, *Policy-Making in the European Union*, 6th edn (Oxford: Oxford University Press, 2010), 458–77; and **U. Uçarer**, 'The Area of Freedom, Security and Justice', in **M. Cini and N. Pérez-Solórzano**

Borragán (eds), *European Union Politics*, 4th edn (Oxford: Oxford University Press, 2013), 281–95. On migration, see **C. Boswell and A. Geddes**, *Migration and Mobility in the European Union* (Basingstoke: Palgrave Macmillan, 2011).

For reviews of the dynamics of the policy area, see: **C. Boswell**, 'Justice and Home Affairs', in **M. Egan, N. Nugent, and W. Paterson (eds)**, *Research Agendas in EU Studies: Stalking the Elephant* (Basingstoke: Palgrave Macmillan, 2010), 278–304; and **A. Geddes**, 'The Politics of European Union Domestic Order', in **K. E. Jørgensen, M. Pollack, and B. Rosamond (eds)**, *Handbook of European Union Politics* (London: SAGE Publications, 2006), 449–62. A useful summary of annual policy developments is provided by **J. Monar** in the special Annual Review edition of the *Journal of Common Market Studies*: for example, 'Justice and Home Affairs', *Journal of Common Market Studies: Annual Review*, 51 (2013): 124–38.

online
resource
centre

Visit the Online Resource Centre that accompanies this book for links to more information on Justice and Home Affairs: http://oxfordtextbooks.co. uk/orc.bache4e/

Chapter 25

Trade and Development Aid

Chapter Overview

Up to now, this part of the book has dealt primarily with the internal policies of the European Union (EU). In this chapter and the next, the focus shifts to policies that concern the relations of the EU with the rest of the world. This chapter looks at the external trade relations of the EU in the context of the wider framework of global trade agreements, and at its related policies on development aid, particularly with the African, Caribbean, and Pacific (ACP) states. It also looks at the combination of trade and aid policies towards the near neighbours of the EU in the rest of Europe and in North Africa. From this examination of policy, it becomes clear that too sharp a distinction cannot be drawn between economic and political aspects of the external relations of the EU.

History

From the outset, the European Economic Community (EEC) aimed to become a major international economic actor. Its main pattern of bilateral and multilateral trade relations was structured through the international institutions that were set up after the Second World War to promote the emergence of the post-war trading system. It also pursued an active policy of cultivating special relations with former European colonies, which sometimes provided a tension with its commitments under the wider trading arrangements. More recently, the EU became concerned to use economic and trade instruments to help to stabilize the economies of its near neighbours in other parts of Europe and in North Africa.

The International Context for EU Policy

When the EEC came into existence, international economic relations were governed by the agreements reached at negotiations in Bretton Woods, New Hampshire, in 1944. These agreements set up several institutions designed to help an international economic system to emerge. At the heart of the structure was a monetary system nominally based on gold, but in practice with the US dollar as the anchor. To assist the development of states' economies, the International Bank for Reconstruction and Development (IBRD), or World Bank, was created. To help states that got into temporary difficulties with their balance of payments, the International Monetary Fund

(IMF) was set up. There was also intended to be an International Trade Organization (ITO), to facilitate the gradual introduction of global free trade agreements, and to regulate trade disputes between states. However, the US Congress would not agree to the ITO, so instead a series of intergovernmental negotiations were initiated, known as the **General Agreement on Tariffs and Trade (GATT)**.

One important feature of the GATT framework was that the EEC, after its formation, had a single representative. This followed from the commitment in the Treaty of Rome to have a common commercial policy that was solely a Community competence (Article 113, now Article 207 TFEU).

Within the GATT framework, a key concept was that of 'most favoured nation' (MFN) treatment. This meant that states would not negotiate more favourable deals with some partners than they were prepared to offer to all of the participants in GATT. Exceptions were allowed to the rule, though, and the EEC received special dispensation from the MFN principle to allow it to dismantle tariffs on internal trade between the member states, because there was provision in the rules to allow the creation of **customs unions** and **free trade areas** that might speed up the process of dismantling barriers to free trade globally. Another area in which the EEC concluded preferential trading deals was in relation to the former colonies of the member states. There were also special agreements with prospective future members of the EEC. These arrangements were not uncontroversial, though, and they became more liable to challenge when the GATT was superseded by the World Trade Organization (WTO) in 1995.

The GATT was a weak organization. It was never intended to stand alone, and only became the arbiter of international trade relations because the ITO failed to appear. Although the GATT had a procedure for resolving disputes, it was easy for a state that was losing a case to block a ruling against it. The arrangements began to collapse in the late 1970s and 1980s with the growth of protectionism in the face of a global economic downturn. In response, GATT launched a marathon round of trade negotiations in 1986, known as the Uruguay Round. The negotiations were scheduled to be completed by 1990, but stretched out until 1994. The difficulty of reaching agreement, and the prospect of having to enforce a much more complex package of arrangements, led to the creation of the WTO, a far stronger body than GATT.

Development Policy

One area of considerable concern to the original EEC was its relations with ex-colonies. When the Treaty of Rome was signed in 1957, the vast majority of independent countries that eventually became the ACP group remained the responsibility of colonial powers. In 1956, France, which of the original EEC member states had the largest number of colonies, requested that its overseas territories be granted associated status with the proposed EEC.

Relations were initially dealt with in an Implementing Convention, which was replaced in July 1963 by the Yaoundé Convention, named after the capital of Cameroon, where it was signed. Both these instruments had the objective of gradually moving towards a free trade area between the EEC and the former French colonies, and there was a European Development Fund (EDF) for the purpose of granting European Community (EC) financial aid to the associated countries and territories to promote their social and economic development (Frey-Wouters 1980: 14).

Neither the Implementing Convention nor the Yaoundé agreements marked a serious attempt to break with the traditional pattern of relations between Europe and the developing world. A. H. Jamal, a former Tanzanian Minister of Communications, described the Yaoundé Convention as providing 'an institutional dependence on the part of some African countries on one particular metropolitan power—France' (Jamal 1979: 134), and the EDFs under the Implementing Convention and Yaoundé were described by another commentator as 'basically a device to offload the costs of French colonial mercantilism on the EEC in return for other EEC states receiving access to their markets and sources of supply' (Green 1976: 50).

Many hoped that the first Lomé agreement would mark a turning point in these relations. Lomé was negotiated in the early 1970s as a result of the accession of Britain to the EC. Like France, Britain was a former imperial power, and the addition of its former colonies brought to forty-six the number of associated states. The Lomé agreement was received by the ACP states more enthusiastically than its predecessors had been. As one observer put it:

> When Lomé 1 was signed, both sides claimed that it was qualitatively different from anything that had gone before; a contract between equal partners and a step towards a New International Economic Order.

(Stevens 1984: 1)

Revised Lomé agreements were reached in the late 1970s and the 1980s. In most respects, the terms of the subsequent Lomé Conventions were disappointing. Although aid was increased in each agreement, it was not by enough to take account of the combined effects of increases in inflation and in population. When inflation and population growth were taken into account, the period leading up to Lomé 3 (1976–85) saw a fall in EC real *per capita* transfers to ACP states of 40 per cent (Hewitt 1989: 291).

In the period 1980–87, Africa's *per capita* gross domestic product (GDP) fell by an average of 2.6 per cent and its returns on investment were substantially down (Glaser 1990: 26). This meant that, on top of the unfulfilled hopes of various aid schemes, many ACP countries were under intense pressure to repay loans. By 1983, the IMF and the World Bank were implementing stabilization and structural adjustment programmes in those countries, and the EC response to ACP problems had to be implemented in close co-ordination with these institutions. This situation placed the IMF in the driving seat 'with its own short-run conditions overwhelming those of all the other partners' (Hewitt 1989: 296).

Thus, by the late 1980s, ACP states believed that Lomé seriously neglected their main concerns: the impossibility of servicing debt, and the increasing demands of the World Bank and the IMF for changes in economic and social policies. By the early 1990s, to these concerns were added concerns over the effect of the completion of the single European market and over the aid demands on the EC from the former Communist countries of eastern Europe.

Relations with Near Neighbours

With the collapse of communism, the EU faced the problem of instability among its near neighbours. At the end of the Cold War, the EC signed technical co-operation agreements with the central and eastern European countries (CEECs). These were subsequently replaced with 'Europe Agreements': Association Agreements that fell short of envisaging full membership. Then, in June 1993, the Copenhagen European Council accepted the legitimacy of the aspirations of the newly independent states to become members (see Chapter 27).

In the Balkans, as part of its stability pact for south-eastern Europe, the EU agreed a Memorandum of Understanding (MoU) on Trade Liberalization and Facilitation with Albania, Bosnia and Herzegovina, Croatia, the Federal Republic of Yugoslavia (Serbia and Montenegro), and the former Yugoslav Republic of Macedonia. This was the first stage in what became known as the Stabilization and Association Process (SAP) which led to formal accession processes in a number of cases (see Chapter 27).

While the governments of France and the southern member states could see the arguments for enlargement to the east, and even accepted them, they were concerned that the problems of the Mediterranean, which affected them more than did instability in the east, would be relegated to a secondary issue. Instability in North Africa, particularly a civil war in Algeria, was already having an impact on them in the form of refugees, and in terms of threats to their companies' investments in the region.

Their concern that attention would be diverted from the problems of the Mediterranean was recognized by the German government when it held the presidency of the EU in the second half of 1994. Agreement was reached at the Essen meeting of the European Council in December 1994 to launch an initiative on North Africa and the Middle East. This assumed more tangible form during 1995 under the successive French and Spanish presidencies, culminating in a major conference in Barcelona on 23–29 November 1995 involving the EU member states, the Maghreb states (Algeria, Morocco, and Tunisia), Israel, Jordan, Lebanon, Syria, Turkey, Cyprus, and Malta. From this emerged the Euro-Med Partnership Agreement.

External Trade Policy

The EU is the world's largest trading entity (see Table 25.1) and as of 2014 its twenty-eight member states accounted for around 20 per cent of total world trade. This makes trade policy central to its external activities.

Table 25.1 Trade in Commercial Goods and Services 2010, € billions

Country or region	Imports	Exports
EU	1956	1882
United States	1762	1358
China	1197	1319
Japan	641	685
South Korea	392	417

Source: http://ec.europa.eu, © European Union, 1995–2014.

The Common Commercial Policy

In the negotiation of multilateral and bilateral trade agreements, the EU operates under the rules of its own common commercial policy. Article 207 TFEU gives the EU exclusive competence in commercial policy, including external trade negotiations. However, this is an EU competence, which is not the same as a Commission competence. Before it can even enter into trade negotiations, the Commission has to get the agreement of the Council of Ministers on a negotiating mandate. The negotiations are then to be conducted 'in consultation with a special committee appointed by the Council' (Article 207(3) TFEU). This committee, known as 'the Trade Policy Committee' since the Lisbon Treaty, consists of senior civil servants of the member states who monitor the position taken by the Commission at every stage of trade negotiations to ensure that it is in line with the negotiating mandate laid down by the Council of Ministers. The senior committee meets monthly throughout the year, and there are weekly meetings of deputies. Once an agreement has been reached in the negotiations, it has to be ratified by the member states meeting in full Council, using **qualified majority voting (QMV)** (see Chapter 12).

For a long time, not only was the Commission bound by the mandate and closely monitored in trade negotiations, but also the EC/EU did not even have formal full competence except for trade in goods. Until the Lisbon Treaty, trade in services and in intellectual products were not included. Originally, this was because they were not the subjects of trade negotiations when the Treaty of Rome was drawn up. In 1994, the European Court of Justice (ECJ) ruled that the EU did not have sole competence in negotiations on such matters, but shared the competence with the member states. In September 1996, the Commission asked the Council of Ministers to extend its remit to these sectors, but met with a cool response.

Young (2000: 101) suggested three considerations that made the member states, and especially the larger of them, reluctant to extend competence in these new trade issues to the EU: the new issues are more sensitive domestically than trade in goods; some member states do not trust the Commission to represent their interests in these areas; and if competence were ceded to the EU, where common agreement was blocked by a coalition of unwilling member states, there would be no possibility of those states that wanted to go further in liberalizing such areas concluding agreements independently of the EU.

In the Treaty of Amsterdam, the member states inserted a clause that allowed them to give the Commission full negotiating responsibility in these sectors for specific future negotiations, without further change to the Treaties, but only if they were unanimous in agreeing to do so. Eventually, they were defined as areas of exclusive EU competence in the Lisbon Treaty, but unanimity remains the voting rule in the Council for agreements in the field of trade in services and the commercial aspects of intellectual property 'where such agreements include provisions for which unanimity is required for the adoption of internal rules', and in the field of trade in cultural and audiovisual services 'where these agreements risk prejudicing the Union's cultural and linguistic diversity' (Article 207(4) TFEU).

Another set of instruments of the common commercial policy are those designed to protect the EU from unfair trade practices by non-members. These instruments include restrictions that can be imposed where non-members are suspected of

> **Insight 25.1 The 1997 Internal Dispute over Measures Against Imports of Unbleached Cotton Cloth**
>
> The measures against China, Egypt, India, Indonesia, and Pakistan were demanded by Eurocoton, the association of European producers of cotton fabrics—but they were opposed by European producers of finished cotton goods, who benefited from the cheaper semi-finished products imported from the non-EU countries. The member states were evenly divided, with Germany abstaining when the first vote was taken in March 1997. This reflected the balance of industrial interests between producers of raw cotton cloth and producers of finished cotton goods in the different member states. Eventually, in May 1997, the German government decided to oppose the anti-dumping measures, to the fury of the French.

dumping produce on the EU market at less than the cost of production, and similar measures to counter unfair subsidies. On these sorts of issue, though, the EU prefers, wherever possible, to work through the WTO.

It is not always easy for the member states to reach common positions on external trade policy. For example, in 1997, there was internal dispute over the imposition of anti-dumping measures against imports of unbleached cotton cloth (see Insight 25.1). The divisions between member states in this case illustrated two aspects of the difficulty in reaching common positions: there was a straight division on the basis of national economic interest, and a more general issue about free trade versus managed trade. Among the EU fifteen (that is, prior to the eastern enlargement), generally the northern member states were more in favour of liberalization, while suspicions of market opening were felt most strongly in the southern member states. France has had particular difficulties with the idea of unmanaged global free trade.

Despite such difficulties, the thrust of EC commercial policy has been consistently in the direction of free trade. In the Doha Round of trade negotiations, which began in 2001, the EU's negotiating position with respect to traditional trade policy was described by Young (2007: 798) as 'aggressive, with a heavy emphasis on increasing market access in non-agricultural products, . . . rather than a preoccupation with protecting European industrial sectors'.

While EC commercial policy had from the late 1990s supported multilateralism via the WTO, since 2006 the EU has once again explicitly pursued bilateral free trade agreements (FTAs) (for reasons that are considered later in the chapter). At the time of writing, the EU had agreements in place with a number of countries and was negotiating agreements with a number of others, including, since 2013, with the United States. While there was clearly some will on both sides to reach a wide-ranging agreement, a history of disputes between the two trading partners threatened to render such talks difficult in certain areas (see Insights 25.2, 25.3, and 25.4).

Disputes within the World Trade Organization

Partly because of the increased complexity of the rules, and partly because of the advent of more effective machinery, recourse to dispute panels has increased

---

Insight 25.2 The WTO Dispute over the EU Banana Regime

This was part of the Lomé Agreements with former French and British colonies. It gave preferential access to the EU market for bananas grown in those Caribbean and Pacific states that were parties to the agreement. The United States objected to the discrimination against bananas produced in Latin America, mainly by US-owned companies. Eventually, in April 1999, the WTO did authorize the imposition of sanctions by the United States, although at a much-reduced level from those originally proposed. The whole issue generated a surprising amount of bitterness and heat considering that it concerned a product that was grown in neither the EU nor the United States. It was eventually settled in December 2009 by an agreement under which the EU would reduce its tariffs on imported bananas progressively over seven years, and the United States and banana-producing countries from Latin America agreed to drop litigation against the EU.

Insight 25.3 Two WTO Disputes over the Application of Biotechnology to Foodstuffs

In 1999, the United States won a complaint to the WTO against a ban by the EU on the import of hormone-treated beef. The ban reflected the strong prejudice of EU consumers against meat that contained hormones, and was first imposed in 1987. The United States maintained that this action was against WTO rules because there was no scientific evidence that there was any risk to human health from eating such meat. The EU insisted that it wanted to complete its own scientific tests before agreeing to lift the ban. Early in 1999, the WTO ruled against the EU, and the United States said that it would impose retaliatory sanctions unless the ban was lifted, but the EU refused to lift the ban in the face of intense consumer opposition. It did offer to allow the import of hormone-treated beef if it was clearly labelled as such, but the United States rejected this compromise because it said that the labelling itself implied that there was something wrong with the beef.

Also in 1999, the EU placed an effective moratorium on the granting of licences for genetically modified (GM) crops. This move was attacked by the United States as imposing a non-tariff barrier on agricultural trade. In 2001, the Commission proposed to introduce rules on the labelling of foodstuffs that contained GM crops, and a requirement that the origins of foodstuffs be traceable back to the crops from which they were produced. The United States considered these to be unreasonable requirements that would probably be impossible to implement, and would certainly be very costly, eliminating any advantage that US farmers gained from adopting the new technology, and requested a WTO panel on the issue.

---

considerably under the WTO, averaging forty disputes a year as compared to six per year under the GATT procedures (McQueen 1998: 436). This has affected the EU because of increased challenges to its practices, particularly from the United States.

Since the WTO began operation in January 1995, the United States and the EU have struggled to dominate the procedures and the agenda, or at least to ensure that the other does not dominate. Each side has brought complaints against the other.

> **Insight 25.4 The WTO Dispute over the US Foreign Sales Corporation Tax Provisions**
>
> The FSC came into effect in 1984, and allowed US corporations to claim exemption on between 15 and 30 per cent of their earnings from exports. The EU maintained that this amounted to an export subsidy in breach of WTO rules. The United States considered that the appeal was simply EU retaliation against its appeals on bananas and beef, pointing out that it had taken the EU fourteen years to get round to protesting about the FSC, and that there was no evidence of pressure on the Commission from European businesses for the complaint to be made at this time (Ahearn 2002: 4). However, in October 1999, a WTO disputes panel found in favour of the EU, and the United States was told to come into compliance with its WTO obligations by October 2000. In November 2000, the FSC was repealed and replaced by the Extraterritorial Income (ERI) provisions. This allowed tax breaks up to the same amount to US corporations on all foreign earnings, including their earnings from foreign investments. By extending the provision beyond export earnings in this way, Congress hoped to redefine the tax provision. Predictably, the EU appealed and the WTO ruled against the ERI, and against the counter-appeal from the Bush Administration (Ahearn 2002: 5). In August 2002, the WTO disputes panel ruled that the EU could impose up to US$4 billion of sanctions in retaliation.

In 1998, a fierce dispute blew up over the EU's banana regime (see Insight 25.2), and, in 1999, two issues arose about the application of biotechnology to agricultural produce (see Insight 25.3). In 1998, the EU launched its own WTO appeal against the foreign sales corporation (FSC) provisions of US tax law (see Insight 25.4).

The result of these moves and counter-moves was that the United States and the EU entered the twenty-first century each armed with the right to impose WTO-approved sanctions on the other. Further tensions emerged over accusations and counter-accusations of illegal subsidies by both sides to their major producers of civil aircraft (Airbus and Boeing). Perhaps because of the awareness of both sides of the potential for damage to themselves as well as to the global trading system, restraint has generally been shown in the application of sanctions.

Relations with the African, Caribbean, and Pacific States

The original ACP states were all former colonies of one or other of the member states of the EU, although, as the Lomé Convention was regularly updated, other states joined that had never been colonies of EU members. When the Cotonou Agreement was signed in June 2000, more ACP states joined, bringing the total to eighty (see Box 25.1).

The Cotonou Agreement

Negotiations on what became Cotonou followed a Commission 'Green Paper' high-lighting the ongoing problems of ACP countries (European Commission 1996*b*). The

---

Box 25.1 The ACP States

African States

Angola, Benin, Botswana, Burkina Faso, Burundi, Cameroon, Cape Verde, Central African Republic, Chad, Comoros, Congo (Republic of), Congo (Democratic Republic of), Djibouti, Equatorial Guinea, Eritrea, Ethiopia, Gabon, Gambia, Ghana, Guinea, Guinea-Bissau, Ivory Coast, Kenya, Lesotho, Liberia, Madagascar, Malawi, Mali, Mauritania, Mauritius, Mozambique, Namibia, Niger, Nigeria, Rwanda, Sao Tome and Principe, Senegal, Seychelles, Sierra Leone, Somalia, South Africa, Sudan, Swaziland, Tanzania, Togo, Uganda, Zaire, Zambia, Zimbabwe.

Caribbean States

Antigua and Barbuda, Bahamas, Barbados, Belize, Cuba, Dominica, Dominican Republic, Grenada, Guyana, Haiti, Jamaica, St Kitts and Nevis, St Lucia, St Vincent and the Grenadines, Suriname, Trinidad and Tobago.

Pacific States

Cook Islands, Federated States of Micronesia, Fiji, Kiribati, Marshall Islands, Nauru, Niue, Palau, Papua New Guinea, Solomon Islands, Timor-Leste, Tonga, Tuvalu, Vanuatu, Western Samoa.

Green Paper identified two main reasons why the Lomé pattern could not continue, as follows:

- The preferences under Lomé were becoming less valuable as the liberalization of global trade proceeded; this was evidenced by a decline in the ACP share of the EU market.

- Lomé was incompatible with WTO rules. Although various waivers had been granted, the rules were quite clear. Article 1 of the WTO Charter requires participants not to discriminate between other WTO members in trade concessions. Exceptions are allowed to this rule for less developed countries (LDCs), but the concessions must apply to all LDCs. There were two problems about the compatibility of Lomé with these WTO rules: first, many of the ACP states covered by Lomé were not classified as LDCs by the WTO; second, there were nine LDCs that were not included in Lomé.

In response to these problems with the existing arrangements, the Commission proposed dividing the ACP states into the LDCs, which could choose to continue to receive non-reciprocal trade concessions that would also be offered to the nine LDC states that had previously been excluded, and the non-LDCs, which would be offered Economic Partnership Agreements (EPAs). The EPAs would involve reciprocity, so the ACP states would have to offer free market access to EU goods. To be WTO-compatible, they would also have to cover 'substantially all' trade, which was generally interpreted as 90 per cent of products, so agricultural produce that had been excluded from Lomé to protect areas that were adjudged 'sensitive' by EU member states would have to be included. The EU agreed that it would conclude such agreements either with individual states or regional groupings, but indicated a strong preference for Regional Economic Partnership Agreements (REPAs). The most significant change from Lomé was the gradual replacement of the system of trade preferences by a series of new economic partnerships based on the progressive and reciprocal removal of trade barriers (European Commission 2000: Chapter 2, Articles 36–8). However, the negotiation of EPAs repeatedly stalled, and at the end of 2013 only the Caribbean region had signed a full EPA (in 2008).

The European Neighbourhood Policy

In 2004, the relations of the EU with neighbouring states were brought together under the European Neighbourhood Policy (ENP). Its objectives were: to share the benefits of the 2004 enlargement with neighbouring countries without offering the perspective of membership, and so to prevent the emergence of stark dividing lines between EU and non-EU states; and to build security in the area surrounding the EU. Although the ENP is not a purely economic arrangement, the provision of financial assistance and economic co-operation, including access for the neighbouring states to the EU's internal market, are central to its operation. In 2013 there were sixteen ENP countries to the south and east of the EU: Algeria, Armenia, Azerbaijan, Belarus, Egypt, Georgia, Israel, Jordan, Lebanon, Libya, Moldova, Morocco, Palestine, Syria, Tunisia, and Ukraine. It does not cover states to the east that already have a prospect of membership—Turkey, and the Western Balkan states of Serbia, Montenegro, Bosnia-Herzegovina, Albania, and the former Yugoslav Republic of Macedonia (see Chapter 27). Nor does it cover Russia.

In line with the objective of avoiding stark dividing lines between the EU and its neighbours, it was intended from the outset that the European Neighbourhood and Partnership Instrument (ENPI) would have a specific focus on cross-border co-operation and intra-regional co-operation. The principles used in the management of the ENPI are those that were pioneered first in the management of the structural funds for regional development in the EU—multi-annual programming, partnership, and co-financing (see Chapter 22)—and later deployed in the context of enlargement policy (see Chapter 27).

Throughout the political and economic dialogue with neighbouring states, the emphasis has been on the development of the rule of law, good governance, respect for human rights—including minority rights—the promotion of good-neighbourly relations, and the principles of the market economy and sustainable development. While the ENP consists in the main of bilateral relations between the EU and partner countries, it co-exists and overlaps with ongoing multilateral regional based initiatives in the 'neighbourhood', such as the Euro-Med Partnership, the Eastern Partnership, and Black Sea Synergy.

In the context of the ENP, the EU has been able to negotiate association agreements with many countries in the EU 'neighbourhood'. These agreements typically provide for the liberalization of trade to various degrees and often (though not necessarily) pave the way to formal accession processes. One of the earliest such agreements was with Turkey in 1973. In recognition of the disappointment of Turkey at not being treated as a candidate for membership of the EU in the enlargement round that ended in 2004, in 1996, the association agreement with it was extended into a special customs union.

In the late 1990s and throughout the 2000s the EU negotiated association agreements with a number of countries in the Mediterranean region geared towards the liberalization of trade in goods. Since the late 2000s and in the context of its Eastern Partnership, the EU has sought to negotiate further such agreements. As of early 2014 it had made significant progress towards the signature of agreements with Georgia and Moldova. Despite having negotiated and initialled an agreement with the EU, Ukraine opted in late 2013 not to sign this in response to Russian pressure. This led to widespread political opposition and upheaval in Ukraine in early 2014 and significant tensions between Russia and the west (for more on these events see Chapter 26). Russia is generally concerned about the extension of EU economic and political influence in the east and particularly into soviet successor states.

Explaining Trade and Development Aid Policies

Theoretical explanations of the external trade and development aid policies of the EU have focused on the politics of formulating a common commercial policy and on the relations of the EU with the ACP states. In both cases, use has been made of the idea of a 'multi-level game', derived from Robert Putnam's concept of a 'two-level game', combined with insights from institutionalist approaches.

Explaining External Trade Policy

Explanations of the external trade policy of the EU have not generally supported supranational theories, although, given the qualms of France and some of the other member states about policies of liberalization, the idea of the Commission playing an autonomous role can be put forward. Most analyses, though, adopt an approach based on the idea of a multi-level game, to which has been added an institutionalist perspective.

One possible explanation of the trade policy of the EU is that the Commission is able to play a role as an autonomous actor (Damro 2007). On this view, divisions within the EU between member states, combined with the need for the Council to approve trade agreements by a qualified majority rather than unanimity, opened up an opportunity for active and committed Commission leadership to influence the direction of policy. Such leadership was provided by a succession of Trade Commissioners, all of whom favoured trade liberalization. In the Santer Commission, Sir Leon Brittan held the portfolio from 1994 to 1999, and set a strong free trade agenda; he was followed by Pascal Lamy (1999–2004), who, despite his French nationality, continued to push the EU in the same direction during the Prodi Commission, as did his successor in the Barroso Commission, Peter Mandelson (2004–08).

485

This does not mean that there were no differences in emphasis between the Commissioners. Meunier (2007a) looked at the differences between the 'managed globalization' favoured by Lamy and the position of his successor, Mandelson, as expressed in the 2006 communication *Global Europe: Competing in the World* (European Commission 2006b). 'Managed globalization' made multilateralism the central doctrine of EU trade policy, and linked trade to political objectives such as social justice and sustainable development. 'Global Europe' argued that the central objective of EU trade policy should be to open markets abroad for European companies. The shift of emphasis involved a downgrading of the political adjuncts to trade negotiations and a retreat from the commitment to multilateralism. Although multilateralism was still to be afforded primacy, an informal moratorium on bilateral agreements until the end of the Doha Round, which Lamy had introduced, was abandoned.

Meunier (2007a) noted that neither the adoption of the approach of managed globalization nor the shift to that of 'Global Europe' involved a new mandate from the member states. This seemed to indicate a degree of autonomy of the Commission in making EU policy on external trade. However, little evidence was found to sustain the argument that the Commission had a significant autonomous effect on the policy. The autonomy of the Commission was judged to be limited to reframing and repackaging the interests of the member states, and perhaps tweaking them at the margins (Meunier 2007a: 922).

Intergovernmental explanations have centred on the idea of trade negotiations as a multi-level game. Putnam (1988) described the making of foreign policy for a state as a 'two-level game'. Moravcsik (1991, 1993, 1998) incorporated this insight into his 'liberal intergovernmental' theorizations of the nature of the relationship between the EC/EU and its member states (see Chapter 1). At one level, the government of each member state has to find a position that will satisfy the balance of pressures in its domestic political arena. It then has to play a game at the level of negotiations with the other member states to try to achieve an agreement that falls within the parameters of what is acceptable domestically.

However, the position in EC trade negotiations is even more complex. The nature of the relationship between the member states, the Commission, and the trade partners means that it is a three-level, rather than a two-level, game (Collinson 1999). The three levels are as follows.

(1) The government of each of the member states has to find a negotiating position that reflects its own domestic constraints.

(2) All of the governments then have to negotiate around these positions in determining together the negotiating mandate for the Commission in the wider trade talks.

(3) The Commission then has to negotiate in the wider talks within the tight parameters of this mandate.

If it is necessary to go beyond these parameters to reach a deal, the Commission has to refer back to its constituency in the Council, and the members of that constituency (the governments of the member states) have to refer back to their domestic constituencies.

Matters are made even more difficult by the multi-issue nature of trade talks. It has already been suggested that when the Treaty of Rome was drawn up, certain issues that are central to contemporary world trade were not considered to be part of the agenda. Trade in the 1950s was predominantly in goods. Today, there is growing trade in services and intellectual property. Foreign direct investment has also grown rapidly and become a matter of concern, with some governments wishing to regulate it and others wishing to embed international rules that ban national discrimination against foreign investment. In addition, agriculture, which was effectively excluded from the earliest rounds of GATT negotiations by a tacit agreement between the participants, has become a central issue.

Young and Peterson (2006) added even more complexity by pointing to the emergence of a new trade agenda that is no longer concerned with restrictions that occur at the border of national economies, but increasingly involves attempts to harmonize or regulate national domestic rules that affect trade, such as state subsidies, and technical barriers to trade.

Young (2000) had earlier advocated supplementing liberal intergovernmental analysis of trade policy with an institutionalist approach. According to this analysis, the three-level game is structured by the institutionalization of the policy sector. Young (2007) used such an approach in an analysis of the EU's positions in the Doha Round, in which the EU was argued to have taken a more liberal position on traditional trade issues than it did on the newer issues. Young explained this variation by examining the different institutionalization of political forces within each set of issues.

On the traditional trade issues, the range of actors was generally limited to national and EU-level officials and companies within the EU that were directly affected, either because they competed with imports and sought protection, or because they were export-oriented and sought the opening of markets in other countries even at the cost of dismantling EU protection. Within this limited policy arena, a growing acceptance among officials that free trade offered the best prospects for high levels of economic growth, combined with the increasing dominance of the export-oriented firms, ensured that since at least the mid-1980s the EU became more committed to trade liberalization.

Because the newer 'deep trade' agenda involves 'behind-the-border' issues, such as the adverse trade effects of national rules, state subsidies, and public procurement, a different range of actors is involved. As well as trade officials, non-trade departments, both of the Commission and the national governments, have central roles, and they are less likely to share the acceptance of the benefits of free trade that forms the ideational context for policy making among trade officials. National governments are more central actors at the EU level because the policies covered involve them directly, as with subsidies that they pay or public contracts that they award, in both cases for domestic reasons. Also, the sorts of issue covered by the new agenda have much wider direct political implications within states. This is particularly true of the 'social trade' agenda, which affects such issues as measures to protect the environment or consumers. Here, both politicians and campaigning interest groups, such as environmental groups and consumer groups, have an incentive to become active within the policy-making process. For all of these reasons, it will be more difficult for the EU to establish a liberalization agenda on these issues than it is for traditional trade issues.

That said, as noted below, some scholars have argued that just such an agenda is nevertheless emerging.

Relations with the ACP States

Using another adaptation of the two-level game model, Forwood (2001), going against treatments of Cotonou as a radical restructuring of Lomé, argued that a closer examination of the negotiations showed 'that the ability of the negotiators to rise to the challenges facing EU–ACP relations was compromised by the complexities of international negotiations' (Forwood 2001: 424).

Member states of the EU took up different positions on the proposals in the Commission's Green Paper. France wanted to continue with the principles of Lomé to maintain the special relationship with the ACP states. It also opposed adjustments to the relationship that might lead to the ending of agricultural exemptions. Germany wanted to see an end to Lomé, which it considered to be a 'colonial relic'. It was most supportive of the proposals in the Green Paper. Denmark, Sweden, and the Netherlands were primarily concerned to protect the interests of the LDCs. They wanted to see the nine LDCs that were excluded from Lomé brought into the new arrangements. They were also concerned about the Commission's idea of REPAs because they believed that they would benefit the non-LDC members of the ACP group at the expense of the LDCs. Britain shared this suspicion of the idea of REPAs, but, like France, wanted to maintain a special relationship with the ACP states as a whole (Forwood 2001: 428–9).

The result of these divided views was a compromise mandate for the Commission to take into the negotiations with the ACP states: the continuation of a special relationship would be available, but those ACP states that were unwilling to continue with the relationship would be offered EPAs, either on an individual basis or as REPAs (Forwood 2001: 431).

During the negotiations with the ACP states, the Commission's hand was weakened by the collapse of the WTO trade talks in Seattle in December 1999. This focused attention on the position of developing countries, making it more difficult for the EU to force through any agreement with which the ACP states were unhappy and about which they might complain publicly, thereby damaging the international image of the EU. It also demonstrated that the developing countries still had the ability to throw a spanner in the works of global liberalization (Forwood 2001: 437), particularly in the context of growing public dissatisfaction with the perceived inequities of global trading arrangements. The principal reason, though, that Forwood (2001: 438) invoked for an outcome that is here characterized as one in which 'all the features of Lomé have fundamentally been rolled over into the new Convention' was the historical institutionalist idea of 'path dependence' (see Chapter 2, New Institutionalism). In the case of Lomé, it was explained thus:

> The legacy of 25 years of Lomé was such that negotiators were not able merely to wipe the slate clean and start afresh. This legacy is more than a legal commitment, but also a moral and political obligation of the EU Member States towards the ACP countries.

(Forwood 2001: 434)

Critiquing Trade and Development Aid Policies

The general orientation of EU trade policy has been, in accordance with its internal single market policy, towards a free trade agenda (agriculture being a notable exception—see Chapter 19). However, just as the single market project has provoked critiques from a critical political-economy perspective (see Chapters 4 and 20), so, increasingly, have trends in EU trade policy. These interventions have tended to focus on the EU's relationship with the developing world, but increasingly they also consider trade and development policy as a whole and the 'deep trade' or 'behind-the-border' issues discussed above.

Deploying a neo-Gramscian perspective Gibb (2000: 477–8) analysed the shift from Lomé to Cotonou. He argued that the Commission, in its Green Paper, had presented the requirements of the WTO as an insuperable barrier to continuation of Lomé, but, in reality, the WTO system was one that the EU had been involved in installing. An alternative to changing the Lomé principles to make them compatible with the WTO would have been to change the WTO rules to make them compatible with the Lomé principles. Some ACP delegations had suggested that the EU and ACP jointly argue for the acceptance by the WTO of a new category of free trade agreement, a 'soft' or 'low' agreement, that would not be subject to the same stringent requirements as were implied by existing WTO rules. The EU chose not even to raise this issue during the Millennium Round of trade negotiations. The conclusion was that, '[t]he WTO is … at the centre of the post-Lomé negotiations because the EU placed it there. And it placed it there because it is in its own best interests to do so' (Gibb 2000: 478).

Hurt (2003) went further by analyzing the aid provisions as well as the trade provisions of the agreement. He drew attention to the similarity of principles underpinning Cotonou to the principles of other institutions of international economic management, including not only the WTO but also the IMF and the World Bank. This similarity was again attributed to the dominance of neoliberal ideas, which served the interests of powerful actors within the developed world.

> **The current neoliberal hegemony of ideas sits broadly compatibly with the self-interests of political élites and the outward-orientated fraction of the capitalist class within the EU member states.**

(Hurt 2003: 174)

More generally, the shift in agenda from multilateralism to bilateralism associated with the 'Global Europe' agenda can also be considered in terms of such a 'neoliberal hegemony of ideas', or what Heron and Siles-Brügge (2012) have termed a shift towards 'competitive liberalization'.

Moves to pursue bilateral agreements which focus on liberalization in areas with significant 'behind-the-border' implications, such as services and investment, have been understood as exemplary of this shift. Heron and Siles-Brügge (2012) emphasized in particular the importance of broader systemic factors in explaining such a shift: in particular, the efforts of competitor nations such as the United States and Japan to pursue such policies themselves. It can also, according to their analysis, be understood in terms of the increasing power and influence of services and investment-industry interest groups, seen as vital to the fortunes of the EU and developed economies more generally. Commentators have similarly warned of the increased significance of certain 'big business' voices in the context of the EU–US trade negotiations (that were ongoing at the time of writing in 2014). These negotiations are focused on a range of 'behind-the-border' issues rather than free trade in a traditional sense, and critics have pointed to the potentially detrimental effects on a range of EU regulatory standards on issues ranging from food safety to the environment (Monbiot 2013; Corporate Europe Observatory 2013). The broader structural political-economy factors identified by Heron and Siles-Brügge perhaps go some way to explaining why, notwithstanding the above-mentioned difficulties in negotiating 'deep trade' agreements highlighted by Young, the Commission has increasingly been given the mandate to negotiate just such agreements.

There are important parallels here with the controversial shifts towards liberalizing services associated with the single market project (see Chapter 20, Beyond 1992). Both trends can be understood within the context of emerging conceptions of competitiveness and the 'knowledge economy', associated for instance with the Lisbon Agenda (2000) (see Chapter 10). Indeed, adopting a 'radical' constructivist perspective (see Chapter 4), Orbie and De Ville (2014) argued that EU discourse had increasingly used internal neoliberal policy to legitimize external trade policy and vice versa.

While these critical political-economy approaches (see Chapter 4) may at times understate the plurality and complexity of competing interests at play in the trade arena, they offer an important alternative perspective to a mainstream approach which does not explicitly question the normative assumptions underpinning EU trade policy. They point to an important liberalizing trend which has been apparently undiminished by the ongoing crisis within the EU (Orbie and De Ville, 2014; Siles-Brügge 2014), and highlight some of its often neglected and sometimes pernicious consequences for groups within and beyond the EU.

CONCLUSION

Examination of the external economic relations of the EU brings to the fore several of the theoretical themes that have appeared throughout this book: the tension between nationalism and supranationalism; the complexities of bargaining within multiple international forums; the dominance of particular ideas across different forums. It also shows the difficulty entailed in clearly separating internal and external policies, and economic and political issues.

The complex decision-making rules for the common commercial policy demonstrate the dangers of any oversimplification of the relationship between intergovernmentalism and supranationalism. The Commission clearly plays an important role, and has a certain autonomy over the conduct of trade negotiations under the Articles of the original Treaty dealing with the common commercial policy. The member states have always been influential, though. They have to agree the negotiating mandate within which the Commission works, and they have to secure sufficient domestic support before their representatives dare vote for the ratification of the agreements, which acts as a further constraint on the Commission's room for making deals. This complexity is well captured by the theoretical concept of the multi-level game, especially when supplemented by an institutionalist analysis that takes into account variations in the constellations of actors, established practices, and ideational contexts of the different issue areas.

From a more explicitly critical perspective, the dominant ideas that underpin EU trade policies have been called into question. The analyses that do this have, in particular, highlighted the free market and increasingly neoliberal bias inherent in recent EU policy. They emphasize the broader power relations that have supported this bias and draw attention to the often adverse consequences that it has for developing countries and other constituencies both within and beyond the EU. In many cases they have also highlighted the close connections between these external policies and the internal EU economic policies discussed in earlier chapters.

Whatever the approach adopted in considering trade policies, it is an area which makes clear that economic and political issues are interrelated in important and complex ways. This makes it difficult to distinguish clearly the economic external relations examined in this chapter from the political external relations discussed in the following chapters, even if they have traditionally operated under different institutional arrangements.

KEY POINTS

History

- When the EEC was set up in the 1950s, world economic relations were governed by the 1944 Bretton Woods agreements. Trade relations were governed by the GATT.

- A key principle of the GATT was MFN: members had to offer to all other member states terms of trade as favourable as the best terms they offered to any other state. The EEC gained exemption from MFN for the internal **common market** and for its relations with former colonies of EEC members.

- Relations with the former colonies initially continued their dependence on France in particular. When Britain joined the EEC, the Lomé Convention provided the ACP states with a fairer deal.

- Following the collapse of communism in eastern Europe, the EU concluded special trade and aid agreements with the CEECs in an attempt to ensure the stability of its near neighbours. For the same reason, special agreements were reached with the states of the southern Mediterranean.

External Trade Policy

- Trade negotiations are conducted by the Commission on behalf of the EU as a whole, working to a mandate agreed by the Council of Ministers and supervised by a committee of national representatives.

- Until the Lisbon Treaty came into force, trade in services and intellectual products were not automatically covered by this arrangement: the governments of the member states had to agree ahead of each round of negotiations to allow the Commission authority in these areas.

- Under the terms of the Lisbon Treaty, trade in services and intellectual products are an EU competence, but unanimity remains the voting rule where sensitive domestic issues are concerned.

- The Commission has the power to impose duties and other restrictions on imports of goods to the EU where dumping or unfair subsidies are suspected.

- Member states are often divided over trade issues both by conflicting economic interests and by their general attitude to free trade.

491

• Since the introduction of the WTO, the EU has been involved in a series of trade disputes, mainly with the United States.

Relations with the African, Caribbean, and Pacific States

• Between 1975 and 2000, the relations of the EC/EU with the ACP states were governed by the Lomé Conventions. The terms of Lomé were more favourable to the ACP states, reflecting the international economic circumstances in which they were negotiated in the 1970s.

• By the end of the 1990s, when Lomé was renegotiated, it was clear that its terms were incompatible with the rules of the WTO in several respects.

• A new agreement was signed in 2000 in Cotonou, Benin. The Lomé system of trade preferences was replaced by a series of new economic partnerships based on the progressive and reciprocal removal of trade barriers. There was also a new emphasis on political, social, and environmental issues.

The European Neighbourhood Policy

• The ENP aims to prevent the emergence of stark dividing lines between EU and non-EU states by offering many of the advantages of association to neighbouring states that do not have a prospect of membership.

• The EU has negotiated association agreements with many 'neighbourhood' states. Such agreements lead to the liberalization of trade between the EU and association countries.

Explaining Trade and Development Aid Policies

• Shared responsibility for trade negotiations produces a complex pattern of bargaining that has been characterized as a 'three-level game'.

• Such rational choice analyses of trade negotiations have been supplemented by institutional analysis.

• Both types of analysis have also been applied to relations with the ACP states.

Critiquing Trade and Development Aid Policies

• Critical political economists have emphasized the increasingly neoliberal bias in EU trade policy and drawn attention to its negative consequences.

FURTHER READING

The most comprehensive review of the external trade policy of the EU is provided by **S. Meunier**, *Trading Voices: The European Union in International Commercial Negotiations* (Princeton, NJ: Princeton University Press, 2007). A useful recent literature review is offered by **A. Poletti and D. De Bievre**, 'The Political Science of European Trade Policy: A Literature Review With a Research Outlook', *Comparative European Politics*, 12 (2014): 101–19.

The common commercial policy of the EU is analysed as a multi-level game in **S. Collinson**, '"Issue Systems", "Multi-Level Games" and the Analysis of the EU's External Commercial and Associated Policies: A Research Agenda', *Journal of European Public Policy*, 6 (1999): 206–24. The increasing complexity of trade policy is well set out in **A. R. Young and J. Peterson**, 'The EU and the New Trade Politics', *Journal of European Public Policy*, 13 (2006): 795–814.

The chapters in **G. Faber and J. Orbie (eds)**, *Beyond Market Access for Economic Development: EU Africa Relations in Transition* (Routledge, 2009), address the emergence of EPAs in the context of the ACP. **G. Siles-Brügge**, *Constructing European Union Trade Policy: A Global Idea of Europe* (Palgrave Macmillan, 2014) offers an up-to-date example of the critical approach enunciated above with reference to recent FTAs.

 online resource centre

Visit the Online Resource Centre that accompanies this book for links to more information on the external economic relations of the EU, including the website of the relevant Directorates-General of the Commission: http://oxfordtextbooks.co.uk/orc/bache4e/

Chapter 26

Common Foreign and Security Policy

Chapter Overview

External political relations were always handled outside of the European Community (EC) framework, and initially were outside of the Treaty framework altogether. From 1993 to 2009, they formed the second pillar of the European Union (EU), on Common Foreign and Security Policy (CFSP) (the Lisbon Treaty abolished the three pillars). Although CFSP was officially an intergovernmental pillar, the Commission came to play an important role, and informally there were some similarities between the way in which the CFSP pillar operated and the way in which the EC pillar operated, even though the formal rules were different. Serious attempts were made to strengthen the security and defence aspects of the CFSP in the face of the threats that faced the EU from instability in its neighbouring territories. However, the EU remains far from having a truly supranational foreign policy and its status as a 'power' in international relations is debatable.

History

Prior to the Lisbon Treaty taking effect in December 2009, the external economic relations of the EC with the rest of the world were covered by the Treaty establishing the European Community (TEC), and generally came within the competence of the Commission—but the member states also separately developed machinery for formulating common positions on political issues of foreign policy. This initially developed outside of the framework of the Treaties under the name of European Political Co-operation (EPC). It entered the Treaties as Title III of the Single European Act (SEA) in July 1987, although still on an intergovernmental basis. Title V of the Treaty on European Union (TEU) (the Maastricht Treaty) set up a Common Foreign and Security Policy (CFSP) as the second pillar of the EU, and some additions were made to the machinery of the CFSP in the Amsterdam Treaty. In the late 1990s, efforts were made to establish a European Security and Defence Policy (ESDP), and this was brought into the EU by the Nice Treaty, which came into effect at the start of 2003. The Lisbon Treaty introduced further institutional reforms in the late 2000s through the creation of the post of 'High Representative of the Union for Foreign Affairs and

Security Policy' and the 'European External Action Service' (EEAS). This Treaty also renamed the ESDP, which became the Common Security and Defence Policy (CSDP) (although it will be referred to as ESDP hereafter).

European Political Co-operation (EPC)

EPC was suggested by French President Pompidou at The Hague Summit in 1969, but was seen at the time as little more than a sop to his Gaullist supporters. Few participants or observers thought that it would amount to anything, because it closely resembled the Fouchet Plan, which had already been rejected (see Chapter 7, Insight 7.2), and because it proposed co-operation in the field of 'high politics' as defined by Hoffmann (1964, 1966), an area in which concerns about national sovereignty would be expected to get in the way of common action (see Chapter 1, International Relations Theories of European Integration). Nevertheless, the initiative led to the setting up of a committee under the chairmanship of the Belgian Étienne Davignon, and its report—the Davignon or Luxembourg Report—recommending increased co-operation on international political issues, was adopted by Foreign Ministers meeting in Luxembourg in October 1970.

The machinery of EPC consisted mainly of regular meetings to co-ordinate national stances to particular areas of the world, or to particular issues. Foreign Ministers met at least twice a year, but in practice much more often. Immediately below the ministerial level, Foreign Office political directors met, on the original plan every three months, but in practice monthly. In addition to the meetings of Foreign Ministers and political directors, other institutional innovations were the COREU (*Corréspondance Européenne*) telex link, and Working Groups on a range of policy and geographical issues. COREU allowed officials in the Foreign Ministries of member states to communicate with each other as frequently as they wished on a confidential line. By the mid-1970s, the Foreign Offices of member states were exchanging an average of 4,800 confidential telexes a year in an intensive process of consultation (Smith 2004: 107). By the time that the EPC was superseded by CFSP in the Maastricht Treaty, there were more than twenty quasi-permanent Working Groups (Smith 2004: 105).

Until 1987, EPC had no Secretariat to provide administrative back-up. This was provided by whichever member state held the presidency of the Council at the time, imposing additional strain on the state holding the presidency, and also working against proper continuity across changes of presidency. Disappointment at the failure of the EC to respond effectively to the Iranian crisis in 1979 led to a review of EPC—the London Report—that recommended improved procedures for use in a crisis, and the creation of a small permanent Secretariat. These recommendations were adopted in October 1981, and led directly to the creation in the SEA of a small Secretariat, situated in Brussels.

EPC was originally set up as a parallel process to that of economic integration within the EC, but the two became closely linked. The distinction between matters proper to EPC and EC matters was rigidly maintained in the early years of the operation of EPC, at the insistence of the French, but it broke down with the opening of the 'Euro–Arab dialogue' in 1974. This was a structured series of regular meetings between representatives of the EC and representatives of the Arab states, prompted by the oil crisis of 1973–74. The Arab participants in the talks insisted on maintaining a clear linkage between trade and political questions, which forced the EC to fudge the lines of demarcation on its side. Once the artificial distinction had broken down here, it soon became less evident elsewhere in the external relations of the EC.

Once the EPC/EC distinction had been eroded, the Commission, originally excluded from meetings under the machinery of EPC, had to be admitted. One of the most compelling reasons for involving the Commission was that it proved difficult to do anything other than make declarations under EPC without having the use of the normal instruments of foreign policy. As military capabilities were unlikely to be made available to EPC, the obvious 'soft' weapon to use was economic sanctions, together with economic rewards such as loans. These economic instruments fell within the competence of the EC, and were administered by the Commission. In theory, national economic mechanisms could have been used to back-up EPC declarations, but this would have been less efficient than using centralized EC mechanisms, and might have worked against EC external economic policies. Consequently the Commission's role in EPC became gradually more significant. The European Parliament (EP), while less significant, was not entirely excluded from the EPC. Reports were made in a full plenary session, usually as part of the same statement on progress in Community affairs that was made by the Foreign Minister of the state holding the Council presidency. Members of the EP were allowed to question the Minister about EPC matters as well as about more strictly Community matters.

Procedurally, then, EPC made big strides in the course of the 1970s, and became intertwined with the institutions and procedures of the EC. These advances were then formalized in the SEA in 1985–86. The SEA gave EPC a written basis for the first time, but the Articles relating to it were not subject to judicial interpretation by the European Court of Justice (ECJ).

Although EPC was at one time described as an example of 'procedure substituting for policy' (Wallace and Allen 1977), it had several substantive successes. For example, the member states achieved a high degree of unity in the United Nations (UN), voting together on a majority of resolutions in the General Assembly, and developing a reputation for being the most cohesive group there at a time when group diplomacy was becoming much more common.

Perhaps even more impressively, EPC formulated a common position on the Middle East. This in itself was quite an achievement, given that prior to EPC there had been wide divergences in the extent of sympathy for Israel and for the Arab states in different member states. Reaching an agreed position allowed the EC, through the Euro–Arab dialogue, to pursue its clear interest in improving trade with the Arab **Organization of the Petroleum Exporting Countries (OPEC)** states in the 1970s. In June 1980, this common policy culminated in the Venice Declaration, which went further than the United States was prepared to go in recognizing the right of the Palestinians to a homeland.

The then nine member states were also extremely successful in formulating a common position at the Conference on Security and Co-operation in Europe (CSCE) in Helsinki in 1975, and at the follow-up conferences in Belgrade in 1977, and Madrid in 1982–83. Indeed, the whole CSCE process was an initiative of the EC states. Again, the common position adopted by the EC ran somewhat contrary to the position of the United States. The Americans regarded the Helsinki process with some suspicion because they thought it risked legitimating Communist rule in eastern Europe. In January 1995, the CSCE took on more permanent form as the Organization for Security and Co-operation in Europe (OSCE).

Admittedly, there were also failures. It proved difficult to find a joint position on the invasion of Afghanistan by the Soviet Union in December 1979. The British government argued strongly for following the lead of the United States in boycotting the Olympic Games in Moscow, while the French in particular were not prepared to do so, and the West German government was unhappy at the way in which the United States used the issue to heighten East–West tension. On balance, though, there were more successes than there were failures.

The Common Foreign and Security Policy (CFSP) and European Security and Defence Policy (ESDP)

At the beginning of the 1990s, the EC failed to respond adequately to two separate international crises. The first was in the Persian Gulf, where Iraq invaded its neighbour, Kuwait, in August 1990. The second was in Yugoslavia, where fighting broke out in June 1991 between the former Yugoslav army and Croat and Slovenian separatist forces. In both cases, the immediate response of the EC was positive, but as the crises developed, differing national interests paralyzed the process of political co-operation, and the United States ended up having to take the lead in resolving both.

While it was struggling to deal with these crises, the EC was also transforming itself into the EU. The intergovernmental conference (IGC) on political union, which began in January 1991, had the future evolution of EPC as a central item on its agenda. The more radical agenda, supported by Commission President Jacques Delors and by the German government, was to bring EPC into the framework of the EC, with the Commission perhaps not having the sole right of initiative but being centrally involved, and **qualified majority voting (QMV)** applying to decisions in the Council of Ministers. Security and defence would be added to the remit of this new mechanism for a common foreign policy. The opposite pole was marked out by the British, who argued against QMV on issues that were central to the sovereignty of the member states, and were particularly concerned that any moves to establish a common policy for security and defence should not undermine the NATO alliance.

The two voices in this debate drew opposite conclusions from events in the Gulf. Both sides agreed that the failure of the EC to respond effectively to the crises indicated how far there still was to travel to a common policy. However, whereas Delors told the EP that the ineffective response indicated the urgency of pushing forward to political union (*Debates of the European Parliament*, 23 January 1991, 3–398/139), British Prime Minister John Major told the House of Commons that this failure clearly indicated that Europe was not ready for a common policy (Hansard, 22 January 1991, col. 162).

In a compromise between these two positions, a three-pillar structure was adopted at Maastricht, with the CFSP and Justice and Home Affairs (JHA) forming intergovernmental pillars of the new EU alongside the EC pillar. Majority voting in the second pillar was restricted to the implementation measures needed to carry through decisions of principle that would have to be taken by consensus, and even then the QMV would only apply if all states were to agree to accept it in a particular case. There were some other enhancements of EPC, including moving the old EPC Secretariat into the Council Secretariat and giving it a larger staff and budget. Overall, though, the TEU really represented a victory for the minimalist position on the CFSP.

The tragedy in former Yugoslavia did have the effect of bringing France and Britain closer together on security and defence. The common experience of operating under UN auspices in Bosnia led to increased co-operation on the ground, which spread into the creation of a joint air-force command unit. Nevertheless, when, in 1998, a further crisis occurred in the Kosovo province of Serbia, the EU again proved unequal to the task of making a rapid response. It was NATO that undertook a bombing campaign against Serbia to force it to retreat from the persecution of the ethnic Albanians in Kosovo. The United States spearheaded the NATO effort.

The failure of the EU to act in Kosovo provided the impetus for a move to extend CFSP to security and defence. In December 1998, at a bilateral Franco–British summit in Saint-Malo, France, French President Jacques Chirac and British Prime Minister Tony Blair jointly announced their support for an ESDP. A year later, the Helsinki European Council announced what was called the 'headline goal' of creating, by the end of 2003, a European Rapid Reaction Force of 50,000 to 60,000 troops, plus naval and air back-up that could be sustained in the field for up to one year. In March 2000, the institutions of the ESDP began provisional operation: a political and security committee, known by its French acronym COPS (standing for *Comité Politique et de Sécurité*); a military committee; and the basis for a joint military command structure.

The Amsterdam Treaty had already made some modifications to the CFSP, particularly in creating the post of High Representative, the holder of which would be the first point of contact for CFSP matters. In November 1999, it was agreed to appoint the then NATO Secretary-General, Javier Solana, to this post. The Commission had argued that the post should go to one of the Commissioners, but the heads of government decided to make it a position within the Council framework, thus storing up potential for problems in the co-ordination of the work of the two institutions.

Amendments to the TEU at Amsterdam drew a distinction between, on the one hand, deciding the principles and general guidelines of the CFSP, and common strategies in pursuit of these, and on the other, the adoption of joint actions, common positions, and implementing decisions. The first category of decision had to be unanimous; QMV could decide the second. Also, a member state could abstain in a vote and make a formal declaration that it would not be bound by the vote. This would allow the EU as a whole to be committed to the decision, but not the individual abstaining state, which would only be obliged not to act in any way that would conflict with the pursuit of the action by the EU.

Amsterdam also incorporated the so-called 'Petersberg Tasks' into the EU. In June 1992, the Western European Union (WEU) Petersberg Declaration had said that member states would allocate armed forces to peace-keeping and humanitarian tasks in Europe (see Insight 26.1). This had committed only the members of WEU, but the 1997 Amsterdam Treaty committed all EU member states to the tasks. ESDP was officially brought into the TEU by amendments made in the 2000 Nice Treaty, which took effect at the start of 2003.

Further amendment was made to the institutions of the CFSP in the Lisbon Treaty. First, the three-pillar structure was abolished, and CFSP became an integral part of an

> ### Insight 26.1 The Revival of Western European Union (WEU)
>
> WEU was set up in 1954 following the collapse of the Pleven Plan for a European Defence Community (see Chapter 6, The Pleven Plan). The original members were Belgium, France, Luxembourg, the Netherlands, Britain, West Germany, and Italy. Portugal and Spain became members in 1990 and Greece in 1995, bringing the membership to ten.
>
> By the 1980s, WEU had apparently become moribund, but proposals to revive it as a vehicle for co-ordinating European positions were made by the Belgian and French governments in 1984.
>
> Prior to the Gulf War of 1990, WEU co-ordinated mine-sweeping operations in the Persian Gulf, which had been mined during the Iran–Iraq war. It was therefore in a strong position to provide a co-ordination mechanism for the member states involved in the Gulf War, which it did, and continued with mine-sweeping operations afterwards.
>
> WEU co-operated with NATO to monitor the embargo against former Yugoslavia in 1993, providing a joint naval task force. It also helped to enforce the sanctions on the Danube, providing patrol boats, vehicles, and personnel to work alongside the national agencies of Bulgaria, Hungary, and Romania. From 1994 to 1996, the WEU provided a police contingent to the EU administration in Mostar in Bosnia-Herzegovina, to assist in the setting up of a Bosnian–Croat joint police force.
>
> These activities, which prefigured the missions later undertaken by the EU under its ESDP, continued with a police mission in Albania from 1997 to 2001, a Demining Assistance Commission to Croatia in 1999, and a General Security Surveillance Mission in Kosovo in 1998–99.
>
> To facilitate closer co-ordination, in 1992 the WEU Secretariat was moved from London to Brussels, where both the European Commission and NATO headquarters were located. In 1999, Javier Solana, the EU High Representative for the CFSP, was appointed Secretary-General of WEU as well.
>
> Following the effective transfer of its crisis-management functions to the EU, the WEU now consists of a small Secretariat with only residual functions related to preparing and preserving archives, and administering pension and other staff liabilities. Until the Lisbon Treaty came into effect, it could be argued that the Brussels Treaty still formed the basis of a mutual defence pact between the ten member states, but Lisbon amended the TEU so as to envisage a possible future common defence under Article 42, which says that should a member state experience armed aggression on its own territory, the other states shall assist it by all means in their power.

EU that now had a consolidated legal personality. However, this does not mean that CFSP has become regular EU business: it is still 'subject to specific rules and procedures' (Article 24(1) TEU).

Second, the 'High Representative for the Common Foreign and Security Policy' became the 'High Representative of the Union for Foreign Affairs and Security Policy'. This was more than a change of name. Whereas the original post was combined with that of Secretary-General of the Council, and there was a separate Commissioner for External Relations, the new post carried with it the position of a Vice-President of the European Commission, and the incumbent was to chair all meetings of the Council of Foreign Ministers, thus making it a position that straddled both institutions, and acted as a bridge between external economic relations and the CFSP/ESDP. At the Brussels European Council in September 2009, the heads of government agreed to appoint Baroness Catherine Ashton, until then the Commissioner for Trade, to the High Representative post with effect from the Treaty coming into force on 1 December 2009.

Finally, the Lisbon Treaty also established the EEAS (which came into operation in 2011) to assist the High Representative. It is formed by staff drawn from the external relations departments of the Council and Commission, with provision for additional staff to be seconded from the national diplomatic services of the member states.

CFSP and ESDP in Action

The start of CFSP did not suggest a great leap forward in either the capabilities or the ambitions of the EU. The first actions undertaken were modest, and were all in areas that built on EPC. Monitors were sent to observe the elections in Russia in December 1993; humanitarian aid for Bosnia was co-ordinated; and a new political framework was developed for aid to the West Bank and Gaza. Subsequently observers were sent to monitor the first non-racial elections in South Africa, and the EU played an active role in the preparations for elections in the Palestinian homeland.

A more ambitious proposal, which originated with French Prime Minister Edouard Balladur, came to fruition in March 1995, when fifty-two states from western and eastern Europe signed a stability pact binding themselves to be good neighbours, and to respect the rights of minorities. Although there were several flaws in the pact, especially the exclusion for one reason or another of all of the Yugoslav successor states, the pattern was adopted later in the year by the Spanish presidency to develop a regional pact for the Mediterranean, in the face of growing concern in southern Europe about Islamic fundamentalism in the Arab world and about illegal immigration from there.

When the 2001 terrorist attack on the United States took place, the EU, as in previous crises, initially reacted positively and decisively. Within 36 hours, declarations in support of the United States had been made by the Commission President, the Commissioner for External Relations, the Special Representative for Foreign Affairs, and the General Affairs Council. The Commission rapidly tabled proposals for a European Arrest Warrant, and agreement on this was reached in December, despite reservations by Italy (Hill 2004: 145–7). While the EU responded with 'an unforeseeable speed, range and flexibility' (Hill 2004: 150) the full nature of its complicity with the US response over the longer term subsequently met with severe criticism (De Goede 2008). EU solidarity was maintained during the subsequent US campaign in Afghanistan to unseat the Taliban government. The one part of the early response that did not reinforce CFSP was the apparent wish of Britain, France, and Germany to act independently of the EU as a whole. Blair, Chirac, and Schröder met to discuss their responses to 'September 11' ahead of the Ghent European Council in October 2001, and intended to do so again in London in early November. On the latter occasion, though, the insistent protests of other member states led to a widening of the invitation, with the result that the meeting was also attended by Italy, Spain, and the Netherlands, by the Belgian presidency, and by the High Representative, Javier Solana. Although the instinct of the leaders of the three large states had not been to work through CFSP, the outcome showed that this was difficult for them to do against the wishes of others.

Problems really began, though, with the identification of an 'axis of evil' by US President George W. Bush in his 2002 State of the Union speech. Three states were identified as part of this axis: Iraq, Iran, and North Korea. The EU was working diplomatically to bring Iran back into full participation in the international community, and had managed to persuade Tehran to associate itself with the 'war against terror', and not to object to the invasion of Afghanistan. Bush's public condemnation was a setback for these efforts of the EU to build a constructive relationship with Iran. Similarly, the reference to North Korea set alarm bells ringing in Brussels because the EU was following a policy of functional engagement of the North Korean regime in the hope of tempting it out of isolation. Again, the bellicose tone of President Bush did not contribute to the success of this effort. In the case of Iraq, the EU was not following a strategy of its own, but the general view of member states was that the existing UN policy was working: the use of military air patrols to contain Saddam Hussein's reach, together with economic sanctions, and the offer of easing sanctions to lever compliant behaviour.

Of its 'axis of evil' states, it was Iraq that the United States chose to tackle first, and this precipitated a serious split within the EU. In the build-up to the eventual invasion, France and Germany led a small group of states that opposed any military action, while Britain, Spain, and Italy were the leading supporters of a larger group (if the accession states are included) that backed the US action. In March 2003, France publicly declared that it would veto any resolution in support of military action against Iraq that might be presented by the United States and Britain to the UN Security Council. This led to a bitter verbal attack on France by Tony Blair in the House of Commons on 18 March 2003.

As Howorth (2003: 179–80) made clear, the tensions had started to rise before this. Blair's response to the attacks on New York had been to reaffirm Britain's attachment to NATO. When the Spanish presidency attempted to reorient the European Rapid Reaction Force to turn it into a weapon that could be used against terrorism, Blair opposed the change, arguing that the war against terror should be handled through NATO. He subsequently supported a US proposal to the November 2002 NATO Summit in Prague for a NATO Response Force to react to terrorist incidents, and in April 2003, he was critical of the French position of rivalry with the United States, which he contrasted with the British position of partnership.

Following the invasion of Iraq by a US-led coalition backed by Britain in March 2003, Franco–British relations were at a very low ebb, and the prospects for ESDP looked poor. Yet, Howorth (2003: 187) reported that there were signs at the end of 2003 of both sides trying to improve matters. In August, at a meeting of European states in Rome, a clash was expected over whether ESDP needed its own planning headquarters, which France insisted it must have, or whether the EU should develop a permanent planning cell within the Supreme Headquarters Allied Powers Europe (SHAPE) of NATO. But the clash did not happen: the meeting agreed that both developments would be useful, and that they would complement one another. Then, in September, Blair agreed in principle that the EU should have the joint planning capacity to conduct operations without the involvement of NATO, a concession that appeared to alarm the United States. So, the signs were that the British wanted to facilitate the relaunch of the ESDP.

There were also three successful international operations under ESDP in the course of 2003 (Allen and Smith 2004: 97). In March, an EU force replaced the NATO force in the former Yugoslav Republic of Macedonia, a move that had been scheduled for

2002 but had been delayed by Greek objections. In the middle of the year, there was a successful EU intervention to restore order in the Republic of Congo. Then, in December, the European Council agreed to provide a replacement for the NATO stabilization force in Bosnia. Subsequently the EU conducted a number of missions. The majority of these were civilian missions, though some involved the deployment of military personnel, albeit not usually in a combat capacity (see Table 26.1).

At the time of writing it was too early to offer a comprehensive or fair assessment of the effectiveness of the post-Lisbon foreign policy architecture. Nevertheless, it faced an early test as a series of popular uprisings unfolded in the Middle East and North Africa in 2011. In some instances these ousted incumbent authoritarian regimes from power (in Tunisia, Egypt, Libya, and Yemen), while in others they led to sustained

Table 26.1 ESDP Missions as of 2014

Name of Mission	Start Date	End Date	Purpose (type)
EUTM Mali	2013	ongoing	To train Malian armed forces in support of the stabilization of the country (military)
EUBAM Libya	2013	ongoing	To strengthen border security capacity in Libya (civilian)
EUAVSEC South Sudan	2012	ongoing	To assist in increasing security at Juba International Airport (civilian)
EUCAP SAHEL Niger	2012	ongoing	To improve capacity of Nigerian Security Forces in the fight against terrorism and organized crime (civilian)
EUTM Somalia	2010	ongoing	To strengthen the Somali security sector by providing military training for Somali recruits (military)
EUNAVFOR Somalia	2008	ongoing	To combat piracy off the Somali coast (military)
EUMM Georgia	2008	ongoing	To contribute to stability in Georgia and the surrounding region, and to monitor the security situation (civilian)
EULEX Kosovo	2008	ongoing	To support and strengthen the judiciary in Kosovo (civilian)
EUPOL Afghanistan	2007	ongoing	To contribute to the establishment of sustainable and effective civilian policing arrangements in Afghanistan (civilian)
EUJUSTLEX Iraq	2005	ongoing	To provide training to senior Iraqi judiciary, police, and prison officers (civilian)

(continued)

Table 26.1 (*Continued*)

Name of Mission	Start Date	End Date	Purpose (type)
EUBAM Rafah	2005	ongoing	To monitor the implementation of the 2005 Agreement between Israel and the Palestinian Authority on movement through the Rafah crossing (Gaza) (civilian)
EUBAM Moldova and Ukraine	2005	ongoing	To improve the capacity of Moldovan and Ukrainian border and customs services to prevent and detect smuggling, human trafficking, and customs fraud (civilian)
ALTHEA BiH	2004	ongoing	To contribute to a stable security situation in Bosnia and Herzegovina (military)
EU SSR Guinea-Bissau	2008	2010	To support security sector reform in Guinea-Bissau (civilian)
EUFOR TCHAD/RCA	2008	2009	To protect civilians and facilitate the delivery of humanitarian aid in eastern Chad and the north-east of the Central African Republic (military)
EUPOL RD CONGO	2007	2013	To provide assistance and advice on police and judicial reform in the Democratic Republic of Congo (DRC) (civilian)
EUFOR RD Congo	2006	2006	To provide sufficiently stable conditions for elections to take place in the DRC. Time-limited military operation (military)
EUPOL Kinshasa	2005	2007	To monitor and advise on the setting up of the Integrated Police Unit of the Congolese National Police and to ensure that it met international standards of best practice (civilian)
EUSEC RD CONGO	2005	2013	To provide advice and assistance on defence reform (civilian)
EUPOL COPPS/ Palestinian Territories	2005	2013	To support police reform in the Palestine Territories (civilian)
EU Support to AMIS (Darfur)	2005	2007	To provide support to the African Union's Mission to Darfur, Sudan (civilian and military)

(continued)

Table 26.1 (*Continued*)

Name of Mission	Start Date	End Date	Purpose (type)
EUPAT	2005	2006	Follow-on mission from PROXIMA/ FYROM (civilian)
Aceh Monitoring Mission—AMM	2005	2006	To monitor implementation of the 2005 peace agreement between the Indonesian government and the Free Aceh Movement (civilian)
EUJUST/Themis Georgia	2004	2005	To advise the Georgian authorities on tackling urgent challenges within the criminal justice system and assist in the reform process (civilian)
EUPM BiH	2003	2012	To establish sustainable policing arrangements in Bosnia and Herzegovina through monitoring, mentoring, and inspection activities (civilian)
CONCORDIA/ FYROM	2003	2003	To contribute to ensuring a stable security environment for the establishment of the former Yugoslav Republic of Macedonia (military)
EUPOL PROXIMA / FYROM	2003	2005	To assist the police in the former Yugoslav Republic of Macedonia by providing monitoring, mentoring, and advice, and to provide specific assistance in the fight against organized crime (civilian)
DRC/ ARTEMIS	2003	2003	To stabilize the security conditions and improve the humanitarian situation in the DRC (military)

Source: **http://ec.europa.eu**, © European Union, 1995–2014.

campaigns of civil resistance (Bahrain), or drawn-out civil war (Syria). The EU response to the so-called 'Arab Spring' was in many respects similar to its response to other crises. Individual member states led the way in terms of crisis diplomacy and military initiatives, and the visibility of EU-level actors, such Catherine Ashton, was limited. For instance, French and British actors—notably President Sarkozy and Prime Minister Cameron—were key players in promoting and enacting the military intervention in Libya in 2011, which supported the opposition movement in ousting Colonel Gaddafi's regime. The EU's role was, in this case, limited to imposing sanctions. In other cases it sought to engage with the new regimes economically, although in practice this did not amount to much more than a reinforcement of existing policy conducted under the auspices of the European Neighbourhood Policy (ENP) (see Chapter 25, The European Neighbourhood Policy). Notwithstanding the new foreign policy architecture, the Arab Spring exposed certain long-standing weaknesses in CFSP, both in terms of horizontal cohesiveness (between EU institutions) and vertical cohesiveness (between member states and the EU).

That said, there has also been some evidence of success since the post-Lisbon architecture was put in place. EU activities (including some missions—see Table 26.1) in the troubled Sahel region of northern Africa and on the Horn of Africa suggested that greater cohesion between various actors in EU foreign policy was starting to emerge. Catherine Ashton also became an important and visible actor in certain international contexts. She played an important role in the Western Balkans, successfully diffusing ethnic tension in Bosnia in 2011 and facilitating the negotiation of an unlikely agreement between the Kosovo and Serbian authorities in 2013, with the latter recognizing the autonomy of the former (which, in turn, paved the way for accession negotiations to commence with Serbia in 2014—see Chapter 27). Baroness Ashton was also involved with the brokering of a deal with Iran in 2013, which led to talks in 2014 on its nuclear programme (ongoing at the time of writing).

A further test for EU foreign policy came in late 2013 when Ukraine decided at the last minute not to sign an already-negotiated Association Agreement with the EU (see Chapter 25, European Neighbourhood Policy). This 'u-turn' prompted widespread, and at times violent, demonstrations in Ukraine in support of its association with the EU and in opposition to its government. These led in early 2014 to the ousting of its President, Viktor Yanukovych. Russia's support for the ousted President and for the separatist ambitions of the Crimea, a strongly pro-Russian region of Ukraine, created significant tensions with the West, including the EU. In March 2014, the EU (as well as the US) agreed to impose sanctions on Russia, although member states only agreed on a limited range of sanctions. This case revealed the difficulty for the EU of pursuing closer relations with countries that the current Russian administration perceived, for various reasons, as an important part of its sphere of influence. At the time of writing, the situation in Ukraine and relations with Russia looked likely to remain a pre-occupation for EU foreign policy.

Explaining CFSP and ESDP

For a long time explanations of political co-operation were rather weakly linked to theory. There were many detailed empirical accounts, some of the best written by practitioners, but although all such accounts were inevitably underpinned by theoretical assumptions, these were rarely made explicit. Most discussion was around the idea of the 'capability–expectations' gap, which was a valid concept, but was explicitly not intended as an explanatory theory (Hill 1993: 306), and which therefore did not address the central question of why political co-operation took place at all.

Perhaps the difficulty was that the academic community that initially emerged around political co-operation was dominated by 'realists' who started their analysis from the assumption that national interest was the sole motivating force of national foreign policy. As Glarbo (1999: 634) observed, although realist analyses differed from one another in detail, they all held to the common core proposition 'that the interests of single European nation states will eternally block integration within the high politics realms of foreign, security and defence policy'. Where common policies were devised, this would be explained by the coincidence of converging national interests; more often, such common positions were dismissed as trivial. Only with the later deployment of social constructivist and other similar perspectives to the understanding of political co-operation did the debate become more theoretically sophisticated.

The Capability–Expectations Gap

Between the agreement of the TEU and its final ratification, Christopher Hill (1993) produced an assessment of political co-operation in which he developed a concept that was to become widely used in the subsequent literature: the 'capability–expectations gap'. Hill (1993: 309) cast doubt on whether the EC should be conceived as an actor in international affairs. It lacked autonomy, and was not distinct from other actors: notably, the member states. Many foreign policy practitioners external to the EC, and some internal practitioners too, had mistaken the EC for an actor. For instance, former US Secretary of State Henry Kissinger is said to have asked: 'Who do I call if I want to call Europe?' The mistake arose because the EC did have a distinct international 'presence'.

To mistake it for an actor, though, was to raise expectations of what it could achieve. It was expected to perform certain functions in the international system, such as acting as a counter-weight to the dominance of the United States. Yet, the EC lacked the capability to meet these expectations. It lacked the resources, and the instruments—but also, because it was not an actor, it lacked the ability to reach agreement internally (Hill 1993: 310–15). This was why the capability–expectations gap existed, and Hill (1993: 315) believed that the gap had only been increased by the SEA and the TEU, which suggested advances in the international activity of the EC/EU that it was incapable of making.

In a review of the factors that have strengthened the 'actorness' of the EU since Hill's 1993 assessment, and those that continued to weaken it, Krotz (2009) argued that the EU was still a long way from being an international actor, although the forces making for 'actorness' were strengthening and those working against it might be weakening, opening up the future possibility of 'a fully grown high-politics actor Europe on the world stage'. It has been claimed in this respect that the Lisbon Treaty's reforms, highlighted above, contributed to increasing EU 'actorness'. For instance, Commission President Barroso claimed in 2009 that, with the appointment of Catherine Ashton as High Representative, 'the so-called Kissinger question is now solved' (Barroso 2009). However, as also noted, it is debatable whether the reforms to CFSP have led to increased supranational authority in this area.

Theoretical Explanations of Political Co-operation

Ginsberg (1989) made an early attempt to apply theory systematically to the explanation of political co-operation, examining seven theoretical perspectives on EC activity in the field of foreign policy. The first four he termed 'classical perspectives': the national interest perspective; the elite actor perspective; the domestic politics perspective; and the bureaucratic politics perspective. The remaining three he called 'alternative perspectives': integration logic; interdependence logic; and 'self-styled' logic.

Ginsberg argued that the national interest perspective was better at explaining the breakdown of joint action than it was at explaining why joint action sometimes occurred. The elite actor perspective, he argued, could work either way: elite actors could favour or oppose political co-operation. A domestic politics perspective offered little theoretical leverage because there was very little input from domestic politics into foreign policy generally, and especially not into the elite-dominated process of EPC. While bureaucratic politics was neither really accepted nor dismissed (Ginsberg 1989: 17–19), he believed integration theories provided some explanatory leverage: the creation of EPC was 'in part an example of neofunctionalist spillover' (Ginsberg 1989: 25) because one of the main drivers of the process was the need for a political complement to the economic policies of the EC. Interdependence theories put the focus on the external environment, and saw EPC as an attempt 'to reduce the adverse costs of global interdependence by deliberately co-ordinating joint policy actions' (Ginsberg 1989: 31). However, while interdependence might be a background condition that could stimulate integration, Ginsberg did not believe that it could explain the why and where of it.

His own favoured perspective was the 'self-styled' logic, a synthesis of elements from all of the other perspectives, which took the EC and the member states seriously as actors responding to their environment. This eclectic approach was not, however, taken up by other contributors to the debate, which tended to fall into the same pattern of division as the wider debates about European integration.

Glarbo (1999) put forward two alternatives to realist approaches. The first was that important developments in political co-operation could only be understood as the outcome not only of national interest, but also of a growing level of communication between national officials. The second was that, contrary to realist analyses, integration *had* occurred within the field of political co-operation; it was a form of social integration stemming from the communication processes that the institutions of EPC and CFSP had set up. This perspective had affinities with social constructivism and sociological institutionalism (see Chapters 4 and 2) inasmuch as it emphasized how institutional cultures can change over time. According to this thesis, the 'continuous communicative process' (Glarbo 1999: 644) that the EPC set going shifted the perceptions of the actors. They became sensitive to the constraints on the other actors, and tried to accommodate them. A code of conduct emerged whereby actors tried not to surprise their partners with *faits accomplis*. They also came to define the national interest differently, taking account of the emerging *acquis politique*, the accumulation of decisions and policy positions adopted through the EPC process. These developments were recognized by the actors, who were quite prepared to acknowledge in interviews with academics that their national practices had been modified as a result of participation in EPC, and who themselves contributed in surprisingly large numbers to the literature on the process, thereby coming to 'participate in the epistemic community surrounding this field' (Glarbo 1999: 659). In public statements, the advantages of EPC were presented in terms of how the process served national interests, but only because this was the language that was expected and understood by the wider public.

In a series of articles, Michael E. Smith (1999, 2000, 2001, 2003, 2004) developed a perspective on political co-operation that drew on the insights of both social constructivism and historical institutionalism. In this perspective, while the process of political co-operation began as an intergovernmental bargain, once the process was under way, it took on a different aspect. There were three linked elements in this transition. In decreasing order of importance, these were: the development of transgovernmental relations; the development and codification of EPC rules; and the forging of links with EC actors, especially the Commission (Smith 1999: 309–10).

Initial negotiations within EPC were conducted on the basis of existing national positions, so that, in its early years, EPC looked like classic intergovernmentalism—but this did not last. The intensive interaction between national representatives that was implicit in the idea of political co-operation constituted a system of transgovernmental relations in which these discrete national positions began to be modified as mutual trust developed (Smith 2004: 114–22). Out of this trust, and the constant process of discussion, emerged a socialization of participants, which led naturally to the gradual displacement of instrumental rationality by social rationality: the replacement of a bargaining approach by a problem-solving approach (Smith 2004) (note the similarities here with Glarbo).

The second aspect of the movement of EPC away from intergovernmentalism was the development and codification of EPC rules. This process, which can be described as the 'institutionalization' of EPC, has been discussed above. The increasingly rich institutional structure provided the forum for intensive interaction between officials from different levels in national Foreign Ministries. The **transgovernmental network** of diplomats and technical experts was thus extended and deepened. Such intensive interaction could not but influence the attitudes of professional diplomatic actors, and through them the process of defining the national interest. It fed back into national institutional structures, too. Political co-operation required the creation of new posts to serve it. This led to the expansion of national diplomatic services, and a reorientation of internal structures, sometimes amounting to complete reorganizations (M. E. Smith 2000: 619–23).

The third element in the transformation of EPC was the forging of links with EC institutions, especially the Commission. The reasons for involving the Commission and the EP in political co-operation have been outlined above. Eventually, the role of the Commission in ensuring the consistency of EPC and EC actions was codified in the SEA (M. E. Smith 2001: 90). From this point on, the involvement of the Commission in political co-operation was not only customary, it was also mandatory.

Explaining ESDP

Can this analysis also be applied to ESDP? Certainly the initiation of the security and defence dimension to CFSP has to be explained in terms of intergovernmental politics. In this case, coinciding national interests, one of the realist/intergovernmental explanations for political co-operation, has to be given a dominant role. The experience of the crises in the Gulf, in Bosnia, and in Kosovo all pointed up the weakness of the EU. From the French point of view, awareness of the gap that had opened up between US and European military capabilities, and especially the dependence of the French armed forces on the United States for reconnaissance and for transport of equipment, pushed towards closer collaboration with NATO in the short term because it was obvious that there was no immediate prospect of these vital gaps being filled by

France without an unsustainable increase in military expenditure. In the longer term, the gaps might be filled by collaboration between European states, but clearly the co-operation of the British would be essential given that Britain was the other main military power in the EU. From the British point of view, the rapprochement between France and NATO was encouraging, and, in the wake of the two Balkan crises, the United States began to pressure the Europeans to get their act together so that they could make a bigger contribution to policing their own hinterland.

It is possible, though, that other factors were at work. Howorth (2004) identified an 'epistemic community' (see Chapter 2, Governance and Networks) that had formed around the issue of defence. He argued that one of the facilitating factors in the determination of Britain and France to take forward the project of ESDP in 2001 was 'the close-knit epistemic community of senior officials in London and Paris who, from the early 1990s onwards, had gradually developed a common mindset around the necessity and legitimacy of ESDP' (Howorth 2003: 175).

Whatever the contribution of these pre-existing transgovernmental links to the start of the ESDP, once collaboration began, the same process identified by Michael E. Smith for political co-operation generally, and outlined above, could be expected to take place. CFSP had been kept firmly under the control of national Foreign Offices. National Ministries of Defence were not given a role. This changed with the ESDP initiatives. New transgovernmental links started to be built between officials of national Ministries of Defence, and between military personnel. Some links already existed, of course, because of co-operation in NATO and the WEU, although the links were less intense for France, which was outside of the NATO command structure, and for those EU member states that were not members of NATO or WEU.

Because it was in its early stages when events changed everything in September 2001, the ESDP process of socialization was particularly prone to being disrupted. In the summer of 2001, the pre-existing alliance of like-minded officials identified by Howorth (2004) had already been disrupted by a major reshuffle of responsibilities in London. The new officials came into office just before the strategic priorities of the government were reordered by the events of 11 September. They were therefore less committed to the ESDP when the political direction changed (Howorth 2003: 177–8). However, by this time, the institutional structure of ESDP was already in place, so the process of intensive interaction of officials was going to continue. As Michael E. Smith (1999) argued, socialization and institutionalization interact with one another. The processes are still new when compared with the parallel CFSP processes for non-military co-operation on foreign policy, and so are particularly vulnerable to being blown off course by events. They operate at a slow pace, beneath the level of current affairs—but once institutionalized, they can be expected to continue, and eventually to have an impact on the way in which national leaders perceive events and respond to them.

EU Power in World Politics

A number of academic discussions of developments in CFSP/ESDP are situated within a broader debate about what kind of power the EC/EU is in international affairs. While at one level this debate is about understanding the nature of the EU as a global power, at another level it is a normative debate about what kind of power the EU should be. The positions taken in this debate are important in terms of how EU external actions and policies are judged.

Duchêne (1973: 19) famously described the EC as a 'civilian power', 'long on economic power and relatively short on armed forces', and argued that it should not seek to increase its military power. As discussed in Chapter 25, the EC/EU has long been influential in global economic governance, and its member states have delegated significant responsibilities to supranational authority in this area. The linking of foreign policy with economic relations has given the EC/EU significant leverage in international affairs and allowed it to pursue European interests and promote ostensibly European values (such as free trade, democracy, and human rights) in the absence of military power. For Duchêne, this commitment to multi-lateral economic diplomacy was characterized as a 'domestication' of international relations and distinct from a then-prevalent Cold War power-politics. This was a welcome feature of EC external relations that the development of a military capa-bility would threaten. His argument had affinities with various liberal approaches to International Relations, which emphasized the importance of economic interdependence.

Bull (1982) countered Duchêne's argument, making the case that the effectiveness of 'civilian power' would always require some form of 'military power', and conse-quently advocated an increase in the EC's military capabilities. In this respect, Bull's argument had affinities with a realist perspective in International Relations, although he was an advocate of international co-operation, so by no means a hard-line realist. As discussed above, the development of a common defence capacity was a long-standing goal of many actors in European affairs, but substantive steps in this direc-tion were only achieved in the late 1990s with ESDP. For some advocates of 'civilian power Europe' such steps were a source of concern because they indicated the con-tinued necessity of military force (K. Smith 2000: 28). However, for others the mis-sions conducted in the context of ESDP (see Table 26.1) were not necessarily incompatible with 'civilian' goals inasmuch as their primary aim was the promotion of sustainable peace (Whitman 2002). Moreover, EU capabilities in this area remained limited.

Manners (2002, 2008) drew attention to a third aspect of EU external power—its 'normative power'—which is rooted in neither its economic nor its military power, but in its ability to promote certain 'norms' or ideas in international affairs. This can refer to the promotion of values such as democracy and human rights, or to the way in which the very evolution and existence of the EU serves as a model for peaceful rela-tions between states based on a set of common values. From this perspective, the nov-elty of the EU as an actor in international affairs means that it is particularly well positioned to promote these ostensibly 'normative' values. The concept of normative power spawned a significant debate. It was criticized for understating the ways in which the EU's 'normative' agendas are in practice tied to strategic economic and geo-political interests (Youngs 2004) and for dangerously (even complacently) overstating the value of the EU as a force for 'good' (Diez 2005; Parker and Rosamond 2013). However, Manners' argument was as much normative as descriptive: it was about pro-moting a cosmopolitan agenda for the EU and in international affairs more generally (see Chapter 4, Critical Social Theory).

CONCLUSION

European co-operation on the political aspects of external relations arose partly out of necessity and partly out of the ambitions of some EC member states, particularly France, to use the EC as a platform to exert greater global influence than any one European state could exercise acting alone. It expanded partly as a result of the process itself generating its own momentum, and partly through the member states trying to learn the lessons of their failures to deal adequately with a series of international crises.

The necessity for EPC came from the inextricable tangling of external economic and external political relations. For the EC to maximize its economic influence, it had to have a coherent relationship between the economic and the political. From an early stage, other states expected the EC to behave as a single unified actor on the world stage, placing a burden of expectation on the member states for which they were partly responsible because they spoke of European integration in terms that represented aspirations rather than realities. The practice of collaboration between national foreign ministries led to a habit of consultation that eroded stark national positions on issues that did not become overtly politicized. However, major crises proved difficult for the Europeans to handle jointly because they had a high domestic profile and senior politicians took control of the decisions. Between crises, though, a web of procedures and a growing *acquis* of joint positions were imperceptibly eroding the separate national foreign policies and slowly putting a European policy in their place.

Paradoxically, the crises themselves contributed to furthering EPC. Each time the EC/EU failed to act decisively in a crisis, each time the United States was able to take the lead or had to do so because of European failings, there was a round of soul-searching and attempts to make future co-operation more effective. This produced the transition from EPC to CFSP and the efforts to create an ESDP. While the 'capability–expectations' gap remained, the weight of international expectations acted as a spur to continued efforts to increase capabilities. The creation of the role of High Representative in the Amsterdam Treaty, and the extension of the role and responsibilities of this post in the Lisbon Treaty, were indicative of a desire to reduce the gap by increasing the 'actorness' of the EU.

Academic discussions of EC/EU foreign policy often have an underlying normative dimension which relates to different visions of the EU's purpose in global politics. In particular, a debate about what kind of international power the EU should be has been ongoing since the 1970s, with some arguing that it should develop its military power and others arguing that it should maintain its focus on its already significant 'civilian' economic power. Recent contributors to this debate have made the case that the EU is well positioned to promote important values such as democracy and human rights and this should be its primary foreign policy focus. Different perspectives in this debate will have different views on the EU's CFSP, both in terms of what it has done and where it should be headed.

KEY POINTS

History

- EPC was set up in 1970. It consisted of regular meetings of Foreign Ministers and of senior Foreign Office officials to try to co-ordinate national foreign policies.

- EPC was incorporated into the Treaties for the first time with the SEA, which also created a small EPC Secretariat.

- Initially, the Commission was excluded from meetings of Foreign Ministers under EPC, but gradually the role of the Commission increased.

- EPC had several substantive successes to its name: achieving a high degree of unified voting at the UN; conducting an effective 'Euro–Arab dialogue'; and launching and sustaining the CSCE process.

- Failures of EPC occurred in responding to the invasion of Afghanistan by the USSR in December 1979, over the Gulf Crisis in 1990–91, and over successive crises in former Yugoslavia.

The Common Foreign and Security Policy (CFSP) and European Security and Defence Policy (ESDP)

- In the run-up to Maastricht, the Commission and the Germans argued for EPC to come under EC rules (including QMV) and to include security and defence issues; the British opposed this, stressing the intergovernmental nature of EPC and the central role of NATO in defence.

- The TEU made CFSP a separate pillar of the EU from the EC; QMV was restricted to implementation of agreed measures, and could only be used if all participants agreed.

- In 1998–99, as a reaction to the failure of the EU to respond effectively to the crisis in Kosovo, the first steps were taken towards the ESDP. The institutions of ESDP began work in 2000. It was incorporated into the EU by the Nice Treaty.

- The Treaty of Amsterdam created the post of High Representative for CFSP, which was later extended in the Lisbon Treaty to the High Representative for Foreign Affairs and Security Policy. Lisbon also created the EEAS.

CFSP and ESDP in Action

- Initial actions under CFSP were modest and built on EPC; subsequently stability pacts for Europe and for the Mediterranean extended the scope of activity.

- The terrorist attacks in the United States in September 2001 caused a series of setbacks to the progress that had been made on the ESDP. Initial support for the United States began to waver in the light of the Bush Administration's identification of an 'axis of evil'. The invasion of Iraq led to an open rift, especially between Britain, which supported the US action, and France and Germany, which condemned it.

- Despite these setbacks, by the end of 2009, ESDP had undertaken some twenty-two crisis-management missions.

- In the post-Lisbon Treaty period the EU faced a series of tests, notably: the 'Arab Spring'; ethnic tension in the Western Balkans; political instability in the Sahel region of Africa; discussions over Iran's nuclear programme; and a dispute with Russia over Ukraine.

Explaining CFSP and ESDP

- Hill (1993) identified a 'capability–expectations gap' in the international activities of the EC, which he expected would only increase when it became the EU.

- Realists assumed that political co-operation would never amount to more than trivial actions or would only achieve success where national interests coincided.

- Social constructivist perspectives emphasize the extent to which social interaction between foreign policy practitioners has led to a changing of their perspectives and the emergence of a common outlook.

- Historical institutionalist perspectives add to the constructivist analysis the insight that pragmatic institutional developments build in 'path dependence' for the process, making it difficult to reverse.

- The process that brought about the approximation of general foreign policy positions may now be repeated for security and defence policy.

EU Power in World Politics

- How the EU's impact in the world is judged from a normative perspective depends to a large extent on what kind of actor or power one thinks the EU should be in international affairs.

- Academics have variously promoted visions of the EU as a civilian (economic), military, and normative (cosmopolitan) power.

FURTHER READING

A clear introduction to the complexity of the EU's external relations is provided by **K. Smith**, *European Union Foreign Policy in a Changing World* (Cambridge: Polity Press, 2008). Also very useful is the second edition of **C. Hill and M. Smith (eds)**, *International Relations and the European Union* (Oxford: Oxford University Press, 2011).

Given its importance to so many later contributions, and the frequency with which the central idea is misunderstood or misused, an article that should certainly be read is **C. Hill**, 'The Capability-Expectations Gap, or Conceptualising Europe's International Role', *Journal of Common Market Studies*, 31 (1993): 305–28; the analysis can then be followed up by looking at **Hill**, *The Actors in Europe's Foreign Policy* (London: Routledge, 1996), and 'Closing the Capability–Expectations Gap', in **J. Peterson and H. Sjursen (eds)**, *A Common Foreign Policy for Europe? Competing Visions of the CFSP* (London: Routledge, 1998), 18–38. A more recent review of the factors that have increased the 'actorness' of the EU, and those that continue to weaken it, is provided in **U. Krotz**, 'Momentum and Impediments: Why Europe Won't Emerge as a Full Political Actor on the World Stage Soon', *Journal of Common Market Studies*, 47 (2009): 555–78. A useful assessment of the progress made by the ESDP can be found in **A. Menon**, 'Empowering Paradise: The ESDP at Ten', *International Affairs*, 85 (2010): 227–46.

For a recent discussion of the 'power' debate with a particular focus on the concept of 'normative power Europe' see the special issue of *Co-operation and Conflict*, 48, 2 (2013), edited by **K. Nicolaïdis and R. Whitman**.

 online resource centre
Visit the Online Resource Centre that accompanies this book for links to more information on the Common Foreign and Security Policy, including to the website of the relevant Directorate-General of the Commission: http:// oxfordtextbooks.co.uk/orc/bache4e/

Chapter 27

Enlargement

Chapter Overview

Starting with six member states originally, the European Community (EC)/European Union (EU) has grown through successive enlargements—from six to nine, then ten, twelve, fifteen, twenty-five, twenty-seven, and now twenty-eight. This chapter looks at each of the main enlargement rounds in turn, outlining what happened and what the effect was on the EC/EU, and at the outstanding applications that were still under consideration at the time of writing. A procedure emerged over the six rounds of enlargement that is being applied to the present applications, and this is explained. Academic explanations of why the various applications for membership were made, and why they were accepted by the EC/EU, are reviewed. Finally, a closer analysis of the controversial case of Turkey is offered and consideration is given to the concept of 'enlargement fatigue'.

History

The EC/EU has preferred to negotiate enlargements with groups of states together. This has produced six distinct rounds of enlargement (see Table 27.1), starting in 1973 when Britain, Denmark, and Ireland became members.

The second enlargement was in 1981, when Greece became a member, and the third was in 1986, when Portugal and Spain joined. For analytical purposes, the second and third enlargements are often treated as a single 'Southern enlargement', as they were undertaken for similar reasons and involved similar issues.

The fourth enlargement was that of 1995, which admitted Austria, Finland, and Sweden. Because the applicants (including Norway, which rejected membership in a referendum) were the leading members of the European Free Trade Association (EFTA) (see Insight 27.1), this is usually referred to as 'the EFTA enlargement'.

The fifth and sixth enlargements, in 2004 and 2007, are often referred to collectively as 'the Eastern enlargement' because most of the new entrants were former communist states in central and eastern Europe. Strictly speaking, this name is inaccurate, because two of the entrants in 2004—Cyprus and Malta—were Mediterranean island states.

The seventh enlargement saw the admittance of Croatia in 2013. It was the first of the Western Balkan states to complete its accession process.

Table 27.1 Enlargements of the EEC/EC/EU

Year	1973	1981	1986	1995	2004	2007	2013
New members	Denmark, Ireland, UK	Greece	Portugal, Spain	Austria, Finland, Sweden	Cyprus, Czech Republic, Estonia, Hungary, Latvia, Lithuania, Malta, Poland, Slovakia, Slovenia	Bulgaria, Romania	Croatia

Source: **http://ec.europa.eu**, © European Union, 1995–2014.

Insight 27.1 EFTA at the End of the 1980s

The European Free Trade Association (EFTA) was set up in 1959 and entered into force in January 1960. It was a response to the setting up of the European Economic Community (EEC) in 1958. The original members of EFTA were Austria, Britain, Denmark, Norway, Portugal, Sweden, and Switzerland.

By the late 1980s, EFTA consisted of seven states of varying size:

Country	Population (000s)
Sweden	8,640
Austria	7,820
Switzerland	6,790
Finland	5,030
Norway	4,260
Iceland	256
Liechtenstein	30

The economies of the EFTA states had been linked with those of the EC since the 1970s by a series of bilateral free-trade agreements.

By the end of the 1980s, EFTA was economically closely integrated with the EC.

The EC did 25 per cent of its trade with EFTA, a higher proportion than with the United States, while the EFTA states sent 56 per cent of their exports to the EC, and bought 60 per cent of their imports from the EC.

The First Enlargement

In August 1961, Britain, Denmark, and Ireland applied for membership of the EC. In April 1962, Norway also applied. The key applicant here was Britain. The other applicants were highly dependent on their economic links with Britain, which were fostered through their membership of EFTA. None of these states could afford to risk the loss of trade with their biggest customer that might result from Britain going into the European Economic Community (EEC) while they remained outside.

Negotiations went on throughout 1962, until, in January 1963, President de Gaulle of France unilaterally announced that France was not prepared to accept British membership. As any member state could veto entry, and as the other applications were dependent on British entry, the enlargement round collapsed.

In May 1967, Britain, Denmark, and Ireland applied again, and Norway joined the second application in July. This time, negotiations did not even get under way: France blocked agreement on opening negotiations in December 1967. Following the replacement of de Gaulle by Georges Pompidou as French President in 1969, a summit meeting at The Hague agreed on a package of measures to 'relaunch Europe' that included opening negotiations with the applicants, the 1967 applications of which remained on the table (see Chapter 7, The Hague Summit). On 1 January 1973, Britain, Denmark, and Ireland became members of the EC. Norway negotiated terms of entry, but the Norwegian people rejected membership in a subsequent referendum in 1972.

The impact of the first enlargement on the EC was profound. In terms of bargaining games, not only did the total number of member states increase by 50 per cent, but there was also another 'big state' among the new members—Britain—which changed the coalition dynamics that had previously been dominated by France and West Germany. In terms of the sense of self-identity of the EC, the admission of two states—Britain and Denmark—that were sceptical of the 'European ideal' made it much more difficult to find a common discourse to conceptualize the mission of the organization.

The Southern Enlargements

As explained above, the second and third enlargements of the EC are often treated as a single 'Southern' enlargement. Greece became a member state in January 1981, and Spain and Portugal in January 1986. In all cases, political considerations overrode economic in the decision to enlarge.

All three of the states concerned had just emerged from periods of dictatorship, and the desire to consolidate democracy and guard against a resurgence of authoritarianism featured strongly in the reasons for the applications and the reasons for their acceptance. It was assumed that EC membership, conditional on democratic government, would help to achieve that. The impact of this enlargement on the EC/EU was in its way as great as that of the first enlargement. Again, it changed the bargaining dynamics of the organization. The three new members shifted the orientation of the EC to the south, and the membership of Greece and Spain ensured that there would be a stronger Mediterranean dimension to policy. In political co-operation, the influence of Spain and Portugal led to a greater emphasis on relations with Latin America.

Perhaps most significantly in the short run, Spain, with the support of the other new entrants, took the lead in demanding larger structural funds (see Chapter 22, Explaining Cohesion Policy) and soon showed itself adept at playing the EC negotiating game to get them.

On the other hand, Greece's membership had some less positive consequences. Its long-standing disputes with Turkey proved an embarrassment to the EC/EU on more than one occasion, and spilled over into a hard line on Cyprus. Also, its position on the edge of the Balkans meant that Greece had sensitivities in the region that were difficult for other EU members to understand. These became particularly pertinent in the early 1990s following the break-up of Yugoslavia (see Chapter 26, The Common Foreign and Security Policy (CFSP) and European Security and Defence Policy (ESDP)).

The EFTA Enlargement

In the early 1990s, several member states of EFTA enquired about membership. At first, they were offered a form of close association that fell short of full membership. Subsequently, though, they lodged formal applications, and eventually Austria, Finland, and Sweden became members of the EU on 1 January 1995. Norway again rejected membership in a referendum in 1994, after terms of entry had been agreed.

Because the new members were wealthy, were already culturally aligned with the prevailing values of the existing member states, and had been closely associated with the EC prior to their membership, the effects of this enlargement were smaller than those of any other enlargement.

One effect was the emergence of a Nordic bloc within the Council of Ministers. From 1995, Denmark received support from Sweden and Finland for positions that it had long defended on issues such as environmental protection and human rights, and the Nordic states combined to press the membership claims of the Baltic states (Estonia, Latvia, and Lithuania) in the Eastern enlargement round. Austria joined the Nordic states in reinforcing the coalition of member states for which environmental protection was a significant issue. Because the new members were all net contributors to the budget, their presence reinforced the coalition in favour of reform of the budgetary rules.

The 'Eastern' Enlargement

With the collapse of communism in 1989, the EC was faced with a large number of potential new members, all of which expressed an aspiration to join. The first response was to conclude 'Europe Agreements', Association Agreements that fell short of envisaging full membership. Then in June 1993 the Copenhagen European Council accepted the legitimacy of the aspirations of the newly independent states to become members, and laid down criteria that they would have to fulfil in order for their applications to be considered. Applications came in rapidly from ten central and eastern European countries (CEECs)—Bulgaria, the Czech Republic, Estonia, Hungary, Latvia, Lithuania, Poland, Slovakia, Slovenia, and Romania—plus Cyprus, Malta, and Turkey.

In December 1997, the Luxembourg European Council agreed that negotiations should open with five of these states—the Czech Republic, Estonia, Hungary, Poland, and Slovenia—plus Cyprus (Malta had withdrawn its application), but hold back on the five others. In December 1999, the Helsinki European Council agreed to open negotiations with the remaining five CEECs, plus Malta, which had resubmitted its application. On 1 May 2004, eight CEECs —the ten listed above not including Bulgaria and Romania—plus Cyprus and Malta, became members of the EU.

The two outstanding applications from former eastern European communist states were from Bulgaria and Romania. Starting from a lower base of both economic development and legal stability than the other applicants, they took longer to satisfy the basic criteria, but both became members in 2007.

The effects of this enlargement were profound. In order to be ready to take as many as twelve new members, the EU had to deal with some difficult issues requiring reforms of both policies and institutions. Two policy issues were particularly crucial to the prospects for enlargement: agriculture (see Chapter 19, Agenda 2000 and the 2003 Reform) and the structural funds (see Chapter 22, The 2006 Reform). In both cases, the existing member states that were beneficiaries from the funds proved very reluctant to surrender their benefits to facilitate enlargement. The institutional questions were those that were already apparent at the time of the EFTA enlargement: the weighting of votes under **qualified majority voting (QMV)**, and the size of the blocking minority; the abandonment of the national veto in more policy sectors; and the size of the Commission.

Croatia

With the completion of the Eastern enlargement, the EU faced the question of how far it would continue to expand geographically. There was no shortage of prospective applicants. In particular there was the prospect of applications from the Yugoslav successor states.

Most of these were not expected to be ready to make applications for some time, but in March 2003, Croatia applied for membership, and was granted candidate status in June. In April 2004, the Commission recommended the opening of negotiations with Croatia, which had made remarkable progress in a short time on both the political and economic fronts. Accession negotiations began in December 2005 and Croatia became a member in 2013.

Further Applications

Beyond Croatia a number of other Yugoslav successor states applied for membership. In March 2004, the former Yugoslav Republic of Macedonia (FYRM) applied, and was granted candidate status in December 2005. Despite Commission recommendations since 2009 that accession negotiations should begin with FYRM, they were blocked by Greece because of a dispute over the applicant country's name. Montenegro applied for membership in December 2008, was granted candidate status in December 2010, and accession negotiations began in June 2012. Serbia applied for membership in December 2009, and became a candidate in March 2012. Following the EU-brokered agreement that was reached on the status of Kosovo in 2013 (see Chapter 11, Other Developments) accession negotiations began in January 2014. Albania submitted a membership application in April 2009. Bosnia and Herzegovina remains a potential candidate for EU membership. However, any prospect of membership is not imminent given ongoing issues of serious corruption, economic underdevelopment, and

Table 27.2 Prospective members (as of 2014)

Accession Negotiations open	Turkey, Iceland (suspended), Serbia, Montenegro
Candidate status	former Yugoslav Republic of Macedonia
Applied	Albania

political instability (see, for instance, European Commission 2013*b*), which in early 2014 led to widespread unrest and protests.

Following the financial crisis of 2008–09, in which Icelandic banks suffered badly, the Icelandic parliament, the Althingi, narrowly voted (by thirty-three votes to twenty-eight with two abstentions) to apply for EU membership. Iceland was granted candidate status in June 2010 and accession negotiations began immediately. However, following elections in April 2013 which brought to power Eurosceptic parties, negotiations with the EU were suspended.

Turkey had been an applicant for membership for longer than any of the states that gained entry in 2004. An Association Agreement envisaging eventual membership had been signed in 1963. It had been suspended in 1970 and again in 1980, following military takeovers of power, but reinstated following elections and a return to civilian government in 1973 and again in 1983. In 1987, Turkey lodged its first formal application for membership of the EU. Two years later, the EU responded by saying that no further enlargement was envisaged in the foreseeable future. In 1995 a **customs union** agreement was signed, the first time that such an agreement had not been part of a process of accession. Then in 1997 came the Luxembourg European Council and the decision to move forward with various applications, but excluding Turkey. In 1999 the Helsinki European Council reversed this decision and recognized Turkey as an applicant. Negotiations began in October 2005, at the same time as those for Croatia (for an overview of the status of prospective members see Table 27.2; for further discussion of Turkey, see this chapter, Turkey).

The Enlargement Procedure

Over the course of the five rounds of enlargement, a procedure gradually evolved. Each of the enlargements added something to this emerging approach.

When a potential applicant approaches the EU, the first step is for the European Council to consider whether the application is acceptable in principle. If it is, then the Commission produces an official Opinion on the application. This consists of a report on the economic and political position of the applicant state, and a recommendation on whether to proceed to negotiations immediately, or whether to delay. Usually, the recommendation to delay is to give the applicant time to strengthen its claim to be ready for membership. If so, then a plan of action is produced to facilitate this, which will normally involve an Association Agreement or the strengthening of existing agreements.

If the decision of the European Council is to proceed with the application immediately, it will set a date for the opening of negotiations. The Commission will then convene meetings of various sectoral groups of experts to work out the detail of the EU's negotiating position. Negotiations then commence with the applicant(s). These are handled on a day-to-day basis by the groups of experts, often by correspondence rather than in formal meetings. They are co-ordinated by the Commission, and overseen by the Council of Foreign Ministers.

When agreement has been reached by the expert working groups in all sectors, and have been pronounced acceptable by the Foreign Ministers, the terms are passed to the European Council for formal approval. Assuming that approval is given, an Accession Treaty is drawn up with each applicant state. The Accession Treaty then has to be ratified by the European Parliament (EP) on the side of the EU, and by either the national parliament of the applicant state, or by referendum depending on the constitutional procedures of each state.

The practice that was established at the time of the first enlargement was that the existing member states would sort out arrangements that suited them before the new members were admitted. The corollary of this was French insistence that accession for the new members could only be on the basis of acceptance of the complete **acquis communautaire** (Preston 1995: 452). This was to ensure that Britain did not try to slip out of the uncomfortable budgetary position into which the French believed that they had manoeuvred it. The implicit understanding that there was a deal in operation here explains the strength of French (and German) resistance to subsequent British demands for a correction of the budgetary imbalance.

The main contribution that the Southern enlargement made to the principles on which future enlargements would be conducted was the precedent set for the acceptance of applications for geostrategic and political reasons even where the economic conditions were not ideal. This was relevant to the applications from a range of CEECs following the collapse of communism in 1989. Although the economies of these states were not strong, the need to ensure their political stability was; the 1975 Council decision to override the Commission's Opinion on Greece, and later to wave aside doubts about the economic preparedness of Portugal for membership for similar political reasons, created a precedent to do the same for these new applicants.

The EFTA enlargement did not produce any new principles, but in the negotiation of the Eastern enlargement, formal criteria were laid down for the first time. These criteria arose from concern about the preparedness of the former communist states for membership, and because they were agreed at the June 1993 Copenhagen European Council, they are known as the Copenhagen criteria (1993). They are:

- a political criterion—that an applicant must have stable institutions guaranteeing democracy, the rule of law, human rights, and the protection of minorities;

- an economic criterion—that an applicant must have a functioning market economy and the capacity to cope with competitive pressures within the single market of the EU;

- a criterion relating to the *acquis communautaire*—that an applicant must be able to take on the obligations of membership, including adherence to the aims of political, economic, and monetary union.

Although these were originally criteria for the acceptance of applications, they also came to structure the negotiations on membership, and were applied in the negotiations with subsequent applicants. Adherence to these criteria on the part of prospective member states amounts to a significant Europeanization of their politics, economy, and institutions (see Chapter 3).

Explaining Enlargement

Schimmelfennig and Sedelmeier (2002) produced a typology of the academic literature on enlargement, classifying it according to the research focus along four dimensions:

- the enlargement policies of the applicants;
- the enlargement policies of the existing member states;
- the enlargement policies of the EU;
- the impact of enlargement.

Structuring existing studies along these dimensions, Schimmelfennig and Sedelmeier (2002: 523–4) were able to conclude that:

- the bulk of the analytical studies were on the last two enlargements;
- the analyses of the EFTA enlargement focused primarily on their first dimension—questioning why the EFTA states applied for membership;
- the analyses of the Eastern enlargement focused primarily on their second and third dimensions—questioning why the applications were accepted, and on what conditions the applicants were offered membership.

Schimmelfennig and Sedelmeier (2002: 508–15) also divided existing studies of enlargement according to whether they emphasized interests or ideas in their analysis. They referred to these as 'rationalist' and 'constructivist' institutionalism (see Chapters 2 and 3).

Explanations which emphasize interests—both economic and geopolitical—are in most cases able at least partially to account for the desire of prospective members to join the EU and the desire of the EU and its constituent states and institutions to permit membership. However, they are liable to understate the costs incurred on both sides: for prospective members in terms of the often domestically unpopular adjustment processes required in order to meet membership criteria and for current members in terms of diminished influence within the EU as well as the potential financial costs of accepting new members (relevant in many enlargement rounds). Constructivist explanations which emphasize the importance of ideas can usefully account for a willingness on all sides to overlook such costs. Such ideas can consist of general normative conceptions about 'Europe', its identity, and its limits (see Chapter 4), and also more specific technical norms associated with policy and law that are 'diffused' during the enlargement process.

Explanations of the First Enlargement

It is generally agreed that to understand why the applicant states of the first enlargement decided to seek entry, it is primarily necessary to consider the reasons for the

British application. The other applicants were so tightly bound economically to Britain that they could not afford to stay outside the EC if Britain went in. There were two main factors behind the British application: economic and geostrategic.

Sluggish economic growth in Britain in the late 1950s was increasingly blamed by economists both inside and outside government on the pattern of trade. Britain, at the end of the 1950s, still did a high proportion of its trade with the countries of its former empire, now voluntarily grouped together as the Commonwealth—but the fastest growth in trade was between industrialized countries. This was reflected in the high rates of growth within the newly formed EEC. The success of the EEC surprised British policy makers, and led to efforts in the late 1950s to conclude a free-trade agreement with the six. When this failed, an application for British entry for economic reasons began to be taken seriously. For Moravcsik (1998: 164), such economic reasons were paramount: 'The British membership bid was … aimed primarily at the advancement of enduring British commercial interests.'

Political considerations started to point in the same direction when de Gaulle began to dominate the EEC, and became especially influential when he made proposals for political co-operation in the Fouchet Plan (see Insight 7.2, The Fouchet Plan). British concern centred on the known hostility of de Gaulle to US hegemony in the capitalist world. Fouchet contained reference to co-operation on defence, but no reference to NATO. Because it was a central doctrine of British defence policy that the United States must be allowed to exercise leadership of the Western defence effort through NATO, Fouchet set alarm bells ringing in London. It did the same in Washington. Camps (1964: 336) recorded that the British government came under increasing pressure from the United States to join the EEC so as to act as a counterweight to French influence, and she believed that this was 'a very important—perhaps the controlling—element in Macmillan's decision to apply'. The same perception seems to have been one of the significant factors in de Gaulle's decision to block enlargement throughout the 1960s.

Initially, the EC member states other than France were interested in British membership for predominantly political reasons. They saw Britain as a future counterweight to French domination of the EC. Concern on this issue was particularly strong where political co-operation was involved. As Ludlow (1997) made clear, the negotiations on British accession in the early 1960s were implicitly linked to the parallel negotiations on the Fouchet Plan. When de Gaulle vetoed British entry, the Fouchet negotiations collapsed (see Chapter 7, The 1963 Crisis). The reason why France finally accepted the British application in 1972 was primarily economic. The post-war economic boom faltered in the late 1960s and British entry offered the prospect of giving a boost to the EC economies. The change of French President cleared the way.

Explanations of the Southern Enlargement

As suggested above, the reasons for the applications of Greece, Portugal, and Spain have not generally been considered problematic. Each emerged from a period of right-wing dictatorship in the course of the 1970s, and the democratic government of each was anxious to embed the democratic constitution by tying in the state to the EC. It seemed equally clear that the existing member states were prepared to accept the applications for essentially the same reason: to stabilize their own southern flank.

This assumption that there was no problem to be explained worked against detailed research on issues that were investigated for other enlargements.

Explanations of the EFTA Enlargement

The EFTA enlargement was the first to be systematically analysed in the literature. As Schimmelfennig and Sedelmeier (2002: 517) put it: 'The key question pursued is: why did the EFTA countries, after a long period of deliberate non-membership in the EC, develop an interest in closer ties with, and membership of, the EC at the beginning of the 1990s?'

At the beginning of the 1980s, the European economies generally experienced an economic downturn. In response to the downturn, the EC launched the '1992 Project' to create the single European market. In the course of the 1980s, the member states of EFTA became concerned about the impact on investment in their economies of the EC's decision to create the single internal market. Export-oriented businesses in the EFTA states experienced difficulties in selling to the EU, with the result that, increasingly, businesses wanted to be inside the single market, and investment began to flow in that direction. Even large national companies of the EFTA states, such as Volvo of Sweden, were locating their investments inside the EC and not in the EFTA countries. This led the EFTA states to enquire about closer links with the EC, despite the unpopularity of the idea of membership inside some of the states concerned.

The other factor that affected the decision was the end of the Cold War. Events in 1989 removed one of the main objections of opponents of membership within the EFTA states. Austria, Finland, and Sweden were all neutral during the Cold War, and there had been doubts about whether membership of an organization that was developing a Common Foreign and Security Policy was compatible with neutrality. The end of the Cold War called into question the meaning of neutrality, and effectively dissipated the doubts on that score.

Sweden is the most studied of the cases from this enlargement. It illustrates well why analysts have considered their main problem to be explaining the reasons for the EFTA states' applications. Sweden was an exemplar of a social-democratic **neo-corporatist** type of state, and its social-democratic governments had previously rejected membership of the EC on the grounds that the free market orientation of the organization would jeopardize the Swedish model of capitalism. Yet, in 1991 a social-democratic government applied for membership at just the time that the EC was taking a major step in a neoliberal direction with the single market programme (Bieler 2002: 576): why?

Ingebritsen (1998) offered a rational-choice explanation for the decision, in the mould of liberal intergovernmentalism. She concentrated on the leading industrial sectors, which in Sweden were export-oriented. The largest firms were also transnational, and in the course of the 1980s began to transfer production abroad. Swedish governments were already concerned about the country's lack of competitiveness, and the internal market programme offered a means of injecting more competitiveness into the economy. So, the combination of the push factor of the loss of investment and the pull factor of achieving domestic economic objectives through taking on external commitments (hand-tying) made the choice for membership of the internal market rational for the Swedish government.

523

> ### Insight 27.2 The European Economic Area
>
> When the EFTA states first enquired about membership of the EC, the reaction from the Commission was to suggest an alternative. In January 1989, Commission President Delors proposed the idea of the European Economic Space (EES), which was later renamed the European Economic Area (EEA). This would give the EFTA states membership of the single market without them becoming full members of the EC. For the governments of the EFTA states, the EEA had the advantage that it might be easier than full membership of the EC to sell to their electorates. The disadvantage was that they would have no voice in the ongoing negotiation of the regulation of the single market. They would be obliged to accept agreements reached in their absence.
>
> The EEA Agreement was signed between the then seven member states of EFTA and the then twelve member states of the EC in May 1992. Switzerland rejected membership in a referendum held in December 1992. The EEA entered into force for the remaining EFTA states on 1 January 1994, but one year later its membership on the EFTA side was reduced again when the accession to the EU of Austria, Finland, and Sweden took effect on 1 January 1995. This left Iceland, Norway, and (after 1 May 1995) Liechtenstein.
>
> The EFTA members of the EEA enjoy the benefits of membership of the single market, but they have to adopt the law of the EU on social policy, consumer protection, the environment, and company law without having any formal voice in the making of those laws. They also have to contribute to the costs of maintaining the single market, including the social costs, but receive no money themselves from the various EU funds.

At first, the EFTA states were offered membership of a new organization called the European Economic Area (EEA) (see Insight 27.2). The Swedish government tried this approach, but it was abandoned in favour of an application for full membership because it did not satisfy the large Swedish manufacturers and did not stop the outward flow of **investment capital**. Essentially, the same analysis was applied to Finland, where the economy was also dominated by capital-intensive manufacturing exporters.

Fioretos (1997) offered a similar analysis. Essentially, Fioretos (1997) argued that globalization had increased the power of corporations in the domestic arena and allowed them to force governments onto paths of policy that they—the corporations—preferred. Like Ingebritsen (1998), Fioretos (1997) offered a rationalist analysis that was compatible with liberal intergovernmentalism.

Liberal intergovernmentalism analyses European integration as an example of a two-level game, in which the first stage is the formation of preferences (see Chapter 1, International Relations Theories of European Integration). At this stage: 'Groups articulate preferences; governments aggregate them' (Moravcsik 1993: 483).

This is exactly the relationship theorized by Fioretos (1997). In response to the economic downturn of the 1980s, Swedish firms took advantage of growing globalization to become transnational. This strengthened their hand in domestic bargaining with government because they had a much stronger option to exit the game than previously—that is, if they did not get their way, they could close down production in Sweden and switch it elsewhere. The firms were kept in Sweden in the 1980s by a series of devaluations that kept the krona at a competitive exchange rate with the economies of the EC, which were the main markets for Swedish manufactured products. This strategy could not be pursued indefinitely, though, and increasingly investment capital did leave Sweden for EC locations that offered lower costs of production and lower transport costs because of greater proximity to the market. Weakened in the domestic bargaining game by the greater ease with which capital could relocate, the Swedish social democrats had to pursue membership of the single market, which meant membership of the EC once it became clear that the EEA was an unsatisfactory compromise for Swedish firms.

Bieler (2000, 2002) offered a neo-Gramscian analysis (see Chapter 4, Critical Political Economy) that placed more emphasis on the role of ideas. Sweden was compared with Austria. Whereas the transnational sectors were the primary economic actors in Sweden, in Austria the dominant economic sector was not transnational. It consisted of internationally-oriented national firms, which were dependent on exports to the EC but did not have the production facilities outside their own country that the larger Swedish firms had acquired during the 1980s. This sector dominated the Austrian Federation of Industrialists.

In order to convince the Austrian government to apply for membership, the Federation had to overcome political opposition. So it undertook what Bieler (2002: 583) called a 'hegemonic project'. This involved issuing a series of studies that not only advanced a strong version of the neoliberal economic argument, but also dealt with the constitutional implications of membership and the issue of what it implied for Austria's post-war neutrality. These arguments then fed into internal debates within the two main political parties—the Social Democratic Party and the People's Party. Although they encountered opposition from representatives of the economic sectors that had been sheltered from foreign competition by the state, and from representatives of the public sector, they eventually won over the leadership of both parties, thus setting the course for the application. By the time of the Austrian referendum in June 1994, a new orthodoxy had emerged around membership, thus ensuring a comfortable 'yes' vote by 66.6 per cent to 33.4 per cent.

In Sweden, Bieler (2002: 586–7) argued that the transnational corporations did not need to build a hegemonic project in favour of membership because they had the option of exit. Instead, they brutally spelt out the implications of not joining: notably, in a series of advertisements in national newspapers in the run-up to the 1994 general election (Fioretos 1997: 316). Swedish membership was pushed most strongly by the Ministry of Finance and the Prime Minister's Office, and Bieler (2002: 585) argued that this showed that 'neo-liberal restructuring had become ... internalized within the Swedish form of state in view of domestic economic recession'. In other words, the Swedish government was looking for a long-term means of solving the country's chronic economic problems, and had accepted the ideological claims of neoliberalism to provide the only such solution. It was therefore trying to tie its own hands by joining the EC, which would provide an external buttress against resistance to the dismantling of the welfare state and neo-corporatist institutions of Sweden.

The initial response of the EU was to offer the prospective applicants a form of relationship that fell short of full membership. This position was then abandoned, and the applications for full membership accepted. So why the change of attitude?

At the time of the initial approach from the EFTA states, the EC was trying to process the legislation that was needed to make a reality of the internal market. It was also looking to the next stage in the process. To prevent another round of enlargement dominating the attention of the organization, and possibly deflecting the course of the spillover from the single market to the single currency, Delors proposed the creation of a European Economic Space. This later became the EEA (see Insight 27.2).

The EEA negotiations were successfully concluded in 1991, and a treaty was signed in 1992—but it became increasingly apparent that businesses were simply not prepared to accept that members of the EEA would be full members of the single market. Investment flows did not revert to previous patterns. The EEA suffered a further blow to its credibility when the Swiss people rejected membership of it in a referendum in December 1992. The government of Austria had already applied for full membership of the EC in July 1989, and Finland, Norway, and Sweden did likewise between July 1991 and November 1992.

By this time, the prospect had emerged of an eventual Eastern enlargement to embrace states that were economically considerably less developed than the existing member states. The EFTA applicants were wealthy and potential net contributors to a common budget that would come under much greater pressure if the CEECs were eventually accepted. So, the EFTA applications were accepted.

Explanations of the Eastern Enlargement

As with the membership applications of Greece, Portugal, and Spain in the 1970s, the wish of the former communist states to become members of the EU has hardly been considered problematic. The states that had emerged from Soviet domination wanted to cement their status as Europeans, and to foreclose any possibility of being drawn back into the Russian sphere of influence. From this point of view, membership of NATO was the more important objective, but membership of the EU was also a guarantee, albeit weaker. The former communist states also saw EU membership as essential to their future economic success, and it fitted with a widespread desire to reaffirm a European identity.

Bieler (2002: 588–9) applied neo-Gramscian concepts to the analysis of why the applications by the former communist states were made. He suggested that the decision to apply was taken by what he called 'cadre élites within state institutions'. These elites had taken advantage of the collapse of the previous regimes to take power and to introduce programmes of neoliberal reconstruction, supported by external forces. When the restructuring programmes precipitated big falls in gross domestic product (GDP), the legitimacy of the elites and of their reform programmes were jeopardized. EU membership was pursued as a buttress against resistance and reversion to anti-capitalist politicians and policies. It was sold to the populations of the CEECs as a historical 'return to Europe'. However, the volatility of society and politics in the CEECs ruled out the construction of a pro-EU historical bloc organized around a hegemonic project such as Bieler had identified in Austria (2002: 582–5). Instead, the process in the CEECs was what Gramsci had described as a 'passive revolution', led from above by the state elites. This had implications for the commitment of socio-economic actors to the project.

The immediate reaction of the EC to the collapse of communism was to offer the Europe Agreements, which did not make a commitment to eventual membership. In explanation of this, Friis (1998) pointed out that the collapse of communism came quickly and was not anticipated. First, the European Commission was preoccupied with the prospect of a sudden increase in the territory of the EC, and the adaptation of common policies to the addition of another 17 million people with a GDP per head well below the EC average.

Second, the negotiation of the EFTA enlargement was still at an early stage in 1989. Indeed, the EC was still following a policy of trying to persuade the EFTA applicants to become part of the single market without becoming members of the EC—that is, the EEA negotiations. Indeed, the deal offered in the original Europe Agreements was similar to that on offer to the EFTA states at that stage: membership of the single market without membership of the EC.

Third, the EC in 1989 was about to embark on the process of agreeing to a monetary union, a further issue that occupied the attention of the member states and the Commission.

Between 1990 and 1995, the three pressing issues identified above were all cleared out of the way. Formal reunification of Germany took place on 3 October 1990. The Treaty on European Union (TEU), setting out the timetable and conditions for monetary union, was agreed at the Maastricht European Council in December 1991, and formally signed by Foreign Ministers in February 1992. Terms of entry for Austria, Finland, and Sweden were agreed in the early hours of 1 March 1994. Once these issues were resolved, removing what Friis (1998: 333) described as 'the negative spillover from internal negotiating tables', there was the possibility of contemplating further enlargement.

The persistence of the CEECs in pressing for entry to the EC/EU was strengthened by the acceptance of the EC that the EEA scheme was not going to work for the EFTA applicants. It would have been difficult to convince the CEECs that membership of the single market without membership of the EU would be any more successful or acceptable for them once the argument had been conceded for the EFTA applicants. It would have looked simply as though the EC/EU was prepared to accept prosperous member states and not those most in need of support.

Security considerations became more urgent in the context of growing instability in Russia (Friis and Murphy 1999: 220). The USSR broke apart rapidly between August and December 1991. It formally ceased to exist on 31 December 1991. The Russian state that emerged after many of the former Soviet republics had proclaimed independence was an insecure place in which nationalist voices received a hearing from the population, and in turn the governments under President Boris Yeltsin came under pressure to talk tough with 'the near abroad'. In these circumstances, the concern of the CEECs for security from an aggressive Russia led to increased demands for membership of both the EC and NATO. These two issues became intertwined. The United States was concerned not to expand NATO membership too precipitately for fear of alarming Russia, so it put pressure on the EC to offer membership as a sort of second-order guarantee of independence to the states most affected. There was particular pressure on the EC to offer membership to the three Baltic states—Estonia, Latvia, and Lithuania—because they were too close to Russia to make NATO membership feasible, but they were also too close to Russia for comfort given the rising nationalist sentiment there. Although it was never likely that the EC would accede directly to any such demand from the United States, it had to show that it was prepared to move some way to contributing to the stabilization of eastern Europe. Also, as Yugoslavia began to disintegrate on the very doorstep of the EC, concerns about security grew in the member states themselves.

The prevarication on whether to proceed with all twelve applications together or whether to prioritize some of the applicants reflected the different stakes that different member states had in the enlargement. Germany was particularly keen to see early enlargement to take in at least its closest neighbours: Poland, Hungary, and the Czech Republic. This was both for security and economic reasons. The security reasons are obvious: reunification rendered Germany once more a central European state itself; and instability in neighbouring states was highly undesirable. The economic motivations reflected the traditional economic links between Germany and its central European neighbours. France, on the other hand, had less of a stake in either consideration, as it had no contiguous land frontier with the central European states, and had fewer economic links. For France and the other Mediterranean member states, there was a real risk that Eastern enlargement would reduce their influence in the EU, shifting the centre of gravity away from them towards Germany. The French government was therefore more prepared to take a leisurely approach, whereas the German government wanted as few obstacles as possible placed in the way of early accession for its favoured candidates.

The European Commission's motivation in proposing to proceed with only some of the applications reflected particularly its concerns about its limited resources. The process of accession is long and complex, and can tie up a lot of the available resources of the Commission. Member states have never been prepared to provide all of the extra resources necessary to allow it to perform efficiently the task set for it, and there was no indication that they would do so on this occasion.

Acceptance of the Commission's proposal to limit the number of applicants with which accession negotiations would begin reflected a temporary meeting of minds between Germany and France. The link to NATO enlargement, and the pressure that the EU had come under from the United States to proceed rapidly on a broad front, made it very attractive for France to agree to a more limited start, to show that the EU was not going to be pushed around by the United States.

The change of tactic at Helsinki, to open negotiations with the remaining applicants, reflected a number of changed circumstances. First, the CEECs that had not been placed in the first group had become increasingly restive about their treatment. Second, the pressure from the United States had receded as the security threat posed by Russia appeared also to recede. Third, the change of heart in Malta opened the prospect to France, Spain, Portugal, Italy, and Greece of having another Mediterranean small state in the first group of members to offset the influx of small and medium-sized CEECs. Of the second six, Malta was the most equipped to catch up with some of the first six applicants and get membership early.

Bieler (2002: 590) also offered an analysis of why the applications were accepted. He identified the key to the acceptance of the applications as the support given after 1997 by the European Round Table of Industrialists (ERT). Bieler maintained that the ERT was recruited as an ally by the Commission, but was willingly recruited because many of the transnational corporations that made up the membership of the ERT had invested heavily in the CEECs and therefore had an interest in consolidating the conditions for profitable production there.

From a constructivist perspective, others have emphasized the way in which certain actors invoked a moral or ideational argument in favour of CEEC membership during the course of the negotiations. Such rhetoric usually referred in some way to the

'European vocation' of the CEECs and their enforced exclusion from the integration project during the Cold War. This rhetoric was particularly prevalent within the Commission, whose 'policy entrepreneurship' under President Prodi and Enlargement Commissioner Verheugen was for many a critical driver of this enlargement.

Explanations of the Western Balkans Enlargement

Croatia became the first Balkan state to join in 2013, by when negotiations with other states in the region were underway. These states had similar motivations to the CEECs in their desire to become members: in short, twin economic and security concerns. The EU is also interested in guaranteeing long-term stability in the Western Balkans. Following the destructive wars in the 1990s, which led to the break-up of Yugoslavia, the EU became an active presence in the region, involved in peace-keeping and policing missions and various forms of reconstruction project (see Chapter 26).

The EU sought to use the prospect of enlargement as leverage to promote peace and reconciliation in the region. Through the so-called Stabilization and Association Process (SAP) it established a set of conditions which largely mirrored those contained in the Copenhagen criteria. In addition, via this process it successfully pressed for co-operation with the International Criminal Tribunal for the Former Yugoslavia (ICTY), the body responsible for prosecuting those accused of serious crimes committed during the conflicts within the former Yugoslavia.

Turkey

Turkey's application for membership of the EU is linked to the attempts of an elite in Turkey, persistently since the early part of the twentieth century, to establish it as a western country. The explanation for Turkey's application therefore lies in its past to some degree.

After the end of the First World War and the collapse of the Ottoman Empire, the modern state of Turkey emerged from a prolonged civil war in which the new nationalists defeated the Sultan. The radicals, led by Mustafa Kemal Atatürk, defeated the more conservative of the nationalist forces and established a republic. The reformists then set about a process of westernizing and modernizing Turkey. This involved legislation to abolish Islamic law and Islamic modes of dress, to institute a new Civil Code modelled on the Swiss example, and to introduce the Roman alphabet (Ahmad 2001: 850; McLaren 2000: 118).

When private business interests failed to respond to the reforms by investing in the modernization of the economy, and in the wake of the world economic crisis of 1930, an ideology of 'Kemalism' was developed that involved the state carrying out economic modernization from the top. The armed forces became associated with this process, setting themselves up as the guardians of the secular state. This role was consolidated after the Second World War, as a semi-modernized Turkey stuttered and staggered away from statism towards democracy. The struggles between the classes that benefited from modernization and those that suffered produced political crises that led to military interventions in 1960 and 1970 (Ahmad 2001: 850–1).

On the Turkish side, the 1959 application for associate membership of the EC, and the post-dictatorship enquiry about full membership, can be understood as an attempt by certain elites and sections of the population to strengthen the contested identity of Turkey as a western European nation rather than as an eastern, Muslim nation. For the EC, the decision in the 1960s to conclude an Association Agreement with Turkey envisaging eventual membership can be explained largely in geostrategic terms. Turkey had just emerged from a period of military rule, and the political scene was volatile. The predominant strategic concern of the period was the Cold War, and Turkey stood on the cusp of the communist world. It was important for the capitalist states to shore up this flank of NATO, and to do that it was important to strengthen the democratic forces that favoured a western and capitalist orientation for the state.

Further military intervention in 1970 indicated that this tactic had not worked, and led to the suspension of the Association Agreement. The restoration of democracy in 1973 reactivated the Agreement, but tensions between the neo-fascist right and the extreme left precipitated a further military intervention in 1980. Democracy was restored in 1983, but it was not until 1987 that Turkey was sufficiently stable for a formal application to the EU to be a credible move.

Müftüler-Bac and McLaren (2003) analysed the reasons for the decision of the EU to exclude Turkey from the list of prospective members in 1997, and for the change of position in 1999. They considered this to be a puzzle because nothing significant had changed in Turkey in the intervening period. In solving the problem, they adopted an intergovernmental perspective, arguing that the explanation lay in the changing preferences of the governments of existing member states, which in turn reflected their national interests. Turkey not only had no champion among the existing member states, but in Greece it had an adversary. Germany also had grave doubts about the acceptability of Turkish entry. The ability of Greece to exercise a veto over moves towards Turkish membership, and the opposition of Germany to any such moves, explained the omission of Turkey from the list of candidates in 1997. By the end of 1999, though, both of these opponents had changed position.

In late 1999, there was a dramatic improvement in relations between Greece and Turkey. Müftüler-Bac and McLaren (2003) offer four explanations for this:

- Theo Pangalos, a long-standing adversary of Turkey, was replaced by the far more pragmatic and accommodating George Papandreou as Greece's Foreign Minister;
- a terrible earthquake in Turkey in August 1999 produced a wave of sympathy among the Greek public, and emergency assistance from the Greek government;
- in trying to gain membership of the European single currency, the Greek government was struggling to cut its budget deficit, and a relaxation of tensions with Turkey offered the prospect of significant savings on defence expenditure;
- Greece was using up a lot of political capital within the EU in causing trouble for the others over Turkey, political capital that it needed to conserve if it was not to lose out in areas such as receipts from the structural funds following the Eastern enlargement.

There was also a change in the German position between 1997 and 1999. For the German government of Helmut Kohl, the main objection to Turkish membership, which was often unspoken, was a concern that it was not culturally compatible with the image that the CDU/CSU parties held of Europe: in other words, Turkey was not Christian. This was also a view held by other Christian Democrat politicians from outside of Germany. The change of position in Germany came about as a result of the replacement of the CDU–CSU government in 1998 with an SPD–Green government under Gerhard Schröder. Müftüler-Bac and McLaren (2003: 23–4) represented the issue for the new government as one of domestic politics: the need to integrate the large Turkish minority more securely into German society. The conversion of Germany meant that Turkey now had the advocate that it had lacked in 1997, a significant factor in the decision to grant it candidate status in 1999.

Moreover, Britain, always sympathetic to Turkey's claims, became a strong advocate of its case during the early 2000s. In the aftermath of a spate of terrorist bombings in Ankara in November 2003, the British Foreign Secretary, Jack Straw, called for Turkish membership 'as soon as possible', and the Europe Minister, Denis MacShane, said, 'Europe is incomplete without Turkey' (Foreign and Commonwealth Office 2004). The dominant reason for British support was geostrategic. Turkey occupied a geographical position between the EU and the Middle East. It bordered Iran, Iraq, and Syria. It had a majority of Muslims among its population, at a time when the EU was increasingly being accused of a bias against Muslims. A stable and western-oriented Turkey was therefore an important strategic goal for the west, and the best way of ensuring the stability and western orientation of Turkey was to admit it to the EU.

As Parker (2009b) noted, changes within Turkey facilitated these pro-Turkish perspectives in the early 2000s. In November 2002 the Justice and Development Party (AKP) came into office. A self-proclaimed moderate Islamic party, it was committed to pursuing Turkey's bid for EU membership. Under the premiership of Recep Tayyip Erdogan, the AKP vigorously set about trying to satisfy the political prerequisites ('Copenhagen political criteria') for the opening of accession negotiations. Within the space of little over a year, the new government had made significant reforms to the political and legal system. In particular it had taken important steps to improve the human rights situation in the country, including the granting of certain cultural rights to its substantial Kurdish population. This progress was acknowledged in the 2002 Copenhagen European Council Conclusions, which stated that:

> If the European Council in December 2004, on the basis of a report and a recommendation from the Commission, decides that Turkey fulfils the Copenhagen political criteria, the European Union will open accession negotiations with Turkey without delay.

This commitment provided a further incentive to the reform process within Turkey. It also delegated an important role to the Commission, which produced largely positive annual progress reports in 2003 and 2004. These certainly paved the way to the positive European Council decision in 2004 and the opening of accession negotiations in 2005. Although member states endorsed the Commission's recommendation to begin negotiations, there remained significant reluctance in certain national contexts. Some have argued that in this instance, as with the CEECs, the EU's collective 'rhetorical entrapment' made it difficult to shun Turkey at this stage (Bürgin 2010). Such rhetoric consisted of commitments to Turkey's 'European vocation', the political

531

criteria as a basis for assessment, and a clear decision-making timeframe which required a decision in 2004.

However, after 2006, negotiations progressed slowly. Formally this was due to the failure of Turkey to open its land and sea ports to the Republic of Cyprus (the Greek-Cypriot controlled part of the island, which Turkey does not recognize but is an EU member state). However, changes in key member states are also relevant. When the Christian Democrats returned to office in Germany in 2004, the German position became far less positive towards Turkish membership, with Chancellor Merkel arguing in favour of a 'privileged partnership' instead of full membership for Turkey; and, before he took office in 2007, French President Sarkozy stated unequivocally that 'Turkey has no place inside the EU' (Parker 2009b: 1095).

The situation in Turkey also changed. Popular support for the EU significantly waned after 2005. Given Turkey's rapid economic growth (and the EU's own simultaneous economic 'crisis'), Erdogan's rhetoric at times suggested that Turkey might no longer perceive EU membership as its primary foreign policy objective (see *The Economist* 2013a). Moreover, Erdogan's hard-line response to a wave of protests during the summer of 2013 served to reinforce the already growing doubts among some within both Turkey and the EU regarding the sincerity of his government's pledges on human rights (*The Economist* 2013b). That said, the accession process limped on, with both sides realizing the importance of continued engagement, and significant actors on both sides continuing to support the goal of membership.

Perhaps more than in any other case, Turkey's bid for membership brought into focus a number of fundamental normative and sociological questions about the limits and nature of the EU. Such questions as: Where do the EU's geographical borders lie? Are identity, culture, and religion relevant factors in the enlargement process and should they be? If they are relevant, what is the 'European' identity against which prospective members are to be judged? And, is this identity a fixed one to which others must adjust or does the EU (and *should* it) adapt itself to its new members? (Parker 2009b).

Enlargement Fatigue?

Following the 2004 enlargement, many scholars invoked the concept of 'enlargement fatigue' to encapsulate the notion that after June 2004, the EU's appetite for further enlargement was diminished. Certainly that seemed to be the case in the immediate aftermath of the CEEC enlargement, although progress was subsequently made in the Western Balkans. However, the economic crisis (see Chapter 11) may have further reduced the attractiveness of enlargement, both for the EU and for prospective members.

Following the CEEC enlargement, the borders of the enlarged EU abutted states that had formerly been part of the Soviet Union itself: Armenia, Azerbaijan, Georgia, Moldova, and Ukraine. However, there was little prospect that they would be accepted as applicants. In May 2004, Enlargement Commissioner Günter Verheugen appeared to rule it out when he said: 'Membership is not on the agenda for these countries. Full stop' (*Financial Times*, 13 May 2004). His statement applied also to North African states such as Morocco and Tunisia which had expressed an interest in eventual membership.

Unlike Turkey, these latter states were defined as beyond Europe, which allowed membership to be ruled out. Reluctance on the EU side at this time to engage in further large-scale enlargements can be related in particular to difficulties encountered in reforming EU institutions (and associated treaties) in preparation for the CEEC enlargement (see Chapter 10, Enlargement).

Relations between the EU and its neighbouring states are conducted in the context of the European Neighbourhood Policy (see Chapter 25). This policy seeks to promote EU norms and policy preferences in a similar way to enlargement policy. However, the potential rewards for those engaging in partnerships with the EU fall short of a clear membership prospect and this reduces EU leverage in those states.

The economic crisis in the EU which dominated the agenda after 2009 further diminished the EU's appetite for significant enlargement (see Chapter 11). The cost implications of future enlargement became a particular concern given the economic situation within certain member states. Concerns that further enlargement would undermine the prospects of pushing forward further and deeper integration (in response to the crisis) also re-emerged in some quarters. O'Brennan (2013) has argued that, while normative and ideational factors were key to driving recent enlargements, in the context of negotiations with Western Balkans states, member state self-interest has become more important and intergovernmental decision making more prominent.

The attractiveness of the EU for prospective members may have also been adversely affected. Public opinion in favour of enlargement diminished not only within the EU but also within a number of prospective members (Di Mauro and Fraile 2012). That said, EU membership remains an attractive long-term proposition for certain prospective states and some populations beyond the EU. For instance, in 2013 and 2014 there was widespread public anger and protest in the Ukraine in response to its government's last minute decision not to sign an Association Agreement with the EU (see also Chapter 26).

CONCLUSION

It was surely never envisaged by the founders of the European Coal and Steel Community (ECSC) and the EEC that these organizations of six states would expand over the next half century to a membership of twenty-eight, with more applicants waiting to join. Perhaps more than any other policy, enlargement demonstrates the stark difference between the EU and a nation state. This is a policy—often described as the EU's most successful policy—which has allowed the EC/EU to expand geographically but without the violence of national empire-building.

The effects of the enlargements have been significant. They have certainly had a major impact both on the EU and on the new members. Within the EU, enlargement has necessitated European institutional reforms and associated treaty change. It has also changed the EU socially and culturally, as has become evident for EU citizens as a consequence of freedom of movement. For new members, processes of Europeanization (see Chapter 3) have significantly altered their economies, politics, and institutions.

The reasons for this expansion have been much debated, both as to why the applications were made and why they were accepted, but they come down to some mix of economic and political considerations. Scholars have considered the motives on both sides in terms of some combination of rational interests and the role of ideas and norms. Rational interests consist of the various perceived economic and geopolitical advantages and disadvantages of enlargement. Ideas and norms refer to the importance of fundamental normative conceptions about the geographical, cultural, and political limits of the EU.

Considered as a whole, and in relation to all enlargement processes, scholarship has attributed importance to a variety of agents, including governments on different sides of the process, supranational actors (particularly the European Commission), and non-governmental entities. The relative importance given to these actors has varied across different enlargement processes, and the emphasis that different scholars have placed on them has also depended on the broader theoretical perspective that each has adopted.

A number of commentators have noted that, in the context of the post-2008 economic crisis (see Chapter 11), the incentives on all sides for further significant enlargement were substantially diminished.

KEY POINTS

History

- There have been seven rounds of enlargement.

- The first enlargement brought into the EC two states, Britain and Denmark, that were sceptical about European integration.

- The second and third enlargements are often treated together as a 'Southern enlargement'. It gave the EC a stronger Mediterranean orientation, and raised the profile of Latin America in external relations. Greece's membership caused some problems for relations with other states in the Balkans.

- As a result of the fourth enlargement, environmental protection became more important, the coalition in favour of budgetary reform was strengthened, and a Nordic bloc was formed.

- The fifth and sixth enlargements are often treated together as an 'Eastern enlargement'. It forced reform of the institutions and of key policies.

- The seventh enlargement saw Croatia become the first Western Balkan country to join.

- In 2014, accession negotiations were underway with Turkey, Montenegro, and Serbia. The FYRM had candidate status and Albania had applied.

The Enlargement Procedure

- A procedure was developed over the seven rounds of application.

- Once an application has been approved by the European Council, the Commission prepares an Opinion. Negotiations proceed in sectoral groups. Agreed terms have to be ratified by the Council of Foreign Ministers and the European Council.

- Existing member states try to sort out problems that might be caused by the new members before the enlargement is completed.

- The Southern enlargement set a precedent for member states to overrule an unfavourable Commission Opinion on political grounds.

- The Eastern enlargement led to the development of a set of criteria for membership that have come to structure negotiations with applicants.

Explaining Enlargement

- The first enlargement was driven by both economic and geostrategic considerations.

- The EFTA enlargement was a response to the success of the single market programme.

- The Eastern enlargement was a result of a wish to consolidate democracy and capitalism in the former communist states.

- The enlargement processes with the Western Balkans were rooted in a desire to guarantee stability in this previously troubled region.

- Turkey's fluctuating EU membership prospects have been driven by both domestic politics and factors within the EU. The case brings into focus a number of questions about the limits of the EU, both geographically and in terms of its identity.

Turkey

- Turkey signed an Association Agreement with the EU in 1963, but only began formal accession negotiations with the EU in 2005. These negotiations are ongoing despite stalling more than once in recent years.

- Perhaps more than in any other case, Turkey's accession process has prompted fundamental normative and sociological questions about the limits and nature of the EU and enlargement.

Enlargement Fatigue?

- After 2004, and certainly in the context of the eurozone crisis, the prospects of further significant enlargements were diminished due to 'enlargement fatigue'.

FURTHER READING

Comprehensive coverage of the first four enlargements is contained in **C. Preston**, *Enlargement and European Integration in the European Union* (London: Routledge, 1997). It contains sections on the accession process for each new member state and information on other applications. It considers the effects of enlargement on each member state, on the EU's policies and on the structure and processes of the EU. A complete narrative of how those enlargement negotiations developed, with copious quotations from official documentation, is provided in **G. Avery and F. Cameron**, *The Enlargement of the European Union* (Sheffield: Sheffield Academic Press, 1998).

For analyses using conditionality and Europeanization interpretations, see **F. Schimmelfennig and U. Sedelmeier (eds)**, *The Europeanization of Central and Eastern Europe* (Ithaca, NY: Cornell University Press, 2005), and **H. Grabbe**, *The EU's Transformative Power: Europeanization Through Conditionality in Central and Eastern Europe* (Basingstoke: Palgrave Macmillan, 2005).

For a full neo-Gramscian analysis, the conscientious student will look at **A. Bieler**, *Globalization and Enlargement of the European Union: Austrian and Swedish Social Forces in the Struggle over Membership* (London: Routledge, 2000), although others may find enough information in **A. Bieler's** later article, 'The Struggle over EU Enlargement: A Historical Materialist Analysis of European Integration', *Journal of European Public Policy*, 9 (2002): 575–97. This analysis can be usefully compared with that of **C. Ingebritsen**, *The Nordic States and European Unity* (Ithaca, NY: Cornell University Press, 1998).

For a discussion of the drivers behind Turkey's EU membership process, see, **A. Bürgin**, 'Cosmopolitan Entrapment: The Failed Strategies to Reverse Turkey's EU Membership Eligibility', *Perspectives: Review of International Affairs*, 18 (2010): 33–56. For a discussion of the political and normative dilemmas associated with this case, see **O. Parker**, '"Cosmopolitan Europe" and the EU–Turkey Question: The Politics of a "Common Destiny"', *Journal of European Public Policy*,

16 (2009b), 1085–101. And **T. Diez**, 'Expanding Europe: The Ethics of EU–Turkey Relations', *Ethics and International Affairs*, 21 (2007): 415–22.

 online resource centre

Visit the Online Resource Centre that accompanies this book for links to more information on the enlargement of the EU, including the website of the relevant Directorate-General of the Commission: http://oxfordtextbooks.co.uk/orc/bache4e/

References

Ackrill, R. and Kay, A. (2011). 'Multiple Streams in EU Policy-making: The Case of the 2005 Sugar Reform'. *Journal of European Public Policy*, 18: 72–89.

Adnett, N. (2001). 'Modernizing the European Social Model: Developing the Guidelines'. *Journal of Common Market Studies*, 39: 353–64.

Ahearn, R. (2002). 'US-European Union Trade Relations: Issues and Policy Challenges'. *CRS Issue Brief for Congress*. http://fpc.state.gov/documents/organization/9546.pdf.

Ahmad, F. (2001). 'Turkey', in J. Krieger (ed.), *The Oxford Companion to the Politics of the World* (2nd edn). New York: Oxford University Press, 850–1.

Allen, D. and Smith, M. (2004). 'External Policy Developments'. *Journal of Common Market Studies: The European Union*, 2003, *Annual Review of Activities*: 95–112.

Allen, D. and Smith, M. (2012). 'Relations with the Rest of the World', *Journal of Common Market Studies: Annual Review of Activities*: 162–77.

Alter, K. (1996). 'The European Court's Political Power'. *West European Politics*, 19: 458–87.

Alter, K. (1998). 'Who Are the "Masters of the Treaty"? European Governments and the European Court of Justice'. *International Organization*, 52: 121–47.

Alter, K. (2001). *Establishing the Supremacy of European Law: The Making of an International Rule of Law in Europe*. Oxford: Oxford University Press.

Amoore, L. (2008). 'Foucault against the Grain'. *International Political Sociology*, 2: 274–76.

Anderson, J. (2002). 'Globalization and Europeanization: A Conceptual and Theoretical Overview'. Paper prepared for the conference on 'Germany and Europe: A Europeanized Germany?', ESRC Future Governance Programme, The British Academy, London, 9-10 May.

Anderson, J. (2003). 'Europeanization in Context: Concept and Theory', in K. Dyson and K. Goetz (eds), *Germany, Europe and the Politics of Constraint*. Oxford: Oxford University Press, 37–54.

Andreou, G. (2007). 'The New EU Cohesion Policy: Enlargement, "Lisbonisation" and the Challenge of Diversity'. *EU CONSENT Annual State of the Art Report, Second Year*. Athens: Hellenic Foundation for European and Foreign Policy (ELIAMEP).

Armstrong, K. and Bulmer, S. (1998). *The Governance of the Single European Market*. Manchester: Manchester University Press.

Avery, G. and Cameron, F. (1998). *The Enlargement of the European Union*. Sheffield: Sheffield Academic Press/University Association for Contemporary European Studies.

Bache, I. (1998). *The Politics of European Union Regional Policy: Multi-Level Governance or Flexible Gatekeeping?*. Sheffield: Sheffield Academic Press/University Association for Contemporary European Studies.

Bache, I. (1999). 'The Extended Gatekeeper: Central Government and the Implementation of EC Regional Policy in the UK'. *Journal of European Public Policy*, 6: 28–45.

Bache, I. (2006). 'The Europeanization of Higher Education: Markets, Learning or Politics?'. *Journal of Common Market Studies*, 44: 231–48.

Bache, I. (2008). *Europeanization and Multi-level Governance: Cohesion Policy in the European Union and Britain*. Lanham: Rowman and Littlefield.

Bache, I. (2010). 'Europeanization and Multi-level Governance'. *Journal of Southeast European and Black Sea Studies*, 10: 1–12.

Bache, I. (2013). 'Measuring Quality of Life for Public Policy: An Idea Whose Time Has Come? Agenda-Setting Dynamics in the European Union'. *Journal of European Public Policy*, 20: 21–38.

Bache, I. (2014). 'Cohesion Policy: A New Direction for New Times?', in H. Wallace, M. Pollack, and A. Young (eds), *Policy-Making in the European Union* (7th edn). Oxford: Oxford University Press.

Bache, I., Bulmer, S., and Gunay, D. (2012). 'Europeanization: A Critical Realist Perspective', in C. RadaelliC and T. Exadaktylos (eds), *Research Design in European Studies*. Basingstoke: Palgrave Macmillan, 64–84.

Bache, I. and Chapman, R. (2008). 'Democracy through Multi-level Governance? The Implementation of the Structural Funds in South Yorkshire'. *Governance*, 21: 397–418.

Bache, I. and Flinders, M. (2004). 'Conclusions and Implications', in I. Bache and M. Flinders (eds), *Multi-Level Governance*. Oxford: Oxford University Press, 195–206.

Bache, I. and George, S. (2006). *Politics in the European Union* (2nd edn). Oxford: Oxford University Press.

Bache, I. and Jordan, A. (2006*a*). 'Europeanization and Domestic Change', in I. Bache and A. Jordan (eds), *The Europeanization of British Politics*. Basingstoke: Palgrave Macmillan, 17–36.

Bache, I. and Jordan, A. (eds) (2006*b*). *The Europeanization of British Politics*. Basingstoke: Palgrave Macmillan.

Bache, I. and Marshall, A. (2004). 'Europeanisation and Domestic Change: A Governance Approach to Institutional Adaptation in Britain'. *Europeanisation Online Papers* No. 5/2004, Queen's University Belfast. http://qub.ac.uk/schools/SchoolofPoliticsInternationalStudiesand Philosophy/Research/PaperSeries/EuropeanisationPapers/.

Bachtler, J. and McMaster, I. (2008). 'EU Cohesion Policy and the Role of the Regions: Investigating the Influence of Structural Funds in the New Member States'. *Environment and Planning C: Government and Policy*, 26: 398–427.

Bachtler, J. and Mendez, C. (2007) 'Who Governs EU Cohesion Policy? Deconstructing the Reforms of the Structural Funds'. *Journal of Common Market Studies*, 24: 535–64.

Bachtler, J. and Michie, R. (1994). 'Strengthening Economic and Social Cohesion? The Revision of the Structural Funds'. *Regional Studies*, 28: 789–96.

Bailey, D. and De Propris, L. (2002). 'EU Structural Funds, Regional Capabilities and Enlargement: Towards Multi-Level Governance?'. *Journal of European Integration*, 24: 303–24.

Barker, A. and Fleming, S. (2014). 'EU Bank Overhaul Pleases Few in Search For Middle Way'. *Financial Times*, 29 January.

Baker, E. (2009). 'The European Union's "Area of Freedom, Security, and (Criminal) Justice" Ten Years On'. *The Criminal Law Review*, 12: 833–50.

Barber, L. (1995). 'The Men Who Run Europe'. *Financial Times: Weekend FT*, 11/12 March: I-II.

Barca, F. (2009). 'An Agenda for a Reformed Cohesion Policy: A Place-based Approach to Meeting European Union Challenges and Expectations'. *Independent Report Prepared at the Request of Danuta Hübner, Commissioner for Regional Policy*. Brussels: Commission, DG Regional Policy.

Barroso, J. (2009). 'State of the Union: Delivering a "Europe of Results" in a Harsh Economic Climate'. *Journal of Common Market Studies, Annual Review*, 57: 7–16.

Baumgartner, F. and Jones, B. (1993). *Agendas and Instability in American Politics*. Chicago: University of Chicago Press.

Baun, M. J. (1996). 'The Maastricht Treaty as High Politics: Germany, France, and European Integration'. *Political Science Quarterly*, 110: 605–24.

BBC Online (2013). 'EU Leaders Agree 3% Budget Cut Deal in Brussels', 8 February. (http://bbc.co.uk/news/world-europe-21386818).

Beach, D. (2005). *The Dynamics of European Integration: Why and When Institutions Matter*. Basingstoke: Palgrave Macmillan.

Beck, U. and Grande, E. (2007). *Cosmopolitan Europe*. Cambridge: Polity Press.

Beetham, D. and Lord, C. (1998). *Legitimacy and the European Union*. London and New York: Longman.

Begg, I. (2010). 'Cohesion or Confusion: a Policy Searching for Objectives'. *Journal of European Integration*, 32: 77–96.

Benson, D. and Jordan, A. (2008). 'A Grand Barg in or an "Incomplete Contract"? European Union Environmental Policy after the Lisbon Treaty'. *European Energy and Environmental Law Review*, 17: 280–90.

Berghahn, V. and Young, B. (2013). 'Reflections on Werner Bonefeld's "Freedom and the Strong State: On German Ordo-liberalism"'. *New Political Economy*, 18: 768–78.

Beyers, J. (2004). 'Voice and Access: Political Practices of European Interest Associations'. *European Union Politics*, 5: 211–40.

Beyers, J. and Dierickx, G. (1998). 'The Working Groups of the Council of the European Union: Supranational or Intergovernmental Negotiations?'. *Journal of Common Market Studies*, 36: 289–317.

Bickerton, C. J., Hodson, D., and Puetter, U. (forthcoming). 'Explaining European Integration in the Post Maastricht Period', in C. J. Bickerton, D. Hodson, and U. Puetter (eds), *European Politics in the Post Maastricht Period: States, Supranational Actors and the New Intergovernmentalism*. Oxford: Oxford University Press.

Bieler, A. (2000). *Globalization and Enlargement of the European Union: Austrian and Swedish Social Forces in the Struggle over Membership*. London: Routledge.

Bieler, A. (2002). 'The Struggle over EU Enlargement: A Historical Materialist Analysis of

European Integration'. *Journal of European Public Policy*, 9: 575–97.

Bieler, A. (2011). 'Labour, New Social Movements and the Resistance to Neo-Liberal Restructuring in Europe'. *New Political Economy*, 16: 163–83.

Bieler, A., Bonefeld, W., Burnham, P., and Morton, D. A. (2006). *Global Restructuring, State, Capital, and Labour: Contesting Neo-Gramscian Perspectives*. Basingstoke and New York: Palgrave Macmillan.

Bigo, D. (2000). 'When Two Become One: Internal and External Securitisations in Europe', in M. Kelstrup and M. C. Williams (eds), *International Relations Theory and the Politics of European Integration: Power, Security, and Community*. London: Routledge, 171–204.

Birch, A. (2001). *Concepts and Theories of Modern Democracy* (2nd edn). London and New York: Routledge.

Blair, A. (2002). 'Adapting to Europe'. *Journal of European Public Policy*, 9: 841–56.

Blyth, M. (2013). *Austerity: The History of a Dangerous Idea*. Oxford: Oxford University Press.

Bomberg, E. and Peterson, J. (2000). 'Policy Transfer and Europeanization'. *Europeanisation Online Papers*, No. 2/2000. Queen's University, Belfast. (http://qub.ac.uk/schools/Schoolof PoliticsInternationalStudiesandPhilosophy/ Research/PaperSeries/EuropeanisationPapers/).

Bonefeld, W. (2012). 'Freedom and the Strong State: On German Ordo-liberalism'. *New Political Economy*, 17: 633–56.

Borras, S. and Jacobsson, K. (2004). 'The Open Method of Co-ordination and New Governance Patterns in the EU'. *Journal of European Public Policy*, 11: 185–208.

Börzel, T. (1998). 'Organizing Babylon: On the Different Conceptions of Policy Networks'. *Public Administration*, 76: 253–73.

Börzel, T. (2000). 'Why There is no "Southern Problem". On Environmental Leaders and Laggards in the European Union'. *Journal of European Public Policy*, 7: 141–62.

Börzel, T. (2002). 'Pace-Setting, Foot-Dragging, and Fence-Sitting: Member State Responses to Europeanization'. *Journal of Common Market Studies*, 40: 193–214.

Börzel, T. and Risse, T. (2003). 'Conceptualising the Domestic Impact of Europe', in K. Featherstone and C. Radaelli (eds), *The Politics of Europeanization*. Oxford: Oxford University Press, 57–82.

Börzel, T. and Risse, T. (2007). 'The Domestic Impact of European Union Politics', in K. E. Jørgensen, M. Pollack, and B. Rosamond (eds), *Handbook of European Union Politics*. London: SAGE Publications, 483–504.

Boswell, C. (2007). 'Migration Control in Europe after 9/11: Explaining the Absence of Securitization'. *Journal of Common Market Studies*, 45: 589–610.

Boswell, C. (2010). 'Justice and Home Affairs', in M. Egan, N. Nugent, and W. Paterson (eds), *Research Agendas in EU Studies: Stalking the Elephant*. Basingstoke: Palgrave Macmillan, 278–304.

Boswell, C. and Geddes, A. (2011). *Migration and Mobility in the European Union*. Basingstoke: Palgrave Macmillan.

Bouwen, P. (2002). 'Corporate Lobbying in the European Union: The Logic of Access'. *Journal of European Public Policy*, 9: 365–90.

Bouwen, P. (2004a). 'Exchanging Access Goods for Access: A Comparative Study of Business Lobbying in the European Union Institutions'. *European Journal of Political Research*, 43: 337–69.

Bouwen, P. (2004b). 'The Logic of Access to the European Parliament: Business Lobbying in the Committee on Economic and Monetary Affairs'. *Journal of Common Market Studies*, 42: 473–95.

Bowler, S. and Farrell, D. (1995). 'The Organizing of the European Parliament: Committees, Specialization, and Co-ordination'. *British Journal of Political Science*, 25: 219–43.

Branch, A. P. and Øhrgaard, J. C. (1999). 'Trapped in the Supranational-Intergovernmental Dichotomy: A Response to Stone Sweet and Sandholtz'. *Journal of European Public Policy*, 6: 123–43.

Bromley, S. (2001). *Governing the European Union*. London: SAGE Publications, 287–303.

Bruszt, L. (2008). 'Multi-level Governance—The Eastern Versions: Emerging Patterns of Developmental Governance in the New Member States'. *Regional and Federal Studies*, 18: 5, 607–27.

Bull, H. (1982). 'Civilian Power Europe: A Contradiction in Terms?'. *Journal of Common Market Studies*, 21: 149–64.

Buller, J. (1995), 'Britain as an Awkward Partner: Reassessing Britain's Relations with the EU'. *Politics*, 15: 33–42.

Buller, J. and Gamble, A. (2002), '*Conceptualising Europeanization*'. *Public Policy and Administration*, 17: 4–24.

Bulmer, S. (1983). 'Domestic Politics and European Policy-Making'. *Journal of Common Market Studies*, 21: 349–63.

Bulmer, S. (1993). 'The Governance of the European Union: A New Institutionalist Approach'. *Journal of Public Policy*, 13: 351–80.

Bulmer, S. (1998). 'New Institutionalism and the Governance of the Single European Market'. *Journal of European Public Policy*, 5: 365–86.

Bulmer, S. (2007). 'Theorizing Europeanization', in P. Graziano and M. Vink (eds), *Europeanization: New Research Agendas*. Basingstoke: Palgrave Macmillan, 46–58.

Bulmer, S. (2009). 'Institutional and Policy Analysis in the European Union: From the Treaty of Rome to the Present', in D. Phinnemore and A. Warleigh-Lack (eds), *Reflections on European Integration: 50 Years of the Treaty of Rome*. Basingstoke: Palgrave Macmillan, 109–24.

Bulmer, S. (2010). 'Germany: From Launching the EU Constitutional Debate to Salvaging a Treaty', in M. Carbone (ed.), *National Politics and European Integration: From the Constitution to the Lisbon Treaty*. Cheltenham, UK and Northampton, MA: Edward Elgar, 51–70.

Bulmer, S. (2011). 'Shop Till you Drop? The German Executive as Venue-shopper in Justice and Home Affairs?', in P. Bendel, A. Ette, and R. Parkes (eds), *The Europeanization of Control: Venues and Outcomes of EU Justice and Home Affairs Cooperation*. Berlin: Lit Verlag, 41–76.

Bulmer, S. and Burch, M. (1998). 'Organising for Europe: Whitehall, the British State, and the European Union'. *Public Administration*, 76(4): 601–28.

Bulmer, S. and Burch, M. (2009). *The Europeanisation of Whitehall: UK Central Government and the European Union*. Manchester: Manchester University Press.

Bulmer, S. and Lequesne, C. (2013). *The Member States of the European Union* (2nd edn). Oxford: Oxford University Press.

Bulmer, S. and Paterson, W. (2010). 'Germany and the European Union: from "Tamed Power" to Normalized Power?'. *International Affairs*, 86: 1051–73.

Bulmer, S. and Paterson, W. (2013). 'Germany as the EU's Reluctant Hegemon? Of Economic Strength and Political Constraints'. *Journal of European Public Policy*, 20: 1387–405.

Bulmer, S. and Radaelli, C. (2013). 'The Europeanization of Member State Policy', in S. Bulmer and C. Lequesne (eds), *The Member States of the European Union* (2nd edn). Oxford: Oxford University Press, 357–83.

Bulmer, S. and Wessels, W. (1987). *The European Council: Decision-Making in European Politics*. Basingstoke: Macmillan.

Bulmer, S., Dolowitz, D., Humphreys, P., and Padgett, S. (2007). *Policy Transfer in European Union Governance: Regulating the Utilities*. Abingdon: Routledge.

Burch, M. and Gomez, R. (2003). 'Europeanization and the English Regions'. Paper presented to the ESRC Seminar Series/UACES Study Group on the Europeanization of British Politics and Policy-Making, Sheffield, 2 May.

Burchell, J. and Lightfoot, S. (2001). *The Greening of the European Union? Examining the EU's Environmental Credentials*. London and New York: Sheffield Academic Press.

Bürgin, A. (2010). 'Cosmopolitan Entrapment: The Failed Strategies to Reverse Turkey's EU Membership Eligibility'. *Perspectives: Review of International Affairs*, 18(2): 33–56.

Burley, A-M. and Mattli, W. (1993). 'Europe Before the Court: A Political Theory of Legal Integration'. *International Organization*, 47: 41–76.

Burns, C. (2004). 'Co-decision and the European Commission: a study of declining influence?'. *Journal of European Public Policy*, 11: 1–18.

Butler, F. (1993). 'The EC's Common Agricultural Policy', in J. Lodge (ed.), *The European Community and the Challenge of the Future* (2nd edn). London: Pinter, 112–30.

Cafruny, A. W. and Ryner, J. M. (2007). *Europe at Bay: In the Shadow of US Hegemony*. London: Lynne Rienner.

Cafruny, A. W. and Ryner, J. M. (2009). 'Critical Political Economy', in A. Wiener and T. Diez, *European Integration Theory* (2nd edn). Oxford: Oxford University Press, 221–40.

Calingaert, M. (1999). 'Creating a European Market', in L. Cram, D. Dinan, and N. Nugent (eds), *Developments in the European Union*. Basingstoke and London: Macmillan, 153–73.

Cameron, D. R. (1992). 'The 1992 Initiative: Causes and Consequences', in A. Sbragia (ed.), *Euro-Politics: Institutions and Policymaking in the 'New' European Community*. Washington, DC: Brookings Institution, 23–74.

Cameron, D. R. (1997). 'Economic and Monetary Union: Underlying Imperatives and Third-Stage Dilemmas'. *Journal of European Public Policy*, 4: 455–85.

Camps, M. (1964). *Britain and the European Community 1955-1963*. London: Oxford University Press.

Camps, M. (1967). *European Unification in the Sixties: From the Veto to the Crisis*. London: Oxford University Press.

Caporaso, J. (1999). 'Toward a Normal Science of Regional Integration'. *Journal of European Public Policy*, 6: 160–4.

Caporaso, J. and Keeler, J. T. S. (1995). 'The European Union and Regional Integration Theory', in C. Rhodes and S. Mazey (eds), *The State of the European Union Vol. 3, Building a European Polity?*. Boulder, CO, and Harlow, Essex: Lynne Rienner and Longman, 29–62.

Carbone, M. (2010). 'Conclusion: Preference Formation, Inter-state Bargaining and the Treaty of Lisbon', in M. Carbone (ed.), *National Politics and European Integration: From the Constitution to the Lisbon Treaty*. Cheltenham, UK; Northampton, MA: Edward Elgar, 215–32.

Cardwell, P. J. (2013). 'New Modes of Governance in the External Dimension of EU Migration Policy'. *International Migration*, 51/6: 54–66.

Cardwell, P. J. and Hervey, T. (forthcoming). 'The Roles of Law in a New Intergovernmentalist EU', in C. Bickerton, D. Hodson, and U. Puetter (eds), *European Politics in the Post Maastricht Period: States, Supranational Actors and the New Intergovernmentalism*. Oxford: Oxford University Press.

Carmin, J. and VanDeveer, S. D. (2004). 'Enlarging EU Environments: Central and Eastern Europe from Transition to Accession'. *Environmental Politics*, 13: 3–24.

Carrubba, C. J. (2003). 'The European Court of Justice, Democracy, and Enlargement'. *European Union Politics*, 4: 75–100.

Cecchini, P. (1988). *The European Challenge 1992: The Benefits of a Single Market*. Aldershot: Gower.

Chakrabortty, A. (2011). 'Q&A: Greece's debt crisis'. *The Guardian*, 31 July. http://theguardian.com/world/2011/jul/31/greece-debt-crisis-how-bad.

Chalmers, D., Davies, G., and Monti, G. (2010). *European Union Law* (2nd edn). Cambridge: Cambridge University Press.

Christiansen, T. (2010). 'The EU Reform Process: From the European Constitution to the Lisbon Treaty', in M. Carbone (ed.), *National Politics and European Integration: From the Constitution to the Lisbon Treaty*. Cheltenham, UK; Northampton, MA: Edward Elgar, 16–33.

Chryssochoou, D. (2007). 'Democracy and the European Polity', in M. Cini (ed.), *European Union Politics* (2nd edn). Oxford: Oxford University Press, 359–74.

Church, C. and Phinnemore, D. (2010). 'From the Constitutional Treaty to the Treaty of Lisbon', in M. Cini and N. Perez-Solórzano Borragán (eds), *European Union Politics* (3rd edn). Oxford: Oxford University Press, 48–68.

Cini, M. and McGowan, L. (1998). *Competition Policy in the European Union*. Basingstoke and London: Macmillan.

Closa, C. (2012). 'Intergovernmentalism as a Previous Step to "Community Method"', in Fundación Alternativas and Friedrich-Ebert-Stiftung, *The State of the European Union: The Failure of Austerity*. http://library.fes.de/pdf-files/bueros/madrid/09840.pdf.

Cocks, P. (1980). 'Towards a Marxist Theory of European Integration'. *International Organization*, 31: 1–40.

Cohen, B. J. (2012). 'The Future of the Euro: Let's Get Real', *Review of International Political Economy*, 19: 689–700.

Coleman, W. D. (1998). 'From Protected Development to Market Liberalism: Paradigm Change in Agriculture'. *Journal of European Public Policy*, 5: 632–51.

Collinson, S. (1999). '"Issue Systems", "Multi-level Games" and the Analysis of the EU's External Commercial and Associated Policies: A Research Agenda'. *Journal of European Public Policy*, 6: 206–24.

Colman, D. (2007). 'The Common Agricultural Policy', in M. Artis and F. Nixson (eds), *The Economics of the European Union: Policy and Analysis* (4th edn). Oxford: Oxford University Press, 77–104.

Committee of the Regions (2009). *The Committee of the Regions White Paper on Multi-Level Governance*. CdR 89/2009 in FR/EXT/RS/GW/ym/ms. Brussels: Committee of the Regions.

Committee of the Regions (2011). 'Opinion of the Committee of the Regions on "Measuring progress-GDP and beyond"'. *Official Journal* C0015, 18/01/2011P. 0017–0022. http://eur-lex.europa.eu/LexUriServ/LexUriServ.do?uri=OJ:C:2011:015:0017:0022:EN:PDF.

Coombes, D. (1970). *Politics and Bureaucracy in the European Community*. London: Allen &Unwin.

Cooper, I. (2013). 'A Yellow Card for the Striker: How National Parliaments Defeated EU Strikes Regulation'. Paper prepared for the European Union Studies Association conference, Baltimore, 9–11 May.

Copsey, N. and Haughton, T. (2009). 'The Gathering Storm: A Drama in Two Acts'. *Journal of Common Market Studies, Annual Review*, 57: 1–5.

Corbett, A. (2005). *Universities and the Europe of Knowledge: Ideas, Institutions, and Policy Entrepreneurship in European Union Higher Education Policy*. Basingstoke: Palgrave Macmillan.

Corbett, R., Jacobs, F., and Shackleton, M. (2003). 'The European Parliament at Fifty: A View from the Inside'. *Journal of Common Market Studies*, 41: 353–73.

Corporate Europe Observatory (2011). *Lobby Planet Brussels: The EU Quarter*. http://corporateeurope.org/sites/default/files/publications/ceolobbylow.pdf (accessed February 2014).

Corporate Europe Observatory (2013). 'Regulation: None of our Business?'. http://corporateeurope.org/trade/2013/12/regulation-none-our-business (accessed 16 March 2014).

541

Council of the EU (2005). *A Strategy for the External Dimension of JHA: Global Freedom, Security, and Justice*. 14366/3/05 REV 3 Brussels: General Secretariat of the Council, 30 November.

Council of the EU (2009a). *List of Council Preparatory Bodies*. Document 11602/09. Brussels: General Secretariat of the Council, 30 June.

Council of the EU (2012). *Programme of Council Activities Prepared by the Lithuanian, Greek, and Irish Presidencies*. 17426/12. Brussels: Council of the EU, 7 December.

Cowles, M. G. (1995). 'Setting the Agenda for a New Europe: The ERT and EC 1992'. *Journal of Common Market Studies*, 33: 501–26.

Cowles, M. G. (2003). 'Non-state Actors and False Dichotomies: Reviewing IR/IPE Approaches to European Integration'. *Journal of European Public Policy*, 10: 102–20.

Cowles, M. G., Caporaso, J., and Risse, T.C (eds) (2001), *Transforming Europe: Europeanization and Domestic Change*. Ithaca, NY, and London: Cornell University Press.

Cox, R. (1981). 'Social Forces, States, and World Orders: Beyond International Relations Theory'. *Millennium: Journal of International Studies*, 10: 126–55.

Cram, L. (1997). *Policy Making in the EU: Conceptual Lenses and the Integration Process*. London and New York: Routledge.

Cram, L. (2001). 'Whither the Commission? Reform, Renewal and the Issue-attention Cycle'. *Journal of European Public Policy*, 8: 770–86.

Crombez, C. (1996). 'Legislative Procedures in the European Community'. *British Journal of Political Science*, 26: 199–228.

Crombez, C. (1997). 'The Co-decision Procedure in the European Union'. *Legislative Studies Quarterly*, 22: 97–119.

Crombez, C. (2000). 'Understanding the EU Legislative Process-Co-decision: Towards a Bicameral European Union'. *European Union Politics*, 1: 363–8.

Damro, C. (2007). 'EU Delegation and Agency in International Trade Negotiations: A Cautionary Comparison'. *Journal of Common Market Studies*, 45: 883–903.

Dang-Nguyen, G., Schneider, V., and Werle, R. (1993). 'Networks in European Policy-Making: Europeification of Telecommunications Policy', in S. S. Andersen and K. A. Eliassen (eds), *Making Policy in Europe: Europeification of National Policy-Making*. London: SAGE Publications, 93–114.

Daugbjerg, C. (2009). 'Sequencing in Public Policy: The Evolution of the CAP over a Decade'. *Journal of European Public Policy*, 16: 395–411.

Daugbjerg, C. and Swinbank, A. (2008). 'Curbing Agricultural Exceptionalism: The EU's Response to External Challenge'. *World Economy*, 31: 631–52.

DeBardeleben, J.C and Hurrelmann, A.C (eds) (2007). *Democratic Dilemmas of Multilevel Governance: Legitimacy, Representation and Accountability in the European Union*. Basingstoke: Palgrave Macmillan.

De Búrca, G. (1998). 'The Principle of Subsidiarity and the Court of Justice as a Political Actor'. *Journal of Common Market Studies*, 36: 217–315.

Dedman, M. (2010). *The Origins and Development of the European Union 1945-2008* (2nd edn). London: Routledge.

De Goede, M. (2008). 'The Politics of Pre-emption and the War on Terror in Europe'. *European Journal of International Relations*, 14: 161–85.

De Gucht, K. (2003). 'The European Commission: Countdown to Extinction?'. *European Integration*, 25: 165–8.

Delanty, G. and Rumford, C. (2005). *Rethinking Europe: Social Theory and the Implications of Europeanization*. Abingdon and New York: Routledge.

Dell, E. (1995). *The Schuman Plan and the British Abdication of Leadership in Europe*. Oxford: Clarendon Press.

Delreux, T. and van den Brande, K. (2013). 'Taking the Lead: Informal Division of Labour in the EU's External Environmental Policy-Making'. *Journal of European Public Policy*, 20: 113–31.

den Boer, M. and Wallace, W. (2000). 'Justice and Home Affairs: Integration through Incrementalism?', in H. Wallace and W. Wallace (eds), *Policy-Making in the European Union* (4th edn). Oxford: Oxford University Press, 493–519.

de Schoutheete, P. (2012). 'The European Council', in J. Peterson and M. Shackleton (eds), *The Institutions of the European Union* (3rd edn). Oxford: Oxford University Press.

Deutsch, K. (1953). *Nationalism and Social Communication: An Inquiry into the Foundations of Nationality*. Cambridge, MA: MIT Press.

Deutsch, K., Burrell, S. A., Kann, R. A., Lee, M. Jr, Lichterman, M., Lindgren, R. E., Loewenheim, F. L., and van Wagenen, R. W. (1957). *Political Community and the North Atlantic Area: International Organization in the Light of Historical Experience*. Princeton: Princeton University Press.

Devuyst, Y. (1999). 'The Community-Method After Amsterdam'. *Journal of Common Market Studies*, 37: 109–20.

Diebold, W., Jr (1959). *The Schuman Plan: A Study in Economic Cooperation, 1950-1959*. New York: Praeger.

Diez, T. (1999). 'Speaking "Europe": The Politics of Integration Discourse'. *Journal of European Public Policy*, 6: 598–613.

Diez, T. (2005). 'Constructing the Self and Changing Others: Reconsidering "Normative Power Europe"'. *Millennium: Journal of International Studies*, 33: 613–36.

Diez, T. (2007). 'Expanding Europe: The Ethics of EU-Turkey Relations'. *Ethics and International Affairs*, 21: 415–22.

Diez, T. and Wiener, A. (2004). 'Introducing the Mosaic of Integration Theory', in A. Wiener and T. Diez (eds), *European Integration Theory*. Oxford: Oxford University Press, 1–21.

Di Mauro, D. and Fraile, M. (2012). 'Who Wants More? Attitudes Towards EU Enlargement in Time of Crisis'. *European Union Democracy Observatory (EUDO)*, Spotlight 04, October. http://eui.eu/Projects/EUDO/Documents/2012/Spotlight4.pdf.

Dimitrakopoulos, D. (2004). *The Changing European Commission*. Manchester: Manchester University Press.

Dinan, D. (1994). *Ever Closer Union? An Introduction to the European Community*. London: Macmillan.

Dobson, A. (2007). *Green Political Thought* (4th edn). London and New York: Routledge.

Dougan, M. (2008). 'The Treaty of Lisbon 2007: Winning Minds not Hearts'. *Common Market Law Review*, 45: 617–701.

Duchêne, F. (1973). 'The European Community and the Uncertainties of Interdependence', in M. Kohnstamm and W. Hager (eds), *A Nation Writ Large? Foreign-Policy Problems before the European Community*. London: Macmillan, 1–21.

Duchêne, F. (1994). *Jean Monnet: The First Statesman of Interdependence*. New York and London: W.W. Norton & Company.

Duff, A. (2009). *Saving the European Union. The Logic of the Lisbon Treaty*. London: Shoehorn Media.

Dullien, S. (2012). 'Why the Euro Crisis Threatens the Single Market'. *European Council of Foreign Affairs*, Policy Memo 64, October.

Dyson, K. (1994). *Elusive Union: The Process of Economic and Monetary Union in Europe*. Harlow: Longman.

Dyson, K. and Featherstone, K. (1999). *The Road to Maastricht: Negotiating Economic and Monetary Union*. Oxford: Oxford University Press.

Dyson, K. and Goetz, K. (2002). 'Germany and Europe: Beyond Congruence'. Paper given to the British Academy Conference, Germany and Europe: A Europeanised Germany? London, 11 March.

Dyson, K. and Goetz, K. (2003). 'Germany and Europe: Beyond Congruence'. Paper given to the British Academy Conference, 'Germany and Europe: A Europeanised Germany?'. London, 11 March.

Eckersley, R. (1993). 'Free market Environmentalism: Friend or Foe?'. *Environmental Politics*, 2: 1–19.

Edquist, K. (2006). 'EU Social Policy Governance: Advocating Activism or Servicing States?'. *Journal of European Public Policy*, 13: 500–18.

Edwards, G. and Pijpers, A. (1997). *The Politics of European Treaty Reform: The 1996 Intergovernmental Conference and Beyond*. London and Washington: Pinter.

Egeberg, M. (2006), *Multilevel Union Administration: The Transformation of Executive Politics in Europe*. Basingstoke: Palgrave Macmillan.

Ehin, P. (2008). 'Competing Models of EU Legitimacy: the Test of Popular Expectations'. *Journal of Common Market Studies*, 46: 619–40.

Eising, R. and Lehringer, S. (2010). '*Interest Groups and the European Union*', in M. Cini and N. Pérez-Solórzano-Borragán (eds), *European Union Politics* (3rd edn). Oxford: Oxford University Press, 189–206.

Ellerman, D. A. and Buchner, B. K. (2007). 'The European Union Emissions Trading Scheme: Origins, Allocation, and Early Results'. *Review of Environmental Economics and Policy*, 1: 66–87.

Ellina, C. (2003). *Promoting Women's Rights: The Politics of Gender in the European Union*. New York: Routledge.

Eriksen, E. and Fossum, J. (2002). 'Democracy Through Strong Publics in the European Union'. *Journal of Common Market Studies*, 40: 401–24.

Eurobarometer (2012). *Eurobarometer Spring 2012: Public Opinion in the European Union*. EB77. Luxemburg: Eurostat.

European Commission (1975). 'Preamble' to 'Regulation (EEC) No. 724/75 of 18 March 1975 establishing a European Regional Development Fund'. *Official Journal*, L73, 21/3/75. Brussels: European Commission.

European Commission (1985). *Completing the Internal Market*. COM(85)310. Brussels: European Community.

European Commission (1987). *Development of the Common Market for Telecommunications, Services, and Equipment*. Brussels: European Community.

European Commission (1989). *Guide to the Reform of the Community's Structural Funds*. Brussels/Luxembourg: European Communities.

European Commission (1992). *Towards Sustainability: A European Community Programme of Policy and Action in Relation to the Environment and Sustainable Development*. COMD (1992) 23 final.

Brussels: Commission of the European Communities.

European Commission (1993). *Community Structural Funds 1994–99, Revised Regulations and Comments*. Brussels/Luxembourg: European Communities.

European Commission (1995). *The Agricultural Situation in the European Union*. Brussels and Luxembourg: European Communities.

European Commission (1996a). *First Report on Economic and Social Cohesion*. Brussels and Luxembourg: European Commission.

European Commission (1996b). *Green Paper on Relations between the European Union and the ACP Countries on the Eve of the 21st Century—Challenges and Options for a new Partnership*. Brussels: European Commission.

European Commission (1998a). 'Proposed Regulations Governing the Reform of the Structural Funds 2000-2006 (Preliminary Version)'. 18 March. *Inforegio*.

European Commission (1999). *Agenda 2000: For a Stronger and Wider Europe*. Brussels/Luxembourg: European Communities.

European Commission (2000). 'Partnership Agreement between the African, Caribbean, and Pacific Group of States of the One Part, and the European Community and its Member States, of the Other Part, signed in Cotonou, Benin, on 23 June 2000'. http://ec.europa.eu/world/agreements/downloadFile.do?fullText=yes&treatyTransId=818.

European Commission (2001a). *European Governance: A White Paper*. COM(2001)428 final, 25 July. Brussels: Commission of the European Communities.

European Commission (2001b). *Environment 2010: Our Future, Our Choice. Sixth Community Environment Action Programme*. COM(2001)31 final. Brussels: Commission of the European Communities.

European Commission (2004a). *First Report on the Implementation of the Internal Market Strategy 2003–2006*. COM(2004)22 final. Brussels: Commission of the European Communities.

European Commission (2004b). 'A New Partnership for Cohesion: Convergence, Competitiveness, Cooperation'. *Third Report on Economic and Social Cohesion*. Luxembourg: European Communities.

European Commission (2004c). *Commission Working Document. Integrating Environmental Considerations into Other Policy Areas: A Stocktaking of the Cardiff Process*. COM(2004)394 final. Brussels: Commission of the European Communities.

European Commission (2005a). *Second Implementation Report of the Internal Market Strategy 2003–2006*. COM(2005)11 final. Brussels: Commission of the European Communities.

European Commission (2005b). *Communication from the Commission to the Council and the European Parliament. The 2005 Review of the EU Sustainable Development Strategy: Initial Stocktaking and Future Orientations*. COM(2005)37 final. Brussels: Commission of the European Communities.

European Commission (2005c). *Communication from the Commission to the Council and the European Parliament. On the Review of the Sustainable Development Strategy: A Platform for Action*. COM(2005)658 final. Brussels: Commission of the European Communities.

European Commission (2006a). *A European Strategy for Sustainable, Competitive, and Secure Energy*. Brussels: European Union.

European Commission (2006b). *Global Europe: Competing in the World*. Brussels: European Commission.

European Commission (2007a). *Cohesion Policy 2007–13: Commentaries and Official Texts*. Luxembourg: Office for Official Publications of the European Communities.

European Commission (2007b). *Communication from the Commission to the European Parliament, the Council, the European Economic and Social Committee, and the Committee of the Regions on the Mid-term Review of the Sixth Community Environment Action Programme*. COM(2007)225 final. Brussels: Commission of the European Communities.

European Commission (2007c). *Financial Instruments and EU Enlargement Projects*. Brussels: DG Enlargement. (http://ec.europa.eu/enlargement/financialassistance/indexen.htm).

European Commission (2010). *Europe 2020: A Strategy for Smart, Sustainable, and Inclusive Growth*. Communication from the Commission 2020 final. Brussels: European Commission.

European Commission (2012). *Proposal for a Decision of the European Parliament and of the Council on a General Union Environment Action Programme to 2020: Living well, within the limits of our planet'*. 710 final. Brussels: European Commission.

European Commission (2013a). *Human Resources Key Figures Card*. Brussels: European Commission, 5 March. http://ec.europa.eu/civil_service/docs/hr_key_figures_en.pdf (accessed February 2014).

European Commission (2013b). *Bosnia and Herzegovina Annual Progress Report*, 16 October. http://ec.europa.eu/enlargement/pdf/key_documents/2013/package/ba_rapport_2013.pdf (accessed April 2014).

European Commission (2009). 'European Council Decision of 1 December 2009 Adopting its Rules of Procedure' (2009/882/EU). *Official Journal of the European Union*, L315/51, 2 December.

European Parliament (1988). *Official Journal of the European Communities*. Annex. Debates of the European Parliament, 1988–9, no. 2–367.

European Union (2005). *From the ECSC to the Constitution: Treaty of Maastricht on European Union*. Brussels: Europa.

Exadaktylos, T. and Radaelli, C. (2009). 'Research Design in European Studies: The Case of Europeanization'. *Journal of Common Market Studies*, 47: 507–30.

Exadaktylos, T. and Radaelli, C. (eds) (2012). *Research Design in European Studies: Establishing Causality in Europeanization*. Basingstoke: Palgrave Macmillan.

Faber, F G. and Orbie, F J. (eds) (2009). *Beyond Market Access for Economic Development: EU-Africa Relations in Transition*. London: Routledge.

Fairbrass, J. (2003). 'The Europeanization of Business Interest Representation: UK and French Firms Compared'. *Comparative European Politics*, 1: 313–34.

Fairbrass, J. (2006). 'Organized Interests and Interest Politics', in I. Bache and A. Jordan (eds), *The Europeanisation of British Politics?*. Basingstoke: Palgrave Macmillan, 135–51.

Faist, T. and Ette, A. (2007). *The Europeanization of National Policies and Politics of Immigration: Between Autonomy and the European Union*. Basingstoke: Palgrave Macmillan.

Falkner, G. (2000). 'The Council or the Social Partners? EC Social Policy between Diplomacy and Collective Bargaining'. *Journal of European Public Policy*, 7: 705–24.

Featherstone, K. and Papadimitriou, D. (2008). *The Limits of Europeanization. Policy Conflict and Reform Capacity in Greece*. Basingstoke: Palgrave Macmillan.

Featherstone, K. and Radaelli, C. (eds), *The Politics of Europeanization*. Oxford: Oxford University Press.

Fioretos, K-O. (1997). 'The Anatomy of Autonomy: Interdependence, Domestic Balances of Power, and European Integration'. *Review of International Studies*, 23: 293–320.

Flockhart, T. (2010). 'Europeanization or EU-ization? The Transfer of European Norms across Time and Space'. *Journal of Common Market Studies*, 48: 787–810.

Follesdal, A. and Hix, S. (2006). 'Why there is a Democratic Deficit in the EU: A Response to Majone and Moravcsik'. *Journal of Common Market Studies*, 44: 533–62.

Foreign and Commonwealth Office (2004). 'Turkey and the EU'. *Enlargement Update*, spring

2004. London: FCO. http://europe.gov.uk/enlargement.

Forster, A. (1998). 'Britain and the Negotiation of the Maastricht Treaty: A Critique of Liberal Intergovernmentalism'. *Journal of Common Market Studies*, 36: 347–67.

Forsyth, M. G., Keens-Soper, H. M. A., and Savigear, F P. (eds) (1970). The Theory of International Relations: Selected Texts from Gentili to Treitschke. London: George Allen & Unwin.

Forwood, G. (2001). 'The Road to Cotonou: Negotiating a Successor to Lomé'. *Journal of Common Market Studies*, 39: 423–42.

Fouilleux, E. (2007). 'The Common Agricultural Policy', in M. Cini (ed.), *European Union Politics* (2nd edn). Oxford: Oxford University Press, 340–55.

Franchino, F. (2007). *The Powers of the Union: Delegation in the EU*. Cambridge: Cambridge University Press.

Freestone, D. (1983). *'The European Court of Justice'*, in J. Lodge (ed.), *Institutions and Policies of the European Community*. London: Pinter, 45–53.

Frey-Wouters, E. (1980). *The EC and the Third World: The Lomé Convention and its Impact*. New York: Praeger.

Friis, L. (1998). 'Approaching the "third half" of EU grand bargaining—The Post-negotiation Phase of the "Europe Agreement game"'. *Journal of European Public Policy*, 5: 322–38.

Friis, L. and Murphy, A. (1999). 'The European Union and Central and Eastern Europe: Governance and Boundaries'. *Journal of Common Market Studies*, 37: 211–32.

Frontex (2009). *Programme of Work 2009*. Warsaw: Frontex. http://frontex.europa.eu/gfx/frontex/files/justyna/programme_of_work_2009_final.pdf.

Fuchs, G. (1994). 'Policy-Making in a System of Multi-Level Governance-The Commission of the European Community and the Restructuring of the Telecommunications Sector'. *Journal of European Public Policy*, 1: 177–94.

Fursdon, E. (1980). *The European Defence Community: A History*. London: Macmillan.

Garrett, G. (1992). 'International Cooperation and Institutional Choice: The European Community's Internal Market'. *International Organization*, 46: 533–60.

Garrett, G. (1995). 'The Politics of Legal Integration in the European Union'. *International Organization*, 49: 171–81.

Garrett, G. and Tsebelis, G. (1996). 'An Institutional Critique of Intergovernmentalism'. *International Organization*, 50: 269–99.

545

Garrett, G. and Weingast, B. (1993). 'Ideas, Interests, and Institutions: Constructing the European Community's Internal Market', in J. Goldstein and R. Keohane (eds), *Ideas and Foreign Policy*. Ithaca, NY: Cornell University Press, 173–206.

Garrett, G., Keleman, R. D., and Schultz, H. (1998). 'The European Court of Justice, National Governments, and Legal Integration in the European Union'. *International Organization*, 52: 149–76.

Geddes, A. (2006). 'The Politics of European Union Domestic Order', in K. E. Jørgensen, M. Pollack, and B. Rosamond (eds), *Handbook of European Union Politics*. London: SAGE Publications, 449–62.

Geddes, A. (2008). *Immigration and European Integration: Beyond Fortress Europe* (2nd edn). Manchester: Manchester University Press.

Geddes, A. (2013). *Britain and the European Union*. Basingstoke: Palgrave Macmillan.

George, S. (1998). *An Awkward Partner: Britain in the European Community* (3rd edn). Oxford: Oxford University Press.

George, S. (2004). 'Multi-level Governance and the European Union', in I. Bache and M. Flinders (eds), *Multi-level Governance*. Oxford: Oxford University Press, 107–26.

Gibb, R. (2000). 'Post- Lomé: the European Union and the South'. *Third World Quarterly*, 21: 457–81.

Gilbert, M. (2008). 'Narrating the Process: Questioning the Progressive Story of European Integration'. *Journal of Common Market Studies*, 46: 641–62.

Gill, S. (1998). 'European Governance and New Constitutionalism: European Monetary Union and Alternatives to Disciplinary Neo-liberalism in Europe'. *New Political Economy*, 3: 5–26.

Gillingham, J. (1991a). *Coal, Steel, and the Rebirth of Europe, 1945-1955*. Cambridge: Cambridge University Press.

Gillingham, J. (1991b). 'Jean Monnet and the European Coal and Steel Community: A Preliminary Appraisal', in D. Brinkley and C. Hackett (eds), *Jean Monnet: The Path to European Unity*. Basingstoke and London: Macmillan, 129–62.

Ginsberg, R. H. (1989). *Foreign Policy Actions of the European Community: The Politics of Scale*. Boulder, CO: Lynne Rienner.

Glarbo, K. (1999). 'Restructuring the CFSP of the EU'. *Journal of European Public Policy*, 6: 634–51.

Glaser, T. (1990). 'EEC/ACP Cooperation: The Historical Perspective'. *The Courier*, 120, March/April.

Gold, M., Cressey, P., and Leonard, E. (2007). 'Whatever Happened to Social Dialogue? From Partnership to Managerialism in the EU Employment Agenda'. *European Journal of Industrial Relations*, 13: 7–25.

Golub, J. (1998). 'New Instruments for Environmental Policy in the EU: Introduction and Overview', in J. Golub (ed.), *New Instruments for Environmental Policy in the EU*. London and New York: Routledge, 1–29.

Grabbe, H. (2001). 'How Does Europeanization affect CEE Governance? Conditionality, Diffusion, and Diversity'. *Journal of European Public Policy*, 8: 1013–31.

Grabbe, H. (2003). 'Europeanization Goes East: Power and Uncertainty in the EU Accession Process', in K. Featherstone and C. Radaelli (eds), *The Politics of Europeanization*. Oxford: Oxford University Press, 303–27.

Grabbe, H. (2005). *The EU's Transformative Power: Europeanization Through Conditionality in Central and Eastern Europe*. Basingstoke: Palgrave Macmillan.

Grant, C. (1994). *Delors: Inside the House that Jacques Built*. London: Nicholas Brealey Publishing.

Grant, W. (1995). 'The Limits of Common Agricultural Policy Reform and the Option of Denationalization'. *Journal of European Public Policy*, 2: 1–18.

Grant, W. (1997). *The Common Agricultural Policy*. Basingstoke and London: Macmillan.

Green, R. H. (1976). 'The Lomé Convention: Updated Dependence or Departure towards Collective Self-Reliance?'. *African Review*, 6: 43–54.

Graziano, P. (2012). 'Consumers Interest and the EU: A Framework for Analysis, with Evidence from the Italian Case'. *European Policy Analysis*, 14 Stockholm: Swedish Institute for Policy Analysis. October.

Greenwood, J. (1997). *Representing Interests in the European Union*. Basingstoke and London: Macmillan.

Greenwood, J. (2003). *Interest Representation in the European Union*. Basingstoke: Palgrave Macmillan.

Greenwood, J. (2007). *Interest Representation in the European Union* (2nd edn). Basingstoke: Palgrave Macmillan.

Greenwood, J. (2011). *Interest Representation in the European Union*. (3rd edn). Basingstoke: Palgrave Macmillan.

Greenwood, J. and Dreger, J. (2013). 'The Transparency Register: A European Vanguard of Strong Lobby Regulation?'. *Interest Groups and Advocacy*, 2: 139–62.

Guild, E., Carrera, S., and Balzacq, T. (2008). 'The Changing Dynamics of Security in an Enlarged European Union' CEPS CHALLENGE Programme (Changing Landscape of European Liberty and Security), Research Paper 12. http://ceps.be/files/book/1746.pdf (accessed 20 March 2014).

Guiraudon, V. (2000). 'European Integration and Migration Policy: Vertical Policy-Making as Venue-Shopping'. *Journal of Common Market Studies*, 38: 251–71.

Guyomarch, A., Machin, H., and Ritchie, E. (1998). *France in the European Union*. Basingstoke: Macmillan.

Haas, E. B. (1958). *The Uniting of Europe: Political, Social, and Economic Forces 1950–57*. London: Library of World Affairs.

Haas, E. B. (1968). *The Uniting of Europe: Political, Social, and Economic Forces, 1950-1957* (2nd edn). Stanford, CA: Stanford University Press.

Haas, E. B. (1970). 'The Study of Regional Integration: Reflections on the Joy and Anguish of Pre-theorizing', *International Organization*, 24: 607–46.

Haas, E. B. (2001). 'Does Constructivism Subsume Neo-functionalism?', in T. Christiansen, K. E. Jørgensen, and A. Wiener (eds), *The Social Construction of Europe*. London: SAGE Publications, 22–31.

Haas, P. (1992). 'Introduction: Epistemic Communities and International Policy Coordination'. *International Organization*, 46: 1–35.

Habermas, J. (2001a). *The Postnational Constellation*. London: Polity Press.

Habermas, J. (2001b). 'Why Europe Needs a Constitution', *New Left Review*, 11. http://newleftreview.org/II/11/jurgen-habermas-why-europe-needs-a-constitution.

Hagemann, S. and Hoyland, B. (2008). 'Parties in the Council?'. *Journal of European Public Policy*, 15: 1205–21.

Hager, S. B. (2008). '"New Europeans" for the "New European Economy": Citizenship and the Lisbon Agenda', in B. Van Apeldoorn, J. Drahokoupil, and L. Horn (eds), *Contradictions and Limits of Neoliberal European Governance: From Lisbon to Lisbon*. Basingstoke and New York: Palgrave Macmillan, 106–24.

Haigh, N. (1999). 'European Union Environmental Policy at 25: Retrospect and Prospect'. *Environment and Planning C: Government and Policy*, 17: 109–12.

Hall, P. and Taylor, R. (1996). 'Political Science and the Three New Institutionalisms'. *Political Studies*, 44: 936–57.

Hallstein, W. (1962). *United Europe: Challenge and Opportunity*. Cambridge, MA, and London: Harvard University Press and Oxford University Press.

Hanf, F K. and Soetendorp, F B. (eds) (1998). *Adapting to European Integration: Small States and the European Union*. London: Longman.

Hantrais, L. (2000). *Gendered Policies in Europe: Reconciling Employment and Family Life*. Basingstoke: Macmillan.

Harmsen, R. (1999). 'The Europeanization of National Administrations: A Comparative Study of France and the Netherlands'. *Governance*, 12: 81–113.

Haverland, M. (2005). 'Does the EU Cause Domestic Developments? The Problem of Case Selection in Europeanization Research'. *European Integration online Papers (EIoP)*, 9(2). http://eiop.or.at/eiop/pdf/2005-002.pdf.

Hay, C. (2002). *Political Analysis: A Critical Introduction*. Basingstoke, Palgrave Macmillan.

Hay, C. and Rosamond, B. (2002). 'Globalization, European Integration, and the Discursive Construction of Economic Imperatives'. *Journal of European Public Policy*, 9: 147–67.

Hay, C. and Wincott, D. (2012). *The Political Economy of European Welfare Capitalism*. Basingstoke: Palgrave Macmillan.

Hayes-Renshaw, F. and Wallace, H. (1997). *The Council of Ministers*. Basingstoke: Palgrave Macmillan.

Hayes-Renshaw, F. and Wallace, H. (2006). *The Council of Ministers* (2nd edn). Basingstoke: Palgrave Macmillan.

Hayes-Renshaw, F., Lequesne, C., and Mayor Lopez, P. (1989). 'The Permanent Representations of the Member States to the European Communities'. *Journal of Common Market Studies*, 28: 121–37.

Héritier, A. (2007). *Explaining Institutional Change in Europe*. Oxford: Oxford University Press.

Héritier, A., Kerwer, D., Knill, C., Lehmkuhl, D., Teutsch, M., and Douillet, A-C. (2001). *Differential Europe. The European Union Impact on National Policymaking*. Lanham, MD: Rowman and Littlefield.

Héritier, A., Knill, C., and Mingers, S. (1996). *Ringing the Changes in Europe: Regulatory Competition and Redefinition of the State. Britain, France, Germany*. Berlin: Walter de Gruyter.

Heron, T. and Siles-Brügge, G. (2012). 'Competitive Liberalization and the "Global Europe" Services and Investment Agenda: Locating the Commercial Drivers of the EU-ACP Economic Partnership Agreements'. *Journal of Common Market Studies*, 50: 250–66.

Hewitt, A. (1989). 'ACP and the Developing World', in J. Lodge (ed.), *The European Community and the Challenge of the Future*. London: Pinter, 285–300.

Heyer, J. A. and Batzoglou, F. (2012). 'When in Doubt, Call Them Nazis: Ugly Stereotypes of Germany Resurface in Greece'. *Spiegel Online*, 29 February. http://spiegel.de/international/zeitgeist/when-in-doubt-call-them-nazis-ugly-stereotypes-of-germany-resurface-in-greece-a-817995.html.

Higgins, A. (2012). 'Protest of Peace Prize for EU Turns Local', *New York Times*, 9 December.

Hill, C. (1993). 'The Capability-Expectations Gap, or Conceptualising Europe's International Role'. *Journal of Common Market Studies*, 31: 305–28.

Hill, C. (1996). *The Actors in Europe's Foreign Policy*. London: Routledge.

Hill, C. (1998). '*Closing the Capability-Expectations Gap*', in J. Peterson and H. Sjursen (eds), *A Common Foreign Policy for Europe?: Competing Visions of the CFSP*. London: Routledge, 18–38.

Hill, C. (2004). 'Renationalizing or Regrouping? EU Foreign Policy since 11 September 2001'. *Journal of Common Market Studies*, 42: 143–63.

Hix, S. (1994). 'The Study of the European Community: The Challenge to Comparative Politics'. *West European Politics*, 17: 1–30.

Hix, S. (1999). *The Political System of the European Union*. Basingstoke and London: Macmillan.

Hix, S. (2006), 'Democracy, Parties and Elections'. (http://lse-students.ac.uk/HIX/working%20Papers/06-Democracy.pdf).

Hix, S. (2008). 'Towards a Partisan Theory of EU Politics'. *Journal of European Public Policy*, 15: 1254–65.

Hix, S. and Høyland, B. (2011). *The Political System of the European Union* (3rd edn). Basingstoke: Palgrave Macmillan.

Hix, S. and Marsh, M. (2007). 'Punishment or Protest? Understanding European Parliament Elections'. *The Journal of Politics*, 69: 495–510.

Hix, S., Kreppel, A., and Noury, A. (2003). 'The Party System in the European Parliament: Collusive or Competitive?'. *Journal of Common Market Studies*, 41: 309–31.

Hix, S., Noury, A., and Roland, G. (2005). 'Power to the Parties: Cohesion and Competition in the European Parliament, 1979–2001'. *British Journal of Political Science*, 35: 209–34.

Hix, S., Raunio, T., and Scully, R. (2003). 'Fifty Years On: Research on the European Parliament'. *Journal of Common Market Studies*, 41: 191–202.

Hodges, F M. and Wallace, F W. (eds) (1981). *Economic Divergence in the European Community*. London: Butterworth.

Hodson, D. and Maher, I. (2001). 'The Open Method as a New Mode of Governance: The Case of Soft Economic Policy Co-ordination'. *Journal of Common Market Studies*, 39: 719–46.

Hoffmann, S. (1964). 'The European Process at Atlantic Cross-purposes'. *Journal of Common Market Studies*, 3: 85–101.

Hoffmann, S. (1966). 'Obstinate or Obsolete? The Fate of the Nation State and the Case of Western Europe'. *Daedalus*, 95: 862–915.

Hoffmann, S. (1989). 'The European Community and 1992'. *Foreign Affairs*, 68: 27–47.

Holland, S. (1980). *Uncommon Market*. Basingstoke and London: Macmillan.

Holzinger, K., Knill, C., and Schäfer, A. (2006). 'Rhetoric or Reality? "New Governance" in EU Environmental Policy'. *European Law Journal*, 12: 403–20.

Hooghe, L. (1996a). 'Introduction: Reconciling EU-Wide Policy and National Diversity', in L. Hooghe (ed.), *Cohesion Policy and European Integration*. Oxford: Oxford University Press, 1–26.

Hooghe, L. (1996b). 'Building a Europe with the Regions: The Changing Role of the European Commission', in L. Hooghe (ed.), *Cohesion Policy and European Integration*. Oxford: Oxford University Press: 89–128.

Hooghe, L. and Marks, G. (2003). 'Unravelling the Central State, But How?'. *American Political Science Review*, 97: 233–43.

Hooghe, L. and Marks, G. (2004). 'Contrasting Visions of Multi-level Governance', in I. Bache and M. Flinders (eds), *Multi-level Governance*. Oxford: Oxford University Press, 15–30.

Hooghe, L. and Marks, G. (2008). 'A Postfunctionalist Theory of European Integration: From Permissive Consensus to Constraining Dissensus'. *British Journal of Political Science*, 39: 1–23.

Horn, L. (2012). *Regulating Corporate Governance in the EU: Towards the Marketization of Corporate Control*. Basingstoke and New York: Palgrave Macmillan.

Hoskyns, C. (1996). *Integrating Gender: Women, Law, and Politics in the European Union*. London: Verso.

Hoskyns, C. (2004). 'Gender Perspectives', in A. Wiener and T. Diez (eds), *European Integration Theory*. Oxford: Oxford University Press, 217–36.

House of Commons (2012). 'The Treaty on Stability, Coordination and Governance in the Economic and Monetary Union: Political Issues', *Research Paper* 12/14, 27 March.

Howell, K. (2003). 'The Europeanization of British Financial Services'. Paper presented to the ESRC

548

Seminar Series/UACES Study Group on the Europeanization of British Politics and Policy-Making, Sheffield, 2 May 2003.

Howorth, J. (2003). 'France, Britain, and the Euro-Atlantic Crisis'. *Survival*, 45: 173–92.

Howorth, J. (2004). 'The Role of Discourse, Ideas, and Epistemic Communities in the Forging of ESDP'. *West European Politics*, 27: 211–34.

Hu, Y. (1981). *Europe under Stress*. London: Butterworth.

Hübner, D. (2004). *Lisbon and Cohesion Policy: Complementary Objectives*. Speech by the member of the European Commission responsible for Regional Policy. UNICE Competitiveness Day, Brussels, 9 December. http://europa.eu/rapid/pressReleasesAction.do?reference=SPEECH/04/535 (accessed October 2009).

Hughes, J., Sasse, G., and Gordon, C. (2004). 'Conditionality and Compliance in the EU's Eastward Enlargement'. *Journal of Common Market Studies*, 42: 523–51.

Hughes, J., Sasse, G., and Gordon, C. (2005). *Europeanization and Regionalization in the EU's Enlargement to Central and Eastern Europe: The Myth of Conditionality*. Basingstoke: Palgrave Macmillan.

Humphreys, P. and Padgett, S. (2006). 'Globalization, the European Union, and Domestic Governance in Telecoms and Electricity'. *Governance*, 19: 383–406.

Hurt, S. R. (2003). 'Co-operation and Coercion? The Cotonou Agreement between the European Union and ACP States and the end of the Lomé Convention'. *Third World Quarterly*, 24: 161–76.

Huysmans, J. (2006). *The Politics of Insecurity: Fear, Migration, and Asylum in the EU*. Abingdon and New York: Routledge.

Ingebritsen, C. (1998). *The Nordic States and European Unity*. Ithaca, NY: Cornell University Press.

Jachtenfuchs, M. (2001). 'The Governance Approach to European Integration'. *Journal of Common Market Studies*, 39: 245–64.

Jachtenfuchs, M. and Kohler-Koch, B. (2004). 'Governance and Institutional Development', in A. Wiener and T. Diez (eds), *European Integration Theory*. Oxford: Oxford University Press, 97–115.

Jamal, A. H. (1979). 'Preparing for Lomé Two'. *Third World Quarterly*, 1: 134–40.

Jehlicka, P. and Tickle, A. (2004). 'Environmental Implications of Eastern Enlargement: The End of Progressive EU Environmental Policy?'. *Environmental Politics*, 13: 77–95.

Jenkins, R. (1977). 'Europe's Present Challenge and Future Opportunity: The First Jean Monnet Lecture Delivered at the European University Institute, Florence, 27 October 1977'. *Bulletin of the European Communities Supplement* 10/77: 6–14.

Jenkins, R. (1989). *European Diary, 1977–1981*. London: Collins.

Joint Transparency Register (2013). *Annual Report on the operations of the Transparency Register 2013*. http://europarl.europa.eu/pdf/meps/transparency_2013.pdf (accessed February 2014).

Jordan, A. (1999a). 'Editorial Introduction: The Construction of a Multilevel Environment Governance System'. *Environment and Planning C: Government and Policy*, 17: 1–17.

Jordan, A. (1999b). 'The Implementation of EU Environmental Policy: A Policy Problem Without a Political Solution?'. *Environment and Planning C: Government and Policy*, 17: 69–90.

Jordan, A. (2001). 'The European Union: An Evolving System of Multi-Level Governance … or Government?'. *Policy and Politics*, 29: 193–208.

Jordan, A. (2002). 'Decarbonising the UK: A "Radical Agenda" from the Cabinet Office?'. *Political Quarterly*, 73: 344–52.

Jordan, A. (2006). 'Environmental Policy', in I. Bache and A. Jordan (eds), *The Europeanization of British Politics*. Basingstoke: Palgrave Macmillan, 231–47.

Jordan, A. and Liefferink, D. (eds) (2004). *Environmental Policy in Europe: The Europeanization of National Environmental Policy*. London: Routledge.

Jordan, A. and Schout, A. (2006). *The Coordination of the European Union: Exploring the Capacities of Networked Governance*. Oxford: Oxford University Press.

Jordan, A., Schout, A., and Unfried, M. (2008). 'The European Union', in A. J. Jordan and A. Lenschow (eds), *Innovation in Environmental Policy? Integrating the Environment for Sustainability*. Cheltenham: Edward Elgar, 159–79.

Jordan, A., Wurzel, R. K. W., and Zito, A. R. (2003). '"New" Instruments of Environmental Governance: Patterns and Pathways of Change'. *Environmental Politics*, 12: 1–24.

Judge, D. and Earnshaw, D. (2002). 'The European Parliament and the Commission Crisis: A New Assertiveness?'. *Governance*, 15: 345–74.

Judge, D. and Earnshaw, D. (2008). *The European Parliament* (2nd edn). Basingstoke: Palgrave Macmillan.

Judge, D., Earnshaw, D., and Cowan, N. (1994). 'Ripples or Waves: the European Parliament in the European Community Policy Process'. *Journal of European Public Policy*, 1: 27–52.

Kaelberer, M. (2003). 'Knowledge, Power, and Monetary Bargaining: Central Bankers and the Creation of Monetary Union in Europe'. *Journal of European Public Policy*, 10: 365–79.

Kaltenthaler, K. (2002). 'German Interests in European Monetary Integration'. *Journal of Common Market Studies*, 40: 69–87.

Kaltenthaler, K. (2006). *Policymaking in the European Central Bank: The Masters of Europe's Money*. Lanham, MD: Rowman and Littlefield.

Kantola, J. (2010), *Gender and the European Union*. Basingstoke: Palgrave Macmillan.

Kapsis, I. (2010). 'The Courts of the European Union', in M. Cini and N. Pérez-Solórzano-Borragán (eds), *European Union Politics* (3rd edn). Oxford: Oxford University Press, 176–88.

Kassim, H. (1994). 'Policy Networks, Networks, and European Union Policy Making: A Sceptical View'. *West European Politics*, 17: 15–27.

Kassim, H. (2003). 'Meeting the Demands of EU Membership: The Europeanization of National Administrative Systems', in K. Featherstone and C. Radaelli (eds), *The Politics of Europeanization*. Oxford: Oxford University Press, 83–111.

Kassim, H. (2008). '"Mission Impossible", But Mission Accomplished: The Kinnock Reforms and the European Commission'. *Journal of European Public Policy*, 15: 648–68.

Katzenstein, P. (1996). *The Culture of National Security*. New York: Columbia University Press.

Kelleher, J., Batterbury, S., and Stern, E. (1999). *The Thematic Evaluation of the Partnership Principle: Final Synthesis Report*. London: Tavistock Institute.

Keohane, R. (1984). *After Hegemony: Co-operation and Discord in the World Political Economy*. Princeton: Princeton University Press.

Keohane, R. (1989). 'Neoliberal Institutionalism: A Perspective on World Politics', in R. Keohane (ed.), *International Institutions and State Power*. Boulder, CO, San Francisco, CA, and Oxford: Westview Press, 1–20.

Keohane, R. and Nye, J. S., Jr (1977). *Power and Interdependence: World Politics in Transition*. Boston: Little, Brown.

Kietz, D. and Parkes, R. (2008). 'Justiz- und Innenpolitik nach dem Lissabonner Vertrag'. Diskussionspapier, Stiftung Wissenschaft und Politik, 13 May. (http://swp-berlin.org/common/get_document.php?asset_id=5000).

Kietz, D. and von Ondarza, N. (2010). 'Wilkommen in der Lissabonner Wirklichkeit'. *SWP-Aktuell*, 29 March. Berlin: Stiftung Wissenschaft und Politik.

Kingdon, J. (2011). *Agendas, Alternatives, and Public Policies* (4th edn). London: HarperCollins College Publishers.

Knill, C. (2001). *The Europeanization of National Administrations: Patterns of Institutional Change and Persistence*. Cambridge: Cambridge University Press.

Kohler-Koch, B. (1996). 'Catching up with Change: The Transformation of Governance in the European Union'. *Journal of European Public Policy*, 3: 359–80.

Kohler-Koch, B. (1997). 'Organized Interests in European Integration: The Evolution of a New Type of Governance?', in H. Wallace and A. R. Young (eds), *Participation and Policy-Making in the European Union*. Oxford: Clarendon Press, 42–68.

Kohler-Koch, B. and Eising, R. (eds) (1999). *The Transformation of European Governance*. London: Routledge.

Kohler-Koch, B. and Rittberger, B. (2006). 'The "Governance Turn" in EU Studies'. *Journal of Common Market Studies: Annual Review*, 44: 27–49.

Kohler-Koch, B. and Rittberger, B. (2007). *Debating the Democratic Legitimacy of the European Union*. Lanham, MD: Rowman and Littlefield.

Koppen, I. (1993). 'The Role of the European Court of Justice', in D. Liefferink, P. Lowe, and A. P. J. Mol (eds), *European Integration and Environmental Policy*. London: Belhaven Press, 126–49.

Kreppel, A. (2000). 'Rules, Ideology, and Coalition Formation in the European Parliament: Past, Present, and Future'. *European Union Politics*, 1: 340–62.

Kreppel, A. (2002). *The European Parliament and Supranational Party System: A Study in Institutional Development*. Cambridge: Cambridge University Press.

Kreppel, A. (2003). 'Necessary but not Sufficient: Understanding the Impact of Treaty Reform on the Internal Development of the European Parliament'. *Journal of European Public Policy*, 10: 884–911.

Kronsell, A. (2005). 'Gender, Power and European Integration Theory'. *Journal of European Public Policy*, 12: 1022–40.

Krotz, U. (2009). 'Momentum and Impediments: Why Europe Won't Emerge as a Full Political Actor on the World Stage Soon'. *Journal of Common Market Studies*, 47: 555–78.

Kuper, R. (1998). *The Politics of the European Court of Justice*. London: Kogan Page.

Ladrech, R. (1994). 'Europeanization of Domestic Politics and Institutions: The Case of France'. *Journal of Common Market Studies*, 32(1): 69–88.

Laffan, B. (1997a). *The Finances of the European Union*. Basingstoke and London: Macmillan.

Laffan, B. (1997*b*). 'From Policy Entrepreneur to Policy Manager: The Challenge Facing the European Commission'. *Journal of European Public Policy*, 4: 422–38.

Laqueur, W. (1972). *Europe Since Hitler*. Harmondsworth: Penguin.

Lavenex, S. (2010). 'Justice and Home Affairs: Communitarization with Hesitation', in H. Wallace, M. Pollack, and A. Young (eds), *Policy-Making in the European Union* (6th edn). Oxford: Oxford University Press, 458–77.

Lenschow, A. (1999). 'The Greening of the EU: The Common Agricultural Policy and the Structural Funds'. *Environment and Planning C: Government and Policy*, 17: 91–108.

Lenschow, A. (2005). 'Environmental Policy: Contending Dynamics of Policy Change', in H. Wallace, W. Wallace, and M. A. Pollack (eds), *Policy-Making in the European Union* (5th edn). Oxford: Oxford University Press, 305–27.

Lenschow, A. (2007). 'Environmental Policy in the European Union: Bridging Policy, Politics, and Polity Dimensions', in K. E. Jørgensen, M. Pollack, and B. Rosamond (eds), *The SAGE Handbook of European Union Politics*. London: SAGE Publications, 413–31.

Leonardi, R. (2005). *Cohesion Policy in the European Union: The Building of Europe*. Basingstoke: Palgrave Macmillan.

Lewis, J. (1998). 'Is the "Hard Bargaining" Image of the Council Misleading? The Committee of Permanent Representatives and the Local Elections Directive'. *Journal of Common Market Studies*, 36: 479–504.

Lewis, J. (2000). 'The Methods of Community in EU Decision-making and Administrative Rivalry in the Council's Infrastructure'. *Journal of European Public Policy*, 7: 261–89.

Lewis, J. (2003*a*). 'Informal Integration and the Supranational Construction of the Council'. *Journal of European Public Policy*, 10: 996–1019.

Lewis, J. (2003*b*). 'The Council of the European Union', in M. Cini (ed.), *European Union Politics*. Oxford: Oxford University Press, 148–65.

Lewis, J. (2010). 'The Council of the European Union', in M. Cini and N. Pérez-Solózano Borragán (eds), *European Union Politics* (3rd edn). Oxford: Oxford University Press, 141–61.

Liefferink, D. and Andersen, M. S. (1998). 'Strategies of the "Green" Member States in EU Environmental Policy-making'. *Journal of European Public Policy*, 5: 254–70.

Lightfoot, S. and Burchell, J. (2005). 'The European Union and the World Summit on Sustainable Development: Normative Power Europe in Action?'. *Journal of Common Market Studies*, 43: 75–95.

Lindberg, B., Rasmussen, A., and Warntjen, A. (2008). 'Party Politics as Usual? The Role of Political Parties in EU Legislative Decision-making'. *Journal of European Public Policy*, 15: 1107–26.

Lindberg, L. (1963). *The Political Dynamics of European Economic Integration*. Stanford: Stanford University Press; London: Oxford University Press.

Lindberg, L. (1966). 'Integration as a Source of Stress on the European Community System'. *International Organization*, 20: 233–65.

Locher, B. and Prügl, E. (2009). 'Gender and European Integration', in A. Wiener and T. Diez, *European Integration Theory* (2nd edn). Oxford: Oxford University Press, 181–97.

Loedel, P. H. (1998). 'Enhancing Europe's International Monetary Power: The Drive Toward a Single Currency', in P-H. Laurent and M. Maresceau (eds), *The State of the European Union: Vol. 4, Deepening and Widening*. Boulder, CO, and London: Lynne Rienner, 243–61.

Lord C. (1998). *Democracy in the European Union*. Sheffield: Sheffield Academic Press/University Association for Contemporary European Studies.

Lord C. (2001). 'Democracy and Democratization in the European Union', in S. Bromley (ed.), *Governing the European Union*. London: SAGE Publications, 165–90.

Lord, C. (2002). 'Comparing Jacques Delors and Jacques Santer as Presidents of the European Commission. Skill in Supranational Context'. *Politics and Policy*, 30: 324–47.

Lord C. and Harris, E. (2006). *Democracy in the New Europe*. Basingstoke: Palgrave Macmillan.

Lord C. and Magnette, P. (2004). '*E Pluribus Unum*? Creative Disagreement about Legitimacy in the EU'. *Journal of Common Market Studies*, 42: 183–202.

Lowe, P., Buller, H., and Ward. N. (2002). 'Setting the Next Agenda? British and French Approaches to the Second Pillar of the Common Agricultural Policy'. *Journal of Rural Studies*, 18: 1–17.

Ludlow, P. (Peter) (1991). 'The European Commission', in R. Keohane and S. Hoffmann (eds), *The New European Community: Decision-making and Institutional Change*. Boulder, CO, San Francisco, CA, and Oxford: Westview Press, 85–132.

Ludlow, P. (Piers) (1997). *Dealing with Britain: The Six and the First UK Application to the EEC*. Cambridge: Cambridge University Press.

Lynggaard, K. (2007). 'The Institutional Construction of a Policy Field: A Discursive Institutional Perspective on Change within the Common Agricultural Policy'. *Journal of European Public Policy*, 14: 293–312.

551

McAleavey, P. (1992). 'The Politics of European Regional Development Policy: The European Commission's RECHAR Initiative and the Concept of Additionality'. *Strathclyde Papers on Government and Politics*, no. 88 Glasgow:University of Strathclyde.

McAleavey, P. (1995). *Policy Implementation as Incomplete Contracting: The European Regional Development Fund*. Florence: European University Institute, PhD thesis.

McAllister, R. (2010). *European Union: An Historical and Political Survey* (2nd edn). London: Routledge.

McCann, D. (2010). *The Political Economy of the European Union*. Cambridge: Polity.

McCormick, J. (2001). *Environmental Policy in the European Union*. Basingstoke: Palgrave Macmillan.

McGowan, L. and Cini, M. (1999). 'Discretion and Politicization in EU Competition Policy: The Case of Merger Control'. *Governance*, 12: 175–200.

McGowan, L. and Wilks, S. (1995). 'The First Supranational Policy in the European Union: Competition Policy'. *European Journal of Political Research*, 28: 141–69.

McLaren, L. M. (2000). 'Turkey's Eventual Membership of the EU: Turkish Elite Perspectives on the Issue'. *Journal of Common Market Studies*, 38: 117–29.

McQueen, M. (1998). 'Lomé Versus Free Trade Agreements: The Dilemma facing the ACP Countries'. *World Economy*, 21: 421–43.

Mair, P. (2004). 'The Europeanization Dimension'. *Journal of European Public Policy*, 11: 337–48.

Mair, P. (2009). 'Political Parties and Party Systems', in P. Graziano and M. P. Vink (eds), *Europeanization: New Research Agendas*. Basingstoke: Palgrave Macmillan, 154–66.

Majone, G. (1993). 'The European Community Between Social Policy and Social Regulation'. *Journal of Common Market Studies*, 31: 153–70.

Majone, G. (1996). *Regulating Europe*. London: Routledge.

Majone, G. (1998). 'Europe's "Democratic Deficit": The Question of Standards'. *European Law Journal*, 4: 5–28.

Majone, G. (2001). 'Two Logics of Delegation: Agency and Fiduciary Relations in EU Governance'. *European Union Politics*, 2: 103–22.

Majone, G. (2002). 'The European Commission: The Limits of Centralization and the Perils of Parliamentarization'. *Governance*, 15: 375–92.

Mamadouh, V. and Raunio, T. (2003). 'The Committee System: Powers, Appointments, and Report Allocation'. *Journal of Common Market Studies*, 41: 333–51.

Mancini, G. F. (1991). 'The Making of a Constitution for Europe', in R. Keohane and S. Hoffmann (eds), *The New European Community: Decision-making and Institutional Change*. Boulder, CO, San Francisco, CO, and Oxford: Westview Press, 177–94.

Manners, I. (2002). 'Normative Power Europe: A Contradiction in Terms?'. *Journal of Common Market Studies*, 40: 235–58.

Manners, I. (2007). 'Another Europe is Possible', in K. E. Jørgensen, M. Pollack, and B. Rosamond (eds), *Handbook of European Union Politics*. London: SAGE Publications, 77–95.

Manners, I. (2008). 'The Normative Ethics of the European Union'. *International Affairs*, 84: 45–60.

March, J. G. and Olsen, J. (1984). 'The New Institutionalism: Organizational Factors in Political Life'. *American Political Science Review*, 78: 734–49.

March, J. G. and Olsen, J. (1989). *Rediscovering Institutions: The Organizational Basis of Politics*. New York and London: Free Press.

March, J. G. and Olsen, J. (1996). 'Institutional Perspectives on Political Institutions'. *Governance*, 9: 247–64.

Marcou, G. (ed.) (2002). *Regionalization for Development and Accession to the European Union: A Comparative Perspective*. Budapest: Local Government and Public Service Reform Initiative.

Marks, G. (1992). 'Structural Policy in the European Community', in A. Sbragia (ed.), *Euro-Politics: Institutions and Policymaking in the 'New' European Community*. Washington, DC: Brookings Institution, 191–224.

Marks, G. (1993). 'Structural Policy and Multilevel Governance in the EC', in A. Cafruny and G. Rosenthal (eds), *The State of the European Community, Vol. 2: The Maastricht Debates and Beyond*. Boulder, CO: Lynne Rienner; Harlow: Longman, 391–410.

Marks, G. and Hooghe, L. (2004). 'Contrasting Visions of Multi-Level Governance', in I. Bache and M. Flinders (eds), *Multi-Level Governance*. Oxford: Oxford University Press, 15–30.

Marks, G., Hooghe, L., and Blank, K. (1996). 'European Integration from the 1980s: State-Centric v Multi-Level Governance'. *Journal of Common Market Studies*, 34: 341–78.

Marsh, D. W. (2009). *The Euro: The Politics of the New Global Currency*. New Haven, CT, and London: Yale University Press.

Marsh, D. W. (2013). *Europe's Deadlock: How the Euro Crisis Could be Solved—and Why it Won't Happen*. New Haven, CT, and London: Yale University Press.

Matlary, J. H. (1993). *Towards Understanding Integration: An Analysis of the Role of the State in EC Energy Policy*. Oslo: University of Oslo, PhD Thesis.

Matlary, J. H. (1997). *Energy Policy in the European Union*. Basingstoke and London: Macmillan.

Mattila, M. (2008). 'Voting and Coalitions in the Council after the Enlargement', in D. Naurin and H. Wallace (eds), *Unveiling the Council of the European Union: Games Governments Play in Brussels*. Basingstoke: Palgrave Macmillan, 23–35.

Mattli, W. and Slaughter, A-M. (1995). 'Law and Politics in the EU: A Reply to Garrett'. *International Organization*, 49: 183–90.

Mawson, J., Martins, M., and Gibney, J. (1985). 'The Development of the European Community Regional Policy', in M. Keating and B. Jones, B.C (eds), *Regions in the European Community*. Oxford: Clarendon Press, 20–59.

Mayne, R. (1991). 'Gray Eminence', in D. Brinkley and C. Hackett (eds), *Jean Monnet: The Path to European Unity*. Basingstoke and London: Macmillan, 114–28.

Mazey, S. (1992). 'Conception and Evolution of the High Authority's Administrative Services (1952–1956): From Supranational Principles to Multinational Practices', in E. V. Heyen (ed.), *Yearbook of European Administrative History 4: Early European Community Administration*. Baden-Baden: Nomos, 31–47.

Mazey, S. and Richardson, J. (1999). 'Interests', in L. Cram, D. Dinan, and N. Nugent (eds), *Developments in the European Union*. Basingstoke and London: Macmillan, 105–29.

Mendez, C. (2013). 'The Post-2013 Reform of EU Cohesion Policy and the Place-based Narrative'. *Journal of European Public Policy*, 20: 639–59.

Mény, Y., Muller, P., and Quermonne, J-L. (1996). 'Introduction', in Y. Mény, P. Muller, and J-L. Quermonne (eds), *Adjusting to Europe: The Impact of the European Union on National Institutions and Policies*. London: Routledge, 1–24.

Merlingen, M. (2007). 'Everything is Dangerous: A Critique of "Normative Power Europe"'. *Security Dialogue*, 38: 435–53.

Metcalfe, L. (1992). 'Can the Commission Manage Europe?'. *Australian Journal of Public Administration*, 51: 117–30.

Metcalfe, L. (2000). 'Reforming the Commission: Will Organizational Efficiency Produce Effective Governance?'. *Journal of Common Market Studies*, 38: 817–41.

Meunier, S. (2007a). 'Managing Globalization? The EU in International Trade Negotiations'. *Journal of Common Market Studies*, 45: 905–26.

Meunier, S. (2007b). *Trading Voices: The European Union in International Commercial Negotiations*. Princeton: Princeton University Press.

Middlemas, K. (1995). *Orchestrating Europe: The Informal Politics of European Union, 1973–1995*. London: Fontana.

Milward, A. S. (1984). *The Reconstruction of Western Europe, 1945-51*. London: Routledge.

Milward, A. S. (1992). *The European Rescue of the Nation State*. London: Routledge.

Mitrany, D. (1943 [1966]). *A Working Peace System*. London: Royal Institute of International Affairs.

Mitrany, D. (1966). 'The Prospect of Integration: Federal or Functional'. *Journal of Common Market Studies*, 4: 119–49.

Mol, A. P. J. and Sonnenfeld, D. A. (eds) (2000). *Ecological Modernisation Around the World: Perspectives and Critical Debates*. London and New York: Frank Cass/Routledge.

Monar, J. (2001). 'The Dynamics of Justice and Home Affairs: Laboratories, Driving Factors, and Costs'. *Journal of Common Market Studies*, 39: 747–64.

Monbiot, G. (2013). 'The Lies behind this Transatlantic Trade Deal'. *The Guardian*, 2 December.

Monnet, J. (1962). 'A Ferment of Change'. *Journal of Common Market Studies*, 1: 203–11.

Monti, M. (2010). 'A New Strategy for the Single Market: At the Service of Europe's Economy and Society'. Report to the President of the European Commission, José Manuel Barroso. http://ec.europa.eu/bepa/pdf/monti_report_final_10_05_2010_en.pdf.

Morata, F. and Munoz, X. (1996). 'Vying for European Funds: Territorial Restructuring in Spain', in L. Hooghe (ed.), *Cohesion Policy and European Integration*. Oxford: Oxford University Press, 195–214.

Moravcsik, A. (1991). 'Negotiating the Single European Act'. *International Organization*, 45: 19–56.

Moravcsik, A. (1993). 'Preferences and Power in the European Community: A Liberal Intergovernmentalist Approach'. *Journal of Common Market Studies*, 31: 473–524.

Moravcsik, A. (1998). *The Choice for Europe: Social Purpose and State Power from Messina to Maastricht*. Ithaca, NY: Cornell University Press; London: UCL Press.

Moravcsik, A. (2002). 'In Defence of the "Democratic Deficit": Reassessing Legitimacy in the European Union'. *Journal of Common Market Studies*, 40: 603–24.

Moravcsik, A. and Nicolaïdes, K. (1999). 'Explaining the Treaty of Amsterdam: Interests, Influences, Institutions'. *Journal of Common Market Studies*, 37: 59–85.

Moravcsik, A. and Schimmelfennig, F. (2009). 'Liberal Intergovernmentalism', in A. Wiener and T. Diez (eds), *European Integration Theory* (2nd edn). Oxford: Oxford University Press, 67–87.

Moschella, M. (2011). 'Getting Hedge Funds Regulation into the EU Agenda: The Constraints of Agenda Dynamics'. *Journal of European Integration*, 33: 251–66.

Moser, P. (1996). 'The European Parliament as a Conditional Agenda Setter: What Are the Conditions? A Critique of Tsebelis (1994)'. *American Political Science Review*, 90: 834–8.

Moser, P. (1997). 'A Theory of the Conditional Influence of the European Parliament in the Cooperation Procedure'. *Public Choice*, 91: 333–50.

Moyer, H. W. and Josling, T. E. (1990). *Agricultural Policy Reform: Politics and Process in the EC and the USA*. Ames: Iowa State University Press.

Müftüler-Bac, M. and McLaren, L. M. (2003). 'Enlargement Preferences and Policy-Making in the European Union: Impacts on Turkey'. *Journal of European Integration*, 25: 17–30.

Mügge, D. (2010). *Widen the Market, Narrow the Competition: Banker Interests and the Making of a European Capital Market*. Colchester: ECPR Press.

Münchau, W. (2014). 'Germany's Constitutional Court has Strengthened the Eurosceptics'. *Financial Times*, 9 February.

National Farmers' Union (1996). *Briefing: 1996 US Farm Bill*. London: National Farmers' Union.

Niemann, A. (2006). *Explaining Decisions in the European Union*. Cambridge: Cambridge University Press.

Niemann, A. and Schmitter, P. (2009). 'Neofunctionalism', in A. Wiener and T. Diez (eds), *European Integration Theory* (2nd edn). Oxford: Oxford University Press, 45–66.

Nousios, P. and Tsolakis, A. (2012). 'The Contested Reconstruction of the Belle Époque? Europe 2020, Transnational Capitalism and the Political Economy of Global Restructuring', in P. Nousios, H. Overbeek, and A. Tsolakis (eds), *Globalisation and European Integration: Critical Approaches to Regional Order and International Relations*. Abingdon and New York: Routledge, 243–68.

Nugent, N. (1995). 'The Leadership Capacity of the European Commission'. *Journal of European Public Policy*, 2: 603–23.

O'Brennan, J. (2008). *The European Union and the Western Balkans: Stability and Europeanization through Enlargement*. Abingdon: Routledge.

O'Brennan, J. (2013). 'Will Europe End in Croatia?'. *Project Syndicate*, 30 June. http://project-syndicate.org/commentary/the-consequences-of-the-eu-s-enlargement-fatigue-by-john-o-brennan (accessed March 2014).

Olsen, J. (2002). 'The Many Faces of Europeanization'. *Journal of Common Market Studies*, 40: 921–52.

Olsen, J. (2003). 'Europeanization', in M. Cini (ed.), *European Union Politics*. Oxford: Oxford University Press, 333–48.

Olsson, J. (2003), 'Democracy Paradoxes in Multi-Level Governance'. *Journal of European Public Policy*, 10: 283–300.

Orbie, J. and De Ville, F. (2014). 'The European Commission's Neoliberal Trade Discourse since the Crisis: Legitimizing Continuity through Subtle Discursive Change'. *British Journal of Politics and International Relations*, 16: 149–67.

Parker, O. (2008). 'Challenging new Constitutionalism in the EU: French Resistance, Social Europe, and Soft Governance'. *New Political Economy*, 13: 397–417.

Parker, O. (2009a). 'Why EU, Which EU? Habermas and the Ethics of Postnational Politics in Europe'. *Constellations: An International Journal of Critical and Democratic Theory*, 16: 392–409.

Parker, O. (2009b). '"Cosmopolitan Europe" and the EU-Turkey Question: The Politics of a "Common destiny"'. *Journal of European Public Policy*, 16: 1085–101.

Parker, O. (2012a). 'Towards an Ambiguous "Cosmopolitics": Citizens and Entrepreneurs in the European Project'. *International Theory*, 4: 198–232.

Parker, O. (2012b). 'Roma and the Politics of EU Citizenship in France: Everyday Security and Resistance'. *Journal of Common Market Studies*, 50: 475–91.

Parker, O. (2013). *Cosmopolitan Government in Europe: Citizens and Entrepreneurs in Postnational Politics*. Abingdon and New York: Routledge.

Parker, O. and Rosamond, B. (2013). '"Normative Power Europe" Meets Economic Liberalism: Complicating Cosmopolitanism Inside/Outside the EU'. *Cooperation and Conflict*, 48: 229–46.

Patomaki, H. (2013). *The Great Eurozone Disaster: From Crisis to Global New Deal*. London: Zed Books.

Pelkmans, J. (1994). 'The Significance of EC-1992', in P-H. Laurent (ed.), *The European Community: To Maastricht and Beyond*. Special Edition of *The Annals of the American Academy of Political and Social Science*, January: 94–111.

Pelkmans, J. and Winters, L. A. (1988). *Europe's Domestic Market*. London: Routledge.

Peters, B. G. (1997). 'The Commission and Implementation in the European Union: Is There an Implementation Deficit and Why?', in N. Nugent (ed.), *At the Heart of the Union: Studies of the European Commission*. Basingstoke and London: Macmillan, 187–202.

Peters, B. G. and Pierre, J. (2004). 'Multi-level Governance and Democracy: A Faustian Bargain?', in I. Bache and M. Flinders (eds), *Multi-level Governance*. Oxford: Oxford University Press, 75–89.

Peterson, J. (1991). 'Technology Policy in Europe: Explaining the Framework Programme in Theory and Practice'. *Journal of Common Market Studies*, 31: 473–524.

Peterson, J. (1992). 'The European Technology Community: Policy Networks in a Supranational Setting', in D. Marsh and R. A. W. Rhodes (eds), *Policy Networks in British Government*. Oxford: Oxford University Press, 226–48.

Peterson, J. (1995a). 'Policy Networks and European Union Policy Making: A Reply to Kassim'. *West European Politics*, 18: 389–407.

Peterson, J. (1995b). 'Decision-making in the European Union: Towards a Framework for analysis'. *Journal of European Public Policy*, 2: 69–93.

Peterson, J. (2004). 'Policy Networks', in A. Wiener and T. Diez (eds), *European Integration Theory*. Oxford: Oxford University Press: 117–36.

Peterson, J. (2009). 'Policy Networks', in A. Wiener and T. Diez (eds), *European Integration Theory* (2nd edn). Oxford: Oxford University Press, 105–24.

Peterson, J. and Bomberg, E. (1993). 'Decision Making in the European Union: A Policy Networks Approach'. Paper prepared for presentation to the annual conference of the UK Political Studies Association, Leicester, 20–22 April.

Pew Research Centre (2013). *The New Sick Man of Europe: the European Union*. Available at: http://pewglobal.org/2013/05/13/the-new-sick-man-of-europe-the-european-union/.

Philippart, E. and Edwards, G. (1999). 'The Provisions on Closer Co-operation in the Treaty of Amsterdam'. *Journal of Common Market Studies*, 37: 87–108.

Phinnemore, D. (2010), 'The European Union: Establishment and Development', in M. Cini and N. Perez-Solórzano Borragán (eds), *European Union Politics* (3rd edn). Oxford: Oxford University Press, 32–47.

Pierson, P. (1996). 'The Path to European Integration: A Historical Institutionalist Analysis'. *Comparative Political Studies*, 29: 123–63.

Pierson, P. (1998). 'The Path to European Integration: A Historical Institutionalist Analysis', in W. Sandholtz and A. Stone Sweet (eds), *European Integration and Supranational Governance*. Oxford: Oxford University Press, 27–58.

Pierre, J. (ed.) (2000). *Debating Governance: Authority, Steering, and Democracy*. Oxford: Oxford University Press.

Poletti, A. and De Bievre, D. (2014). 'The Political Science of European Trade Policy: A Literature Review with a Research Outlook'. *Comparative European Politics*, 12: 101–19.

Pollack, M. (1995). 'Regional Actors in an Intergovernmental Play: The Making and Implementation of EC Structural Policy', in C. Rhodes and S. Mazey (eds), *The State of the European Union Vol. 3, Building a European Polity?*. Boulder, CO, and Essex: Lynne Rienner and Longman, 361–90.

Pollack, M. (1997). 'The Commission as an Agent', in N. Nugent (ed.), *At the Heart of the Union: Studies of the European Commission*. Basingstoke and London: Macmillan, 109–28.

Pollack, M. (2003). *The Engines of European Integration: Delegation, Agency and Agenda Setting in the EU*. Oxford: Oxford University Press.

Pollack, M. (2004). 'The New Institutionalisms and European Integration', in A. Wiener and T. Diez (eds), *European Integration Theory*. Oxford: Oxford University Press, 137–56.

Porter, B. (1983), *Britain, Europe, and the World, 1850–1982: Delusions of Grandeur*. London: Allen & Unwin.

Porter, B. (1987). *Britain, Europe and the World, 1850–1986: Delusions of Grandeur*. London: Allen & Unwin.

Preston, C. (1984). *The Politics of Implementation: The European Community Regional Development Fund and European Community Regional Aid to the UK 1975–81*. Colchester: University of Essex, PhD Thesis.

Preston, C. (1995). 'Obstacles to EU Enlargement: The Classical Community Method and the Prospects for a Wider Europe'. *Journal of Common Market Studies*, 33: 451–63.

Preston, C. (1997). *Enlargement and Integration in the European Union*. London: Routledge.

Princen, S. (2007). 'Agenda-setting in the European Union: A Theoretical Exploration and Agenda for Research'. *Journal of European Public Policy*, 14: 21–38.

Princen, S. (2009). *Agenda-Setting in the European Union*. Basingstoke: Palgrave Macmillan.

Puchala, D. (1975). 'Domestic Politics and Regional Harmonization in the European Communities'. *World Politics*, XXVII: 496–520.

Putnam, R. (1988). 'Diplomacy and Domestic Politics: The Logic of Two Level Games'. *International Organization*, 42: 427–60.

Radaelli, C. (2000), 'Whither Europeanization? Concept Stretching and Substantive Change'. *European Integration Online Papers* 4(8) (http://papers.ssrn.com).

Radaelli, C. (2003). 'The Europeanization of Public Policy', in K. Featherstone and C. Radaelli (eds), *The Politics of Europeanization*. Oxford: Oxford University Press, 27–56.

Radaelli, C. (2004). 'Europeanisation: Solution or Problem?'. Paper presented to the ESRC/UACES Conference on the *Europeanization of British Politics*, Sheffield Town Hall, 16 July.

Radaelli, C. (2006). 'Europeanization: Solution or Problem?', in M. Cini and A. Bourne (eds), *Palgrave Advances in European Studies*. Basingstoke: Palgrave Macmillan, 56–76.

Radaelli, C. (2008). 'Europeanization, Policy Learning, and New Modes of Governance'. *Journal of Comparative European Policy Analysis*, 10: 239–54.

Rasmussen, H. (1986). *On Law and Policy in the European Court of Justice: A Comparative Study in Judicial Politics*. Dordrecht: Martinus Nijhoff.

Rattinger, H. (1994). 'Public Attitudes Towards European Integration in Germany after Maastricht: Inventory and Typology'. *Journal of Common Market Studies*, 32: 525–40.

Raunio, T. (2007). 'Political Parties in the European Union', in K. E. Jørgensen, M. Pollack, and B. Rosamond (eds), *Handbook of European Politics*. London: SAGE Publications, 247–62.

Reif, K. and Schmitt, H. (1980). 'Nine Second-Order National E-elections: A Conceptual Framework for the Analysis of European E-election Results'. *European Journal of Political Research*, 8: 3–45.

Rhodes, R. A. W. (1981). *Control and Power in Central-Local Relations*. Aldershot: Gower.

Rhodes, R. A. W. (1986). *The National World of Local Government*. London: Allen and Unwin.

Rhodes, R. A. W. (1988). *Beyond Westminster and Whitehall: The Sub-Central Governments of Britain*. London: Unwin Hyman.

Rhodes, R. A. W., Bache, I., and George, S. (1996). 'Policy Networks and Policy-Making in the European Union: A Critical Appraisal', in L. Hooghe (ed.), *Cohesion Policy and European Integration*. Oxford: Oxford University Press, 367–87.

Richardson, J. (1996). 'Actor-based Models of National and EU Policy Making', in H. Kassim and A. Menon (eds), *The European Union and National Industrial Policy*. London and New York: Routledge, 26–51.

Rieger, E. (2000). 'The Common Agricultural Policy: Politics against Markets', in H. Wallace and W. Wallace (eds), *Policy-Making in the European Union* (4th edn). Oxford: Oxford University Press, 179–209.

Risse, T. (2003). 'The Euro Between National and European Identity'. *Journal of European Public Policy*, 10: 487–505.

Risse, T. (2004). 'Social Constructivism and European Integration', in A. Wiener and T. Diez (eds), *European Integration Theory*. Oxford: Oxford University Press, 159–76.

Risse, T. (2009). 'Social Constructivism and European Integration', in A. Wiener and T. Diez (eds), *European Integration Theory* (2nd edn). Oxford: Oxford University Press, 144–60.

Risse, T., Cowles, M. G., and Caporaso, J. (2001). 'Europeanization and Domestic Change: Introduction', in M. G. Cowles, J. Caporaso, and T. Risse (eds), *Transforming Europe: Europeanization and Domestic Change*. Ithaca, NY, and London: Cornell University Press, 1–20.

Risse, T. and Wiener, A. (1999). '"Something Rotten" and the Social Construction of Social Constructivism: A Comment on Comments'. *Journal of European Public Policy*, 6: 775–82.

Rittberger, B. (2003). 'The Creation and Empowerment of the European Parliament'. *Journal of Common Market Studies*, 41: 203–25.

Rosamond, B. (2002). 'Imagining the European Economy: "Competitiveness" and the Social Construction of "Europe" as an Economic Space'. *New Political Economy*, 7: 157–77.

Rosamond, B. (2003). 'New Theories of European Integration', in M. Cini (ed.), *European Union Politics*. Oxford: Oxford University Press, 109–27.

Rosamond, B. (2007). 'European Integration and the Social Science of EU Studies: The Disciplinary Politics of a Sub-field'. *International Affairs*, 83: 231–52.

Rosamond, B. (2013). 'Theorizing the European Union after Integration Theory', in M. Cini and N. Pérez-Solórzano Borragán (eds), *European Union Politics* (3rd edn). Oxford: Oxford University Press, 85–102.

Ross, G. (1995). *Jacques Delors and European Integration*. Cambridge: Polity Press.

Roth, S. (2008). *Gender Politics in the Expanding European Union: Mobilization, Inclusion, Exclusion*. New York and Oxford: Berghahn Books.

Ryner, M. (2012). 'Financial Crisis, Orthodoxy, and Heterodoxy in the Production of Knowledge about the EU'. *Millennium: Journal of International Studies*, 40: 647–73.

Sabatier, P. (1988). 'An Advocacy Coalition Framework of Policy Change and the Role of

Policy-Oriented Learning Therein'. *Policy Sciences*, 21: 129–68.

Sabatier, P. (1998). 'The Advocacy Coalition Framework: Revisions and Relevance for Europe'. *Journal of European Public Policy*, 5: 98–130.

Sandholtz, W. (1993). 'Choosing Union: Monetary Politics and Maastricht'. *International Organization*, 47: 1–39.

Sandholtz, W. (1998). 'The Emergence of a Supranational Telecommunications Regime', in W. Sandholtz and A. Stone Sweet (eds), *European Integration and Supranational Governance*. Oxford: Oxford University Press, 134–63.

Sandholtz, W. and Stone Sweet, A. (1998). *European Integration and Supranational Governance*. Oxford: Oxford University Press.

Sandholtz, W. and Zysman, J. (1989). '1992: Recasting the European Bargain'. *World Politics*, 42: 95–128.

Saurugger, S. (2013). *Theoretical Approaches to European Integration*. Basingstoke and New York: Palgrave Macmillan.

Sbragia, A. (1996). 'Environmental Policy: The "Push-Pull" of Policy-Making', in H. Wallace and W. Wallace (eds), *Policy-Making in the European Union* (3rd edn). Oxford: Oxford University Press, 235–55.

Sbragia, A. (2000). 'Environmental Policy: Economic Constraints and External Pressures', in H. Wallace and W. Wallace (eds), *Policy-Making in the European Union* (4th edn). Oxford: Oxford University Press, 293–316.

Sbragia, A. and Damro, C. (1999). 'The Changing Role of the European Union in International Environmental Politics: Institution Building and the Politics of Climate Change'. *Environment and Planning C: Government and Policy*, 17: 53–68.

Scarrow, S. (1997). 'Political Career Paths and the European Parliament'. *Legislative Studies Quarterly*, 22: 253–63.

Scharpf, F. (1989). 'The Joint-Decision Trap: Lessons from German Federalism and European Integration'. *Public Administration*, 66: 239–78.

Scharpf, F. (1997) 'Economic Integration, Democracy and the Welfare State'. *Journal of European Public Policy*, 4: 18–36.

Scharpf, F. (1998). *Governing in Europe: Effective and Democratic?*. Oxford: Oxford University Press.

Scharpf, F. (1999a). 'Review Section Symposium: The Choice for Europe: Social Purpose and State Power from Messina to Maastricht. Selecting Cases and Testing Hypotheses'. *Journal of European Public Policy*, 6: 164–8.

Scharpf, F. (1999b). *Crisis and Choice in European Social Democracy*. Ithaca, NY: Cornell University Press.

Scharpf, F. (2010). 'The Double Asymmetry of European Integration, or Why the EU Cannot Be a Social Market Economy'. *Socio-Economic Review*, 8: 211–50.

Scheinman, L. (1967). 'Euratom: Nuclear Integration in Europe'. *International Conciliation*, no. 563.

Schimmelfennig, F. and Sedelmeier, U. (2002). 'Theorizing Enlargement: Research Focus, Hypotheses, and the State of Research'. *Journal of European Public Policy*, 9: 500–28.

Schimmelfennig, F. and Sedelmeier, U. (2004). 'Governance by Conditionality: EU Rule Transfer to the Candidate Countries of Central and Eastern Europe'. *Journal of European Public Policy*, 11: 661–79.

Schimmelfennig, F. and Sedelmeier, U. (eds) (2005). *The Europeanization of Central and Eastern Europe*. Ithaca, NY: Cornell University Press.

Schmidt, V. (2006). *Democracy in Europe*. Oxford: Oxford University Press.

Schmitt, H. and Thomasen, J. (eds) (1999). *Political Representation and Legitimacy in the European Union*. Oxford: Oxford University Press.

Schmitter, P. (1970). 'A Revised Theory of Regional Integration'. *International Organization*, 24: 836–68.

Schreurs, M. (2004). 'Environmental Protection in an Expanding European Community: Lessons from Past Accessions'. *Environmental Politics*, 13: 27–51.

Scott, J. (1995). *Development Dilemmas in the European Community: Rethinking Regional Development Policy*. Buckingham and Philadelphia: Open University Press.

Scully, R. M. (1997a). 'The European Parliament and the Co-decision Procedure: A Reassessment'. *Journal of Legislative Studies*, 3: 58–73.

Scully, R.M. (1997b). 'The European Parliament and Co-decision: A Rejoinder to Tsebelis and Garrett'. *Journal of Legislative Studies*, 3: 93–103.

Scully, R.M. (2001). 'National Parties and European Parliamentarians: Developing and Testing an Institutionalist Theory'. *EPRG Working Paper*, no.6. http://lse.ac.uk/collections/EPRG/working-papers.htm.

Sedelmeier, U. and Young, A. (2008). 'Editorial: The EU in 2007: Development Without Drama, Progress Without Passion'. *Journal of Common Market Studies, Annual Review*, 46: 1–5.

Servan-Schreiber, J-J. (1968). *The American Challenge*. Harmondsworth: Penguin.

Shackleton, M. and Raunio, T. (2003). 'Co-decision since Amsterdam: A Laboratory for Institutional Innovation and Change'. *Journal of European Public Policy*, 10: 171–87.

557

Sharp, M. (1989). 'The Community and the New Technologies', in J. Lodge (ed.), *The European Community and the Challenge of the Future*. London: Pinter, 223–40.

Sharp, M. (1991). 'The Single Market and European Technology Policies', in C. Freeman, M. Sharp, and W. Walker (eds), *Technology and the Future of Europe: Global Competition and the Environment in the 1990s*. London: Pinter Publishers, 59–76.

Sharp, M. and Shearman, C. (1987). *European Technological Collaboration*. London: Royal Institute of International Affairs/Routledge and Kegan Paul.

Siles-Brügge, G. (2014). *Constructing European Union Trade Policy: A Global Idea of Europe*. Basingstoke: Palgrave Macmillan.

Smaghi, I. B. (2013). 'The European Banking Union is a Disappointment'. *Financial Times*, 19 December.

Smismans, S. (2007). 'How Political Theory Could Deal with the Role of Civil Society Organisations in European Governance: Reflexive Deliberative Polyarchy', in C. Ruzza and V. Della Sala (eds), *Governance and Civil Society in the European Union: Normative Perspectives*. Manchester: Manchester University Press, 73–88.

Smith, A. (1992). 'National Identity and the Idea of European Unity'. *International Affairs*, 68: 55–76.

Smith, J. (1999). *Europe's Elected Parliament*. Sheffield: Sheffield Academic Press/University Association for Contemporary European Studies.

Smith, K. (2000). 'The End of Civilian Power EU: A Welcome Demise or a Cause for Concern?'. *The International Spectator*, 35(2): 11–28.

Smith, M. E. (1999). 'Rules, Transgovernmentalism, and the Expansion of European Political Cooperation', in W. Sandholtz and A. Stone Sweet (eds), *European Integration and Supranational Governance*. Oxford: Oxford University Press, 304–33.

Smith, M. E. (2000). 'Conforming to Europe: The Domestic Impact of EU Foreign Policy Co-operation'. *Journal of European Public Policy*, 7: 613–31.

Smith, M. E. (2001). 'Diplomacy by Decree: The Legalization of EU Foreign Policy'. *Journal of Common Market Studies*, 39: 79–104.

Smith, M. E. (2003). 'The Framing of European Foreign and Security Policy: Towards a Post-modern Policy Framework?'. *Journal of European Public Policy*, 10: 556–75.

Smith, M. E. (2004) 'Institutionalization, Policy Adaptation and European Foreign Policy Co-operation'. *European Journal of International Relations*, 10: 95–136.

Smith, M. P. (1998). 'Autonomy by the Rules: The European Commission and the Development of State Aid Policy'. *Journal of Common Market Studies*, 36: 55–78.

Spierenburg, D. and Poidevin, R. (1994). *The History of the High Authority of the European Coal and Steel Community: Supranationality in Action*. London: Weidenfeld.

Steingart, G. (2010). 'It Takes a Crisis to Make a Continent'. *New York Times*, 22 May.

Stetter, S. (2000). 'Regulating Migration: Authority Delegation in Justice and Home Affairs'. *Journal of European Public Policy*, 7: 80–103.

Stevens, A. and Stevens, H. (2001). *Brussels Bureaucrats? The Administration of the European Union*. Basingstoke: Palgrave Macmillan.

Stevens, C. (1984). *The EEC and the Third World: A Survey. 4: Renegotiating Lomé*. London: Hodder and Stoughton.

Stone Sweet, A. and Sandholtz, W. (1997). 'European Integration and Supranational Governance'. *Journal of European Public Policy*, 4: 297–317.

Stone Sweet, A., Sandholtz, W., and Fligstein, N. (eds) (2001). *The Institutionalization of Europe*. Oxford: Oxford University Press.

Strøby Jensen, C. (2000). 'Neofunctionalist Theories and the Development of European Social and Labour Market Policy'. *Journal of Common Market Studies*, 38: 71–92.

Swift, M. (1978). 'A Regional Policy for Europe'. *Young Fabian Pamphlet 48*. London: Fabian Society.

Swinbank, A. and Daugbjerg, C. (2006). 'The 2003 CAP Reform: Accommodating WTO Pressures'. *Comparative European Politics*, 4: 47–64.

Tallberg, J. (2003). 'The Agenda-shaping Powers of the EU Council Presidency'. *Journal of European Public Policy*, 10: 1–19.

Tallberg, J. and Johansson, K. M. (2008). 'Party Politics in the European Council'. *Journal of European Public Policy*, 15: 1222–42.

The Economist (2013*a*). 'Turkey and the European Union: A Tiny Thaw?'. 23 February. http://economist.com/news/europe/21572244-many-turks-have-given-up-progress-towards-eu-inches-forward-tiny-thaw (accessed March 2014).

The Economist (2013*b*). 'Turkey's Protests: Erdogan Cracks Down'. 22 June. http://www.economist.com/news/europe/21579873-vicious-police-tactics-have-reclaimed-taksim-square-and-other-places-protest-high (accessed April 2014).

Tranholm-Mikkelsen, J. (1991). 'Neofunctionalism: Obstinate or Obsolete? A Reappraisal in the Light of the New Dynamism of the European

Community'. *Millennium: Journal of International Studies*, 20: 1–22.

Traynor, I. (2009). 'Europe has Shown it Wants to be a Supersize Switzerland'. *The Guardian*, 20 November.

Tsakatika, M. (2007). 'Governance vs Politics: The European Union's "Constitutive Democratic Deficit" '. *Journal of European Public Policy*, 14: 867–85.

Tsebelis, G. and Garrett, G. (1996). 'Agenda Setting Power, Power Indices, and Decision Making in the European Union'. *International Review of Law and Economics*, 16: 345–61.

Tsebelis, G. and Garrett, G. (2000). 'Legislative Politics in the European Union'. *European Union Politics*, 1: 9–36.

Tsebelis, G. and Garrett, G. (2001). 'The Institutional Foundations of Intergovernmentalism and Supranationalism in the European Union'. *International Organization*, 55: 357–90.

Tsoukalis, L. (1977). *The Politics and Economics of European Monetary Integration*. London: Allen & Unwin.

Turnbull, P. and Sandholtz, W. (2001). 'Policing and Immigration: The Creation of New Policy Spaces', in A. Stone Sweet, W. Sandholtz, and N. Fligstein (eds), *The Institutionalization of Europe*. Oxford: Oxford University Press, 194–220.

Urwin, D. W. (1985). *Western Europe since 1945: A Short Political History* (4th edn). London and New York: Longman.

Urwin, D. W. (1995). *The Community of Europe: A History of European Integration since 1945* (2nd edn). New York: Longman.

van Apeldoorn, B. (2002). *Transnational Capitalism and the Struggle over European Integration*. London and New York: Routledge.

van Apeldoorn, B., Overbeek, H., and Ryner, M. (2003). 'Theories of European Integration: A Critique', in A. Cafruny and M. Ryner (eds), *A Ruined Fortress? Neoliberal Hegemony and Transformation in Europe*. Lanham, MD: Rowman and Littlefield, 17–46.

van der Eijk, C. and Franklin, M. (1996). *Choosing Europe? The European Electorate and National Politics in the Face of Union*. Ann Arbor, MI: University of Michigan Press.

van der Veen, M. (2010). 'Ireland Votes "No", then "Yes", Once More: The Lisbon Treaty Referenda'. *EUSA Review*, 23(1): 15–18. (European Union Studies Association, USA, http://eustudies.org/publications_review_ winter10.php).

Van Munster, R. (2009). *Securitizing Immigration: The Politics of Risk in the EU*. Basingstoke and New York: Palgrave Macmillan.

Vaughan Williams, N. (2008). 'Borderwork beyond Inside/Outside? Frontex, the Citizen-Detective, and the War on Terror'. *Space and Polity*, 12: 63–79.

Verdun, A. (1999). 'The Role of the Delors Committee in the Creation of EMU: An Epistemic Community?'. *Journal of Common Market Studies*, 34: 531–48.

VoteWatch Europe (2012). *Agreeing to Disagree: The Voting Records of the Member States in the Council since 2009, Annual Report*. Brussels: VoteWatch Europe, July.IR http://votewatch.eu/blog/ wp-content/uploads/2012/07/votewatch-annual-report-july-2012-final-7-july.pdf (accessed February 2014).

VoteWatch Europe (2013). *20 Years of Co-decision: A More (Party) Political Parliament, a Less Consensual Council. Special Report*. Brussels: VoteWatch Europe, December. http://votewatch.eu/blog/ wp-content/uploads/2013/12/votewatch-europe-special-policy-brief-20-years-of-co-decision_final.pdf (accessed February 2014).

Waever, O. (1996). 'European Security Identities'. *Journal of Common Market Studies*, 34: 103–32.

Wall, S. (2008). *A Stranger in Europe: Britain and the EU from Thatcher to Blair*. Oxford: Oxford University Press.

Wallace, H. (1977). 'The Establishment of the Regional Development Fund: Common Policy or Pork Barrel?', in H. Wallace, W. Wallace, and C. Webb (eds), *Policy-Making in the European Communities*. London: John Wiley and Sons, 137–63.

Wallace, H. (1986). 'The British Presidency of the European Community's Council of Ministers'. *International Affairs*, 62: 583–99.

Wallace, H. (1999). 'Piecing the Integration Jigsaw Together'. *Journal of European Public Policy*, 6: 155–79.

Wallace, H. (2005). 'An Institutional Anatomy and Five Policy Modes', in H. Wallace, W. Wallace, and M. Pollack (eds), *Policy-Making in the European Union* (5th edn). Oxford: Oxford University Press, 49–90.

Wallace, H. and Young, A.R. (1997). 'The Kaleidoscope of European Policy-Making: Shifting Patterns of Participation and Influence', in H. Wallace and A. R. Young (eds), *Participation and Policy-Making in the European Union*. Oxford: Clarendon Press, 235–50.

Wallace, W. and Allen, D. (1977). 'Political Co-operation: Procedure as Substitute for Policy', in H. Wallace, W. Wallace, and C. Webb (eds), *Policy-Making in the European Communities*. London: John Wiley and Sons, 227–48.

Walters, W. and Haahr, Henrik J. (2005). *Governing Europe: Discourse, Governmentality, and*

559

European Integration. Abingdon and New York: Routledge.

Warleigh, A. (2003). *Democracy in the European Union: Theory, Practice and Reform*. London: SAGE Publications.

Warleigh, A. (2006). 'Conceptual Combinations: Multi-level Governance and Policy Networks', in M. Cini and A. Bourne (eds), *Palgrave Advances in European Union Studies*. Basingstoke: Palgrave Macmillan, 77–95.

Weale, A. (1999*a*). *Democracy*. London: Macmillan.

Weale, A. (1999*b*). 'European Environmental Policy by Stealth: The Dysfunctionality of Functionalism?'. *Environment and Planning C: Government and Policy*, 17: 37–51.

Weale, A., Pridham, G., Cini, M., Konstadakopulos, D., Porter, M., and Flynn, B. (eds) (2000). *Environmental Governance in Europe: An Ever Closer Ecological Union?*. Oxford: Oxford University Press.

Webber, D. (2014). 'How Likely is it that the European Union will Disintegrate? A Critical Analysis of Competing Theoretical Perspectives'. *European Journal of International Relations*, 20: 341–65

Weiler, J. (1999). *The Constitution of Europe: "Do the New Clothes have an Emperor" and other Essays on European Integration*. Cambridge: Cambridge University Press.

Wendon, B. (1998). 'The Commission as an Image-venue Entrepreneur in EU Social Policy'. *Journal of European Public Policy*, 5: 339–53.

Wessels, W. (1991). 'The EC Council: The Community's Decision-Making Center', in R. Keohane and S. Hoffmann (eds), *The New European Community: Decision-making and Institutional Change*. Boulder, CO, San Francisco, CA, and Oxford: Westview Press, 133–54.

Westlake, M. (1994). *The European Parliament: A Modern Guide*. London: Pinter.

Wettestad, J., Eikeland, P. O., and Nilsson, M. (2012). 'EU Climate and Energy Policy: A Hesitant Supranational Turn?'. *Global Environmental Politics*, 12: 67–86.

Whitman, R. (2002). 'The Fall, and Rise of Civilian Power Europe?'. Australian National University, *National Europe Centre*, Paper No. 16.

Wilson, J. (2012). 'ECB "Ready to do Whatever it Takes"'. *Financial Times*, 26 July.

Wincott, D. (1995). 'Institutional Interaction and European Integration: Towards an Everyday Critique of Liberal Intergovernmentalism'. *Journal of Common Market Studies*, 33: 597–609.

Wincott, D. (2006). 'European Political Development, Regulatory Governance, and the European Social Model: the Challenge of Substantive Legitimacy'. *European Law Journal*, 12: 743–63.

Wishlade, F. (1996). 'EU Cohesion Policy: Facts, Figures, and Issues', in L. Hooghe (ed.), *Cohesion Policy and European Integration*. Oxford: Oxford University Press, 27–58.

Wolf, M. (2011). 'Merkozy Failed to Save the Eurozone', *Financial Times*, 6 December.

Woll, C. (2006). 'Lobbying in the European Union: From *sui generis* to a Comparative Perspective'. *Journal of European Public Policy*, 13: 456–69.

Woll, C. and Jacquot, S. (2010). 'Using Europe: Strategic Action in Multi-level Politics'. *Comparative European Politics*, 8: 110–26.

Young, A. R. (2000). 'The Adaptation of European Foreign Economic Policy'. *Journal of Common Market Studies*, 38: 93–116.

Young, A. R. (2007). 'Trade Politics Ain't What It Used To Be'. *Journal of Common Market Studies*, 45: 789–811.

Young, A. R. and Peterson, J. (2006). 'The EU and the New Trade Politics'. *Journal of European Public Policy*, 13: 795–814.

Young, H. (1998). *This Blessed Plot: Britain and Europe from Churchill to Blair*. London: Macmillan.

Young, J. W. (1993). *Britain and European Unity, 1945-1992*. Basingstoke: Macmillan.

Youngs, R. (2004). 'Normative Dynamics and Strategic Interests in the EU's External Identity'. *Journal of Common Market Studies*, 42: 415–35.

Zito, A. (1999). 'Task Expansion: A Theoretical Overview'. *Environment and Planning C: Government and Policy*, 17: 19–35.

Glossary

acquis communautaire Often abbreviated simply to *acquis*, this is a French phrase for which it is difficult to find a precise English translation. A French–English dictionary would define *acquis* as something like 'acquired knowledge' or 'accumulated experience', but the connotation in this phrase is much more like 'heritage'. The *acquis* is the body of laws, policies, and practices that have accumulated over the lifetime of the European Communities, and now the European Union. Any new member state joining the EU has to accept the *acquis* as part of its terms of entry. The adjective '*communautaire*', when applied to the *acquis* or to other nouns, means more than just 'of the (European) community'. It has connotations of something that is in sympathy with the co-operative spirit that informed the original European Community. The term '*communitaire*', which can be found all too frequently in texts on the European Union, is simply an incorrect piece of 'Franglais'.

balance of trade The difference between the exports and imports of a state, or other economic unit such as the EU.

Benelux This is an acronym made up of the first parts of the names of the member states: *Bel*gium; the *Ne*therlands; and *Lux*embourg. The governments of these three states adopted a **customs union** while in exile in London in 1944, and extended this to an **economic union** on 1 January 1948.

black box of the state The realist tradition in international relations assumed that relations between states could be understood without analysing the internal politics of the states. It was assumed that each state had a clear and abiding national interest, derived largely from its geographical position in the world and from strategic considerations such as the need to prevent neighbouring states from being able to dominate the region, and the need to defend any colonies and overseas territories that the state might possess. This national interest was assumed to be stronger than any differences between political parties within the country, so that changes of government would produce little lasting change in foreign policy. Therefore, the state could be treated as though it were a 'black box' into which the analyst need not peer.

Bretton Woods In 1944, a major economic conference was held at Bretton Woods in New Hampshire, USA. Agreement was reached on the basis of a post-war international economic and monetary system. The key principles were free trade and monetary stability. Monetary stability was to be achieved by tying the value of national currencies to the US dollar, which in turn was tied to the value of gold at the rate of US$35 per ounce. The **International Monetary Fund (IMF)** was set up to assist in the establishment of the system, and to provide short-term and medium-term loans to states experiencing temporary problems with their balance of payments. The system lasted until 1971, when it collapsed because the United States was forced to devalue the dollar against gold. It was temporarily replaced by the **Smithsonian agreements**. (See also Insight 7.3).

common market A **customs union**, but with the addition of free movement of factors of production, including capital and labour.

Community method The predominant form of decision making in the EU, based on a Commission proposal and co-decision with the European Parliament and Council of Ministers (via **QMV**). (See also **Union method**.)

corporatism/corporatist The terms 'corporatist' and 'corporatism' comes from the Latin verb *corporare*, meaning 'to form into a body'. The process of forming individuals into collective bodies produces corporations, which are artificial persons created by individuals, who authorize the corporation to act on their behalf. Between the wars in Europe, the idea of the 'corporate state' emerged in which representation of the people would not be by geographical constituencies, but through vocational corporations of the employers and employees in each trade and industry. It was seen as an alternative 'third way' between capitalism and Communism. In practice, corporatism came to be most closely associated with the Fascist regime in Italy after 1928, and was widely imitated by other authoritarian regimes. This association discredited the term in the eyes of the Anglo-Saxon states, but the idea still held some resonance in Roman Catholic social thought, hence its revival, without the formal title of corporatism, in the post-war constitutions of some western European states.

customs union   A **free trade area** that has a uniform set of rules on trade with the outside world.

dirigiste/dirigisme   A French term that translates literally into English as 'directionism'. It is an economic doctrine that gives a central role to the state in the direction of economic development under capitalism. Typically, the state draws up a national economic plan that acts as a framework within which both state-sector and private-sector enterprises can co-ordinate their decisions on investments. The term 'indicative planning' is often used in English to suggest the same system.

economic union   A **common market** with unified economic and monetary policies.

epistemology   The theory of knowledge; about how knowledge is acquired and validated.

European Investment Bank (EIB)   The EIB is an EU agency that is charged to provide capital at affordable rates to support projects that contribute to the integration, balanced development, and economic and social cohesion of the member states. It does this by raising funds itself on the capital markets, and then loaning the funds at favourable rates of interest to support projects that further these objectives.

It also implements the financial components of agreements under the European development aid policies.

Eurosceptic(ism)   Euroscepticism indicates either qualified or unqualified opposition to the process of European integration.

free trade area   Member states remove all tariff and quota barriers to trade between themselves, but retain independent trade policies with the outside world.

G20   A forum that brings together twenty major advanced and emerging economies to promote the financial stability of the world and to achieve sustainable economic growth and development. It was established in 1999.

General Agreement on Tariffs and Trade (GATT)   The GATT was negotiated in 1947 and started operation on 1 January 1948. It consisted of a standing conference for the negotiation of tariff cuts, and an agreement that all such cuts would be multilateral, not bilateral. This was embodied in the principle of 'most favoured nation treatment' for all signatories of the agreement: any trade concession extended by one member to another had to be extended to all other members. It was originally intended that the GATT would be one part of an overarching International Trade Organization (ITO), but this proposal ran into resistance in the US Congress, and never received ratification. The GATT held eight rounds of multilateral trade negotiations, culminating in the Uruguay Round, which opened in Punte del Este, Uruguay, in 1986 and was not completed until 1994. It was this round that focused attention on the trade-distorting effects of the EU's Common Agricultural Policy. One of the agreements in the Uruguay Round was the creation of a new World Trade Organization (WTO), which began operation on 1 January 1995. Its functions are: to administer WTO trade agreements; to act as a forum for trade negotiations; to handle trade disputes; to monitor national trade policies; to provide technical assistance and training for developing countries; to co-operate with other international organizations. (*Source:* **http://wto.org/**.)

Geneva Convention   The Geneva Convention is the term used for a set of Treaties and protocols that set the standards in international law for humanitarian rights during periods of war. There are, in fact, four conventions. They provide, amongst other things, a set of humanitarian standards for dealing with wounded fighters, prisoners of war, civilians, and medical or religious personnel.

International Monetary Fund (IMF) The IMF was set up in 1944: to promote international monetary co-operation; to facilitate the expansion and balanced growth of international trade; to promote stability in exchange rates; to assist in the establishment of a multilateral system of payments in respect of trade between member states, to contribute to the elimination of foreign exchange restrictions; to provide short-term and medium-term loans to states experiencing temporary balance of payments difficulties. (*Source:* **http://imf. org/external/about.htm**.)

investment capital Refers to assets that are invested in a country in the form of factories, businesses, etc.

liquid capital Refers to assets that are placed into bank deposits or similar sources from which they may quickly be withdrawn and transferred elsewhere.

neo–corporatism/neo–corporatist In the 1970s, academics coined the term 'neo-corporatism' to describe a relationship between the state and organized economic interests that was less formal than **corporatism**, but nevertheless institutionalized patterns of consultation on policy between governments, business, and trade unions in several leading western European states.

ontology Refers to the nature of being; an underlying understanding of the world.

OPEC See **Organization of the Petroleum Exporting Countries**

ordinary legislative procedure (OLP) This term was introduced by the Lisbon Treaty to cover those instances in which the Council of Ministers may decide on legislation by **QMV**, while holding co-decision powers with the European Parliament. The terminology is designed to present this pattern as the default arrangement in EU decision making, while all other arrangements (unanimous voting in the

Council and consent or consultation procedures in the EP) are termed 'special legislative procedures'.

ordo–liberalism Sometimes termed 'German neo-liberalism', this refers to a strand in liberal thinking associated with the so-called 'Freiburg school' founded in 1930s Germany. Thinkers associated with this tradition are said to have had an important impact on post-war German politics and also the design and course of aspects of European integration. Ordo-liberals believe in the free market, but emphasize the role of the state or non-politicized public institutional actors (such as the EU) in ensuring that the market works properly. They have, in particular, championed a role for independent public actors in ensuring fair competition and a 'sound' monetary policy based on low inflation (see for instance Chapter 21, Explaining and Critiquing EMU).

Organization of the Petroleum Exporting Countries (OPEC) OPEC was created at a conference of petroleum-exporting states in Baghdad in 1960. The founder members were Iran, Iraq, Kuwait, Saudi Arabia, and Venezuela. They were later joined by eight other members: Qatar (1961); Indonesia (1962); Libya (1962); the United Arab Emirates (1967); Algeria (1969); Nigeria (1971); Ecuador (1973–92); and Gabon (1975–94). OPEC's objective is to co-ordinate and unify petroleum policies among member countries, in order to secure: fair and stable prices for petroleum producers; an efficient, economic and regular supply of petroleum to consuming nations; and a fair return on capital to those investing in the industry. (*Source:* **http://opec.org/opec**.)

passerelle **clause** A *passerelle* clause permits a procedural reform to take place within the EU without the need for a full Treaty reform process. Typically, such a clause would allow the European Council to agree (unanimously) that a particular area of policy making can move from unanimity to **QMV** in the Council of Ministers. First provided for in the Amsterdam Treaty, the number of provisions was extended in the Lisbon Treaty, as well as the requirement for approval by national parliaments added. The first practical use of a *passerelle* provision came in 2004 when, following a five-year transition period after the implementation of the Amsterdam Treaty, the European Council unanimously agreed to move to introduce QMV rules in asylum and immigration policy.

pluralism/pluralist In a pluralist system, interest groups lobby the formal institutions to try to get their preferred legislative options. It is a competitive system of seeking influence, but although early pluralist theories suggested that there was a level playing field of competition, it is now generally accepted that some groups have greater resources than others, and so benefit more from this form of interest representation.

policy entrepreneur(ship) A policy actor who seeks to exploit favourable political conditions in order to promote a particular initiative or policy.

principal–agent theory A branch of rational choice theory that investigates the relationship between institutions that delegate tasks and authority (the principals) and the institutions to which they delegate (the agents). The main concern of principal–agent theory is to investigate the degree to which agents can 'cut slack' so as to achieve a degree of freedom from their principals, freedom that they can use to follow their own agendas rather than the agendas of the principals. Principal–agent theory has been widely used in the investigation of the degree of freedom available to federal agencies in the United States, and in discussion of the relationship of the European Commission to the governments of the member states.

public procurement Purchases of goods and services by governments or other public agencies for use in the public sector, covering everything from paper clips to major projects of civil engineering such as the construction of highways.

qualified majority voting (QMV) A system of voting practised in the Council of Ministers. Under QMV, each member state is given a weighting, which broadly reflects its population size. For a decision to be approved, it is necessary to reach the specific thresholds set down in the Treaties. The rules have been revised over time as a result of institutional reforms and to reflect successive increases in the number of member states. For details of the rules set down most recently, see Table 12.1. QMV applies to many areas of policy: see Table 12.2. QMV is distinct from unanimous voting. Under the latter, all member states must agree before a decision can be taken. Under QMV, by contrast, it is possible for one or a small number of states to be overruled in the Council.

regulated capitalism A form of capitalism that is characterized by government intervention to influence the shape of the economy. It is best understood in contrast to free-market capitalism, in which governments seek to allow markets to regulate themselves and determine the overall shape of the economy.

roll-call voting This is the term given to the formal record of voting in the European Parliament or other assemblies. It is often used by researchers to investigate patterns of behaviour on the part of individual elected politicians and the coherence of the party or party grouping to which they belong.

Smithsonian agreements In 1971, the **Bretton Woods** system of international payments, which had been set up at the end of the war, collapsed. It was replaced by a new set of agreements that were signed at the Smithsonian Institute in Washington, DC, in December 1971. Under these arrangements, the US dollar was substantially devalued against all other currencies, and the major central banks of all other states agreed to try to hold the value of their currencies in a range of fluctuation of 2.25 per cent either side of the US dollar, a maximum range of fluctuation of 4.5 per cent. This attempt to restore fixed exchange rates collapsed in March 1973 in the face of extreme speculative pressure, and the world then entered the era of floating exchange rates that we have today.

stagflation Economists used to believe that there was a trade-off between economic growth and inflation. Policies could either promote economic growth, at the price of higher inflation, or they could focus on restraining inflation at the cost of lower rates of economic growth. Governments made policy choices based on this assumption: some aimed for lower growth in return for low inflation; others preferred high rates of inflation in order to promote high rates of growth. However, following the oil crisis in 1973, the trade-off no longer seemed to work. States began to experience the worst of both worlds: stagnation with inflation, or 'stagflation' as it became known.

structure and agency debate The debate over structure and agency is a debate in the social sciences about whether or to what extent social structures—such as prevailing ideologies or institutional norms and rules—have primacy over social agency—the ability of individuals or actors to make choices autonomously. Social constructivists and some other critical perspectives (see Chapter 4) would claim that structures and agents are co-constitutive. In other words, structures will place limits on agents, but agents will also sometimes be able to alter particular structures. The position that one takes on this debate relates to the position taken on **ontology** (see also Chapter 4, Critical of What?).

subsidiarity Subsidiarity is an ambiguous concept and is taken to mean different things by different political actors. For example, it is interpreted by the British government to mean that action should not be taken at the EU level unless it can be shown that the objectives of the action can be better achieved at that level than at the national level. This interpretation appears to be supported by the wording of Article 5 (formerly Article 3b) of the TEC. The German government interprets it more generally to mean that decisions should be taken at the lowest level of government at which they can be made effective. This implies a commitment to internal devolution of power within states. This interpretation appears to be supported by the wording of Article 1 (formerly Article A) of the TEU.

supranational institution/organization 'Supranational' literally means 'above the national'. A supranational institution or a supranational organization is one that has power or influence going beyond that permitted to it by national governments. An international institution or organization, in contrast, is one that results from the co-operation of national governments, and has no power beyond that permitted to it by those governments.

transgovernmental and transnational networks Links across national boundaries between interest groups and individuals outside of government (transnational) or between departments of national government and individuals working for governments (transgovernmental), which are not monitored or controlled by national foreign offices or other core departments of the executive.

Union method This term relates to mainstream EU business where the Commission typically has the power of initiative, the Council of Ministers and the EP decide on the legislation, and the Court of Justice holds authority as final arbiter on any disputes arising from the Treaties or EU legislation. Prior to implementation of the Lisbon Treaty, the equivalent term used in the academic literature was the **Community method**, which applied to the practices in the then European Community 'pillar' of the EU's former three-pillar architecture (see Chapter 12, Treaties). The Union method does not apply to foreign and security policy, which is treated on a more intergovernmental basis, and has no role for EU law and the Court of Justice, while the Commission and EP have significantly reduced importance.

variable-geometry Europe A method of differentiated integration that allows for a permanent separation between a group of member states that wish to co-operate more closely in a particular area and those that do not wish to do so.

World Bank (International Bank for Reconstruction and Development or IBRD) The IBRD was founded in 1944 to give loans to states to aid their economic recovery. It is now one of five closely associated institutions that together constitute the World Bank Group: the IBRD, which provides loans and development assistance to middle-income countries and creditworthy poorer countries; the International Development Association (IDA), which is focused on the poorest countries, providing them with interest-free loans and other services; the International Finance Corporation (IFC), which promotes growth in the developing world by financing private sector investments and providing technical assistance and advice to governments and businesses; the Multilateral Investment Guarantee Agency (MIGA), which helps to encourage foreign investment in developing countries by providing guarantees to foreign investors against loss caused by non-commercial risks; and the International Centre for Settlement of Investment Disputes (ICSID), which provides conciliation and arbitration facilities for the settlement of investment disputes between foreign investors and their host countries. (*Source:* **http://worldbank.org/**.)

Abbreviations and Acronyms

AASM	Associated African States and Madagascar
ACP	African, Caribbean, and Pacific
AFSJ	area of freedom, security, and justice
Agfish	Agriculture and Fisheries Council
AMIS	African Union Mission in Sudan
AKP	Justice and Development Party (Turkey)
APEC	Asia–Pacific Economic Co-operation
BBC	British Broadcasting Corporation
BDB	Bundesverband Deutscher Banken
BDI	Bundesverband der Deutschen Industrie
Benelux	Belgium, the Netherlands, and Luxembourg
BkartA	Bundeskartellamt (German Cartel Office)
BSE	bovine spongiform encephalopathy
CAP	Common Agricultural Policy
CBI	Confederation of British Industry
CdP	Commissariat du Plan (French Economic Planning Commission)
CDU	Christian Democratic Union (Germany)
CEE	central and eastern Europe
CEEC	Committee for European Economic Co-operation
CEECs	central and eastern European countries
CEEP	European Centre of Public Enterprises
CEN	European Committee for Standardization
CENELEC	European Committee for Standardization of Electrical Products
CEPOL	the European Police College
CEPS	Centre for European Policy Studies
CET	common external tariff
CFDT	Confédération Française Démocratique du Travail
CFP	Common Fisheries Policy
CFSP	Common Foreign and Security Policy

CGT	Confédération Générale du Travail
CI	Community Initiative
CJD	Creutzfeldt-Jakob disease
CJEU	Court of Justice of the European Union
CNPF	Conseil National du Patronat Français
COGECA	General Confederation of Agricultural Co-operatives
COPA	Committee of Professional Agricultural Organizations of the European Community
COPS	Comité Politique et de Sécurité (see also PSC)
CoR	Committee of the Regions and Local Authorities
COREPER	Committee of Permanent Representatives
COREU	Corréspondance Européenne (Telex link)
COSAC	Conference of European Affairs Committees of the Parliaments of the European Union
CPE	critical political economy
CSCE	Conference on Security and Co-operation in Europe
CSDP	Common Security and Defence Policy
CSFs	Community Support Frameworks
CSU	Christian Social Union (Germany)
DDR	Deutsche Demokratische Republik (East Germany)
DG	Directorate-General
DIHT	Deutscher Industrie- und Handelskammertag
EAFRD	European Agricultural Fund for Rural Development
EAGGF	European Agricultural Guarantee and Guidance Fund
EAP	European Environmental Action Programme
EAW	European Arrest Warrant
EBRD	European Bank for Reconstruction and Development
EBU	European Banking Union
EC	European Community
ECB	European Central Bank
ECHO	European Community Humanitarian Aid Office
ECHR	European Court of Human Rights
ECJ	European Court of Justice
ECO	European Cartel Office
ECOFIN	Economic and Financial Affairs Council
ECSC	European Coal and Steel Community
ecu	European currency unit
EDC	European Defence Community
EdF	Electricité de France

EDF	European Development Fund
EEA	(1) European Economic Area; (2) European Environment Agency
EEAS	European External Action Service
EEC	European Economic Community
EES	European Economic Space
EESC	European Economic and Social Committee
EFC	Economic and Finance Committee
EFF	European Fisheries Fund
EFSF	European Financial Stability Facility
EFSM	European Financial Stabilization Mechanism
EFTA	European Free Trade Association
EIB	European Investment Bank
EMCF	European Monetary Co-operation Fund
EMF	European Monetary Fund
EMI	European Monetary Institute
EMS	European Monetary System
EMU	economic and monetary union
ENP	European Neighbourhood Policy
ENPI	European Neighbourhood and Partnership Instrument
EP	European Parliament
EPA	(1) European Parliamentary Assembly; (2) Economic Partnership Agreement
EPC	(1) European Political Community (until 1952); (2) European political co-operation
EPI	environmental policy integration
EPP	European People's Party
EPP-ED	European People's Party and European Democrats
ERDF	European Regional Development Fund
ERI	Extraterritorial Income
ERM	exchange rate mechanism
ERP	European Recovery Programme ('Marshall Plan')
ERT	European Round Table of Industrialists
ERTA	European Road Transport Agreement
ESC	Economic and Social Committee
ESCB	European System of Central Banks
ESDP	European Security and Defence Policy
ESF	European Social Fund
ESPRIT	European Strategic Programme for Research and Development in Information Technology

ESM	European Stability Mechanism
ETS	emissions trading scheme
ETUC	European Trade Union Confederation
EU	European Union
EUA	European Unit of Account
EUF	European Union of Federalists
EUMS	European Union's Military Staff
Euratom	European Atomic Energy Community
EUREKA	European Research Co-ordination Agency
EURODAC	EU-wide electronic system for the identification of asylum-seekers
Eurojust	EU's judicial co-operation unit
Europol	European Police Office
FDP	Free Democrat Party (Germany)
FIFG	Financial Instrument for Fisheries Guidance
FLN	National Liberation Front (Algeria)
FN	Front National (National Front, France)
Frontex	The European Agency for the Management of Operational Co-operation at the External Borders of the Member States of the European Union
FSC	foreign sales corporation
FTA	free trade agreement
FYROM	former Yugoslav Republic of Macedonia
GAC	General Affairs Council
GAERC	General Affairs and External Relations Council
GATT	General Agreement on Tariffs and Trade
GDP	gross domestic product
GM	genetically modified
GNP	gross national product
HMSO	Her Majesty's Stationery Office
HRUFASP	High Representative of the Union for Foreign Affairs and Security Policy
IAR	International Authority for the Ruhr
IBRD	International Bank for Reconstruction and Development
ICSID	International Centre for Settlement of Investment Disputes
ICTY	International Criminal Tribunal for the Former Yugoslavia
IDA	International Development Association
IFC	International Finance Corporation
IGC	intergovernmental conference
IMF	International Monetary Fund
IMPs	Integrated Mediterranean Programmes

INTUG	Information Technology User Group
IPA	Instrument for Pre-Accession
IPE	international political economy
IR	international relations
ISPA	Instrument for Structural Policies Pre-accession
ITO	International Trade Organization
JHA	Justice and Home Affairs
KFOR	Kosovo Force
LCD	lowest common denominator
LDC	less developed country
LI	liberal intergovernmentalism
LLP	Lifelong Learning Programme
LTRO	Long-Term Refinancing Operations
MAFF	Ministry of Agriculture, Fisheries and Food (Britain)
MEP	member of the European Parliament
MFF	multi-annual financial framework
MFN	most favoured nation
MIGA	Multilateral Investment Guarantee Agency
MLG	multi-level governance
MoU	Memorandum of Understanding
MP	member of Parliament (Britain)
MRP	Mouvement Républicain Populaire (France)
MUA	Monetary Units of Account
NAFTA	North American Free Trade Agreement
NAPs	(1) National Action Plans (for employment) (2) National Allocation Plans (for carbon emissions)
NATO	North Atlantic Treaty Organization
NEPI	new environmental policy instrument
NFU	National Farmers' Union (Britain)
NGOs	non-governmental organizations
NPD	National Democratic Party (Germany)
NRPs	National Reform Programmes
NSRF	national strategic reference framework
NTB	non-tariff barrier
NUM	National Union of Mineworkers (Britain)
OECD	Organization for Economic Co-operation and Development
OEEC	Organization for European Economic Co-operation
OJ	Official Journal

OLAF	European Anti-Fraud Office
OLP	ordinary legislative procedure
OMC	open method(s) of co-ordination
OMT	Outright Monetary Transaction
ONP	Open Network Provision
OPEC	Organization of Petroleum Exporting Countries
OSCE	Organization for Security and Co-operation in Europe
PASOK	Panhellenic Socialist Party (Greece)
PCP	Portuguese Communist Party
Phare	Poland–Hungary: Actions for Economic Reconstruction
PJCCM	police and judicial co-operation in criminal matters
PR	proportional representation
PS	Parti Socialiste (Socialist Party, France)
PSC	Political and Security Committee (see also COPS)
PSOE	Spanish Socialist Workers Party
PSP	Portuguese Socialist Party
PTTs	post, telegraph, and telephone companies
QMV	qualified majority voting
RABITs	Rapid Border Intervention Teams
RDF	Regional Development Fund
RENAVAL	Community Initiative programme for the conversion of shipbuilding areas
REPA	Regional Economic Partnership Agreement
RESIDER	Community Initiative programme for the conversion of steel areas
RPF	Rassemblement du Peuple Français (Gaullist Party, France)
RPR	Rassemblement pour la République
SAA	Stabilization and Association Agreement
SAP	Stabilization and Association Process
Sapard	Special Accession Programme for Agriculture and Rural Development
SARS	severe acute respiratory syndrome
SCA	Special Committee on Agriculture
SDP	Social Democratic Party (Britain)
SDS	sustainable development strategy
SEA	Single European Act
SEM	single European market
SGP	stability and growth pact
SHAPE	Supreme Headquarters Allied Powers Europe
SIRENE	Supplementary Information Request at the National Entry
SIS	Schengen Information System

SNA	sub-national authorities
SPD	Sozialdemokratische Partei Deutschlands (Social Democratic Party, Germany)
Stabex	System for the Stabilization for Export Earnings
TEC	Treaty Establishing the European Community
TENs	trans-European networks
TEU	Treaty on European Union
TFEU	Treaty on the Functioning of the European Union
TSCG	Treaty on Stability Coordination and Governance
UDF	Union pour la Démocratie Française
UK	United Kingdom
UKIP	UK Independence Party
UN	United Nations
UNICE	Union of Industrial and Employers' Confederations of Europe
US(A)	United States (of America)
USSR	Union of Soviet Socialist Republics
VAT	value added tax
WEU	Western European Union
WTO	World Trade Organization

Chronology

1940s

1945

February Yalta Summit between the United States, the Soviet Union, and Britain. Agreed 'spheres of interest' in post-war Europe

May Surrender of Germany ends the war in Europe

September Surrender of Japan. End of the Second World War

1946

September Civil war breaks out in Greece

September Winston Churchill's speech in Zurich in which he calls for a 'United States of Europe'

December European Union of Federalists (EUF) formed

1947

February British government tells US administration that it cannot continue aid to Greece and Turkey

March Truman Doctrine announced in US Congress

March Treaty of Dunkirk signed by Britain and France

April Soviet walkout of Four-Power Council of Foreign Ministers

June Marshall Plan announced

July Committee for European Economic Co-operation (CEEC) set up

1948

January Benelux states commence economic union

March Treaty of Brussels signed by Britain, France, and Benelux states

April Organization for European Economic Co-operation (OEEC) replaces CEEC

May European Congress in The Hague

1949

April Federal Republic of Germany established

April North Atlantic Treaty signed in Washington, DC, setting up NATO

April International Authority for the Ruhr (IAR) established

May Council of Europe formed

1950s

1950

May Schuman Plan for coal and steel announced (Schuman Declaration)

June Korean War begins

October Pleven Plan for a European Defence Community (EDC) launched

November Council of Europe adopts European Convention on Human Rights

1951

April Treaty of Paris signed, establishing the European Coal and Steel Community (ECSC)

1952

May European Defence Community (EDC) Treaty signed in Paris

July ECSC begins operation

1953

March Draft Treaty for a European Political Community (EPC) adopted

September European Convention on Human Rights comes into force

1954

August EDC Treaty rejected by French National Assembly (collapse of EPC)

October Treaty creating Western European Union (WEU) signed

November Monnet announces that he will not stand for a second term as President of the High Authority of the ECSC

1955

April Spaak memorandum to ECSC states proposing an extension of sectoral integration

April Beyen memorandum on behalf of the Benelux states proposing a general common market

June Messina Conference agrees to set up Spaak Committee to consider future of integration

October Monnet sets up Action Committee for the United States of Europe

1956

March Spaak Report published

May Governments agree Spaak Report

June Start of 'Messina negotiations' based on the Spaak Report

October USSR invades Hungary to put down anti-communist uprising

October Suez crisis: Israel, Britain, and France attack Egypt and occupy Port Said, but forced to withdraw their troops in the face of opposition from the United States

1957

March Completion of 'Messina negotiations'

April Treaties of Rome (establishing the EEC and Euratom) signed

1958

January EEC and Euratom begin operations: Walter Hallstein becomes the first President of the EEC Commission, Louis Armand the first President of the Euratom Commission

July CAP system of common prices agreed at Stresa Conference

1959

January Customs duties within the EEC cut by 10 per cent

1960s

1960

May Acceleration agreement on the common market and Common Agricultural Policy between six EC states

December Organization for Economic Co-operation and Development (OECD) supersedes OEEC

1961

February Paris Summit agrees to set up committee under Christian Fouchet to review co-operation

March Fouchet negotiations begin

July Association Agreement signed with Greece

August Britain, Denmark, and Ireland apply for membership of the EC

December Commission convenes first conference on European regional policy

1962

April Norway applies to join the EEC

July CAP system of common prices agreed at Stresa Conference

December Nassau agreement between Macmillan and Kennedy

1963

January De Gaulle announces his veto of British membership

July First Yaoundé Convention comes into effect

September Association Agreement signed with Turkey

1965

April Merger Treaty signed, agreeing to merge the institutions of the ECSC, EEC, and Euratom

July Start of French boycott of the Council of Ministers

1966

January Luxembourg compromise

1967

May Britain, Denmark, and Ireland make a second application for membership of the EC

July Norway makes a second application for membership of the EC

July Sweden applies for EC membership

July Merger Treaty takes effect: Jean Rey is first Commission President for all three communities (ECSC, EEC, Euratom)

December France blocks agreement on opening negotiations with the applicant states

1968

July Customs union completed and common external tariff established

December Commission produces 'Mansholt Plan' for restructuring EC agriculture

1969

December Hague Summit: the 'relaunching of Europe'

1970s

1970

June Membership negotiations begin with Britain, Ireland, Denmark, and Norway

July Franco Malfatti becomes President of the European Commission

October Davignon Report on European political co-operation

1971

January Second Yaoundé Convention signed

February Werner Report on economic and monetary union

March Start of first attempt to move to monetary union with the joint floating of European currencies

March Farmers demonstrate in Brussels against Mansholt Plan. Council of Agricultural Ministers agrees a modified version of the Plan

August Ending of the convertibility of the US dollar into gold marks the collapse of the Bretton Woods international monetary system, closely followed by the collapse of the first experiment with European monetary union

December Smithsonian agreements on international monetary regime to replace Bretton Woods

1972

January Completion of membership negotiations with Britain, Ireland, Denmark, and Norway; Accession Treaties signed

March Sicco Mansholt becomes President of the European Commission

March Start of the 'snake in the tunnel' system of EC monetary co-ordination

March European Parliament accepts Commission proposals for creation of EC regional policy

May Irish referendum in favour of EC membership

June British pound withdrawn from the 'snake in the tunnel'

September Norwegian referendum rejecting EC membership

October Danish referendum in favour of EC membership

October Paris Summit accepts the case for EC regional policy and requests the Commission to prepare a report on the issue

1973

January François-Xavier Ortoli becomes Commission President

January First enlargement of EC from six to nine member states

February Italy forced to leave the 'snake'

May 'Thomson Report' on regional problems presented to the Council of Ministers

December OPEC oil crisis

1974

January France forced to leave the 'snake'

July Turkish invasion of Cyprus

December Paris Summit: agrees to direct elections to the European Parliament, creation of the European Council, and the creation of the European Regional Development Fund (ERDF)

1975

January ERDF comes into operation

February First Lomé Convention comes into effect

March First European Council meeting in Dublin

June British referendum agrees continued membership of EC

June Greek application for membership of EC

July France rejoins the 'snake'

August Signing of the 'Final Act' at the Conference on Security and Co-operation in Europe (CSCE) in Helsinki

1976

January Commission Opinion on Greek application: not very favourable

April France leaves the 'snake' for the second time

July Opening of Greek accession negotiations

1977

January Roy Jenkins becomes President of the European Commission

March Portuguese application for membership of the EC

July Spanish application for membership of the EC

October Jenkins lecture at the European University Institute, Florence: calls for a new attempt at monetary union

1978

July Bremen European Council agrees to pursue proposal from Schmidt and Giscard for a 'zone of monetary stability in Europe'

October Opening of accession negotiations with Portugal

December Bremen European Council agrees to create the European Monetary System (EMS)

1979

February Opening of accession negotiations with Spain

March EMS begins

May Greek Accession Treaty signed

June First direct elections to the European Parliament

June EC makes Venice Declaration recognizing the right of Palestinians to a homeland

November Dublin European Council: Prime Minister Thatcher demands a British budgetary rebate

December USSR invades Afghanistan

1980s

1980

March Second Lomé Convention comes into effect

June Venice Declaration of the EC member states on the situation in the Middle East

December Second stage of the EMS scheme postponed indefinitely

1981

January Gaston Thorn becomes President of the European Commission

January Greece becomes a member of the EC

October London Report on European Political Co-operation (EPC) published

November Genscher–Colombo Plan calls for a new European Charter to replace the Treaties and form a constitution for the European Communities

1982

June EMS currencies realigned; French socialist government agrees to reform its domestic economic policies and to retreat from its attempts to reflate the economy

1983

January Stuttgart European Council signs Solemn Declaration on European Union

March Further realignment of EMS currencies

1984

February European Parliament approves draft Treaty on European Union

March System of quotas for dairy products agreed as part of reform of CAP

June Fontainebleau European Council: British budgetary dispute settled; Dooge Committee on institutional reform set up

June Elections to European Parliament

December Third Lomé Convention signed

1985

January Jacques Delors becomes President of the European Commission

February Brussels European Council: mandates Commission to produce a plan for the single European market

June Cockfield White Paper on the freeing of the internal market

June Portuguese and Spanish Accession Treaties signed

June Milan European Council: 1992 Programme agreed

December Single European Act agreed in principle by heads of government at Luxembourg European Council

1986

January Portugal and Spain join the EC

February Single European Act signed by Foreign Ministers in Luxembourg (nine states) and, subsequently, The Hague (the remaining three states)

1987

April Turkey applies for EC membership

July Single European Act comes into effect

1988

February Brussels European Council: agrees to a doubling of the structural funds; legal limit placed on increases in spending on agricultural support

June Hanover European Council: sets up the Delors Committee on monetary union

July Jacques Delors makes a speech to the EP in which he predicts that, in ten years' time, 80 per cent of economic legislation will be directed from Brussels; infuriates British Prime Minister Thatcher

September Margaret Thatcher's Bruges speech

1989

January Reformed structural funds, with new policy principles agreed during 1988, come into operation

January Start of revived 'social dialogue' between representatives of employers and trade unions

June Delors Report on monetary union; accepted by heads of government at Madrid European Council

June Elections to European Parliament

July German monetary union

July Austria applies for EC membership

September Start of collapse of communism in Eastern Europe

October Delors lectures to the College of Europe in Bruges

December Fourth Lomé Convention signed

December Strasbourg European Council sets up an intergovernmental conference (IGC) to consider institutional changes necessary for completing monetary union

1990s

1990

July Stage 1 of economic and monetary union begins

July Cyprus applies for EC membership

July Malta applies for EC membership

August Iraq invades Kuwait

October Reunification of Germany; five new *Länder* become part of the EC

1991

January Start of IGC on political union

June Start of conflict between federal Yugoslav army and Slovenian separatist forces

July Sweden applies for EC membership

July Agriculture Commissioner MacSharry introduces his proposals for reform of the CAP

November EC imposes sanctions on Yugoslavia

December Maastricht European Council: agrees principles of Treaty on European Union (TEU), and to set up a cohesion fund to assist Greece, Spain, Ireland, and Portugal

1992

January Badinter Commission gives support for recognition of Macedonia and qualified support for Croatian independence

February Maastricht Treaty on European Union signed

March Finland applies for EC membership

May Switzerland applies for EC membership

May MacSharry proposals for reform of CAP agreed by Agriculture Ministers

June Danish referendum rejects TEU

June WEU Petersberg Declaration commits member states to allocate armed forces to peace keeping and humanitarian tasks in Europe

September French referendum accepts TEU

September British forced to withdraw from exchange rate mechanism of EMS

November Norway applies for EC membership

November Blair House agreement between the EU and the USA on trade in agricultural goods: paves the way for the completion of the Uruguay Round of GATT negotiations

December Swiss referendum rejects membership of the European Economic Area: Swiss government withdraws application for membership of EC

December Edinburgh European Council agrees opt-out for Denmark from single currency

1993

May Second Danish referendum accepts TEU

August The ERM's 'narrow bands' have to be widened to 15 per cent to allow it to survive

November TEU comes into effect

December EU monitors observe Russian elections

1994

January Stage 2 of economic and monetary union begins

January Start of European Economic Area (EEA)

January Reforms of structural funds agreed during 1993 come into effect

February Greek government refuses the former Yugoslav Republic of Macedonia access to the port of Salonika

April Hungary applies for EU membership

April Poland applies for EU membership

June Austrian referendum in favour of EU membership

June Corfu European Council agrees to extend internal market to energy and telecommunications

June Elections to European Parliament

October Finnish referendum in favour of EU membership

November Swedish referendum in favour of EU membership

November Norwegian referendum rejects EU membership

1995

January Austria, Finland, and Sweden become members of the EU

January Jacques Santer becomes President of the European Commission

January World Trade Organization (WTO) begins to operate

January CSCE becomes the Organization for Security and Co-operation in Europe (OSCE)

March 'Stability Pact' signed by fifty-two states from western and eastern Europe in an attempt to stabilize the political and security situation in eastern Europe

June Romania applies for EU membership

June Slovak Republic applies for EU membership

October Latvia applies for EU membership

November Estonia applies for EU membership

November Barcelona Conference launches the process that leads to the 'Euro-Med' agreements between the EU and North African and other states bordering the Mediterranean

November Agriculture Commissioner Franz Fischler introduces his proposals for further reform of the CAP; they are subsequently incorporated into *Agenda 2000*

December Lithuania applies for EU membership

December Bulgaria applies for EU membership

December 'New Transatlantic Agenda' agreed between the EU and the USA

December Madrid European Council decides on 'euro' as the name for the single currency

1996

January Czech Republic applies for EU membership

June Slovenia applies for EU membership

March Intergovernmental conference to review TEU officially opens in Turin

September Commission requests that member states extend its mandate in international trade negotiations to cover trade in services; request is refused

December Dublin European Council agrees a 'stability pact' to support monetary union

1997

June Amsterdam European Council: agreement on terms of Treaty of Amsterdam, including to supplement the stability pact with a growth and employment pact. All EU member states commit to the 'Petersberg tasks' as agreed by WEU members in June 1992

July Publication of Commission's *Agenda 2000* on eastern enlargement and the reform of the CAP and structural funds

October Treaty of Amsterdam signed

November Special 'jobs summit' held in Luxembourg to work out the principles of the 'co-ordinated strategy for employment' agreed at Amsterdam in June; effectively the 'Luxembourg process' is the first example of the 'open method of co-ordination' (OMC)

1998

March Opening of accession negotiations with Cyprus, Czech Republic, Estonia, Hungary, Poland, and Slovenia

May Special European Council meeting in Brussels to launch the single currency; Wim Duisenberg chosen to be first President of the European Central Bank

December At the end of a bilateral summit at St Malo in France, French President Chirac and British Prime Minister Blair announce their support for the development of a European Security and Defence Policy (ESDP)

1999

January The euro comes into operation, although national notes and coins remain in circulation until 2002

February Negotiations over *Agenda 2000* proposals for agriculture begin

March Resignation of the Santer Commission

March Berlin European Council agrees on a financial perspective for 2000–06, reform of CAP and structural funds, and to nominate Romano Prodi as the next President of the Commission

May Treaty of Amsterdam enters into force

May Prodi becomes President of the Commission

June Elections to European Parliament

December Helsinki European Council agrees to open accession negotiations with Bulgaria, Latvia, Lithuania, Malta, Romania, and Slovakia, and also recognizes Turkey as an applicant country; adopts the 'headline goal' of creating a European Rapid Reaction Force by the end of 2003

2000s

2000

March Institutions of ESDP begin provisional operation

March Special European Council held in Lisbon agrees to a new EU strategy on employment, economic reform, and social cohesion, and makes a commitment to turn the EU into 'the most competitive knowledge-based economy in the world' by 2010

June Signing of Cotonou Agreement as successor to Lomé

June Greece gains approval to join single currency

September Danish people vote to reject adoption of the euro

December Nice European Council agrees the Treaty of Nice and formally proclaims the Charter of Fundamental Rights of the European Union

2001

January Greece joins single currency

June Irish people vote to reject the Treaty of Nice

September Terrorist attacks in New York and Washington, DC

September European Council votes to support United States and to develop EU response following 11 September terrorist attacks

November In the face of protests from other member states, a planned trilateral meeting in London between Blair, Chirac, and Schmidt, to co-ordinate their countries' responses to the September terrorist attacks, has to be widened to include the EU High Representative for the CFSP, the Belgian Presidency of the Council, and the leaders of Italy, Spain, and the Netherlands

December Laeken European Council adopts the Declaration on the Future of the European Union, preparing the ground for a European Constitution

2002

January Citizens start using euro notes and coins in the twelve participating member states

February Convention on the Future of Europe begins its deliberations in Brussels, chaired by former French President Giscard d'Estaing

December US President Bush identifies an 'axis of evil' that includes Iraq

583

2003

February Treaty of Nice enters into force

March A coalition of states led by the United States and Britain invades Iraq; France and Germany condemn the invasion

March An EU force replaces the NATO stabilization force in the former Yugoslav Republic of Macedonia

April European Parliament assents to the accession of ten new member states

June Agreement in Council of Ministers on final decoupling of agricultural payments from production

June Giscard d'Estaing presents draft EU Constitution to the European Council

September Swedish people vote to reject adoption of the euro

October Rome IGC convenes to consider draft EU Constitution

November Jean-Claude Trichet replaces Wim Duisenberg as President of the ECB

November Eurozone heads of government decide not to impose sanctions on France and Germany for breaching the rules of the stability pact

December Proposals of the Constitutional Convention presented to the European Council

2004

February Commission outlines its proposals for the operation of the structural funds in the period 2007–13

March Terrorist bombings in Madrid

April Adoption of an Internal Market Strategy to improve transposition of EU agreements into national law

May Ten new member states join the EU

June Elections to European Parliament, marked by a record low turnout

June European Council nominates Portuguese Prime Minister José Manuel Durao Barroso as the next President of the Commission

October Treaty establishing a Constitution for Europe signed by the heads of state and government and the EU Foreign Ministers

November Barroso Commission eventually approved by EP, following resignation of controversial nominee Rocco Buttiglione

November Kok Report on the 'Lisbon Agenda' presented to the Commission

December Heads of government agree to open accession negotiations with Turkey

2005

February Spanish people vote to approve the Constitutional Treaty

April Bulgaria and Romania sign Accession Treaties

May French people vote to reject the Constitutional Treaty

June Dutch people vote to reject the Constitutional Treaty

July Luxembourg people vote to accept the Constitutional Treaty

October EU opens accession negotiations with Croatia and Turkey

December The former Yugoslav Republic of Macedonia given official candidate status

2006

June European Council asks the incoming German presidency for proposals on how to end the constitutional impasse

July European Council agrees to Slovenia joining the eurozone as from 1 January 2007

December Finnish Parliament ratifies the Constitutional Treaty

December Services Directive is adopted by the European Parliament and the Council

2007

January Bulgaria and Romania join the EU

January Slovenia adopts the euro

July Beginning of IGC convened to finalize a 'reform treaty'

October EU Summit in Lisbon agrees text on the 'reform treaty'

December 'Lisbon Treaty' formally signed by EU leaders in the Portuguese capital

December Schengen area is extended to include the Czech Republic, Estonia, Hungary, Latvia, Lithuania, Malta, Poland, Slovakia, and Slovenia

2008

January Cyprus and Malta adopt the euro

June Irish people vote to reject the Lisbon Treaty

June European Council urges other member states to continue with the ratification process for the Lisbon Treaty

August Military conflict breaks out between Georgia and Russia

September EU Summit condemns Russia's 'disproportionate reaction' in Georgia

December EU announces the creation of an 'eastern partnership' with six former Soviet states (Armenia, Azerbaijan, Belarus, Georgia, Moldova, and Ukraine)

December European Council gives Ireland reassurances over areas of concern in the Lisbon Treaty and the Irish government agrees to hold a new referendum by the end of 2009

December EU leaders agree to cut greenhouse gas emissions by 20 per cent by 2020

December Montenegro applies for EU membership

2009

January Slovakia adopts the euro

April Albania applies for EU membership

June European Parliament elections held

July Iceland applies for EU membership

September Heads of government appoint Herman Van Rompuy as first President of the European Council and nominate Baroness Catherine Ashton for the post of High Representative of the Union for Foreign Affairs and Security Policy

September European Parliament votes in favour of a second five-year term for Commission President Barroso

October Irish people vote to accept the Lisbon Treaty in a second referendum

October New socialist government in Greece reveals fiscal position worse than thought

December Lisbon Treaty comes into effect

December Serbia applies for EU membership

2010s

2010

February New Commission takes office headed by President Barroso

April Eurozone members agree a financial assistance package for Greece

May EU and IMF agree financial package for Greece

June Formal adoption of Europe 2020 strategy

June Iceland given official candidate status

November Financial assistance package for Ireland agreed

2011

October Second assistance package for Greece

December European Council agrees a new set of fiscal rules, but Britain refuses to sign up

2012

March The Treaty on Stability Coordination and Governance (TSCG, or Fiscal Compact) is signed by all the EU member states except Britain and the Czech Republic.

June Spain requests assistance to recapitalize its banking sector

June Cyprus requests financial assistance

October EU awarded Nobel Peace Prize

2013

January British Prime Minister David Cameron pledges a referendum on membership of EU in 2017

March Financial assistance package given to Cyprus

April Catherine Ashton brokers deal over Kosovo

May Agreement reached on reform of Common Fisheries Policy, covering 2014–20

June Agreement reached between European Commission, European Parliament, and Council of Ministers on reform of the CAP covering 2014–20

July Croatia joins EU

November EU budget for 2014 and the multiannual financial framework for 2014–20 agreed

November Seventh European environmental action programme adopted, covering 2014–20

2014

May Elections to European Parliament

General Index

Diagrams are given in italics

Name Index

603